CHURCH, STATE, AND FREEDOM

# Church
# State
# and Freedom

## REVISED EDITION

*by Leo Pfeffer*

BEACON PRESS    BOSTON

TO FREDA, ALAN, AND SUSAN

# Contents

PART TWO

". . . No Law Respecting an Establishment of
Religion . . ."

# Contents

## Contents

## Contents

# Contents

PART THREE

". . . OR PROHIBITING THE FREE
EXERCISE THEREOF . . ."

# Contents

# Foreword

"CONGRESS SHALL MAKE no law respecting an establishment of religion or prohibiting the free exercise thereof." These sixteen words epitomize a radical experiment unique in human history. It was of this experiment that one great American jurist said:

> The greatest achievement ever made in the cause of human progress is the total and final separation of church and state. If we had nothing else to boast of, we could lay claim with justice that first among the nations we of this country made it an article of organic law that the relations between man and his Maker were a private concern, into which other men have no right to intrude. To measure the stride thus made for the Emancipation of the race, we have only to look back over the centuries that have gone before us, and recall the dreadful persecutions in the name of religion that have filled the world.[1]

And another that:

> The manifest object of the men who framed the institutions of this country, was to have a State without religion and a Church without politics—that is to say, they meant that one should never be used as an engine for the purposes of the other. . . . For that reason they built up a wall of complete and perfect partition between the two.[2]

It is the purpose of this book to examine how this experiment came to be made, what are the implications and consequences of its application to democratic living in America today, and what are the forces seeking to frustrate and defeat that experiment.

The first part of this book deals with the events leading to the launching of the experiment; the second, with that aspect of the experiment which relates to the separation of church and state; and the third, with that aspect which relates to religious freedom.

# PART ONE

# THE EVOLUTION OF A PRINCIPLE

### CHAPTER ONE

# Old World Antecedents

## PRIEST AND KING IN ANCIENT RELIGION

AMERICANS who today generally take it for granted that their religion is a private matter of no concern to the men elected or appointed to run their government are rarely aware how recent an innovation this concept is in the thousands of years of human history. The differentiation between the religious and the secular is itself a comparatively modern development in the evolution of human society. To the primitive savage, all of life may be said to have been religious. Tribal society was kept together and survived because religious sanctions effectively enforced adherence to social customs; one who broke a custom violated a taboo which could bring upon him the wrathful vengeance of a superhuman mysterious power.[1]

Every important event in the life of primitive man, from birth to death, was consecrated and solemnized by religious ceremonies. Obviously, an attempt to differentiate between the religious and the nonreligious would have been meaningless to him. He could not distinguish among the evils which threatened his daily existence, and quite naturally looked to the same person to protect him against the wild beast or the enemy tribe as well as against the lightning or the wind. When the protector and provider was the family head, he naturally performed the religious functions; when it became the head of the clan or the Old Man of the tribe, or the king, it was he who protected his wards against both human and superhuman enemies. In time, the king not only interceded for his people with the divine powers, but he himself was regarded as a divine being and his laws as divine decrees.[2]

It was only when the business of acting as intermediary between human and spiritual powers became sufficiently differentiated from the responsibility of leading the tribe in war and policing it in peace as to require the full-time services of a special priest class that competing claims of king and priest began to present a social and communal problem. It is important to note that from the beginning it was the king and not the priest who was superior. The head of the tribe was the warrior, and although he performed priestly functions as well, he assumed these functions because he was the head and representative of the community.[3]

3

The development of the priesthood as a class did not terminate the king's dominance over religion. The king continued to exercise priestly functions when he chose to do so, as did the Biblical Melchizedek, king of Salem;[4] and his sovereignty included the priests as it did all other members of the community. There were exceptions to this; in ancient India the priesthood attained some independence of the king, and in presenting a new king to the people, the priests proclaimed: "Here, O people, is your king, not ours, for our king is the (god) Soma." Occasionally, too, the priesthood acquired ascendancy over the king and maintained him more or less as a ceremonial puppet.[5] By and large, however, it was the king who dominated and the priest who obeyed.

Since primitive and ancient religions recognized no distinction between the religious and the secular, the same authority that promulgated laws regulating relations between man and man promulgated laws concerning man's obligations to the supernatural. This authority was the king; and though the performance of the sacrifice and other rituals could be delegated to the priests, the source of all law was the head of the state. The Code of Hammurabi, king of Babylonia, imposed penalties for homicide, larceny, perjury, and other crimes; it regulated the fees of surgeons and the wages of masons and tailors and prescribed rules for the inheritance of property.[6] The same Code catalogued the gods and assigned them their places in the divine hierarchy.[7] Some five centuries later, Akhnaton, upon his ascendancy to the throne of Egypt, likewise rearranged the order of the gods, going even further than Hammurabi, who merely promoted his own god to a position of equality with existing gods; whereas Akhnaton sought to replace all existing deities with his own personal god, the sun.[8] All in all, the relationship of religion to the state (king) in the pre-Hebraic period may be described as a union of the two forces, with the state almost universally the dominant partner.

## THE HEBREW THEOCRACY

The relation of the Hebrew state and the Mosaic religion was so different from that of other states and religions that Josephus had to coin a new name to describe it.

> Some legislators have permitted their governments to be under monarchies; others put them under oligarchies and others under a republic form; but our legislator (Moses) had no regard to any of these forms, but he ordained our government to be what, by a strained expression, may be termed a *theocracy*, by ascribing the authority and the power to God.[9]

4

Unlike other religions, the Mosaic creed was not merely the religion of the state, it was (at least until Saul) the state itself. Among the Hebrews alone, patriarch, prophet, and priest preceded king and prince. Moses, man of God, determined when the people should travel and when they should pitch camp, when they should make war and when peace. Saul and David were made kings by the prophet Samuel, disciple of Eli the priest. Like the Code of Hammurabi, the Mosaic code combined what today would be considered civil laws with religious mandates, but unlike the Hammurabi Code, the Mosaic religious laws were not of secondary or subsidiary importance. The religious motivation was primary and all-embracing; sacrifices were to be performed because God commanded them, and for the same reason Israel was prohibited from exacting usury, mistreating aliens, or using false weights.

The ancient kings used religion as an engine to further the purposes of state; Eannatum of Lagas (*ca.* 2800 B.C.) made secure his conquest of Kis by declaring himself the "beloved spouse" of the highly venerated goddess of that community.[10] Hammurabi unified Mesopotamia and established Babylon as its capital by elevating its city-god to a position of primacy over the previous reigning gods.[11] Moses of the Bible acted conversely. He exploited the natural ambitions of the Hebrew slaves for freedom and independence to further the purposes of God. Liberation and exodus were merely preludes to Sinai and the receipt of the Divine Law; and the conquest of Canaan was merely a preparation for the building of the temple and the full worship of God.

(It is, of course, quite possible that like other founders and leaders of nations, Moses actually used the concept of a single all-powerful God as a means of unifying the Hebrews and establishing them as a nation, rather than vice versa. This is not important for our purposes; the monotheism whereon was founded the Christianity of western civilization with its consequences in church-state relations was established and fashioned by the Moses of the Bible, not the Moses of history.)

The theocracy of Israel was founded on the monotheism of Moses, which, more than anything else, determined not only the future of religion in western civilization but equally the future of the relationships between religion and state in that civilization. This fact has been noted by many writers. Northcott points out that

Historically it was the Hebrew and Christian conception of a single and universal God that introduced a religious exclusivism leading to compulsion and persecution in the realm of religion. Ancient religions were regarded as confined to each separate people believing in them, and the question of change from one religious belief to another did not arise. It was not until an exclusive dogma appeared, as in Christianity, with its belief in an exclusive fellowship, that the questions of proselytism, change of belief and liberty of religion arose.[12]

The same point was made earlier by Ruffini in his work on *Religious Liberty:*

> When the idea of a single and universal God was set, first by the Hebrews and then by the Christians, against the ancient polytheism, there arose a new form of religious exclusivism, contrary to the old not less in its basis than in its effects. The gods of the other peoples were said to be false and fallen, and religion lost its national and public character and became on one side cosmopolitan and on the other proper to each single individual. From this followed not only an inextinguishable spirit of proselytism but also the principle that he only could be saved who worshipped the true God, that is to say, the principle of absolute intolerance.[13]

These observations must be qualified to some extent. In the first place, the "spirit of proselytism" was hardly "inextinguishable" among the Hebrews. While proselytism was undoubtedly a powerful force before the dispersion of Jewry after the destruction of the second Temple — indeed, Salo Baron estimates that every tenth Roman was a Jew[14] — it ceased to be a significant element in Judaism thereafter.[15] Nor is it entirely accurate to say that the Jews believed that "he only could be saved who worshipped the true God."[16] Moreover, compulsion and persecution in the realm of religion was not exclusively a Hebraic-Christian invention; one of the two crimes for which Socrates was condemned to death was "neglect of the gods when the city worships and the practice of religious novelties."[17]

For all this, it is substantially true that the problem of compulsion in religion is a heritage of the monotheistic worship which Moses commanded must, under penalty of death, be accorded to a jealous God. The history of religious persecution flows directly from Moses' command to slay the three thousand men who worshipped the golden calf[18] to the Spanish Inquisition and the exiling of Roger Williams and Anne Hutchinson by the Puritan fathers.

The Hebrew theocracy existed in its purity only from Moses to Samuel. During that period religion was not merely superior to state, it was all of state. The Law of God as transmitted through Moses and his successors was the whole of government. With Saul, however, the state became the rival and ultimately the master of religion. Saul and David each received his kingdom from Samuel the prophet and disciple of Eli the priest, but it was not long before king dominated prophet and priest. Saul not only disobeyed the command of God through Samuel, but sought to slay Samuel the prophet of God.[19] The subordination of religion to state became complete under Solomon, who did not hesitate to use religion as an engine to further the purposes of the state. He changed the order of priesthood established by Moses because the high priest under that order had espoused the claim of his rival to the throne.[20] He not only ignored the Mosaic imposition of death as the penalty for idolatry, but, to secure his kingdom among the nations, he established altars for the deities of his many foreign wives.[21]

The subservience of religion to state continued in Israel after the revolt of Jeroboam, who set up new gods, new temples, and a new priesthood, so as to keep the people from going to Judea to worship at the temple in Jerusalem. This incident so clearly illustrates the inevitable corruption of religion when it becomes an engine to further state purposes that it merits recounting here in the vivid language of the Bible:[22]

> And Jeroboam said in his heart, Now shall the kingdom return to the house of David: if this people go up to do sacrifice in the house of the Lord at Jerusalem, then shall the heart of this people turn again unto their lord, even unto Rehoboam king of Judah, and they shall kill me, and go again to Rehoboam king of Judah. Whereupon the king took counsel, and made two calves of gold, and said unto them, It is too much for you to go up to Jerusalem: behold thy gods, O Israel, which brought thee up out of the land of Egypt. And he set the one in Bethel, and the other put he in Dan. And this thing became a sin: for the people went to worship before the one, even unto Dan. And he made an house of high places, and made priests of the lowest of the people, which were not of the sons of Levi. And Jeroboam ordained a feast in the eighth month, on the fifteenth day of the month, like unto the feast that is in Judah, and he offered upon the altar. So did he in Bethel, sacrificing unto the calves that he had made: and he placed in Bethel the priests of the high places which he had made. So he offered upon the altar which he had made in Bethel the fifteenth day of the eighth month, even in the month which he had devised of his own heart; and ordained a feast unto the children of Israel: and he offered upon the altar, and burnt incense.

Yet the theocratic spirit never wholly died even in Israel. The tradition on which kingship was founded could not be wholly extinguished. As Lord Acton observed:

> The throne was erected on a compact; and the king was deprived of the right of legislation among a people that recognized no law giver but God, whose highest aim in politics was to restore the original purity of the constitution, and to make its government conform to the ideal type that was hallowed by the sanctions of heaven. The inspired men who

rose in unfailing succession to prophesy against the usurper and the tyrant, constantly proclaimed that the laws, which were divine, were paramount over sinful rulers, and appealed from the established authorities, from the king, the priests, and princes of the people, to the healing forces that slept in the uncorrupted consciences of the masses.[23]

And rarely did the kings dare to punish these prophets, however subversive to established government was their preaching.[24]

In Judea the theocratic element was even stronger. Shortly before the destruction of the first temple, the high priest produced from it the Book of the Law, and the king made a solemn oath before the people to observe it.[25] Later, the restoration of the kingdom after the Babylonian exile witnessed the re-establishment for a time of a religion-state relationship more clearly approximating the Mosaic theocracy than any since the death of Samuel.[26] This condition did not last long; the last days of the second temple saw the priesthood again an engine of royalty, with the kingship and the high priesthood ultimately becoming joined in one person. The Maccabean kingdom degenerated to such a degree that the Pharisees, the true successors of Moses and the prophets, pleaded with Pompey to put an end to it.[27]

The final victory in Judaism, at least for almost two thousand years, was won by theocracy. It was won when one of the two rivals, the state, was destroyed and the other, religion, took over as the unifying, cohesive force which was responsible for the survival of the Jewish people as an ethnic entity. It was after the temple was razed and the Jews expelled from their land to begin their long exile and dispersion that the laws of Moses and the Pharisees achieved supremacy. The Jewish state almost to the contemporary era was the ghetto; its head was the rabbi; its constitution the Bible of Moses (Torah), and its laws, the Talmud and later rabbinic commentaries. The whole of the life of a Jew in the ghetto was governed by religion; there was no line between the religious and the secular. Marriage, divorce, inheritance, commercial transactions—all were governed by religious laws. The Hebrew theocracy had been pure and complete in the Sinai desert before the Hebrews entered Canaan, and it became again pure and complete in the Diaspora after they had been expelled from Palestine.

## Ancient Greece

In primitive Greece, as elsewhere, there was no distinction between the religious and the secular. The king, in his capacity as head of the state, was also the chief priest and supreme guardian of religion. When monarchy gave way to republic, the unity of religion and state continued, and the republican officials, whether elected or chosen by lot, took over the religious no less than the civil functions of the king. The particular cult practiced by the king passed into the hands of the republican state and became subject to the control of the popular assembly, which later also took over in large degree control of the family cults as well.[28]

The unity of religion and state which characterized the Greek city-republics was that of a dominant state and a subservient religion.[29] The Greek city religion was characterized by the absence of any comprehensive religious organization with a uniform dogma, lack of a strongly established priesthood, and absence of religious instruction.[30] The extent to which religion was used to serve state interests is illustrated by the situation in the Ionian cities, where it was the custom for the government to auction off the priesthood to the highest bidder. Since the office of priest was a highly profitable one and the fees for rendering priestly services were substantial, the bidding was likely to be spirited and the returns to the state high.[31]

By and large the Greeks were tolerant in religious beliefs. The monotheistic exclusiveness of Moses and the Hebrew prophets was absent in Greece, where, on the contrary, a great tolerance was shown to alien gods and religions.[32]

This tolerance in matters of dogma and creed was not unlimited, and must not be confused with religious liberty. Religious liberty was no more possible of achievement in Greece than anywhere else where religion and state are united. In Athens, a resolution was enacted in the popular assembly directed against "those who did not believe in the divine, and promulgated doctrines about the phenomena of the heavens."[33] Anaxagoras was prosecuted on a charge of atheism because he declared the sun to be a glowing mass and the moon a lump of earth no bigger than the Peloponnesus;[34] Socrates was condemned to death for religious heterodoxy.

Moreover, the Athenian citizen, while free to worship his private gods, was under a duty to participate in the worship of Zeus and Apollo in the legally prescribed manner. Neglect to do so disqualified one from holding the office of magistrate; but beyond that, the state officials saw to it that the worship demanded by law was duly rendered even by those having no aspiration for political office.[35] Measured against the Hebrew theocracy or the Christian church-state, the Greek city-republic showed a remarkable degree of religious tolerance to the citizens' private religions, but it was far from the religious liberty which the fathers of the American constitutional republic sought to secure for all time in the new nation they established.

## Pre-Christian Rome

The development of the relationship between state and religion in ancient Rome paralleled the development which has been outlined in respect to other primitive state-religion relationships. On the Italian peninsula, as elsewhere, the first priest was the father of the family. When the social organization expanded, the king as head of the community exercised the priestly functions. Later, the usual pattern unfolded: the king delegated these functions to a chief priest, and gradually there was developed a whole priestly hierarchy headed by the Pontifex Maximus or chief priest.[36]

By the time of Caesar, the expansion of Rome, with the resulting corruption of the state religion by contact with pagan deities and worships, brought about in Rome an extreme skepticism toward religion. Cicero, himself a member of the sacerdotal order of augurs or official diviners, declared publicly that he did not believe in omens; and Cato said he wondered how two members of the augurs' guild could meet without laughing. Caesar, who was not only head of the secular state but also Pontifex Maximus, declared in the Senate that he did not believe in a future life.[37]

When Augustus became sole head of the Roman state and Pontifex Maximus, he determined that the welfare of the state demanded the revival and restoration of religion to its former high estate. Augustus himself may or may not have been a believer; the answer is neither certain nor significant. What is certain, and, for our purpose, deeply significant, is that the religious revival which he instituted was part of a political plan. Its motivation and object were political; in short, it was but another illustration of the use of religion as an engine to further state policy.[38]

Augustus ordered the restoration of the temples and the revival of the old cults with their worship. He went further: he set his great uncle Julius Caesar among the gods, and commanded that the worship of the Divine Julius should not be less than the worship of Apollo, Jupiter, and the other gods. Augustus thus initiated what has been called the real religion of pre-Christian Rome—the worship of the head of the state. At his death Augustus too joined the ranks of the gods, as did other emperors after him.[39]

In its early history, Rome exhibited the same comparative tolerance in religion that Greece did. Worship of the state gods in accordance with the official custom was expected; but in addition, private or family cults were tolerated, as long as they did not intervene in the political arena, where the state religion enjoyed a monopoly. Foreign gods were not merely tolerated, they were welcomed. National gods of conquered nations were admitted into the Roman pantheon, and in return for this courtesy the subject peoples were glad to worship the Roman gods and render homage to the emperor as a divine being.[40]

But by the time emperor-worship was fully established, much of this tolerance disappeared. Refusal to worship Jupiter was tolerated; but refusal to worship Caesar was a manifestation of disloyalty, and brought with it the full force of the state's displeasure.[41] Only the Jews were able to escape. Their adherence to Mosaic monotheism, which prohibited any form of idolatry, made it impossible for them to participate in emperor-worship. The Romans could destroy their temple, burn their cities, and scatter them throughout the empire, but it could not overcome their recalcitrance. Ultimately, a *modus vivendi* was arrived at: the Jews were not required to pray to the emperor, but only for him, and to contribute, like all other citizens, to the upkeep of the public temples.[42]

## CHRISTIANITY OPPRESSED

It took considerably longer for a *modus vivendi* to develop in respect to the new sect of those who called themselves Christians, although, when the adjustment was finally made, its consequences were universal and permanent. The Christians were afflicted with the same dogmatic exclusiveness that prevented the Jews from rendering due homage to the publicly accepted gods.

The first two centuries after the death of Jesus saw the Christians subjected to persecution that varied in extent and duration with the various emperors. Persecution of Christians appears to have begun under Nero, who found in them a convenient scapegoat to bear the odium of the burning of Rome.[43] Under Nero and Domitian the Christians were persecuted not as Christians but as arsonists;[44] but by the time of Trajan, Christians as such were outlaws. Their crime was "hatred of the human race," which placed them in the category of pirates, brigands, and other "enemies of mankind" who were subject to such summary punishments as being devoured by animals or buried alive, without the necessity of formulating a specific charge or holding a trial.[45] Indeed a trial was hardly necessary; if the accused was known not to be a Jew (and therefore exempt from the requirement of emperor-worship) he was directed to perform some act of worship to the emperor's image; if he refused, he was obviously a Christian and therefore an outlaw.

Under Trajan the persecution of Christians was legalized, formalized, and in fact somewhat ameliorated. Trajan declared that to be a Christian was a criminal offense; it was "the name itself" that constituted the offense, not any particular criminal act. Any person therefore convicted of belonging to the sect, and refusing to recant when formally ordered to do so, must be punished. On the other hand there was to be no official hunt for offenders; only if information was formally presented were criminal proceedings to be taken, and in no event was anonymous information to be accepted. Any accused person who denied Christ and gave satisfactory proof that he abjured his errors, by adoring the gods and the emperor's image and cursing Christ, was to be immediately acquitted.[46]

Under Trajan's successors, the status of Christians as outlaws continued, though the number of actual martyrs was relatively small for a century and a half. No general persecution occurred before the middle of the 3rd century.[47] Indeed, even though the Christians were deemed atheists and anarchists — atheists because of their rejection of the old gods and anarchists because of their refusal to join in emperor-worship[48] — and were therefore outlaws, yet their church was apparently a duly licensed corporation entitled to own real property.[49] By the year 250 the legislation outlawing Christianity had become a dead letter; but under Decius and Valerian there was a revival of persecution in that year.

The law for the persecution of Christians was given new life by a decree of Valerian, acting under authority of the emperor, Decius, which required every householder in the empire to obtain a certificate of his devotion to the state religion. The application for such a certificate presents an interesting illustration of the restriction on religious liberty which always occurs when the religion of its citizens becomes a matter of state concern. The application read:

> I have always sacrificed to the gods, and now in your presence I have in accordance with the regulations sacrificed, caused libation, and tasted of the victims; and I request that you shall certify the same.

The police made a house-to-house inspection for certificates, and the Christians thus discovered either were put to death or escaped into exile.

Valerian, who became emperor shortly after the death of Decius, sought not merely to secure the apostasy of individual Christians but to destroy the church as an institution. He promulgated edicts that declared the church to be an illicit corporation. Its property was confiscated, its meetings forbidden, and its clergy declared guilty of conspiracy to commit high treason.[50]

After the death of Valerian the persecution abated, only to be revived in the final struggle under Diocletian, who became emperor in 284. Diocletian set about reorganizing the empire and making its administration more efficient. The closely knit, hierarchically controlled church presented a serious political problem. It was a state within a state, over which he had no control. Two courses lay open: he could either force it into submission and break its power, or enter into an alliance with it and thus procure political control of it. Diocletian chose the first method. By a series of edicts he revived the persecution of Valerian. Churches were ordered destroyed, sacred books confiscated, clergy imprisoned and forced to sacrifice by torture.[51]

These edicts and the persecution they invoked were no more successful than those that preceded them. They represented the last vain effort of the Roman state to solve the serious political problems which the new church brought with it, by trying to destroy the church and its adherents. As history both before and after proved, the state could not conquer religion by force; it could achieve its purpose only by collaboration, alliance, and corruption.

Constantine and his successors tried the second approach. Persecution had practically ceased on the retirement of Diocletian, and in 311 Constantine joined with Galerius and Licinius, his two co-rulers of the empire, in issuing an edict of toleration to Christians "on condition that nothing is done by them contrary to discipline."[52] A year later, after the death of Galerius, Constantine and Licinius joined in issuing the epochal Edict of Milan (312 or 313), a document of primary importance in the history of religious liberty. It provided "that liberty of worship shall not be denied to any, but that the mind and will of every individual shall be free to manage divine affairs according to his own choice." Accordingly all restrictive statutes were abrogated, and it was enacted "that every person who cherishes the desire to observe the Christian religion shall freely and unconditionally proceed to observe the same without let or hindrance." Moreover, it was provided that the "same free and open power to follow their own religion or worship is granted also to others, in accordance with the tranquillity of our times, in order that every person may have free opportunity to worship the object of his choice."[53]

13

## The Church Triumphant

Before long the equality which Christianity thus received became privilege, and privilege became prestige that approached exclusive power. Although not baptized — at least not until he was on his deathbed — Constantine was undoubtedly personally sympathetic to Christianity. But his actions were primarily motivated not by that sympathy, but by political considerations. Again religion became an engine of state policy. For Constantine considered Christianity as a means of unifying his complex empire. As Pontifex Maximus of the non-Christian state religion, he of course had exclusive power to control its administration and determine its course. Constantine and his successors had no hesitation in exercising the same control of the newly recognized religion and according it the same favors previously enjoyed by its predecessor.

Within seven years after the Edict of Milan, great Christian church edifices were erected under imperial auspices, the clergy were freed from the public burdens which others had to bear, and private heathen sacrifices were forbidden. Two years later the Christian Sunday was made a legal holiday, and urban citizens were forbidden to work on that day. In the year 346 the non-Christian temples were ordered closed and the death penalty imposed for sacrifices, and Theodosius' edict of 392 forbade even the simplest offerings to household gods.[54]

With the favors thus accorded Christianity by the state came the price which religion must always pay for state favors — state interference in religious affairs. Constantine and his successors called and dismissed church councils, and enforced unity of belief and practice. The church, which until so recently had been the victim of persecution and repression, now welcomed the state's persecution and repression of the nonconformist and the unorthodox. When Nestor was consecrated Bishop of Constantinople, he preached a sermon to the Emperor Theodosius in which he said: "Give me, my Prince, the earth purged of heretics, and I will give you heaven as a recompense. Assist me in destroying heretics, and I will assist you in vanquishing the Persians."[55]

These pleas were heeded by the emperors. Deviation from orthodoxy was made a crime against the state, often punishable by death. Heretics were forbidden to build churches, hold religious assemblies, or teach their doctrines even privately. Pagans were required to hear instruction in the churches, were subject to exile if they refused baptism, and to death if, after receiving baptism, they lapsed into pagan rites. The partnership between church and state was not an easy one, either in practice or in theory. Pope Gelasius I, writing to the emperor in 496, staked out the church's mighty claim of the future:

> There are two things, most august emperor, by which this world is chiefly ruled: the sacred authority of the priesthood and the royal power. Of these two the priests carry the greater weight, because they will have to render account in the divine judgment even for the kings of men.[56]

There were within the Christian church voices raised in behalf of liberty. Justin Martyr, Tertullian, St. Hilary of Poitiers, Chrysostom, and St. Augustine, among others, pleaded the cause of toleration and condemned constraint as a means of promoting religion. Unfortunately, once Christianity left the region of the oppressed and achieved the status of state patronage, many of these church leaders forgot what they had preached in their youth. Tertullian, when Christianity was persecuted, pleaded that "It is a fundamental human right, a privilege of nature, that every man should worship according to his own convictions. One man's religion neither helps nor harms another man,"[57] and that "It is not in the nature of religion to coerce religion which must be adopted freely and not by force." But years later the same Tertullian argued: "Heretics may properly be compelled, not enticed to duty. Obstinacy must be corrected, not coaxed."[58]

Most significant, in view of his tremendous influence on later Christian thought, was the change in the views of St. Augustine. When he was young and an adherent of orthodoxy in North Africa, an area then controlled by heretics, he was fervent in his pleas for freedom of conscience. Later, however, when orthodoxy was the attitude favored by the state, he called on the civil power to suppress the dissidents in the church. It was better that the heretics should be purged of their error, even by punishment, than that they should die unsaved. Compulsion in such cases was benevolent, "for what is a worse killer of the soul than freedom to err." Augustine made much use of the passage in Luke (14:23): "Go out into the highways and hedges, and compel them to come in, that my house may be filled." His position on religious liberty has been summarized in the maxim commonly (though erroneously) ascribed to him: "When error prevails, it is right to invoke liberty of conscience; but when, on the contrary, the truth predominates, it is just to use coercion."[59]

Augustine's influence on the course of religious liberty and the relationship of church and state can hardly be measured. Fifteen hundred years have passed since his death, yet his teachings remained the most potent factor in the position of the Catholic Church on the subject of religion and government, at least until the promulgation in 1965 of Second Vatican Council's Declaration on Religious Liberty. As a result of his teaching,

> The principle that religious unity ought to be imposed in one way or another dominates the whole of the Christian Middle Ages and finds a concise and rigorous sanction in civil as well as in ecclesiastical legislation.[60]

Because of Augustine, more than any other person,

> the Medieval Church was intolerant, was the source and author of persecution, justified and defended the most violent measures which could be taken against those who differed from it.[61]

### Church and Emperor in the Middle Ages

After the collapse and disintegration of the Roman Empire, and while monarchic states were slowly being consolidated among the numerous feudal holdings, the church represented the one permanent, stable, and universal power. It is therefore not suprising that it should now claim, not merely equality, but superiority to the secular states. The claim first made by Gelasius, and symbolized by Pope Leo's crowning of Charlemagne, became the church's accepted principle of its relationship to the state in the Middle Ages. The union of church and state, as viewed by the church, was now a union of the state in the church. The classic statement of the church's view of the relationship was made by Thomas Aquinas in the 13th century in these words:

> The highest aim of mankind is eternal happiness. To this chief aim of mankind all earthly aims must be subordinated. This chief aim cannot be realized through human direction alone but must obtain divine assistance which is only to be obtained through the Church. Therefore the State, through which earthly aims are obtained, must be subordinated to the Church. Church and State are as two swords which God has given to Christendom for protection; both of these, however, are given by him to the Pope and the temporal sword by him handed to the rulers of the State.[62]

The supremacy claimed by the Church was of course not conceded by the rulers of the states. Charlemagne had received his crown from the Pope, but to nullify the inference of subordination arising from his own crowning, he himself crowned his son as his successor.[63] The whole history of medieval Europe revolved around the continual struggle for supremacy between prince and Pope, and the resulting religious wars and persecution of heretics and nonconformists. This book is obviously not the place for a detailed account of this struggle, but a few incidents may be briefly related to show what the fathers of our Constitution sought to keep from this country when they established the unique experiment of the mutual independence of religious and political sovereignties.

Probably the most dramatic and well-known chapter is the head-on contest between Hildebrand (Pope Gregory VII) and Emperor Henry IV in the 11th century. After the revival in Germany of the Holy Roman Empire, the Popes were often chosen by the German emperors, and the local church officials came under the complete domination of German princes who did not hesitate to sell appointments to the highest bidders. On Hildebrand's ascendancy to the papacy, he reasserted the claim of papal supremacy. Declaring that "the Pontiff alone is able to bind and to loose, to give and take away, according to the merits of each man, empires, kingdoms, duchies, countships, and the possessions of all men,"[64] he ordered Henry to conform to a papal decree that bishops receive their staff of office from the Pope and not from the Emperor. Henry answered by defiantly appointing a cleric of his own choice to the bishopric of Milan, and sought to sustain his act by calling a council of his nobles and bishops which rejected the Pope's authority.

The Pope responded with drastic counteraction. He issued a decree excommunicating Henry and releasing his subjects from their oaths of allegiance to him. The Emperor at first remained defiant; he sent Hildebrand a fierce letter calling him "no pope, but a false monk," and inviting him to "come down, to be damned through all eternity." But his defiance did not last. Henry's nobles gave him a year to obtain release from excommunication and warned him that failure would result in his deposition.

Henry crossed the Alps and followed the Pope to his castle at Canossa, where for three days he stood in the snowy courtyard, barefooted and dressed in penitential white, until the Pope admitted him to an audience, releasing him from his excommunication.

But the Pope's triumph was shortlived. When three years later he again excommunicated Henry, Henry's reply was radically different. He marched on Rome, drove out Hildebrand, and set up a rival as Pope. The contest was temporarily resolved shortly after when, on the death of both Henry and Hildebrand, their successors arrived at a compromise under which the bishops, though appointed by the

Pope, were to be invested in office by the touch of the Emperor's scepter.[65]

Almost as dramatic was the struggle, a century later, between the English kings Henry II and John and the Popes Celestine III and Innocent III. Henry challenged Celestine by enacting laws limiting the application of canon law in ecclesiastical cases, and assumed the power to elect bishops who were required to do him homage. The expression of opposition by Thomas à Becket, Archbishop of Canterbury, resulted in his assassination, and the Pope capitalized on Becket's popularity by canonizing him. Henry was forced to withdraw the offending laws, and as a penitent submitted himself to being scourged before Becket's tomb.[66]

The contest for the control of the English episcopacy was resumed in the reigns of John and Innocent, successors to Henry and Celestine. When, in 1205, the office of Archbishop of Canterbury became vacant, two successors were elected, one by a group of monks and the other by bishops who backed the king's choice. Innocent refused confirmation of both candidates and ordered a new election, at which Stephen Langton, his own nominee, was chosen. When the king countered by banishing the recalcitrant monks, and threatened to prevent any English appeals from being brought to Rome, Innocent placed England under an interdict and excommunicated John.[67]

Innocent had early reiterated the papal claims of supremacy over princes. He had informed the Patriarch of Constantinople that "the Lord left to Peter (the Pope) the government not of the Church only but of the whole world," and advised Philip Augustus of France that

> Single rulers have single provinces and single kings have single kingdoms, but Peter, as in the plentitude, so in the extent of his power, is pre-eminent over all since he is the vicar of Him whose is the earth and fulness thereof, the whole world and all that dwell therein.[68]

When, therefore, John remained obdurate, Innocent invited the king of France to enter England and depose him. This threat proved sufficient; John capitulated and accepted Langton as Archbishop of Canterbury.[69] But that was insufficient to satisfy Innocent, who proceeded to take over the actual sovereignty of England, and governed it effectively by his legatees during the remaining years of John's kingship and the first years of Henry III.

That Innocent's claim of temporal as well as spiritual supremacy had real consequences was evidenced not merely by his victory over John. During his lifetime he was supreme temporal chief of the Italian state, the Spanish peninsula, the Scandinavian states, Hungary, Bohemia, Poland, Servia, Bosnia, Bulgaria, and the Christian state of Syria.[70]

Innocent represents the apex of the Church's supremacy over state in Europe. After him, a number of factors combined to cause the decline of the papacy. Most important among these were the rising tide of nationalism, the growing corruption of the Church which ultimately led to the Protestant revolution, and the rise of commerce and its expansion over the world. By the beginning of the 14th century, the direction of church-state rivalry in Europe in the future became clear. When a conflict arose between Pope Boniface VIII and King Philip the Fair of France, Philip convoked the first French States-General, with representation from clergy, nobility, and commoners. When the States-General pledged its support to the king, Boniface issued his famous bull, *Unam Sanctum*, containing the words: "We declare, say, define and pronounce that to every creature it is absolutely necessary to salvation to be subject to the Roman Pontiff." But the days of Canossa and Canterbury were never to return. Philip called another session of the States-General, during which the Pope was arraigned as a criminal, a heretic, and immoral, and an appeal was issued for a general council of the churches to put the Pope on trial. Philip went so far as to have the Pope imprisoned; and though he was soon released, it was clear that the contest for temporal supremacy between church and state had been finally—at least to the present—won by the state.[71]

Though state ascendancy over the church was predicated on practical considerations, and the princes and emperors did not concern themselves much with procuring theoretic justifications for their struggles with the Popes, one radical voice was heard in defense of the crown over the cross. Marsilius of Padua, whose great book *Defensor pacis* appeared in 1324, denied not only to the Pope, but to the bishops and clergy, any coercive jurisdiction or the right to pronounce interdicts or excommunications. He proposed seizure of most church property by the state, which should have the right to appoint church officers. The Pope's power was to be limited to spiritual pre-eminence.[72]

Marsilius's ideas were destined to have a profound influence not only on those who later were responsible for the Reformation, but also on the founders of modern constitutional democracy.

> Laws [he said] derive their authority from the nation, and are invalid without its assent. As the whole is greater than any part, it is wrong that any part should legislate for the whole; and as men are equal, it is

wrong that one should be bound by laws made by another. But in obeying laws to which all men have agreed, all men, in reality, govern themselves. The monarch, who is instituted by the legislature to execute its will, ought to be armed with a force sufficient to coerce individuals, but not sufficient to control the majority of the people. He is responsible to the nation, and subject to the law; and the nation that appoints him, and assigns him his duties, has to see that he obeys the Constitution, and has to dismiss him if he breaks it.[73]

The close affinity of these ideas to those expressed centuries later by Locke, Montesquieu, Rousseau, and Jefferson is patent and truly remarkable.

## THE INQUISITION

Marsilius was centuries in advance of his age also when he stated that "The rights of citizens are independent of the faith they profess; and no man may be punished for his religion."[74] The sole judge of the divine law is Christ, and the sole sanction for its breach is punishment in the next world. Eternal salvation could not be achieved by compulsion, and the Church has no right to punish heresy.[75]

But the spirit that pervaded the Middle Ages reflected the thinking not of Marsilius but of Augustine and Aquinas, who taught that salvation could be achieved through compulsion, and that oppression and persecution of heretics was not merely the right but the holy duty of the Church. Thus, for example, in Iceland in the year 1000, the entire population was made Christian by law, and all who had not previously accepted baptism were required to do so. The knights who conquered the Baltic seacoast likewise forced Christianity on the natives, in order to insure their salvation in eternity.[76] The bloodbaths and massacres suffered by the Jews at the hands of the Crusaders were motivated partly to effect their conversion to Christianity, but more to avenge Christ—although by and large they were opposed by the Church.

The major victims of church-sanctioned religious persecution were the unorthodox Christians. Augustine preached that heresy was worse than murder, because it destroyed the soul rather than the body. Aquinas added that the counterfeiting of God's truth was worse than forging the prince's coin (which was punishable by death), and that "the sin of heresy separates man from God more than all other sins and, therefore, is to be punished more severely."[77]

Fortified by the justifications of Augustine and Aquinas, the church developed its law against heresy in the Decretals, based on Gratian's collection of the strongest statements against heresy that could be found in Christian writings. The state cooperated by reviving the Roman law, with the severities of Theodosius and the Justinian Code. In one country after another, death was prescribed as the penalty of heresy.

From the latter part of the 10th century to the beginning of the 12th, there were numerous executions of heretics, either by burning or strangling; but it was not until the reign of Innocent III at the beginning of the 13th century that persecution and oppression of heretics really became universal and systematic. Innocent called on the secular princes to organize a crusade against the heretical Albigenses, and the result was mass executions. This was followed by the establishment of the Inquisition about the second quarter of the 13th century.

The purpose of the Inquisition was the discovery and extermination of heresy, and the chief responsibility for its operation was assigned to the Dominican order. The Dominicans travelled from place to place. Arriving in a town, they addressed its inhabitants, called on them to confess if they were heretics, or to denounce those whom they knew to be heretics. A period of grace, not exceeding one month, was given. Those who confessed were treated with varying degrees of leniency, ranging from dispensation of all punishment to exemption from the death penalty.

At the end of the grace period, the inquisition proper began. The procedure was secret and arbitrary. External acts of piety and professions of faith were disregarded. No ordinary rules of procedure or evidence were applied. The accused was surprised by a sudden summons and imprisoned on suspicion. The judge and the prosecutor were the same person, and the accused was presumed to be guilty. While he had the right to demand a written account of the offense with which he was charged, he could not learn the names of the witnesses who denounced him. If a witness who testified against the accused retracted his testimony, he was subject to punishment, but his evidence stood.

If the accused confessed and denounced relatives or friends, he became reconciled to the church and escaped the extreme penalties. If he did not, he was to be subjected to torture, which was officially approved by the church in the bull *Ad extirpanda* issued by Pope Innocent IV in 1252. In addition, it was permissible for the Inquisitor to torture witnesses in order to obtain evidence against the accused. There was, of course, no lawyer for the defense; anyone daring to defend the accused would himself have been held guilty of heresy.

In view of this procedure, it is hardly surprising that no one was ever acquitted. Indeed, though the authoritative textbook for Inquisitors set forth a formula for complete acquittal, it warned that the formula should never or very rarely be employed. Trial was inevitably followed by sentence, which ranged from penances and fasting to life imprisonment and death by fire. Serious punishment always was accompanied by confiscation of the accused's property for division between the secular authorities and the church; and the operation of the Inquisition became highly profitable for both prince and pontiff.

The Inquisition was at its worst in Spain. In its inception it was aimed not at heretics but at the many new Christians who, to escape the wholesale massacres which were endemic in Spain, had relinquished the Mohammedan and Jewish religions and accepted baptism. Many of these, the Jews particularly, were suspected of practicing their old religion in the secrecy of their cellars. In addition, many of them were rich in worldly goods, and their possessions were tempting to both church and state.

Established by Ferdinand and Isabella in 1480, the Spanish Inquisition grew more powerful than any other, and acquired a large degree of autonomy and independence of Rome. When its scope was extended from the new Christians to heretics, it even instituted heresy proceedings against bishops and archbishops. Later it turned its attention to Protestants, and in 1560 three Protestants, two English and one French, were burned at the stake. The Spanish Inquisition lasted centuries longer than any other. As late as 1781 it caused heretics to be burnt at the stake, and it was not finally abolished until 1834.[78]

## THE REFORMATION

Protestants are wont to ascribe to the Reformation the rise of religious liberty, and its acceptance as the principle governing the relations between a democratic state and its citizens. It would be far more accurate to say that the same causes that gave rise to the Protestant revolution also resulted in the widespread acceptance of the principle of religious liberty, and ultimately of the principle of separation of church and state. Certainly it would be inaccurate to say that the leaders of the Reformation were great champions of religious liberty. William Warren Sweet expressed it thus:

> There is a widespread notion among Protestant groups that the separation of Church and State, and thus religious liberty, was one of the immediate products of the Reformation, that the early Protestants were

22

advocates of a large tolerance, and that religious liberty was but the logical development of the principles held by all of the reformers. Just where this notion arose is difficult to say, and no reputable historian of our times would endorse it. The fact is that the rise of Protestantism was accompanied by an unprecedented outburst of intolerance and cruelty in which both Protestants and Catholics participated.[79]

Pleas for tolerance and freedom of conscience can undoubtedly be found in the writings of Luther and Calvin; but, as with Augustine, they were made while the dogma of the pleader was straining for acceptance and had not yet achieved the status of orthodoxy. The situation was best epitomized by John Robinson, pastor of the Pilgrims, who said

> Protestants living in the countries of papists commonly plead for toleration of religions: so do papists that live where Protestants bear sway: though few of either, especially of the clergy . . . would have the other tolerated, where the world goes on their side.[80]

Luther, when he was expecting excommunication and assassination, pleaded that

> Princes are not to be obeyed when they command submission to superstitious errors, but their aid is not to be invoked in support of the Word of God.

Heretics, he said, must be converted by the Scriptures, and not by fire.[81] With passion he asserted:

> I say, then, neither pope, nor bishop, nor any man whatever has the right of making one syllable binding on a Christian man, unless it be done with his own consent. Whatever is done otherwise is done in the spirit of tyranny. . . . I cry aloud on behalf of liberty and conscience, and I proclaim with confidence that no kind of law can with any justice be imposed on Christians, except so far as they themselves will; for we are free from all.[82]

When, however, he had made an effective alliance with the secular powers and was no longer the hunted heretic, his tone was entirely different.

> Heretics are not to be disputed with, but to be condemned unheard, and whilst they perish by fire, the faithful ought to pursue the evil to its source, and bathe their hands in the blood of the Catholic bishops, and of the Pope, who is a devil in disguise.[83]

No government, he argued, could tolerate heresy without being responsible for the souls seduced by it. The mass and monastic life must be suppressed by the state, for it was unlawful to connive at error.

> It will lie heavy on your conscience [he wrote to the Duke of Saxony]

23

if you tolerate the Catholic worship; for no secular prince can permit his subjects to be divided by the preaching of opposite doctrines.[84]

Luther's disciple, Melanchthon, like his master, also opposed at first the use of severe methods against dissenters, but later repented of his earlier clemency. He taught that dissenting sects ought to be put down by the sword, and that any person who started new opinions ought to be punished with death. The state is morally obligated to persecute heretics, not because of the danger to the state arising out of a religiously divided population, but because dissent from orthodoxy is a crime, which is to be declared by the clergy and punished by the prince.[85]

It is to be noticed that the theocratic element — the use of state as an engine to further religion — is stronger in Melanchthon than in Luther. Luther felt that unity among the peoples in the interests of the state was an important consideration. He directed his ministers to keep out of Catholic territory, so as not to interfere with religious unity. He went even further: he declared that the German Protestant princes had no right to resist the Catholic emperor in defense of their religion, since it was "the duty of a Christian to suffer wrong, and no breach of oath or of duty could deprive the Emperor of his right to the unconditional obedience of his subjects."[86]

With Melanchthon, on the other hand, the suppression of error, not the promotion of unity, was the principal duty of government. His view of the relationship of church and state was stated by Lord Acton in these words:

> ... The government of the Church being administered by the civil magistrates, it was their office also to enforce the ordinances of religion; and the same power whose voice proclaimed religious orthodoxy and law held in its hand the sword by which they were enforced. No religious authority existed except through the civil power. The Church was merged in the State; but the laws of the State, in return, were identified with the commandments of religion.[87]

The theocratic motivation was also strong in Zwingli. He conceived of the state as possessing spiritual functions; its foremost duty was the preservation and promotion of the true religion. Civil rulers were bound to establish uniformity of doctrine, and to defend it against papists and heretics. Rulers who did not act in accordance with this duty violated the condition of their office and must be removed.[88]

The theocratic element was strongest in Calvin. Like Augustine and Luther, some tolerance is found in his early writings. The church, he said,

has no power of the sword to punish or to coerce, no authority to compel, no prisons, fines, or other punishments, like those inflicted by the
civil magistrate. Besides, the object of this power is, not that he who has
transgressed may be punished against his will, but that he may profess
his repentance by a voluntary submission to chastisement. The difference therefore is very great; because the Church does not assume to
itself what belongs to the magistrate, nor can the magistrate execute
that which is executed by the Church.[89]

But when he established his theocracy in Geneva, the situation
was entirely different. In his "community of saints," absence from
the sermon was a crime, and to miss partaking of the Sacrament was
penalized by banishment for a year. Criticism of the clergy was included in the crime of blasphemy, and blasphemy was punishable by
death. Indeed, according to Calvin and his close associate Beza, denial that blasphemy is punishable by death was itself the equivalent
of blasphemy.

Whoever shall now contend that it is unjust to put heretics and blasphemers to death, will, knowingly and willingly, incur their very guilt.
This is not laid down on human authority; it is God that speaks and
prescribes a perpetual rule for His Church.[90]

In his passion to extirpate heresy, Calvin did not hesitate to
cooperate with the Inquisition. When Servetus, the anti-Trinitarian
Anabaptist, was tried by the Inquisition in France, Calvin furnished
the Inquisitors with evidence that helped to secure his condemnation. Servetus escaped to Geneva, where he was denounced by Calvin and sentenced to death by the town council.[91]

There were some voices, however, heard in the cause of religious
liberty. These often belonged to persons who never graduated
from heresy to orthodoxy; but their sentiments were occasionally
expressed by adherents of the accepted faith. Erasmus, who belonged
to the Renaissance rather than the Reformation and remained a
Catholic all his life, wrote:

The terrible papal edict, the more terrible imperial edict, the impris-
onments, the confiscations, the recantations, the fagots and burnings,
all these things I can see accomplish nothing except to make the evil
more widespread.[92]

Castellio, a follower of Erasmus, condemned Calvin for his part in
the burning of Servetus. He argued that "to force conscience is
worse than cruelly to kill a man," and that by persecution or violence
"one can no more build the church than one can construct a wall
with cannon blasts."[93]

Ardent advocates of religious liberty were also to be found
among the minority or dissident sects. The Anabaptists, persecuted

25

and despised, taught the supremacy and freedom of the individual conscience. So did the Socinians (Unitarians) and the Friends or Quakers, founded by George Fox in the 17th century. The English Baptists, organizing their church in Amsterdam, proclaimed that

> The magistrate is not to meddle with religion or matters of conscience, nor compel men to this or that form of religion.

A petition presented by a Baptist to James I in 1614 stated:

> Kings and magistrates are to rule temporal affairs by the swords of their temporal kingdoms, and bishops and ministers are to rule spiritual affairs by the Word and Spirit of God, the sword of Christ's spiritual kingdom, and not to intermeddle one with another's authority, office, and function. . . . It is not only unmerciful, but unnatural and abominable, yea, monstrous, for one Christian to vex and destroy another for difference and questions of religion.[94]

Three fairly distinguishable rationalizations of church-state relations can thus be seen arising out of the Reformation: the Erastian (after the German doctor Erastus), the theocratic, and the separatist. The first was predicated on the assumption of state superiority in ecclesiastical affairs and the use of religion to further state policy. The second was based on ecclesiastical supremacy and the use of state machinery to further religious interests. The third, which was to receive its ultimate and complete expression in the New World, is nevertheless clearly discernible in its incipient form in the arguments of some of the dissident minorities that the civil magistrate may not intermeddle in religious affairs.

The premise, espoused by Luther and articulated most extensively and cogently by Hobbes, that civic cohesion could not exist without religious unity and that coercion to achieve religious unity was justifiable, was of course an expansion of Erastian philosophy. The Peace of Augsburg of 1555, whereby Lutherans and Catholics in the German states effected a compromise according to the formula (*cujus regio, ejus religio*) whereby the religion of a province was determined by the religion of its prince, was based on the same Erastian concept. So too, basically, was the Peace of Westphalia, which in 1648 brought an end to the terrible thirty years of religious war, and extended, in a somewhat modified form, the Augsburg principle to Calvinist states.[95] Indeed, with the exception of Calvin's theocratic Geneva, Erastianism pervaded all Europe after the Reformation.

The extent to which religion was considered a servant of state policy can be seen from the action of Henry IV of France, who, though originally a Protestant, became a Catholic in order to rule peaceably a country which was predominantly Catholic. Even

Henry's Edict of Nantes, which, while sanctioning the dominant position of Catholicism in France, assured the Huguenots of security, admission to public office, freedom of conscience, and the right to worship publicly in specified regions, was a manifestation of the same Erastian principle.[96]

The Edict of Nantes was condemned by Pope Clement VIII as "the most accursed thing that can be imagined, whereby liberty of conscience is granted to everybody, which is the worst thing in the world." Under Henry's successors, the limited freedom conferred by the Edict was further limited by successive measures; and in 1685 the Edict was completely revoked by Louis XIV, and a campaign of forced conversion was instituted against the Huguenots.[97] The persecution of Protestants in France finally abated when the Edict was revived in a somewhat less liberal form in 1787 on the eve of the French Revolution.[98]

In England, perhaps more than any other country, Erastianism achieved its greatest triumph. The extent of this triumph and of the use of religion as an engine to further state policy is indicated by a statute enacted by Parliament in 1678, which, to encourage the woolen trade, imposed on all clergymen the duty of seeing to it that no person was buried in a shroud made of any substance other than wool.[99] The breach with Rome effected by Henry VIII was motivated by practical considerations, not theological differences. On the contrary, he sought to retain practically all of Catholicism except the Pope. In 1539 he had Parliament enact the "Bloody Statute," which declared the doctrine of transubstantiation to be the faith of the Church of England, and made denial of the doctrine punishable by burning at the stake and confiscation of goods. It also forbade the marriage of priests, and enjoined private masses and auricular confession. The Reformation really was effected in England under Henry's children, Edward VI and Elizabeth. It was in Elizabeth's reign that the thirty-nine Articles of the Church of England were adopted and English Protestantism reached its present doctrinal status.[100]

Under Elizabeth the supremacy of the crown over the church was complete. Ecclesiastical offices were regulated by her proclamations, which concerned themselves with such purely ecclesiastical matters as the inclusion of music and singing in the Common Prayer and the texture of the bread used in communion.[101] In the early years of Elizabeth's reign recusants were fined and imprisoned, and Jesuits and proselyting priests were subject to death for high treason.[102] Later a temporary settlement of the bloody conflicts among

Catholics, Anglicans, and Reformers was effected, whereby recusants were permitted to indulge in private worship but were deprived of certain civil rights. In the 17th century, however, both Catholics and nonconformist Protestants came to be looked on with increasing suspicion, not only as opponents of the established Anglican church but as a menace to the political order. An important milestone was the constitution established by Cromwell in 1647, which granted full liberty to all Protestant sects, but denied any toleration to Catholics.[103]

The 1647 constitution, supplemented by another constitutional instrument in 1653, provided for a national profession of Christianity, with instruction "in a public way, so it be not compulsive." Error and heresy were to be met only by the spiritual work of a clergy maintained in such a manner as Parliament might determine.[104]

But the constitution made no provision for Catholics. Cromwell's attitude toward their worship is well indicated by his reply to an Irish town which offered to surrender if the inhabitants should be permitted liberty of conscience:

> For that which you mention concerning liberty of conscience, I meddle not with any man's conscience. But if by liberty of conscience you mean a liberty to exercise the mass, I judge it best to use plain dealing, and to let you know, where the Parliament of England have power, that will not be allowed of. . . .[105]

Cromwell's position on religious liberty has been summarized by a historian in these words:

> In Cromwell we discover fused in a peculiar amalgam the sectarian devotion to religious liberty on the grounds of moral right, the lay distrust of clerical bigotry, the latitudinarian conviction that all Christians who profess the fundamentals of the faith are in a substantial unity, and the Erastian determination to preserve to mankind the benefits of intellectual and spiritual freedom through the restraint of clerical arrogance.[106]

During the reign of Charles II, the Declaration of Indulgence issued in 1672 benefited Protestant dissenters, and to some extent even Catholics; and testified to a growing conviction that a cessation of religious oppression was necessary both for internal peace and the interests of commerce, because a large section of the trading class was affiliated with the nonconformist sects. The logical outcome of this conviction was the Act of Toleration issued by William III in 1689, which established a *de facto* toleration for all except Catholics.[107] Religious liberty was not achieved by Catholics until the 19th century, when the Test Acts were repealed and the Roman Catholic

Relief Act of 1829 was adapted. It was not achieved by the Jews until 1858, when they were finally permitted to sit in Parliament.[108]

On the Continent, the enlightened despotism of Joseph II gave to the Austrian dominions, including the Austrian Netherlands and Lombardy, the Patent of Toleration of 1781, which, though it kept Catholicism as the official religion, granted limited rights of worship and civil liberties to dissenting sects. In the Prussia of Frederick II, the territorial law of 1794 guaranteed equal and full civil privileges to the Reformed, the Lutheran, and the Catholic faiths, but withheld from other religious bodies the right to public worship and legal recognition.[109]

In summary, the situation of church-state relations in Europe in 1787, when the representatives of the American States met in Philadelphia to lay the constitutional foundation for the new republic, was briefly this: the theocratic state, which had flourished intermittently in Israel, Judea, the Holy Roman Empire, and Geneva, had completely disappeared. On the other hand, no nation had yet adopted as the basis of its church-state relationship the principle of the mutual independence of religion and political government and the concomitant principle that neither might be used as an engine to further the policies of the other; although expressions of that principle in its first stages were occasionally voiced by dissident sects, and later by the intellectual leaders of 18th century enlightenment. The prevailing rationalization of church-state relationships in Europe in 1781 was Erastianism, and the practical expression of that rationalization was the system of jurisdictionalism which prevailed all over Europe, under which one faith was favored as the official state-supported religion, but other faiths were permitted to exist with varying degrees of freedom.

Individual liberty of worship varied from country to country. Most liberal was Holland, where since the 17th century wide freedom had been allowed all sects, and which became an asylum for the persecuted of all European countries. At the other extreme was Spain, where the Inquisition was still a reality in 1787 and the spirit of medieval intolerance was far from extinguished.

The religious wars which plagued Europe during the 16th and 17th centuries were a matter of history when America declared its independence from the Old World, but their memory was still vivid in the minds of the Constitutional Fathers. As the United States Supreme Court has expressed it:

> The centuries immediately before and contemporaneous with the colonization of America had been filled with turmoil, civil strife, and

persecution, generated in large part by established sects determined to maintain their absolute political and religious supremacy. With the power of government supporting them, at various times and places, Catholics had persecuted Protestants, Protestants had persecuted Catholics, Protestant sects had persecuted other Protestant sects, Catholics of one shade of belief had persecuted Catholics of another shade of belief, and all of these had from time to time persecuted Jews. In efforts to force loyalty to whatever religious group happened to be on top and in league with the government of a particular time and place, men and women had been fined, cast in jail, cruelly tortured, and killed. Among the offenses for which these punishments had been inflicted were such things as speaking disrespectfully of the views of ministers of government-established churches, non-attendance at those churches, expressions of non-belief in their doctrines, and failure to pay taxes and tithes to support them.[110]

James Madison, in 1784, cried out:

Torrents of blood have been spilt in the world in vain attempts of the secular arm to extinguish religious discord, by proscribing all differences in religious opinions.[111]

This statement of Madison epitomizes the entire history of church-state relations in Europe up to the time our Constitution was adopted. It points up sharply the two salient features of that history: (1) With minor exceptions, the history of church-state relationships was a history of persecution, oppression, hatred, bloodshed, and war, all in the name of the God of Love and of the Prince of Peace. (2) With equally minor exceptions, that history was the history of the unscrupulous use of religion by secular powers to promote their purposes and policies, and the willing acceptance of that role by the guardians of religion in exchange for the favors and mundane benefits which ambitious princes and imperialistic emperors conferred in exchange for religion's invaluable service. With this background in mind, we can better appreciate the unique experiment launched by the generation which saw the birth of American constitutional democracy.

### CHAPTER TWO

# The Solution in Other Countries

A TRUE APPRECIATION of the uniqueness and significance of America's solution of the competing claims of church and state requires some knowledge not only of the Old World antecedents of the American experiment, but also of the solution arrived at in the other countries of the world. It is for that reason that a chapter on present-day church-state relationships outside the United States is included in this study of the American experiment.

Logically, this chapter belongs at the end of the book, since the solutions arrived at in many of the countries of the world have been deeply influenced by the birth and evolution of the American principle. Convenience, however, dictates that it be placed here, enclosed as it were in an imaginary great parenthesis.

## COUNTRIES IN THE CATHOLIC TRADITION

### Spain

Church-state relations in Spain are governed by (1) the decree of the Franco government which in 1939 annulled the Law of Religious Confessions and Congregations enacted by the Republic government in 1933 and other measures relating to secularization, expropriation, and freedom of worship; and (2) a concordat entered into in 1953 between the Holy See and the Franco government, affirming the earlier accord between them. The preamble of the 1939 law asserts that the 1933 measure was based on the false premise of a plurality of religious confessions in Spain, whereas the Catholic religion is the only one existing in Spain for many centuries.[1] (According to the Spanish Ministry of Information, Protestants in Spain are less than one-third of one per cent of the total population.[2] Today there are approximately 26,000 Protestants and 1,000 Jews out of a total population of about 30 million.[3])

The accord with the Holy See reaffirmed four articles of the concordat of 1851: (1) Catholicism continues to be the sole religion of the Spanish nation, to the exclusion of any other, and is to be maintained "with all the rights and privileges which it should have in accordance with God's law and the prescriptions of the sacred canons." (2) Instruction in all government schools must conform to the doctrines of the Catholic religion as determined by the bishops and their aides, who therefore shall have full and free supervision over the purity of faith and customs and the religious education of youth. (3) The clergy shall be accorded respect and protection, and shall receive necessary support when they request it to combat "the iniquity of men who attempt to pervert the souls of the faithful and to corrupt customs," or to prevent the publication or circulation of harmful or evil books. (4) In all other matters relative to the exercise of ecclesiastical authority, and the ministry of holy orders, the bishops and clergy shall enjoy full liberty according to the sacred canons.[4]

Spokesmen for the Catholic Church in America and representatives of the Spanish government here bitterly deny that Protestants or other non-Catholics are "persecuted" in Spain.[5] There can be little doubt, however, and indeed it is hardly denied that Protestants and other non-Catholics in Spain do not enjoy full religious liberty. (Nor, for that matter, do Catholics.) The extent to which their religious liberty is restricted is subject to considerable dispute. What is presented here is this writer's estimate of the actual situation in Spain today on the basis of reports from Catholic, Protestant, and secular sources.

Non-Catholics' rights of worship are based on Article VI of *Fuero de los Españoles*, known as the "Spanish Charter," which was issued in July 1945, and reads:

> The profession and practice of the Catholic religion, which is that of the Spanish State, shall enjoy official protection. None shall be molested for their religious beliefs or the private practices of their worship. No other ceremonies or external demonstrations than those of the Catholic religion shall be permitted.[6]

Under the law, as it has been applied in actual practice, Protestants are not persecuted by the government, at least not in the sense of that term as understood in the light of the history of the Spanish Inquisition. Protestants may assemble for worship in their churches, without hindrance from the government. The services are well attended; the singing is full-voiced, and no sense of secrecy attends the meetings.[7]

There can be no doubt that the Spanish bishops consider Protestantism an evil; in 1949 *Ecclesia,* a Catholic publication, said: "The objective right to profess a false religion does not exist";[8] and the vandalism against Protestant chapels which broke out in 1947 and 1948 can be justifiably attributed in large part to the inflammatory pastoral letter of Cardinal Segura of Seville in September 1947.[9] On the other hand, there is no evidence that these riots were instigated or approved by the government. On the contrary, some of the persons responsible were arrested, indemnity was provided by the government, and guards were placed around the chapels to protect them.[10] Indeed, Cardinal Segura, in another pastoral letter, bitterly complained that the government was censoring his ecclesiastical statements denouncing Protestant activities in Spain.[11] The effectiveness of these measures is attested by the fact that the acts of vandalism appear to have ceased,[12] except for one incident in Seville in February of 1952.[13] At that time Cardinal Segura engaged in a bitter controversy with the government over its alleged failure to take sufficiently vigorous action against Protestants.[14] His criticism of the Franco government on this score appears even then to have evoked little sympathy from the Vatican, the Catholic Church in America, or even a substantial section of that Church in Spain.[15]

Protestant ministers have freedom of the pulpit, and do not feel themselves under restraint as to what they may preach. Seminarians may be trained for the ministry, and Protestant children may receive religious instruction in their Sunday schools. Protestants may print religious books for their own use, and in general may do whatever acts come under the head of the private practice of their religion.[16]

But conversely, Protestants may not perform any acts which can be considered the public exercise of their religion. Protestant chapels may not display any exterior evidence that they are places of worship. They may not advertise their existence—not even by a bulletin board. They may not be listed in the public directories,[17] and generally must be situated in narrow side streets. They may not publish or import Bibles or other religious books for general circulation, and they must secure special permits to print such books for their own use. They may not open new churches or reopen closed ones without specific license, which may be, and are, refused without stated reason.[18] Public religious demonstrations, proselytizing, and propagandizing are forbidden.[19] A statement issued by the foreign ministry in September 1952, declared:

> Neither the Bill of Rights, basic constitutional charter of the Spanish people, nor our concordat with the Holy See gives the government power to authorize Protestant proselytism. . . .[20]

Protestants may not conduct schools (other than Sunday schools) for their own children.[21] Protestant children must attend Catholic schools or public schools, and even if they attend the latter they are required to receive instruction in the Catholic religion,[22] and must take part in mass.[23]

33

Marriages performed by Protestant ministers have no legal recognition. Catholic religious ceremony is obligatory on all Catholics. For many years civil marriage was permissible only if the parties produced documents proving that they had never been baptized as Catholics. If they were baptized but were thereafter converted to Protestantism, they could not have a civil marriage without the permission of the local priest.[24] However, in 1955, the Madrid Court of Appeals ruled that Catholics might contract valid civil marriages if they could prove conclusively that they had abandoned the Roman Catholic faith,[25] and in 1961 this privilege was extended to Protestants.[26] Protestants face difficulties in burying their dead with religious services in civil cemeteries;[27] nor may they hold official positions in the government or rise to officer rank in the army unless they conceal their religious beliefs.[28] Attendance at mass is compulsory for all officers and soldiers in the armed forces.[29]

Jews in Spain are regarded as less of a menace than Protestants, but are subject to substantially the same restrictions of their religious liberty. Private worship is unrestricted, but public worship and exterior signs on synagogues are forbidden. Official permits to open new synagogues are required, and these are frequently withheld.[30] In Barcelona, Jews are not permitted to bury their dead, but are required to seal their bodies in vaults in a wall maintained at one side of the civil cemetery; in Madrid this condition does not prevail—the civil cemetery is divided into two parts for Protestants and Jews.[31]

Catholicism is the favored religion of the Spanish government. Franco has restored the benefices of the clergy and religious teaching in the schools. He has rebuilt burnt churches, established new seminaries, and reopened and expanded charitable institutions.[32] But in Spain, as everywhere, religion must pay a price for governmental favor.

It is obvious that Catholics in Spain do not enjoy religious liberty—certainly if the term "Catholic" includes, as it does under Spanish law, everyone ever baptized as a Catholic who has not formally adopted another religion. But beyond that, the Church is subject to restrictions and control which would not be contemplated and, of course, would be completely unconstitutional in America, where it is separated from the state and receives no state favor or aid. Neither the Federal nor any State government in the United States would even consider suppressing a mass, as did the "Catholic" government of Spain in 1950.[33]

Franco exercises vast powers over church organizations. Not only does he receive an oath of submission from the bishops, but he effectively exercises the right to appoint them. By agreement with the Vatican, Franco submits to the Vatican six candidates for any episcopal vacancy. The Pope has the right to veto three, and Franco fills the vacancy from the remaining three. Franco has been able to gain increasing control over the bishops, as one by one their sees become vacant.[34] It is probable that the Vatican's long-time reluctance to enter into a concordat with the Franco government was based on its dissatisfaction with this arrangement, although a concordat was entered into in 1953.[35]

The libertarianism of Pope John XXIII affected Spain perhaps less than any other part of the Roman Catholic world; yet even here it exerted some influence. A number of Protestant places of worship, which had been closed in previous years,[36] were reopened.[37] A Baptist congregation in Madrid was permitted to post outside its chapel door notices giving the times of services.[38] A draft law that would give Protestants somewhat greater freedom was approved by Spain's twelve Roman Catholic archbishops.[39] However, the progress has been slow and small, almost to the point of being negligible. At the present writing the draft law, modest in its terms, has still not been enacted, and the Spanish hierarchy seems to have drawn back from any all-out endorsement of the measure.[40] That restrictions on religious liberty in Spain will be affected and ameliorated as a consequence of the Vatican Council's Declaration on Religious Liberty may be assumed. It is yet, however, too early to predict when and to what extent this will come about. There are today what appear to be growing tensions between the Spanish Church and the Franco government, and these too are likely to influence church-state relations in that country. All that can safely be said now is that there is today considerably less religious liberty in Spain than in any other Western nation.

### Portugal

Portugal, like Spain, is a Catholic nation in the sense that its population is overwhelmingly Catholic, but its solution of the church-state problem is radically different. The relations between the Catholic Church and the Portuguese state are regulated by the 1933 constitution as amended in 1951 and by the 1940 concordat with the Vatican.

The relevant sections of the constitution provide:

The public or private practice of the Catholic faith is free, as the religion of the Portuguese nation. The Catholic Church enjoys juridical existence and may organize in conformity with canonical right, and in this conformity form associations or organizations whose juridical existence is also recognized.

The State maintains the regime of separation from the Catholic Church without prejudice to the relations between the Holy See and Portugal, with reciprocal representation, and with the concordats and agreements . . . which are or may be drawn up concerning matters of common interest.

The principle of separation, liberty of faith and of organization and recognition of the juridical existence of religious associations constituted in conformity with the norms of hierarchy and discipline in the respective faiths, are applicable to the other religions or faiths practiced within Portuguese territory.

Solely excepted from the above are all practice of religious bodies incompatible with the life and physical integrity of the human individual and with good morals, and the diffusion of doctrines contrary to the established social order.[41]

Though the constitution refers to a "regime of separation from the Catholic Church," that "separation" is subject to the state's concordats with the Vatican, and under the 1940 concordat it is clear that church and state are not separated in Portugal, at least not as Americans understand the term. Churches, seminaries, and ecclesiastics in the performance of their sacred office are exempt from taxation. Ecclesiastics in the exercise of their ministry enjoy state protection as if they were public officials. Persons married in accordance with canon law may not be divorced civilly. Bishops, priests, and seminary heads must be Portuguese citizens. The names of proposed bishops must be submitted by the Holy See to the government thirty days before appointment so as to enable it to file objections to the nominations.

The concordat provides for church schools of general education subsidized and fully recognized by the state.[42] Therefore an educational reform bill enacted in 1949 was amended expressly to exclude church schools. One of the deleted provisions would have required priest-teachers to obtain normal professional diplomas before being permitted to teach literature, science, or other specialized subjects. Also rejected by the national assembly was a clause subjecting church schools to government inspection of their teaching, sanitation, and hygienic conditions.[43]

The concordat also confers on the church important powers with respect to education in the public schools. The concordat provides:

The teaching administered by the State in public schools shall be guided by the principles of Christian doctrine and morals traditional to the country. Therefore, the Catholic religion and Catholic morals will be taught in public elementary, complementary, and intermediate schools to pupils whose parents or guardians have not lodged a request to the contrary. . . .

For the teaching of the Catholic religion, the textbooks employed must be passed by the ecclesiastical authorities, and the teachers will be appointed by the State in agreement with the said authorities. In no case shall religious instruction be given by persons not approved by the ecclesiastical authorities as competent.[44]

That the benefits the church receives from the Portuguese government are not gratuitous can be seen not only in the government's participation in the selection of bishops and other ecclesiastical officials but in the provisions of the Colonial Act, which declares that "Portuguese Catholic missions overseas" are "an instrument of civilization and national influence."[45] It is hardly to be expected that a state which confers its favors on a particular church will be able to resist using that church to further its own imperial interests.

*Italy*

Religion in relationship to the Italian state is theoretically governed by the 1947 constitution of Italy. The relevant sections of the constitution provide:

Article 8: All religious confessions are equally free before the law.

Religious confessions other than the Catholic have the right to organize according to their own statutes, insofar as they do not conflict with the Italian juridical order.

Their relationships with the state are regulated by law on the basis of agreement with the appropriate representatives.

Article 19: All have the right freely to profess their own religious faith in whatever form, individual or collective; to propagate it and to conduct worship in private or in public, provided this does not involve rites contrary to morality.

Article 20: The ecclesiastical character and religious purpose or the purpose of worship of an association or institution may not be the cause of special legislative restrictions or of special fiscal burdens upon its constitution, its legal capacity, or any form of its activity.[46]

But the constitution also ratifies and adopts the Lateran Treaty and Concordat entered into by Pope Pius XI and Benito Mussolini in 1929. Article 7 of the constitution reads:

The state and the Catholic Church are, each in its own order, independent and sovereign.

Their relationships are regulated by the Lateran Pacts.

Modifications of the pacts, which have been accepted by the two parties, do not require the procedure of constitutional amendment.[47]

The adoption of the Lateran Pacts as part of the new constitution was opposed by the Protestant and Jewish minorities in Italy, and was effected only because the Communists in the Assembly, in an attempt to win the peasant vote by giving the impression that they were not anticlerical, joined the right wing parties in voting for the adoption.[48] The concordat, which in its first article provides that "Italy recognizes the Catholic Religion as the sole religion of the State,"[49] had been originally signed by the atheist Mussolini and was thus reaffirmed by the atheistic Communist party. When it is remembered that in 1933 Hitler's antireligious Nazi government also entered into a concordat with the Vatican,[50] it becomes clear that neither the totalitarianism of the right nor the totalitarianism of the left is above using religion to further its political purposes.

It is obvious that the establishment of Catholicism as the state religion of Italy by the concordat is inconsistent with the provision in the constitution guaranteeing equality to all sects without discrimination. The Italian courts have therefore ruled that the guarantee of equality in Article 8 must be interpreted in the light of the special preferred status conferred on the Catholic Church by Article 7 and the concordat.[51] Accordingly, only Catholic priests receive a regular nontaxable salary from the government; Protestant pastors not only receive no financial help from the government but must pay income taxes on their salaries.[52] Catholic institutions, but not Protestant, are likewise exempt from taxation, and insults to Catholicism, but not to other faiths, are punishable offenses.[53]

Each Protestant group must be recognized by the government before it can establish churches, and a Protestant church may be opened for worship only after special authorization is obtained from the ministry of the interior. Protestant pastors require the interior ministry's permission to practice in authorized churches. No such authorizations are required for Catholic worship.[54]

Probably the gravest act of discrimination on the part of the postwar government in Italy was its denial of official recognition to the Pentecostal group. Mussolini dissolved the Pentecostal Church, banned its services, and arrested Pentecostals who continued to worship clandestinely. At the end of World War II the Pentecostals applied for recognition, but after six years of dilatory tactics, the interior ministry in 1951 finally rejected the application.[55] Later the Church of Christ was the victim. The government has ordered it to close all its missions in the country, and the police barred the missionaries from conducting religious services in their churches.[56] After considerable protest in the United States and a plea by Protestants for American government intervention, and, most important, several significant libertarian decisions by Italy's constitutional High Court,[57] some amelioration has manifested itself. Nevertheless, the position of this sect as well as other non-Catholic faiths in Italy is by no means secure.

Under the concordat, a non-Catholic may not obtain a divorce in Italy. Under Article 34 an annulment may be granted by an ecclesiastical tribunal, but only to Catholics. The concordat provides also that excommunicated or apostate priests may not receive any government employment which brings them into direct contact with the public.[58]

In a letter sent by Pope Pius XI to the then Cardinal Gasparri shortly after the adoption of the Lateran Pacts, the Pope stated fully and emphatically his interpretation of their provisions. In respect to the provision regarding cults "tolerated, permitted or admitted" in Italy, he stated that:

> the words, "permitted or admitted" are acceptable, provided there is loyal understanding of these words, provided further that it be and remain clearly and loyally understood that the Catholic religion, and it only in accordance with the statute and the Treaty, is the religion of the State with all the consequences logical and juridical deriving from such a situation under constitutional law, especially with regard to propaganda. . . .
>
> It is not admissible that the understanding is that there is to be absolute liberty of discussion including such discussions as might easily mislead the good faith of the less enlightened and readily degenerate into disguised propaganda, damaging to the religion of the State. . . .[59]

Acting on the basis of his interpretation, the Pope made repeated protests against the government's tolerance of Protestant propaganda carried on throughout Italy and in Rome itself as a violation of the concordat.[60] More recently, after World War II some Italian Catholics did not content themselves with protests. In January 1950 a group of young evangelists from Texas constituting the Church of Christ, who conducted Bible classes and a hospital in Rome, were stoned out of Castel Gondolfo, summer home of Pope Pius XII. One of the evangelists declared that "the priests aroused the people against" them,[61] but this was denied by Catholic Church sources.[62]

Probably the most important article of the concordat is Article 36, which deals with education. The article reads:

> Italy considers the teaching of Christian doctrine, according to the form handed down by Catholic tradition, as the foundation and capstone of public education. Therefore, Italy agrees that the religious instruction now given in the public elementary schools shall be further

developed in the secondary schools according to a program to be agreed upon by the Holy See and the State.

This instruction is to be given by teachers and professors who are priests or religious approved by ecclesiastical authority and who will be aided by lay teachers and professors holding for this purpose proper certificates of fitness and capacity, these certificates to be issued by the diocesan Bishop.

Revocation of the certificate by the Bishop immediately deprives the individual of the right to teach.

No texts will be adopted for this religious instruction in the public schools except such as are approved by ecclesiastical authority.[63]

Although the law permits parents to request that their children be exempted from religious instruction in the schools, the influence of the church frequently makes the privilege more theoretical than real;[64] and the Italian Jewish community has vainly appealed to the government to make religious instruction purely optional.[65] Moreover, Protestant children in the public schools are generally not allowed to receive religious instruction in their own faith, and public-school textbooks, based on Catholic principles, often contain references to Protestantism deemed offensive by Protestants.[66] The libertarianism of Pope John XXIII and the increased influence of the Socialists in the government has led to some amelioration of the situation, and in fact the Socialists were able in 1964 to defeat a Catholic sponsored bill for state financial aid to private schools.[67] Here, too, it may be assumed that the 1965 Declaration on Religious Liberty issued by Vatican II will further ameliorate the situation.

## *Ireland*

Ireland presents an instance of an overwhelmingly Catholic nation which in its constitution acknowledges the special position of the Catholic Church, and yet seeks both in constitution and in practice to grant freedom and equality to other faiths. Article 44 of the Irish constitution, entitled "Religion," provides:

1. (1) The State acknowledges that the homage of public worship is due to Almighty God. It shall hold His Name in reverence, and shall respect and honour religion.

    (2) The State recognises the special position of the Holy Catholic Apostolic and Roman Church as the guardian of the Faith professed by the great majority of the citizens.

    (3) The State also recognises the Church of Ireland, the Presbyterian Church in Ireland, the Methodist Church in Ireland, the Religious Society of Friends in Ireland, as well as the Jewish Congregations and the other religious denominations existing in Ireland at the date of the coming into operation of this Constitution.

2. (1) Freedom of conscience and the free profession and practice of religion are, subject to public order and morality, guaranteed to every citizen.

(2) The State guarantees not to endow any religion.

(3) The State shall not impose any disabilities or make any discrimination on the ground of religious profession, belief or status.

(4) Legislation providing State aid for schools shall not discriminate between schools under the management of different religious denominations, nor be such as to affect prejudicially the right of any child to attend a school receiving public money without attending religious instruction at that school.

(5) Every religious denomination shall have the right to manage its own affairs, own, acquire and administer property, movable and immovable, and maintain institutions for religious or charitable purposes.

(6) The property of any religious denomination or any educational institution shall not be diverted save for necessary works of public utility and on payment of compensation.[68]

It is true that the liberal provisions of this article were required by Article 16 of the 1921 treaty with England creating the Irish Free State, which provided that:

Neither the Parliament of the Irish Free State nor the Parliament of Northern Ireland shall make any law so as either directly or indirectly to endow any religion or prohibit the free exercise thereof or give any preference or impose any disability on account of religious belief or religious status, or affect prejudicially the right of any child to attend a school receiving public money without attending the religious instruction at the school, or make any discrimination as respects state aid between schools under the management of different religious denominations, or divert from any religious denomination or any educational institution any of its property except for public utility purposes and on payment of compensation.[69]

It is true also that Article 41 of the Irish constitution prohibits divorces even among non-Catholics, and that there have been complaints of other discriminatory treatment of Protestants,[70] particularly when the Irish courts ruled in 1950 that they would enforce a prenuptial agreement providing for the Catholic upbringing of the children of a mixed marriage and would therefore prevent the Protestant father from rearing the children in his own faith.[71] This decision was especially resented by Irish Protestants, in view of another decision by the Supreme Court of Ireland a few months earlier that the custody of the child of a mixed marriage was to be given to the Catholic father rather than the Protestant mother, because it could not otherwise guarantee that the child would be brought up as a Catholic in accordance with Irish law,[72] although the force of these decisions was somewhat weakened by a 1956 decision by the same court.[73]

41

On the whole, the available evidence indicates clearly that by and large Ireland has been faithful to the obligations undertaken in the treaty and constitution, and has not restricted the religious liberty or equality of non-Catholics.[74] Indeed, a resolution by the Westmeath County Council in February 1950, calling on the government to amend the constitution so as to put the Roman Catholic Church "on a plane above the man-made religions of the world," was roundly denounced and has been unheard of since that time.[75]

## Latin America

The present-day relations of Latin American governments to religion can be appreciated only with an understanding of the historic attitude of the Catholic Church to the revolutionary movements which swept South and Central America in the 19th and early 20th centuries. Colonization by Spain and Portugal brought to the southern American countries not only the Catholic culture and religion but also the Catholic Church, which almost everywhere became a wealthy and powerful institution among the ignorant, poverty-stricken masses. With the outbreak of revolutions against the established orders, it was natural that the Church should be identified with the oppressors, and its privileges greatly abridged or completely eliminated in the new system. Indeed, it may fairly be said that the status of the church in many Latin American countries stands in inverse proportion to the extent of the revolution in that country.

Mexico presents an extreme case; yet the factors that brought about its solution of the church-state problem were present to some degree in all the other countries. The revolutionary forces attributed to the church a large measure of responsibility for the underprivilege, illiteracy, and destitution of the masses. A report of the National Council of Evangelical Churches stated:

> The critics of religion in Mexico point significantly to the fact that, after more than three centuries of practically complete domination by the Church, the country came to the beginning of the present revolutionary period with a population eighty-five per cent illiterate and submerged in poverty. The pitiful condition of its multitude of believers contrasted eloquently with the wealth and power of organized religion as represented by the Church. Not only had the Church been guilty of neglecting educating the masses, but of opposing efforts put forth by the State and by other agencies in their behalf.[76]

The church itself had the largest interest in the established order; before the revolutionary reforms of Juarez in the second half of the 19th century, it may well have owned as much as one-fourth of all the wealth of Mexico.[77] The church moreover did not hesitate to use its religious influence and power in a vain attempt to prevent the disruption of the social and economic *status quo*. In 1921 the Archbishop of Jalisco, who directed the National Catholic Labor Foundation, admonished his flock in a pastoral letter:

> What poor are they upon whom God looks with compassion? Certainly not those poor who are discontented with their fate. . . . Much less are they the poor who envy the rich only because they are rich, and only await the time when they can fling themselves against them with lighted torch or fratricidal dagger in hand, with the vehement desire for an unjust distribution of riches. The Savior loves the poor who are resigned and submissive, long-suffering and patient; who have not put their desires in the things of this world, but who try to lay up treasure in heaven.[78]

With this background in mind, we can understand the antireligious campaign conducted by successive Mexican governments in the two decades after the adoption of the 1917 constitution. While the constitutional and statutory provisions do not specify the Catholic Church as the adversary, they are obviously directed at that Church. In 1935 the intersectarian American Committee on Religious Rights and Minorities sent a deputation to Mexico to investigate conditions in that country. Its report, based on the investigation, estimated that more than seventy-five per cent of the 16,000,000 Mexicans were Catholic; only 150,000 were Protestants and 16,000 Jews.[79] The Protestants generally supported wholeheartedly the revolutionary movement; their condition was immeasurably improved after 1917. Nevertheless, they too were restricted in the free exercise of their religion by the operation of the antireligious laws.[80]

The present Mexican constitution (promulgated in 1917) guarantees that

> Every man is free to profess the religious belief which is most pleasing to him and to practice the ceremonies, rites, or acts of the respective cult in places of worship or in his private residence.

But the same article (24) provides that

> Any religious rite of public worship shall be confined entirely within places of worship, which shall always be under the supervision of the authorities.[81]

The constitution also provides for the confiscation and nationalization of all church real property. Under Article 27,

> Religious associations called churches, whatever may be their belief,

in no case have the capacity to acquire, possess or administer real estate or capital invested therein; the properties that they hold at present directly or through some intermediary, shall pass to the domain of the Nation, the people allowed to denounce properties that they find in such case. . . . Churches being dedicated to public worship are the property of the Nation, represented by the federal Government, which shall determine those that should continue in use.[82]

By virtue of this article and the laws promulgated in 1926 to implement it, all churches, convents, and monasteries were nationalized by the mid-thirties. Although in most cases the confiscation and nationalization of title was only of symbolic significance, since the government permitted the church properties to continue to be used for worship, nevertheless, between 1931 and 1935, 266 churches and rectories were restrained from religious uses by decree of the president.[83]

Article 130 of the constitution provides that

Only the legislatures of the States shall have the power to determine the maximum number of ministers of denominations necessary to local needs.[84]

During the period from 1926 to 1935 legislatures in fifteen states either fixed the number of priests at one or two or entirely prohibited any priests from functioning. Before 1926 there were about 5,000 priests functioning in Mexico; by 1935 the number had been reduced to not much more than 200.[85]

The constitution forbids the establishment of monastic orders; it disqualifies the minister of any religious sect from becoming a deputy of congress or a senator; it disqualifies anyone belonging to an ecclesiastical body or a minister of any religious sect from becoming president. The law recognizes no corporate existence of the religious association known as a church; and ministers of religious creeds are considered persons exercising a profession, directly subject to the law governing the professions, and must be Mexican by birth. Clergymen may not criticize the fundamental laws of the country, the authorities, or the government, either in public or private. They are not entitled to vote or hold office, and may not wear clerical garb outside church premises. Religious publications may not comment on political affairs, nor may a political association have a name indicating any relation to any religious sect or belief.[86]

Restrictions on religious education are equally severe. The constitution not only prohibits religious instruction in state schools, but seeks to prohibit all religious education at the primary or secondary level in private as well as public schools. Article 3 of the constitution provides that private institutions at the primary, secondary, and normal educational level (and also any institution providing education for workers and peasants) "must . . . without exception" adjust their program so as to maintain "complete freedom from any religious doctrine." In addition, "religious corporations, ministers of faiths . . . and associations or societies connected with the propagation of any religious belief may not intervene in any form in any educational institutions in which is imparted primary, secondary or normal education and in those intended for workers and peasants."[87]

The constitution of 1917 and the laws of 1926 have not been substantially changed and modified; they are still the law of Mexico. Nevertheless, the year 1937 saw the beginning of a period of reconciliation between church and state. In that year Pope Pius XI appointed the leader of the liberal element in the Church as Archbishop of Mexico. In the following year the church expressed its complete support of the government program of expropriating foreign oil companies. In 1941 President Comacho protested that though public education "should be kept apart from all religious doctrines . . . it cannot be converted into an antireligious system."[88] In 1952 the government party's candidate for president compaigned on a platform that included the declaration that the "Religion of the people is sacred."[89]

The language of the antireligious laws has not been changed, but there have been great changes in their enforcement. There is a gentlemen's agreement between church and state not to cause provocations and not to enforce the legal provisions strictly. A number of church buildings that had been expropriated have been returned, though the exact number is not known. The seminaries have been reopened, and some of them are large and flourishing. Garbed clerics are seen in the public streets in small towns, and the government has contributed substantially to the construction of a large new plaza in front of the Shrine of Our Lady of Guadalupe. New churches are being built. Clergymen of varying denominations, priests, pastors, and missionaries, have come to Mexico from the United States and are working openly. There have been many religious parades and manifestations during recent years without anyone being punished. Private schools are teaching religious subjects. The situation has thus been summarized by Mexico's primate, Archbishop Martinez:

> The general state of affairs prevent formal reconciliation at the moment, but there is an understanding and an effort to get along on both sides.[90]

Peru represents the other pole from that on which Mexico stands. It is probably the Latin American country in which the Roman Catholic Church retains most influence and privilege. In the words of Mecham,[91] the Peruvian "system of interdependence of State and Church is one of the most comprehensive and absolute in Latin America." Even there the revolutionary movement left its imprint in constitutional provisions which disqualify clerics from holding the office of legislator (Article 100) or president (Article 137).[92] Nevertheless under the constitution Catholicism is the state religion (Article 232), and relations with the church are governed by a concordat with the Holy See (Article 234). "Other religions enjoy freedom for the exercise of their respective faiths" (Article 232), "Freedom of conscience and belief is inviolable," and "No one may be persecuted by reason of his ideas" (Article 59).[93]

Despite these guarantees, Peru requires mass every morning in all public schools. Non-Catholic children may be excused at the risk of ostracism and petty persecution. The Catholic religion must be taught in all schools, public and private, with textbooks approved by the hierarchy. According to Mecham, the "exclusive privilege of giving religious instruction in public schools virtually assigns the youth of the land to be cast in the Catholic mould." A decree of 1929 prohibited the teaching of non-Catholic faiths in any school, and required the teaching of Catholicism even in Protestant schools, though the efforts of the church to require such teaching in the Protestant schools to be done by Catholic teachers has apparently not yet succeeded. In many other respects the laws of Peru protect and confer special privileges on the Catholic Church, particularly in restrictions on non-Catholic proselytizing and propaganda.[94] When and to what extent this situation will be affected by the Vatican Council's Declaration on Religious Liberty remains to be seen.

The Catholic Church in Peru pays for the privileged status conferred on it by the state. The laws that protect it also regulate it. The constitution which makes it the state religion authorizes the state not only to create new archbishoprics and bishoprics, but also to suppress those already existing (Article 123). Archbishops and bishops "must be Peruvian by birth and shall be designated by the President of the Republic in the Council of Ministers. The chief of State shall make the presentation before the Holy See, and authorize the respective bulls" (Article 154).[95]

Chile and Cuba present Latin-American solutions of the church-state problems which most closely resemble the solution arrived at in the United States. Chile is neither antagonistic to religion like Mex-

46

ico, nor does it establish the Catholic Church as does Peru. Both the government and the people manifest a sincere respect for freedom of conscience, and missionaries of all faiths are protected and respected.[96]

Cuba, too, provides for the separation of church and state and complete religious freedom. Marriage is civil, and public education is secular. The religious education in private schools is guaranteed as a right, but may not receive government subsidies.[97] Under Castro there have been incidents of hostility, not only to the Catholic Church but also to some Protestant groups as well.[98] Despite this, on the whole, the basic relationship between church and state remains unchanged.[99]

These four countries, Mexico, Peru, Chile, and Cuba, represent the varying approaches which have been made in Latin America to arrive at a satisfactory solution of the conflicting claims of religion and government. The other countries follow more or less the patterns set by these four. Colombia, for example, is, like Peru, hostile to Protestant missionaries, who have been subject to suppression and oppression bordering on persecution.[100] In Argentina, Peron, after falling out with the Catholic Church, abolished tax exemption, certain religious holidays, religious teaching in government schools, and certain other privileges of the church.[101] His successor, however, restored most of these, although religious teaching is still not permitted in government schools.[102] Half of the twenty Latin American countries provide for church-state separation; the other half continue to confer a privileged status on the Roman Catholic Church. All twenty have constitutional provisions guaranteeing religious liberty, but there are wide variances among the countries in the extent to which these guarantees are honored in practice.

### Quebec

Canada is the only country in the Western Hemisphere whose constitution, the British North America Act of 1867, contains no guaranty of religious freedom. The constitution contains no provision guaranteeing any civil liberties, but leaves the protection of these rights to the individual provinces. None of the provinces, not even Quebec, has an established church in the strict sense; and outside Quebec, there is no serious problem of religious liberty, with the exception of the prevailing practice of conducting religious exercises and instruction in the public schools,[103] and some controversy in the western provinces on governmental support of Catholic schools.[104]

The province of Quebec stands in the Catholic tradition — Catholics outnumber Protestants almost six to one, and the Jewish minority is even smaller. The political authority of the Catholic hierarchy, the entrenched position of their schools in the public educational system, the subsidies that church welfare enterprises receive from the provincial treasury, amount to many aspects of a state church, though establishment in the literal sense is absent.[105] A few instances may be cited to show that this relationship tends toward the infringement of the religious freedom of non-Catholics, and even of Catholics.

In many of the cities and towns of the province, including Montreal and Quebec City, religious worship may not be conducted without a special permit. In Quebec City, in the 1930's and '40's, the Jews were prevented for more than ten years from building a much-needed new synagogue because of their inability to obtain permission from the City Council, and were ultimately compelled to sue to obtain the right to conduct synagogue service in an existing structure.[106] In Montreal in 1951 an immigrant rabbi from Hungary, who spoke neither French nor English, innocently conducted Sabbath services in his home on two Saturdays at which a dozen persons attended. He was prosecuted for violating a Montreal law requiring a special permit to use any building for worship. The rabbi was found guilty, as he obviously was, but justice was tempered with mercy and he received a suspended sentence.[107]

In 1951 the Montreal City Council adopted a law requiring retail stores, with certain exceptions, to remain closed on six Catholic holy days. Previously the law required closing only on Christmas and New Year's Day, but the 1951 law added Epiphany, Ascension, All Saints', and Immaculate Conception days. At the opening of the City Council meeting at which the resolution was adopted, copies of a letter from the archbishop to the mayor requesting its passage were distributed among the members of the Council.[108]

The action of the Montreal Council was protested by the Montreal Presbytery of the Presbyterian Church in Canada. One member of the Presbytery inquired whether the Protestants were not on shaky grounds in view of their own reliance on the civil law to compel Sunday observance by Jews and other non-Christians. The Presbytery, however, adopted a resolution stating that the law "cannot but lead to the destruction of equality in religion in this country and the erection of one body into the position of a State Church, if not in law, at least in fact." Perhaps to compensate the Jews, the Presbytery simultaneously adopted a resolution protesting the law under which the immigrant rabbi was convicted for holding religious services in his home.[109] A number of Protestant storekeepers decided to defy the law, and more than 500 of them opened their stores on Immaculate Conception Day, in December 1951, and more than 200 on Ascension Day in May 1952. Many of them were prosecuted, convicted, and fined, but their conviction was reversed by the Montreal Superior Court in June 1952, and the law declared an illegal infringement on the exclusive legislative power of the federal parliament.[110]

Ordinary nonreligious laws may also be used to restrict religious liberty. In the early 1950's the town of Val d'Or in Quebec prosecuted Baptist evangelists holding religious street meetings for obstructing traffic. By the end of October 1950, 37 arrests had been made and 34 jail sentences meted out. The regular week-end meetings which the Baptists conducted were suspended, because all able-bodied evangelists who could conduct them were in jail.[111] By August of 1951 some of the evangelists had completed their sentences and were again attempting to hold street meetings, only to be arrested and sent to jail again.[112]

The Quebec educational system presents a particularly serious problem of religious liberty, particularly as it affects Jewish children. The educational system in Quebec is frozen in the pattern that existed in 1867.[113] The British North America Act of 1867 conferred on the provinces exclusive power over education, but specifically preserved "any right or privilege with respect to denominational schools which any class of persons have by law."[114] There are no public schools, as Americans understand the term, in the province. All schools are either Protestant-controlled or Catholic-controlled; and though the Protestant schools are similar by and large to the public schools in the other provinces, the Catholic schools are conducted like Catholic parochial schools in the United States—though of course both school systems are maintained by tax-raised funds. The authority of the province department of education is limited to maintaining liaison with the local school commission, the Catholic and Protestant school committees, and the government. The immediate direction of education is left in the hands of the religious authorities. As stated by the superintendent of education in 1950:

> Our teaching is clearly confessional. With us, school life is impregnated with religion. The doctrine of the Church in regard to the training of children is scrupulously observed.[115]

The Catholic schools are maintained by taxes paid by Catholics, and the Protestant schools by the taxes of Protestant taxpayers. In addition, the school systems share proportionately in the "neutral" fund, consisting of taxes paid by corporations. In 1846 the Jews were given the option of paying their taxes into either the Protestant or Catholic fund or panel. They chose the Protestant and were accordingly admitted to the Protestant schools.[116]

By 1885 the Jewish population had become a substantial minority in Montreal, and the Protestant School Board suggested that Jews be considered "Protestants," and that the term should be construed to include any person not confessing the Roman Catholic faith. Such interpretation would enable the Protestants to collect money from Jewish real estate and from the neutral panel. In 1903 an amendment to the Quebec Education Act conferred on Jews "the same rights to be educated in the public schools of the Province as Protestants," and that for all school purposes Jews should be considered Protestants.

The validity of this act was not questioned for twenty years, but by 1924 the Protestant School Board asserted that the substantial increase in the Jewish population of Montreal made the arrangement burdensome, and accordingly brought suit to declare the law invalid or prejudicial to its position as it had existed in 1867. The case reached the Privy Council in London, the highest court of the British Commonwealth, which decided that: (1) Jews might not be appointed to the Protestant School Board, which also might not be compelled to employ Jewish teachers; (2) except in the cities of Montreal and Quebec, Jewish children had no right to admission to the Protestant schools, and the legislature might not compel the schools to accept them; but (3) the legislature might, if it wished, set up separate schools for Jews.

On the basis of this decision a Jewish school commission was appointed to set up a separate school system or to enter into contracts with Protestant school boards for the education of Jewish children. The Jewish community, after considerable discussion, came to the conclusion that further fragmentization of education would be harmful, and voted against setting up a separate Jewish school system. Instead the Jewish commissioners entered into contracts with Protestant boards for the education of Jewish children.

One such contract was entered into with the Protestant school board of Outremont, a suburb of Montreal, which by 1945 was predominantly Jewish in its population. The agreement called for the admission of Jewish children on the same terms as Protestants. It forbade segregation of Jewish children in the schools, and permitted them to be excused from participating in religious instruction or exercises. The agreement also allowed the Jewish children to absent themselves on Jewish holy days. The board also agreed to consider Jewish applicants for its teaching staff, though it did not specifically agree to employ any, and in fact did not.

In 1945 the fifteen-year contract was due to expire, and shortly before then the Protestant board gave notice that it did not intend to renew it. Upon being pressed for an explanation it stated that the contract was financially burdensome, and that in addition the absence of Jewish children on their holy days disrupted the regular school procedure. Thus in 1945 the Jewish school children of Outremont were faced with the prospect of not receiving any school education. After a good deal of public protest, the board renewed the contract for two years, and in 1947 renewed it for another five years. The new contract, however, cut down to two the holy days on which Jewish children may absent themselves as a matter of right. Moreover, the prohibition against segregating Jewish children was omitted. The contract has since then been renewed from time to time.

Jewish children are not the only ones to suffer from the archaic Quebec educational system. Children of Jehovah's Witnesses, a sect which is particularly anti-Catholic, are in an even more difficult situation. Some relief was obtained by them in 1956 when a court ruled that they were to be considered Protestants and hence entitled to enter the Protestant schools.[117] However, in many of the rural communities there are not enough non-Catholic children to maintain a Protestant school, and all the children must therefore attend the Catholic schools. In these schools, participation in Catholic instruction and practices is compulsory, at least for the Catholic children; and children who had been born and baptized as Catholics but whose parents had converted to the Jehovah's Witness sect have been expelled for refusing to participate in Catholic religious instruction and exercises.[118]

Dissatisfaction with church-state relationships in Quebec is growing even among Catholics. In 1963, four priest-professors urged legislation to authorize civil marriages in the province and permit witnesses in civil courts to make a solemn declaration instead of taking an oath on the Bible.[119] Earlier, a government commission recommended changes in law to permit atheists, agnostics, and non-Christians who are not Jews to testify in courts,[120] but neither proposal has as yet been adopted. Dissatisfaction with the educational system has led to proposals to limit the present unlimited censorial powers of the Catholic and Protestant church officials over texts and curricula so as to apply only when religion and morals are involved.[121] Substantial reforms, however, are still difficult of achievement, in large part because the question of clericalism is inextricably intertwined with that of French separatism and nationalism.

## PROTESTANT COUNTRIES

### Great Britain

Great Britain is frequently pointed to as a country which maintains complete religious freedom alongside an establishment of religion.[122] It is of course true that there is a large measure of religious liberty in England; whether there is complete religious liberty depends largely on one's viewpoint. Many, for example, would say that a child in the English common school who must make a specific request to be excused from participating in instruction in which he is taught at home and in church to disbelieve is not enjoying complete religious liberty.[123] So, too, Jefferson, who drafted the Virginia Statute of Religious Freedom, to assure that "no man shall be compelled to . . . support any religious worship, place, or ministry whatsoever,"[124] would hardly agree that the English taxpayer who is required to support the Anglican establishment enjoys complete religious freedom. Within our own generation, certain dissenting ministers have gone to jail one day each year for refusing to pay local taxes from which were drawn subsidies for Church of England schools.[125]

Certainly the established church does not enjoy religious freedom — at least that is the testimony of the two English archbishops. In the preface to his *Church and State in England,* Dr. Cyril Garbett, then Archbishop of York, stated that "except possibly in the early days, the Church of England never has had complete freedom. In the Middle Ages it was controlled by the Pope and the Crown; later by the Crown, and eventually by Parliament."[126] The most liberal interpretation of the term "religious freedom" can hardly encompass a situation in which a government prohibits a church from praying out of the prayer book the church wishes to use. Government dictation of how God is to be worshiped cannot be equated with religious liberty, even by the most ardent supporter of establishmentarianism.

Yet that is exactly what happened in England in 1927 and 1928. In each of those years a proposal to revise the Anglican Prayer Book was rejected by a Parliament in which a majority were not members of the Anglican Church, and many of whom were Catholics, Jews, and even non-believers. The first measure was passed by the House of Lords, but both were rejected by the House of Commons. For fourteen years the church had been engaged in revising its prayer books; the proposed revision had been accepted by large majorities in the House of Bishops, the House of Clergy, and the House of Laity. In 1927 it took the House of Commons but a few hours to dispose of this work of fourteen years. In 1928 Parliament was more charitable, and devoted two full days to debate the issue; but the result was the same. In the words of Archbishop Garbett, "Parliament refused legal authority to the Church to worship God in the manner its bishops, clergy and laity thought most fitting."[127] A commission of the Church of England summed up the situation neatly when it said that the rejection of the prayer book "revealed in unmistakable fashion the subordination of the Church to a Parliament which might consist largely of non-Christians, and does consist largely of persons who are not members of the Church of England."[128]

When Parliament was considering the proposed revision of the prayer book, Dr. Garbett was a young man, and upon being asked by the then Archbishop of Canterbury what action the Church should take if the proposal were rejected, he answered with the courage of youth, "we should ask for disestablishment."[129] Twenty-five years later, when he was older, wiser, and the Archbishop of York, he believed disestablishment would be interpreted by the world "as the national repudiation of Christianity," and therefore opposed it.[130] A special commission set up by the church in 1949 to propose changes in the existing relationship between the church and the state reached the same conclusion. In January of 1952 it recommended that the church should have more freedom (as does the established Presbyterian Church in Scotland),[131] but felt that "the unique relationship between Church and State in England is regarded by the world as a sign that the country has preserved a continuous Christian tradition," and that if "this relationship were broken it would be considered as a sign that England had abandoned Christianity."[132] *The Christian Century* commented on this that it would be hard to find a better example of the presumptuous nonsense on which much modern argument for the principle of state churches rests.[133]

Occasional demands for disestablishment continue to be heard today, both within and without the Anglican Church. In 1955, Parliament rejected a motion by some Labor members that a royal commission be appointed to examine the question of separating the Church of England from the state.[134] A similar motion was made in 1961, and again rejected.[135] Within the church, suggestions for disestablishment continue to be opposed on the ground that it might be construed as a repudiation of Christianity and lead to secularization of the state.[136]

Disestablishment might or might not be construed as a repudiation of Christianity, but there can be no question that it would mean the loss by the church of certain tangible benefits which can hardly be considered unsubstantial. Under the establishment, the Church of England enjoys material advantages. First is the prestige which comes with being the national church. The reigning monarch must be a member of that church, and is crowned by the Archbishop of Canterbury. Secondly, the church as such participates in the governing of the country. The two archbishops and twenty-four bishops sit in the House of Lords as regular voting members, a privilege not accorded to the churchmen of any other religious denomination.[137] Third, the duly rendered sentences of the ecclesiastical courts are enforced by the state, even to the extent of imprisoning those who disobey its lawfully issued judgments. Finally, under the establishment, the church enjoys properties and endowments amounting to several million pounds annually, which it would unquestionably lose on disestablishment.[138]

But for these benefits the church pays dearly. The coin of payment is freedom, and the price is state control. The crown appoints all bishops and deans; and all bishops, incumbents, and curates must take an oath of allegiance to the crown before their consecration or ordination. No changes may be made legally in the doctrine or public worship of the church without an act of Parliament, with the result that Anglicans must choose between praying in a manner not consistent with church doctrine[139] or clandestinely violate the law.[140] In July 1964, the church had to apply to Parliament for the enactment of a measure permitting the clergy to wear ritual vestments at Holy Communion services. (Translate that into our terms, and imagine an America in which the change of the mass promulgated at Vatican II Council could not be effected without an act of Congress.) The convocations may meet only when summoned to do so by royal writ. The final court of appeal in ecclesiastical matters is a secular court. And lastly, the state exercises considerable control over the property and administration of the church.[141]

The price for governmental aid is paid in Britain not only by the Anglican Church but by the other denominations which, though not the established church, nevertheless receive such aid. Roman Catholic schools, like Anglican, are financed out of tax-raised funds, but in return are subject to strict supervision and control by the local public authorities.[142] What this can lead to is indicated by the fact that in 1962 the Roman Catholic School of St. Mary and St. John in Wolverhampton found itself saddled with a local Communist Party official on its board of management.[143] This situation is not uncommon in Communist countries,[144] but few non-Communists claim that religious freedom prevails in these countries.

## The Scandinavian Countries

When Protestants raise the cry of religious persecution in Spain, Catholics frequently counter with "What about Scandinavia?"[145] Though the situations are far from equal—a Catholic church, for instance, need not conceal its identity in any Scandinavian country— there is nevertheless much validity to the countercharge. Protestants cannot in good faith assert that complete or substantially complete religious freedom prevails today in the Scandinavian countries, particularly in Sweden. All that can be said is that the restrictions on non-Lutherans are much less severe today than before January 1, 1952, the effective date of Sweden's first freedom of religion law since the establishment of the Lutheran Church in the 16th century.[146]

Under the Swedish constitution the king and all his ministers must belong to the Lutheran church,[147] although the 1951 law amended the constitution so as to eliminate the religious test for members of the government.[148] Freedom from constraint is assured to everyone "in the free exercise of his religion, provided he does not disturb public order or occasion general offense." Under the constitution, the king appoints the archbishops and bishops from among three persons nominated by the church for each vacancy. A general assembly of the church is provided for, to be convened by the king and to consider business which he presents. Decisions of the general assembly are merely petitions to the king and parliament, and have no effect until approved by them, though the general assembly may veto religious bills passed by parliament.[149]

Religious instruction is compulsory in elementary, secondary, and teacher-training schools, although in recent years efforts have been made by governmental authorities to de-emphasize school prayers and substitute "objective" for doctrinal teaching of religion.[150] If parents who are not members of the state church do not wish to have their children taught the Lutheran faith, they may have their children excused if they can demonstrate to the school board that they provide adequate religious training.[151] Catholic Church spokesmen in this country, however, have complained that university admission officers do not give credit for non-Lutheran religious education.[152]

Since January 1, 1952, a person born into the state church may leave it without having to join any other denomination, thus nullifying an 1873 law which required everyone to belong to some religious body. Children automatically become members of the state church at birth if either of their parents is a member, but after reaching eighteen any person may file in his registrar's office notice of intention to leave the church. Persons not belonging to the state church are relieved of paying one-half the church fees now imposed to cover the civic work of the clergy. The new law eliminated the requirement of membership in the state church for the holding of public office. It recognized marriages performed by non-Lutheran clergy as having the same legal status as state church or civil marriages. Under the law, convents and monasteries may be established, for the first time since the Reformation, though government approval is still required in each case.[153]

Few persons, perhaps not much more than 1% of the population, have availed themselves of the opportunity to leave the Lutheran Church.[154] The result is that practically all non-Catholic and non-Jewish children born in Sweden become members of the church and are required to participate in prayers and religious instruction in the public schools. Despite this only about 3% attend religious services regularly, although most are married, have their children christened, and are buried by the church;[155] or, as has been somewhat irreverently remarked, their contact with the church during their lives is limited to the times they are hatched, matched, and dispatched.

In Norway and Denmark, as in Sweden, the Lutheran Church is established as the state church, and is both supported and controlled by the state. The king appoints the bishops and other high church officers. Freedom of worship is granted to non-Lutherans, but until 1956 Jesuits were excluded from Norway. In that year, Article 2 of the Norway constitution, which provided:

> The Evangelical-Lutheran religion shall remain the public religion of the State. The inhabitants professing it shall be bound to bring up their children in the same. Jesuits shall not be tolerated.[156]

was amended to delete the last sentence.[157]

Article VII of the Danish constitution reads:

The constitution of the Established Church shall be laid down by law.

The citizens shall have a right to join together in communities to worship God in the way that is in accordance with their convictions, provided that nothing is taught or done that is at variance with good morals or public order.

No person is bound to make personal contributions to any religious community other than the one to which he or she belongs.

The details of the religious communities other than the Established Church shall be regulated by law.

No person shall, on account of his or her religious belief, be excluded from the full enjoyment and privilege of civil and political rights or evade the fulfillment of any common duty as a citizen.[158]

Religious instruction is obligatory in the schools of both Norway and Denmark, with a partial exemption to non-Lutheran children, who are excused from classes in dogma, but not Bible or church history. All teachers giving religious instruction must be approved by the bishop, and since most teachers do give such instruction, the practical effect is to close the teaching staff to non-Lutherans.[159]

## OTHER WEST EUROPEAN COUNTRIES

The relationship between religion and the state prevailing in France closely approximates that prevailing in the United States. Ever since 1905 there has been practically complete separation of church and state, together with full freedom to all religions. The first article of the French constitution states simply, "France is a republic, indivisible, secular, democratic and social."[160] The preamble to the constitution provides that "The establishment of free, secular, public education on all levels is a duty of the State."[161]

Consistent with this declaration, the French government is neutral to all religions and allows complete freedom to all. The public schools are entirely secular, and devoid of all religious instruction or exercises. In this respect France goes further than probably any other country, including most American states. It does not even permit members of religious orders to teach in the public schools. Since the question whether nuns and brothers may teach in the American public schools is a subject of considerable controversy in this country,[162] it is appropriate to quote here the justification for this prohibition expressed by a French educational administrator:

Considerations of two kinds have influenced Parliament to exclude members of congregations from teaching. In the first place laicity of courses of study implies laicity of staffs. "The mission which the sectarian teachers believe themselves called upon to fulfill, the vows they

57

have uttered, compel them to give the first place to the teaching of their religion." (Report to the Chamber of Deputies). Added to this fact is another of a legal nature. The State cannot maintain in its civil hierarchy functionaries belonging to another hierarony independent of it, to which they owe absolute obedience in all their actions. It can no more put up with this in education than it could in the army, for example, or in law.[163]

As in the United States, the church is free to establish parochial schools as long as they maintain minimum secular requirements. Until 1951 these schools received no financial support from the government, either directly or indirectly. In that year, however, after a bitter political controversy, two bills were adopted to provide some financial aid to the impoverished Catholic school system. One bill gave indirect aid by making state scholarships available to students in Catholic schools, while the other provided for financial allotments to Catholic parents' associations for educational purposes.[164] In 1959 aid was further extended by enactment, after considerable controversy, of a bill providing for payment of teachers' salaries in private schools which undertook to admit "all children, regardless of origins, opinions and beliefs" and give them instruction "with full respect for freedom of conscience."[165]

Belgium couples a constitutional guaranty of religious liberty to all with a grant of substantial government aid to the churches. Article 117 of the constitution provides that "the salaries and pensions of the ministers of religion shall be paid by the State."[166] Under an agreement with the Catholic school authorities entered into in 1958, and a law enacted the next year to carry out the agreement, two hours of religious or moral instruction is required in all public schools, and the teachers must be approved by ecclesiastical authorities. The law also gives parents the right to request and obtain a new school, public or parochial, if they do not live reasonably close to the type of school they desire. The government pays teachers' salaries in all schools, but pays only for the buildings of the public schools.[167] While the privilege of maintaining government-supported religious schools is available to all denominations, the Catholic Church is, with slight exceptions, the only one to exercise it.[168]

The Netherlands constitution likewise provides for religious freedom and equality, with provision for public aid to the various sects. The constitution imposes on the state the obligation to pay adequate salaries to all ministers of religion.[169]

For almost half of a century, ever since 1920, the Netherlands has provided public support for confessional schools equally with public schools. In view of the contention frequently made by Catholic sources in this country that the Netherlands' adjustment of the claims of the church schools on the state treasury is a fair solution of the problem that might well be emulated here, it may be well to examine the effect of the government's action of the Netherlands' public school system. In 1850, of students enrolled in the primary schools, 77 per cent were in the public schools and 23 per cent in the private schools. In 1958 the percentages were almost exactly reversed—28 per cent in the public schools and 72 per cent in the private schools.[170]

According to Theodore L. Reller, dean of the school of education at the University of California at Berkeley, who has made a special study of the situation in Holland, the division of tax-raised funds between public and confessional schools has resulted in a segmented society. It has also adversely affected education. Surprisingly, rather than achieving diversity and experimentation, the pursuit of equality in government support has resulted in standardization and in uniformity and in lack of initiative by public and private schools and by the municipalities. Public schools find it difficult to move because the municipality constantly notes that anything done for any public school must be provided in all private schools on request.[171]

Moreover, because of the limited perspectives of the confessional schools, social sciences are taught inadequately. Each religious school system teaches the facts of history strictly from its own view. There is practically no cooperation among teachers or schools in the development of common understanding. Each group lives within its own circle. When teachers of different schools meet, they discuss only technical matters such as salaries, technical aids, etc.[172] All in all, Dean Reller concludes that the Dutch system is not one to be emulated in the United States.[173]

Switzerland presents a variety of church-state arrangements among its many cantons. Some have one established church, some two, some three, and some none. The present trend seems to be toward separation. The relationships in the cantons are, however, subject to the limitations of the federal constitution, which guarantees freedom of conscience, requires that the "public schools shall be such that they may be frequented by adherents of all religious confessions," prohibits taxing any person for the specific benefit of a church to which he does not belong,[174] and bars entry of the Jesuit order in the country, though individual Jesuits are at liberty to engage in their work.[175]

West Germany ("The Federal Republic of Germany") adopted a constitution in 1949. Before that, relations between the churches and the states or "Laender" were principally a matter for determination by each state. Relations with the Catholic Church were governed by concordats entered into with the Vatican. Under these concordats the states, while guaranteeing freedom of religion and self-administration, undertook to contribute to the upkeep of the diocese, whose property was made free from taxation, to maintain religious instruction in schools under church supervision, and to provide theological training in the universities. For its part, the church acknowledged the right of the states to pass on church appointments. These concordats were not affected by the 1949 constitution and are still effective.[176]

In addition to these separate concordats, the Vatican entered into a concordat with Adolph Hitler in 1933 under which the Nazi government agreed to pay the salaries of some of the Catholic clergy, permit religious orders to establish schools freely and with rights equal to those of equivalent state institutions, allow freedom of communication between the Pope and the German bishops, and permit Catholics in youth organizations the opportunity to perform their religious duties. According to Vatican sources, this concordat created a moral and legal obligation which remains binding on the new West German government.[177] In 1957, the Constitutional Court agreed that the 1933 concordat was still valid and binding upon the West German government, but because of the independence of the Laender they could not be compelled to support Catholic institutions and schools.[178]

The Lutheran and Reformed churches in the states are subject to state supervision and receive state subsidies. They enjoy the right to levy church taxes on their members, which are collected by the state. The Methodists and the Baptists, though entitled to the same privilege, prefer to do their own collecting, but the Jews have regularly levied church taxes.[179]

Because of the close relation of church and state in Germany, church influence on education was strong even under the Nazis. Generally speaking, three types of schools developed: (1) The secular school, which was legally exempt from including religion in the course of study. No pupil could be required to take part in religious instruction unless his parents consented. (2) The interdenominational school, which divided children along denominational lines for religious instruction. Class work in other subjects was given to all pupils in common. (3) The denominational school, which included only teachers and pupils of the same religious confession.[180]

These relations continue substantially unchanged under the new constitution. This constitution guarantees freedom of faith and conscience, including the right to refrain from combatant war service for reasons of conscience (Article 4). Article 7 places the entire education system under state supervision, with the right in the parents to determine whether their children shall receive religious instruction, which is made part of the curriculum of the state schools. No teacher in the state schools may be required to give religious instructions against his will, and the right to establish private schools is guaranteed.[181]

## COMMUNIST EUROPE

The passions which events in Communist-controlled Europe arouse in an era of mutual hostility, and the inevitable propagandistic nature of almost everything written about Communist Europe whether written east or west of the "iron curtain," make it impossible to present a complete, reasonably accurate account of the relationship of religion and state in Communist Europe. Such an account must await a day when communications between east and west will be considerably freer than they are today. Nevertheless, the broad outlines of the pattern are discernible, and substantiated by sufficiently objective and impartial testimony to warrant inclusion here.

The picture is clearest in Soviet Russia, the oldest Communist state and the fountainhead of Marxian dogma. There can be little doubt that there has been no basic retreat in principle from the views on religion of the Communist trinity expressed in the statement by Marx that "Religion is the opiate of the people," by Lenin that "Religion is one of the aspects of spiritual oppression," and by Stalin that "All religion is contrary to science."[182] The Communist Party, which controls the Soviet state, has never abandoned that part of its program which looks toward the ultimate elimination of all religious influence from the Socialist society. "The Party," in its own words, "strives for the complete destruction of the connection between the exploiting classes and the organizations of religious propaganda, aiding the actual release of the working masses from religious prejudice, and organizing the very broadest scientific enlightenment and anti-religious propaganda."[183]

It is important to note that the enmity of the Bolshevist revolution to religion was based on two separate considerations: the theoretical, indicated in the quoted statements of Marx, Lenin, and Stalin, and the practical, arising from the fact that the church in Russia (as generally elsewhere) was a powerful ally of the imperial Russian despotism and had a huge material stake in the defeat of the revolution and the maintenance of the *status quo*. Until the Revolution had achieved a state of more or less stable security, there remained the real danger of counter-revolution, in which the church would probably play a prominent role. For some two decades after 1918 the Soviet state engaged in a program of persecution and repression aimed at exterminating religion as a social force.

By the end of the '30's, however, it became clear that the goal of extermination could not be achieved through force. In addition, external aggression rather than counter-revolution seemed to present the major threat, and the support of the church was highly valuable if not indispensable in meeting that threat. Accordingly, shortly before the outbreak of the German-Russian war, the Soviet state worked out an agreement with the Russian Church. The latter agreed to give its wholehearted support to the Soviet regime, and in return the government stopped its program of antireligious propaganda, disbanded the League of Militant Atheists, allowed the reopening of some 8,000 churches, authorized the training of priests in theological seminaries, and permitted believers to worship without molestation.[184]

A number of factors have tended to encourage this policy on the part of the Soviet government towards reconciliation with religion. Among others were the death of Stalin and the onset of a determined effort by the government, particularly under Khrushchev, to improve relations with the United States and other western nations, and the brief but extremely influential reign of Pope John XXIII, whose encyclical *Pacem in Terris* manifested a strong commitment to peace, even between east and west.

The effects of this reconciliation have been noted by many observers. The people are flocking to the churches, which find it difficult to accommodate all worshipers.[185] Churches multiplied and monasteries were reopened with governmental help. Clergymen have been liberated from the obligation of military service, and monks have been exempted from the bachelor tax. Special services may be held for women and children, and Christian instruction may be given to children in preparation for communion.[186]

It would be completely erroneous to assume either that the rulers of Soviet Russia have abandoned the principle of the irreconcilability of Communism and religion, or that religious liberty exists in

Russia today. Article 124 of the present (1947) Constitution of the Union of Soviet Socialist Republics provides that

> In order to insure to citizens freedom of conscience, the church in the USSR is separated from the state, and the school from the church. Freedom of religious worship and freedom of anti-religious propaganda is recognized for all citizens.[187]

The constitution thus does not guarantee the right to engage in religious propaganda, without which religious freedom can hardly be said to exist, and in addition clearly indicates its lack of neutrality. Moreover, while it does purport to guarantee freedom of worship, and the prevailing evidence seems to indicate that the government is honoring the guaranty, the actual situation would be more accurately described as a toleration of worship. For the continued adherence of the rulers of the Soviet state to the basic views of Marx, Lenin, and Stalin on religion makes it fairly certain that persecution and outright warfare will return when expediency ceases to dictate a temporary policy of tolerance.

In the countries of East Europe under Communist domination, the stage of relative stability which the Russian revolution has reached has not yet been as fully attained. As a result, actual persecution and repression still prevail, with the Roman Catholic Church and its bishops and priests as the chief victims. Just as the Orthodox Church in Russia was for a long time an enemy of the Revolution and an ally, actual or potential, of the counter-revolution, so in Poland, Hungary, Czechoslovakia, and the other East European countries in the Soviet sphere, the Catholic Church is an unreconciled enemy of Communism, and its priests are considered potential traitors and spies for capitalism and reaction.

There is one significant difference between the persecution of the Orthodox Church in the early days of the Russian Revolution, and the persecution of the Catholic Church today in eastern Europe outside Russia: present-day persecution is almost completely practical and nonideological. The church is fought not primarily because religion is an "opiate" for the masses or inconsistent with the science of the Communist new world, but because churchmen such as Stepinacz and Mindszenty represent the leadership of a force whose enmity to Communism is so intense that it did not hesitate to deprive of eternal salvation all who adhered to it.

The purpose of the persecution in Communist Europe outside Russia is not to destroy the church; the impossibility of accomplishing this within the foreseeable future is recognized. Its purpose is to use it to aid state purposes, just as Soviet Russia uses the Orthodox Church and as Fascist Italy used the Catholic Church. The atheism of the rulers of Poland and Hungary proved no more serious an obstacle to their entering into agreements with the church in which they bartered material support for political subservience than the atheism of Mussolini or Stalin constituted an obstacle to similar arrangements in their countries. Alliances between church and state are not limited to religious states; they are just as likely in antireligious states.

Poland in April 1950 entered into an agreement with the Polish Catholic hierarchy under which the Church undertook to teach loyalty to the government, to oppose antigovernment activities, and to request the Vatican to recognize the permanence of Poland's annexation of the territories acquired from Germany at the end of World War II. In return, the State guaranteed the continuance of religious instruction in the schools and of financial support to the Catholic schools. In addition, the state guaranteed the right of the church to continue its charitable, welfare, and educational work, and agreed to furnish financial aid to the bishops and church institutions.[188]

But this reconciliation between the Polish state and the church appears to have been short-lived. In September 1950 the church, in a letter to the president of Poland, protested the State's unilateral denouncement of the agreement, its ban on the reactivation of Catholic institutions, the gradual but steady liquidation of Catholic schools and similar elimination of religious teaching practices. The government replied that the church had itself not lived up to the agreement but had in fact violated every promise made by it.[189] This breakdown was followed by a period of violent attack on the church and a resumption of active persecution, which closed, though temporarily, just as suddenly as it began, after the hierarchy recognized the validity of the government's appointment of vicars in five dioceses in the so-called Regained Territories in western Poland.[190]

In 1956 the resumed cordial relations between church and state in Poland was reflected in an agreement providing for restoration of religious instruction in the public schools, permission for chaplains to work in hospitals and prisons, the return of exiled priests and nuns, and, on the other hand, the recognition by the church of the state's voice in ecclesiastical appointments.[191] But again, tension and mutual recrimination returned, each party charging the other with breach of faith,[192] particularly after complaints by non-Catholic children of pressure and oppression because of their refusal to participate in religious instruction in the public schools.[193] Today, the relationship between church and state in Poland is best described as an armed truce, with mutual hostility and suspicion barely concealed by a formal *modus vivendi*.[194]

Communist Hungary also entered into an agreement with the Catholic Church about the same time as Poland's first agreement. The Hungarian Church undertook to support the government and its "five-year plan," to support the peace movement, and to condemn warmongering and the use of atomic weapons. In exchange, the government agreed to return eight Catholic schools, permit the religious orders to work, guarantee freedom of religion to the church, and support the church financially for 18 years.[195] Similar agreements had been entered into between the state and the Hungarian Reformed Church, the largest Protestant body in the country, two years earlier.[196]

At the time of this writing, similar agreements have not yet been worked out in the other Soviet dominated countries, Romania, Czechoslovakia, Bulgaria, and Albania. The situation in these countries is still one of active persecution and oppression.[197] That the end sought by the state in all these countries is not destruction of the church but an alliance with it as in Russia, Poland, and Hungary, is evidenced by the fact that in these countries active persecution is coupled with continued subsidization and other government material assistance.[198] The pattern is similar in Yugoslavia, a Communist state which has freed itself from Soviet domination,[199] and in East Germany.[200]

## COUNTRIES IN THE MOSLEM TRADITION

The constitutions in most of the Moslem countries have borrowed from the West the usual guarantees of religious freedom, yet it is doubtful that substantial religious freedom prevails in any of them. *Sharia*, or religious law, is the law of society and of the state. Limited rights are conferred on non-Moslem religious minorities, Christian and Jewish; but by and large church and state are identical, and Islam controls the entire life of the citizens of Moslem lands. Apostasy is forbidden under dire penalties, which—at least theoretically—include death. It is thought inconceivable that a Moslem should change his faith, and any attempt to persuade him to do so is considered an affront to both national and religious solidarity.[201]

The Egyptian constitution is typical. It confers liberty of conscience to all, but declares Islam to be the religion of the state. Persons belonging to non-Islamic religious communities are subject to the personal law of their own community in regard to marriage and family rights; but the heads of these communities are appointed by the Moslem state, and if members of different non-Islamic communities marry, the legal problems arising out of the marriage are determined by the Moslem courts under the *Sharia*. Non-Islamic religious radio programs are not permitted, and government permits are required in order to build new churches.[202] In 1950 a government order was promulgated requiring all private schools, even if operated by Catholic or Protestant churches, to provide Islamic religious teaching for their Moslem students,[203] a decree which was reissued and strengthened in 1955.[204] But in 1951 the government also provided for Christian religious instruction to Christian students in the public schools during the period in which Moslem students receive instruction in the Koran.[205]

In Turkey, somewhat as in Mexico, a revolutionary nationalist government, seeking to liberate the people from autocracy and feudalism and to westernize its culture, adopted an antireligious policy; but with the passing of years and the disappearance of the imminent danger of counter-revolution it has begun to adopt a more conciliatory attitude toward religion. Alone among the Moslem countries, the Turkish constitution declares that the Turkish state is *"Laique,"* and guarantees religious freedom for all.[206]

In 1924 Kemal Ataturk initiated a program of Westernization which included the banning of the veil for women and the fez for men, shifting the weekly holiday from Friday to Sunday, barring all religious teaching from the public school system, closing the Moslem schools, and suppressing the religious order of dervishes, though tolerating normal public forms of worship. Within the past several years, however, this policy has been relaxed. Religion has been reintroduced into the public school as an optional study. Schools for the training of the clergy have been reopened, and the national budget contains an item for maintaining religion.[207] •

## ASIAN COUNTRIES

An interesting picture of one nation's struggle toward a solution of the problem of church-state relationships is present in the young republic of Israel. Before the establishment of Israel, Palestine was governed under the 1922 mandate to Great Britain, implemented by the Palestine Order in Council of that year. Complete freedom and equality with reference to race, religion, and language were guaranteed. Article 15 of the mandate also provided:

The right of each community to maintain its own schools for the education of its own members in its own language, while conforming to such educational requirements of a general nature as the Administration may impose, shall not be denied or impaired.

Article 83 of the Order in Council provided for autonomy in the internal affairs of each religious community recognized by the government, subject to general ordinance by the High Commissioner. Articles 51 to 56 continued the law and custom which prevailed under the prior Turkish rule, the entrusting to the courts of the religious communities (Moslem, Jewish, and various Christian) of jurisdiction in matters of personal status: marriage, divorce, guardianship, legitimation, adoption, legal incompetence, succession, and wills and legacies. Article 56 provided that "The judgments of the Religious Courts shall be executed by the process and offices of the Civil Courts."[208]

The resolution of the United Nations which on November 29, 1947, divided Palestine into an Arab and a Jewish state, required each state to preserve the rights of its minority communities as they existed under the British mandate. The resulting perpetuation of the religious courts which existed under Turkish and British rule has caused the continuation of laws that are grotesquely anachronistic and out of place in a modern, democratic republic with a distinctly western orientation. For instance, civil marriage does not exist in Israel today, and under the law as administered in the religious courts, "Enoch Arden" laws terminating a marriage if a spouse disappears for many years are not allowed; a wife can be divorced without cause and without her consent; a "kohen" or member of the priestly tribe (*i.e.*, anyone presumably descendant from Aaron) may not marry a divorced woman; polygamy is permissible; women and non-Jews are not permitted to testify in the religious courts; and parents may validly contract binding marriages for their minor children without the children's consent.

The obsolete character of these laws is widely recognized in Israel, and their rigor is rapidly being ameliorated. In the first place, the rabbis themselves have been studying the religious codes with a view toward modernizing them and reconciling them with modern living conditions.[209] In the second place, the state has by various devices sharply restricted the effect of these laws. Thus, while polygamy is theoretically permissible to a small percentage of Israelis under certain circumstances, for all practical purposes it is forbidden and has practically disappeared.[210] The rule against the violation of the Sabbath has been held not applicable to a YMCA which exhibited motion pictures on Saturdays.[211] The Ministry of Education has ruled that Christian missionary schools are entitled to complete freedom, and may not be restricted to educating only non-Jewish children,[212] and efforts by the Orthodox to curb their activities have been resisted by the government.[213] Public busses operate on Saturday in some cities,[214] and the jurisdiction of religious courts has been challenged by the Israel High Court.[215]

At present it is impossible to foretell the exact ultimate outcome of the struggle for the control of the Jewish state between secularism and clericalism. The trend, however, is clearly toward increasing liberalization and religious freedom.

The American experiment of religious liberty and separation of church and state has exercised a great influence in the constitutions of the other new Asian democratic republics, as well as Israel. The Indian constitution, adopted in 1949, is like the American, a purely secular document. Like the American constitution, it contains no reference to God, a motion to begin the preamble with the words "In the name of God" having been overwhelmingly defeated in the Constitutional Assembly.[216]

The constitution provides that, "subject to public order, morality and health," all persons are equally entitled to freedom of conscience and the right freely to profess, practice, and propagate religion. Every religious denomination has the right to establish and maintain institutions for religious and charitable purposes, to manage its own affairs in religion, to own and acquire property and to administer such property; and no person is compelled to pay any taxes whose proceeds are specifically used to promote or maintain any particular religion or religious denomination.

Religious education is barred in any educational institution maintained wholly by state funds, except when an institution is administered by the state on behalf of an endowment or trust which requires that religious instruction shall be given. Even in such cases, students will not be required to receive religious instruction or attend worship services at state-recognized or -supported institutions, though they may receive the instruction and attend services with the consent of their parents or guardians.

Citizens must not be denied admission into any state-supported educational institution on grounds of religion, race, caste, or language. All minority groups have the right to establish and administer educational institutions of their choice. The state must not, in granting aid, discriminate against any institution because it is managed by a minority.[217]

China today is one of the countries under Communist control.

Information of the actual state of affairs there, as in other Communist countries, is impossible to obtain, and the relationship of the government to religion there can only be inferred from pre-Communist practices in China and from practices in other Communist-controlled countries. China is a country in which no one religion has dominated others or enjoyed any working relationship with the state. The diffusion and diversity of religions has resulted in an essentially secular state and a large degree of religious liberty.[218]

Reports on the fate of religion under the Communist government vary. Catholic sources claim oppression and persecution of priests and nuns, and these claims are substantiated by United States Government reports. Protestant missionaries, on the other hand, report a high degree of religious freedom.[219] The secularity of the public educational system inherited from the Kuomintang regime has undoubtedly been intensified. In the 1930's the Kuomintang had banned Bible study as a required course, and the Communists completely eliminated it as part of the curriculum even as an elective course, but have not interfered with such study on a voluntary basis after school hours.[220] Unlike the other countries which succumbed to Communism, religion in China has not been a powerful counter-revolutionary force, and it is therefore likely that the pre-Communist attitude of tolerance has not been substantially changed.

Japan, possibly more than any other country, reflects the American influence on church-state relations. The change from the state religion of imperial Japan to the secularism of democratic Japan has been dramatic and thorough. Before 1945, state Shinto required devotion at public shrines and teaching in the public schools. It considered the land, the nation, and above all the continuing imperial family to be religiously sacred, and indeed to be the offspring of the gods. The position of the emperor in imperial Japan has been described in the following words:

> He is . . . the Supreme Being in the Cosmos of Japan, as God is in the universe of the pantheistic philosopher. From him everything emanates, in him everything subsists.

A private religion might be cherished in addition to the state religion provided it did not conflict with Shinto.[221]

Contrast this with the constitution of Japan promulgated on November 3, 1946, and made effective on May 3, 1947. Article 20 provides:

> Freedom of religion is guaranteed to all. No religious organization shall receive any privileges from the State, nor exercise any political

authority. No person shall be compelled to take part in any religious act, celebration, rite or practice. The state and its organs shall refrain from religious education or any other religious activity.[222]

## Summary

A number of conclusions can reasonably be drawn from this brief summary of contemporary solutions to the problem of reconciling the rival claims of church and state:

(1) Religious liberty is generally most secure where church and state are most completely separated. Conversely, religious liberty suffers where the state seeks to make the church an engine to further national policy, or the church seeks to utilize the compulsive arm of the state to further religious interests.

(2) This proposition is true not only in totalitarian countries, but to a lesser extent in democracies as well.

(3) Antireligious and atheistic government finds little difficulty in entering into alliances with churches.

(4) A church receiving special state favors invariably pays for them in the loss of religious freedom.

(5) Revolutionary governments of countries in which the churches were politically powerful and aligned with the exploiting classes exhibit strong antireligious tendencies and impose severe restrictions on religious liberty.

(6) The newer democracies have been greatly influenced by the American experiment, and make constitutional provision for complete religious liberty and the separation of church and state.

### CHAPTER THREE

# The Colonial Period in America

## OLD WORLD PATTERNS TRANSPLANTED

THE EARLY COLONIZATION of the New World gave no indication of the evolutionary process which ultimately culminated in the separation and religious liberty principle of the Constitution. On the contrary, the Old World patterns of church-state union and religious oppression were transplanted to the New World with all their rigor. Religion was an important motivation in the colonization of America. Catholic and Protestant missionaries braved the dangers of the unknown continents to spread their respective forms of Christianity. Many were the religious laymen of a multitude of sects who fled to the wilderness to find a haven where they might practice their own version of Christianity.[1] Whoever came, and for whatever reason, always brought with him the system of church-state relationship with which he was familiar and under which he had lived his religious life.

Indeed, in some cases the rigor of church-state union was more severe in the New World than in the Old. The Jews of New Amsterdam were able to obtain some amelioration of the oppression they suffered under Peter Stuyvesant only by invoking the intervention of the Dutch government in Europe.[2] A royal commission from England expressed concern over the treatment Dissenters were receiving in New England;[3] and the association of church and state in Spanish America was closer than in Spain itself.

In the Spanish colonies, as in the mother country, conformity in religion was considered essential, and immigration was strictly controlled in order to secure a religiously homogeneous population. To make doubly sure, the Holy Inquisition was brought over to deal with such heritical immigrants as might have slipped through. As in the mother country, the church paid for the favors it received from the state in the form of material resources and the use of its secular arm for the repression of heritics. Major ecclesiastical ap-

71

pointments were made on presentation by the king or his representatives, and ecclesiastics who accepted appointment without royal permission were subject to banishment. Royal consent was required for the establishment of churches or convents, the circulation of papal bulls, and the holding of church assemblies or the publication of their decisions.[4]

In the Protestant English colonies, as in Catholic New Spain, the Old World traditions of church-state union and religious oppression took root quickly. The situation was well summarized by the United States Supreme Court in 1947:[5]

> These practices of the old world were transplanted to and began to thrive in the soil of the new America. The very charters granted by the English Crown to the individuals and companies designated to make the laws which would control the destinies of the colonials authorized these individuals and companies to erect religious establishments which all, whether believers or nonbelievers, would be required to support and attend. An exercise of this authority was accompanied by a repetition of many of the old world practices and persecutions. Catholics found themselves hounded and proscribed because of their faith; Quakers who followed their conscience went to jail; Baptists were peculiarly obnoxious to certain dominant Protestant sects; men and women of varied faiths who happened to be in a minority in a particular locality were persecuted because they steadfastly persisted in worshipping God only as their own consciences dictated. And all of these dissenters were compelled to pay tithes and taxes to support government-sponsored churches whose ministers preached inflammatory sermons designed to strengthen and consolidate the established faith by generating a burning hatred against dissenters.

There were, however, two differences between the treatment of dissenters by the Catholic motherlands of Spain and France and the Protestant motherland of England, differences which were later to prove of great significance in the evolution of the American experiment.

In the first place, unlike the Spanish and French monarchs — who strove to keep the heretics out of the New World as they sought to destroy them in the Old — the English statesmen opened the gates of their American colonies to every kind of religious faith that could be found in Europe. Freedom of immigration was accorded not only to Catholics, Separatists, Puritans, Quakers, Presbyterians, and Baptists from the British Isles, but no less to Lutherans, Dunkards, Moravians, Mennonites, Huguenots, and Salzburgers from the continent. Even Jews were not excluded, particularly after they were allowed into England under Cromwell.[6]

In the second place, no significant change in church-state relationships in Spain or France occurred during the entire period of American colonization. On the other hand, the Anglo-American colonies were explored and populated during two centuries of religious changes in England, which ranged from the Catholicism of Mary to the Puritanism of Cromwell.

The greatly desired uniformity of religion and the principle of *cujus regio, ejus religio,* which, it was believed, would alone secure that objective, were brought over to the new continent, but as a result of these two differences in colonization the objective of uniformity was achieved only in Catholic Mexico and Catholic Quebec (until the English took over). Between these two Catholic provinces a multiplicity of sects arose, established themselves, multiplied, and flourished. Heretics and dissenters were oppressed and persecuted in Protestant as in Catholic America, and the union of church and state was no less prevalent there. But in Mexico and Quebec Catholicism was the sole state religion, whereas in the English colonies there was no single faith which dominated the others throughout all the colonies. The Calvinists who governed New England and oppressed Anglicans were themselves persecuted in Virginia, and forced to pay taxes for the support of the hated Anglican establishment from which they had fled. Under Stuyvesant the Reformed Church was the state church in New Amsterdam; the Quakers dominated Pennsylvania, the Baptists Rhode Island, and, for a short time, the Catholics Maryland. In the colonies which later became the United States, religious uniformity was severely limited both geographically and chronologically.

For the purposes of our study, the colonies may be divided into four groups. In New England, Calvinist Congregationalism was the established church. Massachusetts, Plymouth, Connecticut, and New Hampshire belonged to this group. In the southern colonies of Virginia and the two Carolinas, the Church of England was established. A third group consisting of New York, New Jersey, Maryland, and Georgia experienced changes in church-state establishments. In the fourth group of Rhode Island, Pennsylvania, and Delaware no single church ever attained the status of monopolistic establishment.[7]

## PURITAN NEW ENGLAND

The Pilgrims, who in 1620 established the Plymouth colony, brought with them a liberality in church-state relations that contrasted greatly with the unmitigated Calvinism of the Puritans, who, a decade later, founded the Massachusetts Bay Colony. The Pilgrims' liberality may be explained partly by their stay in tolerant Holland, where diverse sects lived together in peace and harmony;[8] and partly by the teachings of their leader John Robinson, who argued that: "Neither God is pleased with unwilling worshippers, nor Christian societies bettered, nor the persons themselves neither, but the plain contrary in all three,"[9] and who noted trenchantly that: "Protestants living in the countries of papists commonly plead for toleration of religions; so do papists that live where Protestants bear sway: though few of either, especially of the clergy . . . would have the other tolerated where the world goes on their side."[10]

Whatever the reason, Plymouth, though founded primarily for religious reasons, never established Congregationalism by any civil law, nor made membership in the church a condition of citizenship. (Myles Standish, a leading citizen of the colony, was not a member of the church.) Dissenters like Anne Hutchinson and Roger Williams were treated with tolerance after their expulsion from Massachusetts Bay. In the early days of the colony there was a conspicuous absence of legislation on matters of religion, and contributions for the support of the church were voluntary.[11]

When, however, the founders of neighboring Massachusetts Bay adopted the Congregational system of church government, the differences between the Plymouth Pilgrims and Massachusetts Puritans faded. By 1651 a presentment was made by the Plymouth grand jury against a person "for not frequenting the public assemblage on the Lord's Day." Magistrates were authorized to enforce contributions for the support of the church; voters had to be certified as "orthodox in the fundamentals of religion"; and legislation was enacted against Quakers and other heretics. By the time Plymouth was united with Massachusetts in 1691 all major differences between the two had disappeared.[12]

The Puritans who came to Massachusetts Bay in 1628 brought with them the principles of theocratic church-state relationships which Calvin had put into effect in Geneva. Their expressed purpose in coming to New England was to establish a Bible commonwealth, a community "under a due form of government both civil and ecclesiastical." They were not long in establishing their own church-state, which differed from the English church-state they had fled from primarily in that it soon became Congregational rather than Anglican and was basically theocratic rather than Erastian.

It was quickly established by the General Court, the legislature of the colony, that the privilege of voting was to be limited to members of the church. The Puritan tests for church membership were so exacting that many religious persons, including those in general sympathy with Calvinist doctrine and Congregational church discipline, were unable or unwilling to qualify, with the result that the colony was governed by a small church oligarchy in the best theocratic tradition.[13]

By 1635 the General Court assumed the power of regulating the affairs of the local churches and passing on the qualifications of preachers and elders. This action was based on the principle formally adopted by the General Court in 1641:

> The civil authority . . . hath power and liberty to see the peace, ordinances, and rules of Christ observed in every Church, according to His word. . . . It is the duty of the Christian magistrate to take care that the people be fed with wholesome and sound doctrine.

Accordingly, in 1650 a pastor who preached to an unauthorized church was fined £10, and the county courts were instructed to bring further "abuses and neglects of this kind" to the attention of the grand juries for appropriate action.[14]

In 1646 the General Court declared that "no human power be lord over conscience, yet because such as being in damnable heresies . . . ought to be duly restrained," it adopted the Act against Heresy. This law imposed banishment on any person denying the immortality of the soul, or the resurrection, or sin in the regenerate, or the need of repentance, or the baptism of infants, or "who shall purposely depart the congregation at the administration of that ordinance" or endeavor to reduce others to any of these heresies. In the same year contemptuous conduct toward preachers and nonattendance on divine service were made punishable, the former by "standing on a block four feet high" having on the breast a placard with the words "An Open and Obstinate Contemner of God's Holy Ordinances."[15]

The extent to which theological differences were deemed punishable heresy is indicated by the treatment accorded to Anne Hutchinson. Mrs. Hutchinson was not a Catholic or Quaker, or even a Baptist, Lutheran, or Episcopalian; like the other residents of Boston she was a Congregationalist.[16] She persisted, however, in holding meetings in her home in which she advocated the preaching of a "covenant of grace," a religion based on the individual's direct intuition of God's grace and love, as opposed to the preaching of a "covenant of works"—a religion based on obedience to the laws of church and state.[17] After unsuccessful attempts by the leaders of the church-

state to induce her to discontinue her heretical and seditious teachings, she and her doctrines were tried in 1638 and both condemned—
she as a blasphemer and seducer of the faithful, and her doctrines as
error.[18]

As a result of her trial and excommunication she fled with her
children to Rhode Island and thereafter migrated to New York,
where in 1642 she and most of her children were killed by the Indians.[19] When Governor Winthrop of the Massachusetts colony heard
of this, he remarked piously:

> God's hand is the more apparently seen therein, to pick out this woe-
> ful woman to make her, and those belonging to her, an unheard-of
> heavy example of their [the Indians'] cruelty.[20]

Anne Hutchinson was but one of many who incurred the terri-
fying displeasure of the leaders of the colony for expressing theological dissent. Her brother-in-law, a minister named John Wheelwright,
who also claimed to teach the pure covenant of grace, was similarly tried as a menace to the community. He was found guilty, dis-
franchised, banished, and denied the right to appeal to the king.[21]
Earlier, in the winter of 1635–1636, Roger Williams had also been
banished because he "broached and divulged divers new and
dangerous opinions, against the authority of the magistrates."[22]

The treatment accorded to Quakers was even worse. A series of
legislative acts was adopted against the "cursed sect of heretics which
are commonly called Quakers" and their "pestilent Heresy." Under
these laws, any Quaker coming into the colony was to be thrown into
jail, whipped with twenty stripes, and kept at work until banished or
transported.[23] A group of king's commissioners sent from London to
investigate conditions in the colonies reported in 1661 that

> Puritans have put many Quakers to death, of other provinces. First
> they banished them as Quakers upon pain of death, and then executed
> them for returning. They have beaten some to jelly and been exceed-
> ingly cruel to others.[24]

(Actually, four Quakers were executed.)[25]

Catholics were not more welcome in Massachusetts. In 1647 the
General Court decreed that

> No Jesuit or spiritual or ecclesiastical person ordained by the pope or
> see of Rome shall henceforth come into Massachusetts. Any person not
> freeing himself of suspicion shall be jailed, then banished. If taken a
> second time he shall be put to death.

Tempering justice with mercy and commercial considerations, exceptions were made for shipwrecked Jesuits and priests transiently in

the colony on business.[26] Proscription of Catholic dogma and worship continued in Massachusetts long after restrictions on non-Congregational worship had been removed. In 1691 a new charter was granted to Massachusetts (by which Plymouth was merged with the larger colony) decreeing that "forever thereafter there shall be liberty of conscience allowed in the worship of God to all Christians (except Papists)."[27]

The other two members of the New England confederation, New Haven and Connecticut, did not differ substantially from Massachusetts in their church-state relations. New Haven, during the quarter century of its independent existence, was possibly more extreme in its theocracy than Massachusetts. Connecticut, under Thomas Hooker, was not much more liberal. Though there was no formal church-membership qualification for suffrage, the governor had to be a member of "some approved congregation." After the coming of the Quakers, Connecticut joined the other colonies of the confederation in barring them from the colony, although it did not follow the example of Massachusetts in applying the death penalty.[28]

## THE ANGLICAN ESTABLISHMENTS

Although economic and social considerations were the principal motivating factors in the colonization of Virginia and the other southern colonies, religious motivations were also present. The royal charters emphasized the missionary aim of colonization, and Captain John Smith declared that the first duty of Virginians was to

> preach, baptise into the Christian religion and by the propagation of the Gospel to recover out of the arms of the devil, a number of poor and miserable souls wrapt up unto death in almost invincible ignorance.[29]

The Anglican Church became a state church in Virginia, much as the Puritan Church later became the established church of Massachusetts, but with this difference: in the Massachusetts theocracy the church tended to control the state; in Virginia the state controlled the church. There was no resident bishop, and the governor exercised both the ecclesiastical prerogatives of the crown and the supervisory functions of the episcopacy.[30] But lest it be assumed that the Anglican establishment in Virginia was more liberal in religious legislation than the Calvinist theocracy in Massachusetts, the substance of the religious sections of the "Lawes Divine, Moral and Martial" decreed by Governor Thomas Dale in 1612 is set forth here.[31]

1. To speak impiously of the Trinity or one of the Divine Persons, or against the known articles of Christian faith, was punishable with death.

2. The same penalty of death was to avenge "blaspheming God's holy Name."

3. To curse or "banne"—for the first offense some severe punishment; for the second a "bodkin should be thrust through the tongue"; if the culprit was incorrigible, he should suffer death.

4. To say or do anything "to the derision or despight of God's holy word," or in disrespect to any Minister, exposed the offender to be "openly whipt 3 times, and to ask public forgiveness in the assembly of the congregation, 3 several Sabath daies."

5. Non-attendance on religious services entailed a penalty, for the first offence, of the stoppage of allowance; for the second, whipping; for the third, the galleys for six months.

6. For Sabbath-breaking the first offence brought the stoppage of allowance; the second, whipping, and the third, death.

7. Preachers and ministers were enjoined to faithfulness in the conduct of regular services on pain "of losing their entertainment."

8. Every person in the colony, or who should come into it, was required to repair to the Minister for examination in the faith. If he should be unsound, he was to be instructed. If any refused to go to the minister, he should be whipt; on a second refusal he should be whipt twice and compelled to "acknowledge his fault on Sabath day in the assembly of the congregation"; for a third refusal he should be "whipt every day until he makes acknowledgment."

It is true that on appeal to England, the "Lawes Divine, Moral and Martial" were abrogated,[32] and the laws thereafter enacted in the colony in support of the Anglican establishment were considerably less severe. Nevertheless, fines were imposed for nonattendance at church service, and payment of tithes was made compulsory on all and a first lien on every resident's tobacco. Besides the tithes, every parson was entitled to a piece of land, called the glebe. Parish churches were built by local taxation, and all ministers had to "conform themselves in all things according to canons of the Church of England." Puritan clergy were banished for failing to conform to the Anglican services; Quakers were fined, imprisoned, and banished. Catholics were disqualified for public office, and any priest who ventured to enter the colony was subject to instant expulsion. Penalties were imposed on those who, having scruples against infant baptism, neglected to present their children for that purpose.[33]

As in New England, the Act of Toleration adopted in England in 1689 resulted in alleviating the condition of Protestant dissenters in Virginia and the granting of liberty of conscience to all orderly persons. As in New England, too, toleration was not to be extended unreasonably; the formula "Papists excepted" was used in Virginia also.[34]

In the Carolinas, the Anglican Church was established in much the same way as it was in Virginia. The need for settlers, however, induced the proprietors to try to attract Puritans from New England and elsewhere. Accordingly Protestant dissenters were accorded freedom of conscience, and were permitted to form congregations with ministers of their own choice.[35]

## New York's Multiple Establishments

Under Peter Stuyvesant the Dutch Reformed Church was established and supported by the state. Residents were compelled, under penalty of arrest and imprisonment, to contribute to the support of the church minister.[36] In addition, the law required baptism of all children, and the rite might be performed only by the Reformed minister and in the Reformed church.[37] At first only the Reformed religion could be practiced publicly, but English Presbyterians and Congregationalists were shortly permitted to build their own churches.[38] Other sects, however, were not so favorably treated. When in 1653 the Lutherans petitioned for liberty of worship and permission to send for a Lutheran minister, the petition was rebuffed; and some of the Lutherans who persisted in holding religious services in their houses without a minister were thrown into prison.[39] Baptists who held religious services in their homes were also subject to arrest, fine, whipping, and banishment.[40]

As in the English colonies, the Quakers were particular victims of persecution. Called "instruments of Satan," they were subject to arrest and expulsion if they entered New Netherlands, and the ship that brought them was liable to confiscation. The penalty for harboring a Quaker for a single night was £50 and one Quaker was sentenced to two years' hard labor for the crime of preaching.[41]

With the surrender of New Amsterdam to the English in 1664, the Reformed Church fell from its position of exclusive establishment. Substituted therefor was what has appropriately been called "multiple establishments."[42] The "Instructions" from the Duke of York prescribed that

> In all the territories of his Royal Highness liberty of conscience is allowed, provided such liberty is not converted to licentiousness or the disturbance of others in the exercise of the protestant religion. Every township is obliged to pay their minister, according to such agreement as they shall make with him, and no man shall refuse his proportion; the minister being elected by the major part of the householders, inhabitants of the town.

The "Duke's laws," as they concerned religion, further provided for the erection of a church building in every parish, with the cost, as well as the minister's support, raised by public tax; that "every inhabitant shall contribute to all charges both in Church and State"; that preachers, duly ordained by some Protestant bishop or minister, should present their certificates of ordination to the governor, who should induct them into their pastorates; that the minister must administer the Lord's Supper at least once a year, and must not refuse baptism to a child of Christian parents; "nor shall any person be molested, fined or imprisoned, for differing in judgment in matters of religion, who professes Christianity."

As Cobb emphasizes, it is important to note that the disestablishment of the Reformed Church did not result in the separation of church and state. On the contrary, the state extended its jurisdiction over all sects. No individual church was established, but the legal effect was to establish the Protestant religion by whatever sect it might be represented. The head of the state was also the head of every church in the province, a situation unprecedented in the history of church-state relationships (with the possible exception of Great Britain, where the same monarch is head of both the Anglican Church of England and the Presbyterian Church of Scotland). Elsewhere the idea of civil power over the church always involved the legal preference of one church, accompanied by either the persecution or the toleration of others. Here for the first time all churches were established.[43]

The "Charter of Liberties" adopted by the assembly of the colony in 1683 reaffirmed the system of multiple establishments, by decreeing that

> No person professing faith in God by Jesus Christ is to be molested or called in question for any difference of opinion in matters of religion, [and that] the Churches already in New York do appear to be privileged Churches. . . . Provided also that all other Christian Churches, that shall hereafter come and settle in the province, shall have the same privileges.

When, however, the Duke of York ascended to the throne of England, attempts were made to confer preferential status upon the Church of England; but these succeeded in only four counties in the colony.[44]

In New Jersey agitation by Episcopal clergy for the legal establishment of the Church of England failed to attain even the partial success achieved in New York.[45] In Georgia the original charter of 1732, which guaranteed liberty of conscience to all persons "except Papists," was voided in 1752, and the Church of England was formally established.[46]

## CATHOLIC MARYLAND

Even during the early English colonial period there were some places where the restrictive policies and practices of Puritan New England and Anglican Virginia were, if not absent, at least substantially ameliorated. In Maryland, Rhode Island, and Pennsylvania attempts were made to establish communities in which at least all Christians if not all men could live together with a reasonable degree of harmony.

Maryland was colonized in large part as an economic venture,[47] but also to provide a refuge for a persecuted religious minority. The Calverts, father and son, who founded the colony, were converts to Catholicism, and sought to provide an asylum for English Catholics and opportunities for Catholic missions among the Indians. Since, however, most English Catholics preferred to risk the penalty of intermittent fines for nonattendance at Anglican religious services rather than the dangers and rigors of colonial life, Protestants as well as Catholics were recruited for settlement.[48] Moreover, the second Calvert received his charter from a Protestant king in a nation in which the tide of Puritanism was rising high, and he could not possibly hope to erect a purely Catholic community in Maryland.[49]

Undoubtedly the Calverts had, for their times, a liberal outlook; but it is also true that practical considerations played a major part in the generous policy to non-Catholic Christians practiced in Maryland under Catholic proprietorship. The original charter, drawn by the first Lord Baltimore, expressly provided that the churches built in the colony were to be consecrated "according to the ecclesiastical laws of England." The second Baltimore, in his instructions to the first governor and commissioners, warned them that they should suffer no offense or scandal to be given to any of the Protestants, to "cause all acts of Roman Catholic Religion to be done privately as may be," and to "instruct the Roman Catholics to be silent upon all occasions of discourse concerning matters of religion."[50] The third Baltimore was both realistic and frank when he stated that there were many who were willing to go as colonists

> so as they might have a General Toleration . . . by a Law by which all of all sorts who professed Christianity in General might be at liberty to worship God in such manner as was most agreeable with their respective judgments and consciences . . . without the complying with these conditions in all probability, this Province had never been planted.[51]

Whether, like Roger Williams and William Penn, Baltimore was motivated by a sincere belief in religious liberty for its own sake or by the demands of expediency, he succeeded in establishing an oasis of tolerance in a desert of religious persecution. In 1636 he prescribed an oath to be taken by all Maryland governors which stated that "if any person or officer shall molest any person, professing to believe in Jesus Christ, on account of his religion, I will protect the person molested and punish the offender."[52] During the fifteen years between the establishment of the colony and the Act of Toleration of 1649 there does not appear to have been a single incident of persecution for religious belief.[53] Moreover, Baltimore exercised a substantial restraining influence on Jesuit priests who sought to procure for the Catholic Church the preferred position which it possessed in Catholic countries in Europe and which Congregationalism was then enjoying in New England and Anglicanism in Virginia.[54] A demand by the priests to introduce the canon law and ecclesiastical courts for cases involving priests was met by a law enacted in the colony in 1638 that all laws should be "equally enforced against and concerning all persons, lay and ecclesiastical, without distinction, exemption or privilege of any."[55]

The Act of Toleration of 1649 has been lauded as "the first decree granting complete religious liberty to emanate from an assembly."[56] Though even a superficial examination of the law shows quite clearly that it is far from a grant of "complete religious liberty," it nevertheless is an important landmark in the history of the evolution of the American principle of separation and religious liberty. And this is so even though its adoption may well have been the result of the exigencies of the situation rather than any deep-felt commitment to any principle of tolerance.

The practice of toleration established by the Baltimores had brought into Maryland a mixture of religious sects, with the Protestant elements increasing more rapidly than the Catholic. Moreover, in 1648 Charles I, in fear of the ascendant Puritan power, begged Baltimore to take measures to avoid the charge that his colony was in reality a Catholic stronghold. Baltimore accordingly replaced his Catholic governor and council with Protestants, and submitted to his dominion a draft of his Toleration Act which was shortly thereafter passed by the Maryland Assembly.[57] Whether, as has been stated, the majority of the Assembly were Catholics is not certain,[58] nor is it of much significance one way or the other. As the Beards point out, "a general freedom of conscience had not been up to that time a cardinal principle proclaimed by Catholics, Anglicans or Puritans wherever they were in a position to coerce."[59] It is hardly unfair to assume that but for the perilous situation at home the Act would not have been adopted by a Catholic assembly in Maryland in 1649.

The statute itself, entitled, "An Act concerning Religion," was only partly an act of toleration. It had four principal provisions, the first three of which were denials rather than grants of religious liberty; only the last dealt with toleration. The first section imposed the penalty of death and forfeiture of estate on any person who "shall hence forth blaspheme God, that is curse Him, or deny our Savior Jesus Christ to be the Son of God, or shall deny the Holy Trinity the Father the Son and Holy Ghost, or the Godhead of any of the said three persons of the Trinity or the unity of the Godhead, or shall use or utter any reproachful speeches, words or language concerning the Holy Trinity, or any of the three persons therein." Utterance of "reproachful words and speeches" concerning the Virgin Mary, or the "holy apostles or evangelists," was punishable only by fine, whipping, imprisonment, and banishment.

The second section imposed fines, whipping, and imprisonment on any person calling another "an heretic, schismatic, idolator, Puritan, Independent, Presbyterian, papish priest, Jesuit, Jesuited papist, Lutheran, Calvinist, Anabaptist, Brownist, Antinomian, Barrowist, Roundhead, Separatist, or any other name or term in a reproachful manner relating to matter of religion."

The third section imposed fines or imprisonment for profaning the Lord's Day.

The fourth section read in part as follows:

And whereas the enforcing of the conscience in matters of religion hath frequently fallen out to be of dangerous consequence in those commonwealths where it has been practiced, and for the more quiet and peaceable government of this province and the better to preserve mutual love and unity among the inhabitants, no person or persons whatsoever within this province ... professing to believe in Jesus Christ, shall henceforth be in any ways troubled, molested or discountenanced for or in respect of his or her religion, nor in the free exercise thereof ... nor any way compelled to the belief or exercise of any other religion against his or her consent. . . .[60]

Measured by the standards of liberty prevailing today—or during the Revolutionary era—the Act of Toleration obviously leaves much to be desired, even disregarding the blasphemy and Sabbath profanation provisions. Its protection was limited not merely to Christians but to Trinitarian Christians; Jews and infidels were of course excluded. But beyond that, the ban on any slight to the apostles, Mary, or Jesus threatened to suppress any discussion deviating from orthodox theology.

The extent to which the blasphemy prohibition was a restriction on religious liberty is evidenced by the prosecution in 1658 of a Jew,

Jacob Lumbrazo, "for uttering words of blasphemy against our Blessed Savior Jesus Christ." In answer to some questions provocatively put by a Christian, Lumbrazo stated that a mere man had been crucified at Jerusalem, that he performed miracles by magic, and that his disciples stole his body. For reasons which have never been clearly explained, the prosecution was dropped before it reached trial.[61]

The Maryland Act must in fairness be judged in the light of the times in which it was promulgated. Blasphemy of God or the Trinity was punishable by death under laws which had previously been promulgated in England, Massachusetts, and Virginia,[62] and strict Sunday laws were common in the colonies.[63] Measured by the standards prevailing in most of the colonies at the time, the Maryland Act represented a great advance in the struggle toward the achievement of religious liberty.

Unfortunately the advance was only temporary. Within a few years the Puritans obtained control of England, Maryland was taken away from the Baltimores, and the Act was repealed. In 1658 the province was restored to Lord Baltimore and the Act again put in force;[64] but thirty years later James II was driven from his throne. Thereafter Anglicans had the upper hand, and used it as they did in Virginia. The Church of England was established in Maryland, and the collection of taxes for its support was decreed. The public exercise of Catholic worship was proscribed, and the admission of Catholic immigrants was forbidden.[65]

## ROGER WILLIAMS' "LIVELIE EXPERIMENT"

The policy of limited toleration that was practiced in Maryland under the Calverts was based on practical considerations; there is no evidence that ideological considerations played any significant role. In Rhode Island, on the other hand, religious liberty was not a practice forced on an unwilling leader by the accident of history, but an ideal founded on the concept which a century and a half later was to achieve its fullest expression in the American Constitution—the concept of the mutual independence of religion and government.

Roger Williams, who founded the colony, was banished from Massachusetts in the winter of 1635—1636 because he "broached and divulged divers new and dangerous opinions"[66]—among others, the doctrine of the two tables, i.e., that it was the business of the civil magistrate to enforce the injunctions of the second table of the Decalogue which concerned man's dealings with his fellow men, but that the punishment of offenses against the first table, governing one's relations with God, was not within the proper sphere of the state.[67] Fleeing with four companions, Williams settled at Providence, where he established a community for Baptists, Quakers, and other nonconformists. Williams personally disliked the Quakers, but refused to bar them from his colony. In the plantation covenant of the Providence settlers, obedience to the state was expressly limited to "civil things"; and when Rhode Island was called on by the New England confederation to enact penal legislation against the Quakers it refused, and pointed out that it had no law for punishing people because of their utterances "concerning the things and ways of God, as to salvation and an eternal condition."[68]

In 1663 a charter was obtained from the British crown, which recited that settlers have it "much on their hearts to hold forth a livelie experiment that a most flourishing civil state may best be maintained . . . with full libertie in religious concernments." It decreed that

> no person within the said colony . . . shall be in any wise molested, punished, disquieted or called in question, for any differences in opinion in matters of religion, and do not actually disturb the civil peace of our said colony.[69]

Throughout the 17th century Rhode Island seems to have acted in accord with this policy. Later, however, a law was enacted that limited citizenship and eligibility to public office to Protestants.[70] (Williams had argued that to limit civil magistrates to church members was like permitting only church members to assume "the office of a Doctor of Physic, a Master or a Pilot of a Ship, or a Captain or Commander of a Band or Army of men; for which services, the children of God may be no ways qualified, though otherwise excellent for the fear of God, and the knowledge and Grace of the Lord Jesus.")[77] This law was not always strictly enforced, and some Jews and Catholics were actually admitted to citizenship by special acts of the assembly; but in 1762 the Superior Court of the colony enforced the restrictive law by refusing the application of two Jews for citizenship. There was, however, no penal legislation against either Catholics or Jews, and the latter were sufficiently numerous in Newport to maintain a synagogue.[72]

More than a century before the Declaration of Independence declared that governments derive their just powers from the consent of the governed, Williams wrote that "the Sovereign power of all Civil Authority is founded in the consent of the People."[73] But the extent to which, as Vernon Parrington put it, "the gods were pleased to have their jest with Roger Williams by sending him to earth before his time,"[74] can best be gauged by contrasting his statement that "No civil state or country can be truly called Christian, although the Christians be in it,"[75] with a dictum of a justice of the United States Supreme Court, deciding a case under a Constitution which prohibited any "establishment of religion," that the United States "is a Christian nation."[76] Or we may contrast the action of the United States Supreme Court in 1961 upholding the conviction of Jewish Sabbatarians for violation of a state Sunday law,[77] with the following extract from the journal of Governor Winthrop of Massachusetts Bay in 1631:

> At a court holden at Boston . . . a letter was written from that court to Mr. Endecott to this effect: That . . . Mr. Williams . . . had declared his opinion, that the magistrate might not punish the breach of the Sabbath, . . . as it was a breach of the first table.[78]

It is not too much to say that American principles of religious liberty have not yet caught up with Roger Williams.

In 1654 Williams wrote his famous letter to the Town of Providence, in which he said:

> There goes many a ship to sea, with many hundred souls in one ship, whose weal and woe is common, and is a true picture of a commonwealth, or a human combination or society. It hath fallen out sometimes, that both papists and protestants, Jews and Turks, may be embarked in one ship; upon which supposal I affirm, that all the liberty of conscience, that ever I pleaded for, turns upon these two hinges — that none of the papists, protestants, Jews, or Turks, be forced to come to the ship's prayers or worship, nor compelled from their own particular prayers or worship, if they practice any. I further add, that I never denied, that notwithstanding this liberty, the commander of this ship ought to command the ship's course, yea, and also command that justice, peace and sobriety, be kept and practiced, both among the seamen and all the passengers.[79]

Williams' pamphlet, *The Bloudy Tenent of Persecution for cause of Conscience, discussed in a Conference between Truth and Peace*,[80] is an epochal milestone in the history of religious freedom and the separation of church and state. Along with Jefferson's *Act for Establishing Religious Freedom*, Madison's *Memorial and Remonstrance*, and the First Amendment, it stands as one of the cornerstones of the American experiment. The purpose of the pamphlet is to support twelve principles, of which the following are typical:

> First, that the blood of so many hundred thousand souls of Protestants and Papists, spilt in the Wars of present and former Ages, for their respective Consciences, is not required nor accepted by Jesus Christ the Prince of Peace. . . .
> Fifthly, All Civil States with their Officers of justice in their respec-

tive constitutions and administrations are proved essentially Civil, and therefore not Judges, Governors or Defenders of the Spiritual or Christian State and Worship.

Sixthly, It is the will and command of God, that (since the coming of his Son the Lord Jesus) a permission of the most Paganish, Jewish, Turkish, or Antichristian consciences and worships, be granted to all men in all Nations and Countries: and they are only to be fought against with that Sword which is only (in Soul matters) able to conquer, to wit, the Sword of God's Spirit, the Word of God. . . .

Tenthly, An enforced uniformity of Religion throughout a Nation or civil state, confounds the Civil and Religious, denies the principles of Christianity and civility, and that Jesus Christ is come in the Flesh. . . .

Twelfthly, lastly, true civility and Christianity may both flourish in a state or Kingdom, notwithstanding the permission of divers and contrary consciences, either of Jew or Gentile. . . .

The significance of the *Bloudy Tenent* lies not so much in its argument for religious liberty as in the philosophic basis for that argument. In view of contemporary attempts to justify a severable dichotomy of religious freedom and separation of church and state,[81] it is important to note that to Williams (as to Jefferson and Madison 150 years later), not two but one principle was involved. Religious persecution is wrong because it "confounds the Civil and Religious" and because "States . . . are proved essentially Civil." The "power of true discerning the true fear of God" is not one of the powers that the people have transferred to Civil Authority.[82]

All lawful Magistrates in the World, [Williams said] both before the coming of Christ Jesus, and since, (excepting those unparalleled typical Magistrates of the Church of Israel) are but Derivatives and Agents immediately derived and employed as eyes and hands, serving for the good of the whole: Hence they have and can have no more Power than fundamentally lies in the Bodies or fountains themselves, which Power, Might, or Authority, is not Religious, Christian, etc. but natural, humane and civil.[83]

To Williams, taxation for religious purposes was unjust:

It is reasonable to expect and demand of such as live within the State a civil maintenance of their civil officers, and to force it where it is denied. It is reasonable for a School-master to demand his recompense for his labor in his School: but it is not reasonable to expect or force it from strangers, enemies, rebels to that City, from such as come not within, or else would not be received into the School. What is the Church of Christ Jesus, but the City, the School, and Family of Christ? The Officers of this City, School, Family, may reasonably expect maintenance from such [as] they minister unto, but not from strangers, enemies, etc. . . .

Williams disposes of the argument that religion requires the aid

87

of the state, in the same way that the opponents of Virginia's Assessment Bill were to do 140 years later:[84]

> ... the Scriptures of Truth and the Records of Time concur in this, that the first Churches of Christ Jesus, the lights, patterns, and precedents to all succeeding Ages, were gathered and governed without the aid, assistance, or countenance of any Civil Authority, from which they suffered great persecutions for the name of the Lord Jesus professed amongst them.[85]

Seventeenth century America was not ready for Roger Williams. In view of the still current attack on the principle of separation of church and state,[86] and the continued civil enforcement of Sunday laws, we are perhaps even now not ready for those ideas. Nevertheless, they do represent the great contribution of American democracy to civilization.

## PENNSYLVANIA

Pennsylvania, like Maryland, was colonized partly as a substantial business venture and partly as a "holy experiment," conceived in a liberal yet distinctly religious spirit.[87] Its proprietor, William Penn, inherited from his father a large claim against Charles II, which was settled by a grant to Penn of the land that became Pennsylvania.[88]

Long before he received his charter Penn had been an ardent advocate of toleration, having himself suffered imprisonment for his religious convictions. While still a student at Oxford, he had joined the despised and persecuted sect of Friends, commonly called the Quakers. In his early writing, *The Great Case of Liberty of Conscience ... Briefly Debated and Defended* (1670), he opposed coercion in matters of conscience on the ground that

> imposition, restraint and persecution for conscience sake, highly invade the Divine prerogative.

On another occasion he wrote:

> Let the tares grow with the wheat, errors of judgment remain till removed by the power of light and conviction. . . . For my part, I frankly declare that I can not think that God will damn any man for the errors of his judgment.[89]

In 1677, even before the establishment of Pennsylvania, Penn had an opportunity to give practical effect to his ideals. As one of the coproprietors of West Jersey, before control passed in 1692 to a group belonging to the Church of England, Penn was largely responsible for the "Concessions and agreements of the Proprietors,

Freeholders, and inhabitants of West Jersey, in America." This document was a great forward step in the history of civil liberty, providing as it did not only for liberty of conscience, but also for security from illegal arrest, trial by jury, and control of taxation by representatives elected by the secret ballot of the entire body of proprietors, freeholders, and inhabitants of the colony.[90]

On his acquisition of Pennsylvania, Penn set down as "the first fundamentall" of his government freedom of faith and worship "in such a way and manner as every Person shall in conscience believe is most acceptable to God." Under the Great Law, enacted in 1682, no person who acknowledged one God and agreed to live "peaceable and justly under the civil government" was to be disturbed because of his religious faith or worship, or compelled to attend any religious service other than that of his own choice. Nevertheless, profanity was penalized, and Sunday observance was required with rest from "common toil," not merely for "the ease of the creation," but also in order to prevent the growth of "Looseness, irreligion and Atheism . . . under pretence of Conscience," and that there might be time for reading the Scriptures either at home or in a place of public worship. But though the grant of freedom of faith and worship to all who believed in God was theoretically broad enough to encompass not only Catholics but Jews as well, political privileges were limited to Christians;[91] and in practice it appears that neither Catholics nor Jews enjoyed complete freedom of worship, at least at the beginning of the enterprise.[92] Yet it remains true that on the eve of the Revolution Pennsylvania was the only one of the thirteen colonies in which the services of the Roman communion were publicly held.[93]

Undoubtedly toleration in Pennsylvania was based on Penn's idealism, but, as in Calvert's Maryland, it also coincided with the proprietor's desire to reap substantial profits from his province, and this necessitated attracting large numbers of settlers. Penn's widespread advertisements for settlers prominently promised religious toleration. These brought immigrants from the continent as well as from Britain, and resulted in a more rapid population growth than in any of the older colonies. In none of the other colonies at the end of the colonial period was there so great a variety of religious groups as in Pennsylvania. In 1776 the Christian congregations in Pennsylvania included German Reformed, Presbyterian, Lutheran, Quaker, Episcopalian, Baptist, Moravian, Mennonite, Dunker, Catholic, and Dutch Reformed.[94]

Summarizing the colonial period, we may note that the proprietary regimes permitted a considerable degree of toleration, at least in comparison with the other colonies. This difference may be explained partly by the idealism of the proprietors and partly by the economic necessity of attracting large numbers of settlers in order to preserve and make profitable the proprietor's substantial investment.

Even in the proprietory colonies, however, the death of the idealistic founder, Calvert, Williams, or Penn, resulted in considerable backsliding, and the imposition of restrictions on civil and religious rights, particularly of non-Protestants. The limited tolerance which did exist did not include Catholics, Jews, Unitarians, or Deists. The variety and degree of discrimination against them varied. Primarily, the discrimination was political—the non-Protestants could not vote or hold office. But the restrictions were not always limited to political disabilities. Public performance of Catholic worship was prohibited almost everywhere, and as late as 1756 the colony which had been founded by the Catholic Calverts enacted a law subjecting Catholics to double taxation.[95] Perhaps the incident that most ironically illustrates the turnabout after the death of the idealistic founder is the action of a Rhode Island court which in 1762 denied the petition of two Jews for naturalization on the ground that to grant the petition would be "inconsistent with the first principles on which the colony was founded."[96]

### CHAPTER FOUR

# The Principle Is Born

## INFLUENCES LEADING TO FREEDOM AND SEPARATION

IN AUGUST 1700 the province of New York enacted a law under which any Jesuit, priest, or other ecclesiastic ordained by the Pope who remained in the province after November 1, 1700, teaching or practicing Catholic doctrines or rites or granting absolutions "shall be deemed and accounted an incendiary and disturber of the public peace and safety and an enemy of the true Christian religion and shall be adjudged to suffer perpetual banishment."[1] In 1704 Maryland forbade Roman Catholic priests to baptize children, and in 1716 imposed severe penalties on public officials who participated in the mass after taking an oath of office.[2] As late as the eve of the Revolution, the governor of Pennsylvania, the only colony that did not interfere with the public exercise of Catholic rites,[3] expressed the opinion that such practice was illegal even in that colony.[4]

Nor were Catholics the only victims of colonial restrictions on religious liberty. In Virginia up to the time of the Revolution, denial of the Trinity was punishable by imprisonment for three years, and a Unitarian or freethinker could be adjudged an unfit custodian of his own children. Baptists, particularly during the "period of the Great Persecution," 1768 to 1774, were whipped, beaten, arrested, fined, and imprisoned, sometimes on bread and water.[5] In 1774 Madison wrote to a friend:

> That diabolical, hell-conceived principle of persecution rages among some. . . . This vexes me the worst of anything whatever. There are at this time in the adjacent county not less than five or six well-meaning men in close jail for publishing their religious sentiments, which in the main are very orthodox. I have neither patience to hear, talk, or think of anything relative to this matter; for I have squabbled and scolded, abused and ridiculed, so long about it to little purpose, that I am without common patience. So I must beg you to pity me, and pray for liberty of conscience to all.[6]

In the same letter Madison complained that "ecclesiastical establishments tend to great ignorance and corruption; all of which facilitates the execution of mischievous projects . . . ," but compulsory support of religion was the rule rather than the exception, and Virginia by law required church attendance several times yearly.[7] At the outbreak of the Revolution some type of establishment existed in most of the thirteen colonies,[8] and eighteen dissenters were in jail in one Massachusetts community for declining to pay ministerial rates in support of the established worship.[9]

In 1787 a constitution was created for the new republic in which was implicit the principle that the government had no power to legislate in the domain of religion either by restricting its free exercise or providing for its support. In 1791 this principle was made explicit with the adoption of the First Amendment. By and large the principle was accepted by the states about the same time, even though Massachusetts did not formally disestablish the Congregational Church until 1833. The American principle of separation and religious liberty may then accurately be said to have been born in the last quarter of the 18th century.

The establishment of the American experiment cannot be attributed to any single event or cause; a number of factors combined to bring forth this result. Practical considerations, such as the multiplicity of sects spreading over all the colonies, and the advance of trade and commerce, were undoubtedly of vital significance. But it would be a complete misreading of American history if these were to be considered the sole reasons for disestablishment and freedom—ideological considerations were equally important. The American experiment rests as much on the social contract as it does on the mutual suspicions and rivalries of Anglicans, Congregationalists, and Presbyterians.

Insistence on the recognition of the ideological bases of separation is not merely a matter of academic history; it has practical consequences. This point will be discussed more fully in the next chapter. Here we need note only that acceptance of separation as the necessary price paid for religious pluralism leads to an interpretation of separation that permits government support of religion if it can be accomplished in a manner that is fair and equitable to all sects. On the other hand, if separation is conceived as government disability to intervene in religious affairs by reason of the people's withholding of that power from those delegated to govern, the support of religion violates the principle of separation even if all sects agree on the manner of sharing in the state's favors.

The American experiment was the result of the happy coincidence of a number of interdependent practical and ideological factors, each of which must be accorded its due weight. Among these, the most important were probably the English Act of Toleration of 1689, the multiplicity of sects, the lack of church affiliation on the part of most Americans, the rise of commercial intercourse, the exigencies of the Revolutionary War, the Williams-Penn tradition and the success of their experiments, the writings of Locke, the social contract theory, the Great Awakening, and the influence of European rationalism and deism.

## PRACTICAL CONSIDERATIONS

### The English Act of Toleration

In England, Protestant dissenters who had cooperated with Anglican churchmen in the revolution of 1688 were rewarded by the Act of Toleration of 1689, which conferred on them the right to hold public services subject to the registration of their ministers and places of worship. The Anglican Church retained its special privileges, and Dissenters were still disqualified from public office. Moreover, Catholics and Unitarians were completely excluded from the benefits of the statute.[10] Measured by the practices then prevailing not only in Rhode Island, but even in New York, this could hardly be considered an advance of religious liberty. Indeed, it is possible that its enactment had the reverse effect in Rhode Island, and was responsible for the removal of Catholics from those entitled to religious liberty under the laws of that colony.[11] It was, nevertheless, an advance over the practices prevailing in most of the colonies, and its enactment had a salutary influence on them.

Colonial policy in general followed the pattern of the English Act of Toleration,[12] though its applicability to the colonies was occasionally disputed. In 1748, the attorney general of Virginia argued before the General Court that the Act did not extend to Virginia, and therefore the "New Side Presbyterians," applying for a license for meetinghouses, were not entitled to its benefits. The court, however, decided to the contrary,[13] and when ten years later a new lieutenant governor was appointed, he assured the Presbytery of Hanover that he "would secure to them the continued enjoyment of the liberties and immunities granted by the Act of Toleration."[14]

In the other colonies the applicability of the Act appears to have been assumed; at least, toleration was accorded to Protestant dissenters who qualified under its terms.[15] Modest an advance as it was, it nevertheless constituted a factor of some influence in the evolution of the American experiment.

### Multiplicity of Sects

It was indeed a matter of great good fortune that England did not follow the example of Spain in closing its colonies to schismatics and heretics. England adopted the opposite policy, and opened the gates of the American colonies to every kind of religious faith that could be found in the old world.[16] The result of this policy is observable today in the difference between the religious complexion of the peoples of Latin America and of the United States. In Latin America the religious origin of the population is almost exclusively Roman Catholic,[17] whereas in the United States there are at least 256 different sects and denominations.[18] The result is equally observable in the different solutions arrived at in Latin America and the United States of the problem of the relationship of religion and government.

It is of course true that, as we have seen, the English policy was motivated by solid practical considerations. The colonies represented large financial investments which would be profitable only if people would settle there. With an Erastian tradition going back at least to Henry VIII, the English lords decided to forgo the luxury of protecting at the expense of their pocketbooks whatever at the moment happened to be the true and eternal church. But the motivation of the policy is of secondary importance to its consequence—a religious diversity unique in the New World.

The extent of the diversity in but one colony as early as 1687 can be gauged from the report made that year by Governor Dongan of New York, in which he stated:

> New York has first a chaplain . . . of the Church of England; secondly, a Dutch Calvinist; thirdly, a French Calvinist; fourthly, a Dutch Lutheran. Here be not many of the Church of England; few Roman Catholics; abundance of Quaker preachers, men, and women especially; Singling Quakers; Ranting Quakers; Sabbatarians; Anti-Sabbatarians; some Ana-baptists; some Jews; in short, of all sorts of opinion there are some, and the most part none at all.[19]

In Pennsylvania there were to be found Quakers, Mennonites, Dunkers, Moravians, Schwenkfelders, Lutherans, German and Dutch Reformed, several varieties of Presbyterians, Baptists, Anglicans, and Roman Catholics, with no one group having a majority.[20] Similar religious diversity was to be found in the other colonies. At the time of the Revolution there were at least ten major denominations, with substantial numbers of churches and clergymen.[21]

The influence of the multiplicity of sects in colonial America on the growth of religious freedom has been recognized by all students of the subject.[22] Even in the 18th century Jefferson, Madison, Voltaire, and others recognized this. Voltaire said:

If there were one religion in England, its despotism would be terrible; if there were only two, they would destroy each other; but there are thirty, and therefore they live in peace and happiness.[23]

To this Madison added:

Security for civil rights must be the same as that for religious rights; it consists in the one case in a multiplicity of interests and in the other in a multiplicity of sects.[24]

The influence of diversity on freedom and separation was effected in a number of ways. In the first place, since there were too many dissenting sects to be extirpated, there was no alternative but to learn to live together. In the second place, daily exposure to different religions weakened that passionate conviction in the exclusive rightness of one's own faith which is a necessary prerequisite of persecution for the sake of religion. Finally, the great diversity of sects made religious uniformity impossible, and without such uniformity establishment could not long survive.

## The Unchurched

Another important practical factor influencing the growth of religious freedom was the fact that during the period between the Revolution and the adoption of the First Amendment, only a small minority of Americans were affiliated with any church. There was a multiplicity of denominations, but paradoxically a paucity of adherents.

Exact figures do not exist on church affiliation or lack of church affiliation in the second half of the 18th century. Authorities do agree, however, that affiliation was extremely small. According to Sweet, colonial America contained "the largest proportion of unchurched in Christendom."[25] Even in New England, the most churched section of the thirteen colonies, there was not more than one church member to every eight persons in the total population at the close of the colonial period.[26] In respect to the population of the total country, the best estimate is that church affiliation at the founding of the republic was limited to four per cent of the population.[27] Today almost two out of every three Americans are church members.[28]

A variety of reasons may be ascribed for this small percentage of church membership at the close of the colonial period. Undoubtedly some of the skepticism that accompanied the European enlightenment traveled westward over the ocean to American shores. Doubtless, too, economic considerations pre-empted much of American life. But lack of church affiliation does not necessarily mean an

95

equal lack of religious motivation. Frontier conditions made formal church membership difficult if not impossible for many. The individualism of the American colonist, which manifested itself in the great number of sects, also resulted in much unaffiliated religion. It is probably true that religion was widespread but was mostly a personal, noninstitutional matter.

Whatever the reasons, the prevalence of the lack of formal church affiliation obviously contributed to the growing movement toward religious liberty and disestablishment. Persons not themselves connected with any church were not likely to persecute others for similar independence. Nor were they likely to countenance for long compulsory taxation to support a church to which they did not belong.

### The Rise of Commerce

It is no accident that the proprietary colonies, which were developed largely for commercial purposes, manifested on the whole a larger degree of toleration than did the other colonies. Nor is it any accident that the two greatest commercial powers of the 17th century, England and Holland, were the ones that showed the largest measure of religious tolerance in their colonial laws.[29] The value of toleration to the advancement of commerce was recognized by the rulers of these countries.

It was the growing influence of the merchants which accounts at least in part for the writing of liberty-of-conscience clauses into the charters of New York, New Jersey, the Carolinas, and Georgia.[30] The toleration accorded to Jews by England in the 17th and 18th centuries was expressly stated to be motivated by considerations of trade and commerce. Stokes and Sweet both refer significantly to a request made in 1750 by the lords of trade to the president of the council, which begins:

> With regard to the affair of Mr. Davies the Presbyterian, as Toleration and a free exercise of religion is so valuable a branch of true liberty, and so essential to the enriching and improving of a Trading Nation, it should ever be held sacred in his Majesty's Colonies. . . .[31]

Besides the difficulty of engaging in trade with persons one seeks to destroy for difference in religious belief, commerce, as Ruffini points out, tended to distract the colonies from their absorbing preoccupations and their exclusiveness in the matter of religion, encouraging them "to think less of the Church and more of the State and of commerce."[32] Another student states:

> The growth of trade and commerce which were especially prominent

in New England and the middle colonies was a further important factor in inducing toleration; not only did it, by taking man away from home to lands practicing other religions, breed an indifference to sectarian differences, but it also made religion in general seem less important. Business and wealth tended to replace salvation as the main interest of man. To some extent this was encouraged by the Calvinistic tendency to equate worldly success with salvation.[33]

## The Revolutionary War

The War of Independence exercised a significant influence on the development of religious freedom. Wars generally have a unifying effect on the population, and tend to submerge internal differences. This was particularly true of the Revolutionary War, based as it claimed to be on ideological grounds. Thoughtful persons could not fail to see the inconsistency between the practices of religious discrimination and the natural-rights doctrines of freedom and equality set forth in the Declaration of Independence.[34] It was difficult to justify inequality in religious treatment by a nation which severed its political bonds with the king of England because he violated the self-evident truth that all men are created equal.

The practical exigencies of the war itself played an important part in liberalizing the treatment of dissenters and nonconformists. Concessions had to be made to the dissenting churches to insure their cooperation in the over-all struggle. What may have been the first break in the exclusive privileges of the Anglican establishment in Virginia came with the organization of the Revolutionary Army. The convention of Richmond in 1775 granted to each dissenting denomination the privilege of performing divine service in the army "for the ease of such scrupulous consciences as may not choose to attend divine services as celebrated by the [Anglican] chaplain."[35] In addition, petitions for relief from compulsory tithes were more sympathetically received.

The liberalizing effect of the Revolutionary War was most clear in the treatment of Catholics. They had been specifically excluded from the Toleration Act of 1689, and the colonial charters and legislative acts thereafter promulgated followed the pattern of the Toleration Act, using the standard phrase, "Papists excepted." As we have seen, at the outbreak of the Revolution only Pennsylvania allowed public performance of the mass.

Though there were probably not more than 18,000 Catholics in the United States when the War broke out,[36] the Continental Congress felt that their cooperation was necessary for the successful outcome of the conflict. Even more important was its desire to win the cooperation or at least neutrality of Catholic Canada. In 1774 Congress sent a conciliatory "Letter to the Inhabitants of Quebec," in which it referred to the Swiss Confederation as a "union . . . composed of Roman Catholic and Protestant States, living in the utmost concord and peace with one another, and thereby enabled . . . to defy and defeat every tyrant that has invaded them."[37] The next year, when Congress was planning an expedition to Canada, Washington warned his army at Cambridge against participating in the observance of "Pope's Day," the New England commemoration of the Gunpowder Plot, by "that ridiculous and childish custom of burning the effigy of the Pope," in view of the "impropriety of such a step at this juncture; at a time when we are soliciting, and have really obtained the friendship and alliance of the people of Canada. . . ."[38]

In 1776 Congress sent a committee, which included the Catholic layman Charles Carroll, a signer of the Declaration of Independence, and the free-thinking Benjamin Franklin, to confer with the Canadian Catholics. Though the mission failed of its object, it was a significant episode in the evolution of religious freedom in view of the instructions given to the delegation by Congress. These read in part:

> You are further to declare that we hold sacred the rights of conscience and may promise to the whole people, solemnly in our name, the free and undisturbed exercise of their religion; and, to the clergy, the full, perfect and peaceable possession and enjoyment of all their estates. That the government of everything relating to their religion and clergy, shall be left entirely in the hands of the good people of that province and such legislature as they shall constitute; provided, however, that all other denominations of Christians be equally entitled to hold offices and enjoy civil privileges and the free exercise of their religion and be totally exempt from the payment of any tithes or taxes for the support of any religion.[39]

The alliance with Catholic France and informal cooperation with Catholic Spain furthered the movement toward religious freedom for Catholics. There were Catholics in the Continental Army ministered to by Catholic chaplains. In fact, the animosities toward Catholics lessened to such an extent that on occasions members of Congress attended the services of the Catholic Church.[40]

## IDEOLOGICAL INFLUENCES

### The Williams-Penn Tradition

The experiments of Rhode Island and Pennsylvania in religious freedom and separation proved of great value in the final evolution of the American principle. They were bold experiments, but they were successful, and, all in all, permanent.[41] When the Constitutional fathers convened in Philadelphia in 1787, and when Congress and the states adopted the First Amendment in 1791, they were fully familiar with, and greatly influenced by, the success of these experiments,[42] which they contrasted with the practices of religious persecution and oppression that—as the Supreme Court said—had "become so commonplace as to shock the freedom-loving colonists into a feeling of abhorrence,"[43] and which had led to the adoption of the First Amendment.[44]

As important as the practical example of Rhode Island and Pennsylvania was the influence of the ideas of the fathers of these experiments. The Baptists who followed Williams and the Quakers who came after Penn remained faithful to the tradition articulated by the leaders of these denominations.[45] In the case of the Baptists especially there was, besides the teachings of Williams, a European background of separatism and of hostility to the association of Church and State.[46] The Baptists were the most active of all the colonial religious bodies in their unceasing struggle for religious freedom and separation.[47]

Williams' associate, John Clarke, though much less known than Williams, was equally forthright in his views on liberty of conscience. In his petition to Charles II in 1662 for a charter for Rhode Island, he stated: "A most flourishing Civil State may stand, yea, and best be maintained . . . with full liberty in religious concernments."[48] It is largely through his efforts that the charter obtained from the king in 1663 provided that "no person within the said colony . . . shall be in any way molested, punished, disquieted, or called in question, for any differences in opinion in matters of religion. . . ."[49]

By far the most active and effective Baptist follower of Williams in the struggle for religious freedom and separation of Church and State was the pastor Isaac Backus. From 1772, when he became agent to represent Baptists in their relations with the state in Massachusetts, until his death in 1806 he continually prayed, pleaded, and petitioned for freedom and separation. The petitions written by or under his direction in behalf of the Baptists are important documents in the evolution of the American experiment. Their importance lies in the fact that their plea for freedom is not predicated exclusively or even primarily on practical grounds, but on the ideological ground of the state's incapacity to intermeddle in matters of religion. This concept, as we have seen,[50] had been expressed by Williams in less explicit form, and was to be later stated even more clearly by Jefferson and Madison. It is on this concept that the American experiment is founded; and its acceptance by those who framed and adopted the Constitution and First Amendment is the reason for the uniqueness of the American solution of the problem of the relationship of church and state.

This concept was, of course, not the personal view of Backus. It was an official Baptist principle. Samuel Stillman, pastor of the First Baptist Church in Boston, delivered the election sermon in May 1779, in which he presented the Baptist view that the "jurisdiction of the magistrate neither can nor ought to be extended to the salvation of souls."[51] In 1791 John Leland, Baptist leader in Virginia, wrote a tract entitled *Rights of Conscience and therefore Religious Opinions not cognizable by law,* in which he stated that "Government has no more to do with the religious opinions of men than it has with the principles of mathematics."[52] The Baptists in opposing the Virginia Assessment Bill[53] did so on the ground that "religion was a thing apart from the concerns of the state."[54]

Backus fought and remonstrated in support of the tradition. His conscientious scruples against the support of religion by the civil authorities resulted in his arrest in Massachusetts for refusal to pay a precinct tax in support of the establishment.[55] In 1774 he presented a memorial against the Massachusetts tax in which he stated:

> The free exercises of private judgment, and the unalienable rights of conscience, are of too high a rank and dignity to be submitted to the decrees of councils, or the imperfect laws of fallible legislators . . . religion is a concern between God and the soul with which no human authority can intermeddle. . . .[56]

In the same year Backus wrote to John Adams:

> I fully concur with your grand maxim, that it is essential to liberty that representation and taxation go together. Well, then, since people do not vote for representatives in our legislature from ecclesiastical qualifications, but only, by virtue of those which are of a civil and worldly nature, how can representatives thus chosen have any right to impose ecclesiastical taxes? Yet they have assumed and long exercised such a power. For they assume a power to compel each town and parish in this Province to settle a minister, and have empowered the majority of the inhabitants to give away as much of their neighbor's estates as they please to their minister; and if they refuse to yield it to them, then to take it by force. And I am bold in it that taxes laid by the British Parliament upon America are not more contrary to civil freedom, than these taxes are to the very nature of liberty of conscience, which is an essential article in our character. . . .[57]

Later, in approving the provision in the Federal Constitution against any religious test, he stated:

. . . nothing is more evident, both in reason and the Holy Scriptures, than that religion is ever a matter between God and individuals, and therefore no man or men can impose any religious test without invading the essential prerogatives of the Lord Jesus Christ.[58]

Although the Baptists were the denomination by far most vigorous in the struggle for religious freedom and separation of church and state, they were not alone in the struggle. As we have seen, the Quakers also participated actively. Besides these, the Presbyterians made an effective contribution to the evolution of separation and freedom. Madison was quite likely influenced by the teachings of the Presbyterian president of Princeton, John Witherspoon, who strongly advocated separation of church and state,[59] and taught that every church should be supported by its own members or funds without help from the taxing power of the state.[60] Samuel Davies, leader of the Presbyterians of Virginia, was likewise an ardent advocate of separation.[61] It was the Presbytery of Hanover, founded largely by Davies, which remonstrated against the Virginia Assessment Bill on the ground that

The end of Civil Government is security to the temporal liberty and property of Mankind; and to protect them in the free Exercise of Religion — Legislators are invested with powers from their Constituents, for these purposes only; and their duty extends no farther — Religion is altogether personal, and the right of exercising it unalienable; and it is not, cannot, and ought not to be, resigned to the will of the society at large; and much less to the Legislature, — which derives its authority wholly from the consent of the People; and is limited by the Original intention of Civil Associations. . . .[62]

### Locke and the Social Contract

The petitions and remonstrances of the religious groups against establishment contained many arguments, such as the dangers of establishments and their futility. It is, however, deeply significant that so many of them — like the one just quoted — stressed the concept that religion is a natural right that is entirely personal and not within the scope of the powers of a political body. This was no accident; it was but an application of the social contract theory which had been popularized by John Locke and was so widely accepted as to be deemed a self-evident truth to the signers of the Declaration of Independence.

Locke's influence on America's solution of the church-state problem is recognized by most students.[63] Locke defined a church as a "voluntary society of men, joining themselves together of their own accord in order to engage in the public worship of God, in such a manner as they judge acceptable to Him, and effectual to the salvation of their souls."[64] On the other hand, he defines the commonwealth as "a society of men constituted only for the procuring, preserving, and advancing their own civil interests."[65] The idea that religion is outside the jurisdiction of civil government is expressed in his epochal first *Letter Concerning Toleration:*

> Now that the whole jurisdiction of the magistrate reaches only to these civil concernments; and that all civil power, right and dominion, is bounded and confined to the only care of promoting these things; and that it neither can nor ought in any manner to be extended to the salvation of souls, these following considerations seem to me abundantly to demonstrate,
>
> *First,* Because the care of souls is not committed to the civil magistrate, any more than to other men. It is not committed unto him, I say, by God; because it appears not that God has ever given any such authority to one man over another, as to compel any one to his religion. . . .
>
> *In the second place,* The care of souls cannot belong to the civil magistrate because his power consists only in outward force, but true and saving religion consists in the inward persuasion of the mind. . . .[66]

The influence of Locke and the social contract theory on the development of religious freedom and separation in America can be clearly seen from the memorial presented by the Baptists to the Continental Congress in 1774:

> Men unite in society, according to the great Mr. Locke, with an intention in every one the better to preserve himself, his liberty and property. The power of the society, or Legislature constituted by them, can never be supposed to extend any further than the common good, but is obliged to secure every one's property. To give laws, to receive obedience, to compel with the sword, belong to none but the civil magistrate; and on this ground we affirm that the magistrate's power extends not to the establishing any articles of faith or forms of worship, by force of laws; for laws are of no force without penalties. The care of souls cannot belong to the civil magistrate, because his power consists only in outward force; but pure and saving religion consists in the inward persuasion of the mind, without which nothing can be acceptable to God.[67]

Locke himself did not pursue his ideas to their logical conclusion. His view of toleration did not find room for Catholics and atheists; and implicit in his thinking is the contradiction that though no church should be established, yet the establishment of Protestant Christianity was quite proper.[68] The logical extension of his ideas was, however, effected by Jefferson, Madison, and the others responsible for the American experiment.

It was largely on the basis of Locke's ideas that Madison predicated his arguments against religious assessments. Since religion from its very nature lies outside the authority of civil society, it cannot be within the jurisdiction of any legislative body whose powers, being derivative, are necessarily limited. Representatives of government, therefore, who presume to regulate religion transcend their powers, and violate the inalienable rights of the people.[69]

The concept that religion was outside the jurisdiction of civil government was acceptable to and accepted both by the religionist and the rationalist. To the religionist, God or Christ did not desire the magistrate to have such jurisdiction ("render unto Caesar that which is Caesar's"; "my kingdom is not of this world," etc.); to the rationalist, the power to act in religion was not one of the powers conferred on government as part of the social contract. It is irrelevant that the social contract is today generally considered to be a historical fiction. What is important is that it was generally accepted as historical truth when American democracy was launched, and that it exercised a vital influence on the evolution of the American experiment in church-state relations.

## The Great Awakening

The middle of the 18th century saw an evangelical religious revival, originating in New England, which became known as the Great Awakening. The movement, associated with Jonathan Edwards, the New Light Presbyterians, and the Methodist George Whitefield, emphasized an emotional, personal religion. It appealed directly to the individual, stressing the rights and duties of the individual conscience and its answerability exclusively to God.[70]

Most of the revivalist groups who participated in the Great Awakening had no quarrel with orthodox Christian theology. On the contrary, they were generally fundamentalists, in the present-day meaning of that term. But the movement constituted a break with formal church religion, and developed a resistance to coercion by established churches. The result was that the ardent revivalist groups which formed the movement became staunch partisans of the separation of church and state.[71]

## Rationalism and Deism

It is paradoxical that separation in America came as the result of an alliance between the theological orthodoxy of the Great Awakening, and the deism and skepticism of the enlightenment that came to America primarily from France. As Mecklin notes:

It was the pressure of circumstances that brought the leaders of the dissenting sects into sympathetic contacts with Paine and Jefferson. . . . When the battle for religious and national liberty was finally won and the great principle of separation of state and church was safely embodied in the Constitution, Paine and Jefferson speedily lost their attraction for the dissenting sects.[72]

Many of the political leaders of the Revolutionary and post-Revolutionary period had come under the influence of deism and enlightenment, and not a few were apathetic if not antagonistic to formal religious worship and institutionalized religion. As the Beards put it:

When the crisis came, Jefferson, Paine, John Adams, Washington, Franklin, Madison and many lesser lights were to be reckoned among either the Unitarians or the Deists. It was not Cotton Mather's God to whom the authors of the Declaration of Independence appealed; it was to "Nature's God." From whatever source derived, the effect of both Unitarianism and Deism was to hasten the retirement of historic theology from its empire over the intellect of American leaders and to clear the atmosphere for secular interests.[73]

It is significant, indeed, that the first four presidents of the United States were either Deists or Unitarians. But liberalism in religion was not limited to the leaders. In the opinion of Harold Laski:

There was, indeed, far more likelihood than the evidence permits us to affirm with certainty that, by the end of the eighteenth century, rationalism had made a good deal of progress among the urban masses; it is not easy, otherwise, to account for the popularity of Paine's *Age of Reason*, or of Volney's *Les Ruines*.[74]

The Deists and Unitarians exerted a great influence even on the orthodox theologians. Lelands's *Rights of Conscience Inalienable* (1791) shows clearly the influence of Jefferson and Paine. Before the publication of his *Age of Reason* in 1793, Paine was consistently praised by Baptists and Presbyterians.[75] In 1776 he wrote, in his *Epistle to the Quakers*, that "To God, and not to man, are all men accountable on the score of religion." In *Common Sense* he wrote:

As to religion, I hold it to be the indispensable duty of government to protect all conscientious professors thereof, and I know of no other business which government hath to do therewith.[76]

The evidence we have makes it reasonable to believe that this represented the view of the overwhelming majority of Americans when our republic was founded.

## THE REVOLUTION IN VIRGINIA

The effect of these influences was revealed most dramatically in Virginia. The change in that state from an establishment probably more severe and oppressive than any other in the country to a condition of almost complete separation and freedom was so swift—taking as it did little more than a decade—that it may properly be called revolutionary. The events leading to freedom and separation in Virginia were of vital importance in the establishment of the American experiment in the Constitution a few years later. The Supreme Court has on several occasions recognized that the provisions of the First Amendment had the same objectives and were intended to provide the same protection against government intrusion on religious liberty as the Virginia Statute of Religious Liberty which marked the culmination and climax of the Virginia revolution.[77]

There were a number of reasons why the revolution occurred in Virginia, and why it became "the first state in the history of the world to proclaim the decree of absolute divorce between church and state."[78] Many of the liberalizing factors discussed in this chapter were present there. The dissenting sects, particularly the Baptists and Presbyterians, were numerous and well organized; from half to two-thirds of the population were dissenters.[79] The Great Awakening had won many converts. The Revolutionary War played a particularly important role, since, unlike Massachusetts—where the leaders of the established (Congregational) church were staunch supporters of the revolution—most of the clergy of the established (Anglican) church of Virginia opposed it and found themselves on the losing side.[80] Even before the Revolution, the clergy had alienated many influential laymen when they invoked the intervention of the British government to invalidate an act of the Virginia Assembly whose effect was to devalue the stipends received by the clergy. The controversy culminated in the famous "Parson's Cause," in which Patrick Henry, as attorney for the laity, eloquently identified the clergy's conduct with the king's tyranny.[81] Above all, perhaps, was the presence in Virginia of a group of political leaders who were devoted to and fought for the cause of liberty generally, accepted the social contract as self-evident, and were greatly influenced by Deism and Unitarianism. The group included Washington, Patrick Henry, George Mason, James Madison, and—towering above the rest—Thomas Jefferson.

Throughout his adult life Jefferson never swerved from his devotion to the principle of complete independence of religion and government.[82] Shortly after he wrote the Declaration of Independence, he jotted down a few *Notes on Religion:*

> The care of every man's soul belongs to himself. But what if he neglect the care of it? Well, what if he neglect the care of his health or estate, which more clearly relate to the state. Will the magistrate make a

law that he shall not be poor or sick? Laws provide against injury from others; but not from ourselves. God himself will not save men against their wills. . . .

If the magistrate command me to bring my commodity to a publick store house I bring it because he can indemnify me if he erred & I thereby lose it; but what indemnification can be given one for the kingdom of heaven?

I cannot give up my guidance to the magistrate, because he knows no more of the way to heaven than I do, & is less concerned to direct me right than I am to go right.[83]

Perhaps Jefferson's most eloquent defense of religious liberty and separation is to be found in his *Notes on Virginia:*

But our rulers can have no authority over such natural rights, only as we have submitted to them. The rights of conscience we never submitted, we could not submit. We are answerable for them to our God. . . . Reason and free inquiry are the only effectual agents against error. Give a loose to them, they will support the true religion by bringing every false one to their tribunal, to the test of their investigation. They are the natural enemies of error, and of error only.

. . . Subject opinions to coercion: whom will you make your inquisitors? Fallible men; men governed by bad passions, by private as well as public reasons. And why subject it to coercion? To produce uniformity. . . .

Is uniformity attainable? Millions of innocent men, women and children, since the introduction of Christianity, have been burnt, tortured, fined, imprisoned; yet we have not advanced one inch towards uniformity. What has been the effect of coercion? To make one half the world fools, and the other half hypocrites. To support roguery and error all over the earth.[84]

Establishment in Virginia was accompanied by persecution and oppression up to the eve of the Revolutionary War. Denial of the Trinity was punishable by imprisonment and loss of the custody of one's children.[85] Baptist preachers were whipped, arrested, fined, imprisoned on bread and water, although the authorities sanctimoniously denied that punishment was for "preaching"; the crime, they said, was "breach of the peace."[86] The law requiring church attendance was strictly enforced against dissenters. Though the Baptists were the chief victims, other dissenting groups, particularly those most affected by the Great Awakening, also felt the oppressive hand of the establishment.[87]

The Anglican establishment in Virginia appeared secure as the Revolution approached; at least it was carefully guarded by protective statutes. These provided for: religious services according to the laws and orders of the Church of England; a ministry conformable to the canons; compulsory attendance at religious services; the regulation of nonconformists; glebe lands for the support of the clergy; closed, corporate and nonresponsible vestries empowered to levy tithes for ministers' salaries, upkeep of the church, and support of the poor, and occupied by vestrymen subscribing to the doctrine and discipline of the church and bound by the oath of supremacy.[88]

Nevertheless, the jury's verdict of one cent in the "Parson's Cause" in 1763 foretold events that became inevitable when the protective arm of the home government could no longer be invoked. The first breach occurred when the Richmond Convention allowed dissenting chaplains to minister in the army.[89] At about the same time the Baptists resolved to circulate petitions "that the church establishment should be abolished and religion left to stand on its own merits;"[90] and Jefferson, while in Philadelphia writing the Declaration of Independence, still had time to draft a proposed constitution for Virginia with a provision that

> All persons shall have full and free liberty of religious opinion; nor shall any be compelled to frequent or maintain any religious institution.[91]

Both Jefferson and the Baptists were premature; but the first major step was taken when the Virginia Convention of 1776 adopted, as part of the Bill of Rights of the state's first constitution, the provision drafted by George Mason and amended by Madison, reading:

> That religion, or the duty which we owe to our Creator, and the manner of discharging it, can be directed only by reason and conviction, not by force or violence; and therefore, all men are equally entitled to the free exercise of religion according to the dictates of conscience; and that it is the mutual duty of all to practice Christian forbearance, love, and charity towards each other.[92]

The adoption of the Bill of Rights marked the beginning of the end of the establishment. Petitions came pouring in to the first legislative assembly from Baptists, Presbyterians, and Lutherans praying for its abolition. The Presbytery of Hanover urged that it was unjust to force the people of the frontier counties, where there were few Episcopalians, to pay taxes in support of an establishment, contending that

> There is no argument in favor of establishing the Christian religion but what may be pleaded with equal propriety for establishing the tenets of Mahoment. [Moreover, the] gospel needs no such civil aid, [because Christ declared that his kingdom is not of this world; and because] . . . the only proper objects of civil government are the happiness and protection of men in the present state of existence. . . . But . . . the

duty which we owe to our Creator, and the manner of discharging it, can only be directed by reason and conviction; and is nowhere cognizable but at the tribunal of the universal Judge.[93]

Jefferson wrote that

the first republican legislature . . . was crowded with petitions to abolish . . . spiritual tyranny. These brought on the severest contest in which I have ever been engaged. . . . Though the majority of our citizens were dissenters . . . a majority of the Legislature were churchmen.

The legislature compromised. A bill was enacted abolishing the more oppressive features of the establishment and granting exemption to the dissenters. Enacted in December 1776, it repealed the laws punishing heresy and absence from worship and requiring dissenters to contribute to the support of the establishment.[94] Though a compromise, the bill sounded the death knell of the Anglican establishment; but it did not guarantee separation. As Jefferson reported:

. . . in the bill . . . was inserted an express reservation of the question whether a general assessment should not be established by law on every one to the support of the pastor of his choice; or whether all should be left to voluntary contributions.[95]

This was the crucial issue: was the support of religion the concern of the state, or was it a matter to "be left to voluntary contribution"? The lines were clear; to one group, liberty meant disestablishment and separation and voluntariness, because man's relation to his Maker was not within the jurisdiction of civil government; to the other, establishment meant "order and internal tranquility, true piety and virtue . . . peace and happiness," and was therefore quite properly a state responsibility.[96]

The issue was well recognized by the people of Virginia. The Baptists, the Presbyterians, the other dissenters, and the libertarians were not content with the 1776 act which abolished the requirement that they support the established church. They opposed the compulsory support of their own religions, as well as others. Within six months after the 1776 act, the Hanover Presbytery again memorialized the assembly that

. . . as it is contrary to our Principles and Interest; and as we think, subversive of Religious Liberty, we do again and most earnestly intreat, that our Legislature would never extend any Assessment for Religious purposes to us or to the Congregations under our Care.[97]

Similar petitions were received from the Baptists and other dissenters. From 1776 to 1779 the assembly was engaged almost daily in the desperate contests between the contending factions. Finally, in

1779, the campaign that had been led principally by the Baptists was successful, and in that year the assembly repealed all laws requiring members of the Episcopal Church to contribute to the support of their own ministry.[98]

Jefferson sought to press the advantage, and introduced his Bill for Establishing Religious Freedom, but Virginia was not quite ready to formalize the separation which had in effect taken place, and the bill was not voted on. The act of 1776, besides eliminating permanently the payment of tithes by dissenters, had temporarily suspended the payment of tithes even by members of the established church; and the act of 1779 had made permanent the establishment's loss of its exclusive status and power to tax its members. But many of the Episcopalians who had voted for the 1779 disestablishment law had done so expecting that it would be succeeded by a general assessment for all religions.[99] Without a general assessment bill the establishment was doomed, for any attempt to levy tithes on Anglicans alone would drive many of them into the ranks of dissent.[100] Accordingly, a bill was introduced in 1779 which declared that

> the Christian Religion shall in all times coming be deemed and held to be the established Religion of this Commonwealth.

The bill required every person to enroll his name with the county clerk and indicate which "Society for the purpose of Religious Worship" he wished to support. The county clerk was to present the names to the trustees of the appropriate religious society, who were to determine the assessment rates; these were then collected by the sheriff and turned over to the clergymen and teachers designated by the trustees. The assessment of any person failing to enroll in a society was to be divided proportionately among the societies.[101]

Between 1779 and 1784 the assembly contented itself with receiving petitions and listening to debates. In 1784, however, it called up a "Bill Establishing a Provision for Teachers of the Christian Religion."[102] The purpose of the bill, according to its chief sponsor, Patrick Henry, was to require all persons

> to pay a moderate tax or contribution annually for the support of the Christian religion, or of some Christian church, denomination or communion of Christians, or for some form of Christian worship.[103]

The bill was predicated on the legislative determination in its preamble that

> the general diffusion of Christian knowledge hath a natural tendency to correct the morals of men, restrain their vices, and preserve the

peace of society; which cannot be effected without a competent provision for licensed teachers. . . .[104]

The preamble is of great significance, because it recognized the widely held belief that religion was not within the competence of civil legislatures. It sought to justify intervention not on any theocratic ground but on what today would be called the "police" or "welfare" power. Government support of religion is required to restrain vice and preserve peace, not to promote God's kingdom on earth.

It should be noted too that the bill was limited to Christians. A motion was made and passed in committee to substitute the word "religious" for "Christian," but the committee's action was reversed by a narrow vote of the assembly and the word "Christian" was reinserted.[105] This, however, was little more than a semantic difference; for all practical purposes Christianity and religion were synonymous in Virginia in 1784. There were no non-Christian teachers of religion; indeed, there were probably not a half-dozen Jewish families in the whole state.[106] Moreover, Washington, at least, interpreted the bill as permitting persons to "declare themselves Jews, Mohametans, or otherwise" and thus obtain exemption.[107]

Finally the bill, which gave to each taxpayer the privilege of designating which church should receive his share of the tax, in its final form allowed the nonreligious taxpayer to elect that his tax be used "for the encouragement of seminaries of learning within the Counties where such sums shall arise, and to no other use or purpose whatsoever." This was a radical change from the 1779 bill, which had provided for the division among the denominations of taxes not designated to any particular church.

The 1784 measure aroused the same opposition evoked by the earlier measure. As usual, the Baptists were most vocal and active, reiterating their deeply held principle that "religion was a thing apart from the concerns of the state,"[108] and that "no human laws ought to be established for this purpose, but that every person ought to be left entirely free in respect to matters of religion."[109] The Presbyterians temporarily faltered, but soon returned to their original position of strong opposition. The memorial presented by the Hanover Presbytery in 1785 set forth the same arguments as those presented in its petitions in 1776 and 1777. It rejected the attempted justification in the preamble, and argued that the bill was wrong, among other reasons, because:

> Religion is altogether personal, and the right of exercising it unalienable; and it is not, cannot and ought not to be resigned to the will of the society at large; and much less to the Legislature which derives its au-

thority wholly from the consent of the People; and is limited by the Original intention of Civil Associations; [and] we never resigned to the control of Government our rights of determining for ourselves in this important article. . . .[110]

Madison, who led the opposition, was able to obtain a postponement of consideration of the bill from December 1784 to November 1785. Before adjournment the legislature enacted a bill incorporating the Protestant Episcopal Church, which was deemed necessary in order to regulate the status of that church in view of the severance of its subordination to the Church of England that had resulted from the Revolution. The bill gave the Episcopal ministers title to the churches, glebes, and other property, and prescribed the method of electing vestrymen.[111]

Even Madison voted for the incorporation bill, though reluctantly and only in order to stave off passage of the assessment bill. Nevertheless, the incorporation bill aroused a good deal of opposition. The Hanover Presbytery presented a memorial protesting the bill, in which it urged that

> The real ministers of true religion derive their authority to act in the duties of their profession from a higher source than any Legislature on earth.[112]

The widespread antagonism to the incorporation law is evidenced by the fact that it was repealed two years later, and that even today the Virginia constitution prohibits the incorporation of "any church or religious denomination."[113] Much of this opposition reacted against the assessment bill. In addition, Henry's elevation to the governorship in 1784 deprived the assessment bill of its ablest legislative leader. But the most telling blow against the bill was the "Memorial and Remonstrance against Religious Assessments," written by Madison at the suggestion of George Mason and George Nicholas, and widely distributed by them before the reconvening of the legislature in the fall of 1785.

The "Memorial" is one of the great documents in the history of human liberty, but one which, until revived by Justice Rutledge in his dissent in the Everson case, was known to only a few historical students. Even today it does not receive the attention it merits, and is greatly overshadowed by Jefferson's Virginia Statute of Religious Liberty, which, though undoubtedly an equally great document in the history of liberty, was made possible by the "Memorial."[114] Both should be required reading in every American school.

The "Memorial" presents fifteen arguments against the assessment bill, which may be summarized as follows:

(1) Religion is wholly exempt from the cognizance of Civil Society, and in matters of religion no man's right is abridged by the institution of Civil Society, whose authority is necessarily subordinate to the individual's allegiance to the Universal Sovereign.

(2) Since religion is exempt from the authority of the Society at large, still less can it be subject to that of the Legislative Body whose jurisdiction is both derivative and limited.

(3) The same authority which can establish Christianity, in exclusion of all other religions, may establish with the same ease, any particular sect of Christians in exclusion of all other sects, and the same authority which can force a citizen to contribute three pence only of his property for the support of any one establishment, may force him to conform to any other establishment in all cases whatsoever.

(4) All men are to be considered as entering into Society on equal conditions and retain equally their natural rights, and the bill denies this equality to those who do not embrace . . . profess and . . . observe the Religion which we believe to be of divine origin.

(5) The bill implies either that the Civil Magistrate is a competent judge of Religious truth; or that he may employ Religion as an engine of Civil policy. The first is a false arrogant pretension; the second an unhallowed perversion of the means of salvation.

(6) The bill is unnecessary because religion does not need the support of human laws; on the contrary, the bill fosters a suspicion that the friends of religion are too conscious of its fallacies to trust to its own merits.

(7) Experience shows that ecclesiastical establishments, instead of maintaining the purity and efficacy of Religion have resulted in pride and indolence in the Clergy; ignorance and servility in the laity; in both, superstition, bigotry and persecution.

(8) Since Religion is not within the cognizance of Civil Government . . . its legal establishment cannot be said to be necessary to civil government.

(9) The bill degrades from the equal rank of Citizen all those whose opinions in Religion do not bend to those of Legislative authority. Distant as it may be, in its present form, from the Inquisition it differs from it only in degree. The one is the first step, the other the last in the career of intolerance.

(10) The bill will add a fresh motive to migration by revoking the liberty which the citizens now enjoy.

(11) The bill will destroy that moderation and harmony which the forbearance of our laws to intermeddle with Religion, has produced among its several sects. Torrents of blood have been spilt in the old world in vain attempts of the secular arm to extinguish Religious discord by proscribing all differences in Religious opinions. . . . The very appearance of the Bill has transformed that "Christian forbearance, love and charity" which of late mutually prevailed into animosities and jealousies which may not soon be appeased. What mischiefs may not be dreaded should this enemy to the public quiet be armed with the force of law?

(12) The many who have not yet accepted the truth of Christianity

will be discouraged from doing so.

(13) The inevitable difficulty of enforcing a law obnoxious to so great a proportion of the citizens will tend to enervate the laws in general, and to slacken the bonds of Society.

(14) It is not sufficiently clear that a majority of the citizens approve the bill.

(15) Since the equal right of every citizen to the free exercise of his Religion is equal in weight to all other natural rights, acceptance of a legislative infringement of this right means that the legislature may likewise infringe the freedom of the press or abolish trial by jury. The alternatives are clear and unescapable. Either . . . the will of the Legislature is the only measure of their authority; and that in the plenitude of this authority, they may sweep away all our fundamental rights, or . . . they are bound to leave this particular right untouched and sacred.

It is important to note the emphasis the "Memorial" places on ideological factors. Though it does not omit such practical considerations as the loss of population through migration, its stress is on natural rights, the government's lack of jurisdiction over matters of religion, the social contract, etc. These were not ideas original to Madison; on the contrary, Madison was merely articulating, eloquently and forcefully, beliefs that were widely held in 1785. This quickly became clear from the great numbers of signatures appended to the "Memorial," including, in the words of Madison, "a considerable portion of the old hierarchy."[115]

The overwhelming opposition to the assessment bill from all sects and regions — petitions were received from 48 counties in opposition, as against 7 counties which favored it — resulted in the speedy defeat of the measure. Pressing his advantage, Madison called up Jefferson's Bill for Establishing Religious Freedom, which had first been introduced in 1779, and finally obtained its passage in January 1786.

The Virginia statute[116] consists of three sections. The first is a preamble setting forth the reasons for its enactment, which may be summarized as follows:

(1) God made man's mind free, and deliberately chose that religion should be propagated by reason and not by coercion.

(2) Legislators and rulers have impiously assumed dominion over faith, and have established and maintained false religions.

(3) It is sinful and tyrannical to compel a man to furnish contributions for the propagation of opinions which he disbelieves and abhors; and it is also wrong to force him to support this or that teacher of his own religious persuasion.

(4) Our civil rights have no dependence on our religious opinion, and therefore imposing religious qualifications for civil office tends to corrupt religion by bribery to obtain purely external conformity.

(5) The opinions of men are not the object of civil government, nor under its jurisdiction. It is a dangerous fallacy to restrain the profession of opinions because of their ill tendency; it is enough for the rightful purpose of Civil Government for its officers to interfere when principles break into overt acts against peace and good order.

(6) Truth is great and will prevail if left to herself. Truth has nothing to fear from the conflict with error.

The second section, which is the operative part, reads as follows:

Be it therefore enacted by the General Assembly of Virginia that no man shall be compelled to frequent or support any religious worship, place or ministry whatsoever, nor shall be enforced, restrained, molested or burdened in his body or goods, nor shall otherwise suffer on account of his religious opinions or beliefs, but that all men shall be free to profess, and by argument to maintain, their opinions in matters of religion, and that the same shall in no wise diminish, enlarge or affect their civil capacities.

The last section acknowledges that any later legislature has the power to repeal the statute, but declares that if it does so such "act will be an infringement of natural right."

Jefferson's autobiography contains an interesting comment on the passage of the bill;

The bill for establishing religious freedom, the principles of which had, to a certain degree, been enacted before, I had drawn in all the latitude of reason and right. It still met with opposition; but, with some multilations in the preamble, it was finally passed; and a singular proposition proved that its protection of opinion was meant to be universal. Where the preamble declares that coercion is a departure from the plan of the holy author of our religion, an amendment was proposed, by inserting the words "Jesus Christ," so that it should read, "a departure from the plan of Jesus Christ, the holy author of our religion"; the insertion was rejected by a great majority, in proof that they meant to comprehend, within the mantle of its protection, the Jew and the Gentile, the Christian and the Mahometan, the Hindoo, the infidel of every denomination.[117]

Some vestiges of the Virginia establishment remained until 1802, when a law was finally enacted providing that whenever glebe lands became vacant by reason of the death or removal of the Episcopal minister, they were to be sold by the overseer of the poor for the support of the poor, or for any other nonreligious purpose which a majority of the voters might decide.[118] Nevertheless, for all practical purposes, the passage of Jefferson's bill marked the culmination of the successful struggle in Virginia to achieve full religious freedom and separation of church and state.

## THE OTHER STATES

The struggle in Virginia was the most dramatic, and exercised the most influence in the acceptance by the new national government of the principle of freedom and separation. It therefore merits the extended treatment it has received here. A summary survey of the situation in the other twelve of the original states when the American Constitution was adopted may suffice.

Massachusetts declared in its constitution of 1780 that it "is the right as well as the duty of all men in society, publicly and at stated seasons, to worship the Supreme Being," but that no person should be molested "for worshipping God in the manner and season most agreeable to the dictates of his own conscience . . . provided he does not disturb the public peace or obstruct others in their religious worship."

The constitution then provided:

As the happiness of a people, and the good order and preservation of civil government, essentially depend upon piety, religion, and morality; and as these cannot be generally diffused through a community but by the institution of the public worship of God, and of public instructions in piety, religion, and morality: Therefore, to promote their happiness, and to secure the good order and preservation of their government, the people of this commonwealth have a right to invest their legislature with power to authorize and require, and the legislature shall, from time to time, authorize and require, the several towns, parishes, precincts, and other bodies politic, or religious societies, to make suitable provision, at their own expense, for the institution of the public worship of God, and for the support and maintenance of public Protestant teachers of piety, religion, and morality, in all cases where such provision shall not be made voluntarily.

And the people of this commonwealth have also a right to, and do, invest their legislature with authority to enjoin upon all the subjects an attendance upon the instructions of the public teachers aforesaid, at stated times and seasons, if there be any on whose instructions they can conscientiously and conveniently attend. . . .

And all moneys paid by the subject to the support of public worship, and of the public teachers aforesaid, shall, if he require it, be uniformly applied to the support of the public teacher or teachers of his own religious sect or denomination, provided there be any on whose instructions he attends; otherwise it may be paid towards the support of the teacher or teachers of the parish or precinct in which the said moneys are raised.

And every denomination of Christians, demeaning themselves peaceably, and as good subjects of the commonwealth, shall be equally under the protection of the law: and no subordination of any one sect or denomination to another shall ever be established by law.[119]

115

New Hampshire's constitution of 1784 shows the effect of the intervening four years. Modeled after the Massachusetts constitution of 1780, it nevertheless manifests some liberalization. Worship of God is stated to be a right, but not a duty; the legislature is empowered to authorize, but not to require, the towns to make provision for Protestant teachers; there is no provision authorizing or requiring the towns to provide and support the public worship of God; nor is there any provision authorizing the legislature to compel attendance on Protestant instruction.[120]

Connecticut adopted its first constitution in 1818. In 1784, however, a Toleration Act was adopted which provided that persons who were not members of the established Congregational Church could obtain exemption by establishing to the satisfaction of the justice of the peace that they regularly worshipped and supported a dissenting church.[121]

Rhode Island, like Connecticut, did not adopt its first constitution until well into the 19th century. Unlike Connecticut, which was founded on establishment and restraint, colonial Rhode Island was founded on the principle of separation and freedom. By 1787 the disabilities imposed on Catholics after the death of Roger Williams had largely if not entirely disappeared, and Rhode Island was the only state besides Virginia which at the adoption of the Federal Constitution enjoyed full religious liberty and separation.[122]

New York, in its 1777 constitution, abrogated all laws which "may be construed to establish or maintain any particular denomination of Christians or their ministers," and guaranteed forever the "free exercise and enjoyment of religious profession and worship without discrimination or preference."[123] In 1784 the legislature repealed the "Settling Act" of 1693 and all subsequent acts granting privileges to the Episcopal Church. Two restrictions were retained: first, all persons naturalized by the state were required to take an oath of abjuration of all foreign allegiance in all matters, "ecclesiastical as well as civil" (i.e., disqualifying Roman Catholics from naturalization); and second, clergymen were excluded from civil office, because they "ought not to be diverted from their great duties of the service of God and the care of souls."[124]

The New Jersey constitution of 1776 guaranteed freedom of worship, and prohibited compulsory attendance at or support of any church or ministry. Although it decreed that "There shall be no establishment of any one religious sect . . . in preference to another," it limited public office to Protestants.[125]

Delaware's constitution of 1776 forbade the "establishment of one religious sect in this State in preference to another," but disqualified clergymen from holding civil office, and required every public officer to take an oath professing faith in the Trinity and in the Old and New Testaments.[126]

Pennsylvania, by its constitution of 1776, likewise secured freedom of worship and prohibited compulsory attendance at or support of churches. But it also imposed a religious test for public office which required belief in God and the divine inspiration of the Old and New Testaments.[127]

The Maryland constitution of 1776 assured equal protection to all persons professing the Christian religion, and forbade compulsory church attendance or support. "Yet the legislature may in their discretion lay a general and equal tax for the support for the Christian religion, leaving to each individual the power" of designating the church to which his tax is to be paid, or directing that it be used for the aid of the poor.[128]

North Carolina's constitution of 1776 prohibited the establishment of any church or sect in preference to any other, and compulsory church attendance or support. On the other hand, it barred clergymen from holding legislative office, and limited public office to Protestants.[129]

South Carolina's constitution of 1778 represented an elaborate attempt to establish the "Christian Protestant" faith. After excluding clergymen from holding elective office, it decreed that all persons and religious societies acknowledging God, a future state of rewards and punishments, and the duty of public worship should be tolerated. It provided that "the Christian Protestant religion shall be deemed and is hereby constituted and declared to be the established religion of this State," and assured equal privileges to all Protestant denominations. Ownership of property by the Protestant Episcopal Church was secured, and provision was made for the incorporation of every religious society of fifteen or more adult males. It provided, however, that every such society

> shall have agreed to and subscribed in a book the following five articles, without which no agreement or union of men, upon pretence of religion, shall entitle them to be incorporated and esteemed as a church of the established religion of this State:
> 1. That there is one eternal God and a future state of rewards and punishments.
> 2. That God is publicly to be worshipped.
> 3. That the Christian religion is the true religion.
> 4. That the Holy Scriptures of the Old and New Testaments are of divine inspiration, and are the rules of faith and practice.

5. That it is lawful, and the duty of every man, being thereunto called by those that govern, to bear witness to the truth.

The constitution then provided that pastors were to be chosen by a majority of the church, but that no minister might enter on his pastorate until he had subscribed to a declaration (taken almost verbatim from the answers of the minister to the bishop in the ordination services as contained in the Anglican *Book of Common Prayer*)[130]

> That he is determined by God's grace out of the holy scriptures to instruct the people committed to his charge, and to teach nothing as required of necessity to eternal salvation, but that which he shall be persuaded may be concluded and proved from the scripture; that he will use both public and private admoniion, as well to the sick as to the whole within his cure, as need shall require and occasion shall be given; and that he will be diligent in prayers and in reading of the same; that he will be diligent to frame and fashion his own self and his family according to the d ctrine of Christ and to make both himself and them, as much as in him lieth, wholesome examples and patterns to the flock of Christ; that he will maintain and set forward, as much as he can, quietness, peace, and love among all people, and especially among those that are, or shall be committed to his charge.

The article concluded by providing that no person should be obligated toward the support of any religious worship which he does not freely join and engage to support.[131]

Georgia, by its constitution of 1777, guaranteed freedom of conscience, limited membership in the legislature to Protestants, and forbade clergymen from sitting in the legislature.[132]

The relationship of religion to government in the original state constitutions or organic laws at the time of the adoption of the Federal Constitution may be summarized as follows:

> Two out of thirteen, Virginia and Rhode Island, conceded full freedom;
> One, New York, gave full freedom except for requiring naturalized citizens to abjure foreign allegiance and subjection in all matters ecclesiastical as well as civil;
> Six, New Hampshire, Connecticut, New Jersey, Georgia, North and South Carolina, adhered to religious establishments;
> Two, Delaware and Maryland, demanded Christianity;
> Four, Pennsylvania, Delaware, North and South Carolina, required assent to the divine inspiration of the Bible;
> Two, Pennsylvania and South Carolina, imposed a belief in heaven and hell;
> Three, New York, Delaware, and South Carolina, excluded ministers from civil office;
> Four, Maryland, Virginia, North Carolina, and Georgia, excluded ministers from the legislature;

Two, Pennsylvania and South Carolina, emphasized belief in one eternal God;

One, Delaware, required assent to the doctrine of the Trinity;

Five, New Hampshire, Massachusetts, Connecticut, Maryland, and South Carolina, insisted on Protestantism;

One, South Carolina, still referred to religious "toleration."[133]

## RELIGION AND THE CONTINENTAL CONGRESS

As can be seen from this summary of the Revolutionary consitutions, their makers, while promising religious liberty, did not expect the states to be wholly neutral in matters of religion, and generally assumed a consensus of opinion in support either of Protestantism or some form of Christianity.[134] The same assumption was implicit in the activities of the Continental Congress, from its first meeting in 1774 to its replacement by the Congress provided for in the Federal Constitution. The Continental Congress began its activities before the onset of the revolutionary change from establishment and restraint to separation and freedom. It was therefore quite natural that the scope of its legislative activities included religious matters. It is significant that when, in 1774, Isaac Backus presented to the Continental Congress the Baptists' complaint against the Massachusetts establishment, it apparently did not occur to Massachusetts to question the jurisdiction of the Congress to consider the issue.[135]

The proclamations and other state papers of the Continental Congress were replete with references to religion, unabashedly exhibiting a belief in Protestantism. Congress continually invoked, as sanction for its acts, the name of "God," "Almighty God," "Nature's God," "God of Armies," "Lord of Hosts," "His Goodness," "God's Superintending Providence," "Providence of God," "Providence," "Supreme and Universal Providence," "Overruling Providence of God," "Creator of All," "Indulgent Creator," "Great Governor of the World," "The Divinity," "Supreme Disposer of All Events," "Holy Ghost," "Jesus Christ," "Christian Religion," and "Free Protestant Colonies" and other expressions of devout Christian Protestantism. Humphrey suggests, possibly with tongue in cheek, that this "extreme insistence upon the religious sanction may be explained in part by the fact that the government was without definite legislative authority; this deficiency could be remedied in no other way so well as by a reliance upon religion."[136]

The pre-eminent position held in the Congress by leading Protestant clergymen undoubtedly exercised an important influence in this direction. In any event, since there was no constitutional limitation on the scope of Congressional legislation, the Congress did not hesitate to legislate on such subjects as morality, sin, repentance, humiliation, divine service, fasting, prayer, reformation, mourning, public worship, funerals, chaplains, true religion, and Thanksgiving. The Sabbath was recognized to a degree rarely exhibited in other countries; Congress adjourned and all official business was suspended, as it was on Good Friday.[137]

As was to be expected, immediately on its assembling Congress adopted a resolution calling for prayer at the opening of each daily session, and designated an Episcopal clergyman to act as chaplain of Congress. The choice of an Episcopalian was not dictated by religious considerations; it was felt politically expedient to give the position to an Anglican. Unfortunately the person selected, after serving as chaplain two years, resigned, went over to the British, and departed to England.[138]

In June 1775 Congress adopted a resolution setting aside July 20, 1775, as a day of national "humiliation, fasting and prayer." In the same year it provided for chaplains in the army, with pay equivalent to that of captains. Finding that religion was an excellent weapon with which to keep the Indians friendly, Congress in 1776 directed the employment of a minister to instruct them in the principles of Christianity. According to Humphrey, Congress made extensive use of religion and the churches as instruments of propaganda for the Revolutionary War and the new nation.[139] In 1778 it recommended to the states that they encourage religion and suppress vice. A few years later it officially endorsed an American edition of the Bible, and recommended it to the people as a careful and accurate work. And in 1783 it proclaimed the peace treaty with England "In the name of the Most Holy and Undivided Trinity."[140]

In 1785 a committee of Congress drew up a proposal for the disposition of the western lands which Congress had acquired from the states. The plan proposed that the 16th section of each township should be set aside for the use of public schools, and another section for the support of the ministry, according to the practice of town establishment current in Massachusetts and Connecticut. In the course of committee action the latter proposal was defeated, and evoked the following comment from Madison in a letter to James Monroe:

> How a regulation so unjust in itself, so foreign to the Authority of Congress, so hurtful to the sale of the public land, and smelling so strongly of an antiquated Bigotry, could have received the countenance of a Committee is truly a matter of astonishment.

When, however, the Northwest Ordinance of 1787 was adopted

it contained a declaration that

> Religion, morality and knowledge, being necessary to good government and the happiness of mankind, schools and the means of education shall forever be encouraged.

Moreover, notwithstanding the committee's action in 1785, Congress granted tracts of land for the support of religion, as well as for schools, though it is important to note that after the Constitution and the First Amendment were adopted no more public land was granted for the support of religion under the Ordinance.[141]

In one instance did the Continental Congress manifest rather surprising scruples against intervention in religious affairs. In 1783 the papal nuncio at Paris addressed a note to Benjamin Franklin suggesting that since it was no longer possible to maintain the previous status whereunder American Catholics were subject to the Vicar Apostolic at London, the Holy See proposed to Congress that a Catholic bishopric be established in one of the American cities. Franklin transmitted the note to Congress, which directed Franklin to notify the nuncio "that the subject of his application to Doctor Franklin, being purely spiritual, it is without the jurisdiction and powers of Congress, who have no authority to permit or refuse it, these powers being reserved to the several States individually."

This unique compunction may have been due to the fact that the nuncio's note suggested that since there might be no American Catholic qualified to act as bishop, it might be necessary to appoint a French prelate to the post, a suggestion quite incompatible with the growing nationalism of Americans, Protestant and Catholic alike.[142]

Certainly, as Humphrey points out,

> It is clear that Congress rested heavily upon a religious authority and intended in every way possible to promote as a basis for a well-ordered government a dependence upon Protestant Christianity. There is no evidence that it for a moment contemplated a possible separation of the state and religion. This makes all the more intense the process by which, so soon after the adoption of the Federal constitution and its new government, separation of church and state became a national characteristic.[143]

## THE FRAMING OF THE CONSTITUTION

It is perhaps symbolic of the difference in the relationship of state and religion between the Continental Congress and the new government established by the Constitutional Convention of 1787, that whereas the Continental Congress instituted the practice of daily prayers immediately on first convening, the Convention met for four months without any recitation of prayers. After the Convention had been in session for a month, the octogenarian Franklin, who in earlier years had been pretty much of a Deist, moved "that henceforth prayers imploring the assistance of Heaven, and its blessings on our deliberations, be held in this Assembly every morning before we proceed to business, and that one or more of the Clergy of this City be requested to officiate in that service." The motion was received politely though not without embarrassment. According to the records of the Convention, "After several unsuccessful attempts for silently postponing the matter by adjourning, the adjournment was at length carried, without any vote on the motion."[144]

More than symbolic, it is deeply significant that whereas there was scarcely a document or promulgation issued by the Continental Congress that did not contain an invocation to "God" or one of the numerous synonyms of the Deity,[145] the Constitution emerging from the Convention contained no such invocation or reference. The omission was not inadvertent; nor did it remain unnoticed. A delegate to the Connecticut ratifying convention stated in a letter to Oliver Ellsworth (later Chief Justice of the United States) that he would have required

> . . . an explicit acknowledgment of the being of God, his perfections and his providence, . . . in the following or similar terms, viz. "We the people of the United States, in a firm belief of the being and perfections of the one living and true God, the creator and supreme Governor of the world, in his universal providence and the authority of his laws . . . do ordain, etc."

And at a meeting of Congregationalists in June 1788 a request was presented "that some suitable Testimony might be borne against the sinful omission in the late Federal Constitution in not looking to God for direction, and of omitting the mention of the name of God in the Constitution."[146]

In the early days of the Continental Congress, John Adams had expressed the vain hope that "Congress will never meddle with religion further than to say their own prayers, and to fast and to give thanks once a year."[147] The Philadelphia convention had no doubts that the new Congress would not be authorized to "meddle with religion"—certainly not beyond the minimal extent suggested by Adams. As Madison forcefully put it later, the Constitution was not to create "a shadow of right in the general government to intermeddle with religion."[148]

Edmund Randolph, addressing the Virginia ratification convention, pointed out that "no power is expressly given to Congress over religion."[149] Charles Pinckney of South Carolina had sought to make the absence of power specific and explicit. He proposed a provision that ". . . the Legislature of the United States shall pass no law on the subject of religion; nor touching or abridging the liberty of the press; nor shall the privilege of the writ of Habeas Corpus ever be suspended, except in the case of rebellion or invasion."[150] Though none of these express prohibitions were acted on by the Convention, they were to reappear without change in substance in the Bill of Rights.[151] There can be little doubt that the Convention's failure to adopt the proposal resulted not from disagreement with its purpose but from a strong belief that it was unnecessary.[152]

What was considered necessary, however, was so much of Pinckney's proposal as related to a subject within the jurisdiction of the Federal government. Obviously, the government would have jurisdiction to fix the qualifications for Federal office, and might arguably have power to impose a religious test as a qualification for such office. As Madison wrote to Randolph, it might be implied that "without [an] exception, a power would have been given to impose an oath involving a religious test as a qualification for office."[153] To prevent this, the Convention adopted Pinckney's motion (now the last clause in Article VI of the Constitution) that ". . . no religious test shall ever be required as a qualification to any office or public trust under the United States."[154]

The breadth of this prohibition is clear. Even Joseph Story, a vigorous opponent of separation,[155] recognized that

> This clause is not introduced merely for the purpose of satisfying the scruples of many respectable persons who feel an invincible repugnance to any religious test or affirmation. It had a higher object: to cut off forever every pretense of any alliance between church and state in the national government.[156]

Nor were the framers of the Constitution unaware of the broad scope of the prohibition. Luther Martin, addressing the Maryland legislature, related:

> The part of the system which provides that no religious test shall ever be required as a qualification to any office or public trust under the United States was adopted by a great majority of the Convention and without much debate: however, there were some members so unfashionable as to think that a belief in the existence of a Deity, and of a state of future rewards and punishments would be some security for the good conduct of our rulers, and that, in a Christian country, it would be at least decent to hold out some distinction between the professors of Christianity and, downright infidelity or paganism.[157]

Ellsworth explained the basic reason for the prohibition. The clause, he said, was not "unfavorable to religion," as some feared. "If any test-act were to be made, perhaps the least exceptionable would be one requiring all persons appointed to office to declare, at the time of their admission, their belief in the being of God, and in the divine authority of the Scriptures." But, Ellsworth continued, such a declaration would be useless, since an unprincipled man would have no hesitation in making such a declaration. The "true principle by which this question ought to be determined" is this: "the business of civil government is to protect the citizen in his rights, to defend the community from hostile powers, and to promote the general welfare. Civil government has no business to meddle with the private opinions of the people."[158]

In Massachusetts, it was feared, in the words of Madison, "that the constitution by prohibiting religious tests, opened a door for Jews, Turks and infidels."[159] Isaac Backus, though opposed to ratification, defended the prohibition on the ground that "nothing is more evident, both in reason and the Holy Scriptures, than that religion is ever a matter between God and individuals." The same view was expressed by a Congregational minister delegate, who urged that "God alone is the God of conscience, and, consequently, attempts to erect human tribunals for the conscience of men, are impious encroachments upon the prerogatives of God."[160]

In North Carolina, too, the fear was expressed "that if there be no religious tests required, pagans, deists and Mohametans might obtain office among us, and that the senators and representatives might all be pagans." To this James Iredell replied that while it was possible that the people may "choose representatives who have no religion at all . . . how is it possible to exclude any set of men, without taking away that principle of religious freedom which we ourselves so warmly contend for. . . . It would be happy for mankind if religion was permitted to take its own course, and maintain itself by the excellence of its own doctrines. The divine Author of our religion never wished for its support by worldly authority. . . . It made much greater progress for itself than when supported by the greatest authority upon earth." To the suggestion that "in administering an oath, it is only necessary to inquire if the person who is to take it, believes in a Supreme Being and in a future state of rewards and punishments," Iredell replied: "We may, I think, very safely leave religion to itself."[161] Governor Samuel Johnston also warned "that it would have been dangerous if Congress could intermeddle with the subject of religion, although he conceded that Jews, Pagans, etc. might emigrate to the United States."[162]

## THE FIRST AMENDMENT

Omission of an invocation to God and the proscription of religious tests for office in the proposed constitution were thus acceptable to the American people when they were called on to pass on them in the ratifying conventions. On the other hand, omission of an express guaranty of religious freedom and other natural rights almost prevented ratification. In the ratifying conventions of almost every state some objection was expressed to the absence of a restriction on the Federal government with respect to legislation regarding religion.[163] Six states ratified but proposed amendments for a guaranty of religious liberty.[164] Two, North Carolina and Rhode Island, would not ratify until a bill of rights including religious freedom and disestablishment was adopted.[165] Jefferson wrote to Madison from Paris:

> I will now add what I do not like. First, the omission of a bill of rights providing clearly and without the aid of sophisms for freedom of religion, freedom of the press, protection against standing armies, restriction against monopolies, the eternal and unremitting force of the habeas corpus laws, and trials by juries. . . . [A] bill of rights is what the people are entitled to against every government on earth, general or particular, and what no just government should refuse or rest on inference.[166]

No one justified the omission of a bill of rights on the ground that the Federal government should have the power to restrict religious liberty or the freedom of speech or press; the omission was justified on the ground that a bill of rights was unnecessary. A provision prohibiting Congress from establishing religion or prohibiting its free exercise was unnecessary because, as Madison said, "the government has no jurisdiction over it [religion]."[167] James Wilson argued that "all is reserved in a general government which is not given," and that since the power to legislate on religion or speech or press was not given to the Federal government, the government did not possess it, and there was therefore no need for an express prohibition.[168] Replying to the charge "that there is no security for the rights of conscience," Wilson queried:

> . . . what part of this system puts it in the power of Congress to attack those rights? Where there is no power to attack, it is idle to prepare the means of defence.[169]

Alexander Hamilton argued that a bill of rights, not only was unnecessary, but would be dangerous, since it might create the inference that a power to deal with the reserved subject was in fact conferred. Writing in the *Federalist* he said:

I go further and affirm that bills of rights in the sense and to the extent in which they are contended for, are not only unnecessary in the proposed Constitution, but would even be dangerous. They would contain various exceptions to powers not granted; and, on this very account, would afford a colorable pretext to claim more than was granted. For why declare that things shall not be done which there is no power to do?[170]

But neither Jefferson nor the people were satisfied with these assurances. Jefferson felt that a bill of rights should not "rest on inferences." Patrick Henry, eloquent as ever, pleaded before the Virginia convention, "That sacred and lovely thing, religion," ought not to rest on "the ingenuity of logical deduction."[171] The "public clamor" for a bill of rights was so great that Madison and the other proponents of the Constitution could persuade several states to ratify only after promising to work for the addition of a bill of rights.[172] Madison had been skeptical concerning the necessity or desirability of a bill of rights, but after the Constitution was ratified by the requisite number of states he changed his mind, and stated that he now favored amendment to provide for "all essential rights, particularly the rights of Conscience in the fullest latitude, the freedom of the press, trial by jury, security against general warrants, etc."[173] Accordingly, shortly after his election to the House of Representatives in 1789, Madison introduced his compilation of proposals for amendments to the Constitution to meet the demands for a bill of rights. In a notable address delivered in support of his proposal, he stated that many Americans, "respectable for their talents and respectable for the jealousy which they have for their liberty," were dissatisfied with the Constitution as it stood because it "did not contain effectual provisions against encroachments on particular rights, and those safeguards which they have been long accustomed to have interposed between them and the magistrate who exercises the sovereign power." "We ought not to disregard their inclination," he urged, "but, on principles of amity and moderation, conform to their wishes and expressly declare the great rights of mankind secured under this Constitution."[174]

The discussion which surrounded Madison's proposed bill of rights, and the amendments that were made to the proposed First Amendment, will be discussed in the next chapter. Here it may be sufficient to record that the proposed amendments were in substance agreed to by the House of Representatives and were sent to the Senate. Discussion of differences between the two Houses followed, and on September 25, 1789, the Senate concurred "in the amendments proposed by the House of Representatives to the amendments of the Senate."[175] The Bill of Rights, approved by the requisite number of states in 1791, began with a guaranty of religious freedom. The First Amendment reads in full:

> Congress shall make no law respecting an establishment of religion, or prohibiting the free exercise thereof; or abridging the freedom of speech, or of the press; or the right of the people peaceably to assemble and to petition the Government for a redress of grievances.

Other amendments in the Bill of Rights guaranteed the right to keep arms and to be free of compulsory quartering of soldiers in peace, security of person and home against unreasonable searches and seizures, the right to a fair, speedy, and public trial by jury, and prohibitions against deprivation of life, liberty, or property without due process of law, and against cruel and unusual punishments.

What, however, is particularly significant to our study is that the last words of the last article of the Constitution (except for the purely formal article specifying when the Constitution should become effective) prohibit any religious test "as a qualification to any office or public trust under the United States," and the first words of the first article of the Bill of Rights prohibit "any law respecting an establishment of religion." The significance of this ending and beginning is more than symbolic; it indicates unmistakably that in the minds of the fathers of our Constitution, independence of religion and government was the alpha and omega of democracy and freedom.

### CHAPTER FIVE

# The Meaning of the Principle

## THE CONSTITUTION AND THE FIRST AMENDMENT

STRICTLY SPEAKING, the American experiment of freedom and separation was not established in the First Amendment command that "Congress shall make no law respecting an establishment of religion or prohibiting the free exercise thereof." That experiment had been launched four years earlier, when the founders of the republic carefully withheld from the new national government any power to deal with religion. As Madison said, the national government had no "jurisdiction" over religion or any "shadow of right to intermeddle" with it.[1]

The First Amendment, then, did not take away or abridge any power of the national government; its intent was to make express the absence of power. The historian George Bancroft, in a letter to Philip Schaff, stated:

> Congress from the beginning was as much without the power to make a law respecting the establishment of religion as it is now that the amendment has passed.[2]

Charles Beard made the same point:

> The Constitution does not confer upon the Federal government any power whatever to deal with religion in any form or manner. . . . The First Amendment merely confirms the intention of the framers.[3]

## THE FIRST AMENDMENT AS A RESTRICTION ON
## PRESIDENTIAL AND JUDICIAL POWERS

This distinction between an abridgment of existing power and a declaration of the nonexistence of power has important theoretic and practical consequences, as will appear from time to time in this volume. Here it may be sufficient to point out briefly but one of these consequences.

The First Amendment, it will be noted, provides only that

> *Congress* shall make no law respecting an establishment of religion or prohibiting the free exercise thereof.

The amendment expresses no restriction upon action by the President or the Federal judiciary. This omission was emphasized by the late Professor Edward S. Corwin and others in defending the constitutionality of an American ambassador to the Vatican.[4] The appointment of an ambassador, Professor Corwin argued, is an act of the President, and therefore cannot violate the mandate of the First Amendment that "Congress shall make no law respecting an establishment of religion."

The logic of this argument is predicated on the assumption that but for the First Amendment the Federal government, in its legislative, executive, and judiciary divisions, would have power to act in the area of religion. It follows from this assumption that since the power was taken away only from Congress, it still remains with the President and the Federal courts. But, as we have seen, the power to deal with religion was never delegated to the Federal government or to any part of it. Madison used the terms "government" and "general government," not "Congress," in denying "jurisdiction" over religion and the right to "intermeddle" with it. If no branch of the national government has any inherent or delegated power under the Constitution to intermeddle with religion, the fact that the First Amendment expresses a restraint only upon Congressional action may not be construed as an implied grant of power to the President or the judiciary.

It was the possibility of just such "a colorable pretext to claim more than was granted" that Hamilton warned against when he asked "why declare that things shall not be done which there is no power to do?" And it was to meet this threat that the Bill of Rights included the Ninth and Tenth Amendments, which provide respectively, that

> The enumeration in the Constitution of certain rights, shall not be construed to deny and disparage others retained by the people, [and] The powers not delegated to the United States by the Constitution, nor prohibited by it to the States, are reserved to the States respectively, or to the people.

The Bill of Rights was added to the Constitution to satisfy the demands of Jefferson and his Republicans, who above all else were fearful and suspicious of a strong executive. It seems highly unlikely that they would have agreed to an amendment which left the executive free to abridge a right so carefully withheld from legislative interference. This becomes even clearer when it is remembered that the First Amendment is not limited to a prohibition on laws respecting religion; it provides also that "Congress shall make no law . . . prohibiting the free exercise" of religion, "or abridging the freedom of speech, or of the press; or the right of the people peaceably to assemble, and to petition the government for a redress of grievances." If the President and the Federal courts are free to disregard the prohibition of laws respecting an establishment of religion, they must be equally free to disregard the other prohibitions.

Only the First Amendment mentions Congress; the other seven amendments use passive verbs without limiting the subject of the restraint: ". . . the right to keep and bear arms shall not be infringed," "no soldier shall . . . be quartered in any house," the right to be secure against "unreasonable searches and seizures shall not be violated," etc. The First Amendment as originally drafted by Madison was in the same passive form, and it too did not mention Congress. It read:

> The civil rights of none shall be abridged on account of religious belief, nor shall any national religion be established, nor shall the full and equal rights of conscience in any manner or on any pretext be infringed.[5]

During the course of its travels until its final adoption (discussed more fully below) the grammatical structure was changed to the active and the word "Congress" was inserted. There appears, however, to be no indication in any of the debates or writings that the purpose of the stylistic change was to leave the executive and judicial branches of the government free of the restriction imposed on the Congress.

How this change came about can only be a matter of speculation. In colonial days establishments of religion were effected by the colonial legislatures; and, as we have seen, the Continental Congress, in the period immediately preceding the adoption of the Constitution, busied itself with religious matters. It was therefore natural that in restricting the national government's activities in the field of religion, the framers of the First Amendment in the form it was finally adopted thought in terms of Congress. The change may also be explained by the fact that Madison's original version contained a provision that "No *state* shall violate the rights of conscience, or the freedom of the press, or the trial by jury in criminal cases." When it was decided to eliminate this restriction on state action, it was natural to change the sentence structure. This seems highly probable when it is noted that the word "Congress" first appears in the third version of the amendment, and that the second version read: "No religion shall be established by law, nor shall the equal rights of conscience be infringed." Retention of the passive style might have been construed as an intent to encompass state action, and it was natural in the third version to indicate expressly that "*Congress* shall make no laws, etc."

Whatever the reason for the change, it is a reasonable assumption that its purpose was not to confer on the President and the Federal courts power to deal with religious affairs. As will be seen later,[6] the Supreme Court in 1872 ruled that under the Constitution the Federal courts have no power to determine controversies of ecclesiastical dogma. The logic of that decision, as well as of the history of the First Amendment, leads necessarily to the conclusion that the President and the Federal courts are as constitutionally incapable of engaging in acts "respecting an establishment of religion or prohibiting the free exercise thereof" as is the Congress. That the interpretation represents the view of the Supreme Court would seem to be indicated by its use of the words "Federal Government" rather than "Congress" in its carefully phrased explanation of the meaning of the "establishment" clauses stated in the Everson case, repeated in other cases, and quoted later in this chapter. It is clear that Jefferson and Madison, at least, so interpreted the First Amendment, as can be seen from their stated reasons for opposing Presidential Thanksgiving proclamations.[7]

## THE FIRST AMENDMENT AND "SEPARATION OF CHURCH AND STATE"

In the Everson case in 1947 and in the McCollum case in 1948 the Supreme Court stated that the First Amendment was intended to erect a "wall of separation between church and state."[8] This statement has been severely criticized, particularly by Catholic spokesmen and writers. Immediately after the Everson decision was announced, Father John Courtney Murray described the phrase "separation of church and state" as a "negative, ill-defined, basically un-American [sic] formula."[9] After the McCollum decision the Catholic bishops of the United States, in a statement issued through the National Catholic Welfare Conference in November 1948,[10] called the phrase "separation of church and state" the "shibboleth of doctrinaire secularism." Father Robert I. Gannon, former president of Fordham University, in an address delivered in St. Louis in November 1951, used the phrase "the current fraud of separation of church and state."[11] James M. O'Neill, a Catholic writer whose interpretation of the First Amendment was adopted by the Catholic bishops, termed "spurious" the so-called "great American principle of complete separation of church and state," and affirmed that "There is no such great American principle and there never has been."[12] Father Thomas F. Coakely, on the front cover of a pamphlet, "Separation of Church and State," published by the Catholic Truth Society, said unqualifiedly: "Church and State have never been separated in

America." Even the then Attorney General of the United States, in an address before the National Catholic Educational Association, charged that the Supreme Court had "distorted" the First Amendment in referring to "a wall of separation of Church and State."[13]

Recently, even Protestants have expressed some dissatisfaction with the term "separation of church and state." In February 1964, the National Council of Churches of Christ in the United States conducted a national study conference on church and state at Columbus, Ohio, attended by some 400 delegates representing 24 Protestant denominations. While the conference was not authorized to issue any pronouncements binding either the National Council or the denominations, it was authorized and did issue recommendations in the form of "General Findings." These, adopted with but one voiced dissent, probably reflected faithfully the tenor of the conference. These findings contained the following statement:

> In the American experience, relations between church and state have generally been affirmative, friendly and marked by mutual respect. In view of the nature of these relationships, any attempt to express church-state relations in terms of an absolute and complete separation or of a wall of separation between church and state serves only to obscure the fullness of their relationship rather than offering a fruitful basis for an understanding of the present situation. The history of church-state relations in the United States refutes such a rigid conception.

Critics of the Supreme Court's use of the phrase "separation of church and state" as expressing the intent of the First Amendment emphasize that the phrase does not appear in the Amendment. Professor Corwin points out that

> Actually, the Constitution does not mention this principle. In fact, it does not contain the word "church," nor yet the word "state," . . . even the word "separation" fails to put in an appearance. These singular omissions—singular if what the Framers wanted was "Separation of Church and State" in the Court's understanding of it—are now supplied by the Court by the interpretation which it affixes to the "establishment of religion" clause of the First Amendment.[14]

At first glance there would seem to be little value in much of the argument around the phrase "separation of church and state." No magic attaches to the particular verbalization of an underlying concept. Indeed, the concept at issue here is more accurately expressed in Madison's phrase "separation between Religion and Government,"[15] or in the popular maxim that "religion is a private matter." Nevertheless, much of the controversy surrounding the Everson and later cases[16] has centered in the phrase "separation of church and state," and the opponents of the broad interpretation of the First Amendment contained in these cases have strenuously urged that identification of the phrase with the Constitution is a recent invention of what might be called the Everson-McCollum court; for these reasons, their contention merits consideration.

It is true, of course, that the phrase "separation of church and state" does not appear in the Constitution. But it was inevitable that some convenient term should come into existence to verbalize a principle so clearly and widely held by the American people. For example, the phrase "Bill of Rights" has become a convenient term to designate the freedoms guaranteed in the first ten amendments; yet it would be the height of captiousness to argue that the phrase does not appear in the Constitution. Similarly, the right to a fair trial is generally accepted to be a constitutional principle; yet the term "fair trial" is not found in the Constitution. The phrase "interstate commerce," used innumerably by every constitutional writer including Professor Corwin, does not appear in the Constitution—neither does the phrase "self-incrimination," or "right of privacy," or "freedom of association." To bring the point even closer home, who would deny that "religious liberty" is a constitutional principle? Yet that phrase too is not in the Constitution. The universal acceptance which all these terms, including "separation of church and state," have received in America would seem to confirm rather than disparage their reality as basic American democratic principles.

In view of the acrimony evoked by the Everson-McCollum court's use of the phrase, it is perhaps not entirely unnecessary to note that that court neither invented the phrase nor originated its identification with the First Amendment. It was Jefferson who, only a decade after the First Amendment was adopted, conceived the phrase. Replying to an address of the Danbury Baptists Association, he wrote:

> Believing with you that religion is a matter which lies solely between man and his God, that he owes account to none other for his faith or his worship, that the legitimate powers of government reach actions only, and not opinions, I contemplate with sovereign reverence that act of the whole American people which declared that their legislature should "make no law respecting an establishment of religion, or prohibiting the free exercise thereof," thus building a wall of separation between church and state.[17]

Valiant attempts have been made to minimize this letter. Professor O'Neill referred to it as a "little address of courtesy,"[18] and Professor Corwin sought to dispose of it by remarking that it "was not improbably motivated by an impish desire to heave a brick at the

Congregationalist-Federalist hierarchy of Connecticut," and suggested that it was not a "deliberate" or "carefully considered evaluation by Jefferson of the religious clauses of the First Amendment."[19]

This facile disposal is, however, historically inaccurate. We have Jefferson's own testimony that the letter was prepared with extreme care and deliberation, and that in fact he merely seized upon the Danbury Baptists' address as a long-awaited opportunity to express the thoughts contained in the letter. Indeed, he went further: he actually consulted his attorney general before sending the letter. Submitting the letter to Levi Lincoln, he wrote:

> Averse to receive addresses, yet unable to prevent them, I have generally endeavored to turn them to some account, by making them the occasion, by way of answer, of sowing useful truths & principles among the people, which might germinate and become rooted among their political tenets. The Baptist address, now enclosed, admits of a condemnation of the alliance between Church & State, under the authority of the Constitution. It furnishes an occasion, too, which I have long wished to find, of saying why I do not proclaim fastings and thanksgivings, as my predecessors did.
> The address, to be sure, does not point at this, and its introduction is awkward. But I foresee no opportunity of doing it more pertinently. . . . Will you be so good as to examine the answer, and suggest any alterations which might prevent an ill effect, or promote a good one among the people?[20]

In the light of this evidence it is difficult to characterize the letter as lacking in deliberation and care.

Furthermore it was not the Everson-McCollum court that first introduced Jefferson's metaphor into a judicial opinion and accepted Jefferson's identification of it with the First Amendment. When the Everson-McCollum court stated that, in the words of Jefferson, the clause against establishment of religion by law was intended to erect "a wall of separation between church and state," it was merely following an 1878 opinion of a unanimous Supreme Court, speaking through Chief Justice Waite, which quoted the Danbury letter and stated that "Coming as this does from an acknowledged leader of the advocates of the measure, it may be accepted almost as an authoritative declaration of the scope and effect of the amendment. . . ."[21]

If, then, identification of the phrase "separation of church and state" with the First Amendment was error, the error was shared by Jefferson and a unanimous Supreme Court which wrote three-quarters of a century before the Everson case. Moreover, in view of the leading role that the Catholic Church has played in the attack on the Jefferson phrase, it is not unfair to suggest that the church shared in the error; and to point out that possibly the most authoritative Catholic text on church and state in America, published four years before the Everson decision, stated:

> Our Federal and State constitutions forbid the legal establishment of any form of religion thereby insuring the separation of Church and State. . . .[22]

Nevertheless, as will be seen,[23] the four-year verbal barrage loosed against the phrase "separation of church and state" was not without effect. In the Zorach case Justice Douglas, speaking for a majority of the Court, did indeed reaffirm that "the First Amendment reflects the philosophy that Church and State should be separated," but for the first time he propounded a "common sense" approach to the problem, and expressed the view that the "First Amendment . . . does not say that in every and all respects there shall be a separation of Church and State."

## THE UNITARY GUARANTY OF THE FIRST AMENDMENT

The language of the First Amendment encompasses two prohibitions: it forbids laws respecting an establishment of religion, and laws prohibiting the free exercise of religion. Spokesmen for those sectarian groups which condemn as "error" the concept of separation as developed by American democracy, or at best "the shibboleth of doctrinaire secularism," have naturally emphasized this formal dichotomy, and have viewed the establishment bar as of secondary importance and meriting only the narrowest construction. Father Murray, for instance, expressed the opinion that "separation of church and state . . . put in its proper grounds in its true relation to the free exercise of religion . . . [is] instrumental to freedom, [and is] therefore . . . a relative, not an absolute right."[24] George E. Reed, in *Catholic Action,* called "error" the tendency to treat "separation of Church and State" as being synonymous with religious liberty rather than as a means of securing it.[25]

The same thought has been expressed by Protestants. A Congregationalist spokesman has written: "Separation of church and state . . . is simply a means, a technique, a policy to implement the principle of religious freedom. . . . As a method, separation of church and state can never be an absolute."[26] Another prominent Congregationalist, Erwin Griswold, dean of Harvard Law School, has expressed the same thought.[27] So, too, has Professor Paul Kauper,[28] who attended the Columbus Conference as a representative of the Lutheran Church, and Professor Wilber Katz,[29] an Episcopalian delegate to the same conference. Thus, Professor Katz has written:

> Except for occasional flights of rhetoric, no one contends either that absolute separation of church and state is required by the First Amendment or that such a rule would be desirable. Nor does the concept of separation provide its own principle of limitation. In determining the limits of constitutional separation, it is the concept of religious freedom which provides the criterion. The principle of church-state separation is an instrumental principle. Separation ordinarily promotes religious freedom; it is defensible so long as it does so, and only so long.[30]

Father Parsons, too, viewed the separation aspect of the First Amendment to be no more than a "policy," a means to an end — an end less idealistic than security of religious freedom. Indeed, he all but suggested that it was little more than a necessary evil, a price unwillingly paid by Madison.

> It was not [said Father Parsons] a doctrine or "principle" of separation of church and state that motivated those who proposed the First Amendment. It was a policy to be adopted. It was found that, unless the Federal Government were inhibited from establishing any church, it would be extremely difficult, if not impossible, to get the Constitution ratified by many States. If the people of a State could not have their church established nationally, they were not going to allow any other to be established. . . . The First Amendment was the price that Madison and others paid to secure ratification of the Constitution.[31]

Professor Corwin, too, found a dichotomy in the First Amendment. He expressed the view that contemporary England manages to maintain alongside an establishment as complete freedom of religion as exists in this country.[32] As we have previously remarked, this begs the question. It assumes that Jefferson, for instance, who drafted the Virginia Bill for Establishing Religious Freedom in order to assure that "no man shall be compelled to . . . support any religious worship, place or ministry whatsoever," would agree that the English taxpayer enjoys "complete freedom of religion" even though he is required to support the Anglican establishment. Moreover, as we have also seen,[33] even the established Anglican church does not believe it enjoys "complete freedom of religion."

The result is the same in other countries. Wherever the church or state seeks to use the other as an engine for its own purpose — that is, wherever a state or church pierces the wall of separation between them — religious freedom inevitably suffers. Mussolini, a confirmed atheist most of his life and the father of modern totalitarianism, found no difficulty in according state support to religion, for he effectively used the church as an engine for his purposes. The Soviet government, equally totalitarian and equally atheistic, finds no difficulty in conferring on its church state support, for it also uses the church as an engine for state purposes. Conversely in Spain, another totalitarian state, the church uses the state as an engine to further its own purposes. In all these countries religious freedom has been the inevitable victim.[34]

The fathers of our democracy reached the same conclusion. The draftsmen of the First Amendment regarded freedom of religion as incompatible with an establishment. Nothing in American constitutional history or tradition justifies an apportionment of values between disestablishment and freedom or indeed the dichotomy itself. The struggle for religious liberty and for disestablishment were parts of the same single evolutionary process that culminated in the First Amendment.

Roger Williams opposed an "enforced uniformity of religion" (freedom concept) because it "confounds the Civil and Religious" (separation concept); and Madison fought a bill establishing a provision for teachers of the Christian religion (separation concept) because it violated the "fundamental and undeniable truth 'that religion . . . can be directed only be reason and conviction, not by force or violence'" (freedom concept). Virginia's statute for establishing "religious freedom" was enacted because of "the impious presumption of legislators and rulers" who had "established and maintained false religions" (separation concept). The proposed versions of the First Amendment submitted by the states and considered by Congress before it adopted the Amendment in its final form,[35] combined both aspects of the dual prohibition without any indication that one was superior and the other subordinate. Jefferson refused to proclaim days of fasting and prayer because of "the provision that no law shall be made respecting the establishment or free exercise of religion."[36] It was in a case involving an attack (on a statute proscribing bigamy) under the religious freedom clause that the Supreme Court in 1878 first judicially stated that the First Amendment was intended to erect "a wall of separation between church and state."[37] That all the fifty states guarantee religious freedom and not one maintains an establishment of religion would appear to be convincing evidence that in American tradition the concepts are correlative and unitary. In the words of Justice Rutledge in his dissent in the Everson case,

"Establishment" and "free exercise" were correlative and coextensive ideas, representing only different facets of the single great and fundamental freedom.[38]

Or, in the words of Professor Ruffini,

. . . Religious liberty and separatism have become in America two terms which, ideally, historically and practically, are inseparable.[39]

Although the guaranty of the First Amendment is unitary, it does have a dual aspect, and in most cases one or the other aspect is more conspicuous. Thus, in a case involving public aid to religious education, the separation aspect is more obvious than the freedom aspect, and such cases can be conveniently considered in this volume under the separation rubric. Conversely, in other cases the freedom facet is more conspicuous, as in statutes prohibiting polygamy, or requiring all children to attend secular public schools. Sometimes both aspects are equally prominent, as in cases involving compulsory Sunday observance laws, particularly when enforced against seventh-day observers. Cases like these will be treated more or less arbitrarily under one rubric or the other. But whichever facet is the more obvious, the other is ever-present. This statement is made with all due respect to Justice Douglas, who, in the Zorach released time case, expressed the view that "it takes obtuse reasoning to inject any issue of the 'free excercise' of religion into the present case."[40] The Zorach case will be considered more fully in the chapter dealing with released time, but here it may be said that Justice Douglas was neither charitable nor just to his three dissenting colleagues, who saw clearly in the case a religious freedom issue.

There are, nevertheless, situations in which the two aspects of the First Amendment appear to conflict. As we have seen, constitutions and statutes disestablishing state churches frequently had provisions disqualifying clergymen from holding all public office or from serving in the legislature, and Jefferson at first agreed that this disqualification was necessary to protect separation. Madison, however, believed—and he was ultimately able to convince Jefferson of the correctness of his view—that such disqualification constituted an infringement of religious freedom.[41] So, too, Madison vetoed a bill to incorporate the Episcopal Church in Washington because he believed it violated the constitutional prohibition of religious establishment.[42] Yet it is fairly arguable today that a refusal to allow persons to incorporate for religious purposes under a law permitting incorporation for all other legitimate purposes would violate their religious freedom.

Tax exemption of religious organizations is another illustration of the apparent conflict of the two aspects. Does a grant of exemption impair separation, or does denial infringe on religious freedom? Again, may a city, consistently with the principle of separation, permit missionary activities in municipally owned parks; or may it, consistently with the principle of religious freedom, deny such permission?[43] Furnishing the services of a government-paid chaplain to members of the armed forces may violate the mandate of separation; but depriving a conscripted sailor of the opportunity to obtain spiritual comfort from a pastor of his faith may unnecessarily violate the mandate of freedom.

The conflict may be more apparent than real. Madison opposed the disqualification of clergymen from public office not only because it infringed on their religious freedom, but also because "it violate[s] another article of the plan which exempts religion from the cognizance of Civil power . . . ," thus indicating his opinion that both aspects were impaired.[44] It is, however, true that in most cases the conflict appears irreconcilable, and that it is a difficult task to determine where "establishment" ends and "free exercise" begins.[45] The difficult task of drawing lines and weighing apparently conflicting values is not unique in the subject under study in this volume; it can hardly be avoided in any area of constitutional law.

## THE FIRST AMENDMENT AND THE STATES

The First Amendment contains no restriction on action by the states. It provides only that "*Congress* shall make no law," etc. Madison felt that a bill of rights should bind the states as well as the Federal government, and when he introduced his draft of proposed amendments, he included a provision that "No State shall violate the equal rights of conscience, or the freedom of the press, or the trial by jury in criminal cases." He argued in its behalf that

> It is proper that every Government shall be disarmed of powers which trench upon these particular rights. . . . [It] must be admitted, on all hands, that the State Governments are as liable to attack these invaluable privileges as the General Government is, and therefore ought to be as cautiously guarded against.

A select committee, consisting of one Representative from each state, approved the proposal and reported it favorably, merely adding the phrase "freedom of speech." The amendment was opposed in debate by Thomas Tucker of South Carolina, who argued that: "It will be much better, I apprehend, to leave the State Governments to themselves, and not to interfere with them more than we already do, and that is thought by many to be too much." Madison persisted, saying that he "conceived this to be the most valuable amendment of the whole lot. If there were any reason to restrain the Government of the United States from infringing these essential rights, it was equally necessary that they should be secured against the State Governments. He thought that if they provided against the one, it was necessary to provide against the other." On motion of Samuel Livermore of New Hampshire, the amendment was rephrased slightly so as to read: "The equal rights of conscience, the freedom of speech or of the press, and the right of trial by jury in criminal cases, shall not be infringed by any State." In this form the amendment was passed by the House of Representatives; but it was stricken out by the Senate when it considered the seventeen amendments adopted by the House, and the House later concurred in the Senate action.[46]

Only the First Amendment specifically mentions Congress; the other seven constituting the Bill of Rights contain unqualified prohibitions. The Fifth Amendment, for instance, provides simply that "No person shall be . . . deprived of life, liberty or property without due process of law," without express indication of an intent to prohibit deprivation only by the Federal Government. By 1833 the omission was cured by the Supreme Court. In Barron vs. Baltimore[47] the Court held that no part of the Bill of Rights, not merely the First Amendment, restrained the states. Speaking through Chief Justice John Marshall, the Court said:

> Had Congress engaged in the extraordinary occupation of improving the constitutions of the several states by affording the people additional protection from the exercise of power by their own governments in matters which concerned themselves alone, they would have declared this purpose in plain and intelligible language. . . .
>
> These amendments contain no expression indicating an intention to apply them to the State governments. This court cannot so apply them. . . . The fifth amendment is intended solely as a limitation on the exercise of power by the government of the United States and is not applicable to the legislation of the States.

This holding was repeatedly reaffirmed by the Supreme Court.[48] In 1845 it was specifically applied to the religious freedom clause of the First Amendment. In Permoli vs. First Municipality of New Orleans[49] the Court ruled that

> The Constitution makes no provision for protecting the citizens of the respective States in their religious liberties; this is left to the state constitutions and laws; nor is there any inhibition imposed by the constitution of the United States in this respect on the states.

Though not required by the First Amendment either to separate church and state or to secure freedom of religion, all the states assumed the dual obligation in their own constitutions. At the time of the adoption of the First Amendment in 1791, all the states guaranteed substantial religious liberty, though some vestiges of colonial intolerance—chiefly political disabilities of Catholics and Jews—remained for a while in a few states. But even in those states the constitutional and statutory restrictions were dead letters for many years before they were formally repealed. It was not until 1868 that a provision of the North Carolina constitution disqualifying for public office any person who "shall deny the being of God or the truth of the Christian religion" was eliminated; yet as early as 1808 a Jew had been elected to the legislature and a challenge to his right to sit was overwhelmingly rejected.[50]

Nor was disestablishment in the states long in coming. When the First Amendment was adopted in 1791, only four of the thirteen States—Massachusetts, Connecticut, New Hampshire, and Maryland—retained any substantial establishment in their basic laws, and in none of these was the establishment exclusive; in each case the taxpayer could choose the religious denomination that was to receive his tax.[51] Typical of these states was Massachusetts, whose constitution of 1780 (Article 3) read:

> And all moneys paid by the subject to the support of public worship, and of the public teachers aforesaid, shall, if he require it, be uniformly applied to the support of the public teacher or teachers of his own religious sect or denomination, provided there be any on whose instruction he attends; otherwise it may be paid towards the support of the teacher or teachers of the parish or precinct in which the said moneys are raised.

Massachusetts was the last state to give up its establishment. It was not until 1833 that a constitutional amendment was adopted which restricted religion to voluntary support.[52]

The evolution of the American principle may, then, be said to have been completed in 1833. The rate of its development was not uniform in all states. Massachusetts arrived in 1833 at the point from which neighboring Rhode Island had started almost two centuries earlier. But by and large a general pattern is discernible: a gradual extension of the areas of religious liberty, first to include all Protestant sects, then all Christians, then all believers in God, and finally elimination of all religious tests. Starting and culminating later, but following more or less the same pattern, was the progress of disestablishment: a gradual extension of the area of tax support, first to include all Protestant sects, then all Christians, then a provision allowing non-Christians to assign their tax to general education or charity (which was the only practicable method in view of the minute number of professed non-Christians), and finally the abolition of all tax support.

It is important to note that in no case did the development end until complete disestablishment was arrived at: no state stopped with according freedom of worship, or indeed with less than complete prohibition of tax support of any and all religions. Moreover, every state that entered the union after the Constitution was adopted incorporated both prohibitions in its constitution or basic laws. In no case was there any attempt to establish any denomination or religion; on the contrary, in varying language but with a single spirit, all states expressly forbade such attempt. This deliberate decision was not motivated by indifference to religion: most of the states had been settled by deeply religious pioneers. Nor was it dictated by purely practical considerations; many of the states had a population far more homogeneous religiously than Canada, Holland, or even England. Nor was the decision required by the Federal government: up to 1868 at least, nothing in the Constitution prevented any state, after its admission to the union, from establishing a religion or indeed from restricting freedom of worship. The decision was in all cases voluntary; and it was made because the unitary principle of separation and freedom was as integral a part of American democracy as republicanism, representative government, and freedom of expression.

It is clear, therefore, that by 1868, when the Fourteenth Amendment was adopted, the principle of freedom and separation was firmly established in American life. The Fourteenth Amendment was directed specifically at the states, and in its relevant part (Section 1), reads:

> All persons born or naturalized in the United States, and subject to the jurisdiction thereof, are citizens of the United States and of the State wherein they reside. No State shall make or enforce any law which shall abridge the privileges or immunities of citizens of the United States; nor shall any State deprive any person of life, liberty, or property without due process of law; nor deny to any person within its jurisdiction the equal protection of the laws.

The Amendment makes no express reference to religion or to any of the other freedoms guaranteed in the Bill of Rights. But the Supreme Court, in Barron vs. Baltimore, had expressly ruled that the Bill of Rights did not apply to the states, and the deliberations that preceded the passing of the Fourteenth Amendment in Congress make it clear that the purpose of the Amendment, as understood by some of the Congressional leaders most responsible for its drafting and adoption, was to overrule Barron vs. Baltimore and to make the Bill of Rights applicable to the states. Representative John A. Bingham of Ohio, who drafted the first section of the Fourteenth Amendment, and whose relationship to it was not unlike Madison's relationship to the First, repeatedly referred to Barron vs. Baltimore in the debates, and urged the adoption of his proposed Amendment to overcome this decision and make the Bill of Rights applicable to the states. Representative Thaddeus Stevens, in introducing the proposed amendment into the House in behalf of the drafting committee, on which he and Bingham served, stated:

> The first section prohibits the States from abridging the privileges and immunities of citizens of the United States, or unlawfully depriving them of life, liberty, or property, or of denying to any person within their jurisdiction the equal protection of the laws.
> I can hardly believe that any person can be found who will not admit that every one of these provisions is just. They are all asserted, in some form or other, in our Declaration or organic law. But the Constitution limits only the action of Congress, and is not a limitation on the States. This amendment supplies that defect, and allows Congress to correct the unjust legislation of the States, so far that the law which operated upon one man shall operate equally upon all.[53]

The leader of the proposed amendment in the Senate, J. M. Howard, stated expressly that the "privileges and immunities" clause of the amendment included "the personal rights guaranteed and secured by the first eight amendments to the Constitution."[54] The author of a comprehensive analysis of the historical origins of the Fourteenth Amendment comes to the conclusion that

> Congress, the House and the Senate, had the following objects and motives in view for submitting the first section of the Fourteenth Amendment to the States for ratification:
> 1. To make the Bill of Rights (the first eight Amendments) binding upon or applicable to, the States.
> 2. To give validity to the Civil Rights Bill.
> 3. To declare who were citizens of the United States.[55]

On the other hand, these conclusions have been seriously challenged by other constitutional historians, who say that the available evidence does not support the assertion that Congress, in adopting the Amendment, intended thereby to make the first eight amendments applicable to the states, or to do anything beyond protecting the civil rights of Negroes.[56]

Whatever may have been the intent of the framers and adopters of the Fourteenth Amendment—if indeed there was any consensus of intent at all—a majority of the Supreme Court in the Slaughter-House Cases in 1873 ruled that the phrase "privileges and immunities" did not include the rights secured against Federal infringement by the first eight amendments, nor any civil rights "which belong to citizens of the States as such," but only those "privileges and immunities" applicable to national citizenship, *e.g.*, the privilege of voting for Congressmen or President.[59] Despite Justice Black's valiant attempt to turn the tide in his dissent in Adamson vs. California,[58] this holding in the Slaughter-House Cases has been consistently followed by the Supreme Court.[59] As late as 1922 the Supreme Court stated that

> The Constitution of the United States imposes upon the States no obligation to confer upon those within their jurisdiction . . . the right of free speech. . . .[60]

But though the restricted interpretation of the "privileges and immunities" clause by the decision in the Slaughter-House Cases has not been disturbed by the Court, most of the force of that decision was gradually dissipated by the Court's expansion of the word "liberty" in that part of the Fourteenth Amendment which prohibits states from depriving "any person of life, liberty, or property, without due process of law." The framers of the Fourteenth Amendment may have intended the "privileges and immunities" clause to be the vehicle for prohibition of state impairment of the liberties secured by the First Amendment. This intent was frustrated by the decision in the Slaughter-House Cases, but ultimately the Court reached substantially the same result by interpreting the word "liberty" in the "due process" clause.

The expanded interpretation of "liberty" began in 1923 when the Court, in holding unconstitutional a Nebraska statute forbidding the teaching of foreign languages to schoolchildren,[61] stated:

> Without doubt it ["liberty" in the Fourteenth Amendment] denotes not merely freedom from bodily restraint but also the right of the individual to contract, to engage in any of the common occupations of life, to acquire useful knowledge, to marry, establish a home, and bring up children, *to worship God according to the dictates of his own conscience,* and generally to enjoy those privileges long recognized at common law as essential to the orderly pursuit of happiness by free men.[62]

This case was followed two years later by a decision invalidating an Oregon statute outlawing private schools.[63] The same year the Court, in a case in which a New York antisedition law was attacked as a violation of freedom of speech, said:

> For present purposes we may and do assume that freedom of speech and of the press—which are protected by the First Amendment from

abridgment by Congress—are among the fundamental personal rights and "liberties" protected by the due process clause of the Fourteenth Amendment from impairment by the States.[64]

This statement was followed in case after case beginning with the 1930's,[65] and the extension of the Fourteenth Amendment to include the guaranty against laws "prohibiting the free exercise" of religion followed logically. Beginning with the many Jehovah's Witnesses cases at the close of the 1930's, the Court held in case after case that a state was barred by the due process clause of the Fourteenth Amendment from infringing on religious freedom.[66]

It has been pointed out that the use of the "liberty" of the Fourteenth Amendment to transfer to the states the freedoms of the First Amendment leads to a logical difficulty. The prohibition in the First Amendment of laws prohibiting the free exercise of religion and abridging freedom of the speech, press, or assemblage is absolute and unqualified; the prohibition of the "liberty" clause of the Fourteenth is qualified by the term "without due process of law."[67] Logically, then, a state could abridge freedom of religion, press, or speech if it did so with "due process of law." The Court, however, has disregarded the "due process" phrase, and has treated the freedoms equally whether abridged by the Federal or state governments.[68] It should be noted that this disregard of logic was required by the Court's earlier frustration of what may well have been the framers' intent to use the absolute and unqualified "privileges and immunities" clause as the vehicle for transfer into the Fourteenth Amendment of the freedoms of the First Amendment. It sometimes requires an illogical decision to undo the work of a previous illogical decision.

In the Everson parochial bus case, the Supreme Court in 1947 ruled that the First Amendment prohibition of laws respecting an establishment of religion was made applicable to the states by the Fourteenth Amendment; in later cases this ruling was expressly reaffirmed. This ruling has been subject to criticism. Some have criticized it on the ground that no part of the First Amendment, either "establishment" or "free exercise," is incorporated in the Fourteenth;[69] but it should be noted that unless the religious freedom aspect of the First Amendment is deemed incorporated into the Fourteenth, it is difficult to justify the Supreme Court decision in the Pierce case, which invalidated an Oregon law outlawing parochial schools and on which the constitutional security of the parochial school system depends today.

Possibly for that reason, most Catholic spokesmen do not criticize the incorporation of the "free exercise" guaranty into the Fourteenth Amendment, but do criticize the incorporation of the "establishment" prohibition.[70] Others, non-Catholics, have likewise limited their criticism to the incorporation of the "establishment" prohibition.[71] Semantically, a good argument can be made for the distinction. A ban on the deprivation of "liberty" might well be construed to include religious liberty. But the inclusion of the prohibition against establishment is more difficult. That aspect of the First Amendment does not superficially concern or protect "liberty," but regulates government relations. A person deprived of the liberty of religious belief or nonbelief may reasonably be held to have been deprived of "liberty . . . without due process of law"; but such deprivation is not as clear when the only issue apparently involved is the use of a small measure of public funds to pay for the transportation of children to parochial schools, or the release of public school children for religious instruction during school hours.

Professor Corwin expressed this criticism as follows:

> . . . the Fourteenth Amendment does not authorize the Court to substitute the word "state" for "Congress" in the ban imposed by the First Amendment on laws "respecting an establishment of religion." So far as the Fourteenth Amendment is concerned, States are entirely free to establish religions, provided they do not deprive anybody of religious liberty. It is only liberty that the Fourteenth Amendment protects. And in this connection it should not be overlooked that contemporary England manages to maintain as complete freedom of religion as exists in this country alongside an establishment of religion, although originally that establishment involved a ban upon all other faiths.[72]

Some,[73] including the present writer,[74] have inferred from the unsuccessful attempt to enact the Blaine amendment in 1875–1876, that the Fourteenth Amendment was not intended to incorporate the "establishment" prohibition of the First. In his annual message of 1876, President Grant recommended an amendment to the United States Constitution forbidding the teaching in any public school of religious tenets, and further prohibiting "the granting of any school funds, or school taxes, or any part thereof, either by legislative, municipal, or other authority, for the benefit or in aid, directly or indirectly, of any religious sect or denomination."[75] One week later James G. Blaine introduced a resolution for a constitutional amendment providing that

> No State shall make any law respecting an establishment of religion or prohibiting the free exercise thereof; and no money raised by taxation in any State for the support of public schools, or derived from any public fund therefore, nor any public lands devoted thereto, shall ever

be under the control of any religious sect or denomination nor shall any money so raised or lands so devoted be divided between religious sects or denominations.[76]

The amendment was overwhelmingly passed by the House, but failed to obtain the necessary two-thirds vote in the Senate.

The inference that the introduction of the Blaine amendment manifested a belief that the Fourteenth Amendment did not prohibit the states from making laws respecting an establishment of religion or prohibiting its free exercise (else why would a specific amendment be introduced for that purpose?) is predicated on the assumption that the situation in 1875 when the Blaine amendment was introduced was the same as in 1868 when the Fourteenth Amendment was adopted. This, of course, is not so. In the interim the Slaughter-House Cases were decided and the Supreme Court had ruled that the Bill of Rights, including the First Amendment, was not made applicable to the states by the "privileges and immunities" clause of the Fourteenth. That amendment itself was probably adopted in part to overrule a Supreme Court decision—Barron vs. Baltimore—and the Blaine amendment may well have been introduced to overrule another—the Slaughter-House Cases.

The defeat of the amendment does not necessarily mean that the Supreme Court decision in the Slaughter-House Cases was correct, or that Congress wished the state legislatures to have the power to make laws establishing religion or prohibiting its free exercise. The Blaine amendment was—or at least became—a partisan measure. All but one of the 27 Senators who voted for it were Republicans, and all the 16 who voted against it were Democrats.[77] Moreover, defeat of the amendment was based, at least in part, on the belief that the provisions of the state constitutions were adequate.[78] The extent to which the principle of separation had become part of the American constitutional system, state as well as Federal, is indicated by the fact that every state admitted into the union since 1876 was compelled by Congress to write into its constitution a requirement that it maintain a school system "free from sectarian control."[79]

Professor Corwin argued from English experience that religious liberty and establishment are not necessarily incompatible, and that therefore the "liberty" of the Fourteenth Amendment may include the "free exercise" aspect of the First Amendment—but not the "establishment" aspect. Even if we were to accept his appraisal of England's religious freedom, that country's constitutional history is very different from ours. In England there has been no substantial struggle for disestablishment—only an evolution of religious liberty.

147

In our country, as we have seen, the struggle for religious liberty was a facet of the struggle for disestablishment, and vice versa; there were not two struggles, but one. By 1868 the final victory had long been won in all the states, and in no state had the struggle ended with the attainment of freedom of worship; in all states it continued until separation was achieved.

The Blaine amendment stated both aspects of the First Amendment—again indicating their disseverability as an American constitutional principle. None of the Jehovah's Witnesses decisions, which held the "free exercise" provision applicable to the states, intimated that it alone was incorporated into the Fourteenth Amendment. Several contain language indicating a clearly contrary intent. Thus, the Court said in Cantwell vs. Connecticut:

> The fundamental concept of liberty embodied in the [Fourteenth] Amendment embraces the liberties guaranteed by the First Amendment. The First Amendment declares that Congress shall make no law *respecting an establishment of religion* or prohibiting the free exercise thereof. The Fourteenth Amendment has rendered the legislatures of the states as incompetent as Congress to enact such laws.[80]

In Minersville School District v. Gobitis[81] the Court said:

> Centuries of strife over the erection of particular dogmas as exclusive or all-comprehending faiths led to the inclusion of a guarantee for religious freedom in the Bill of Rights. The First Amendment, and the Fourteenth through its absorption of the First, sought to guard against repetition of those bitter religious struggles by prohibiting *the establishment of a state religion* and by securing to every sect the free exercise of its faith. So persuasive is the acceptance of this precious right that its scope is brought into question, as here, only when the conscience of individuals collides with the felt necessities of society.

In Murdock vs. Pennsylvania[82] the Court stated:

> The First Amendment, which the Fourteenth makes applicable to the states, declares that "Congress shall make *no law respecting an establishment of religion*, or prohibiting the free exercise thereof; or abridging the freedom of speech, or of the press. . . ."

But clearest of all, and earliest in time, is the following statement from Justice Cardozo's concurring opinion in the 1934 case of Hamilton vs. Regents of the University of California:[83]

> The First Amendment, if it be read into the Fourteenth, makes invalid any state law "respecting an establishment of religion, or prohibiting the free exercise thereof." *Instruction in military science is not instruction in the practice or tenets of a religion.* Neither directly nor indirectly is government establishing a state religion when it insists upon such training.

Thus, fourteen years before McCollum, not only did Justice Cardozo assume that the ban on establishment was made applicable to the states to the same extent as the free exercise clause, but, perhaps even more significant, that "instruction in the practice or tenets of a religion" would violate that ban.

In view of these statements and the direct holdings of the Everson and later cases, it may safely be said that it is now securely part of our constitutional law that the states under the Fourteenth Amendment are as committed to the requirement of the separation of church and state as the Federal government is under the First. Indeed, in one respect the commitment might be deemed even more severe. The First Amendment in its language prohibits only laws by "Congress"; the Fourteenth prohibits a "State" from depriving any person of life, liberty, or property without due process of law. As we have seen, Professor Corwin argued that the First Amendment does not prohibit action by the President or the judiciary; but the Fourteenth Amendment has been uniformly construed to control action by all departments of the states, executive and judiciary, as well as legislative.[84] As has been indicated above, however, it is more reasonable to hold that the constitutional disability to establish religion or prohibit its free exercise is no less applicable to the President and the Federal courts than it is to Congress; and for practical purposes it may therefore be assumed that the Federal Government and the States are equal in all respects in regard to the limitations imposed by the Constitution on "laws respecting an establishment of religion or prohibiting the free exercise thereof."

## THE MEANING OF SEPARATION

It was in the Everson case in 1947 that the Supreme Court first gave complete consideration to the meaning and scope of the "establishment" provision of the First Amendment. Although the Court, by a vote of five to four, held that a New Jersey town ordinance providing for the reimbursement of bus fares expended by parents sending their children to public high schools or Catholic parochial schools did not constitute a "law respecting an establishment of religion," all the justices agreed that the First Amendment was to be given a broad interpretation, and that its intent was not merely to prohibit the establishment of a state church but to preclude any government aid to religious groups or dogmas. In words which have now become well-known, Justice Black, speaking for the Court, said:

The "establishment of religion" clause of the First Amendment means at least this: Neither a state nor the Federal Government can set up a church. Neither can pass laws which aid one religion, aid all religions, or prefer one religion over another. Neither can force nor influence a person to go to or to remain away from church against his will or force him to profess a belief or disbelief in any religion. No person can be punished for entertaining or professing religious beliefs or disbeliefs, for church attendance or non-attendance. No tax in any amount, large or small, can be levied to support any religious activities or institutions, whatever they may be called, or whatever form they may adopt to teach or practice religion. Neither a state nor the Federal Government can, openly or secretly, participate in the affairs of any religious organizations or groups and *vice versa*. In the words of Jefferson, the clause against establishment of religion by law was intended to erect "a wall of separation between church and State."[85]

The decision aroused a storm of controversy, particularly along sectarian lines. Catholic spokesmen hailed the decision as a victory for religious liberty,[86] while Protestants criticized it as impairing the principle of separation of church and state.[87] The significance of the Court's interpretation of the First Amendment was overshadowed by the attention attracted by the specific holding of the case. Professor O'Neill was one of the few who saw that the broad principle on which the Court had agreed was far more important than the majority ruling that the First Amendment was not violated by the law under attack. His book, *Religion and Education under the Constitution*, was written to establish his contention that the Court's definitive announcement of the broad interpretation of the First Amendment was "historically and semantically indefensible," and that the Amendment did not prohibit nonpreferential government aid to all religions.

Several months after the Everson decision was announced, the Supreme Court was again required to pass on a state law which had been challenged under the "establishment of religion" clause of the First Amendment. In the McCollum case a system of released time for religious education in operation in the public school system of Champaign, Illinois, was attacked as violating the principles announced in the Everson case. It was clear that unless these principles were repudiated the Champaign system could not stand. Counsel for the Champaign Board of Education used the manuscript of Professor O'Neill's book,[88] and urged the Court to reinterpret the Amendment to conform to Professor O'Neill's thesis. The Court, however, was not convinced, and by a vote of eight to one invalidated the released-time program. In doing so it made its position clear by quoting at length the Everson decision's definitive interpretation of the First Amendment.[89] The Court held that, in the words of Justice

Frankfurter's concurring opinion, "separation means separation, not something less."

Although rejected by the Court, the narrow interpretation found ready acceptance in sectarian circles, and marked the basis of an all-out effort to persuade the American people and ultimately the courts that separation does mean something less. The leadership in the attack was taken by the Catholic Church; and it probably is not unfair or inaccurate to say that the narrow interpretation is the official position of the Catholic Church in America. On November 20, 1948, it issued, through the National Catholic Welfare Conference, an important statement which declared:

> To one who knows something of history and law, the meaning of the First Amendment is clear enough from its own words: "Congress shall make no laws [sic] respecting an establishment of religion or forbidding [sic] the free exercise thereof." The meaning is even clearer in the records of the Congress that enacted it. Then, and throughout English and Colonial history, "an establishment of religion" meant the setting up by law of an official Church which would receive from the government favors not equally accorded to others in the cooperation between government and religion — which was simply taken for granted in our country at that time and has, in many ways, continued to this day. Under the First Amendment, the Federal Government could not extend this type of preferential treatment to one religion as against another, nor could it compel or forbid any state to do so.
>
> If this practical policy be described by the loose metaphor "a wall of separation between Church and State," that term must be understood in a definite and typically American sense. It would be an utter distortion of American history and law to make that practical policy involve the indifference to religion and the exclusion of cooperation between religion and government implied in the term "separation of Church and State" as it has become the shibboleth of doctrinaire secularism. . . .
>
> We, therefore, hope and pray that the novel interpretation of the First Amendment recently adopted by the Supreme Court will in due process be revised. To that end we shall peacefully, patiently and perseveringly work. . . .
>
> We call upon our Catholic people to seek in their faith an inspiration and a guide in making an informed contribution to good citizenship. We urge members of the legal profession in particular to develop and apply their special competence in this field. We stand ready to cooperate in fairness and charity with all who believe in God and are devoted to freedom under God to avert the impending danger of a judicial "establishment of secularism" that would ban God from public life.[90]

Other Catholic writers and spokesmen who took the same position included Father John Courtney Murray,[91] Father Wilfred Parsons, Charles Fahy,[92] Joseph H. Brady[93] and former Attorney General J. Howard McGrath, who evoked an editorial demand from *The*

*Christian Century* for his removal[94] by the statement in his address before the National Catholic Education Association that

> A [constitutional] amendment, which was intended to prevent the creation of an established church, and a phrase in a letter of Thomas Jefferson have been distorted to create, in the words of United States Supreme Court Justice Black . . . "a wall between the church and state which must be kept high and impregnable." . . . If anything, the state and church must not have any fences between them.[95]

It must, however, by no means be assumed that support of this narrow interpretation of the First Amendment was limited to Catholics. Even before the bishops issued their statement, a group of prominent Protestant clergy and laymen issued a statement in which they criticized the Court's decision and broad interpretation of the principle of separation. The late Professor Edward S. Corwin, a noted non-Catholic constitutional authority, and Professor Alexander Meiklejohn, also a non-Catholic, adopted the same position.[96]

The principal premises of Professor O'Neill's thesis can be divided into the following elements:

(1) "Separation of church and state" or "a wall of separation of church and state" is only a "metaphor," a "figure of speech," a "spurious slogan," or a "shibboleth" which is not part of our American tradition or constitutional history. Its promulgation as constitutional law is a recent invention of the Everson-McCollum court. (This contention has already been discussed and requires no further consideration.)

(2) The First Amendment ban on any law by Congress respecting an establishment of religion does not in any way restrict the enactment of such laws by the states, and is not incorporated into the Fourteenth Amendment. (This contention too has already been considered.)

(3) The First Amendment does not require government neutrality between believers and nonbelievers, and the assertion that it does is a recent invention of the Everson-McCollum court.

(4) The First Amendment was not intended to divorce religion from government, but only to meet in practical manner the problems raised by a multiplicity of competing sects by prohibiting Congress from establishing any one sect, *i.e.*, granting it "monopolistic recognition" or conferring on it a preferred or privileged status.

(5) There was no intent on the part of those who drafted and adopted the First Amendment to bar the general support of religion by the Federal government, and the First Amendment therefore

does not prohibit the nonpreferential expenditure for religious purposes of funds raised by general taxation.

(6) The First Amendment, however, does bar the preferential treatment of a particular religion or sect short of according it monopolistic recognition of formal dominant status. A law, for instance, imposing a general tax for the support of Episcopalian schools would violate the Amendment, even though the Episcopal Church were not otherwise accorded the monopolistic status it enjoys in England.

Before considering the basis of this narrow interpretation, its implications should be clearly understood. In the first place, if the "establishment" clause is limited to requiring neutrality among sects, but not as between believers and nonbelievers, the clause forbidding laws "prohibiting the free exercise" of religion likewise protects only believers. In other words, the Constitution does not guarantee freedom of nonbelief.

Father Parsons recognized this:

> As for those who profess no religion, or who repudiate religion, it is difficult to conceive how they can appeal to the First Amendment, since this document was solely concerned with religion itself, not its denial. By its very nature as regards what it says about religion, they are outside its ken.[97]

This concept has been put in the form of a maxim that for a time gained wide acceptance in sectarian circles,[98] and was adopted by at least two courts, which stated that the First Amendment guarantees "freedom *of* religion, not freedom *from* religion."[99] Since almost half of our population today are not members of any church,[100] there is a real danger that under the narrow interpretation a substantial part of the American people may be adjudged beyond the pale of constitutional protection in respect to religious matters.

Acceptance of the narrow interpretation would permit direct use of Federal funds and property for religious purposes, as long as a practicable method could be evolved for the nonpreferential distribution of these benefits among the various sectarian groups. Though state constitutions generally prohibit the use of public funds for sectarian purposes, any state could, without violating the Federal Constitution, eliminate or amend the state constitutional prohibition, and open the treasury to churches seeking to use public funds to spread their sectarian beliefs.

In 1930 the United States Supreme Court ruled that a state could constitutionally provide parochial schools with secular textbooks, since the children and not the parochial schools were the direct beneficiaries of the state's bounty.[101] Similarly, in the Everson case, the majority of the Court allowed New Jersey to expend public funds to transport children to parochial schools in part because secular subjects were also taught there. Under the narrow interpretation the limitations implicit in these decisions would be abandoned; public funds could be used to benefit sectarian schools directly, to pay for their books, sectarian as well as secular, to transport children to schools in which only religious subjects were taught, and to pay the salaries of the teachers in such schools.

Far more important, the doctrine threatens the secular nature of the American public school by depriving it of Federal constitutional protection against compulsory religious instruction. Consequences as grave as these should not be accepted without careful consideration of the premises on which they are based.

### Neutrality a Recent Invention

As we have seen, the claim that identification of the First Amendment with the concept of the separation of church and state is the recent invention of the Everson-McCollum court is contradicted by historical fact. Nor is there more merit to the claim that government neutrality as between religion and irreligion is a recent invention.

The idea of neutrality is implicit in Jefferson's remark that "it does me no injury for my neighbor to say there are twenty Gods or no God."[102] The idea of neutrality is also the basis of the prohibition in Article VI of the Constitution against all religious tests, a prohibition which it was clearly realized would make it possible for an atheist to become President or Congressman. Philip Schaff, a devout Protestant clergyman, remarked in his *Church and State in the United States*,[103] that in America "the state must be equally just to all forms of belief and unbelief which do not endanger the public safety."

Francis Lieber, an authority cited by the Supreme Court in Reynolds vs. United States,[104] in his work *Civil Liberty and Self-Government*, published in 1859, stated:

> It belongs to American liberty to separate entirely that institution which has for its object the support and diffusion of religion from the political government. We have seen already what our constitution says on this point. . . . No worship shall be interfered with, either directly by persecution, or indirectly by disqualifying members of certain sects, or by favoring one sect above others; and no church shall be declared the church of the state, or the established church; *nor shall the people be taxed*

*by the government to support the clergy of all churches,* as is the case in France.[105]

James Bryce in 1889 said:

> It is accepted as an axiom by all Americans that civil power ought to be not only neutral and impartial as between different forms of faith, but ought to leave these matters entirely on one side, regarding them no more than it regards the artistic or literary pursuits of the citizens. There seem to be no two opinions on this subject in the United States.[106]

Four years before the Everson decision, Charles A. Beard wrote in language anticipatory of the Everson-McCollum paragraph interpreting the First Amendment:

> Congress can make no law respecting an establishment of religion. This means that Congress cannot adopt any form of religion as the national religion. It cannot set up one church as the national church, establish its creed, lay taxes generally to support it, compel people to attend it, and punish them for nonattendance. Nor can Congress any more vote money for the support of all churches than it can establish one of them as a national church. That would be a form of establishment....
> The Constitution is a purely secular document....
> The Constitution does not confer upon the Federal Government any power whatever to deal with religion in any form or manner....
> The First Amendment merely confirms the intentions of the framers.[107]

## The Semantic Argument

In support of the narrow interpretation it is argued that the term "establishment of religion" as used in the First Amendment had and has a well-defined meaning:

> A single Church or religion, enjoying formal, legal, official monopolistic privilege through a union with the Government of the State.[108]

The definition of "establishment" as appearing in the *Encyclopædia Britannica* is cited, as follows:

> Establishment, a word applied to certain religious bodies in their relation to the State. Perhaps the best definition which can be given and which will cover all cases, is that establishment implies the existence of some definite and distinctive relation between the State and a religious society (or conceivably more than one) other than that which is shared in by other societies of the same general character. It denotes any special connection with the State, or privileges and responsibilities before the law, possessed by one religious society to the exclusion of others; in a word, establishment is of the nature of a monopoly.

It is argued that if the framers of the First Amendment had wished to bar nonpreferential aid to religion they would have done so in express language and would not have used the well-defined term "establishment."

The argument is subject to a number of basic difficulties. In the first place, it would appear to prove too much. It would permit an outright grant of public funds, property, or other aid to a single sectarian group as long as the assistance given falls short of the grant of formal dominant status contemplated by the quoted definitions. Yet, as we have seen, those urging the narrow interpretation agree that such a grant is forbidden by the First Amendment. In the second place, it ignores the word "respecting." The Amendment does not say "Congress shall make no law establishing religion," but "no law respecting an establishment of religion." It may reasonably be argued that the latter phraseology imposes a broader prohibition than the former.[109]

Third: The term "establishment" or "establish" was used much more frequently and loosely in 1791 than it is today. The short preamble to the Constitution itself uses the word "establish" twice ("establish justice" and "establish this Constitution"). It was used by Jefferson in the title of his Statute for Establishing Religious Freedom. It was used in describing a measure as closely approximating nonpreferential aid to religion as could practicably be conceived—the Virginia Bill Establishing a Provision for Teachers of the Christian Religion. (There were, as we have seen, no teachers of non-Christian religion in Virginia in 1784, and taxpayers not desiring that their money go to any Christian sect could direct that it be used for general educational purposes.) Justice Story spoke of "establishing funds for the support of ministers."[110] Madison used the term "establishment" to denote chaplaincy in Congress and chaplaincy in the armed forces, stating:

> The *establishment* of the chaplainship [in Congress] is a palpable violation of equal rights, as well as of Constitutional principles . . . Were the *establishment* to be tried by its fruits, are not the daily devotions conducted by these legal Ecclesiastics, already degenerating into a scanty attendance, and a tiresome formality? Better also to disarm in the same way, the precedent of Chaplainships for the army and navy, than erect them into a political authority in matters of religion. The object of this *establishment* is seducing; the motive to it is laudable.[111]

In 1817 Jefferson drafted a "Bill for the Establishment of District Colleges and University,"[112] and the Regulations of the University of Virginia of 1824 provided that the students "will be free and expected to attend religious worship at the establishment of their respective sects."[113]

Moreover, during the debates preceding the adoption of the First Amendment and after its adoption, the term "establishment of religion" was used synonymously with "religious establishment." Roger Sherman argued that the First Amendment was unnecessary because "Congress had no authority whatever delegated to them by the Constitution to make religious establishments."[114] Later, in vetoing two separate measures, Madison twice referred to the First Amendment as prohibiting any law respecting "a religious establishment."

In vetoing a bill to incorporate the Episcopal Church in the District of Columbia, Madison said:

> . . . the bill exceeds the rightful authority to which governments are limited by the essential distinction between civil and religious functions, and violates in particular the article of the Constitution of the United States which declares that "Congress shall make no law respecting *a religious establishment* . . ." This particular church, therefore, would so far be a *religious establishment* by law, a legal force and sanction being given to certain articles in its constitution and administration.

A week later he vetoed a bill giving certain land to a Baptist church,

> because the bill in reserving a certain parcel of land of the United States for the use of said Baptist Church comprises a principle and a precedent for the appropriation of funds of the United States for the use and support of religious *societies,* contrary to the article of the Constitution which declares that "Congress shall make no law *respecting a religious establishment.*"[115]

A constitutional prohibition against laws "respecting religious establishments" is obviously not far removed from a prohibition of laws supporting or aiding religious establishments. More important, Presidents Jefferson, Madison, and Jackson interpreted the First Amendment ban on laws "respecting an establishment of religion" as prohibiting such nonpreferential and nonmonetary aid as Presidential proclamations of thanksgiving to God.[116]

But perhaps the most important evidence indicating that the term "establish" was given a far wider meaning in the last quarter of the 18th century than contended for by those asserting a narrow interpretation of the First Amendment is to be found in the American reaction to the Quebec Act of 1774. The purpose of this Act was to accord some privileges to the Catholic Church, principally the right to sue for the collection of tithes. This obviously did not accord a monopolistic status to the Catholic Church; it did not even put it at parity with Protestantism, which still retained principal government favor. Yet the Act was widely attacked in the Colonies on the ground that its effect was to "establish the Popish religion." Samuel Adams, for example, in an address to the Mohawk Indians, charged the English with having "made a law to establish the religion of the Pope in Canada which lies so near to you." In 1774 the Continental Congress in listing its grievances against Parliament, included the act "for establishing the Roman Catholic religion in the province of Quebec." Later, in an Address to the People of Great Britain, it asserted that "the Legislature of Great Britain is not authorized by the constitution to establish a religion fraught with sanguinary and impious tenets."[117]

Fourth: It is true that Congress did not expressly bar nonpreferential aid to religion, but it is also true that it did not expressly limit the bar to preferential establishment. It had two occasions to do so, and refused both times. When the First Amendment as adopted by the House was debated in the Senate, the following proceedings took place:

> The resolve of the House of Representatives . . . was read, as followeth: "Art. III. Congress shall make no law establishing religion, or prohibiting the free exercise thereof; nor shall the rights of conscience be infringed."
>
> The Senate resumed the consideration of the resolve of the House of Representatives on the amendments to the Constitution of the United States.
>
> On motion to amend Article the third, and to strike out these words: "Religion, or prohibiting the free exercise thereof," and insert "No religious sect or society in preference to others":
>
> It passed in the negative.
>
> On motion for reconsideration:
>
> It passed in the affirmative.
>
> On motion that Article the third be stricken out:
>
> It passed in the negative.
>
> On motion to adopt the following, in lieu of the third Article: "Congress shall not make any law infringing the rights of conscience, or establishing any religious sect or society":
>
> It passed in the negative.
>
> On motion to amend the third Article, to read thus: "Congress shall make no law establishing any particular denomination or religion in preference to another, or prohibiting the free exercise thereof, nor shall the rights of conscience be infringed":
>
> It passed in the negative.
>
> On the question upon the third Article as it came from the House of Representatives:
>
> It passed in the negative.

On motion to adopt the third Article proposed in the resolve of the House of Representatives, amended by striking out these words, "Nor shall the rights of conscience be infringed":
It passed in the affirmative.[118]

It can be seen that the purpose of the proposed changes was to have the First Amendment read:

Congress shall make no law establishing one Religious Sect or society in preference to others, or prohibiting the free exercise thereof, nor shall the rights of conscience be infringed; [and:] Congress shall make no law establishing any particular denomination or religion in preference to another, or prohibiting the free exercise thereof, nor shall the rights of conscience be infringed.

The rejection of these versions, each of which expressly and unambiguously spells out the narrow interpretation of the First Amendment, would seem to indicate that Congress did not intend such narrow interpretation.

## The Practices in the States

It is argued that the First Amendment must be read in the light of the prevailing practices among the states when the First Amendment was proposed and adopted; and that these practices were to use tax-raised funds for religious purposes. Justice Story particularly is cited as authority for the argument. He stated that

Every American colony, from its foundation down to the revolution, with the exception of Rhode Island, if, indeed, that State be an exception, did openly, by the whole course of its laws and institutions, support and sustain in some form the Christian religion, and almost invariably gave a peculiar sanction to some of its fundamental doctrines. And this has continued to be the case in some of the States down to the present period without the slightest suspicion that it was against the principles of public law or republican liberty. . . . Probably at the time of the adoption of the Constitution, and of the amendment to it now under consideration, the general if not the universal sentiment in America was, that Christianity ought to receive encouragement from the state so far as was not incompatible with the private rights of conscience and the freedom of religious worship. An attempt to level all religions, and to make it a matter of state policy to hold all in utter indifference, would have created universal disapprobation, if not universal indignation. . . .
The real object of the amendment was not to countenance, much less to advance, Mahometanism, or Judaism, or infidelity, by prostrating Christianity; but to exclude all rivalry among Christian sects, and to prevent any national ecclesiastical establishment which should give to an hierarchy the exclusive patronage of the national government. It thus cuts off the means of religious persecution (the vice and pest of

former ages), of the subversion of the rights of conscience in matters of religion, which had been trampled upon almost from the days of the Apostles to the present age.[119]

Story, it may be suggested, is hardly a disinterested authority on the meaning of separation. His decision in Terrett vs. Tayler[120] sought to undo disestablishment in Virginia by ruling unconstitutional the statutes repealing the act of incorporation of the Episcopal Church. In a state which defeated a bill for the support of religious teachers and then enacted Jefferson's religious liberty statute, it is difficult to accept as an accurate interpretation of the Virginia constitution Story's statement that

> Consistent with the constitution of Virginia the legislature could not create or continue a religious establishment which should have exclusive rights and prerogatives, or compel the citizens to worship under a stipulated form or discipline or to pay taxes to those whose creed they could not conscientiously believe. But the free exercise of religion cannot be justly deemed to be restrained by aiding with equal attention the votaries of every sect to perform their own religious duties, or by establishing funds for the support of ministers, for public charities, for the endowment of churches, or for the sepulture of the dead.[121]

If anything in American history is clear it is that Jefferson, Madison, and the other fathers of separation and freedom in Virginia did earnestly believe that the "free exercise of religion" would be restrained "by establishing funds for the support of ministers" or "the endowment of churches."

There is little reason to assume that Story's interpretation of the Federal Constitution was more consistent with the framers' intent than his interpretation of the Virginia constitution. Moreover, the entire argument based on contemporary state practices proves either too little or too much. If the practice in Virginia is reckoned, it proves too little, for that state, as a result of the defeat of the Assessment Bill, did not aid religion even on a nonpreferential basis. If, on the other hand, the practices in Massachusetts or North Carolina are considered, the argument proves too much; for these states maintained just the type of preferred establishment which, according to the narrow interpretation, it was the limited intent of the First Amendment to prevent on a national scale.

In any case, it must be remembered that the First Amendment had no application to the states at the time it was adopted. It established the principle of freedom and separation only for the Federal government. It is reasonable to assume that Congress did not then believe it desirable or practicable to impose these principles on those states which still maintained an establishment.

By 1868, however, when the Fourteenth Amendment was adopted, the situation had changed. As noted by Justice Frankfurter in his concurring opinion in the McCollum case:

> ... long before the Fourteenth Amendment subjected the States to new limitations, the prohibition of furtherance by the State of religious instruction became the guiding principle, in law and feeling, of the American people. ...
>
> In this respect the Fourteenth Amendment merely reflected a principle then dominant in our national life. To the extent that the Constitution thus made it binding upon the States, the basis of the restriction is the whole experience of our people. Zealous watchfulness against fusion of secular and religious activities by Government itself, through any of its instruments but especially through its educational agencies, was the democratic response of the American community to the particular needs of a young and growing nation, unique in the composition of its people.[122]

The Blaine amendment, which received a majority in both houses of Congress in 1876, expressly prohibited the nonpreferential aid to religion which the protagonists of the narrow interpretation contend the First Amendment permits on the part of the Federal government. But the Blaine amendment was specifically limited to the states; it did not impose any restrictions on the Federal government beyond what was imposed by the First Amendment. It is difficult to believe that a more severe restriction would be imposed on the states than governed action by the Federal government, whose powers were derived from the states. The sponsors of the Blaine amendment did not so construe it. Senator Christancy, arguing for the amendment, stated that "it is simply imposing on the States *what the Constitution already imposes on the United States.*" Equally significant was Senator Frelinhuysen's statement that

> the article as amended by the Senate prohibits the States, for the first time, *from the establishment of religion,* from prohibiting its free exercise, and from making any religious test a qualification to office.[123]

It thus appears that not only was it believed that the First Amendment barred nonpreferential aid to religion, but also that such aid constituted an "establishment of religion."

### The Prior Versions

The versions of the First Amendment proposed by the states and considered by Congress before adoption of the Amendment in its present form are offered as evidence that the intent of the states and of Congress was only to prevent Congress from establishing a national religion and according it the preferential dominant status implied in the term "establishment of religion." Thus, the first version submitted by Madison and considered by Congress read:

> The civil rights of none shall be abridged on account of religious belief, *nor shall any national religion be established,* nor shall the full and equal rights of conscience in any manner or on any pretext be infringed.[124]

The second version considered by Congress read:

> *No religion shall be established by law,* nor shall the equal rights of conscience be infringed.[125]

It is argued that these prior versions of the First Amendment should be considered as evidence of what Congress intended; but it would seem that unaccepted versions of a bill or constitutional amendment would be more probative of what the legislature intended *not* to adopt than of what it did adopt. But even if we consider unaccepted prior versions as possessing evidentiary value, the weight of the evidence is small.

In the first place, it helps little to point out that the first version submitted by Madison provided that no "national religion be established," or that the second version provided that "no religion shall be established by law," unless the meanings of these terms are clear — which they are not. It is fairly arguable that "no religion shall be established by law" means what the Everson-McCollum court interpreted "no law respecting an establishment of religion" to mean. The sponsors of the Blaine amendment so interpreted the term "establishment of religion." Adding the word "national" does not remove the ambiguity. Madison himself used the term "establishment of a national religion" in expressing his opposition to chaplaincies in Congress.[126]

In the second place, if the meaning of the First Amendment is to be found in versions which Congress failed to adopt, all such versions should be considered, not just some of them. The first and second versions do not present the whole picture. At the Constitutional Convention itself Charles Pinckney, who was second only to Madison in his contributions to the framing of the Constitution, proposed that "The Legislature of the United States shall pass no law on the subject of religion." The proposal was referred to committee and was apparently dropped — which is not surprising in view of the general agreement that Congress in any event had no jurisdiction over religious matters.[127]

If we consider only prior versions of the First Amendment and not of the Constitution itself, certainly at least evidentiary weight equal to that given the first two versions should be accorded to the third version, which was requested by New Hampshire and proposed in the House of Representatives by Samuel Livermore. This version, strikingly similar to Pinckney's original version, read:

> Congress shall make no laws touching religion, or infringing the rights of conscience.[128]

Canon Stokes's comment on the Livermore proposal is significant:

> This, it will be noticed, is in its first half a more inclusive prohibition than that proposed by Madison, and it had its important influence on the ultimate wording of the First Amendment. Livermore wished not only to prevent a national Church but also the adoption of any federal laws touching religion. Some remarks by Mr. Gerry followed, criticizing Mr. Madison's proposal, principally because he considered the government a federal rather than a national one. Then comes this epoch-making entry: "Mr. Madison withdrew his motion, but observed that the words 'no national religion shall be established by law,' did not imply that the government was a national one, the question was then taken on Livermore's motion, and passed in the affirmative, thirty-one for, and twenty against it." *And so the general form which the religious-freedom guarantee later took in our Federal Bill of Rights was largely due to Samuel Livermore.*[129]

### Congressional Debates

The debates in Congress on the proposed First Amendment are offered as proof that the limited interpretation was intended. Most frequently quoted is the following extract from the *Annals of Congress:*

> Mr. Madison said, he apprehended the meaning of the words to be, that Congress should not *establish a religion,* and enforce the legal observation of it by law, nor compel men to worship God in any manner contrary to their conscience. Whether the words are necessary or not, he did not mean to say, but they had been required by some of the State Conventions, which served to entertain an opinion that under the clause of the Constitution which gave power to Congress to make all laws necessary and proper to carry into execution the Constitution, and the laws under it, enabled them to make laws of such a nature as might infringe the rights of conscience and *establish a national religion;* to prevent these effects he presumed the Amendment was intended, and he thought it was as well expressed as the nature of the language would admit.[130]

This passage is no freer of ambiguity than the prior versions of the Amendment on which the proponents of the narrow interpretation rely. Madison's phrases "establish a religion" and "establish a national religion" cannot be assumed to have the limited meaning assigned by these proponents.

Nor can the Madison extract from the *Annals* be understood without reference to the remark which evoked it. Justice Rutledge relates the incident and comments as follows:

> At one point the wording was proposed: "No religion shall be established by law, nor shall the equal rights of conscience be infringed." 1 *Annals of Congress* 729 . . . Representative Huntington of Connecticut feared this might be construed to prevent judicial enforcement of private pledges. He stated "that he feared . . . that the words might be taken in such latitude as to be extremely hurtful to the cause of religion. He understood the amendment to mean what had been expressed by the gentleman from Virginia; but others might find it convenient to put another construction upon it. The ministers of their congregations to the Eastward were maintained by the contributions of those who belonged to their society; the expense of building meeting houses was contributed in the same manner. These things were regulated by by-laws. If an action was brought before a Federal Court on any of these cases, the person who had neglected to perform his engagements could not be compelled to do it; for a support of ministers or building of places of worship might be construed into a religious establishment." 1 *Annals of Congress* 730.
>
> To avoid any such possibility, Madison suggested inserting the word "national" before "religion," thereby not only again disclaiming intent to bring about the result Huntington feared but also showing unmistakably that "establishment" meant public "support" of religion in the financial sense. 1 *Annals of Congress* 731.[131]

It is undoubtedly true that fear of the attainment by a single church or denomination of the privileged status of an established church in the narrow sense played a prominent role in the debates within and without Congress at the time of the framing and adopting of the First Amendment. This was natural, inasmuch as it presented the fear most common and most real in the minds of Americans, and it can be assumed that proponents of the Amendment would emphasize that danger. It does not follow, however, that the evil most feared and emphasized is the only one sought to be guarded against. To cite a contemporary analogy, one of the arguments most frequently cited by civil libertarians against restricting Communists' freedom of expression is the danger of the restriction spreading to Socialists and liberals. That, however, does not mean that if this danger could be avoided, civil libertarians would favor restricting Communists' freedom of expression. Another contemporary analogy is the argument that discrimination against racial minorities aids the propaganda efforts of Communists. Assertions of that argument can hardly be evidence of the approval of discrimination if there were no Communists. Similarly, the fear of an exclusive national establishment was cited as a leading argument for adoption of the First Amendment; but that is far from proof that it was the only fear that the Amendment sought to allay and the only evil it sought to prevent.

### Friends of Religion

It is argued that Americans are and always have been a religious people, that those who framed and adopted the First Amendment were the friends of religion, not its enemies, and that they therefore could not have intended to harm religion by depriving it of government support.

The basic weakness of this argument is that it confuses friendship for religion with friendship for government aid to religion. Madison himself exposed the fallacy of this reasoning during the debate on the Virginia Assessment Bill. The issue, he said, was "not is religion necessary—but are Religious Establishments necessary for Religion."[132] In a letter to Edward Livingston in 1822, Madison referred to "the old error, that without some sort of allegiance or coalition between government and Religion neither can be duly supported."[132] According to Madison, government support was not only unnecessary for religion but detrimental thereto. In the same letter to Livingston he referred to the "lesson that Religion flourishes in greater purity, without than with the aid of government." He presented the same argument in the Remonstrance against the Assessment Bill, and the same argument was made in the several petitions of the Presbytery of Hanover and of the Baptists.

That the principle of strict separation is based on friendliness to religion rather than on enmity, is evident from its warm espousal by these religious bodies. Even more persuasive is the overwhelming opposition by organizations of all religious faiths to proposals, such as the Becker resolution, for an amendment to the Constitution to overrule the Supreme Court decisions barring state-sponsored prayer and Bible reading in the public schools.[134] It is most evident from the position of strength and influence that religion has achieved in the United States under the protection of the guaranty of religious liberty and the separation of church and state.

By and large, the American people have been faithful to the unique and radical experiment formalized in the "establishment" and religious liberty provision of the First Amendment.[135] So conclusive was Madison's victory in the Virginia legislature and in the adoption of the First Amendment, that in the more than a century and a half since the Amendment was adopted Congress has never enacted—nor indeed been called upon to consider—a bill for the support of teachers of religion. The latest expressions of the national will on this principle are the acts of Congress in admitting to statehood Alaska and Hawaii, both of whose constitutions forbid appropriation of public funds for religious education institutions.[136]

Under this system of mutual independence of church and government, religion has flourished in this country to an extent unparalleled elsewhere. By 1830 DeTocqueville could note that

> there is no country in the whole world in which the Christian religion retains a greater influence over the souls of men than in America.[137]

A half century later, Lord Bryce remarked that while the

> legal position of a Christian church is in the United States simply that of a voluntary association or group of associations corporate or unincorporate, under the ordinary law, [yet] the influence of Christianity seems to be . . . greater and more widespread in the United States than in any part of western Continental Europe, and I think greater than in England.[138]

Schaff, too, noted that

> the American nation is as religious and as Christian as any nation on earth, and in some respects even more so, for the very reason that the profession and support of religion are left entirely free.[139]

But the best evidence of the beneficial effect on religion of America's adherence to the principle of strict separation lies in the simple statistic that whereas in 1790 not more than one out of eight Americans and possibly as few as one out of twenty-five belonged to any church, today more than one out of every two Americans is a church member.[140] Moreover, as Professor Sweet has pointed out,

> It is significant that the churches which had the least proportional gain in membership were the Congregationalist and the Episcopal, the two state churches of the colonial period.[141]

Justice Rutledge was clearly right when he stated that complete separation between religion and the state is best, not only for the state, but for religion as well.[142]

### Virginia's Dissatisfaction

When the First Amendment in the form in which it was finally adopted was presented for ratification it was opposed by eight members of the Virginia Senate on the ground that

> The . . . amendment recommended by Congress does not prohibit

the rights of conscience from being violated or infringed; and although it goes to restrain Congress *from passing laws establishing any national religion, they might, notwithstanding, levy taxes to any amount for the support of religion or its preachers;* and any particular denomination of Christians might be so favored and supported by the general government, as to give it a decided advantage over the others, and in the process of time render it powerful and dangerous as if it was established as the national religion of the country.

Notwithstanding this argument, the Virginia legislature ratified the Amendment. From this it is inferred that the Amendment had only the limited intent seen by the eight Virginia senators and the states in adopting the amendment accepted that limited interpretation.[143]

Unsuccessful arguments against a measure on the ground that it would have certain consequences may give rise to the inference that those who adopted the measure wanted or at least were willing to accept those consequences. But it is at least equally inferrible that those who adopted the measure did not agree that the consequences would follow. As the United States Supreme Court has said: "The fears and doubts of the opposition are no authoritative guide to the construction of legislation."[144] In other words, the Virginia legislature may have ratified the amendment, not despite the fact that they believed it would permit Congress to support a particular creed and suppress religious freedom, but because they believed it would have no such effect.

The latter inference seems more probable. For even under the narrow theory, the authors of the quoted statement were wrong in saying that "any particular denomination of Christians might be so favored and supported by the general government, as to give it a decided advantage over the others. . . ." It was exactly this consequence that the proponents of the narrow theory assert the First Amendment was framed to avoid. The authors were also obviously wrong in arguing that the "amendment recommended by Congress does not prohibit the rights of conscience from being violated or infringed." Is it not more probable that the Virginia legislature deemed them wrong not merely in most part but entirely, than that it was willing to accept from the Federal government consequences which but a few years earlier had been rejected when proposed in the state legislature? That this inference is more probable is evidenced by the fact that the Baptists' Central Committee of Virginia, which fought so vigorously against all governmental aid to religion and for strict separation, was entirely satisfied with the First Amendment and enlisted the cooperation of other Baptist committees to secure its adoption.[145]

## Practical Construction

By far the most frequently cited and undoubtedly the most potent argument in support of the narrow interpretation is the practical construction argument, *i.e.*, that numerous instances of government support of religion at the time of the adoption of the Amendment and since then indicate that it could not have been the intent of the Amendment to prohibit such support. Conversely, it is argued that if these practices are unconstitutional, Presidents, Congressmen, and other government officials have been violating their oaths of office — which is unthinkable. Many examples are cited; and most of these will be considered in detail separately throughout this volume. For the purpose of the present discussion, only the most frequently mentioned instances need be cited. (They are typical, and the comments on them are equally applicable to the others.) They are: chaplaincies in Congress; chaplaincies in the armed forces; presidential Thanksgiving proclamations; tax exemption for religious institutions; compulsory chapel attendance at West Point and Annapolis; and the presence of "In God We Trust" on our coins. The following comments may be made:

(1) The argument that participation in these practices must be construed as a deliberate violation of an oath of office is equally applicable to the many laws passed by Congress and approved by the President which are subsequently declared unconstitutional by the Supreme Court. The logical application of this argument would require the impeachment of Congress and the President whenever a law passed by them is adjudicated by the courts to be violative of the Constitution. The defeat of the attempt to impeach President Andrew Johnson should have put an end to the proposition that an erroneous interpretation of the Constitution necessarily constitutes a violation of an oath of office.

(2) Some of the cited practices would seem to be unconstitutional even under the narrow interpretation of the First Amendment, or even without considering the Amendment. Thus, compulsory chapel attendance at West Point and Annapolis would seem to be violative of the mandate of Article VI of the Constitution that "no religious test shall ever be required as a qualification to any office or public trust under the United States." Similarly, though President Washington's proclamation recommending a day of Thanksgiving was consistent with the restricted interpretation because it embraced all who believed in a supreme ruler of the universe, President Adams's proclamation calling for a Christian worship cannot be reconciled even with the narrow interpretation.[146]

One Supreme Court justice once cited these same practices—and indeed the text of the First Amendment—to support not the nonpreferential theory, but the proposition that this is a Christian nation. In the case of Church of Holy Trinity vs. United States,[147] Justice Brewer completed a long recitation of religious invocations in official documents with the statement that

> These, and many other matters which might be noticed, add a volume of unofficial declarations to the mass of organic utterances that this is a Christian nation.

(3) Many unconstitutional acts stand undisturbed because of the legal incapacity of anyone to challenge them, or because of the serious consequences frequently befalling anyone daring to challenge them. As will be seen later,[148] in some states and in Federal courts a government expenditure of public funds for a direct, sectarian purpose is not subject to judicial attack by a citizen or taxpayer. Similarly, it would require a cadet of rare devotion to principle who would risk his career in a judicial attack on West Point's regulation requiring chapel attendance.

(4) Items such as the reference to God on coins, a practice dating since 1864,[149] are insignificant to the point of being trivial. Government expenditures of tax-raised funds for religious institutions cannot easily be justified on the basis of so meaningless an act of ceremonial obeisance. (It is difficult to understand why true religionists do not resent, rather than approve, this marriage of God and Mammon.)

(5) Some of the cited practices may be constitutional under any view of the First Amendment. Chaplains in the armed forces may be necessary under the constitutional guarantee of freedom of conscience. A soldier drafted into the armed forces and sent to camp far from home is deprived of the opportunity to visit his church. To the extent that such deprivation is necessary to the overriding consideration of national defense, it is constitutional.[150] But the deprivation is constitutional only to the extent that it is necessary; and if the government can practicably furnish a substitute in the form of a traveling church, the soldier may well have a constitutional right thereto. So, too, much of the exemption that religion enjoys under tax laws may likewise be justified under the "free exercise" clause.[151]

(6) The probative weight of any of these items is by no means as great as many would have it. The value of practices under a statutory or constitutional provision as evidence of the framers' intent lies in the uncontroverted acceptance of those practices. The value is

greatly decreased, if not completely vitiated, if the statutory or constitutional validity of these practices is seriously contested by persons having responsibility for the enforcement of the statute or constitution.

Long before the Everson-McCollum decisions, the constitutional validity of most of these practices was seriously controverted by persons whose views are entitled to great weight in interpreting the First Amendment. Thus Presidents Jefferson, Madison, and Jackson all considered presidential Thanksgiving proclamations to be violative of the First Amendment. Madison considered "the appointment of chaplains to the two Houses of Congress" as an "establishment" not "consistent with the Constitution." These practices were a carry-over from the days of the Continental Congress, which, as we have seen, exercised plenary jurisdiction in matters of religion; and ceremonial practices such as these are not easily dislodged after becoming so firmly established. Madison viewed chaplaincies in the armed forces as an "establishment" prohibited by the Constitution. He referred to a proposal "to exempt Houses of Worship from taxes" as an "encroachment" on "the separation between Religion and Government in the Constitution of the United States."[152]

(7) The practices cited by the proponents of the narrow interpretation, when considered alone, present an incomplete and misleading picture. Contrary practices with respect to other matters are of at least equal evidentiary consequence. The Continental Congress had dealt with a myriad of religious matters, including sin, repentance, humiliation, divine service, fasting, reformation, mourning, public worship, funerals, true religion, and many others. With the exception of an isolated few, such as Thanksgiving proclamations and chaplaincies, these matters were never even considered, much less legislated on, by the Congress established by the Constitution. (And even the practices continued by the new Congress were challenged on constitutional grounds.) Much significance too should be attached to the fact that the Constitution contains no invocation to God, nor even mention of God. Indeed, the only mention of religion in the text of the Constitution is the negative one contained in the prohibition of religious tests for office—a prohibition difficult to reconcile with the theory of nonpreference, since the Constitution does not even permit a requirement of belief in God as a condition of Federal office. Most significant of all is that in the 175 years since the First Amendment was adopted Congress has never enacted a general appropriation bill for religion on the nonpreferential basis which

proponents of the narrow interpretation hold constitutionally permissible.

(9) Anyone familiar with the American political scene can readily appreciate that what holders of political office do is not an infallible guide to what they believe. Madison felt it politically unwise to refuse to proclaim a day of thanksgiving, even though he believed such a proclamation inconsistent with the constitutional prohibition of establishment.[163] A contemporary of Jefferson commented on the President's attendance at chaplain's services in Congress: "The political necessity of paying some respect to the religion of the country is felt."[154]

(10) Finally, the area of religion and government is not the only one in which practice lags behind principle. The validity of the constitutional principle of freedom of expression is not vitiated by the widespread limitations on that freedom in actual practice. The Congress that framed the First Amendment's ban on laws abridging freedom of speech or press was pretty much the same Congress that enacted the Alien and Sedition Laws. Similarly, the validity of the principle of equality in the Fourteenth Amendment is not destroyed by the widespread unequal treatment accorded to Negroes. Indeed, the gap between principle and practice is far narrower in the area of government-religion relations than in the area of civil liberties and race relations. If the practical construction argument is to be applied universally, not only the "establishment" clause but all of the First Amendment and the Fourteenth as well might fall.

## The Virginia Bill and Madison's Remonstrance

A basic difficulty of the whole nonpreference theory is the historical fact that Madison, who played so leading a role in the drafting and adoption of the First Amendment, had only a few years earlier successfully led the opposition to a general appropriation bill in Virginia for the support of religion. During the course of this struggle he wrote the great Remonstrance setting forth his arguments against establishment.

Madison's role in the drafting and adoption of the First Amendment is not disputed by the proponents of the narrow interpretation. They seek to meet the difficulty in two ways: they argue first, that Madison opposed the Assessment Bill because it would establish the Christian religion, and that he would not have opposed it if it had been truly nonpreferential; and second, that his opposition to a general assessment bill in Virginia is not evidence that he opposed similar action by the Federal legislature. The Remonstrance is therefore not to be considered relevant in ascertaining his intent with respect to the First Amendment.

In support of the first argument, the following passage in the Remonstrance is stressed:

> Who does not see that the same authority which would establish Christianity, in exclusion of all other Religions, may establish with the same ease any particular sect of Christians, in exclusion of all other Sects? That the same authority which can force a citizen to contribute three pence only of his property for the support of any one establishment, may force him to conform to any other establishment in all cases whatsoever.

Madison's Remonstrance, however, presented fifteen arguments against the Assessment Bill. Only this one can be viewed as referring to the exclusive establishment of Christianity; the other arguments are germane whether one or all religions were to be supported by the Assessment. For example, the second argument in the Remonstrance was that "if religion be exempt from the authority of the society at large, still less can it be subject to that of the legislative body." There is no reason to assume that this argument was considered by Madison of less importance than the argument that establishing Christianity permits the establishing of a particular Christian sect. The position taken by Madison, Jefferson, and their supporters during this period was that religion was exempt from and entirely outside of state authority. Their objection to the fact that the Assessment Bill provided for the support of the "Christian Religion" stemmed at least as much from that reason as from opposition to preferential treatment.

Nor can the Assessment Bill realistically be viewed as preferential. Eckenrode in 1910 called it a proposal for "taxing all citizens for the general support of religion."[155] As we have seen, Washington did not regard the bill as supporting Christianity only, but believed that its terms permitted grants to non-Christian religious teachers, if any such should ever come to Virginia.[156] And the bill provided even for those who professed no religion, Christian or non-Christian, by permitting them to direct that their tax be used for general educational purposes.

If the Jefferson-Madison group had favored the general support of religion, and objected to the bill only because it was preferential, they would not have opposed it *in toto*. It would have been a simple matter to propose amending the bill to provide for all religions, particularly since none other than the Christian religion existed in Virginia. Instead they opposed the fundamental theory of the bill, as is clear from the fact that they followed the successful campaign against it by bringing about the enactment of Jefferson's Statute for Establishing Religious Freedom. The preamble of that act asserts, *inter alia,* that "Forcing [a person] to support this or that teacher of his own persuasion, is depriving him of the comfortable liberty of giving his contributions to the particular pastor whose morals he would make his pattern." The act then provides "that no man shall be compelled to frequent or support any religious worship, place or ministry whatsoever."

Jefferson's statute, and the struggle against the Assessment Bill that preceded it, were incidents that showed the growing Amercian tradition of voluntary support of religion that culminated in the adoption of the First Amendment. The tradition can be traced back to Milton and Locke in England. Roger Williams, Benjamin Franklin, and George Mason were some of the better-known molders of public opinion in America who expressed the same tradition. It was because the Assessment Bill violated the principle of voluntariness rather than because Christianity was selected as the exclusive beneficiary of the state's bounty that Jefferson and Madison opposed it so strenuously.

The difficulty is also sought to be met by the assertion that even if Madison opposed nonpreferential support by the Virginia legislature, he did not oppose such support by the Federal legislature; the considerations he set forth in the Remonstrance are therefore not relevant to a determination of his intent in respect to the First Amendment. In the words of Professor O'Neill:

> Even if Madison had advocated legislation in the State of Virginia which totally prohibited any contact between government and religion, any support of religion by public money (which he never did), it would not follow that he believed in similar provisions in the Constitution and laws of the United States.[157]

There is, however, no reason to believe that Madison favored a narrower restriction on the powers of the Federal legislature than on the Virginia legislature. The arguments presented in the Remonstrance would hardly have been less relevant if the Assessment Bill had been introduced in Congress. There is no evidence that Madison changed his views between 1784 and 1791; all the evidence is to the contrary. In 1790 Madison explained that his omission of clergymen from the proposed national census was because "the general government is proscribed from interfering in any manner whatever in matters respecting religion; and it may be thought to do this in ascertaining who [are] and who are not ministers of the gospel."[158] As Father Murray says:

> For Madison, as for John Locke, his master, religion could not by law be made a concern of the commonwealth as such, deserving in any degree of public recognition or aid, for the essentially theological reason that religion is of its nature a personal, private interior matter of the individual conscience having no relevance to the public concerns of the state.[159]

Nor is there any reason to believe that the Baptists changed their position between the time they opposed the Virginia Assessment Bill in 1785 and the time they supported the First Amendment in 1791.

### The First Amendment and the Constitution

Another basic difficulty with the narrow interpretation lies in the admitted purpose and express language of the First Amendment. It is conceded by all that before the First Amendment was adopted, it was generally accepted that Congress had no jurisdiction or power to deal with religion on a preferential or nonpreferential basis.[160] The proponents of the First Amendment were not content with inferences, and demanded an express prohibition. Acceptance of the nonpreferential theory means that instead of receiving an assurance of nonpower they received a conferral of power theretofore absent, and that such conferral was not in the form of an express grant, but in the form of a prohibition. Hamilton appears to have been right in his prophetic warning against declaring "that things shall not be done which there is no power to do."

### The Zorach Decision

All the above arguments in support of the narrow interpretation of the First Amendment were presented to the Supreme Court in the briefs and argument in the McCollum case. After noting that "counsel for respondents . . . argue that historically the First Amendment was intended to forbid only government preference of one religion over another, not an impartial governmental assistance of all religions," the Court said summarily: "After giving full consideration to the arguments presented, we are unable to accept this contention."[161]

Nothing additional by way of research was uncovered in the four years between McCollum and Zorach. Nevertheless, the arguments so summarily rejected in the McCollum case appear to have been accepted, at least in part, in the Zorach case. Of the eight justices who agreed to the result in the McCollum case, two, Justices Murphy and Rutledge, had died and had been succeeded by Justices Clark and Minton. Of the remaining six, three—Justices Black, Frankfurter, and Jackson—dissented in the Zorach case. The remaining three, Chief Justice Vinson and Justices Douglas and Burton, clearly retreated from their position in the McCollum case. The retreat cannot be explained in terms of new historical discoveries or new legal arguments. It is difficult to explain it in terms other than the unceasing four-year campaign against the McCollum principles and the justices who propounded them.[162]

The specific holding in the Zorach case will be discussed in the section dealing with the released time program; here we are concerned only with the Court's interpretation of separation and the First Amendment. That interpretation lies not only in what the Court said but also in what it left unsaid. The Court refrained from reiterating the definitive interpretation of the Amendment, set forth in the Everson case and repeated in the McCollum case in the paragraph beginning "Neither a State nor the Federal Government can set up a church," and ending with Jefferson's reference to the "wall of separation between church and state." Omitted also is the statement asserted in both the Everson and McCollum cases that the Amendment required government neutrality as between religion and irreligion, believers and disbelievers. Instead the Court said only that "We sponsor an attitude on the part of government that shows no partiality to any group . . ." and that "the government must be neutral when it comes to competition between sects."[163]

What the Court said in the Zorach case also indicated a retreat from the Everson-McCollum principle. In the McCollum case only Justice Reed in his dissent argued on the strength of the oft-cited practices of government aid to religion (chaplains in Congress and the armed forces, compulsory chapel at West Point and Annapolis, etc.) that

> the prohibitions of enactments respecting the establishment of religion do not bar every friendly gesture between church and state. It is not an absolute prohibition against every conceivable situation where the two may work together. . . .

In the Zorach case the majority of the Court adopted that argument. Speaking for the majority, Justice Douglas stated:

> . . . There cannot be the slightest doubt that the First Amendment reflects the philosophy that Church and State should be separated. And so far as interference with the "free exercise" of religion and an "establishment" of religion are concerned, the separation must be com-

plete and unequivocal. The First Amendment within the scope of its coverage permits no exception; the prohibition is absolute. The First Amendment, however, does not say that in every and all respects there shall be a separation of Church and State. Rather, it studiously defines the manner, the specific ways, in which there shall be no concert or union or dependency one on the other. That is the common sense of the matter. Otherwise the state and religion would be aliens to each other — hostile, suspicious, and even unfriendly. Churches could not be required to pay even property taxes. Municipalities would not be permitted to render police or fire protection to religious groups. Policemen who helped parishioners into their places of worship would violate the Constitution. Prayers in our legislative halls; the appeals to the Almighty in the messages of the Chief Executive; the proclamations making Thanksgiving Day a holiday; "so help me God" in our courtroom oaths — these and all other references to the Almighty that run through our laws, our public rituals, our ceremonies would be flouting the First Amendment. A fastidious atheist or agnostic could even object to the supplication with which the Court opens each session: "God save the United States and this Honorable Court. . . ."

We are a religious people whose institutions presuppose a Supreme Being. . . . We sponsor an attitude on the part of government that shows no partiality to any one group and that lets each flourish according to the zeal of its adherents and the appeal of its dogma. When the state encourages religious instruction or cooperates with religious authorities . . . it follows the best of our traditions. For it then respects the religious nature of our people and accommodates the public service to their spiritual needs.

## The Return to Everson-McCollum

That the Zorach decision represented a retreat from the forward position taken in the Everson and McCollum cases is hardly open to question. There was, however, considerable dispute among lawyers and scholars as to the extent of the retreat. The holding in the Zorach case was quite narrow: that the McCollum decision did not bar releasing children for off-school religious instruction where the public school in no way participated in that instruction or did anything other than adjust its schedule so as to accomodate the religious needs of the children. Moreover, Justice Douglas went out of his way to say, "We follow the McCollum case," and that "Government may not finance religious groups nor undertake religious instruction. . . ," a statement hardly consistent with any interpretation of the First Amendment other than that of Everson-McCollum. But these statements were largely overlooked, and there was undoubtedly a good deal of support for the view expressed by Professor Paul Kauper that "all students of this subject may well agree that Zorach for all practical purposes overruled McCollum."[164]

The dispute continued until 1961, when the court handed down two decisions proving quite clearly that the retreat in the Zorach case, whatever its extent, was a temporary one.

In the first of these decisions, McGowan vs. Maryland,[165] Chief Justice Warren, speaking for six members of the Court in a decision upholding a state Sunday law, went out of his way to do what was not done in the Zorach decision—reiterate verbatim the Everson-McCollum definitive paragraph. And Justice Douglas used the occasion of his dissent in this case to explain his statement in the Zorach case that "we are a religious people whose institutions presuppose a Supreme Being." Its purpose, he said, was only to indicate that the "Puritan influence helped shape our constitutional law and our common law" in that it "put individual conscience and individual judgment in the first place."[166]

In the second of the cases, Torcaso vs. Watkins,[167] the Court's opinion was written by Justice Black, the author of the opinions in the Everson and McCollum cases. In invalidating under the First Amendment a state requirement that holders of public office qualify by taking an oath expressing their belief in the existence of God, Justice Black again reiterated in full the definitive Everson-McCollum paragraph. He pointed out that although in the McCollum case the Court had been urged to repudiate the paragraph as dictum, it "declined to do this, but instead strongly reaffirmed what had been said in *Everson,* calling attention to the fact that both the majority and minority in *Everson* had agreed on the principles declared in this part of the Everson opinion." Referring specifically to the court below but undoubtedly having in mind also many others, he stated:

> The Maryland Court of Appeals thought, and it is argued here, that this Court's later holding and opinion in *Zorach* v. *Clauson,* 343 U.S. 306, . . . had in part repudiated the statement in the *Everson* opinion quoted above and previously reaffirmed in *McCollum.* But the Court's opinion in *Zorach* specifically stated: "We follow the McCollum case."

It should be noted that only three of the Justices who participated in the Everson and McCollum decisions (Black, Frankfurter, and Douglas) were still on the Court when McGowan vs. Maryland and Torcaso vs. Watkins were decided and that the cases were passed upon by six new Justices, all of whom indicated their concurrence in the Everson-McCollum interpretation of the First Amendment. It might therefore have been expected that in view of this latest expression of the Court, two-thirds of whose members were appointed after the Everson and McCollum decisions, the issue would be put to rest and it would be accepted by all that the First Amendment was to be broadly interpreted as barring not only preferential aid but all aid to religion and erecting a wall of separation between church and state.

Alas, this was not to be. In the Schempp-Murray cases,[168] Justice Clark, speaking for the Court, found it necessary again to repeat the broad Everson-McCollum interpretation of the Amendment and say, "we affirm it now." In the hope that he might finally end that controversy, he added:

> While none of the parties to either of these cases has questioned these basic conclusions of the Court, both of which have been long established, recognized and consistently reaffirmed, others continue to question their history, logic and efficacy. Such contentions, in the light of the consistent interpretation in cases of this Court, seem entirely untenable and of value only as academic exercises.

"Academic exercise" or not, it is safe to assume that the contention for a narrow interpretation of the First Amendment will continue to be made.

### Religion as a Means and End

On the whole, the decisions of the Supreme Court, with the exception of Zorach vs. Clauson, have been consistent in interpreting the meaning of the no-establishment clause. Under these decisions, the First Amendment, which merely makes explicit what is implicit in the Constitution itself, requires government in the United States to be secular. Its ends must be exclusively secular and, in achieving them, it may use only secular means. The Preamble to the Constitution sets forth the purposes for which the new republic in the Western Hemisphere was established, all of them secular: "to form a more perfect union, establish justice, insure domestic tranquility, provide for the common defense, promote the general welfare, and secure the blessings of liberty. . . ."

When government effects its secular purposes, its action may, as an incidental by-product, affect religion, either beneficially or detrimentally—indeed, one would assume that this would generally be so—and that fact, the Court has consistently held, does not restrict government in the manner in which it effects its purposes. Thus, as in the Everson case, a state may seek to achieve its secular purpose of protecting children from the hazards of traffic by providing them with free transportation to the schools they attend, and the fact that an incidental by-product benefits religion by relieving parochial schools of what might otherwise be a necessary part of their budget, the Court held, does not render its action unconstitutional. So, too, in pursuing its secular purpose of assuring to every person one day a week for rest, relaxation, and family togetherness, the Court held that the state may require businesses to close down on Sundays, even though the Christian religion, or that part of it which observes Sunday as the Sabbath, is incidentally benefited thereby, while those faiths which observe Saturday as the Sabbath are detrimentally affected.[169]

On the other hand, if the governmental purpose is to aid religion, its action transgresses the limits of its power prescribed by the Constitution and the First Amendment. Unlike the secular purpose in the Everson case, the purposes in the McCollum, Engel, and Schempp-Murray cases were religious—to promote devotional Bible reading and prayer recitation—and the practices therefore were declared unconstitutional.[170]

The principle was thus expressed by the Court in the Schempp-Murray decisions:

> . . . As we have indicated, the Establishment Clause has been directly considered by this Court eight times in the past score of years and, with only one Justice dissenting on the point, it has consistently held that the clause withdrew all legislative power respecting religious belief or the expression thereof. The test may be stated as follows: what are the purpose and the primary effect of the enactment? If either is the advancement or inhibition of religion, then the enactment exceeds the scope of legislative power as circumscribed by the Constitution. That is to say that to withstand the strictures of the Establishment Clause there must be a secular legislative purpose and a primary effect that neither advances nor inhibits religion.

Moreover, in pursuing secular ends, government may use only secular means. One of the arguments stated by Madison in his *Memorial and Remonstrance* in opposition to taxation for religious purposes, was the government's employment of "Religion as an engine of Civil policy . . . [is] an unhallowed perversion of the means of salvation."[171] The great statesman and jurist, Jeremiah S. Black, stated that the fathers of our Constitution "built up a wall of complete and perfect partition" between church and state in order that "one should never be used as an engine for the purpose of the other."[172]

To hold that government may employ religion as a means to effect secular ends which are properly within governmental competence would go far toward making the First Amendment meaningless. Practically every defense of religious instruction in public schools is predicated on the not unreasonable assertion that religious education leads to morality and good citizenship. If religion could be used to achieve the obviously secular goals of morality and good citizenship, it would follow not only that religion could constitutionally be taught in the public schools, but also that tax-raised funds could be used to finance religion and religious education. (As we have seen, the preamble of the Virginia Assessment Bill stated that its purpose was "to correct the morals of men, restrain their vices, and preserve the peace of society.") Moreover, the government could reasonably find that some religions, such as Protestantism, Catholicism, and Judaism, are more likely to inculcate good citizenship than others (Jehovah's Witnesses or the Black Muslims, for example) and, therefore, could aid the former and not the latter, a conclusion rejected even by those who hold that the Amendment goes no further than forbidding government from preferring some religions over others.

This principle, though somewhat qualified, was stated by Justice Brennan in his concurring opinion in the Schempp-Murray case as follows:

> ... the teaching of both Torcaso and the Sunday Law Cases is that government may not employ religious means to serve secular interests, however legitimate they may be, at least without the clearest demonstration that nonreligious means will not suffice.

In summary, therefore, it may be said that under our Constitution, government may seek to achieve only secular ends, and in doing so may employ only secular means. This is the meaning of the principle epitomized in the words "Congress shall make no law respecting an establishment of religion," and this is the standard by which the cases discussed in Part Two of this volume should be tested.

PART TWO

"... NO LAW RESPECTING AN ESTABLISHMENT
OF RELIGION ..."

### CHAPTER SIX

# State Aid to Religion

## COURT ATTACKS ON FINANCIAL GRANTS TO RELIGIOUS BODIES

THE MOST OBVIOUS FORM of government aid to religion is the direct grant of public funds. Such grants are unconstitutional under both state and Federal law. Many state constitutions expressly prohibit the grant of public funds or property to religious bodies. The breadth of some of these prohibitions is typified by Section 30 of Article IV of the California constitution, which reads:

> Neither the Legislature, nor any county, city and county, township, school district, or other municipal corporation, shall ever make an appropriation, or pay from any public fund whatever, or grant anything to or in aid of any religious sect, church, creed or sectarian purpose, or help to support or sustain any school, college, university, hospital or other institution controlled by any religious creed, church, or sectarian denomination whatever; nor shall any grant or donation of personal property or real estate ever be made by the State, or any city, city and county, town or other municipal corporation for any religious creed, church, or sectarian purpose whatever. . . .[1]

Even in the absence of an express prohibition against religious subsidies in a state constitution, constitutional prohibitions of the grant of state funds or property for private purposes would preclude grants for religious purposes.[2] Under the American principle of the separation of church and state, religion must be deemed a "private" matter. A state, said Justice Jackson, has

> great latitude in deciding for itself, in the light of its own conditions, what shall be public purposes in its scheme of things. It may socialize utilities and economic enterprises and make taxpayers' business out of what conventionally had been private business. It may make public business of individual welfare, health, education, entertainment or security. But it cannot make public business of religious worship or instruction, or of attendance at religious institutions of any character. . . . The effect of the religious freedom Amendment to our Constitution was to take every form of propagation of religion out of the realm of things which could directly or indirectly be made public business and thereby be supported in whole or in part at taxpayers' expense.[3]

It is clear today that the First Amendment of the Federal constitution, as applied to the states by the Fourteenth, forbids both Federal and state governments from making grants of public funds or property to religious groups or for religious purposes. "Government," said the Supreme Court in the Zorach case, "may not finance religious groups. . . ."[4]

Ever since Massachusetts disestablished religion in 1833, litigation or other public controversy concerning direct public financial subsidies or donations of public properties to churches has been relatively infrequent. The problems that have arisen have concerned themselves largely with appropriations to sectarian-controlled welfare institutions (hospitals, orphans' homes, etc.), use of public property by religious bodies, and public aid to religious education. (Each of these subjects will be considered separately later in this volume.) The infrequency of direct donations of public funds or property to church bodies is attributable to the strength of the tradition of separation, which, as we have seen, manifested itself most clearly in the victorious struggle in Virginia against taxation for religious purposes.

Even less frequent than direct donations to denominations has been the successful judicial attack on such donations. There are a number of reasons for the lack of success of litigation to prevent grants of public funds to churches; and since the reasons are equally applicable to the more usual instances of government aid to religion (grants to church-controlled welfare institutions and to religious education and church use of state property), they merit some discussion here. These are: (1) the reluctance of citizens to sue to prevent illegal grants to religion; (2) the lack of legal standing to sue on the part of the citizen willing to sue; and (3) the frequent reluctance of courts and judges to invalidate grants to religion.

### Reluctance to Sue

It takes a rare combination of qualities to make up a suitor willing to invoke court action to prevent an unconstitutional expenditure of public funds for sectarian purposes or other government aid to religion. In the first place, litigation is expensive, and the would-be litigant must possess financial resources sufficient to pay court expenses and lawyers' fees, and sufficient devotion to the constitutional principle he seeks to vindicate to expend those sums for that purpose. If—as is sometimes necessary—the decision of a lower court is appealed to the state's highest court or to the United States Supreme Court, the expense runs into thousands of dollars, an expenditure prohibitive to the ordinary citizen.

In recent years, the financial difficulty has in many cases been met by organizational contributions to the financing of litigation.

Protestants and Other Americans United for Separation of Church and State (POAU) has helped finance some litigation involving the incorporation of Catholic parochial school systems into the public school system.[5] The General Conference of Seventh Day Adventists and the American Jewish Congress have financed litigation concerning the rights of Sabbatarians.[6] A number of Jewish organizations financed the Zorach suit. Other suits have been financed by the Catholic Church[7] and the American Civil Liberties Union.[8] Sometimes the expense of litigation is met in whole or in part by contributions from indignant citizens; the Dixon (N.M.) suit[9] was in large part financed in that way.

At least as serious as the financial burden is the communal displeasure frequently incurred by litigants seeking to bar government aid to religion. Of course missionary atheists like Joseph Lewis, who employ litigation at least partly as a propaganda device, are no more deterred by such displeasure than by their singular lack of success in their numerous suits.[10] The occasional litigant, however, is likely to face at the very least charges of atheism, and often neighborhood hostility amounting to social ostracism and occasionally manifesting itself in threats of violence to the litigant and his family. Vashti McCollum, in her book *One Woman's Fight,*[11] has described the experiences of herself and her family after her decision to bring suit to enjoin the released-time program in the Champaign public schools. Esta Gluck, one of the plaintiffs in the Zorach released-time case, suffered similar experiences. The 16-year-old son of Mrs. Madalyn Murray, a plaintiff in the Schempp-Murray cases, was subjected to harrassment and even assault in his home town of Baltimore to such an extent that a police captain remarked: "They haven't left him alone since this thing started. This is a bad city for that boy."[12] Even the present writer, whose relationship to the Zorach and other cases has been exclusively that of counsel, has received many anonymous letters and telephone calls charging him with atheism and threatening him and his family with physical violence. It is therefore not surprising that there are not too many persons with hardy temperament and devotion to principle sufficiently strong to induce them to brave the wrath of their neighbors in order to vindicate a constitutional principle.

## Taxpayers' Standing to Sue

Even if a citizen is found with sufficient financial resources and fortitude to challenge legally an attempted unconstitutional grant of public funds or property to a religious group, the judicial invalida-

185

tion of the attempt is frequently frustrated by the rule prevailing in the Federal and some state courts that an ordinary citizen-taxpayer has no legal standing to sue to enjoin the grant. A plaintiff, in order to sue, must show an injury to himself resulting from the action attacked, and that injury must be different from the injury suffered alike by all taxpayers when public funds are illegally expended. A person seeking to invoke judicial power to invalidate a legislative act must, in the words of the United States Supreme Court,

> be able to show not only that the statute is invalid but that he has sustained or is immediately in danger of sustaining some direct injury as a result of its enforcement, and not merely that he suffers in some indefinite way in common with people generally.[13]

By reason of this rule, a taxpayer's suit to enjoin payment of the salaries of Congressional and army chaplains on the ground that employment of chaplains violated the First Amendment's ban on laws respecting an establishment of religion was dismissed.[14] For the same reason, a suit in New York attacking a state grant of $128,000 to Canisius College in Buffalo, a Jesuit institution, was dismissed, even though the grant was a patent violation of both state and Federal constitutional prohibitions;[15] and the same disposition was made of a suit to restrain the use of a state hall for a Jesuit missionary's lecture under the auspices of a Catholic college.[16] When in 1951 President Truman announced his intention of appointing an ambassador to the Vatican,[17] there was much talk of seeking a judicial determination of the constitutional validity of the appointment; but constitutional scholars were unanimous in pointing out that under present law as expressed in decisions of the United States Supreme Court an ordinary citizen would have no standing to bring suit to prevent the appointment.[18]

The reasons for the rule disallowing taxpayers' suits have been expressed by the Supreme Court in Massachusetts vs. Mellon[19] in the following words:

> [The interest] of a taxpayer of the United States in the moneys of the Treasury — partly realized from taxation and partly from other sources — is shared with millions of others; is comparatively minute and indeterminable; and the effect upon future taxation, of any payment out of the funds, so remote, fluctuating and uncertain, that no basis is afforded for an appeal to the preventive powers of a court of equity.
>
> The administration of any statute, likely to produce additional taxation to be imposed upon a vast number of taxpayers, the extent of whose several liability is indefinite and constantly changing, is essentially a matter of public and not of individual concern. If one taxpayer may champion and litigate such a cause, then every other taxpayer may

do the same, not only in respect of the statute here under review but also in respect of every other appropriation act and statute whose administration requires the outlay of public money, and whose validity may be questioned. The bare suggestion of such a result, with its attendant inconveniences, goes far to sustain the conclusion which we have reached, that a suit of this character cannot be maintained. It is of much significance that no precedent sustaining the right to maintain suits like this has been called to our attention, although, since the formation of the government, as an examination of the acts of Congress will disclose, a large number of statutes appropriating or involving the expenditure of moneys for non-federal purposes have been enacted and carried into effect.

It can be seen from this quotation that judicial disapproval of taxpayers' suits is predicated on two grounds: first, that the injury suffered by the taxpayer litigant is so small as to be negligible; and second, that acceptance of such suits would open the door to wholesale suits by officious intermeddlers to the great inconvenience of the orderly administration of the laws.

The first ground is an expression of the ancient legal maxim, *de minimis non curat lex* — the law does not concern itself with trifles. This maxim has been often used, expressly or implicitly, in sustaining the sectarian use of public property. In the McCollum case the Supreme Court of Illinois ruled that the incidental expense incurred by the state through the use of its public school facilities in the course of released-time religious instruction was so small as to fall within the *de minimis* rule.[20] In a brief presented to the United States Supreme Court on the appeal from the Illinois court's decision in the McCollum case, the present writer argued that in cases involving religious liberty and establishment the *de minimis* doctrine is inapplicable.[21] This argument was criticized by Professor Arthur E. Sutherland, Jr., in the following language:

> . . . to say . . . that there is no place at all for *de minimis* may turn out to be embarrassingly extreme, for the number of small instances of government support, or at least favorable recognition, of religious activity is so great and they are so pervasive that they go unnoticed until attention is drawn to them.
>
> Among mankind there are always enthusiasts for all causes, and it is well that this is so; but one conquest only adds zeal for the next, and the Supreme Court may yet be glad to have available a doctrine that some matters are really so trifling that they do not set in action the somewhat ponderous machinery of the Federal Government. A few months after the McCollum decision was handed down, a member of the board of education in an upstate New York village had occasion to visit his school. Christmas was coming, and small children had pasted up in their classrooms various pictures — laden camels, and wise men,

and a star with spreading rays, and cut-outs of a canonized Lycian bishop of the early Christian church, named Nicholas, white bearded and dressed for sleighing in red garments. As the trustee had learned of the McCollum case he fell to thinking about these clearly sectarian manifestations to which the children of the district, under threat of the truancy laws, were unavoidably subjected. He wondered curiously whether a federal court, if asked, would send a marshal, heavy with the power and majesty of these United States, to scrape the children's pasted pictures from the schoolroom walls.[22]

Yet what is "trifling" or *de minimis* to a dominant sect may be of vital importance to a minority sect. To the Christian, Jewish concern over Christological Christmas and Easter observances in the public school may appear "trifling," as it does to Professor Sutherland; but, as we shall see later,[23] to many Jews it is not "trifling." Protestant judges have decided that the differences between the King James and the Douay versions of the Bible are so small as to be negligible or "trifling"; yet Catholic children have been expelled, flogged, and otherwise persecuted, and indeed lives have been lost, because to Catholics the differences are not *de minimis*.[24] Children of Jehovah's Witnesses have suffered persecution for refusing to engage in the "trifling" ceremonial act of saluting the American flag;[25] and, as we have seen, dissenting Christians were jailed for refusing to contribute "trifling" sums to the established state churches.[26] To an atheist all Christianity—and indeed all religion—would be categorized *de minimis*.

The rule of *de minimis* is a rule of convenience. The monetary loss suffered by a taxpayer as the result of a slight waste of public funds may be too insignificant to warrant invoking the judicial process to obtain redress. The expense to government incurred in judicially determining whether a particular government expenditure of a small sum of money is legal, may so far exceed the attacked expenditure that it is more economical to allow the unlawful expenditure to go unchallenged. But different considerations underlie an expenditure attacked under the separation or religious liberty guaranty. The right sought to be vindicated is a religious right, not an economic one, and it is therefore inappropriate to measure it in economic terms. When the Federal or state government makes any appropriation, no matter how slight, for religious purposes, religion has come "within the cognizance of Civil Government."[27] It is for that reason that Madison warned

That the same authority which can force a citizen to contribute three pence only of his property for the support of any one establishment, may force him to conform to any other establishment in all cases whatsoever.[28]

It is true that it would be impracticable to send a Federal marshal into every schoolroom to enforce observance of the constitutional mandate of the separation of church and state. But it is equally impracticable to send a marshal into every southern public school or college to make sure that Negro students are not segregated in violation of the Constitution.[29] It would be a surrender to anarchy and lawlessness if constitutionality were determined by the pervasiveness of disobedience and the difficulty of compelling obedience.[30] Our system of the judicial determination of constitutional issues rests on the assumption that public officials, sworn to uphold the Constitution, will voluntarily abide by such judicial determinations. This is particularly true where the mandate of restraint is imposed by the Court on religious bodies which preach and teach the moral and religious requirements of good citizenship and obedience to law.

The fear expressed by Professor Sutherland, and earlier expressed by Justice Jackson in his concurrence in the McCollum case, that Mrs. McCollum's victory would unloose on the Supreme Court a torrent of litigation by zealous enthusiasts has proved to be groundless. Four years elapsed after the McCollum case before the Court was again called to pass on the question of religion in public education in the Zorach and Doremus cases, and another decade before it was again called on to do so in Engel vs. Vitale. This paucity of litigation is hardly surprising in view of the deterring effects of the financial burden and communal displeasure consequent on an appeal to the Supreme Court in such cases.

Even though the allowance of taxpayers' suits should entail "inconvenience" to the administration of appropriation laws, as the Court feared in Massachusetts vs. Mellon, that inconvenience must be weighed against the consideration that unless taxpayers' suits are allowed flagrant violations of the Constitution will remain unremedied. Theoretically, the state attorney general could sue to enjoin an illegal grant, such as was involved in the Canisius College case; but—as is usually true—the attorney general there defended rather than attacked the grant. The result was that the unconstitutional grant was not disturbed.

That the fear of a multitude of baseless suits if taxpayers' actions are allowed is exaggerated is shown by the fact that most states do not follow the restrictive policy of the Federal and New York courts, and do allow suits by taxpayers to enjoin illegal expenditures of state funds;[31] and the courts in these states have not found the resulting inconvenience burdensome. Indeed, on occasion even the Federal courts have accepted taxpayers' suits.[32] Moreover, until the Doremus decision[33] in 1952, it was the rule that the United States Supreme Court would review an appeal from a decision in a taxpayer's suit brought in a state allowing such suits, even though such a suit could not be brought originally in the Federal courts. It was on this basis that the Supreme Court reviewed a suit by a Louisiana taxpayer to prevent the state from furnishing free textbooks for the use of children attending parochial schools.[34] On the same basis, the Court in the Everson case reviewed a decision of the New Jersey courts in a taxpayer's suit to prevent the payment of public funds for the expense of transporting children to parochial schools.[35]

The Doremus decision, however, appears to be a retreat from that position—or at least a qualification of what was assumed to be the Supreme Court policy. In the Doremus case a suit to prevent Bible reading in the New Jersey public schools was brought by two plaintiffs, one a parent of a public school child and the other a taxpayer. By the time the suit was argued in the Supreme Court the child had graduated; and the Court held that the issue as to her parent was academic and therefore not subject to judicial determination. With respect to the taxpayer's claim, the Court held that it would review such a suit only where, as in the Everson case, there was "a measurable appropriation or disbursement of [public] funds occasioned solely by the activities complained of." In the case before it, said the Court, "the grievance which it is sought to litigate . . . is not a direct dollars-and-cents injury but . . . a religious difference," although, the Court continued, "if appellants established the requisite special injury necessary to a taxpayer's case or controversy, it would not matter that his dominant inducement to action was more religious than mercenary." The present rule, therefore, appears to be that the Supreme Court will review a taxpayer's attack upon state financial aid to religion if a measurable appropriation of public funds is proved, but not a similar suit against Federal aid. It is for that reason that vigorous, though ultimately unsuccessful, efforts were made to include in the 1963 College Aid Bill and 1965 Elementary and Secondary Education Act[36] provisions to allow judicial review so as to make possible a taxpayer's suit challenging the inclusion of church-related institutions in these programs.[37]

Where, however, the basis of the constitutional challenge is not that the state has expended public funds for a religious purpose, but that it has sponsored or engaged in a religious exercise or practice,

190

the principle of *de minimis* is inapplicable. An action by the parent of a child in the public school in which religious exercises are conducted will not be defeated because these exercises are minimal in time. If there ever was an occasion for the Court to avail itself of the protection afforded by the *de minimis* rule, as suggested by Professor Sutherland, it was in Engel vs. Vitale. Nothing could be more *de minimus* than the inoffensive 22-word prayer that took less than ten seconds to recite. Yet the Court quite firmly refused the protection. Its opinion stated:

> It is true that New York's establishment of its Regents' prayer as an officially approved religious doctrine of that State does not amount to a total establishment of one particular religious sect to the exclusion of all others — that, indeed, the government endorsement of that prayer seems relatively insignificant when compared to the governmental encroachments upon religion which were commonplace 200 years ago. To those who may subscribe to the view that because the Regents' official prayer is so brief and general there can be no danger to religious freedom in its government establishment, however, it may be appropriate to say in the words of James Madison, the author of the First Amendment:
>
> [I]t is proper to take alarm at the first experiment on our liberties. . . . Who does not see that the same authority which can establish Christianity, in exclusion of all other religions, may establish with the same ease any particular sect of Christians, in exclusion of all other sects? That the same authority which can force a citizen to contribute three pence only of his property for the support of any one establishment, may force him to conform to any other establishment in all cases whatsoever?"[38]

### Judicial Reluctance to Decide against State Aid to Religion

This rather technical discussion of taxpayers' suits has been included to show that acts of state aid to religion are frequently attributable not to their constitutionality but to the difficulty of attacking them judicially. Besides the legal difficulty of standing to sue, the social difficulty of incurring communal displeasure by suing, and the economic burden of financing such a suit, another factor must be recognized. This factor is not usually discussed; it is almost indelicate to suggest that it exists. Yet it would be totally unrealistic to disregard judicial reluctance to decide against religious groups. Few students of church-state litigation can fail to be aware of the potent effect of such reluctance on the law of church-state relationships. This does not mean that the court never decides against religious bodies; it means only that the courts will frequently use all available means to avoid a decision that might be construed as hostile to religion.

This is particularly true where the litigant is an avowed atheist. It is difficult to explain on other grounds the consistent lack of success on the part of Joseph Lewis in New York.[39]

Several reasons may be offered for the courts' reluctance to invalidate state aid to religion. More or less, these reasons are the same as those that motivated the legislature in the first instance in making the grant. In the first place—and probably most important—judges, like legislators, are generally religious people, and frequently may feel that religion is benefited by state aid, particularly where the opponent to state aid is an avowed atheist who obviously is hostile to religion. Even where the plaintiff is not an atheist, the attorneys defending state aid are likely to cast their argument in terms of a struggle between the forces of religion and atheism.

The Zorach case is a good illustration of this point. There neither of the plaintiffs suing to invalidate the New York City released-time program was an atheist; each was the parent of children regularly attending religious schools on Sundays and after public school hours. Yet the briefs of the attorneys for the New York City Board of Education and of the attorneys for the Greater New York Coordinating Committee on Released Time sought to convey the impression that the plaintiffs' opposition to released time was motivated by opposition to religion or to religious education. The brief of Charles H. Tuttle and Porter R. Chandler, attorneys for the Coordinating Committee—the former a prominent Protestant lay church leader and the latter attorney for the Roman Catholic archdiocese of New York—asserted that the plaintiff's attack on the released-time system was merely one phase of the battle launched by Joseph Lewis, and sought to identify the plaintiffs with that avowed atheist. The brief of the Board of Education stated that "unmistakably the cause pleaded by petitioners is a cause of irreligion. Secularism to the exclusion of religion under any and all conditions is their theme. They would do away with the American tradition that 'this is a religious people.'" That these arguments were not without effect is shown by the statement in the opinion of Justice Di Giovanna in the first court that decided the case, that the granting of the plaintiffs' petition "would be a step in the direction of and be consonant with totalitarianism and communistic philosophies existing in jurisdictions wherein atheism and the suppression of all religions are preferred to the freedom of the individual to seek religious instruction and worship."[40] Similar overtones are found in the opinions of Judges Froessel and Desmond in the Court of Appeals,[41] and even in the opinion of Justice Douglas in the United States Supreme Court.[42]

The same assertion was made by the attorney for the Baltimore school authorities in his argument before the Supreme Court in the Schempp-Murray cases until Chief Justice Warren called his attention to the fact that the Synagogue Council of America had filed a brief *amicus curiae* against public school Bible reading and prayer recitation, and asked whether he considered that organization to be antireligious.

So pervasive has this identification of opposition to state aid to religion with opposition to religion become that the Supreme Court found it necessary to contradict it in each of the three major decisions against state aid. In the McCollum case the Court said:[43]

> To hold that a state cannot consistently with the First and Fourteenth Amendments utilize its public school system to aid any or all religious faiths or sects in the dissemination of their doctrines and ideals does not, as counsel urge, manifest a governmental hostility to religion or religious teachings. A manifestation of such hostility would be at war with our national tradition as embodied in the First Amendment's guaranty of the free exercise of religion. For the First Amendment rests upon the premise that both religion and government can best work to achieve their lofty aims if each is left free from the other within its respective sphere.

In Engel vs. Vitale, the Court said:[44]

> The history of man is inseparable from the history of religion. And perhaps it is not too much to say that since the beginning of that history many people have devoutly believed that "More things are wrought by prayer than this world dreams of." It was doubtless largely due to men who believed this that there grew up a sentiment that caused men to leave the crosscurrents of officially established state religions and religious persecution in Europe and come to this country filled with the hope that they could find a place in which they could pray when they pleased to the God of their faith in the language they chose. And there were men of this same faith in the power of prayer who led the fight for adoption of our Constitution and also for our Bill of Rights with the very guarantees of religious freedom that forbid the sort of governmental activity which New York has attempted here. These men knew that the First Amendment, which tried to put an end to governmental control of religion and of prayer, was not written to destroy either. They knew rather that it was written to quiet well-justified fears which nearly all of them felt arising out of an awareness that governments of the past had shackled men's tongues to make them speak only the religious thoughts that government wanted them to speak and to pray only to the God that government wanted them to pray to. It is neither sacrilegious nor antireligious to say that each separate government in this country should stay out of the business of writing or sanctioning official prayers and leave that purely religious function to the people themselves and to those the people choose to look to for religious guidance.

In the Schempp-Murray decision the Court said:[45]

> It is insisted that unless these religious exercises are permitted a "religion of secularism" is established in the schools. We agree of course that the State may not establish a "religion of secularism" in the sense of affirmatively opposing or showing hostility to religion, thus "preferring those who believe in no religion over those who do believe." Zorach vs. Clauson, supra, at 314. We do not agree, however, that this decision in any sense has that effect.

The overwhelming opposition to proposed amendments to the Constitution to overrule the Engel vs. Vitale and Schempp-Murray decisions on the part of spokesmen for all major faiths[46] undoubtedly did much to mitigate the strong feeling that only antireligionists oppose government aid to religion. Yet it remains true today that lower courts, at least, are generally reluctant to decide against such aid.

Judicial reluctance to decide against state aid to religion manifests itself in a number of ways. The most direct, of course, is to decide on the merits in favor of the grant. This does not mean that the judge consciously decides a case in a manner inconsistent with correct law and precedent: it does mean that in doubtful or borderline cases these motivations may exert a significant if unrecognized influence on the ultimate decision.

Decision on the merits sustaining state aid to religion is frequently achieved by what has been called the "adroit manipulation of fiction."[47] Legal fictions serve a useful and possibly necessary purpose in jurisprudence; they enable courts to reach decisions inconsistent with statutory law or previous decisions, without appearing to disobey the statute or disregard the precedents. The law of church-state relations abounds with legal fictions, as will be seen from time to time in this volume. Only a few instances need be cited here.

State constitutional prohibitions against sectarian teachings in the public schools were often held not to be violated by readings from the King James version of the Bible on the ground that it is not a sectarian book[48] — this though the mere possession of the book by a Catholic may constitute a "mortal sin." A prayer recited in public school ending with the words, "These things we ask for Christ's sake," has likewise been held to be nonsectarian.[49] Equally fictional was the public school teacher's statement, accepted by a Kansas court, that she read the Lord's Prayer and the Twenty-Third Psalm to her pupils not as a religious exercise, but only to quiet them in preparation for regular studies,[50] an assertion also made by the attorney for the Baltimore school authorities in the Schempp-Murray cases. (One of the Justices asked him why the teachers did not distribute tranquilizers to the children.) The act of a board of a county poor farm in permitting erection of a Catholic chapel on the premises was upheld in Illinois by viewing the transaction as the gift of a building to the county by the church rather than a forbidden gift by the commissioners of the land or its use to the church[51] — although, it will be remembered, it was just such a permanent use of public land for a church that Madison declared violative of the First Amendment.[52] As will be seen below, the grant of Federal funds to a hospital controlled by the Catholic Sisters of Charity could be sustained only by accepting the fiction that the corporation formed by the Sisters to hold title to the hospital was a secular entity distinct from the Sisters;[53] the supplying of textbooks for use in parochial schools could be sustained only by accepting the fiction that the children, rather than the parochial schools, were the beneficiaries, even though the parochial schools would have been required to purchase the books if they had not been supplied gratuitously by the state;[54] the validity of paying the transportation expenses of children attending Catholic parochial schools depends, according to Justice Jackson, on the fiction that such schools are merely secular schools in which religion is taught as one subject among many;[55] the validity of the New York City released-time system depends, according to the dissenting justices, on the fiction that the basic purpose of the plan is to release the children desiring to attend religious instruction, rather than the confinement of the children not desiring to attend;[56] and, finally, according to not a few scholars, the Court's upholding of Sunday closing laws is based on the fiction that they are secular rather than religious laws.[57] It is fairly inferable from these and many other similar instances that the ubiquity of legal fictions in church-state cases is a manifestation of the frequent judicial reluctance to invalidate state aid to religion.

Another way judicial reluctance to decide against grants to religion manifests itself is in the treatment accorded by the courts to technical defects in cases involving state aid to religion. Where the court can decide on the merits in favor of the grant it frequently disregards technical defects; on the other hand, where the court finds that it cannot make such a decision, it will not infrequently avoid such a decision by deciding the case on some procedural technicality.[58]

A few cases may be cited to illustrate this point. In Bradfield vs. Roberts[59] a taxpayer's action was brought to enjoin the payment of Federal funds to a sectarian-controlled hospital. The Supreme Court disregarded the technical defect that a taxpayer could not sue, and upheld the validity of the payment. On the other hand, in the Doremus case the Court could not uphold the validity of the New Jersey Bible-reading statute without overruling the holding in the McCollum case that barred religious teaching in public schools—which, as the Zorach case made clear, it was not then prepared to do. Instead, however, of disregarding the same technical defect present in Bradfield vs. Roberts, the Court dismissed the appeal because of just that technical defect. Another illustration is the treatment accorded by the New York courts to two taxpayer's suits. In Lewis vs. Spaulding[60] a suit was brought to invalidate the New York City released-time system. The plaintiff, Joseph Lewis, was not the parent of any child in the public school; indeed, he was not even a resident of New York City, and therefore had no standing to sue even if a taxpayer's suit were to be allowed. Nevertheless the court disregarded this serious defect, and decided the case on its merits, upholding the released-time program. On the other hand, in Bull vs. Stichman[61] the courts avoided invalidating a patently unconstitutional grant of public moneys to a sectarian educational institution by ruling that the plaintiff, a taxpayer, had no standing to sue.

## GOVERNMENTAL GRANTS TO DENOMINATIONAL WELFARE INSTITUTIONS

Instances of the direct grants of money or property to institutions exclusively devoted to worship, such as churches, are rare, and their unconstitutionality is clear. More frequent and more difficult of constitutional determination are Federal and state grants to welfare institutions under sectarian control. It is common practice to make government grants and subsidies to hospitals, homes for orphaned or neglected children or for the aged, and for similar welfare institutions. The constitutional problem arises when, as frequently happens, these institutions are controlled and operated by denominational groups.

Christianity has a long tradition of concern for the ill, the neglected, and the aged. As early as the Middle Ages, church hospitals were widespread.[62] With the industrialization of American life, the need for hospitals and other social welfare institutions grew continually, and denominational institutions likewise increased.[63] It soon became clear, however, that religious bodies could not carry the burden alone, and both governments and secular private organizations entered the field. Large American cities today frequently have municipal hospitals, private nonsectarian hospitals, and Protestant, Catholic, and Jewish hospitals as well. It was natural, however, that where a privately controlled hospital or orphans' home was in existence in a smaller county or municipality the local government would make arrangements to pay a specified sum for each person helped or housed, rather than erect its own similar municipal institutions.

Where the private social welfare institution is entirely secular in operation and control, no church-state problem arises; where the institution is under denominational auspices, constitutional difficulties arise. One method of meeting the problem is by simply banning grants of public money to any welfare institution not under state control. Such a provision is suggested by the National Municipal League, whose Model State Constitution provides (Section 10):

> No public money or property shall ever be appropriated, applied, donated or used directly or indirectly, for the use, benefit or support of any sect, church, denomination, sectarian institution or association, or system of religion, or for charitable, industrial, educational, or benevolent purposes not under the control of the State.[64]

A few states, such as Colorado (Article V, section 34), Montana (Article V, section 35), and Wyoming (Article III, section 36), embody the substance of this provision in their constitutions. Others, such as Pennsylvania (Article III, section 18), bar only appropriations for charitable or educational purposes "to any denominational or sectarian institution, corporation or association," allowing appropriations to secular private institutions.

Provisions like these would appear to be sufficiently clear to preclude state appropriations for hospitals, asylums, or other welfare institutions operated under sectarian auspices. Nevertheless, in a number of cases state courts have used legal fictions to evade the spirit if not the letter of such constitutional prohibitions. One example is the ruling of an Illinois court that a prohibition against public expenditures "in aid of any church or sectarian purpose" was not violated by an appropriation to a Catholic institution for children, where the costs of the institution's services were less than that of comparable secular costs. "It is contrary to fact and reason," said the court, "to say that paying less than the actual cost of clothing, medical care and attention and training in useful arts and domestic science is aiding the institution where such things are furnished."[65] It should be noted that acceptance of this reasoning would permit state payment of the costs of secular education in parochial schools, as long as the sums paid are less than the amounts necessary to provide secular education for the affected children if they were to attend public schools.

A later case[66] was decided in Mississippi, where an appropriation of state funds to the Mercy-Hospital-Street Memorial as part of the state's hospital expansion program under the Hill-Burton Act was attacked as violating the state constitutional provision barring any "donation or gratuity . . . for a sectarian purpose or use." The majority of the court followed the reasoning of the Illinois case, that in agreeing to take a number of patients on a free, nonsectarian basis the hospital was not receiving a "donation or gratuity," but rather was rendering services that the state itself would otherwise be compelled to render. Nor, said the majority of the court, could ministering to the sick be deemed a "sectarian use," even though the hospital was operated by the Catholic Sisters of Mercy, and crucifixes were exhibited in all rooms. A cruficix, said the court, "is a cross bearing an effigy of Christ crucified—a Christian emblem—its use is not confined to one Church alone. Its presence could neither cause a Protestant or a Jew to embrace the Catholic faith, nor could its absence cause a Catholic to relinquish his beliefs in favor of the Protestant or Jewish religion. No patient would likely stay so long." The court pointed out that the hospital admitted patients of all faiths and creeds, and that the hospital was the property of a corporation whose powers were determined by its charter rather than by the sectarian beliefs of the stockholders, members of the Sisters of Mercy.

The minority opinion argued that the crucifix is a peculiarly Catholic "symbol of . . . faith," and that members of the Sisters of Mercy who constitute the hospital's board of directors were subject to the "authority and jurisdiction of the Diocesan Bishop," who thus had absolute dominion and control over the hospital. To accept the argument, the minority continued, that "administering to the sick is not sectarian" would logically lead to the holding that "the public treasury may be opened to religious orphanages and schools."

There are many state court cases involving the issue presented in this case, and different courts have reached different results. In 1962, when this case was decided, the highest court in Kentucky arrived at the same result in a similar case, and the United States Supreme Court refused to review the decision.[67] But, according to the writer of a note summarizing and analyzing the numerous cases, "the weight of authority is to the effect that a contract between a state, city or other political subdivision and a sectarian institution, whereby the former agrees to pay the latter for services rendered or expenditures incurred thereunder, is within the meaning of a constitutional provision inhibiting the use of public funds in aid of sectarian institution, and void."[68]

Aside from the restrictions imposed by state constitutions, any appropriations of public funds, Federal or state, to charitable institutions under denominational control are subject to attack under the First Amendment ban on laws respecting an establishment of religion. This issue was presented to the United States Supreme Court in 1899 in the case of Bradfield vs. Roberts.[69] In that case a taxpayer sued to enjoin the Federal government from consummating a contract under which it agreed to erect a building on the property of the Providence Hospital in Washington, D.C., and to pay a specified sum for each poor patient sent by the Commissioners of the District of Columbia. The Court, in a unanimous opinion, sustained the validity of the contract on the ground that, though the hospital was owned by a corporation consisting exclusively of Catholic Sisters of Charity, the corporation was an entity separate and distinct from its stockholders, and was secular and nonsectarian, though its stockholders were all nuns. The Court said:

> . . . Assuming that the hospital is a private eleemosynary corporation, the fact that its members . . . are members of a monastic order or sisterhood of the Roman Catholic Church, and the further fact that the hospital is conducted under the auspices of said church, are wholly immaterial, as is also the allegation regarding the title to its property. . . . The facts . . . do not in the least change the legal character of the hospital, or make a religious corporation out of a purely secular one as constituted by the law of its being. Whether the individuals who compose the corporation under its charter happen to be all Roman Catholics, or all Methodists, or Presbyterians, or Unitarians, or members of any other religious organization, or of no organization at all, is of not the slightest consequence with reference to the law of its incorporation, nor can the individual beliefs upon religious matters of the various incorporators be inquired into.
>
> Nor is it material that the hospital may be conducted under the auspices of the Roman Catholic Church. To be conducted under the auspices is to be conducted under the influence or patronage of that church. The meaning of the allegation is that the church exercises great and perhaps controlling influence over the management of the hospital. It must, however, be managed pursuant to the law of its being. That the influence of any particular church may be powerful over the members of a non-sectarian and secular corporation, incorporated for a certain defined purpose and with clearly stated powers, is surely not sufficient to convert such a corporation into a religious or sectarian body. That fact does not alter the legal character of the corporation, which is incorporated under an act of Congress, and its powers, duties and character are to be solely measured by the charter under which it alone has any legal existence.
>
> There is no allegation that its hospital work is confined to members of that church or that in its management the hospital has been conduct-

ed so as to violate its charter in the smallest degree. It is simply the case of a secular corporation being managed by people who hold to the doctrines of the Roman Catholic Church, but who nevertheless are managing the corporation according to the law under which it exists. . . .

In theory, the decision in Bradfield vs. Roberts is completely consistent with the test for constitutionality suggested earlier in this volume:[70] government may pursue only secular ends and in doing so may use only secular means. Healing the ill is obviously a secular end and, as emphasized in the Court's opinion, since the hospital had been incorporated it was a secular institution, so that a secular means was being used to achieve the secular ends. Nonlawyers might consider it a pure fiction to hold that an order of nuns becomes a secular body by incorporating themselves, and Justice Rutledge, in his dissent in the Everson case, characterized the Court's reasoning in Bradfield vs. Roberts as "highly artificial." Nevertheless, the decision is the law of the land, and it is on the basis of this decision that the Hill-Burton Act rests. The Act—technically the Hospital Survey and Construction Act—was passed originally in 1946, and has since been renewed from time to time. It has provided many hundred millions of dollars from Federal funds to assist "public and non-profit" hospitals in the expansion of their facilities. Current reports of the Department of Health, Education and Welfare indicate that more Hill-Burton funds go to private than to public hospitals and that among the denominational groups, Roman Catholic institutions are the chief beneficiaries of the act, although Protestant and Jewish hospitals have received substantial sums as well.

Though Protestant and Jewish religious bodies overwhelmingly oppose government aid to denominational schools,[71] no such consensus exists in respect to the Hill-Burton Act or other laws providing government aid to denominational hospitals. By and large, opposition has been limited to the Disciples of Christ,[72] some Presbyterians,[73] and the Baptists, many Baptist institutions having declined government grants.[74] On the other hand, most Protestant bodies have applied for and accepted funds for their hospitals, though occasionally with some reservations and reluctance.[75]

Jewish hospital organizations, too, have availed themselves of the benefits of the Hill-Burton Act. Representatives of Jewish organizations, in conversations with the present writer, have argued that their action is not inconsistent with their opposition to government funds for denominational schools. A Jewish hospital is such only by reason of the fact that it is financially maintained primarily by contributions from Jews and Jewish community chests. Unlike Jewish cemeteries—which are frequently affiliated with or owned by synagogues and congregations—Jewish hospitals have no congregational affiliation; they are operated by lay directorates completely free of rabbinic control, and only a small percentage are Jewish. On the other hand, it is also true that Jewish hospitals usually serve kosher food prepared under the supervision of a rabbi, paid for out of hospital funds. They frequently have a rabbi on their staff, also paid out of hospital funds, to minister to the religious wants of the patient; and likewise frequently maintain a Jewish chapel for religious services. Thus, though a Jewish hospital cannot be said to be sectarian in the same sense as one owned and operated by an order of nuns who owe complete fealty to their ecclesiastical superiors, it would seem to be no less sectarian than a Methodist or Baptist affiliated hospital.

Aside from the fiction that corporations are secular even though their stockholders may be clerics or religious organizations, a fair argument can be presented for the inclusion of denominational hospitals in programs of government aid. Though such hospitals are motivated by considerations of Christian charity and are a part of the church's healing ministry, it is nevertheless true that healing the sick is not generally deemed a sectarian act. Under our Constitution government may not undertake religious instruction, and therefore the payment of public funds to parochial schools cannot be justified on the ground that these schools are performing a function that the state would otherwise be required to perform. But the state may, and indeed must, care for the destitute ill; and denominational hospitals that accept poor patients of all faiths and of no faith are performing a service the state would otherwise be required to perform. The Constitution prohibits government from aiding religious organizations; it does not prohibit it from dealing with them on fair and equal terms. As long as the sum paid to the denominational hospital does not exceed the amount the state would be required to expend to care for the patients unable to pay, the hospital is not really receiving government aid.

On the other hand, it may well be argued that denominational hospitals are not truly nonsectarian in their admissions policy. In the Mississippi case, the court disposed of the presence of crucifixes in all rooms, on the implicit basis of the rule of *de minimis non curat lex;* their presence during the short time a non-Catholic remains in a hospital is not likely to convert anybody to Catholicism. But the presence of a crucifix may not be a trival matter to non-Catholics. An orthodox Jew, for example, would consider it sinful to remain, and particularly to pray, in a room with a crucifix on the wall; and that fact may well exclude him from the hospital. So, too, a patient whose religious convictions do not forbid the therapeutic abortion she requires—possibly for her survival—is effectively barred from a Catholic hospital, where such treatment is prohibited exclusively for religious reasons.

Moreover, a patient requiring hospital care may frequently find that the physician he wishes to care for him is barred from the hospital solely for religious reasons. In 1952 St. Francis Hospital, a Roman Catholic institution in Poughkeepsie, N.Y., required seven visiting physicians to sever their connections with the Planned Parenthood Association or be barred from entry into the hospital.[76] The hospital's action was editorially defended by *America,* national Jesuit weekly, in the following words:

> The hospital's stand is not a new departure in Catholic practice, nor is it a deviation from the standards of private institutions in general. The courts have always upheld the rights of private institutions to choose their own staffs, and the medical profession holds as a basic principle that a hospital administration is free to choose the type of doctor it wants.[77]

This is, of course, undoubtedly true. Yet it is equally true that when a hospital receives public funds out of taxes paid by persons whose religious convictions do not include the prohibition of birth control, these persons should not be excluded from that hospital (or be treated by physicans not of their choice) because of religious considerations which they do not share. At the time the physicians were excluded from St. Francis Hospital that institution had just completed a large addition financed out of public funds received under the Hill-Burton Act.[78] It may well be urged that—to paraphrase Justice Jackson's dissent in the Everson case—St. Francis Hospital "cannot have it both ways." Hospital operation "cannot be a private affair when the state seeks to impose regulations which infringe on it indirectly, and a public affair when it comes to taxing citizens of one faith to aid another, or those of no faith to aid all." St. Francis Hospital could justifiably complain if it were to be compelled to extend its facilities to physicans advising therapeutic abortion and birth control; but it cannot logically accept government funds if it bars such physicians and their patients exclusively for religious reasons.

## Peace Corps and Anti-Poverty Programs

Related to the question of governmental aid to sectarian hospitals is the use of church-related institutions in programs on the part of the government to alleviate the sufferings of poverty at home and abroad. The first in time was the Peace Corps program established by President Kennedy in 1961. Its purpose, in the words of its Fact Book, was to have "individual citizens work directly with the people of other countries to provide economic, social or educational assistance and to further the cause of peace through personal relationships and the development of mutual understanding." It sought to accomplish this by setting up a panel of trained men and women to be sent to foreign lands under the auspices of the United States government to help the people to meet their urgent needs for skilled manpower.

Shortly after the program was established, its director, R. Sargent Shriver, announced that twelve of its initial projects would be carried on through private agencies and organizations, half of them religious.[79] The announcement evoked sharp protests, initially by the United Presbyterian Church in the United States and the American Jewish Congress,[80] but thereafter also by other major Protestant organizations and spokesmen.[81] The statement issued by the American Jewish Congress said, in part:

> The involvement of religious bodies in the government's Peace Corps program represents just that type of partnership between church and state that the First Amendment to the Constitution was intended to prevent.
>
> The Government of the United States was formed to achieve political and secular ends. Churches were formed to meet religious objectives. In pursuance of its ends and as part of its foreign policies our government has established the Peace Corps program. The churches' long tradition of missionary activities in foreign lands has independent objectives which must be pursued independently. Any attempt to combine them or to merge the operations of government and church will prove detrimental to the achievement of both objectives.
>
> If church groups participate in the Peace Corps projects there is a grave danger that they may be used as "an engine for the purpose of the other"—that the churches may be used to further American foreign policy or that the government may be used to further the churches' missionary activities. Such a result would corrupt both objectives. To avoid this danger, church and government must pursue their separate ends independently of each other.
>
> It would be unfortunate indeed if the Peace Corps' effectiveness in fulfilling the vital purposes and noble objectives it has been designed to serve should be imperiled by the ill-conceived notion of involving religious groups in a governmental operation.

On the other hand, Peace Corps contracts with religious groups were warmly defended by the National Catholic Welfare Conference and other spokesmen for the Catholic Church.[82] Fears that the beneficiaries of the programs might look at it with suspicion as a missionary effort were dismissed by F. Robert Melina, executive secretary of the Peace Corps Desk of the National Catholic Welfare Conference, with the statement that: "There should be no difficulty in seeing the difference between welfare and humanitarian projects carried on by people of religious conviction and activities which are strictly concerned with conversion, catechetics, and so forth."[83]

The protests of the Protestant and Jewish groups proved effective, however. In December 1961, Mr. Shriver announced at a press conference that it would be a mistake for the Peace Corps to sponsor projects conducted by church-related groups, and accordingly no contracts would be signed with church-related agencies.[84]

The relationship of the Anti-Poverty program initiated by Congress in 1964 to the Peace Corps program is indicated by the fact that President Johnson appointed Mr. Shriver to head the Anti-Poverty program too. The Anti-Poverty Bill, known officially as the Economic Opportunity Act of 1964, stated that its purpose was "to eliminate the paradox of poverty in the midst of plenty in this nation by opening to everyone the opportunity for education and training, the opportunity to work, and the opportunity to live in decency and dignity." Among the means to achieve this purpose was the establishment of Youth Programs (Title I) and Urban and Rural Community Action Programs (Title II). The first created a Job Corps to train youths for employment, and the second sought to utilize the public and private resources of communities in attacking poverty.

Church-state problems arise in connection with both Titles. Under Title I sectarian institutions and organizations are included, with the proviso only that government funds shall not be used for the construction, operation, or maintenance of any facility used "solely" for religious instruction or worship. Title II includes sectarian organizations as community action organizations, and testimony before the House Education and Labor Committee indicated that this was understood to mean that government aid would be given to sectarian organizations conducting health and welfare programs, so long as the government funds were not used for specifically religious purposes.

As originally drafted, Title II excluded direct government aid to sectarian schools by providing that any elementary school education program assisted should be administered by public educational authorities. This provision aroused considerable opposition from Catholic sources, which were not satisfied by a provision in effect endorsing the "shared-time" plan[85] by providing that children attending nonpublic schools were not to be denied the benefits of any such Federally assisted program.

As will be seen later in this volume,[86] general Federal aid to elementary and secondary schools had been frustrated for many years by the fact that Catholic forces were sufficiently powerful to prevent enactment of any measure which did not include parochial schools and non-Catholic forces were able to prevent enactment of any measure which did include them. This pattern was repeated in the Anti-Poverty Bill. As finally enacted it specifically forbade "general aid to elementary or secondary education in any school or school system." The bill as enacted does, however, authorize special remedial and noncurricular educational assistance through programs carried out by either public or church-related schools, provided no sectarian emphasis is placed and the programs are open to the public generally. This provision, as well as the one allowing use of Federal funds for church-related welfare institutions, has evoked criticism from some Protestant and Jewish sources on the ground that it would weaken the church-state separation provisions of the Constitution.[87]

The Office of Economic Opportunity, which administers the Act, has made numerous contracts with religious organizations, particularly those of the Catholic Church, to operate specific projects (such as preschool training) under the Act. It has justified these contracts on the ground that they seek to provide welfare benefits for children, rather than financial aid to church education, and therefore are not barred by the First Amendment. Its efforts, through regulations, to minimize church-state violations in the administration of the Act will be related in the chapter dealing with Federal aid to education, where the subject will be considered further.

## CHURCH USE OF STATE PROPERTY

As we have seen, there are frequent instances where the separation and freedom aspects of the First Amendment appear to be in conflict, and full effect cannot apparently be given to one aspect without sacrificing in part the completeness of the other. The use of publicly owned property for religious purposes frequently presents this seeming dilemma. The refusal by a municipality to allow its streets and parks to be used for religious meetings and missionary activities constitutes an interference with religious liberty in violation of the "free exercise" guaranty.[88] But the free use of government-owned buildings for religious purposes would equally clearly consti-

tute unconstitutional aid to religion in violation of the "establishment" guaranty.

The distinction between public parks and streets on the one
hand and public buildings on the other may appear to be arbitrary,
but it has some historical basis. Supreme Court Justice Roberts noted
in one case that "streets and parks . . . have immemorially been held
in trust for the use of the public and, time out of mind, have been
used for purposes of assembly, communicating thoughts between citizens and discussing political questions."[89] They have similarly been
used immemorially for religious discussions and missionary endeavors; and although, as we shall see,[90] such use is subject to reasonable regulation in the interests of the community as a whole, it
may not be absolutely barred to religious groups.

Buildings, on the other hand, whether privately or publicly
owned, are generally considered property whose use constitutes a
salable economic asset. Though public authorities may allow the free
use of public buildings for certain communal purposes, such as lectures, civic meetings, entertainments, etc., neither the liberty guaranty, nor the guaranty of the "equal protection of the laws" contained in the Fourteenth Amendment, requires them to allow their
free use for religious purposes. This has been repeatedly held by the
courts, which have consistently refused to compel boards of education to allow religious groups the free use of school buildings even
though other groups in the community are accorded that privilege.[91]

The problem of the church use of public buildings has become
acute in recent years, with the modern trend of using public school
buildings as community centers when they are not in use for school
purposes. (The incorporation of parochial schools into the public
school system and other instances of simultaneous use of public
school plants for secular and sectarian instructions will be discussed
later in this volume.[92] Here we are concerned only with the use of
public school buildings after school hours, on Saturdays and Sundays, and during the summer vacation period.) In earlier days the
courts frequently held that local boards of education had no authority to allow the use of public school buildings for any purpose other
than public instruction.[93] Today, however, boards of education and
school superintendents generally are empowered in their discretion
to allow the use of school buildings for lectures, entertainments, political meetings, and other communal uses. As a Kansas court states:

> It is not an essential part of our school system that the public obtain
> no benefit from the buildings it has erected except during the hours

they are occupied by the pupils. The movement for the use of school buildings for civic centers is generally recognized as a wholesome one.[94]

Typical of modern statutes is the Pennsylvania act which provides that

The board of school directors of any district may permit the use of its school ground and buildings for social, recreational and other proper purposes under such rules and regulations as the board may adopt. . . .[95]

It is under such laws as these that the question arises whether a board of education may permit the use of school buildings by sectarian groups without violating the separation guaranty.

In seeking an answer to this question, we should note that if the use by the sectarian group is regular and extended in duration, no constitutional distinction can logically be drawn between such use and an outright grant of public funds or property to the sectarian group.[96] It can hardly be of constitutional significance that the state furnishes gratuitously premises having a definite rental value rather than a sum of money with which the church group could rent the premises. Occasionally such a distinction has been attempted, as where the use in parochial schools of textbooks bought out of public funds is justified on the ground that ownership of the books remains in the public school authorities. When the Cochran case[97] reached the Supreme Court of the United States it said, in upholding the Louisiana statute:

The [Louisiana] Court also stated, *although the point is not of importance in relation to the Federal question,* that "it was only the use of the books that is granted to the children, or, in other words, the books are lent to them."

The Court thus recognized that a state's power to lend the use of state property is not constitutionally distinguishable from its power to give the property, and that the sole test was whether the parochial school or the child was the actual beneficiary of the state aid. A similar distinction was sought to be made by the Supreme Court of Illinois in the McCollum case,[98] and was likewise held erroneous by the Supreme Court of the United States.[99]

On the other hand, an irregular, occasional use of a public building by a sectarian group can be justified if one accepts the view of Professor Sutherland that the rule of *de minimis non curat lex* is applicable to constitutional prohibitions against government aid to religion. A number of state cases have adopted this view. As one court said:[100]

... we incline to think that the use of a public school building for Sabbath schools, religious meetings, debating clubs, temperance meetings and the like, *and which of necessity must be occasional and temporary,* is not so palpably a violation of the fundamental law as to justify the courts in interfering. Especially is this so where ... abundant provision is made for securing any damages which the taxpayer may suffer by reason of the use. ... With such precaution, the amount of taxes anyone could be compelled to pay by reason of such use would never amount to any appreciable sum. We may further say that the use for the purposes named is but temporary, occasional, and liable at any time to be denied by the district electors, and such occasional use does not convert the schoolhouse into a building for worship within the meaning of the Constitution [which prohibits compulsory taxation to support places of worship].

Justification for such irregular and occasional use is even stronger in cases of emergency, as where a church has been damaged by fire or otherwise has been rendered temporarily unusable.[101] It is not an uncommon practice in such cases for the municipal authorities to allow the congregation to use some public building until repairs are completed. Such temporary use of a town fire house was upheld as valid by a court in New York in a suit by Joseph Lewis in December 1951.[102] The practice is reciprocal, and it is not uncommon for churches and parochial schools to permit the use of their premises for public school purposes where the public school building has been rendered temporarily unusable.

Such use of a public building by a religious group raises no constitutional church-state problem if the group pays a fair rental; indeed, no church-state problem is raised even by regular use if a fair rental is paid. The Constitution bars government aid to religion; it does not prohibit government from leasing a public building to a church for a fair rental, any more than it prohibits government from selling a public building to a church at a fair price. The difficulty with such arrangements is not that they violate the limitation of the church-state provisions of the Constitution, but that such rental of school buildings is frequently beyond the power of school boards. In the words of a ruling by the University of the State of New York, "There is no power given to a board to become a landlord and rent its property."[103]

The usual constitutional case, therefore, is not of the rental of school buildings but permission to use them gratuitously; and the use is gratuitous even though — as is frequently the case — a nominal fee is charged to cover heat or lighting expense. Such use is clearly a benefit to the group using it, and would appear to be barred by the prohibition against government aid to religion which is part of the constitutional guaranty of separation of church and state. Occasionally courts have sought to draw a distinction between the use of a school building by a religious group and its use for a religious purpose, to uphold the former and invalidate the latter. Thus, in one of Joseph Lewis's many suits, a New York court refused to bar the use of public school buildings by sectarian groups, saying:

> The manifest vice of plaintiff's position is that he has confused the racial and religious affiliations of the users of the school buildings with the purpose for which the buildings are used. . . . It is the use to which the school buildings are put, and not the identity of the users, that is decisive of the lawfulness of the use.[104]

That this distinction is open to question is evidenced by the New York statute itself, which makes no distinction. Section 414 of the New York Education Law permits the use of school buildings after school hours for educational purposes, library purposes, social, civic, and recreational meetings, civic forums and community centers, and for fund-raising meetings or entertainment by educational or charitable groups, but expressly excludes their use by any "religious sect or denomination." The legal test is not the nature of the use alone, but also the identity of the beneficiary. The issue was presented to a New York court in another of the Lewis suits,[105] in which an injunction was sought against the Commissioner of Education to prevent the use of a state building by a sectarian college to present a lecture by a Jesuit missionary on the subject "Cliff Dwellers of the Far North." Though the subject of the lecture itself was obviously nonreligious, admission fees were to be charged and the proceeds were to be paid over to the sectarian college. The court dismissed the suit on the ground that as a mere taxpayer the plaintiff had no standing to sue, and thus avoided passing on the legality of the proposed use.

It can hardly be denied that to permit the free use of public buildings by a civic group or a reading circle but not to a church appears to be discriminatory and to evince a hostility to religion. But the seeming discrimination is required by a Constitution under which a state "may make public business of individual welfare, health, education or entertainment or security," but "cannot make public business of religious worship or instruction,"[106] either to support or to regulate it. Nor is this law motivated by hostility to religion, but by a conviction that religion inevitably suffers rather than is benefited by accepting the material favors of secular government.

## Tax Exemption

### *The Background*

Tax exemption of church property presents another instance of an apparent conflict between the "establishment" and "free exercise" aspects of the First Amendment. Taxation of religious activities constitutes an unconstitutional abridgment of religious liberty, whereas exemption from taxation of property owned by religious groups is at least arguably that type of material aid to religion that is barred to government as a law respecting an establishment of religion. That phase of the subject of taxation that emphasizes the religious freedom guaranty will be considered in the third part of this volume; here we shall concern ourselves only with the establishment facet, though this division of the problem for convenient treatment is no doubt largely arbitrary.

The tax exemption of church property is probably as ancient as taxation itself. It dates back at least to early Biblical days. When Joseph bought the Egyptians' land for the food he had stored during the seven years of plenty, he turned back to each Egyptian his land, and "made it a law over the land of Egypt unto this day that Pharaoh should have the fifth part [of the produce]; except the land of the priests only, which became not Pharaoh's."[107] When Artaxerxes, king of Persia, authorized Ezra to levy a tax for the rebuilding of the temple in Jerusalem, he specifically directed "that touching any of the priests and Levites, singers, porters, Nethinims, or ministers of the house of God, it shall not be lawful to impose toll, tribute or custom upon them."[108] With the establishment of the Jewish theocracy after the return from Babylon, it was natural that this exemption should be continued, and, with the rise of the rabbinic class, to be extended to the rabbis.[109] By the time Judea became a province of the Roman Empire it had become a maxim in the Talmud that "he that takes upon himself the yoke of the Law [Torah] from him shall be taken away the yoke of the kingdom."[110]

The exemption from taxes enjoyed by Christian churches dates back to the 4th century, when Constantine, in the process of establishing Christianity as the state church of Rome, accorded this privilege to church buildings and the land about them used for church purposes.[111] It is, however, not to be assumed that religious institutions have everywhere been exempt from taxation. The English church was often required to contribute to the support of the government.[112]

With the close relationship of church and state existing in most of the American colonies it was natural that church property should be exempt from taxation. The church was a government agency, supported and regulated by government, and taxing it would have been an idle ceremony.[113] As one New England court said, "so long as towns . . . exercised parochial functions, and raised taxes for supporting and maintaining houses of public worship, those places of worship were exempt from taxation as public property by the nature of things. . . ."[114] When the exclusive establishments gave way to multiple establishments, and the favors accorded a single church were extended to dissenting churches, it was likewise in the "nature of things" that they too should be exempt from taxation.

But the custom of exempting church property continued uninterruptedly after disestablishment, and was later given the force of law by express provisions in state constitutions and statutes.[115] It is this widespread prevalence of the tax exemption of church property that is most often cited to support the position that the Constitution does not require the absolute separation of church and state, nor bar nonpreferential aid to religion. Almost every list of illustrations of governmental aid to religion cited by proponents of the narrow interpretation of the First Amendment contains the tax exemption item.[116]

The universality of the exemption of church property from taxes in the United States is hardly open to doubt; constitutional or statutory provision for such exemption exists today in all states as well as in the District of Columbia. Churches, other houses of worship, and the land on which they stand are everywhere freed from tax levies, as is personal property devoted to religious uses. The property of religious schools and colleges is likewise accorded exemption,[117] though in California the exemption was extended only fairly recently to religious schools below the college level. Denominational colleges in California achieved tax-exempt status in 1914. Attempts to extend it to secondary and primary schools were defeated in 1926 and 1933. In each case, after enactment by the legislature the proposal was defeated by the electorate at the polls. The exemption measure was again approved by the legislature in 1951, and was finally ratified at the polls in the November 1952 elections. However one feels about the constitutionality or desirability of exempting church properties from taxes, the fact that the Catholic Church would be the chief beneficiary of the exemption of secondary and primary schools, whereas Protestant institutions benefited most by the exemption long accorded to denominational colleges, when considered together with some of the arguments used in the 1926 and

1933 campaigns, leads almost necessarily to the conclusion that anti-Catholic feeling played a substantial role in the previous limiting of the exemption to colleges.[118]

Under the earlier statutes and cases, exemption in most states was determined by the use to which property was put. If it was used for religious purposes it was exempt, even though not owned by a church or religious body. Conversely, church-owned property used for secular purposes was not exempt. The modern tendency is to impose both requirements—ownership and use.[119] Typical of the modern trend is the language of the New York State constitution and statute, under which tax exemption is accorded to "real or personal property *used* exclusively for religious, education or charitable purposes as defined by law *and owned* by any corporation or association organized or conducted exclusively for one or more of such purposes and not operating for profit."[120] In addition to church-owned property, most states also exempt, in whole or part, the residences of clergymen.[121]

Real property taxation is the concern of states and municipalities, and religious exemptions are governed by state laws. Also under state laws, testamentary bequests to religious organizations are exempt from inheritance taxes, and sales by or to them are exempt from sales taxes.[122] In the Federal tax system, religious organizations are exempt from the income tax. This exemption is broader than the exemption accorded by state real property tax laws, since it includes income producing real property as long as the income is paid over to the religious organization. In addition, gifts by individuals and business firms to religious organizations are exempt from Federal gift and estate taxes; and the amounts of such gifts, subject to percentage limitations, may be deducted from the donor's gross income in determining his own income tax.[123]

### The Justification

Those who believe that the separation of church and state is at best an unfortunate necessity in a country of religious heterogeneity, and that it is the right and indeed the duty of government to aid religion, face no problem of justification. They recognize, as does practically everyone else, that exemption is the substantial equivalent of direct subsidy; but they find nothing undesirable or unconstitutional in direct subsidy as long as it is granted without discrimination. One court expressed this approach in the following statement.[124]

It is presumed that in the nineteenth century, in a Christian land, no argument is necessary to show that church purposes are public purposes. . . . To deny that church purposes are public purposes is to argue that the maintenance, support, and propagation of the Christian religion is not a matter of public concern. Our laws, although they recognize no particular religious establishment, are not insensible to the advantages of Christianity, and extend their protection to all in that faith and mode of worship they may choose to adopt.

Under such an approach, justification of tax exemption would appear supererogatory.

Those who strongly oppose direct government subsidies to churches find the justification of exemption a necessary and not entirely simple task. More by way of explanation than justification, they urge that the economic loss to the community resulting from the tax exemption of church property is small, and the added burden to any single taxpayer is negligible.[125] In New York, for example, tax exempt realty in 1930 constituted about 23% in value of all the taxable real property, but church-owned exempt property constituted only about 10% of all exempt property, or about 2% of the total real estate valued for taxation.[126]

Obviously, so small an exemption would not be felt by the individual taxpayer. Nor is its effect on the community as a whole significant. In 1927 a New York legislative committee examined twenty-one cities, towns, and villages which showed an abnormal amount of tax-exempt property. The committee's research staff discovered no serious tax hardship to those municipalities. In addition, a statistical examination of government costs and tax rates revealed no correlation between the amount of tax-exempt property in a given city or town and either the cost of government or the local tax rate.[127] In New York City, the books of the tax assessors showed that in 1956 only 5% of the tax-exempt property was owned by religious organizations. Approximately the same percentage was found in 1961 in Boston and Washington, D.C.,[128] and in 1964 in Buffalo, Baltimore, and Denver,[129] indicating that this is probably the approximate percentage for the nation as a whole.

The argument that the economic burden on the community resulting from tax exemption for churches is small is being challenged with increasing frequency. In many communities, the withdrawal of private property from the tax rolls on its acquisition by a religious organization has caused a substantial increase in the burden carried by the remaining property owners. Government officials are struggling with this problem all over the nation.[130]

Moreover, the statement that only 5% of all tax-exempt property is owned by churches is misleading, since included in such property is that owned by the public itself through some governmental agency, Federal, state, or local. To tax such property would simply be taking money out of one pocket and putting it into another, and calling such property tax exempt is meaningful only for bookkeeping purposes. Publicly owned property constitutes about 85% of all tax-exempt property, and if this is deducted it will be seen that the percentage of church-owned property—which heads the list of tax-exempt property—will generally be between 30 and 40 per cent.

Argument based on the smallness of the economic consequences of tax exemption is but another aspect of the principle of *de minimis non curat lex*. That principle, however, has little relevance to a consideration of principle; rightness or wrongness in principle is not measured by the dollar value of exemption.[131] This is implicitly recognized by most defenders, who rest their justification primarily on the asserted equivalence of charitable, educational, and religious organizations. Tax exemption statutes do not usually distinguish among the three types, but almost invariably list them together as a single class. In the defense of exemptions to religious groups it is therefore convenient and advantageous to treat all three types as a single class. Charles W. Eliot, when president of Harvard, made the classic justification when he stated:

> To tax lands, buildings or funds which have been devoted to religious or educational purposes, would be to divert money from the highest public use,—the promotion of learning and virtue,—to some lower public use, like the maintenance of roads, prisons or courts, an operation which cannot be expedient until too large an amount of property has been devoted to the superior use.[132]

Or, as one court stated:

> Exemptions are granted on the hypothesis that the association or organization is of benefit to society, that it promotes the social and moral welfare, and, to some extent, is bearing burdens that would otherwise be imposed upon the public to be met by general taxation.[133]

There can be no quarrel with this reasoning insofar as it relates to social welfare institutions operated by churches, as long as they are operated entirely on a nonsectarian basis. The tax exemption of a denominational hospital operated as a secular institution is as unobjectionable as direct financial grants to such institutions. The hypothesis has no relevance, however, to a church building or religious school. It is undeniable that if private organizations will not care for orphaned children or the destitute ill, the state will be required to do so; and thus the private organizations are performing a function that the government would be required to perform. It is therefore as proper for the state to exempt such organizations from taxation as it is to make direct subsidies to them.

Under our system of separation of church and state, however, it is not within the jurisdiction of government to provide worship or religious instruction if private groups fail to do so. To say that churches perform a public function is therefore misleading. And if it is urged — as it frequently has been — that the promotion of morals and ethics by churches is beneficial to the public and is necessary to the advancement of civilization and the welfare of society,[134] it is inconsistent to argue that the same considerations do not justify direct grants to churches. John C. Bennett is correct in his statement that tax exemption is "the most remarkable of all forms of aid to religious bodies,"[135] and Canon Stokes's opinion that though "exemption is an indirect form of subsidy . . . it seems a far wiser one than direct financial grants,"[136] is undoubtedly acceptable to most Protestant groups; Catholics may suggest with some justice that the distinction is one of expediency rather than wisdom.

### Opposition to Exemption

Universal and long-standing as is tax exemption for religious organizations, it is not to be assumed that its desirability as a matter of policy or its validity as a matter of constitutional law has not been seriously disputed. Madison cited the proposal in Kentucky "to exempt Houses of Worship from taxes" as an illustration of "encroachment by Ecclesiastical Bodies" inconsistent with constitutional "separation between religion and government."[137] Nor is opposition limited to organizations or individuals motivated by what might be construed as anticlerical considerations. *The Christian Century,* the nation's leading Protestant publication, has recognized the inconsistency between opposing direct aid to churches and approving indirect aid in the form of exemption, and urges that church groups should bear their share of the cost of government.[138] A similar position has been taken by other religious leaders and groups,[139] particularly the United Presbyterian Church[140] and its Stated Clerk, Dr. Eugene Carson Blake, now general secretary of the World Council of Churches.[141] These of course are isolated voices; the great majority of religious groups do not oppose tax exemption. Either, like the Catholic Church, they affirmatively defend it,[142] or, like the Jewish and many Protestant organizations, they accept the exemption and maintain a prudent silence.[143]

Opposition to the tax-free position of the church has been based on both ideological and economic grounds. In the first category are arguments that churches should bear a fair share of the burden of government; that the acceptance of exemption is inconsistent with the claimed support of separation and opposition to direct grants to parochial schools; that the acceptance of exemption makes it difficult for churches to criticize the governments that aid them; that non-believers should not be forced to contribute to the church, even indirectly; and that exemption encourages the construction and maintenance of more churches than are needed.[144]

The economic argument was stated by President Grant in a message to Congress in 1875:[145]

In 1850, I believe, the church property of the United States which paid no tax, municipal or State, amounted to about $83,000,000. In 1860 the amount had doubled; in 1875 it is about $1,000,000,000. By 1900, without check, it is safe to say this property will reach a sum exceeding $3,000,000,000. So vast a sum, receiving all the protection and benefits of Government without bearing its proportion of the burdens and expenses of the same, will not be looked upon acquiescently by those who have to pay the taxes. In a growing country, where real estate enhances so rapidly with time, as in the United States, there is scarcely a limit to the wealth that may be acquired by corporations, religious or otherwise, if allowed to retain real estate without taxation. The contemplation of so vast a property as here alluded to without taxation may lead to sequestration, without constitutional authority and through blood.

I would suggest the taxation of all property equally, whether church or corporation, exempting only the last resting-place of the dead, and possibly, with proper restrictions, church edifices.

As we have seen, the severe economic consequences of exemption have been disputed; and the studies made indicate that exemptions of religious properties and organizations add but little to the community's tax burden, although the extent of the burden is increasing steadily, and voices of concern are being heard with growing frequency. Nothing, of course, came from President Grant's suggestion; and the frequent attacks on exemption during the ninety years since President Grant's address have had no concrete effects. A report of a New Mexico commission in 1920 reveals the hopelessness with which some public bodies approach the problem:

The exemption from the property tax . . . while in our opinion quite illogical and provocative of much abuse, has apparently met with the general public approval and the support of churchgoers and other beneficiaries who are instrumental in the formation of public opinion. It seems useless to criticize these exemptions although it should be obvious that whatever reason may exist for holding this property as private property is equally good reason for paying taxes thereon.[146]

As one writer put it: "the tax-exemption battle of the churches seems to have been won by exhaustion."[147]

## The Constitutional Issue

Long before the Everson and McCollum decisions, the constitutionality of tax exemption for churches was seriously questioned.[148] Madison, as has been noted, doubted its constitutionality. Zollman, a writer favorable to state aid to religion, pointed out that

> This exemption is not so easily justified on principle as it is supported by authority. . . . While charity and education may be said to be established in the policy of the state, an establishment of religion is expressly prohibited by the Federal Constitution and impliedly by all but one of the State Constitutions. The strictly religious features of church societies can therefore furnish no valid reason for this exemption.[149]

Some of the older state court decisions evinced the same doubts of the constitutionality of tax exemption for churches. One court stated:

> It is easier to admire the motives for such exemption than to justify it by any sound argument. . . . Only let the theory be carried a little further; let a specific tax be levied to support houses of worship, and it will speedily attract public attention. Yet the one is precisely the same in principle as the other. . . . To say that such is the practice of civilized nations, is not sound. It is rather an apology for a departure from principle.[150]

Nevertheless, before the Everson and McCollum decisions defined the limitations imposed by the establishment clause on Federal and state governments alike, tax exemption for religious bodies was universally upheld under state constitutions. In 1877 the Supreme Court of Iowa, without giving any reasons, ruled that such a statute did not violate state constitutional provisions that

> the General Assembly shall make no law respecting the establishment of religion . . . nor shall any person be compelled to . . . pay . . . taxes, or other rates for . . . the maintenance of any minister, or ministry.[151]

In 1928 the Illinois Supreme Court sustained a similar statute on the grounds that the states in a Christian nation such as ours should encourage religious establishments to build up "the moral character and better impulses of the heart," and that the constitution is not violated if all religions are benefited without discrimination.[152]

Objective consideration of the opinions in the Everson and

McCollum cases leads to the conclusion that tax exemption for churches violates the First Amendment as interpreted by these decisions. This is the conclusion reached in two carefully considered articles.[153] This conclusion can hardly be avoided if the language of these opinions is to be given its fair meaning. Under these decisions, government aid to religion, even if not preferential or discriminatory, is barred by the Constitution, and few would deny that exemption of church property constitutes government aid. Indeed, according to Dean Sperry of the Harvard Divinity School, the tax exemption of churches is "the most important governmental recognition of religion in America,"[154] a view echoed, as we have seen, by President Bennett of Union Theological Seminary.

The real question is whether the Zorach case has made a difference. The Everson and McCollum decisions recognized no qualifications to the absoluteness of the separation between church and state. According to the Zorach decision, however, "the First Amendment . . . does not say that in every and all respects there shall be a separation of Church and State." Moreover, "we are a religious people," and therefore the state may encourage religious education.[155] Language such as this may well be construed as a qualification of the scope of the Everson-McCollum principles, and as the creation of an opening in the wall between church and state sufficiently large for tax exemption to creep through.[156]

Yet it is significant that while Justice Reed in his dissent in the McCollum case referred to the tax exemption of churches as an illustration of permissible government aid to religion, Justice Douglas did not include tax exemption in his list of instances illustrating the qualified nature of separation (which included prayers in legislative halls, presidential Thanksgiving proclamations, etc.). On the contrary, he suggested, not that absolute separation would bar exemption, but that it would bar requiring churches to pay property taxes. Moreover, Justice Douglas was careful to state that "Government may not finance religion . . . ," and, as we have seen, it is generally agreed that exemption is a form of financing.

Whatever the Court said in the Everson and McCollum cases or did not say in the Zorach case, it is fairly safe to predict that the Supreme Court will not invalidate tax exemption to churches in the near future. The considerations (discussed earlier in this chapter) that make courts reluctant to decide against religious groups are particularly applicable and potent where the stakes to religion are so high. In 1956 the Court refused to review a decision by the California Supreme Court upholding the state's constitutional amendment extending tax exemption to parochial elementary and secondary schools.[157] Six years later it again refused to review a state court decision, this time from Rhode Island, upholding the constitutionality of tax exemption for church-owned property.[158] At the present writing (June 1966) the Supreme Court has before it an application by Mrs. Madeline Murray (now Mrs. O'Hair) to review a decision by Maryland's highest court upholding that state's law exempting church-owned property from taxation,[159] and it is probable that the appeal will suffer the same fate as its predecessors. All in all, the tax exemption of church properties may safely be said to be a feature of American church-state relations for a long time to come.

## OTHER GOVERNMENT AID TO CHURCH AND CLERGY

Besides tax exemption of their property, churches and clergymen obtain a number of other benefits from government or pursuant to government authority. An example of direct government benefit is the exclusion of "religious, educational or scientific publications designed specifically for use in school classrooms or in religious instruction classes" from the increase in second-class postage rates prescribed by Congress in 1951.[160] Examples of the benefits conferred not directly by government but pursuant to government authority are the reduced rates that many public utilities fix for churches, reduced rates paid by the clergymen on trains and airplanes, etc.

Occasionally these special benefits to clergymen arouse criticism,[161] but such criticism is rare. Reduced rates granted clergymen by government, public utility, and private organizations are merely tokens of the esteem in which men of God are held by the community. The economic consequences of the practice are too trivial and the practice itself is too deeply ingrained in the social pattern to be seriously affected by occasional criticisms and questionable constitutionality where government bodies grant or authorize the benefit.

Far more serious is the frequent practice of exempting churches and other religious organizations from laws regulating the relationship between employers and workers. The consequences to employees of religious organizations of their exclusion from workmen's compensation or minimum wage or social security laws are not trivial. These laws, however, generally relate more to religious activities than to the ownership of property, and the inclusion of churches in such laws is more likely to be subject to attack as an unconstitutional restriction on religious activities than their exclusion as an unconstitutional aid to religion. It is therefore more convenient to treat this aspect of the problem in the section devoted to religious liberty.[162]

### CHAPTER SEVEN

# Church Intervention in State Affairs

## THE CHURCH IN POLITICS

CHURCHMEN IN POLITICS are a familiar characteristic of the American scene. From Charles H. Parkhurst to John Haynes Holmes and Stephen S. Wise, from Elijah Lovejoy and Lyman Beecher to Martin Luther King, clergymen have played significant roles in combating the corruption of government; and have frequently entered the political arena to lend vigorous support to the cause of political, social, and economic reform. Obviously, a clergyman is neither more nor less a citizen than anyone else; and like anyone else, he has the right and duty to strive for the political cause in which he believes. No church-state problem is raised by such participation in politics.

The fact that clergymen are likely to support the candidates and parties favorable to religion in general or to their particular church is no legitimate cause for concern: that is a natural and inevitable part of American life. Veterans are likely to support candidates and parties favorable to their claims; union members are likely to favor candidates supporting the claims of labor; manufacturers will support candidates sympathetic to the interests of industry; and there is no reason for criticizing clergymen for supporting candidates favorable to organized religion.

A different situation is presented when support of or opposition to a political candidate or measure is expressed through the pulpit or the confessional. In such cases, it is not citizens who happen to be clergymen who are exercising their political right; it is the church as an institution that is entering politics and exercising an institutional influence on government. Here real church-state conflicts arise. When the church possesses religious sanctions which are meaningful to its adherents, and expressly or impliedly threatens to exercise those sanctions to obtain the government action it favors, the conflict is even more clear and real.

The church is not necessarily wrong in entering politics. Trade unions have long adhered to the policy of rewarding their friends and punishing their enemies at the polls, and there may be no valid reason why churches should not do the same. The issue depends to a large extent on what one conceives the church's responsibility to the kingdom of this world. Nor is the issue necessarily legal or constitutional in a technical sense. There is nothing in our laws which does or indeed constitutionally can prevent ministers from using their Sunday sermons to urge their parishioners to vote against a bingo referendum or to urge the President not to send an ambassador to the Vatican. Nor is there anything in the laws which can constitutionally prevent priests from denying the sacraments to citizens who vote for Communist candidates, or even to legislators who vote in favor of birth control legislation. Nevertheless, it can hardly be denied that such situations as these present real problems in church-state relationships that are not simple of solution.

It is the purpose of this section to explore some of the church-state implications and consequences of the church in politics. But before considering the aspects of the broad problem, something should be said concerning the more limited problem of clergymen in government.

### Churchmen in Government

During the colonial era, before the onset of disestablishment and separation, clergymen were prominent in government. In theocratic New England, clergymen were often more than in government—they were the government. It was therefore almost inevitable that the advance of separation should bring with it a movement to exclude clergymen from political office, particularly in view of the wave of anticlericalism that traveled westward over the ocean from prerevolutionary and revolutionary France. As early as 1778 a resolution was offered in the Continental Congress "that the sense of the house be taken, whether it is proper that Congress should appoint any person of an ecclesiastical character to any civil office under the United States." Since the Continental Congress was dominated by clergymen and preoccupied with religion, it is hardly surprising that nothing tangible came from the motion.[1]

A different situation prevailed in the states. At the time the Constitution was adopted, seven, or a majority of the original states, had constitutional provisions barring clergymen from serving in the legislature or, in some cases, from holding any political office.[2] By the end of a half century after independence the number had increased to thirteen.[3] North Carolina, in its constitution of 1776, was the first state to adopt a bar against the election of a clergyman to the legislature, but the New York constitution of the following year contained a broader exclusionary provision, adopted purportedly for the benefit of the clergymen themselves. Article 31 provided:

And whereas the ministers of the gospel are by their profession, dedicated to the service of God and the care of souls, and ought not to be delivered from the great duties of their function; therefore, no minister of the gospel or priest of any denomination whatsoever, shall at any time hereafter, under any pretence or deception whatever, be eligible to, or capable of holding any civil or military office or place within this State.[4]

How seriously this expressed desire to protect ministers from the base temptations of political ambition was intended to be taken can be only a subject of conjecture. It is at least reasonable to believe that the need to police clergymen for their own good was not the real motive for these constitutional exclusionary provisions. The South Carolina constitution of 1778, for example, contained the same expression of purpose, yet it barred not only practicing clergymen but also retired clergymen for two years after the discontinuance of their exercise of the pastoral function.[5] On the other hand, the desire to secure disestablishment and separation could not have been the sole reason, for, as we have seen,[6] the South Carolina constitution of 1778 contained elaborate provisions for the establishment of Trinitarian Protestantism as the state religion. Probably a number of motivating factors were responsible—the trend toward separation, the anticlericalism of Continental Europe, and possibly the activity of some clergymen in behalf of the emancipation of slaves.[7]

In the draft of a constitution for Virginia that Jefferson prepared in 1778, he included a provision barring ministers of the Gospel from holding political office, because he believed that such an exclusion was required by the principle of separation of church and state. Madison, on the other hand, felt that the same principle prohibited such an exclusion. Commenting on Jefferson's proposal, he said:

> Does not the exclusion of ministers of the Gospel as such violate a fundamental principle of liberty by punishing a religious profession with the deprivation of a civil right? Does it not violate another article of the plan itself which exempts religion from the cognizance of Civil power? Does it not violate justice by at once taking away a right and prohibiting a compensation for it? Does it not in fine violate impartiality by shutting the door against Ministers of one Religion and leaving it open for those of every other?[8]

The fact that the two persons most responsible for the American principle of separation could reach diametrically opposite conclusions as to the implications of that principle in a particular instance indicates how difficult it is for courts to decide many of the bitterly contested church-state cases that come before them.

223

Madison, rather than Jefferson, was correct in this instance; at least Jefferson came around to Madision's view and later gave up his opposition to civil office for clergymen.[9] An attempt by Congress to exclude clergymen from Federal office would probably violate the clause (Article VI) barring any religious test for office, without considering the separation or religious guaranty of the First Amendment. Most of the states dropped their constitutional exclusion of clergymen from legislative or other public offices at varying times during the 19th century. Maryland and Tennessee, however, still bar "ministers of the gospel" from serving in their legislatures.[10] The constitutionality of these exclusionary provisions is at least doubtful, not only under the First Amendment as made applicable to the states by the Fourteenth, but also under that provision of the Fourteenth which prohibits states from denying to any person "the equal protection of the laws."

Notwithstanding the absence of exclusionary provisions in the Federal and all but two state constitutions, comparatively few clergymen have held political office either in the Federal or state governments. Clergymen do frequently serve on special or temporary governmental citizens' committees, usually without compensation. For instance, three of the fifteen members of President Truman's Committee on Civil Rights were practicing members of the clergy—an Episcopal bishop, a Catholic priest, and a Jewish rabbi.[11] Occasionally a clergyman is elected to the House of Representatives, and at least once to the Senate; but by and large, churchmen have been conspicuously rare in Federal office, elective or appointive. When this rarity is compared with the frequency with which clerics have occupied political office in Europe, the conclusion is inevitable that the constitutional exclusionary provisions expressed a real American tradition which can best be explained as an aspect of the principle of the separation of church and state. To put the matter in another, and perhaps a paradoxical way, a constitutional or statutory bar on clergymen's serving in political office would be violative of the principle of the separation of church and state, whereas the voluntary abstinence on the part of clergymen from seeking political office would appear to be consistent and in harmony with that same principle.

Although the appointment or election of clergymen to government office has not given rise to any church-state problem since the adoption of the Federal Constitution, one aspect of the subject has evoked bitter controversy and difficult decision. The question whether clergymen and members of monastic orders may, consistently with the separation guaranty, serve as teachers in the public school, or, consistently with the religious liberty guaranty, be barred from teaching in the public school, presents difficult problems that are more conveniently considered in the chapter dealing with religion in the public school.[12]

## The Social Gospel

In the days of Hezekiah and the other kings of decadent Judea a man of God exhorted the rulers and the people:

> To what purpose is the multitude of your sacrifice unto me? saith the Lord: I am full of the burnt offerings of rams, and the fat of fed beasts; and I delight not in the blood of bullocks, or of lambs, or of he goats. . . .
> Bring me no more vain ablutions; incense is an abomination unto me; . . .
> Your new moons and your appointed feasts my soul hateth; they are a trouble unto me; I am weary to bear them. . . .
> Wash you, make you clean; put away the evil of your doings from before mine eyes; cease to do evil;
> Learn to do well; seek judgment, relieve the oppressed, judge the fatherless, plead for the widow.[13]

But centuries before Isaiah, the voice of the prophet crying justice could be heard in the temples amid the chantings of the priests over the incense and the sacrifices and the oblations. Indeed, it is probable that the rivalry of prophet and priest is as old as recorded history; there always must have been some preachers who invoked the name of God to exhort rulers to correct the inequities and injustices of social life, as the priests invoked the same name of God in ceremonies and incantations.

The prophetic tradition of Isaiah, Amos, and Hosea and Jesus of Nazareth has become the social gospel of the Judaic-Christian religious culture of contemporary America. Clergymen with liberal theological views are more likely to emphasize the concern of the church with the evils of poverty, corruption, racial injustice, and war than are their more orthodox brethren; but even the orthodox sects—Catholicism, Evangelical Protestantism, and Orthodox Judaism—do not wholly disregard the evils of the kingdom of this world. For example, in his encyclical *Rerum Novarum*, Pope Leo XIII urged a program of labor reform that included guaranteeing workers the right to organize, placing a floor under wages and a ceiling on the hours of labor, and protecting the young and weak against exploitation. Forty years later, Pope Pius XI, in his encyclical *Quadragesimo Anno*, was even more specific in urging labor reforms, stating that when civil authority adjusts ownership to meet the needs of public good it acts not as an enemy, but as a friend of private owners; for thus it effectively prevents the possession of private property . . . from creating intolerable burdens and so rushing to its own destruction.[14]

Perhaps more than any other pope, John XXIII, particularly in the encyclical, *Mater et Magistra,* showed recognition of the obligation of the church to help ameliorate social ills.

Nevertheless, the burden of the social gospel is generally borne by the church groups who are less concerned with theological dogma and ecclesiastical ritual, and who follow in the tradition of Isaiah rather than that of Aaron. Among the Protestants, it is the churches represented in the National Council of Churches of Christ rather than the fundamentalist American Council of Christian Churches that has been active in campaigns looking toward labor reform, the abolition of war, and general social advance.[15] Among the Jews, it has been the Central Conference of American Rabbis, representing the Reform or Liberal wing of religious Jewry, that has been most articulate and active in social and economic reform. Its "Declaration of Social Principles," adopted in 1930, is almost encyclopedic in its categorization of the social evils to the elimination of which religion must be dedicated. The first section of the declaration sets forth the justification for religious concern with the ills of society, stating:

> It is part of the great social message of the prophets of our faith that salvation can be achieved only through the salvation of society as a whole. It is therefore incumbent upon all men to study the ills of the existing social order and to form intelligent opinions on the subject of social reconstruction. Instead of questioning God's goodness because of the evils in individual and communal life, we should address our God-given intelligence to the extermination of those circumstances which allow slums, vice, feeble-mindedness, poverty, degeneracy and the like to continue, with only palliative efforts for their improvement.

The list of social problems to which the declaration addressed itself included industrial democracy, the right of unionization, unemployment, working conditions, child labor, lynching, civil liberties, the outlawing of war, and birth control.[16]

It is therefore not surprising that the most prominent exponent of the social gospel among American rabbis was the foremost of American Reform rabbis, Stephen S. Wise. Yet, considered from another angle, the concern of the Reform rabbinate with the claims of the economically underprivileged is remarkable, and difficult if not impossible to reconcile with the Marxian view that religion is merely a device used by the capitalist exploiters to keep the masses content and submissive. For the Reform rabbis generally are by far the best paid not only among rabbis but among clergymen of all sects, and their congregants are almost always the wealthiest members of the Jewish community.

The same pattern, though possibly not to the same marked extent, exists among the Protestants. The pietist and fundamentalist wing of the American Protestant clergy, representing churches of lower economic class membership, have predominantly favored "free enterprise" and conservative economic and political practices. On the other hand, those Protestant clergymen who represent the dominant economic and social strata in America have been most articulate and effective in furthering social and economic reform.[17]

Stephen Wise expressed the rationale of the church in politics when he said in his autobiography that

> Religion is a vision or ideal of life. Politics is a method, or *modus vivendi*. To say that the minister should not go into politics is to imply that ideal and reality are twain and alien. Politics is what it is because religion keeps out of it.[18]

Reinhold Niebuhr expressed a more practical consideration when he said:

> For every person who disavows religion because some ancient and unrevised dogma outrages his intelligence, several become irreligious because the social impotence of religion outrages their conscience.[19]

In recent years the major thrust at the social gospel in America — at least in respect to domestic issues — has been in the struggle for racial equality. All the religious groups, the Catholic perhaps somewhat less than the Protestant and Jewish, have involved themselves deeply in this issue and have exerted influence in support of the enactment of such measures as the Civil Rights Act of 1964 and the Voting Rights Act of 1965.

On the other hand, there are many who argue that politics and religion have nothing to do with each other; that religion should deal with general principles and not their daily application; that pastors should concentrate their energies on preparing their flock for a kingdom that is not of this world; and that ministers should not make people discontented with their lot and thus encourage them to render unto Caesar less than that which God ordained rightfully belongs to Caesar.

A critic of "mixing religion with politics" has thus editorialized:

> What then is the duty and role of the church? The answer is that the influence of the church must be wholly individual and not institutional. . . . To attempt to speak of what should or should not be done in the "larger community" . . . is to speak of the State itself. . . . Let the

church endeavor to make individuals care more for the church, let man be brought closer to his spiritual responsibilities as an individual, let the churchmen inspire respect and even awe, but let us not drag the church into the political or economic arena. When the church does come in, let it come in as a mediator with unsullied hands and a clear conscience and without political purpose or factional preoccupation.[20]

## Past Battles

Whatever the arguments pro and con, the social gospel and politics are a major aspect of religious concern in our country today, as can easily be seen by noting how much space religious magazines like the *The Christian Century, The Churchman,* and *America* devote to sociopolitical issues. The church in America has always been knee deep in politics.[21] During the period of the establishment, politics was part of the life of the churches, particularly in theocratic New England. The constitutional provisions barring clergymen from legislative or other governmental offices, which found their way into many state constitutions, sought to keep the church out of politics; but the attempt was vain. Throughout American history the social gospel has been an expressed or implicit part of the religious scene.

The church played an active part in the Revolution. The Congregationalist, Presbyterian, and Baptist Churches generally supported the Revolution ardently. Indeed, one Tory commentator was quite bitter about church intermeddling in politics:

> The few that pretend to preach are mere retailers of politics, sowers of sedition and rebellion, serve to blow the coals of discord and excite the people to arms. The Presbyterian clergy are particularly active in supporting the measures of Congress from the rostrum, gaining proselytes, persecuting the unbelievers, preaching up the righteousness of their cause, and persuading the unthinking populace of the infallibility of success.[22]

On the other hand, the Episcopal clergy generally remained loyal to England. According to Professor Sweet,

> the colonial Anglican clergy became the most effective anti-revolutionary propagandists and produced . . . a large proportion of the writings in the Loyalist cause.[23]

In one case Episcopal devotion to the British cause proved embarrassing. The first chaplain appointed by the Continental Congress was an Episcopalian minister who later resigned, and — like Benedict Arnold — threw in his lot with the British.[24]

Even more prominent than its participation in the politics of the Revolution was the church's participation in the long and ultimately bloody struggle against slavery. This was the social gospel par excellence, and church intervention goes back to the 17th century. The first published protest against slavery was by the Monthly Meeting of Quakers in Germantown, in 1688;[25] and five years later the Monthly Meeting in Philadelphia adopted "An Exhortation" that

> . . . in true Christian Love, we earnestly recommend it to all our Friends and Brethren, Not to buy any Negroes, unless it were on purpose to set them free, and that such who have bought any . . . after a reasonable time of service . . . they may set them at Liberty, and during the time they have them, to teach them to read, and give them a Christian Education. . . . [26]

By the close of the Revolution the leaders of the new nation were practically united in their opposition to slavery. This antislavery opinion was shared by the churches, and was expressed in frequent and strong resolutions. In 1789 the General Committee of Virginia Baptists resolved that "slavery is a violent deprivation of the right of nature and inconsistent with a republican government." The Methodist Conference of 1800 directed the Annual Conference to

> draw up addresses for the gradual emancipation of the slaves, to the legislatures of those States in which no general laws have been passed for that purpose. . . . Let this be continued from year to year till the desired end be accomplished.

For years the passing of resolutions continued. Antislavery societies were organized in the churches. Church leaders took their place in the abolitionist forces. Henry Ward Beecher, Reverend Andrew Foss, and numerous other ministers poured forth fiery sermons from their pulpits. Not content with propaganda from pulpit and platform, some three thousand New England clergymen sent a protest to the Senate against the Nebraska Bill as "a great moral wrong" which exposed the nation "to the righteous judgments of the Almighty."

As was to be expected, proslavery partisans protested vigorously and frequently against "political preaching." The reaction of some Senators to this clerical excursion in troubled political waters can be gathered from the response of Stephen Douglas:

> The sovereign right of the people to manage their own affairs, in conformity with the Constitution of their own making, recedes and disappears when placed in subordination to the authority of a body of men, claiming, by virtue of their offices as ministers, to be a divinely-appointed institution for the declaration and enforcement of God's will upon earth.[27]

The slavery issue was settled finally at Appomattox, but the passionate interest of the church in the Negro question did not abate.

The church continued to take an active part in politics during the Reconstruction periods.[28] At the present time church groups are in the forefront of the struggle against racial discrimination and segregation.[29] Of course the churches in the South did not join the abolitionist movement; generally they were loyal to the Confederacy, and issued many antiabolitionist resolutions. But even in the South the church has been far in the lead of the general community in seeking to attain justice and equality for the Negro.

The political war against alcoholism was even more a struggle of the churches. The short-lived Prohibition Amendment was almost exclusively the work of a well-financed and highly effective church lobby, the Anti-Saloon League. The League was organized in the Calvary Baptist Church in Washington in 1895, and grew to be a powerful force in American political life. Its budget reached as much as $2,500,000 a year, contributed by as many as 60,000 cooperating agencies. From the beginning to the end of its career as an effective force on the national scene, the League was a church organization. Although temperance societies unaffiliated with religious groups cooperated, the churches were the source of its mass strength and its controlling leaderships. Between 1911 and 1925 an annual average of 30,000 churches were affiliated with the League, with the Methodists, Baptists, Presbyterians, and Congregationalists outstanding in its support.

The League did not deny that it was a political machine; confronted with that charge, the League answered: "The Church is a machine and the League is a machine within a machine." Its effectiveness as a machine, as of any political machine, is measured by the fruits thereof; and the fruit of the League was the adoption of the Eighteenth Amendment within six years after the League formally launched its campaign for national prohibition. Though the League was less successful in retaining the victory it had won, its influence was respected and feared by many, and was undoubtedly a substantial factor contributing to the defeat of Alfred E. Smith in his bid for the Presidency in 1928.[30]

Birth control legislation presents an instance of the social gospel in operation in the political arena in which church efforts have been extended to defeat rather than to enact legislation. Many non-Catholic religious groups, including the Protestant Episcopal Church, the Methodist Episcopal Church, the General Conference of the American Unitarian Association, and the Central Conference of American Rabbis, have expressed themselves in favor of allowing physicians and clinics to convey medical information concerning birth control. None of them, however, has made any special effort to obtain the enactment of permissive legislation. The Catholic Church, on the other hand, has, at least until very recently, made the defeat of such legislation a major political issue.

According to Catholic dogma, artificial interference with conception is intrinsically evil and sinful. The *New Catholic Dictionary* states that

> the Catholic doctrine that birth control is essentially wrong, is not a mere disciplinary measure, like the law of clerical celibacy, which can be abrogated or modified by the Church. It is a definition of the law of God, which no power, not even the Church itself, can abrogate. . . .[31]

Catholic dogma does permit, under specified conditions, "natural" birth control or "Rhythm," *i.e.,* restriction of intercourse to the sterile period between menstrual cycles. The United States Customs authorities have ruled that books or publications containing information regarding "rhythm" may be imported into the United States, but that information of artificial birth control must be excluded.[32]

For many years only Massachusetts and Connecticut had laws which barred even physicians from giving information regarding birth control. Numerous attempts to amend the laws so as to permit the prescription of contraceptive devices by a physician to married persons "for protection of life or health" were made, but every time such a measure was introduced into the legislature or found its way on the referendum ballot the Catholic Church sprang into action. Advertisements by the Church were carried in the newspapers, sermons were preached at mass, church vestibule walls were covered with placards and posters, priests and delegations from the Knights of Columbus, Catholic War Veterans, and other Catholic organizations visited legislators to make it clear that an affirmative vote would incur the displeasure of the Catholic electorate, and would not be forgotten on the first Tuesday after the first Monday in November. Until 1966 these measures proved uniformly successful, and Protestant physicians in Massachusetts and Connecticut violated the law if they prescribed a contraceptive drug or device to their married Protestant patients even if necessary for the life or health of the patient. Perhaps this was poetic retribution visited on the two states which longer than any others retained their Protestant establishments.

In recent years there have been strong indications that the Catholic Church is becoming increasingly concerned with what has been called the population explosion and the concommitant question of birth control. Influential voices within the Church have been raised urging at least exploration of the possibility of finding a less rigid yet dogmatically acceptable approach to the problem. There has been a significant lessening of Catholic opposition to measures seeking to repeal or liberalize anti-birth control laws, and almost no significant Catholic adverse reaction to the Supreme Court's 1965 decision, Griswold vs. Connecticut, declaring unconstitutional Connecticut's law forbidding the sale or use of contraceptives. Even more significant was the Church's dramatic change of position when a bill was introduced into the Massachusetts legislature in 1966 to permit physicians to advise and prescribe contraception for married couples. The Church's expressed neutrality led to the passage of the bill. All in all a more liberal official Catholic position on the subject of birth control within the near future can be predicted with reasonable safety.

### The Church in Politics

Negro emancipation, prohibition, and birth control are but three of the many instances of the operation of the social gospel on the American political scene. Some of the others include the pacific settlement of international disputes, particularly through American participation in the League of Nations, the World Court, and the United Nations, the liberalization of immigration laws and procedures (a campaign in which Lutheran, Catholic, and Jewish groups have been especially active), opposition to compulsory military training, particularly in peace time, and nuclear bomb manufacture, and opposition on the part of the Catholic Church to the adoption of the Child Labor Amendment.[33]

Unlike the controversies around Federal aid to education or an ambassador to the Vatican (which will be discussed in detail later in this volume), these issues are tangential to our main theme and may only be mentioned. More space has been given to slavery, prohibition, and birth control because they illustrate the three principal ways in which the church operates in politics.

The slavery controversy presented a great moral issue into which the churches entered with fervor and passion but without organization or planning. Whatever organization existed among the churches was informal, spontaneous, and *ad hoc;* when the issue was apparently finally determined, the loose ties that bound the churches dissolved. The prohibition episode also represented a single issue, but here the churches created a powerful and effective instrumentality to achieve their end. Here too, however, once the issue was determined—this time adversely to the churches—the instrumentality was allowed to die. The birth control struggle illustrates the church permanently in politics, organized and prepared to leap into effective action whenever any issue arises that concerns it.

It is the third type of the church in politics which is prevalent today. The Anti-Saloon League was a single-purpose organization: it supported those candidates who favored prohibition and opposed those unfavorable to prohibition no matter how they voted on other issues. Today churches have organized themselves politically to act instantaneously on a variety of issues. The legislator cannot be assured of the "Catholic vote" by suppporting a Federal aid to education bill that makes provision for children attending parochial schools; he must also vote right on an ambassador to the Vatican, censorship of pornography, Vietnam, and a myriad of other issues. Conversely, the legislator who would please the Protestant churches must also vote right (*i.e.*, frequently contrary to the Catholic Church's conception of right) on all issues.

Today the church is in politics not now and then, but continuously. Its constant presence is a political reality to the legislator, who must weigh carefully each measure he would sponsor in the light of church reaction to it. Further, the experience of the Anti-Saloon League taught the churches not only that politics cannot be entered on a part-time basis, but also that to be effective they must operate very much the same way as do the National Association of Manufacturers, the trade unions, or any other group seeking to exercise political power—that is, through experienced, adequately financed political arms, sometimes called legislative representatives, but more commonly known as "lobbies."

Many of the major Protestant bodies maintain organizations, or departments, usually in Washington, with the avowed purpose of influencing legislation on a continuing basis. For example, ever since 1943 the Quakers have maintained in Washington the Friends Committee on National Legislation, with an office and paid staff. Its purpose is frankly to help in "shaping important decisions by Congress and other agencies of the Federal government in causes that Friends have at heart." The Congregational Christian Council for Social Action, formed in 1934, established its Legislative Committee two years later, and long maintained a full-time staff and office in Washington. The Presbyterians, the Baptists, the Methodists, the Lutherans, and other Protestant denominations maintain offices and paid staff in the capital.

On an interdenominational scale, the Federal Council of the Churches of Christ in America, until its merger in the National Council of the Churches of Christ in the United States, spoke on a variety of topics, showing a fairly broad interpretation of the requirements of the social gospel. Some of the issues on which it expressed itself during the four-year period between 1944 and 1948 included trade agreements, overseas relief, prisoners of war, income tax, Japanese prisoners, displaced persons, civil rights, United Nations, and full employment.[34] The scope of activities of the National Council of Churches, successor to the Federal Council, has been somewhat more limited; race relations and church-state questions have been the major areas of its concern. Protestant organizational activities in the political arena have of course been the subject of frequent criticism, on the conventional ground that the business of the church is exclusively God; but it has also been severely attacked for seeking to lead America down the road to socialism.[35]

More closely related to the subject of this book is the organization Protestants and Other Americans United for Separation of Church and State (POAU). The organization was launched in January 1948 by the issuance of a manifesto, signed by John A. Mackay, president of Princeton Theological Seminary; Edwin McNeill Poteat, president of Colgate-Rochester Divinity School, Methodist Bishop G. Bromley Oxnam, Louie D. Newton, president of the Southern Baptist Convention, and Charles Clayton Morrison, former editor of *The Christian Century*. The immediate objectives of the organization were summarized in the manifesto as follows:

1. To enlighten and mobilize public opinion in support of religious liberty as this monumental principle of democracy has been embodied and implemented in the Constitution by the separation of church and state.

2. To resist every attempt by law or the administration of law further to widen the breach in the wall of separation of church and state.

3. To demand the immediate discontinuance of the ambassadorship to the papal head of the Roman Catholic Church.

4. To work for the repeal of any law now on the statute books of any state which sanctions the granting of aid to church schools from the public school treasury.

5. To invoke the aid of the courts in maintaining the integrity of the Constitution with respect to the separation of church and state, wherever and in whatever form the issue arises, and, specifically, to strive by appropriate constitutional means to secure a reconsideration of the two decisions of the Supreme Court upholding the use of tax funds (a) for providing the pupils of parochial schools with free text books and (b) for the transportation of pupils to parochial schools.

6. To call out and unite all patriotic citizens in a concerted effort to prevent the passage of any law by Congress which allots to church schools any portion of a federal appropriation for education, or which explicitly or implicitly permits the states to make such allotment of federal funds. This purpose in no wise prejudices pro or con the propriety of a federal grant in aid of public education.

7. To give all possible aid to the citizens of any community or state

who are seeking to protect their public schools from sectarian domination, or resisting any other assault upon the principle of separation of church and state.

8. In seeking these objectives we are determined to pursue a course that cannot be justly characterized as anti-Catholic, or as motivated by anti-Catholic animus. As Protestants, we can be called anti-Catholic only in the sense in which every Roman Catholic is anti-Protestant. Profound differences separate us in the area of religious faith, but these differences have no relevancy in the pursuit of our objectives as clearly defined in this manifesto. The issue of separation of church and state has arisen in the political area and we propose to meet it there.[36]

POAU grew out of a meeting of Protestant churchmen held in Washington in May 1947 under the leadership of Joseph M. Dawson, executive director of the Baptist Joint Conference Committee on Public Relations (now "Public Affairs"). It was undoubtedly motivated by the Supreme Court's decision in the Everson bus case. The Federal Council of Churches was represented at this meeting by its general secretary, Dr. Samuel McCrea Cavert, who, however, stated that the Federal Council could not become a party to the proposed organization because of diversity of opinion within the Council.[37] Since then POAU and the Federal Council (and its successor the National Council) have pretty much gone their separate ways, though President Truman's announced intention to appoint an ambassador to the Vatican later brought them together temporarily.

In the years since its formation POAU has made tremendous strides. It owns a spacious, well-equipped building in Washington and maintains a full-time paid staff headed by Glenn Archer, formerly dean of the Law School of Washburn University in Kansas. It publishes a monthly newsletter, and has established local POAU chapters in most of the major cities of the country. It is bitterly attacked by spokesmen for the Catholic Church, who maintain that it is motivated largely by anti-Catholic prejudices and represents the modern successor to the Know-Nothing movement of the 19th century. The spirit of ecumenism evoked by the liberal policies of Pope John XXIII has resulted in significant loss of support of POAU within the National Council of Churches and some of its constituents, a loss which may be in some measure overcome by the somewhat more conservative views of Paul VI and the diversion of large amounts of Federal funds to Catholic parochial schools as a consequence of the enactment of the Anti-Poverty Act and the Elementary and Secondary Education Act of 1965.

The Jewish religious bodies speak out frequently on political issues. The Synagogue Council of America, representing all three branches of Judaism — Orthodox, Conservative, and Reform — has been taking an increasingly active role in political affairs, by issuing statements and by testifying before Congressional committees. In addition, Reform Judaism has set up an office in Washington, D.C., under the direction of a rabbi whose principal function is to keep an eye on developments at the Capitol and to present to Congress and the Executive department the views of Reform Judaism on current issues.

Of all the church groups in the United States, by far the most powerful politically is the Catholic Church. Few legislators in Washington or in any but the Southern and Southwestern states will knowingly incur its wrath. Its influence is particularly strong along the Atlantic seaboard and in cities with large Catholic populations. In New York, for example, the official residence of the archbishop, St. Patrick's Cathedral, is colloquially known to politicians as "the Powerhouse." By any standard Cardinal Francis Spellman is one of the most powerful men politically in the country.

The Catholic Church is not always able to obtain the enactment of measures which it favors — direct Federal aid to parochial schools and an ambassadorship to the Vatican testify to this; but the church is almost always able to defeat the enactment of measures which it strongly opposes.[38] Two incidents illustrating the power of the church in New York may be cited. In March of 1947 a bill to prohibit racial and religious discrimination in colleges and universities was on the verge of passage by the New York Legislature when a public denunciation of it by the New York hierarchy caused it to be killed in committee. Besides the church, the only important opponent of the bill was an association of college presidents, who understandably did not welcome government regulation of their admission practices. During the ensuing year sponsors of the bill entered into negotiation with the church, and certain provisions were rewritten to satisfy its objections, particularly by dropping a statement in the declaration of purposes that education is a function of the state, and by insuring the right of denominational colleges to prefer members of their own denomination. In 1948 these negotiations bore fruit; Catholic Church opposition was withdrawn, and the bill passed the legislature with hardly a dissenting vote.

The second incident occurred during the 1952 legislative session in New York. A Southern oil magnate had made a gift to a college conditioned on its abstaining from teaching the equality of the races. This aroused nationwide comment, and occasioned the introduction in the New York legislature of a bill prohibiting colleges in the state from accepting any gift conditioned on the teaching of any theory of racial supremacy or the practicing of discrimination in its admission policies. The bill had been drafted by the same association of college and university presidents that had unsuccessfully opposed the bill against discrimination; and it had the support of the state department of education. It passed the lower house of the legislature unanimously; but when it reached the floor of the upper house a memorandum was read from the State Catholic Welfare Committee terming the bill "an insult" to the colleges of the state and urging its defeat. As a result the bill was defeated in the upper house after having passed the lower house without a dissenting vote.[39]

There are, however, occasions when public pressure for a particular bill is so strong that the Church finds it imprudent to exercise its veto power. Such was the case in New York in 1963 when the legislature enacted a limited Sabbatarian exemption to the state Sunday closing law, and in Massachusetts the following year when a similar exemption was enacted. Such was also the case in New York in 1966 where, after many years of unsuccessful effort, the legislature enacted a measure liberalizing the state's divorce laws.

The political arm of the Catholic Church on the national scene is the National Catholic Welfare Conference, organized during World War I. The Conference occupies a ten-story modern office building in Washington. Its Washington staff consists of about 250 persons distributed among eight departments. The policies of the Conference are determined by the bishops of the United States, and its immediate direction is by an administrative board consisting of the American cardinals and ten bishops elected by all American bishops. The scope of interest of the National Catholic Welfare Conference is indicated by a statement issued by it in its early days:

> Just as soon as we begin to talk about such subjects as Catholic Education, the Catholic Press, Immigration Aid, Americanization, the Industrial Problem, the Divorce Evil, Social Justice, Birth Control, Girls' and Boys' Welfare, Lay Organizations, the Stage and the Screen, Legislation, Rural Welfare, Training for Social Service, and topics of kindred character, we are compelled at once to regard them in the light of their interest to the whole Catholic body as well as to the public at large.[40]

It will be noted that the subjects of interest to the Catholic Church are substantially the same as those of interest to the Protestant churches — although, of course, different positions are taken on many of these issues. As Luke Ebersole indicates in his useful study, *Church Lobbying in the Nation's Capital,* the methods employed by church groups to attain their political objectives are also very much the same. These methods include helping to draft party platforms, watching and reporting legislative proceedings, making friends in

Congress, drafting legislation, furnishing information to legislators, working with Congressional committees, bringing direct pressure to bear on legislators, keeping records of attitudes on votes of Congressmen, working with administrators, and making contacts with the White House.[41] The wide diversity of the church's interests in sociopolitical affairs, and of the methods used to achieve its objectives in those affairs, indicate fairly clearly that the church in America is very much in politics and will continue to be there for a long time to come.

## REFERENCES TO GOD IN OFFICIAL UTTERANCES

Another aspect of church intervention in government affairs is found in references and invocations to God or Christ in official or semiofficial government utterances. References to Christ are comparatively rare today; even the formal phrase "the year of our Lord" is gradually disappearing from modern official documents. References to God are, however, fairly common. All but six of the state constitutions have preambles invoking the name of God. Typical of these is the preamble to the Ohio constitution, reading:

> We, the people of the State of Ohio, grateful to Almighty God for our freedom, to secure its blessings and promote our common welfare, do establish this Constitution.

In addition, oaths used in courts and by government officials taking office frequently end with the phrase "So help me God"; proclamations of days of thanksgiving or prayer of course contain references to God; and "In God We Trust" has been on our coins for a century.

Separation purists like Jefferson might have theoretic objections to these, but even he recognized that as a practical matter such ceremonial verbalizations could frequently not be avoided; both his Declaration of Independence and his Virginia Religious Freedom statute invoked God. The problems raised by such references are not intrinsic but extrinsic; that is, of themselves they are of no practical significance, but their importance lies in their facile and frequent use to justify practices that raise substantial and practical church-state problems.

Three cases out of many may be cited to illustrate this point. In 1947 the Supreme Court of Illinois referred to "such recognition [of God] in the very preamble of our State constitution" to support its holding that the Champaign released-time program was constitutional.[42] The Supreme Court of the United States was not convinced by this reasoning. Again, in Burstyn vs. Wilson[43] the issue was the constitutionality of a state law under which a motion picture ("The Miracle") was banned by state censors because it allegedly caricatured the virgin birth of Christ. To support its holding that the statute was constitutional, the New York Court of Appeals pointed out that "the preamble to our State Constitution expresses our gratitude as a people to Almighty God for our freedom." Here too the United States Supreme Court did not deem this adequate ground to sustain the statute. Yet only a few weeks earlier the Supreme Court had used the same type of argument to justify its decision upholding the New York released-time system. In the Zorach case the Court said:

> ... the appeals to the Almighty in the messages of the Chief Executive; ... "so help me God" in our courtroom oaths — these and all other references to the Almighty that run through our laws, our public rituals, our ceremonies would be flouting the First Amendment. A fastidious atheist or agnostic could even object to the supplication with which the Court opens each session: "God save the United States and this Honorable Court."

There are several basic difficulties with this type of reasoning. In the first place, it assumes that those who initiated or accepted the references to God in any particular document anticipated and were willing that the reference be taken as authority justifying the particular practice in controversy. There is rarely any evidence to support such an assumption; on the contrary, it is reasonable to assume that many of the original framers of the document would have opposed the reference if they had anticipated the use to which it was later put. For example, Justice Brewer, in Church of Holy Trinity vs. United States,[44] cited the reference to Providence in the Declaration of Independence as one of the items in his long list of religious references and practice to support his conclusion that "this is a *Christian* nation." In view of Jefferson's strong opposition to the maxim that "Christianity is part of the common law,"[45] and to a reference to Christ in the Virginia Act Establishing Religious Freedom,[46] it is quite unlikely that he would have approved this use by Justice Brewer of the reference to Providence in the Declaration of Independence.

In the second place, these references to God that are used to justify concrete practices are themselves assumed to be constitutional only because they have not been adjudged unconstitutional. But there is no practical way in which they can be adjudged unconstitutional. As we have seen, a taxpayer cannot sue to delete references to God from the coins of the realm. (Notwithstanding his opinion in the Zorach case, Justice Douglas today apparently deems such references unconstitutional.[47]) If a public official or a court witness does not wish to use the phrase "So help me God," he need not; but obviously he cannot effectively sue to prevent others from using the phrase if they wish. These various ceremonial references are too trivial to provoke legal action except by rare extremists, and these have no way of effectively challenging the references. As a result, a practice of unproved constitutionality is used to prove the constitutionality of another practice.

Finally, and most important, the question whether particular acts are constitutional must be determined by the Constitution of the United States, and that document does not contain any reference to God. This omission was not accidental or inadvertent, and was the basis of much opposition to the Constitution. Citing references to God in court oaths, legends on coins, Presidential proclamations, and the like would appear to be relying on secondary evidence where the primary evidence does not sustain the contention sought to be proved. Put somewhat differently, when Justice Douglas in the Zorach case or Justice Stewart in Engel vs. Vitale cited references to God in Presidential proclamations and courtroom oaths to prove that the Constitution does not require "that in every and all respects there shall be a separation of Church and State" nor prohibit released-time religious instruction or public school sponsored prayer recitation, the omission of reference to God in that Constitution might be cited with at least equal force and logic for the direct reverse of the proposition.

The omission of reference to God in the Constitution had, as we have seen,[49] evoked criticism when the document was presented for ratification. Two small religious bodies, the Associated Presbyterian Church and the Associated Reform Church, went so far as to resolve to abstain from all voting until the Constitution was amended to remedy the defect.[50] More recently, in August 1964, twelve Senators introduced a resolution to amend the Preamble to the Constitution so that the last phrase would read ". . .do ordain and establish, under God, this Constitution for the United States of America."[51] While this proposal is considerably less controversial than the proposed Christian Amendment, discussed in the next section, there is at the present writing no indication that it is likely to be adopted.

### REFERENCES TO CHRIST IN OFFICIAL UTTERANCES

Although almost all of the state constitutions contain an invocation to God, none makes any reference to Jesus. Many of the resolutions and documents of the Continental Congress did make reference to Christ; for example, the treaty of peace with Britain was proclaimed "in the name of the Most Holy and Undivided Trinity";[52] but no reference to Christ was contained in the most important document of the Congress, the Declaration of Independence, and none, of course, in the Constitution. Though Christ was invoked occasionally in official documents in the early days of our nation, such references are rare today.

There are some who have never accepted this omission and have continually striven to rectify it. An attempt to add a reference to Christ in the preamble of the Virginia Statute for Religious Freedom was barely defeated.[53] In 1863 representatives from eleven Protestant denominations organized the National Reform Association, one of whose principal purposes was

> to secure such an amendment to the Constitution of the United States as will declare the nation's allegiance to Jesus Christ and its acceptance of the moral laws of the Christian religion, and so indicate that this is a Christian nation, and place all the Christian laws, institutions, and usages of our government on an undeniably legal basis in the fundamental law of the land.[54]

Accordingly the next year the Association formally petitioned Congress to amend the preamble of the Constitution so as to read:

> We, the people of the United States, *humbly acknowledging Almighty God as the source of all authority and power in civil government, the Lord Jesus Christ as the Ruler among the nations, His revealed will as the supreme law of the land, in order to constitute a Christian government,* and in order to form a more perfect union, establish justice, insure domestic tranquillity, provide for the common defense, promote the general welfare, *and secure the inalienable rights and the blessings of life, liberty, and the pursuit of happiness to ourselves, our posterity, and all the people,* do ordain and establish this Constitution for the United States of America.[55]

The leaders of the Association had no doubts as to what they wanted. According to one, "the existence of a Christian Constitution would disfranchise every logically consistent infidel." Another argued that just as "Constitutional laws punish for false money, weights and measures, and of course Congress establishes a standard for money, weights and measures, so Congress must establish a standard of religion . . .", and presumably punish for false religion. The historian of the National Reform Movement suggested that if the Christian amendment were adopted, those who "do not see fit to fall in with the majority . . . must abide the consequences, or seek some more congenial clime." But another man of God was somewhat less subtle in indicating the shortest way with dissenters. If, he said, "the opponents of the Bible do not like our government and its Christian features, let them go to some wild, desolate land, and in the name of the devil, and for the sake of the devil, subdue it, and set up a government of their own on infidel and atheistic ideas; and if they can stand it, stay there till they die."[56]

One Congressional committee, a House Judiciary Committee in 1874, passed on the proposed amendment and recommended that it be rejected, stating:

> That, upon examination even of the meager debates by the fathers of the Republic in the convention which framed the Constitution, they find that the subject of this memorial was most fully and carefully considered, and then, in that convention, decided, after grave deliberation, to which the subject was entitled, that, as this country, the foundation of whose government they were then laying, was to be the home of the oppressed of all nations of the earth, whether Christian or pagan, and in full realization of the dangers which the union between church and state had imposed upon so many nations of the Old World, with great unanimity that it was inexpedient to put anything into the Constitution or frame of government which might be construed to be a reference to any religious creed or doctrine.[57]

Notwithstanding this rebuff, the National Reform Movement— now known as the Christian Amendment Movement—is still in business, with its national office in Topeka, Kansas, and with three ministers registered with Congress as regular lobbyists.[58] In 1951 Senator Ralph Flanders of Vermont introduced a proposal to amend the Constitution to add an article reading:

> Section 1. This nation devoutly recognizes the authority and law of Jesus Christ, Saviour and Ruler of nations through whom are bestowed the blessings of Almighty God.
> Section 2. This amendment shall not be interpreted so as to result in the establishment of any particular ecclesiastical organization, or in the abridgment of the rights of religious freedom or freedom of speech and press, or of peaceful assemblage.
> Section 3. Congress shall have power, in such cases as it may deem proper, to provide a suitable oath or affirmation for citizens whose religious scruples prevent them from giving unqualified allegiance to the Constitution as herein amended.[59]

The resolution was reintroduced by Senator Flanders in 1953[60] and again by two Representatives in 1959.[61] In 1954, the Senate Judiciary Committee conducted public hearings on the proposal[62] but did not report the measure out.

## The United States a Christian Nation?

The Christian Amendment Movement has never succeeded in obtaining the approval of Congress and the states to the proposal to amend the Constitution so as to declare in effect that the United States is a Christian nation. There has been considerable controversy about the question whether we are or are not "a Christian nation." The issue is largely theoretical, and also largely semantic. If the term "Christian nation" means that the majority of Americans come from families with a Christian background and that the Christian religion played an important part in shaping American culture and tradition, there can of course be no dispute over its correctness. On the other hand, if the term means that the political apparatus of the nation is subject to any of the mandates of the Christian religion, the statement is very much open to question.

In 1797 the United States entered into a treaty with Tripoli in which it was declared that:

> As the government of the United States is not, in any sense, founded on the Christian religion; as it has in itself no character of enmity against the laws, religion or tranquillity of Musselmen . . . it is declared . . . that no pretext arising from religious opinion shall ever produce an interruption of the harmony existing between the two countries.

Paradoxically the treaty was approved by the Federalist Senate on submission by the Federalist President John Adams; and when, eight years later, a somewhat more extensive superseding treaty was made in the administration of the Republican Jefferson, the words "is not, in any sense, founded on the Christian religion" were omitted.[63]

About a century later the United States Supreme Court, in the case of Church of Holy Trinity vs. United States,[64] ruled that an act of Congress prohibiting the importation of foreigners "under contract or agreement to perform labor in the United States" is not intended to prohibit a church from contracting with an English clergyman to migrate to the United States and act as the church's rector and pastor. As the Court pointed out, the evil at which the act was aimed was the breakdown of domestic wage standards by the importation of large numbers of foreign manual laborers under contract to work off their passage at an agreed substandard rate; the act, as one student noted, was no more intended to affect clergymen than bank presidents or university deans.[65] The court therefore found "that the title of the act, the evil which was intended to be remedied, the circumstances surrounding the appeal to Congress, the reports of the committee of each house, all concur in affirming that the in-

243

tent of Congress was simply to stay the influx of cheap unskilled labor."

Justice David J. Brewer's opinion might well have ended at that point. But — presumedly as an added reason — he argued that "we are a religious people" and that therefore "no purpose against religion can be imputed to any legislation, state or national." To establish this proposition, Justice Brewer cited a long list of religious acts and expressions, going as far back as the commission Columbus received from Ferdinand and Isabella, wherein "God's Assistance" is invoked. Other items listed included the Mayflower Compact, the charters of the colonies, the Declaration of Independence, the state constitutions, the provision in the Federal Constitution excepting Sunday from the ten days in which the President may veto a bill, and court decisions stating that Christianity is part of the common law. Justice Brewer then concluded:

> If we pass beyond these matters to a view of American life as expressed by its laws, its business, its customs and its society, we find everywhere a clear recognition of the same truth. Among other matters note the following: The form of oath universally prevailing, concluding with an appeal to the Almighty; the custom of opening sessions of all deliberative bodies and most conventions with prayer; the prefatory words of all wills, "In the name of God, amen;" the laws respecting the observance of the Sabbath, with the general cessation of all secular business, and the closing of courts, legislatures, and other similar public assemblies on that day; the churches and church organizations which abound in every city, town and hamlet; the multitude of charitable organizations existing everywhere under Christian auspices; the gigantic missionary associations, with general support, and aiming to establish Christian missions in every quarter of the globe. These, and many other matters which might be noticed, add a volume of unofficial declarations to the mass of organic utterances that this is a Christian nation.

Though the Church of Holy Trinity case is frequently cited to support the argument that "we are a religious people" and that accordingly the Constitution does not prohibit government aid to religion,[66] the statement that "this is a Christian nation" is rarely referred to — except, of course, by the Christian Amendment Movement. Yet, logically, if the case is authority for the proposition that government aid to religion is permissible, it is equally authority for the proposition that the government may aid the Christian religion exclusively. Indeed, among the cases which Justice Brewer cited was a New York decision[67] by Chancellor Kent designating Mahomet and the Grand Lama as "imposters," and the statement in the opinion of Justice Story in Vidal vs. Girard's Executor[68] that "the Christian religion is a part of the common law."

The Vidal case and the proposition for which it was cited by Justice Brewer merit further consideration. In 1830 Stephen Girard, a native of France who migrated to America during the anticlerical period preceding the French Revolution, died leaving a will in which his substantial estate was bequeathed for the purpose of establishing an educational institution for orphans, with the proviso, among others, "that no ecclesiastic, missionary, or minister of any sect whatsoever, shall ever hold or exercise any station or duty whatever in the said college; nor shall any such person ever be admitted for any purpose, or as a visitor, within the premises appropriated to the purposes of the said college."

Girard explained that "in making this restriction" he did not "mean to cast any reflection upon any person or sect whatsoever; but as there is such a multitude of sects, and such a diversity of opinion amongst them," he desired "to keep the tender minds of the orphans . . . free from the excitement which clashing doctrines and sectarian controversy are so apt to produce." He directed, however, that the students should receive instruction in "the purest principles of morality, so that, on their entrance into active life, they may, from inclination and habit, evince benevolence toward their fellow-creatures, and a love of truth, sobriety, and industry, adopting at the same time such religious tenets as their matured reason may enable them to prefer."

The will was attacked by Girard's heirs, whose attorney, Daniel Webster, argued that the "plan of education is derogatory to the Christian religion, tending to weaken men's respect for it and their conviction of its importance. It subverts the only foundation of public morals, and therefore it is mischievous and not desirable." He argued, further, that the bequest was contrary to the law and policy of Pennsylvania, where Girard resided, since Christianity was part of the common law of that state.

The United States Supreme Court, in an opinion by Justice Story, upheld the will on the ground that Girard had not impugned or repudiated Christianity, nor had he barred the teaching of the Christian religion. On the contrary, the will directed the teaching of "the purest principles of morality," and "where can the principles of morality be learned so clearly or so perfectly as from the New Testament?" All Girard did was to provide that the teaching not be done by clergymen; and there is no reason why the Christian religion cannot be taught adequately and competently by lay teachers.

What is of particular interest here is Justice Story's treatment of the contention that Christianity is part of the common law. He stated:

> It is also said, and truly, that the Christian religion is a part of the common law of Pennsylvania. But this proposition is to be received with its appropriate qualifications, and in connection with the bill of rights of that state, as found in its constitution of government. The constitution of 1790 . . . expressly declares, "That all men have a natural and indefeasible right to worship Almighty God according to the dictates of their own consciences; no man can of right be compelled to attend, erect, or support any place of worship or to maintain any ministry against his consent; no human authority can, in any case whatever, control or interfere with the rights of conscience; and no preference shall ever be given by law to any religious establishments or modes of worship." Language more comprehensive for the complete protection of every variety of religious opinion could scarcely be used; and it must have been intended to extend equally to all sects, whether they believed in Christianity or not, and whether they were Jews or infidels. So that we are compelled to admit that although Christianity be a part of the common law of the state, yet it is so in this qualified sense, that its divine origin and truth are admitted, and therefore it is not to be maliciously and openly reviled and blasphemed against, to the annoyance of believers or the injury of the public. . . . It is unnecessary for us, however, to consider what would be the legal effect of a devise in Pennsylvania for the establishment of a school or college for the propagation of Judaism, or Deism, or any other form of infidelity. Such a case is not to be presumed to exist in a Christian country; and therefore it must be made out by clear and indisputable proof. . . .

Justice Story's position on separation of church and state has already been referred to;[69] and it is therefore hardly surprising that he should find Christianity to be part of the common law. In view of the "Miracle" decision,[70] it is unlikely that the Supreme Court today would expressly accord Christianity greater protection than "Judaism, or Deism, or any other form of infidelity."[71] But even in Story's day Jefferson strongly disputed the accuracy of the maxim that Christianity is part of the common law. In a memorandum, probably written as early as 1768, he made a careful historical study of the origin of the maxim.[72] Many years later, in a letter to John Cartwright, dated June 5, 1824, he wrote:

> I was glad to find in your book a formal contradiction, at length, of the judicial usurpation of legislative powers; for such the judges have usurped in their repeated decisions that Christianity is a part of the common law. The proof of the contrary, which you have adduced, is incontrovertible; to wit, that the common law existed while the Anglo-Saxons were yet pagans, at a time when they had never yet heard the name of Christ pronounced, or knew that such a character had ever existed. [Then, after summarizing his early memorandum and chal-

lenging] the best-read lawyer to produce another script of authority for this judicial forgery, [he concludes:] What a conspiracy this, between Church and State![73]

Today the assertion that ours is a Christian nation is heard considerably less frequently than in earlier years. We hear instead that we are a pluralistic society, but almost invariably we find that the term Judeo-Christian is used synonymously for pluralistic. The frequent use of this term indicates the great influence that the Jews, notwithstanding their small percentage of the population, have exercised on American political and cultural values. Yet, to say that the United States is a Judeo-Christian nation is as inconsistent with the spirit of the First Amendment as to say it is a Christian nation. Roger Williams, as we have seen,[74] asserted that "no civil state or country can be truly called Christian, although the Christians be in it." And no civil state or country committed to the First Amendment, it may be added, may be called Judeo-Christian, although Christians and Jews be in it.

## CONGRESSIONAL CHAPLAINS

Reference has already been made to the practice of appointing Congressional chaplains to open daily sessions with prayer. The practice started in the Continental Congress before the onset of the revolution in church-state relationships that saw establishment give way to separation in a period of no more than fifteen years. The Continental Congress devoted so much of its time to religious matters that it was hardly deemed improper to appoint a permanent chaplain to pray and preach regularly to Congress. The only objection raised was based on the difficulty of satisfying all the varying denominations represented in the Congress. This difficulty was resolved by selecting a chaplain on political rather than religious considerations.[75]

When the Continental Congress was replaced by the Congress under the Constitution, the chaplaincy continued as a matter of course. It will be remembered that the Constitutional Convention of 1787 had neither daily prayers nor a chaplain; and it is at least possible that if the Congress created by that Convention had not been preceded by the Continental Congress it would likewise have started without benefit of chaplain or prayer. This, of course, is purely speculative. What is certain is that the new Congress took naturally to the chaplaincy. Indeed, Madison himself was a member of the committee of the House of Representatives that arranged for Congressional chaplaincies,[76] and even Jefferson — hardly an adherent of orthodox

Christianity—found it politicially advisable to attend a service conducted by the Congressional chaplain.

The first chaplain of the Continental Congress was selected on the basis of political considerations, and politics has never been entirely absent from the institution. On the one hand, politics rather than godliness not infrequently determined the choice of chaplains.[77] On the other hand, the chaplains have used their priestly office to further their political objectives. One Senator during the Civil War period felt it necessary to introduce a resolution

> That the Chaplain of the Senate be respectfully requested hereafter to pray to and supplicate Almighty God in our behalf, and not to lecture Him . . . [nor] under the form of prayer, to lecture the Senate in relation to questions before the body.[78]

The visitor to the capital today can hardly fail to notice how often the chaplain's prayers are made to empty seats. This has been a long-standing complaint of chaplains. The esteem that some members of Congress held for the chaplaincy is indicated by the fact that in one election Thomas Paine, author of *The Age of Reason,* received three votes for the office of Congressional Chaplain.[79] Today the institution of the chaplaincy has reached a station of permanence and respect, even though a candid observer might doubt that any significant spiritual feeling is inspired by the chaplain's daily prayer. Madison complained that in his day "the daily devotions conducted by these legal Ecclesiastics [were] already degenerating into a scanty attendance and a tiresome formality."[80] Only a charitable observer would say that the situation has substantially improved since Madison wrote.

Despite the secure position of the chaplaincy in the American government pattern, it must not be supposed that the constitutionality of paid Congressional chaplains has never been questioned. Madison, who himself participated in the selection of the first Congressional chaplain, later expressed the view that the institution was inconsistent with the First Amendment. In his *Detached Memoranda* he set forth the classic argument against Congressional chaplains, which, though long, merits inclusion here:

> Is the appointment of Chaplains to the two Houses of Congress consistent with the Constitution, and with the pure principles of religious freedom?
> In strictness the answer on both points must be in the negative. The Constitution of the U.S. forbids everything like an establishment of a national religion. The law appointing Chaplains establishes a religious worship for the national representatives, to be performed by Ministers

of religion, elected by a majority of them; and these are to be paid out of the national taxes. Does not this involve the principle of a national establishment, applicable to a provision for a religious worship for the Constituent as well as of the representative Body, approved by the majority, and conducted by Ministers of religion paid by the entire nation?

The establishment of the chaplainship to Congress is a palpable violation of equal rights, as well as of Constitutional principles: The tenets of the chaplains elected (by the majority) shut the door of worship agst the members whose creeds & consciences forbid a participation in that of the majority. To say nothing of other sects, this is the case with that of Roman Catholics & Quakers who have always had members in one or both of the Legislative branches. Could a Catholic clergyman ever hope to be appointed a Chaplain? To say that his religious principles are obnoxious or that his sect is small, is to lift the evil at once and exhibit in its naked deformity the doctrine that religious truth is to be tested by numbers, or that the major sects have a right to govern the minor.

If Religion consist in voluntary acts of individuals, singly, or voluntarily associated, and it be proper that public functionaries, as well as their Constituents shd discharge their religious duties, let them like their Constituents, do so at their own expense. How small a contribution from each member of Congs wd suffice for the purpose? How just wd it be in its principle? How noble in its exemplary sacrifice to the genius of the Constitution; and the divine right of conscience? Why should the expense of a religious worship be allowed for the Legislature, be paid by the public, more than that for the Ex. or Judiciary branch of the Govt.?[81]

The late Canon Stokes observed that Madison "proved a poor prophet in thinking that no Roman Catholic could be elected a Congressional chaplain."[81] Yet the prophecy was only slightly wrong; in the period of almost two centuries since chaplains were first appointed by the Continental Congress only two Catholics (and no Jews, Jehovah's Witnesses, or Black Muslims) served briefly as chaplains, one in each house.[83]

Under the Everson and McCollum decisions there would seem to be little doubt that employment of paid chaplains by Congress violates the First Amendment. In the Zorach opinion, however, Justice Douglas referred to "prayers in our legislative halls" as one of the accepted practices that show that the Amendment "does not say that in every and all respects there shall be a separation of Church and State," thus indicating his view that the practice is not unconstitutional. But it should be noted that in the same opinion Justice Douglas states that "Government may not finance religious groups"; and it is unlikely that he intended to overrule the holdings of the Everson and McCollum cases that tax-raised funds may not be employed for religious purposes—which, of course, is what is involved in the employment of paid chaplains. Moreover, in his concurring opinion in Engel vs. Vitale,[84] he expressed the opinion that use of tax-raised funds to pay the salaries of Congressional chaplains violated the First Amendment.

In any event, under present Federal court decisions, it appears that the issue cannot be directly determined in the courts. In 1928 a suit was brought in a Federal court to enjoin the United States Treasurer from paying the salaries of government chaplains on the ground that their employment violated the First Amendment. The court dismissed the suit on the ground that the plaintiff was merely a citizen and taxpayer and as such had no standing to sue.[85]

Like references to God in official documents, Congressional chaplaincies are important primarily for their use as precedents for more serious encroachments on church-state separation, as by Justice Douglas in upholding the New York released-time system in the Zorach case. Madison recognized that the expenditure of funds was small; but feared, with prophetic vision, "that this step beyond the landmark of power [might] have the effect of a legitimate precedent."[86]

## CHAPLAINS IN THE ARMED FORCES

Madison opposed chaplains in the armed forces as in the halls of Congress. In his *Detached Memoranda* he set forth his arguments against the practice:

> Better also to disarm in the same way, the precedent of Chaplainships for the army and navy, than erect them into a political authority in matters of religion. The object of this establishment is seducing; the motive to it is laudable. But is it not safer to adhere to a right principle, and trust to its consequences, than confide in the reasoning however specious in favor of a wrong one? Look thro' the armies & navies of the world, and say whether in the appointment of their ministers of religion, the spiritual interest of the flocks or the temporal interest of the Shepherds, be most in view: whether here, as elsewhere, the political care of religion is not a nominal more than a real aid. If the spirit of armies be devout, the spirit out of the armies will never be less so; and a failure of religious instruction & exhortation from a voluntary source within or without, will rarely happen: and if such be not the spirit of armies, the official services of their Teachers are not likely to produce it. It is more likely to flow from the labours of a spontaneous zeal. The armies of the Puritans had their appointed Chaplains; but without these there would have been no lack of public devotion in that devout age.
>
> The case of navies with insulated crews may be less within the scope of these reflections. But it is not entirely so. The chance of a devout officer, might be of as much worth to religion, as the service of an ordi-

nary chaplain (were it admitted that religion has a real interest in the matter). But we are always to keep in mind that it is safer to trust the consequences of a right principle, than reasonings in support of a bad one.[87]

It should be noted that Madison recognized, although he rejected, a possible exception in the "case of navies with insulated crews." Today, soldiers serving far away from their home towns are practically as "insulated" as navies, and it is because of this insulation that chaplains in the armed forces may be justified under the First Amendment's guaranty of religious freedom. This point has already been discussed,[88] and need not be repeated here. Military chaplains can also be justified constitutionally on a ground that is basically Erastian. As will be shown in Part III of this volume, the religious freedom guaranteed in the First Amendment may constitutionally be restricted where necessary for the protection of an interest deemed more important to the community than the unrestricted exercise of religion. Thus, since the protection of the country from its warring enemies is more important to the community than the right to abstain from warfare on religious grounds, religious conviction need not constitutionally be accepted as an excuse for refusal to serve in the armed forces.

The same reasoning is applicable to all the other guaranties of the Bill of Rights; speech, for example, may be restricted during wartime to an extent not permissible in times of peace.[89] It is equally applicable to the First Amendment's guaranty against religious establishments. If, therefore, the expenditure of government funds for religious purposes is militarily necessary, it is constitutionally permissible.

The importance of religious exhortation as a morale factor in war was recognized as far back as Biblical times. Moses commanded the Israelites that:

> When thou goest out to battle against thine enemies, and seest horses and chariots, and a people more than thou, be not afraid of them; for the Lord thy God is with thee, which brought thee up out of the land of Egypt.
> And it shall be, when ye are come nigh unto the battle, that the priest shall approach and speak unto the people,
> And shall say unto them, Hear, O Israel, ye approach this day unto battle against your enemies: let not your hearts faint, fear not, and do not tremble, neither be ye terrified because of them;
> For the Lord your God is he that goeth with you, to fight for you against your enemies, to save you.[90]

It may reasonable be argued that the army chaplain of today serves essentially the same purpose as the Israelite priest. On that basis, the higher urgency of military defense constitutionally permits the expenditure of public funds to pay the salaries of chaplains in the armed forces.

## RELIGIOUS TEST FOR PUBLIC OFFICE

A state united with or closely related to a church would be expected to require its officials to be members of that church and swear their allegiance to its doctrines. When the Anglican Church was finally established as the official church of England by the Act of Supremacy of 1558, it was natural that holders of state office would be required to subscribe to an oath accepting the Queen as supreme governor of all things, ecclesiastical as well as temporal.[91] In 1562 this oath was extended to teachers, lawyers, court officials, sheriffs, and members of the House of Commons.[92] Under James I, "popish recusants," convicted under one of the uniformity or supremacy acts, were denied access to the courts, and "thereby disabled to exercise any public office or charge in the commonwealth."[93] Under Charles II, a sacramental test "according to the rites of the church of England" was imposed on all municipal officials, and all officeholders, civil and military, were required to take the sacrament and make a declaration against the Roman Catholic doctrine of transubstantiation.[94]

As the American colonies inherited from their mother country the general pattern of the relations of church and state, so too did they on the whole inherit the subsidiary pattern of religious tests for public office. For a short time Rhode Island was an exception, following as it did the philosophy of its founder, Roger Williams, who, as we have seen[95] had asserted that to limit civil magistrates to church members was like permitting only church members to assume "the office of a Doctor of Physic, a Master or a Pilot of a Ship, or a Captain or Commander of a Band or Army of men." However, by the beginning of the eighteenth century, Rhode Island had adopted the pattern prevailing among the other colonies and had enacted a law that limited citizenship and eligibility for public office to Protestants.[96]

At the time the colonies declared their independence of England and established themselves as independent states, religious tests for office, either through a test oath or specific disqualification, were widespread, if not practically universal. The most liberal was that prescribed by Pennsylvania which required of officeholders a belief that God was "the rewarder of the good and the punisher of the wicked," and thus was broad enough to encompass most theists. At the other extreme was the North Carolina constitution of 1776 which provided: "That no person who shall deny the being of God or the truth of the Protestant religion, or the divine authority of either of the Old or New Testaments, or who shall hold religious principles incompatible with the freedom and safety of the State, shall be capable of holding any office or place of trust or profit in the civil department within this State." Belief in the Protestant religion was also required by the constitutions of New Hampshire, New Jersey, and South Carolina. Between these extremes was the Delaware constitution which required "Faith in God the Father and in Jesus Christ, His only Son, and in the Holy Ghost, one God, blessed for evermore." Maryland and Massachusetts likewise required only a belief in the Christian religion.

Since religious tests for public office were an incident of state-church union, it was natural and inevitable that the assault on such unions, which culminated with the final disestablishment of the Congregationalist Church in Massachusetts in 1833, would bring with it and as part of it an assault on religious tests.

Thus, for example, while the major issue which brought on disestablishment in Virginia was taxation for religious purposes, the Bill for Establishing Religious Freedom, by which disestablishment was effected in 1786, had as its purpose not only the prohibition of taxation of citizens for the support of churches, but also a ban on disqualification for public office based on religious beliefs. This is indicated clearly by the preamble to the Bill, part of which reads:

> That our civil rights have no dependence on our religious opinions, any more than on our opinions in physics or geometry; that therefore the proscribing of any citizen as unworthy of public confidence by laying upon him an incapacity of being called to offices of trust and emolument, unless he profess or renounce this or that religious opinion, is depriving him injuriously of those privileges and advantages to which in common with his fellow citizens he has a natural right; that it tends only to corrupt the principle of that religion it is meant to encourage by bribing with a monopoly of worldly honor and emoluments, those who will externally profess and conform to it.

At the Federal Constitutional Convention which met in Philadelphia in 1787, Charles Pinckney of South Carolina introduced what was in slightly modified form to become the last clause of Article VI of the United States Constitution. It was, he told the convention, "a provision the world will expect from you in the establishment of a System founded on Republican principles and in an age so liberal and enlightened as the present."[97] Roger Sherman of Connecticut thought the prohibition unnecessary as he could not conceive that anyone would seek to impose a religious test for public office under the Federal government.[98] Luther Martin of Maryland was later to relate that when the clause was under consideration "there were some members so unfashionable as to think that a belief in the existence of a Deity, and of a state of future rewards and punishments would be some security for the good conduct of our rulers, and that, in a Christian country, it would be at least decent to hold out some distinction between the professors of Christianity and downright infidelity or paganism."[99] However, when the vote was taken after a short debate, it was unanimous, and the clause was added to provide that "no religious Test shall ever be required as a Qualification to any Office or public Trust under the United States."[100]

This ban on religious tests for public office aroused some controversy in the state legislatures and ratification conventions, since most of the states retained some form of religious tests for state office. Accordingly, proponents of the new Constitution found it necessary to justify the prohibition of religious tests for Federal office.

Thus, Oliver Ellsworth, later Chief Justice of the United States, dealt with the religious test clause in one of a series of published letters on the proposed Federal Constitution. He explained that the sole purpose of the clause was to exclude persecution and to provide religious liberty, a right of human nature which few other people in the world shared. He pointed out that if any test oath were to be imposed, the least exceptionable would be one requiring all persons appointed to office to declare, at the time of their admission, their belief in the being of a God, and in the divine authority of the Scriptures. In favor of such a test, he explained, it might be said that one who believed these great truths would not be so likely to violate his obligations to his country as one who disbelieved them. However, he rejected this argument. The making of a declaration of such a belief, he said, would be no security at all. For an unprincipled man believing in neither the work nor the being of God and governed merely by selfish motives would easily make a public declaration of his belief in the creed which the law prescribed, and excuse himself by calling it a mere formality. Test oaths, he continued, would bar from public office honest men, men of principle, who would rather suffer an injury than act contrary to their consciences. It is within the authority of the people to choose their officers, he stated, and if they wished to insure that those appointed to public offices would be sincere friends of religion, they should take care to choose such persons and not rely upon "cob-web barriers as test-laws are."

Connecticut, he said, had never thought it expedient to adopt a test-law and yet religion and morality were as extensive in that state as in England, where "every person who holds a public office must either be a saint by law or a hypocrite by practice."[101]

Ellsworth's views represented the consensus of the generation that wrote and approved the Constitution,[102] and while Article VI was by its terms limited to Federal offices it was only a question of time before its mandate spread to the states by their voluntary actions in writing their own constitutions. By about the middle of the nineteenth century the last vestiges of religious tests based upon belief in or adherence to Protestantism or even Christianity had disappeared. However, the constitutions of eight states (Arkansas, Maryland, Mississippi, North Carolina, Pennsylvania, South Carolina, Tennessee, and Texas) either required or authorized the legislature to require an oath or declaration of a belief in God as a qualification for public office. Typical of these was Article 37 of the Declaration of Rights of the Maryland Constitution, which provided that "no religious test ought ever to be required as a qualification for any office of profit or trust in this State, other than a declaration of belief in the existence of God."

It was not until 1961 that the United States Supreme Court had occasion to pass on the validity of these provisions under the Federal Constitution. Roy Torcaso, a resident of Maryland, had been appointed to the office of notary public by the governor of Maryland, but was refused a commission to serve because he would not make an oath or declaration that he believed in the existence of God. He then brought suit to compel the issuance of the commission on the ground that the state's requirement that he declare this belief violated the First Amendment, which bans laws respecting an establishment of religion or prohibiting the free exercise thereof, and the Fourteenth Amendment, which, as we have seen,[103] had on numerous occasions been interpreted by the Supreme Court as making the provisions of the First Amendment applicable against the states. Unsuccessful in the Maryland state courts, he appealed to the United States Supreme Court.

In a unanimous decision (Torcaso vs. Watkins)[104] the Supreme Court in 1961 upheld Torcaso's contentions and declared the Maryland religious oath requirement to be unconstitutional. While the language of the Court's opinion is not precise as to the exact basis of its decision, it seems reasonably clear that the Court relied on both the no-establishment and the free-exercise clauses of the First Amendment. As to the former, the Court reiterated its interpretation that the clause does not merely bar preferential treatment of one religion over other religions (although even such limited interpretation would require invalidation of Maryland's oath requirement since it preferred theistic faiths over nontheistic faiths such as "Buddhism, Taoism, Ethical Culture, Secular Humanism and others"), but also preferential treatment of religion as against nonreligion. "We repeat and again reaffirm," the Court's opinion, written by Justice Hugo Black, said, "that neither a State nor the Federal Government can constitutionally force a person 'to profess a belief or disbelief in any religion.' Neither can constitutionally pass laws or impose requirements which aid all religions as against non-believers, and neither can aid those religions based on a belief in the existence of God against those religions founded on different beliefs."

The Court concluded its opinion by stating: "This Maryland religious test for public office unconstitutionally invades the appellant's freedom of belief and religion and therefore cannot be enforced against him."

## RELIGION IN COURT PROCEEDINGS

Religious intervention in judicial proceedings involves principally the use of the Bible to swear witnesses, and the disqualification as witnesses of persons who do not believe in God or a future life of rewards and punishments. Litigation in the family courts, such as cases of divorce and the custody and upbringing of children, gives rise to special problems, which are treated in more detail elsewhere in this volume.[105] Here we deal with the problem as it affects courts generally.

The use of the Bible in many courts to swear witnesses is in most cases little more than a ceremonial act similar to the use of the expression "So help me God." The version generally used is the King James edition, though Catholics and Jews would today rarely encounter difficulty in using either the Bible acceptable to their respective faiths or no Bible at all. The real problem is the qualification or disqualification of witnesses who reject the proffered Bible not because of its specific version but because they do not believe in the tenets of any religion.

Under the common law no person might qualify as a witness or affiant in a judicial proceeding unless he believed in a Supreme Being and in a future life of rewards and punishments. Though the purported justification for this rule was that only the fear of punishment by a supernatural force could assure veracity in testimony, it is likely that the rule was at least partly one of the consequences of the established church-state relation in England. According to Lord Coke not only atheists but nonconformists as well were deemed *perpetui inimici,* eternal enemies, not worthy of belief and therefore disqualified as witnesses. Practical considerations of domestic and international commercial relations required the modification of this doctrine, and at the time of the American Revolution the English courts admitted the testimony of Jews and other non-Christians at least in commercial cases.[106] It was, however, not until 1869 that Parliament, by statute, removed the disqualification of nonbelievers.[107]

The American courts, as part of their inheritance of the English common law system, naturally adopted the rule disqualifying disbelievers.[108] Under the Federal Judiciary Act of 1789, no witness could testify who "did not believe that there is a God who rewards truth and avenges falsehood." This rule was changed by an amendment enacted by Congress in 1906, providing that the competency of a witness to testify is to be determined by the laws of the state in which the court is held. By that time most of the states, by constitution, statute, or decision, had removed the disqualification of nonbelievers. Typical of the constitutional provisions is the mandate of the New York constitution of 1846 that "no person shall be rendered incompetent to be a witness on account of his opinions on matters of religious belief." Today at least forty-one of the fifty states have removed the disqualification of nonbelievers as witnesses in courts.[109]

It is quite likely that even in the states[110] that do not have specific constitutional or statutory modification of the common law disqualification of nonbelievers, the rule would not be followed. A constitutional provision, such as is contained in the constitution of New Jersey, forbidding the denial of any civil right because of religious principles, would seem to preclude disqualification of witnesses on grounds of religious nonbelief. Aside, however, from state law, the Federal constitutionality of the disqualification is at least questionable. The issue has never been squarely decided by the United States Supreme Court, although in 1900 the Court upheld a Federal statute that required that the testimony of Chinese, in certain cases, be corroborated by that of white men, because of the "loose notions entertained by [Chinese] witnesses of the obligation of an oath."[111] It would seem clear that if a defendant in a criminal case or a party in a civil case could not take the stand in his own behalf because of his religious beliefs or disbeliefs, he would be deprived of his liberty or property without due process of law and would be denied the equal protection of the laws in violation of the Fourteenth Amendment. Moreover, as we shall see later, the "free exercise" clause of the First

Amendment protects religious disbelief as well as belief, and the disqualification would appear to violate that provision as well. Even if the disbeliever is a witness rather than a party, it is fairly arguable that both the witness and the party seeking to use his testimony are deprived of constitutional rights. It need hardly be added that willingness to profess a belief in God and a future state of rewards and punishments is not considered by any state as an adequate assurance of testimonial veracity; perjury, under all state statutes, is punishable in this world. In any event, the Supreme Court's decision in Torcaso vs. Watkins[112] would probably require that nonbelievers be permitted to testify equally with believers.

## THE CHURCH AND THE DIVORCE COURT

Two aspects of church intervention on divorce litigation deserve brief consideration here. The first item concerns an address delivered by Pope Pius XII, November 7, 1949, before the Union of Catholic Italian Lawyers. In this address the Pope outlined the obligations of Catholic civil judges under ecclesiastical law. The Catholic judge, he said, may not issue a decision that "would oblige those affected by it to perform . . . an act which in itself is contrary to the law of God and of the Church." The judge "cannot shirk responsibility for his decisions and place the blame on the law and its authors. When he delivers a judgment in accordance with the law, the judge becomes an accessory to the fact and therefore is equally responsible for its results."

The case in which this conflict between the law of the Catholic Church and the law of the state is most likely to occur is divorce litigation; and as to this the Pope was clear and specific. "The Catholic judge," he said, "cannot pronounce, unless for motives of great moment, a decision of civil divorce (where it does exist) in a marriage valid before God and the Church." The Vatican made it clear that the Pope's mandate was applicable to divorces between non-Catholics as well as between Catholics. The National Catholic Welfare Conference issued a statement explaining the Pope's address in the following words:

> The quote attributed to the Holy Father does not represent a newly arrived at position of the Catholic Church. The common view of theologians holds that the judge in pronouncing a divorce is merely making an official declaration that the state regards the civil effects of the marriage as no longer existing.
> Since this declaration is in itself a morally indifferent action, it can be

permitted, at least in certain circumstances. In developing this point, Father Francis J. Connell, distinguished moral theologian, in his volume, "Morals and Politics in Professions," published in 1946, makes the following statement:

"The Catholic judge knows that the marriage itself cannot be dissolved by the state, and in granting a divorce he has no intention of exempting the parties from anything more than the legal recognition of the effects of their marriage. Nevertheless, when the judge foresees the probability or the certainty of an attempted remarriage, his act of granting the divorce is material cooperation toward this sin. Hence, according to the principles of cooperation, there must be a good reason for performing this act—a reason sufficiently weighty to justify the permitting of the evil effect. Such a reason would seem to be present if the judge were in danger of losing his office in the event that he refuses to accept a divorce suit, or even if serious antagonism and loss of prestige ensued. But if, without any grave inconvenience, he can avoid a divorce case which will probably be the occasion for an invalid remarriage, he is bound to do so."[113]

It is at least arguable that even as qualified by this statement, a Catholic judge's adherence to the Pope's dictate would require him to violate his oath of office. This was the view of a Catholic judge of a New Mexico district court, Luis Amijo, who said he would refuse to be bound by the Pope's ruling because his oath of office and his duty as a citizen of the United States took precedence over his obligations as a Catholic.[114] Glenn L. Archer, Executive Director of Protestants and Other Americans United for Separation of Church and State, called for the resignation of all other Catholic judges who refused to make similar affirmations.[115] As far as is known, no other Catholic judge made such an affirmation, nor did any resign. But lawyers practicing in the divorce courts have not noticed that any of the many Catholic judges evidenced any noticeable reluctance to grant divorces after the Pope's address.

The second aspect of this problem of religion in the divorce courts was raised by section 12 of the Illinois Domestic Relations Court Act of 1949, which provided that

In any hearing by the Divorce Division, the master shall ascertain the possibility of effecting a reconciliation of the parties, and, where deemed feasible, may invite the assistance of representatives of religious denominations to which the parties belong.

The Act in its entirety was declared void by the Supreme Court of Illinois for a variety of reasons. What concerns us here is its invalidation of the provision for attempted reconciliation. In doing so, the court stated:

. . . Section 12 admits of the construction . . . that a master, in his sole discretion, may invite the representatives of religious denominations to any hearing without the acquiescence of the parties. It may well be that a person seeking a divorce does not desire attempts at reconciliation. Indeed, a party may, for reasons sufficient to himself or herself, oppose such an effort. Section 12 does not require, as a prerequisite, the consent of the parties to an attempt to effect a reconciliation. There is no statutory restraint as to the number of persons who may be called in by the master in his attempt to reconcile the parties. Reconciliation attempts could easily develop into inquisitions. . . .

We are of the opinion that the situation presented in Illinois ex rel. McCollum v Board of Education, 333 U.S. 203, is similar. . . . [The released-time] arrangement, the Supreme Court of the United States held, violated the constitutional principle of separation of church and State guaranteed by the first amendment to the Federal Constitution and made applicable to the States by the fourteenth amendment. "This," the court said, "is beyond all question a utilization of the tax established and tax supported public school system to aid religious groups to spread their faith." In like manner and to a greater degree than in the *McCollum* case, by permitting a master in chancery to summon the minister, priest, rabbi, or other representative, to a hearing for the purpose of effecting a reconciliation, the statute utilizes a tax established and tax supported instrumentality for the administration of justice to aid religious groups to spread their faith. It is a matter of common knowledge that divorce is more abhorrent and reprehensible to some religious faiths than to others. Indeed, some religious groups do not recognize the validity of a divorce decree rendered by a civil court. Petitioner raises the legitimate query as to how representatives of those religious faiths can be expected to respond to an invitation to repair to and aid a civil court when their religion considers the proceedings a nullity. On the other hand, if they do cooperate, the representatives of those religious faiths may be more successful in effecting reconciliations than the representatives of other groups; but apart from the fact that the Divorce Division might find itself serving as the vehicle for spreading a particular faith, there would be an element of compulsion present which our basic law does not sanction.[116]

The decision was severely criticized by Archbishop (later Cardinal) Richard J. Cushing of Boston on the ground that "the First Amendment . . . has nothing to do with the separation of a man from his wife any more than it has to do with a clergyman preventing them from separating."[117] This is no doubt very much of an overstatement; nevertheless, consultation by courts with clergymen in cases involving family relations are quite common, and while this fact is not proof of the unconstitutionality of the practice, a reasonable argument can be made that the interest of the state in preserving the family justifies such consultation, provided the parties to the proceeding consent thereto.

## RELIGION IN THE CENSUS

Article I of the Constitution requires the taking of a census of the population every ten years. The scope of questions asked expanded throughout the years so that by the year 1950 it included sex, age, occupations, educational attainment, and agricultural and industrial activities. At no time, however, did a decennial census include any inquiry on religious affiliation and belief. Madison had in fact expressed reservations regarding the propriety of inquiring as to professions on the ground that "As to those who are employed in teaching and inculcating the duties of religion, there may be some indelicacy in singling them out, as the General Government is proscribed from interfering, in any manner whatever, in matters of religion; and it may be thought to do this, in ascertaining who are and who are not ministers of the Gospel."[118]

However, beginning in 1926, the Census Bureau, under Congressional authority, did take a Census of Religious Bodies. This provided detailed statistics on the number of churches and church members, religious education, church finances, and related items. Covering all organized churches, it was taken by questionnaires mailed to church officers. It was always carried out with the cooperation of central church organizations, and no attempt was ever made to request information from individuals as to their beliefs and affiliations.

The Census of Religious Bodies was taken again in 1936, but was not taken in 1946, in part because of objection by the Christian Science Church,[119] even though the Census Law had been amended to exempt from compulsory disclosure any denomination whose "doctrine, teaching or discipline" prohibited "the disclosure of information relative to membership."[120]

In 1956, the Census of Religious Bodies was again passed up, but in April of that year the director of the Bureau of the Census announced that inclusion in the 1960 decennial census of a question on religious affiliation was under consideration. Although not announced publicly, the Bureau had tentatively decided that the form of the question would be "What is your religion," and the person questioned would be requested to answer in one of five categories: Catholic, Jewish, Protestant, other, or none. To meet possible objections it was first thought to make answering to this question voluntary, but the idea was given up as impracticable. The announcement at first evoked no significant public reaction, but in May 1957, the American Jewish Congress officially took the position that it opposed the religious inquiry as unwise and unconstitutional, and undertook leadership in a public educational campaign against the proposal.[121]

This action by the Jewish organization brought the issue into the arena of public discussion. Organizations expressed themselves pro and con, and newspapers editorialized on the subject. Favoring inclusion of the question in the 1960 census were organizations and publications associated with the Roman Catholic Church and demographers and other social scientists, who deemed the information sought to be elicited by the inclusion to be valuable for their studies. Opposed to the inclusion were, besides the American Jewish Congress and other Jewish groups, the Seventh Day Adventist organizations, the Baptists Joint Committee on Public Affairs, and the American Civil Liberties Union.

The arguments in favor of inclusion were that (1) church groups would be helped in church planning and recruitment if information on the religious complexion of the American community were obtained; (2) the information would be useful to social scientists; (3) it would constitute a recognition that, as the Supreme Court said in the Zorach case, "we are a religious people."

The case against inclusion was set forth in a letter signed by Dr. Israel Goldstein, president of the American Jewish Congress, to the New York *Times* and reprinted in a number of other leading newspapers throughout the nation.[122] The letter read in part:

> This innovation, if adopted, would represent a radical breach of tradition that goes back to the very first census conducted in 1790. At that time James Madison, father of our Constitution and author of the Bill of Rights, opposed the inclusion of any questions in the census that might elicit the religion of the person questioned.
>
> Since that time our Government has studiously refrained from including in the census questions regarding religious affiliation and belief. The Census Bureau has consistently refused requests of church groups on the ground that inclusion of such questions would violate the constitutional provision for the separation of church and state.
>
> There are many reasons why our Government should abide by this long-standing tradition. In the first place, inclusion of such questions would violate the constitutional guarantee of freedom of religion. Under Federal law persons questioned by census takers are subject to conviction and imprisonment as criminals should they refuse to answer the census taker.
>
> The Supreme Court has expressly and repeatedly held that under the First Amendment to the Constitution, which guarantees the free exercise of religion, the Government has no power to compel any person to profess a belief or disbelief in any religion.
>
> In the second place, it is alien to our concepts and traditions to di-

vide and classify Americans in categories of religious and nonreligious and sub-categories of sect and denomination.

Third, it would violate the constitutional guarantee for the separation of church and state since it would make out of the Federal Government an agent of religious groups and would employ Government instrumentalities for church purposes.

Fourth, it would constitute an unwarranted impingement upon the privacy of Americans. In a totalitarian society no interest of the people is deemed outside the jurisdiction and concern of the state. A democracy, on the other hand, is predicated upon the assumption that the state has only such powers and jurisdiction as are freely granted to it by the people, and that certain areas of the people's lives are too sacred to be assigned to the state, and that chief among these is the relationship of man to his Maker.

The Supreme Court has only recently held that congressional investigating committees may not inquire into areas in which they are forbidden by the Constitution to legislate. What is true of Congress is true of all other branches of the Federal Government. Under our Constitution, the Government is prohibited from acting in the area of religion. In the words of Madison, religion is outside its jurisdiction. Since the Government cannot act in the area of religion it has no power to conduct inquiries in that area.

Finally, inclusion of such questions in the Federal census would create a dangerous precedent, the full extent of whose portentous consequences and implications cannot be anticipated. If Americans can be compelled to disclose to Government officers their religious beliefs they can equally be compelled to disclose their political, economic, social and all other beliefs.

For a century and three quarters our Government has scrupulously refrained from compelling Americans to disclose their religious beliefs. Abandonment of this tradition at the present time by inclusion of questions on religion in this Federal census will inevitably lead to further encroachments upon the liberties of Americans.

To require, under penalty of law, an individual to disclose his religion, would seem to be inconsistent with the statement made by Jefferson that: "I never will, by any word or act, bow to the shame of intolerance, or admit a right of inquiry into the religious opinion of others."[123] It would also seem inconsistent with what may well be described as the universal American consensus that "religion is a private matter."

In any event, and whatever the reason, the opposition to inclusion proved effective. On December 12, 1957, the Bureau of Census issued a statement that the 1960 Census of Population would not include an inquiry on religion. The reason, according to the statement, was "recognition of the fact that at this time a considerable number of persons would be reluctant to answer such a question in the

Census where a reply is mandatory. Under the circumstances it was not believed that the value of the statistics based on this question would be great enough to justify overruling such an attitude."[124]

Whether this finally disposed of the matter, or whether, as indicated on a supplementary statement issued by the Census Bureau in January 1958, the issue would be revived before the 1970 census, will shortly be seen.[125]

### CHAPTER EIGHT

# State Intervention in Church Affairs

## PROCLAMATION OF THANKSGIVING, FASTS, AND PRAYERS

GOVERNMENT PROCLAMATIONS of days of thanksgiving and occasionally prayer are another illustration of ceremonial acts of government which are of slight intrinsic significance but are of great importance in the use to which they are put as precedents to justify far more substantial encroachments of government on religious affairs or religion on government affairs. As a practical matter there is no way in which the constitutionality of such proclamations can legally be tested, assuming there were a defender either of separation or secularism sufficiently zealous to undertake litigation. Accordingly their constitutionality is generally taken for granted, and they become another item of evidence in the "common sense" interpretation of the First Amendment.

It would, however, be entirely erroneous to assume that the constitutionality of government proclamations of thanksgiving and prayer has always been accepted without question. The practice began during the period of the Continental Congress, which legislated on such religious matters as sins, repentance, humiliation, divine service, reformation, mourning, public worship, funerals, true religion, chaplains, etc.[1] Among this myriad of religious matters were naturally included resolutions fixing days for thanksgiving, prayer, and fasting. On the establishment of the new Constitution, with its concept of religion being beyond the ken of the Federal government, most of these items disappeared from the scope of Congressional or other government action. Comparatively few were continued by the new Congress. Congressional chaplaincy was, as we have seen, one of these; government proclamation of Thanksgiving Day was another. But though the chaplaincy was retained without protest, objection was raised to Thanksgiving. When, in the first Congress after the adoption of the Federal Constitution, a resolution was offered to request the President to "recommend to the People of the United States a day of Thanksgiving and Prayer, to be observed by acknowledging with grateful hearts the many signal favours of Almighty God," objection was raised by another member of Congress that "it is a business with which Congress has nothing to do; it is a religious matter, and as such is proscribed to us."[2]

Notwithstanding this objection the resolution carried, and in 1789 Washington proclaimed a day of national thanksgiving, which he followed with several others during his administration. Although Washington took pains to frame his proclamations in language acceptable to all faiths, his successor, Adams, called for Christian worship. Jefferson refused to issue any religious proclamations; but Madison, though "disinclined to such interpositions of the Executive," nevertheless could not resist the demands, and compromised by using "general terms," for which he was "reproached" by those who thought he should have inserted "particulars according with the faith of certain Christian sects."[3] With one exception, Madison's successors followed his example, and issued thanksgiving and prayer proclamations in nonsectarian terms. The exception was Andrew Jackson, who shared Jefferson's views and steadfastly refused to issue any thanksgiving proclamation.[4]

In a letter to a Presbyterian clergyman, written in 1808, Jefferson explained his reasons for refusing to issue proclamations for prayers or fasts:

> . . . I consider the government of the United States as interdicted by the Constitution from intermeddling with religious institutions, their doctrines, discipline, or exercises. This results not only from the provision that no law shall be made respecting the establishment or free exercise of religion, but from that also which reserves to the States the powers not delegated to the United States. Certainly, no power to prescribe any religious exercise, or to assume authority in religious discipline, has been delegated to the General Government. It must then rest with the States, as far as it can be in any human authority. But it is only proposed that I should recommend not prescribe a day of fasting and prayer. That is, that I should indirectly assume to the United States an authority over religious exercises, which the Constitution has directly precluded them from. . . . I do not believe it is for the interest of religion to invite the civil magistrate to direct its exercises, its discipline, or its doctrine; nor of the religious societies, that the General Government should be invested with the power of effecting any uniformity of time or manner among them. Fasting and prayer are religious exercises; the enjoining them an act of discipline. Every religious society has a right to determine for itself the times for these exercises, and the objects proper for them, according to their own particular tenets; and the right can never be safer than in their hands, where the Constitution has deposited it.[5]

This letter shows fairly conclusively that Jefferson interpreted the First Amendment as restricting not only Congress but the President as well.[6] Madison clearly shared this view.

Madison was unable to resist the demands to proclaim a day of thanksgiving, but after retiring from the Presidency he set forth five objections to the practice: (1) an executive proclamation can be only a recommendation, and an advisory government is a contradiction in terms; (2) in any event, it cannot act in ecclesiastical matters; (3) a Presidential proclamation implies the erroneous idea of a national religion; (4) the tendency of the practice is "to narrow the recommendation to the standard of the predominant sect," as is evidenced by Adams's calling for a Christian worship; (5) "the liability of the practice to a subserviency to political views, to the scandal of religion as well as the increase of party animosities."[7]

That the last fear was not entirely without foundation is indicated by the bitterness engendered among pro-French Republicans by Adams's proclamation of a day of fasting and prayer for protection from "the dangers which threaten it" from "the unfriendly disposition, conduct and demands of a foreign power."[8] Jackson refused to issue a proclamation for prayer because he believed he would be "transcending the limits prescribed by the constitution for the President," and "might disturb the security which religion now enjoys in the country, in its complete separation from the political concerns of the General Government," and this refusal aroused a storm of controversy throughout the nation.[9]

During the Civil War period Presidential proclamations of prayer and thanksgiving likewise aroused controversy and ill will because of the political use to which they were put; but it remained for a later generation to witness a Presidential proclamation of thanksgiving serving not only politics but Mammon as well. In 1939 the department store industry felt that commercial interests would be furthered if a longer buying period intervened between Thanksgiving and Christmas. Yielding to its demands, President Franklin D. Roosevelt decided to advance the holiday, and, breaking the tradition which went back to Lincoln's day, he proclaimed Thanksgiving for one week earlier than the last Thursday in November. This action aroused widespread resentment, and there was much bitter editorial criticism. As a result, in the fall of 1941 the President announced that he planned to return to the traditional last Thursday in November. This of course disappointed the commercial interests, which were able to induce Congress to adopt by resolution at least part of what the President was so bitterly criticized for doing by proclamation. Accordingly, by direction of Congress, Thanksgiving is now celebrated on the fourth instead of the last Thursday in November.[10] Editorial criticism of this act of Congress was conspicuously absent from the country's leading newspapers, which gives rise to the reasonable inference that politics played a not inconsiderable role in this very nonspiritual misalliance of government, profit, and religion.

## CLOSING PUBLIC BUILDINGS ON RELIGIOUS HOLIDAYS

The practice of closing government offices, public schools, and other public offices on Sundays, Christmas, Thanksgiving, New Year's Day, and—increasingly—Good Friday, may be interpreted as government recognition of these religious holidays and an assumption of their religious obligations. Sunday observance presents a special problem of its own, which will be considered in the next section. New Year's Day has long lost its Christological significance, and if it has any relation to religion today it is to the cult of Bacchus rather than of Jesus. Thanksgiving retains something of its spiritual origin, and many Americans observe it religiously; but the religious element is almost pantheistic and the nationalist element so dominant that it is closer to Washington's Birthday or Independence Day than it is to a religious holiday.

Christmas, despite its commercialization and occasional Dionysian celebrations, and Good Friday are clearly religious holy days, and their observance as government holidays might be deemed inconsistent with the principle of the separation of church and state. Moreover, since they are Christian holy days, such observance could not be justified even under the narrow interpretation of the principle of separation which allows the nonpreferential recognition of religion.

There is a basic distinction between a ceremonial observance by government of a religious holiday and the closing of public buildings on that day. The former includes such acts as executive proclamations, legislative prayers, special celebrations in the public schools, and the placing of religious symbols like crucifixes, holy mangers, etc., in public buildings. Such acts as these would seem to violate the spirit, if not the letter, of the First Amendment, by a commingling of the secular and the sacred. An illustration of this type of ceremonial observance by government is the following special Good Friday proclamation issued by the mayor of Waco, Texas, in 1941:

> I urge that business houses join in a cessation of all activities on Good Friday between the hours of 12 noon and 3 P.M., and urge everyone to take advantage of this pause from official duties for prayer and observance of this day. I urge all citizens to lend their wholehearted support to the observance of this day through meditation and prayer, in holy remembrance of the crucifixion of our Lord, and reflect upon the

greatest message of love mortals have ever heard—"For God so loved the world, that He gave His only begotten Son, that whosoever believeth in Him should not perish, but have everlasting life."[11]

Waco is a large city with many Jewish residents, and even many non-Jews who do not believe in Jesus in the sense intended by the mayor. It would seem less than Christian charity for a mayor elected by all the citizens, whose salary is paid by all the citizens, to assign a good portion of his constituents by official proclamation to the deprivation of everlasting life.

This proclamation is far from unique. An increasing number of state and municipal heads are issuing Good Friday proclamations only slightly less sectarian in tone. In Washington, in 1952, a "cross of lights" decorated many government buildings as part of the capital's observance of Good Friday.[12] In 1951 a resolution was introduced in Congress providing that the flag of the United States be flown at half staff between noon and three o'clock in the afternoon on Good Friday.[13]

Ceremonial observances like these are surely improper in a country founded on the principle of the independence of church and state. A different case, however, is presented by the closing of public buildings on religious holidays, including Good Friday. Government employees whose religious convictions require them to abstain from work or to attend church on religious holidays may, consistently with the First Amendment, be excused on those days—at least if the time so lost is made up or accounted for as permissible absence for personal reasons. The religious freedom clause of the First Amendment would prohibit the penalization of children absenting themselves from school on religious holidays. If, in a specific community, the number of children and teachers adhering to a certain faith is so large that keeping the public schools open on a holy day of that faith for a small minority would be economically wasteful—particularly as the work covered on that day would have to be repeated—it is quite proper for the public school authorities, as an administrative matter, to keep the schools entirely closed on that day. This thought was expressed in the *St. Louis Register,* official organ of the Catholic archdiocese, in criticizing a court decision that certain parochial schools were illegally incorporated into the public school system:[14]

> The judge objects to the closing of school on days of obligation in the Catholic Church. And yet it is a universal public school practice to allow Jewish children and others to be absent from school on their sacred days. If, as in Franklin County schools, Catholic school children so dis-

missed are so numerous as to render impractical the holding of classes on those days, this is but the recognition of a fact, not subservience to a Church.

This reasoning, which appears valid, is equally applicable to the closing of public schools on Jewish holy days in localities where Jews constitute a substantial segment of the population. Thus, in many sections of New York City, as well as in the Jewish sections of many other large cities, classrooms are practically deserted, by both children and teachers, on Rosh Hashonnah and Yom Kippur. It is for this reason that the New York City Board of Education authorizes the closing of New York City public schools on these days.[15] It is this administrative recognition of a fact that justifies the closing of public schools and other public buildings on Sundays, Christmas, and, in some communities, Good Friday.

<h3 style="text-align:center">SUNDAY LAWS</h3>

<h4 style="text-align:center">Historical Background</h4>

Compulsory observance of the Sabbath goes back, of course, to Mount Sinai, and the command that

> Ye shall keep the sabbath therefore; for it is holy unto you: every one that defileth it shall surely be put to death: for whosoever doeth any work therein, that soul shall be cut off from among his people. Six days may work be done; but in the seventh is the sabbath of rest, holy to the Lord; whosoever doeth any work in the sabbath day, he shall surely be put to death.[16]

The Sabbath of Sinai was the seventh day of the week; the earliest recognition of Sunday by Christians is recorded by Justin Martyr, who reported that in the 2nd century the Christians of Rome gathered on that day to hear readings from the Scriptures, participate in common prayer, and dine together, in the manner in which the Jews celebrated the Biblical Sabbath.[17] Sunday was selected as it was the day of the resurrection of Jesus; but it was also the day observed by the Mithraists, another popular cult, as the day of the Sun-god. Constantine, as part of his program of empire unification, promulgated the first compulsory Sunday law in the year 321. The law read:

> All judges and city people and the craftsmen shall rest upon the venerable Day of the Sun. Country people, however, may freely attend to the cultivation of the fields, because it frequently happens that no other days are better adapted for planting the grain in the furrows or the vines in the trenches. So that the advantage given by heavenly providence may not for the occasion of a short time perish.

At about the same time soldiers in the army were commanded to worship on the Lord's day; law suits were prohibited on that day, and circus spectacles and theatrical shows were likewise forbidden.[18]

Thereafter Sunday observance laws were promulgated in Gaul under the Merovingian kings and Charlemagne, and in England under the Anglo-Saxon kings. One American court epitomized the history of Sunday legislation as follows:

> All Sunday legislation is the product of pagan Rome; the Saxon laws were the product of Middle Age legislation of the Holy Roman Empire. The English laws are the expansion of the Saxon, and the American are the transcript of the English. . . . During the Middle Ages, the civil authorities exercised the right to legislate in religious matters after the manner of the Jewish theocracy.[19]

Most Sunday laws in the United States are based on the English statute of 1697 in the reign of Charles II. The statute provided:

> For the better observation and keeping holy the Lord's Day commonly called Sunday, bee it enacted . . . that . . . all and every person . . . shall on every Lord's Day apply themselves to the observation of the same by exercising themselves thereon in the dutyes and piety and true religion publiquely and privately and that no tradesman, artificer, workman, labourer or other person whatsoever shall doe or exercise any wordly labour . . . [or] publicly cry, shew forth or expose to sale any wares, merchandise, fruit, herbs, goods or chattells whatsoever upon the Lord's day.[20]

The thirteen original American colonies anticipated this statute, and based their Sunday laws on its predecessors. The first Sunday law to be promulgated in what is now the United States was the Virginia law of 1610. The law, a product of the church-state union of that colony, as its antecedents were products of church-state union in Judea, Rome, Gaul, and England, provided:

> Every man and woman shall repair in the morning to the divine service and sermons preached upon the Sabbath day, and in the afternoon to divine service, and catechising, upon pain for the first fault to lose their provision and the allowance for the whole week following; for the second, to lose the said allowance and also be whipt; and for the third to suffer death.[21]

There is no record of any person suffering death for violation of the Sunday law in Virginia or elsewhere in America. But there is no doubt that enforcement was strict in colonial America, particularly in Puritan New England with its theocratic church-state union. In Massachusetts, for example, John Baker was whipped "for shooting at fowl on the Sabbath day."[22]

In colonial New York, too, there was a union of church and state, and the Sunday laws promulgated both by the Dutch and the English were likewise religious measures. The primary purpose of the laws was to insure attendance at church. The first prosecution for Sunday law violation in New York of which we have a record occurred in 1655, while the colony was still under Dutch rule. Abraham de Lucena, a Jewish merchant, was charged with violating the law by keeping his store open during the Sunday sermon.[23] In 1664, on the conquest of the colony by the English, a new law was adopted which combined the requirement of public preaching and prohibitions of Sabbath breaking.[24] The immediate predecessor of the present New York Sunday law was an act, passed in 1695, "against profanation of the Lord's Day called Sunday," with a preamble declaring:

> Whereas the true and sincere worship of God according to His will and commandments is often profaned and neglected by many of the inhabitants and sojourners . . . who do not keep holy the Lord's Day but in a disorderly manner accustom themselves to travel, labor, walking . . . and the using of many other unlawful exercises and pastimes to the great scandal of the Holy Christian faith.[25]

After this preamble, the act proceeded to prohibit, under criminal penalty, conduct very similar to that proscribed by the present New York statute.

Two conclusions are clear from this summary of the historical background of American Sunday laws. First: Sunday laws were the product of church-state unions; and second, they were always religious laws. In the days before the constitutional requirement of strict separation of church and state became binding on the states as on the Federal government, and when the states were more religiously homogeneous than they are today, the courts quite frankly recognized the religious nature of Sunday laws. The relationship of the Sunday law to the Christian religion (as interpreted by the majority of its adherents) was not deemed something to be denied. A New York court in 1861 found it quite proper that

> the Christian religion and its ordinances [are entitled] to respect and protection as the acknowledged religion of the people. . . . It would be strange that a people, Christian in doctrine and worship . . . should in their zeal to secure to all the freedom of conscience which they valued so highly, solemnly repudiate and put beyond the pale of the law, the religion which is as dear to them as life. . . . Religious tolerance is entirely consistent with a recognized religion. Christianity may be conceded to be the recognized religion, to the qualified extent mentioned. . . .[26]

Another New York court was equally frank when it said:

The Legislature has authority to protect the Christian Sabbath from desecration by such laws as it may deem necessary. . . . Our laws for the observance of the Sabbath are founded upon the command of God at Sinai that we should "Remember the Sabbath Day to keep it holy."[27]

One final quotation may be cited. In upholding the conviction of a grocer for keeping his place of business open on Sunday, an act which the court called "highly vicious and demoralizing," the court said:

. . . Sunday or the Sabbath is properly and emphatically called the Lord's day, and is one amongst the first and most sacred institutions of the Christian religion. This system of religion is recognized as constituting a part and parcel of the common law, and as such all of the institutions growing out of it or in any way connected with it, in case they shall not be found to interfere with the rights of conscience, are entitled to the most profound respect, and can rightfully claim the protection of the law-making power of the State. We think it will readily be conceded that the practice against which the act is directed, is a great and crying vice, and that, in view of its exceedingly deleterious effects upon the body politic, there cannot be a doubt that it falls appropriately under the cognizance of the law-making power.[28]

### A Typical Present-day Sunday Law

With the exception of Alaska and Nevada, every one of the states of the union makes it a crime to perform at least certain business or labor on the first day of the week. Minor restrictions are imposed in seven other western states; California prohibits only boxing on Sunday; Hawaii forbids entertainment during certain hours on Sunday; Montana and Oregon prohibit barbering; Arizona prohibits both boxing and barbering; and Idaho and Wyoming put all Sunday legislation on a local option basis. For practical purposes these nine states may be said to have no compulsory Sunday laws; the other forty-one have Sunday laws of varying degree of severity, with those of Connecticut, Maryland, Massachusetts, and New Jersey the most stringent.[29]

New York's Sunday law is neither the most stringent nor the most liberal; its approach is probably typical of most states, and its provisions therefore warrant more detailed study. The law was amended in 1952 to allow municipalities local option in deciding for themselves whether or not to permit amusements and sports, other than boxing, wrestling, and horse racing, after two o'clock in the afternoon,[30] and minor amendments have been added since then. But since we are considering the New York law as a type rather than for

273

itself, the 1952 amendment may be disregarded for the purposes of the present discussion.

New York's Sunday law constitutes Article 192 of the state's Penal Law, and consists of sixteen sections (reduced to fourteen by consolidation under the 1952 amendment). The substance of these sections follows:

1. The first section, entitled "The Sabbath," states that the law prohibits the doing of certain acts "which are serious interruptions of the repose and religious liberty of the community."

2. The second section declares that a violation of the foregoing prohibition is "Sabbath breaking."

3. Sabbath breaking is declared to be a misdemeanor punishable by fine or imprisonment.

4. All labor, except "works of necessity and charity," is prohibited on Sunday.

5. Persons observing a day other than Sunday as holy time may assert that fact as a defense to a prosecution for work or labor on Sunday, provided the labor performed did not interrupt or disturb other persons observing Sunday as holy time. By an amendment adopted in 1965 this exemption applies to retail selling by Sabbatarians in family-owned stores.

6. All sports are prohibited on Sunday, except that by local option municipalities may permit baseball, basketball, soccer, hockey, and football after two o'clock in the afternoon.

7. All trades, manufacturers, agricultural, or mechanical employments other than works of necessity are prohibited.

8. Public selling or offering for sale of any property is prohibited — with numerous exceptions, noted below.

9. Legal process may not be served on Sunday.

10. All property exposed for sale on Sunday shall be forfeited and sold, "and the proceeds paid to the overseers of the poor for the use of the poor of the town or city."

11. Maliciously serving civil process on Saturday on a person observing that day as holy time constitutes a misdemeanor.

12. Processions and parades, other than funeral and religious processions, are prohibited.

13. Theatrical, dancing, circus, and similar performances are prohibited.

14. By local option, however, municipalities may permit concert and recital dances after two o'clock in the afternoon.

15. Barbering on Sunday is prohibited.

16. By local option, motion pictures and dramatic and musical

productions may be permitted after two o'clock in the afternoon.

This summary of the New York law has been set forth here to show that the law is a mass of inconsistencies and self-contradictions. But the absurdities of the present law can perhaps best be shown by the following chart of permissible and impermissible Sunday conduct, based on the statute, court decisions, and authoritative interpretations by the state's attorneys general:

Sale of Foods

| | |
|---|---|
| Bread and cakes | Permitted |
| Milk and eggs | Permitted |
| Butter and cheese | Prohibited after 10 A.M. unless sold in a delicatessen store, in which event permitted between 4 and 7:30 P.M. |
| Fruits | Permitted |
| Vegetables | Prohibited after 10 A.M. |
| Uncooked meat and fish | Prohibited |
| Cooked meat and fish | Permitted before 10 A.M. to everybody but between 4 and 7:30 P.M. only to delicatessen dealers |

Sale of Drinks

| | |
|---|---|
| Soda water | Permitted |
| Ice (presumably to cool the soda water) | Permitted |
| Beer for on-premises consumption | Prohibited |
| Beer for off-premises consumption | Permitted before 3 A.M. and after 1 P.M. |
| Wine and whiskey for on- or off-premises consumption | Prohibited |

Sale of Other Items of Personal Pleasure

| | |
|---|---|
| Candy and flowers | Permitted |
| Prepared tobacco | Permitted |
| Pipe to smoke the tobacco | Prohibited |
| Souvenirs | Permitted |

Sale of Items for Intellectual Enjoyment

| | |
|---|---|
| Newspapers | Permitted |
| Books and periodicals | Prohibited |

Sale of Items for Travel

| | |
|---|---|
| Gasoline, oil, tires | Permitted |
| Automobiles | Prohibited |
| Hub caps, road maps, tire jacks | Prohibited |

Sale of Other Items

| | |
|---|---|
| Personal property generally | Prohibited |
| Real property | Permitted |

Sports (before 1952 Amendment)

| | |
|---|---|
| Wrestling | Prohibited |
| Boxing | Prohibited |
| Horse racing | Prohibited |
| Baseball | Permitted after 2 P.M. if local law permits |
| Basketball | Permitted after 2 P.M. if local law permits |
| Football | Permitted after 2 P.M. if local law permits |
| Hockey | Permitted after 2 P.M. if local law permits |
| Polo (horse or water) | Prohibited |
| Shooting and hunting | Prohibited |
| Billiards | Prohibited |
| Athletic exhibition | Prohibited |
| Aviation exhibition | Prohibited |
| Bowling | Permitted after 2 P.M. if local law permits |
| Bicycle races | Prohibited |

Amusement and Entertainments

| | |
|---|---|
| Motion pictures | Permitted after 2 P.M. if local law permits |
| Dramatic and musical productions | Permitted after 2 P.M. if local law permits |
| Amusement park | Prohibited |
| Concert and recital dances | Permitted after 2 P.M. if local law permits |
| Other dances | Prohibited |
| Processions and parades | Prohibited |

Other Occupations

| | |
|---|---|
| Barbering | Prohibited |
| Auto washing | Prohibited |
| Factory work | Prohibited except if necessary to keep blast furnace running, in which case permitted |
| Instruction | Prohibited |

It seems impossible to find rhyme or reason in this pattern. There is no reason discernible to the present writer for permitting the sale of bread, milk, and eggs on Sunday but not meat or fish; or for permitting the sale of gasoline, oil, and tires, but not antifreeze, tire jacks, or batteries; or the sale of beer, but not butter; or of real property but not personal property; or (before the 1952 amendment) permitting professional football and hockey, but not bicycle or roller-skate racing. The test cannot be importance to the community, for it can hardly be said that it is more important to attend a professional football game than to have one's hair cut. Nor can the test be disturbance of the rest and repose of the neighborhood, for barbering and retail selling are prohibited, whereas professional football and baseball in large stadiums within the heart of residential districts may be permitted. Nor is perishability the test; if the sale of milk, eggs, ice, fruit, and flowers are allowed because they are perishable, there appears no valid reason to prohibit the sale of equally perishable vegetables, uncooked meat, or fish.

Actually, the only plausible explanation for this maze of inconsistencies is one that does not reflect much credit on the legislature. Originally the law prohibited all forms of labor, trade, and commerce. Its history since its first enactment, however, has been a succession of amendments creating exceptions and amendments based not on the necessity or desirability of the exempted trade, but on the lobbying power of the pressure group seeking the particular amendment. How else can one explain, for instance, the 1941 amendment that permitted the retail sale of beer before three o'clock in the morning and after one o'clock in the afternoon?

Not only does the law as written on the books appear devoid of rational plan, but its enforcement likewise lacks the semblance of consistency or justice. It is enforced fitfully, with long periods of acquiescence in flagrant violation. When enforced at all, it is almost always enforced exclusively against small merchants or individual laborers, while large offenders are ignored. For example, the law does not exempt radio or television broadcasts on Sunday. Yet each

Sunday these commercial entertainment media enjoy full operation free from prosecution. As one writer has noted:

> It is difficult to understand why the sale of Kosher meat[31] ... on Sunday is a more serious threat to the public health, welfare and morals than "The Shadow" or "The Faye Emerson Show." If financial or personnel limitations require selective prosecution, the rational course is to proceed against that activity having the most far-reaching consequences. In practice the opposite seems to be the rule.[32]

The Sunday laws are probably the most frequently violated and least often enforced statutes in the law books. Occasionally a judge, with rather refreshing honesty, calls them "dead letter laws," and remarks that it "is not the business of the police to revive them. They are not employed and paid by the citizens for any such purpose."[33] More often, however, the judge merely shrugs his shoulders and says: "As long as it remains on the statute books, it should be enforced."[34]

The legislature refuses to repeal the Sunday law, yet it is doubtful that it wishes the law to be enforced. Consistent enforcement would completely alter the social and economic habits of the community. It would, for instance, put an end to radio and television broadcasting on Sunday. It would halt the publication of newspapers and magazines on the first day of the week, thus depriving most citizens of their Monday morning newspaper. The law provides that goods unlawfully exhibited for sale on the Sabbath shall be forfeited. It is almost frightening to imagine what would happen if this provision were enforced against all chain drug and cigar stores which, in effect, operate miniature department stores on Sunday. It may well be that the only way to obtain repeal of the Sunday law is to engage in a campaign of strict enforcement. Attorney General (later United States Senator) William Langer thus obtained substantial modification of the North Dakota laws in 1917.[35]

It is far from certain that the use of the state's police power to enforce Sabbath observance is either necessary or effective. There is no reason to believe that voluntary observance of the Sabbath in the western states, which do not have compulsory Sunday laws, is less than enforced observance in New York or New Jersey.

## Sabbatarians and the Sunday Law

Enforcing Sunday laws against those observing Saturday or some other day than Sunday would seem clearly to be discriminatory and inconsistent with the American tradition of fair play. Moreover, it seems as clearly to restrict the religious liberty of one whose conscience requires him to observe a day other than Sunday as holy time; and it is hardly a sufficient answer to say—as some courts have—that the law does not compel him to violate his conscience by working on Saturday. By requiring him to abstain from engaging in his trade or business two days a week while his Sunday-observing competitor need abstain only one day a week, it obviously imposes on him a competitive disadvantage, and thus penalizes him for adhering to his religious beliefs. The sanction imposed by the state for observing a day other than Sunday as holy time is certainly more serious economically than the imposition of a license tax for preaching, which the United States Supreme Court has held to be an unconstitutional restriction on religious liberty.[36]

The inequity of this discriminatory treatment has been recognized in part by the legislature of New York and many other states. The New York law permits a person prosecuted for "work or labor" on Sunday to prove as a defense that he regularly observes a day other than Sunday as his holy day of rest, and that the work performed on Sunday did not interrupt or disturb other persons observing Sunday as holy time. Under this provision, an Orthodox Jewish physician in 1951 was acquitted after being brought into court for erecting a Succoh, or ritual tabernacle, in his back yard on Sunday in preparation for the Tabernacle holiday. Since the charge was laboring on Sunday, the fact that the defendant regularly observed Saturday as his holy day of rest was held a good defense.[37] But in an early Louisiana case a similar provision was interpreted not to apply to a prosecution for engaging in *selling* on Sunday, because to permit Hebrews to open their stores on Sunday while their Sunday-observing Christian neighbors could not would be preferential to Hebrews and therefore unconstitutional.[38]

It needs little consideration to note the speciousness of this reasoning. The argument might be valid if Hebrews, Seventh Day Adventists, or other seventh day observers were entirely exempt from the statute and could keep their stores open seven days each week. The law, of course, does not allow that, nor does anyone argue that this should be permitted. All that is claimed is the right to select—at least on religious grounds—the one day in seven on which to rest, and not to be compelled to select the orthodox Christian day of rest. Nevertheless, the Louisiana court's interpretation has been followed in a number of states,[39] although a few have adopted the more equitable interpretation and applied the statutory exemption to retail selling as well as to laboring.[40]

In People vs. Friedman[41] an attempt was made to induce the

New York courts to abandon the old Louisiana holding. In the Friedman case two orthodox Jews, Sam Friedman and Sam Praska, retailers of kosher meat, were prosecuted for selling uncooked meat on Sunday. The stores were located in a predominantly Jewish neighborhood, the lower east side of New York, and it was conceded by the arresting officers that there were not more than one or two persons in each store at the time the sales took place, and that the businesses were conducted quietly without causing any noise or disturbance. The evidence also established without contradiction that both defendants were pious, Orthodox Jews who never engaged in any secular occupation on Saturday but spent the entire day, with the exception of mealtime, in synagogues praying and studying.

The criminal court refused to accept these facts as defense, and held that the defense permitted by the statute was applicable only in prosecutions for work and labor, but not for selling, and convicted Sam Friedman and Sam Praska of the crime of Sabbath-breaking. The state's highest court upheld this interpretation; and to the plea that the statute so interpreted was discriminatory, the Court of Appeals said: "A plea that a statute imposes inconvenience or hardship upon a litigant should be addressed to the legislature; we may not usurp its functions by legislating judicially."

After the United States Supreme Court refused to review the decision, the advice of the Court of Appeals was taken, and in 1952 a bill was introduced in the state legislature to remove the hardship and inequity by extending the exemption to retail trade. At the request of Governor Thomas E. Dewey, the legislature appointed a committee to consider a revision of the Sunday law. Unfortunately the committee apparently felt that the hardship suffered by professional sports promoters was more serious than that suffered by Orthodox Jews or Seventh Day Adventists. In any event, its report to the legislature recommended only that the law be amended to allow municipalities to permit all professional sports on Sunday after two o'clock in the afternoon. It ignored entirely the plea of the Jewish community which supported the bill for the relief of seventh-day observers. The legislature adopted the recommendations of the committee, and adjourned after enacting legislation to relieve professional sports promoters.

A similar measure was introduced the following year, and each succeeding year for more than a decade. Each year the proposal was defeated because of the opposition of the Roman Catholic Church. Finally, in 1963, the legislature enacted a measure which empowered cities of over a million in population (which, therefore was limited to

New York City) to enact local laws exempting from the operation of the Sunday law stores owned and conducted by an individual and his family who observed religiously a day of rest other than Sunday. The following year a similar exemption statute was enacted in Massachusetts, and in 1965 the New York City exemption was made statewide. All in all some fifteen states today exempt Sabbatarians from laws prohibiting selling on Sundays.[42]

## The Constitutionality of Sunday Laws

Before the Friedman case the United States Supreme Court had never passed on the constitutionality of Sunday laws as a violation of the First Amendment's guaranty of the separation of church and state and the freedom of religion. The Court had, on two occasions, determined the constitutionality of such laws under different sections of the Constitution. In 1896 the Court ruled that the state of Georgia did not unconstitutionally interfere with interstate commerce by a statute that regulated the movement of freight trains within the state on Sundays.[43] In 1900 the Court held that the state of Minnesota had not acted arbitrarily in refusing to classify barbering as an act of necessity or charity that could legally be performed on Sundays.[44]

These cases were decided long before the series of cases holding that the ban of the First Amendment on laws respecting an establishment of religion or prohibiting its free exercise were applicable to the states, and before the Everson and McCollum decisions, in which the meaning of the ban on laws respecting an establishment of religion was clearly spelled out. Moreover, in neither of these cases was the litigant a person whose religious convictions compelled him to keep his place of business closed on Saturday. When, therefore, Friedman and Praska were arraigned for violating the New York Sunday law by selling kosher meat, the present writer, in his capacity as counsel for the American Jewish Congress, believed that their case presented the first real opportunity to test the constitutionality of Sunday laws under the First Amendment, and the organization accordingly undertook to defend the two butchers and appeal their case to the United States Supreme Court.

The basis of the appeal was that the law violated the establishment clause of the First Amendment, infringed upon the defendants' freedom of religion, particularly since their religious conscience compelled them to refrain from business on Saturday, and denied them the equal protection of the laws by reason of lack of any reasonable justification for the classification of businesses permitted or forbidden to operate on Sunday. It took the Court but one brief sentence to dispose of all the defendants' contentions: "Appeal dismissed for the want of a substantial federal question,"[45] meaning that the arguments presented to support the appeal were so obviously lacking in merit that the Court would not waste its time in allowing an oral hearing. A decade later, it took the Court 220 printed pages of its printed Reports to pass upon the same contentions. But the net result was exactly the same: the contentions were overruled and the statutes upheld.

All in all, four cases known collectively as the Sunday Law Cases, were before the Court. Two of them, McGowan vs. Maryland[46] and Two Guys from Harrison-Allentown, Inc. vs. McGinley,[47] concerned owners of highway discount department stores which were open for business seven days a week. The other two, Gallagher vs. Crown Kosher Super Market of Massachusetts[48] and Braunfeld vs. Brown[49] concerned stores owned (as in the Friedman case) by Orthodox Jews who abstained from all business activities on Saturdays.

The four cases involved three statutes — those of Maryland, Massachusetts, and Pennsylvania. As has been indicated, all the statutes were attacked on three principal grounds: (1) that Sunday laws violated the constitutional prohibition against establishment of religion; (2) that they violated the constitutional protection of religious liberty; and (3) that they denied to the merchants equal protection of the laws in violation of the Fourteenth Amendment.

The two cases involving the discount houses were decided by a vote of eight to one, with only Justice Douglas voting to declare the statutes unconstitutional as to all parties. In the two cases involving the Jewish Sabbath observers, Justices Brennan and Stewart also dissented and joined Douglas in voting to declare the laws unconstitutional as against them.

In all four cases the prevailing opinions were written by Chief Justice Warren. In meeting the attack based upon the principle of separation of church and state he said that if the present purpose of a Sunday law is to use the state's coercive power to aid religion it would be unconstitutional and in violation of the no-establishment clause of the First Amendment. He conceded further that this indeed was the original purpose of the three Sunday laws under attack. There was no question, he said, that historically these Sunday laws were enacted during colonial times as religious laws whose purpose was to insure the observance of the Christian Sabbath as a religious obligation. However, he held, the religious origin of these statutes did not require that they be held invalid today, if in fact, the religious purpose was no longer in effect.

This, he said, was the case in respect to these laws. The present purpose of the legislation is to set aside a day not for religious observance, but for rest, relaxation, and family togetherness, and the motivation is therefore secular rather than religious. As evidence to support this conclusion the Chief Justice pointed out, for example, that the Maryland statute permits such Sunday activities as the operation of bathing beaches, amusement parks, and even pin ball and slot machines as well as the sale of alcoholic beverages and the performance of professional sports. Such exemptions from the law obviously are directly contrary to the religious purpose of the Sabbath and thus indicate clearly that the present purpose of the statutes is not religious but secular.[50]

Since these are today welfare or secular statutes, the fact that to a certain extent their operation coincides with religious purposes did not make them religious laws, according to the Chief Justice. In this respect, he referred to the Everson case in which the use of public funds to transport children to parochial schools was upheld. The purpose of that statute, the Chief Justice said, was to protect children from the hazards of traffic and the fact that indirectly the parochial schools benefited thereby did not transform what was basically a secular or welfare law into a prohibited law respecting an establishment of religion. For the same reason, he said, the fact that the Christian religion may benefit by the state's decision to choose Sunday as the day in which people are required to abstain from labor and to rest and relax, does not transform these purely secular and welfare laws into laws prohibited by the First Amendment.

It should be noted parenthetically that the public generally still considers Sunday laws as religious laws. For this reason they are still colloquially known as "blue laws." In the Friedman case the defendants shared this common understanding, as is indicated by the following extract from the record in the case relating to the district attorney's cross-examination of the defendant Friedman.

Q. Mr. Friedman, have you ever been convicted of a crime?
A. No, sir.
Q. Have you ever sold meat on Sunday before this?
Mr. Pfeffer: I object to that, Your Honor.
Q. Before this Sunday?
A. Before this Sunday? Yes, sir.
Mr. Pfeffer: Just a moment. Excuse me, I object to that testimony.
Justice Morrissey: Overruled.
Justice Flood: He said, "Yes, sir."
Q. Were you not convicted of selling meat on Sunday sometimes

before this summons was served on you?

A. I said yes, sir.

Mr. McNeill: Oh, all right, no further questions.

Justice Paige: You said "No" before.

Justice Flood: You said you were never convicted of a crime, but you said you did sell meat on Sunday before this.

The Witness: Oh, that is a crime?

Justice Flood: That is a crime.

The Witness: I am sorry. I didn't. . . . Excuse me. I didn't know what you meant by that.

Justice Flood: All right. You were convicted of a crime, then.

The Witness: I mean, I was. . . .

Justice Flood: You were convicted of selling meat.

The Witness: Yes.

Justice Flood: Were you fined, was sentence suspended, or what?

The Witness: That's right.

Justice Flood: How much?

The Witness: Five dollars.

Justice Flood: That is a conviction of a crime.

The Witness: Oh, oh. I thought when you make a holdup, that is a crime.

Mr. Pfeffer: Your Honor, apparently the witness seems to confuse religious and civil crimes.

Justice Paige: They are both crimes—holdup and selling meat.

With the exception of Justice Douglas, all of the members of the Court also rejected the claim of the two discount houses that the Sunday laws violated their religious liberty. The Chief Justice asserted that the discount houses could not even raise the issue of religious liberty. They alleged only economic injury, not any infringements of their own religious freedoms due to Sunday closings; in fact, there was nothing in the record to show what their religious beliefs were.

The Court did concede that the Jewish Sabbath observers had standing to assert violation of religious freedom since the operation of the compulsory Sunday law hindered their observance of their own Sabbath by imposing upon them an economic hardship. Nevertheless, six of the nine Justices held that the statutes were constitutional even as against the Jewish merchants.

The freedom to hold religious beliefs and opinions, the Chief Justice said, is absolute. However, he continued, what was involved in the present cases is freedom to act, and this, even when motivated by religious convictions, is not totally free from legislative restrictions. Thus, for example, the fact that polygamy may be a positive command of the Mormon religion does not prevent the government from declaring it illegal and making its practice criminal.[51] Similarly, the Court in the past had upheld a statute making it a crime for a girl under the age of eighteen years to sell newspapers or periodicals in public despite the fact that a child of the Jehovah's Witnesses faith felt that it was her religious duty to perform this work.[52]

In the present case, Chief Justice Warren asserted that the statutes did not even go as far as those involved in the polygamy and child labor cases, for there they forbade conduct which religion commanded, whereas the Jewish religion does not command engaging in business on Sunday. The restriction on religious freedom is merely indirect and consequential and the Court should not strike down what it found to be a welfare law merely because of this indirect burden on the exercise of religion. "If the State regulates conduct by enacting a general law within its power, the purpose and effect of which is to advance the State's secular goals," he said, "the statute is valid despite its indirect burden on religious observance unless a State may accomplish its purpose by means which do not impose such a burden."

It was argued in the briefs that the states of Pennsylvania and Massachusetts could in fact accomplish their purpose of securing one day of rest in every seven without imposing such a burden upon Sabbatarians. For example, the state could enact a law requiring one day of rest each week for all workers but leaving it up to each employer to decide which day shall be the day of rest. Or the state could, as a number of states do in fact, designate Sunday as the day of rest but provide an exemption for those whose religious convictions compel them to observe a day other then Sunday as their day of rest. The majority of the Court, however, rejected this argument, stating that the Court could not adjudge arbitrary and unreasonable the refusal of the states to use this method of achieving their purpose.

The third ground upon which the Sunday laws was challenged in all the cases was that the crazy-quilt pattern of exclusions, exceptions, and exemptions in the various statutes bore no semblance of reason and, being arbitrary, constituted a denial of due process and of the equal protection of the laws. For example, in Massachusetts it is legal on Sunday to sell fish and food stuffs at wholesale but not at retail; to dig for clams but not to dredge for oysters. In Pennsylvania it is permissible to fish from public waters but not on private property without the consent of the owner. In Maryland merchandise customarily sold at beaches and amusement parks may be sold there on Sundays, but the same articles may not be sold on Sundays in places other than beaches and amusement parks. These and many other illustrations were cited to support the argument that the

Sunday laws are completely irrational and act unequally, all of which make them unconstitutional and in violation of the Fourteenth Amendment.

Justice Douglas did not address himself to this challenge, since he held the statutes unconstitutional on the other grounds. All the other Justices, however, considered the challenge and rejected it. The Chief Justice's majority opinion reflects the almost unbroken practice of the Supreme Court since the Roosevelt court reform campaign in 1937, not to interfere with state social welfare legislation on the ground that it is arbitrary or a deprivation of property without due process of law.[53] Once the Court determined that Sunday laws are not religious laws but social laws, it was almost inevitable that it would not interfere with the legislature's discretion on which practices should be prohibited and which permitted in these laws. The Court felt that it could not say without a shadow of doubt that there could be no reason or rationale underlying the inclusions and exclusions of the various statutes.

Justices Brennan and Stewart dissented only in the two Sabbatarian cases, and in these only on the ground that the statutes unconstitutionally infringed upon the religious liberty of the Sabbatarians. Acknowledging that the Sunday laws were in fact social welfare statutes, they contended nevertheless, that they unnecessarily infringed upon the constitutional rights of persons who observe a day other than Sunday as their day of rest.

Writing for himself and Justice Stewart, Justice Brennan asserted that "the values of the First Amendment, as embodied in the Fourteenth, look primarily towards the preservation of personal liberty, rather than towards the fulfillment of collective goals." A statute which infringes upon personal liberty, particularly religious liberty, should be subject to a far more exacting standard than is applied to a law which concerns only economic interests. Religious freedom has classically been one of the highest values of our society. He criticized what he believed was the Court's action in holding that "any substantial state interest will justify encroachments on religious practice, at least if those encroachments are cloaked in the guise of some nonreligious public purpose." The majority's sanctioning of the states' refusal to exempt Sabbatarians merely because enforcement of the law might thereby be rendered somewhat more difficult exalts "administrative convenience to a level high enough to justify making one religion economically disadvantageous."

Justice Douglas dissented in all four cases and asserted that he deemed the statutes unconstitutional both as an establishment of religion and as a prohibition of the free exercise thereof.

The Court, it should be noted, did not completely close the door to all judicial attacks on Sunday laws. The Chief Justice, speaking for the majority, concluded one of the opinions with the statement:

> We do not hold that Sunday legislation may not be a violation of the "Establishment" Clause if it can be demonstrated that its purpose—evidenced either on the face of the legislation, in conjunction with its legislative history, or in its operative effect—is to use the State's coercive power to aid religion.[54]

While it is unlikely that the demonstration called for in this quotation can be made to the Court's satisfaction in the proximate future, nevertheless, the Court has left the door slightly ajar. If, as may well be, the Court will at some future time be prepared to invalidate Sunday laws, it may, because of this sentence, be able to do so without repudiating these decisions.

As has been indicated, over the years the Sunday laws have gradually approached the status of being dead letter laws. The trend was interrupted by the recent intervention of two completely different and unrelated forces, both of which undertook to press for vigorous enforcement of Sunday laws. The first is the commercial class represented by owners of stores within cities selling merchandise generally sold in department stores. This class faces competition by highway discount stores which do their best business on Sundays. (In two of the four Sunday Law Cases of 1961 the defendants were owners of highway discount stores.) The second is the Roman Catholic Church, which seems to have taken over from Protestantism leadership in the effort to maintain Sunday law observance. The combination of these two forces revived Sunday law enforcement. Nevertheless, it is probable that the revival is only temporary, and that before long the steady and almost uninterrupted trend of Sunday laws becoming dead letter laws will be resumed. The Supreme Court decisions of 1961 may retard somewhat this development, but they will not likely be able to defeat it. The social, cultural, political, and economic development of the American society inevitably leads to the ultimate discard of compulsory Sunday laws.

## State Intervention in Ecclesiastical Controversies

In a country with an established church, like England, no constitutional problem is raised by government intervention to settle ecclesiastical controversies. The English Parliament determines what is and what is not to be contained in the authorized prayer book of the Anglican Church; and obviously there is no difficulty in invoking the jurisdiction of the English secular courts to decide which of two factions in a church represents the true faith. Ecclesiastical controversies are litigated in the first instance in special ecclesiastical courts, but the decisions of these courts may be appealed to the government tribunals in the same manner as a lower court decision is appealed to an appellate court in the United States.

It seems clear that such a system is not in harmony with the American system of the mutual independence of religion and government. It is quite foreign to our concept of the functions of secular courts that they should, for instance, be called on to decide whether Cardinal Spellman correctly interpreted a particular papal encyclical or a provision of the canon law. It is not that interpretation of ecclesiastical law is too difficult for lay determination, though this has been suggested as a reason for judicial reluctance to intervene. The Supreme Court has decided many patent-law cases involving technical engineering or chemical questions that were at least as difficult as ecclesiastical disputes. It decided these cases in the same way it would decide ecclesiastical disputes, *i.e.*, with the assistance of expert technical consultants. In fact it is not an infrequent occurrence in the law courts of our country for a jury of twelve ordinary citizens to decide whether a surgeon was negligent in performing a complicated operation.

The reason for the refusal of courts to pass judgment in disputes on church dogma and discipline is to be found in the spirit of the unitary guaranty of the First Amendment. The freedom and independence of churches would be in grave danger if the state undertook to define religious heresy or orthodoxy. This thought was thus expressed by the United States Supreme Court in the leading case of Watson vs. Jones:[55]

> In this country the full and free right to entertain any religious belief, to practice any religious principle, and to teach any religious doctrine which does not violate the laws of morality and property, and which does not infringe personal rights, is conceded to all. The law knows no heresy, and is committed to the support of no dogma, the establishment of no sect. The right to organize voluntary religious associations to assist in the expression and dissemination of any religious doctrine, and to create tribunals for the decision of controverted questions of faith within the association, and for the ecclesiastical government of all the individual members, congregations, and officers within the general association, is unquestioned. All who unite themselves to such a body do so with an implied consent to this government, and are

bound to submit to it. But it would be a vain consent and would lead to the total subversion of such religious bodies, if any one aggrieved by one of their decisions could appeal to the secular courts and have them reversed. It is of the essence of these religious unions, and of their right to establish tribunals for the decisions of questions arising among themselves, that those decisions should be binding in all cases of ecclesiastical cognizance, subject only to such appeals as the organism itself provides for.

Nevertheless, government intervention has frequently been invoked in the United States to settle intrachurch disputes. Generally it is the judicial arm of the government that enters the controversy, and the court cases are legion;[56] occasionally the legislature or even the executive department is involved. In this section the facts of several of these controversies, historic and contemporary, will be briefly summarized, and on the basis of these summaries a number of conclusions will be suggested.

### The Presbyterian Church Schism Cases

In 1861, at the outset of the Civil War, the General Assembly of the Presbyterian Church, reversing a *responsa* of 1845 that slavery was not sinful, became an articulate advocate of the Union cause; Southern and border state members objected vainly that it was violating an article of the Confession of Faith that "Synods and councils are to handle or conclude nothing but that which is ecclesiastical, and are not to intermeddle with civil affairs which concern the Commonwealth. . . ." When Lincoln issued the Emancipation Proclamation, the Assembly expressed thanks to Almighty God. At the end of the war the Assembly directed that persons from Southern states seeking employment as missionaries or ministers were to be questioned concerning their views on slavery. If they were found to be sympathetic to the Confederate cause or believed in slavery, they were to be required to repent and forsake these sins as a prerequisite to employment.

This action on the part of the Assembly caused the Presbytery of Louisville to issue a "Declaration and Testimony against the erroneous and heretical doctrines which have obtained and been propagated in the Presbyterian Church in the United States during the last five years." The General Assembly in 1866 condemned this document "as a slander against the Presbyterian Church, schismatical in its character and aims, and its adoption by any of our church courts as an act of rebellion." Since Kentucky is a border state, it was inevitable that the "Declaration and Testimony" split the State Synod and many of the local churches within the state. In each church one faction expressed adherence to the State Synod and its "Declaration and Testimony," and the other to the General Assembly. In each case the issue arose as to which faction was entitled to possession of the church property, and a number of these disputes reached the courts for adjudication.

In one case, involving the Bethel Union Church, a compromise was proposed whereby each faction was to have use of the church for half the time each week. The faction adhering to the General Assembly rejected the compromise and claimed exclusive possession. The Kentucky Court of Appeals wrote an opinion that was thoroughly political in tenor. It deemed slavery to be sanctioned by God, Christ, and the Bible, and averred that "President Lincoln's proclamation of emancipation had aggravated the horrors of war, and perverted it from a defense of the Union into a military crusade against slavery." It reached the not surprising conclusion that the General Assembly had exceeded its authority in entering the arena of politics and imposing a loyalty test and requirement of repentance; that the attempted expulsion of the faction adhering to the "Declaration and Testimony" was void, that this faction represented the true Presbyterian Church and was entitled to at least alternate if not exclusive enjoyment of the Bethel church.[57]

In the previous year, a dispute for the possession of the Walnut Street Presbyterian church in Louisville had similarly been decided by the Kentucky courts in favor of the proslavery faction;[58] but the antislavery faction, realizing that their cause was hopeless in the state courts, brought another suit in the Federal court on the ground of diversity of citizenship, in that some of the congregants of the church resided across the Ohio river in Indiana.[59] The latter case reached the United States Supreme Court and resulted in the landmark decision of Watson vs. Jones, from which we have already quoted. The Court held that under the American system of jurisprudence and the limitations of the Constitutional requirement of the separation of church and state, it had no power to decide for itself which of the two factions contesting for the Walnut Street building represented the true Presbyterian Church, and that it was required to abide by the decision of the appropriate ecclesiastical tribunal. In the case of strictly independent congregations, as in Congregational and Baptist churches, this appropriate tribunal is the majority of the congregants; in the case of hierarchal church systems the tribunal is the highest ecclesiastical judiciary to which the particular church is subject, whether it be priest, bishop, pope, synod, or general assembly. Since in the present case the supreme church body was the General Assembly, and it had determined that the antislavery faction alone represented the true faith, that faction was legally entitled to the possession of the Walnut Street Church property.

But the Watson vs. Jones decision by no means settled the controversy. Two years later the Supreme Court of Missouri, in a dispute concerning the First Presbyterian Church of St. Charles, refused to follow the United States Supreme Court's decision. Judicial refusal to disturb ecclesiastical decisions, the Missouri court held, is proper where the controversy is ecclesiastical or religious; but where it is civil or political, the church tribunal is without jurisdiction, since "Christ authoritatively declared that His kingdom was not of this world. [As] the Presbyterian Church is a part of [Christ's] spiritual kingdom, it had no right as such to interfere in civil matters. [Since it] must be conceded on all hands that questions of slavery and loyalty are merely political and civil, and not ecclesiastical or religious in their nature," the General Assembly's action in excluding the proslavery faction was a legal nullity.[60] (Of course it was not conceded "on all sides" that slavery is not a religious issue.)[61]

### Lay Trustees in the Catholic Church

The early days of Catholicism in the United States witnessed a long and ofttimes bitter internal struggle for the control of church property and appointments of parish priests. The pervading spirit of democracy and nationalism that characterized the first half of the 19th century in America could not fail to have its effect on the Catholic Church. On the other hand, the Church was a hierarchal institution headed by an absolute monarch, jealous of his absolutism and fearful of the rise of national churches. Under Catholic dogma, the obligation of the faithful is an obligation exclusively of obedience; an obligation due from subjects to rulers. The concept that "the faithful might have a wider field of thought and action in religious matters" was condemned by Pope Leo XIII under the name of "Americanism," as inconsistent with the spirit of the Vatican Council's declaration of papal infallibility, and as giving rise to a suspicion that some American Catholics "conceive and desire a Church in America different from that which is in the rest of the world."[62]

The controversy within the Catholic Church in America centered on the position of lay trustees. This device, which American Catholics conceived in an attempt to effect some congregational participation in ecclesiastical affairs, received legal sanction in a general incorporation law enacted in New York in 1784 and followed in a number of other states. What aroused the acrimony between the hierarchy and many congregations was not the fact that legal title was held by the lay trustees — the practice of holding title to church property in the names of lay administrators goes back to European precedents long antedating the American republic. The bitterness arose out of the attempt by some lay trustees to take their office seriously. According to canon law, the church is a judicial person which owns all the temporalities that are required for divine worship. Consequently the real owner of the parish church is the parish itself. As stated by an authority in canon law:

> . . . Especially must the false notion be eliminated that the parishioners are *the* owners of the parish church. Such an idea may suit a Protestant community, but does not agree with the fundamental principles of the Catholic Church.[63]

In New York City, at the end of the 18th century, the five lay trustees of St. Peter's claimed the right "not only to choose such a parish priest as is agreeable to them, but [of] discharging him at pleasure, and that after such election, the bishop or other ecclesiastical superior cannot hinder him from exercising the usual function." Father John Carroll, prefect apostolic, replied that

> If ever the principles then laid down should become predominant, the unity and catholicity of our Church would be at an end; and it would be formed into distinct and independent societies, nearly in the same manner as the congregation Presbyterians of our neighboring New England States.[64]

Even this attempt on the part of laymen to participate in the selection of a priest was not without European precedent. According to an eminent Catholic historian:

> . . . Practically speaking, all the dissensions which arose in the system during Dr. Carroll's episcopate (1790 – 1815) came from the presumption on the part of certain trustees in New York, Philadelphia, Baltimore, Norfolk and Charleston, S.C., that the trustees exercised the old *jus patronatus*. Patronage has also existed in the Church from time immemorial. It is a quasi-contract between the Church and a benefactor, whereby among other privileges the latter has the legally granted right of presenting a name of a suitable person to the vacant benefice or living. During the Middle Ages, this right was exercised, even to excess, by lay patrons . . . In the old canon law patronage was acquired in any one of three ways — the *dos, aedificatio,* or *fundus.* By *fundus* is meant the land on which the church stands; by *aedificatio,* the building of the church itself; and by *dos,* the endowment for the upkeep of the church. . . .[65]

Apparently the dispute between the Catholic laymen and the hierarchy revolved not on the existence of a right of patronage, but in whom such right may vest under Catholic dogma. The right to nominate and in fact control the selection of priests, bishops, and other ecclesiastical officers could be possessed by princes, dictators (as in Spain), and wealthy patrons; the Roman Church, however, could not concede that such a right might reside in the members of the congregation. Bishop Carroll in 1797 excommunicated a priest who maintained that "the power of ecclesiastical ministry and government is derived from the community or congregation of the people."[66]

Although invoking court intervention against the Catholic Church violates canon law and subjects the complainant to the penalty of excommunication, legal suits by the faithful against the church have been numerous — far too numerous for extended examination here. A few cases arising in Pennsylvania will be considered; these are typical of many of the cases that have come into the courts all over the country, and the determination of these cases is fairly typical of the solution arrived at in most states.

In 1820 the lay trustees of St. Mary's Cathedral in Philadelphia, who had elected one Reverend William Hogan as their pastor, met an attempt of the newly arrived bishop, Henry Conwell, to remove him, by petitioning the legislature to pass a law prohibiting hierarchal interference with the lay election of pastors. The passions arising out of the "Hogan schism" were so intense that the Vatican summoned the bishop to Rome, and directed him to stay out of America until the situation was again calm.[67] Although the legislature enacted the bill, which had wide Protestant support, the governor vetoed it.[68] But in 1855 Pennsylvania enacted another statute providing that all property "devised or conveyed to any ecclesiastical corporation, bishop, ecclesiastic or other person [for religious purposes] shall be . . . taken and held . . . subject to the control and disposition of the lay members. . . ." In Scranton in 1905 church property was conveyed to the bishop for a special purpose. After the purpose was completed, the ten lay trustees of the church demanded that the bishop reconvey the title to them, which the bishop refused to do because under canon law the title to church property must be in the bishop. The trustees brought suit to compel reconveyance, and were excommunicated for this action. Nevertheless they continued the suit, and the Pennsylvania Supreme Court ruled that ecclesiastical law is subordinate to the state statute; accordingly the bishop was enjoined to reconvey the property to the trustees.[69]

The bishop complied with the decree; but at the same time he placed the church under an interdict which closed its doors against the congregation "until the members of the congregation shall turn these faithless men out and place the Church once more under the care of the Bishop of the Diocese of Scranton, according to the laws of the Catholic Church." As result of this interdict the congregation split; an uproarious meeting was held at which a resolution was finally adopted designating the bishop as trustee to hold "all the property of said congregation and the title thereto in accordance with the laws, rules and usages of the Catholic Church." This resolution was immediately attacked in the courts; and the trial judge, feeling that the evidence was inconclusive, ordered another election to be held in open court.

The election in court resulted in a victory for the bishop's party; but an appeal was taken to the state Supreme Court, which reversed on the ground that the trial judge had abdicated his judicial functions by ordering the election, and sent the case back to the trial judge for determination without considering the results of the election.[70] The judge reconsidered the case and came up with the same result as before. Again the trustees appealed; and the state Supreme Court held that the action of the congregation was taken either in total misapprehension of the requirements of the 1855 statute or in an attempt to evade it. In either event, the court held, it would not direct the trustees to reconvey to the bishop.[71]

The situation was now a stalemate. Title to the church remained in the lay trustees, but the bishop's interdict prevented the congregation from worshiping in it. To resolve the stalemate, some of the congregants decided to call in a priest who was not in communion with the Roman Catholic Church. Again the controversy came into the courts in a suit to enjoin the foreign priest from officiating in the church. Again the bishop triumphed in the lower court and again he was defeated on appeal. The Supreme Court held that since the purpose of the interdict was to evade the 1855 statute and the previous decisions, the court would not give effect to it by prohibiting the use of the church in violation of the interdict.[72]

Faced with this situation, the bishop decided to revoke the interdict and reinstate the trustees. The congregation, however, apparently preferred the new non-Catholic priest and continued his worship. Again the expedition into the secular courts; but this time the bishop was successful both in the lower court and before the Supreme Court. Since the bishop's party now came into court with clean hands, an injunction against the non-Catholic worship was sustained.[73]

The victory for congregationalism in the Scranton Catholic Church cases was short-lived. In 1922 the Supreme Court of Pennsylvania was faced with a suit by members of a congregation in the town of Shenandoah who had been transferred to another parish against their will by the bishop's decree dividing the parish. As in the Scranton cases, the congregants took to the courts, and as in those cases they were promptly excommunicated. This time the bishop was immediately and conclusively successful. The court ruled that while under the 1855 statute the congregation is the owner of the church property, the decree of the bishop excommunicating the plaintiffs was conclusive on the secular courts; since under the excommunication decree they were no longer members of the church, they had no standing to sue.[74] The effect of this decision was obviously to destroy all meaning of the 1855 statute and the Scranton cases, since excommunication immediately prevents the congregation from obtaining judicial assistance in vindicating the rights conferred by the statute. In any event, the final solution was effected by a sympathetic legislature, which in 1935 repealed the 1855 law and provided that all property conveyed for religious purposes, whether before or after 1935, is to be held in accordance with the appropriate church or canon law. Thus the bishops finally triumphed.

A number of states allow the incorporation of a Catholic bishop as a "corporation sole," a procedure favored by the Catholic Church.[75] New York and a number of other states maintain a semblance of lay participation by requiring that two of the five incorporators and trustees shall be laymen.[76] This, however, is little more than a pretense of congregationalism, for the two laymen are to be selected by the bishop, the vicar general of the diocese, and the church rector; which means that for all practical purposes control is vested exclusively in the bishop.

## The Russian Church Schism

For more than a third of a century the courts of New York have been concerned with litigation arising out of the establishment of an autonomous Russian Orthodox Church body in the United States in 1924. This action was taken at a "sobor," or convention, held in Detroit in that year. The sobor reaffirmed its spiritual ties with the Russian Church, but declared that, in view of the severance of communications with the mother church in Moscow as a result of the

Bolshevik revolution, it was necessary to establish the "Russian Church in America" to administer church affairs and care for the faithful until such time as "a future sobor of the Russian Orthodox Church which will be legally convoked and legally elected, will sit with the participation of representatives of the American Church under conditions of political freedom guaranteeing the fullness and authority of its decisions for the entire Church, and will be recognized as a true Sobor of the Russian Orthodox Church."

Not all the Russian churches in America joined the new group, and by a court decree issued in 1924, the rightful possession of the seat of the Russian Church, St. Nicholas Cathedral in New York City, was declared to be in a priest who was appointed archbishop for America by a sobor held in Russia in 1923. In 1945 the son of this now-deceased archbishop surrendered the premises to the Metropolitan Benjamin, who had been sent to America by the Moscow Patriarchate as archbishop of the Diocese of North America. But in the same year the state of New York by statute gave official recognition to the Russian Church in America, and the representatives of that faction brought suit to obtain possession of the cathedral from Benjamin.

Under the principles of Watson vs. Jones it would seem clear that the court should have ruled that the Metropolitan Benjamin was entitled to possession. The Russian Orthodox Church is a hierarchal church under the Patriarch of Moscow, who, as its supreme head, has exclusive power to appoint archbishops; and it was not disputed that he appointed Benjamin as the archibshop of North America. The New York Court of Appeals, in a four to three decision,[77] held that Watson vs. Jones was not applicable. That decision, the court said, was predicated on the assumption that the highest church judicatory was independent of government control and free to act in accordance with the true doctrines of the church. In the present case, however, the court could take judicial notice that religion in Communist Russia is not free, and that the Moscow Patriarchate is unable to act "except as an arm of the Russian government to further its domestic and foreign policy." Moreover, the court held, the effect of the 1945 statute was to confer exclusive recognition on the church established by the Detroit sobor; this statute was motivated by the legislature's conviction that the Moscow Patriarchate was dominated by the Soviet government, and accordingly the purpose of the statute was to transfer to the American Church all the properties held for worship in accordance with the Russian Orthodox creed, even if held by congregations, priests, or bishops averring allegiance to the Moscow Patriarch and his appointee Benjamin. The court said:

> . . . For the public good, the Legislature decreed that the trustees of religious corporations, irrespective of the wishes of the majority of the local congregation, must administer the temporalities in accordance with the discipline, rules and usages of the ecclesiastical body, if any, to which the corporation was subject. (Religious Corporations Law Sec. 5.) As a broad guide this rule undoubtedly has worked well, but it is by no means a constitutional doctrine not subject to change or modification by the same Legislature which announced it, in cases where literal enforcement would be unreasonable and opposed to the public interest. The Legislature, in the exercise of its extensive and acknowledged power to act for the common welfare, may find as a fact that a situation has arisen of such novelty and uniqueness that existing law is incapable of performing its avowed function—the preservation of religious temporalities for the use of their original and accustomed beneficiaries. If the Legislature find as a fact that, because of drastically changed circumstances the accustomed beneficiaries of religious properties are thus threatened with their loss, and if there be a basis for such finding, we perceive no constitutional objection to a legislative attempt to trace and identify, as of today, the authentic group entitled to the administration of such properties.

The dissenting judges did not deny "that the present Russian government is frankly and grossly anti-religious and irreligious." They dissented because they felt "that this decision is an unlawful intrusion into the internal affairs of a religious body contrary to the first principles of American government, violative of the First Amendment's guaranty of freedom of religions from such governmental interference, and in conflict with the controlling decisional law as set forth in *Watson v Jones*. . . ." To the argument that the Moscow Patriarch "is not acting independently but is obeying commands of his communist masters," the dissenting judges said that even if "the Patriarch's appointment of this archbishop was made for the most unholy reasons, or because of the meanest accommodation to brute power, we still would not, as a court, strike down the appointment or refuse to give it credit. The Patriarch, like all men, must account for his stewardship, but not to the New York courts."

According to the dissenting judges, the 1945 statute was intended merely to regularize the American church and those churches or parishes adhering to it; it was not intended to nor could it constitutionally take away all the property held by parishes loyal to the Patriarch and turn it over bodily to the schismatic American church. So "strange and ruthless a plan" could not have "been intended by the legislature."

The dissenting opinion concluded with a "final comment":

> In the long run, communist repression and abuse of religion will make religion stronger, for "the blood of the martyrs is the seed of the Church." And so with government interferences with churches in our country. But with us the loser will be the traditional principle of American government: that the inner affairs of religious bodies are no concern of the State.

An appeal was taken to the United States Supreme Court, which, in November 1952 reversed the New York Court of Appeals decision, with only Justice Jackson dissenting.[78] The Supreme Court, in an opinion written by Justice Reed, held that "Legislation that regulates church administration, the operation of the churches, the appointment of clergy, by requiring conformity to [specified] church statutes . . . prohibits the free exercise of religion." To the argument that the Russian Church is but an arm of the hostile Soviet government, the Court said:

> . . . Legislative power to punish subversive action cannot be doubted. If such action should actually be attempted by a cleric, neither his robe nor his pulpit would be a defense. But in this case no problem of punishment for the violation of law arises. There is no charge of subversive or hostile action by any ecclesiastic. Here there is a transfer by statute of control over churches. This violates our rule of separation between church and state. . . .

The Court followed the decision of Watson vs. Jones, of which it said:

> The opinion radiates . . . a spirit of freedom of religious organizations, an independence from secular control or manipulation, in short, power to decide for themselves, free from state interference, matters of church government as well as those of faith and doctrine. Freedom to select the clergy, where no improper methods of choice are proven, we think, must now be said to have federal constitutional protection as a part of the free exercise of religion against state interference.

The Court concluded its opinion saying:

> Ours is a government which by the "law of its being" allows no statute, state or national, that prohibits the free exercise of religion. There are occasions when civil courts must draw lines between the responsibilities of church and state for the disposition or use of property. Even in those cases when the property right follows as an incident from decisions of the church custom or law on ecclesiastical issues, the church rule controls. This under our Constitution necessarily follows in order that there may be free exercise of religion.

The significance of this decision (Kedroff vs. Saint Nicholas Cathedral) lies not alone in its reaffirmance of the nonintervention principle of Watson vs. Jones and its according to that principle a firm constitutional base in the First Amendment. It lies also in the clear identification of separation of church and state with religious freedom. Superficially, the case involves only separation of church and state. As Justice Jackson emphasized in his dissent, "New York has not interfered with anyone's exercise of his religion." No one is prevented from worshiping as he sees fit; the sole issue is the internal administration of the Russian Orthodox Church in America. Yet, the Court's majority opinion, though it also referred to separation of church and state, placed by far its major emphasis on religious freedom. Since intervention such as exercised by the New York legislature is taken for granted in England, it is difficult to reconcile this decision with the frequently asserted claim that England has complete religious freedom without separation of church and state.

## Other Intra-Church Controversies

Another church controversy which evoked considerable public attention and dragged on for more than a decade involved the Melishes, father and son, and the Church of Holy Trinity in the heart of downtown Brooklyn.[79] The controversy arose out of the dissatisfaction on the part of the vestry of the church, a Protestant Episcopal parish, with the political and allegedly pro-Communist activities of the assistant rector, the Rev. William Howard Melish, son of the rector, Dr. Howard Melish.

In May 1948, the vestry adopted a resolution calling upon the assistant to resign and upon the rector, to whom alone the assistant was responsible, to direct him to resign. Both refused, and the vestry thereupon invoked the jurisdiction of the local bishop, Dr. James P. De Wolfe, an Anglo-Catholic conservative in both his theology and politics. After conducting a hearing, Bishop De Wolfe issued a decree removing the rector (but not the assistant rector, who could be removed only by the rector) from the church. The congregation, the majority of which strongly favored the Melishes, responded by seeking to oust the vestry and to replace it with a new vestry whose members would be sympathetic to the Melishes. The members of the vestry brought suit in the New York State Supreme Court. After a trial, Supreme Court Justice Meir Steinbrink issued a decision in favor of the bishop and the old vestry, ruling that Dr. Melish had been legally removed and enjoining any interference with the vestry. The tenor of the decision indicated clearly the justice's sympathy with the bishop and the anti-Melish forces. Actually his decision was based on the rule of Watson vs. Jones and the cases that followed it—that, since the bishop was the highest ecclesiastical judicatory, his removal of Dr. Melish could not be interfered with by the secular courts. Since the basis of the decision was that the court could not interfere with the bishop's decision, the justice's extended remarks on the political indiscretions of the younger Melish were obviously irrelevant. What in substance Justice Steinbrink did was to rule that he had no power to review the action of the bishop, while at the same time he reviewed and approved the action.

The pro-Melish force appealed the decision to the state's highest court, which affirmed Justice Steinbrink.[80] A petition was filed with the United States Supreme Court to review the decision.[81] The basis of the petition was that, since under the canon law of the Protestant Episcopal church the only penalty suffered by a congregation that disobeys its bishop is its loss of diocesan representation, the use of the court's injunctive powers to compel compliance violated the congregation's constitutional right of religious liberty.

The Supreme Court, without giving any reasons, refused to review the decision of the New York court. This left the situation in a state of frustrating and paradoxical stalemate. The entire purpose of the original vestry's action was to get rid of the younger, not necessarily the elder Melish. The rector's refusal to dismiss his assistant necessitated his removal so that he might be replaced by a rector who would remove the younger Melish. After Dr. Melish was removed, but before his successor was named, the old vestry was replaced by a pro-Melish vestry. Under canon law a rector must be nominated by the vestry and approved by the bishop. The new vestry refused to nominate anyone but either the older or younger Melish, and Bishop De Wolfe naturally refused to approve such a nomination. The matter dragged on for a decade or so and finally ended by reason of the fact that because of changes in the racial and ethnic character of the neighborhood the Holy Trinity Church was closed down entirely.

Another intra-church controversy which reached the courts arose out of the merger of the Congregational Christian Church with the Evangelical and Reformed Church. In a suit brought by a Congregationalist church which opposed the merger, Justice Steinbrink, who had refused to permit judicial intervention in the Melish case, intervened in this case and issued an injunction against the merger.[82] The decision was reversed by the higher New York courts[83] on the basis of the same principle of Watson vs. Jones that Justice Steinbrink had applied in the Melish case, and the United States Supreme Court, without writing an opinion, refused to review the decision.[84]

Finally, mention should be made of a type of intra-church dispute brought into the civil courts by Jewish litigants. According to Orthodox Jewish principles men and women may not sit together in synagogues but must sit in separate sections with a partition separating the two sections. Reform and Conservative Jewry follow the custom, familiar to most Americans, of having the family sit together. In many communities, the younger generation of Orthodox Jews have, upon acquiring a majority in the membership of an Orthodox congregation, passed resolutions for introduction of mixed seating. In a number of instances the older members have gone to court to seek a decree against mixed seating. The issue has not yet reached the Supreme Court, but on the basis of the principle of Watson vs. Jones, the state courts have in the main refused to intervene in the disputes and have ruled that the majority of members, being the highest authority in the Jewish congregation system, have the legal right to effectuate the change to mixed seating.[85]

### Summary Observations on State Intervention in Ecclesiastical Controversies

The cases which have been summarized here are fairly typical of the many which have reached the courts. On the basis of these cases, a number of observations may be suggested:

(1) Controversies culminating in court intervention are of all kinds, including those arising out of the social gospel (Melish), the church in politics (the Watson cases), the struggle for power between priest and congregation (the Pennsylvania cases), or between two factions within the church (the Russian Church cases).

(2) Court intervention rarely settles the controversy which invoked it; more often than not, it hinders and frustrates a satisfactory solution.

(3) Political considerations frequently motivate or are believed to motivate the court actions. In the Watson cases diametrically opposite results were reached by the proslavery state courts and the antislavery Supreme Court. In the Russian Church and Melish cases many of the defeated congregants believed that the "cold war" was an important factor in the decisions reached.

(4) Both the separation and freedom clauses of the First Amendment require the avoidance of court intervention in ecclesiastical disputes. Intervention frequently is unavoidable, as where the ownership and control of property depends on the determination of an ecclesiastical dispute. Where intervention is required, constitutional and practical policies dictate that the civil court refrain from

determining the issue on its own but defer to the judgment of the appropriate ecclesiastical tribunal. This may result in abandoning the congregation to the mercies of an arbitrary and despotic priest-hood. It may be that this is the price that must be paid for separation; yet careful consideration should lead to the conclusion that, aside from the requirements of the First Amendment, this result is far preferable to the conversion of secular courts into ecclesiastical tribunals in which, for example, Protestant, Jewish, or even atheistic judges might overrule a cardinal's, or, conceivably, even a Pope's interpretation of Catholic dogma.

## AMBASSADOR TO THE VATICAN

### The Background

Few events in the history of our country divided the people along religious lines as dangerously as the act of President Harry S. Truman on Saturday, October 20, 1951, in submitting to the Senate the nomination of General Mark Clark to be Ambassador Extraordinary and Plenipotentiary to the State of Vatican City. This act catapulted all of American Protestantism into politics with a unanimity and a bitterness not matched even by the issue of including parochial schools in legislation for Federal aid to education. Hardly a Protestant church group in the country failed to express its opposition formally and often acrimoniously to the President's proposal.

The background of the controversy can be traced to 1779, when John Adams, writing to the Continental Congress, expressed his opinion that

> Congress will probably never send a Minister to His Holiness who can do them no service, upon condition of receiving a Catholic legate or nuncio; or in other words, an ecclesiastical tyrant which, it is to be hoped, the United States will be too wise ever to admit into their territories.[86]

Except for a twenty-year period between 1848 and 1867 — and possibly for the period of the anomalous status of Myron C. Taylor as personal representative of President Franklin D. Roosevelt and President Truman — Adams's prediction was accurate up to the present writing.

Consular relations, however, are different. Consuls are not recognized in international law as diplomatic officials, but are commercial agents concerned exclusively with affairs of business and travel, and are frequently citizens of the country in which they reside and transact business, rather than of the country in whose behalf they act. Indeed, the first two American consuls in the Papal States were both native Romans; and the first of these, Giovanni Battista Sartori, served simultaneously as United States consul to Rome and as consul general of the Papal States in America.[87] Consular relations between the United States and the Papal States were begun in 1797, and between that date and the fall of the Papal States in 1870 eleven persons served as American consuls in Rome.[88]

Although consuls are only commercial agents, the American consuls in Rome appear to have been accorded special treatment. A number of them reported that they were received by the Pope and other Vatican officials with the honor ordinarily accorded only to diplomatic officials. Even Nicholas Brown, a democrat whose sympathies were outspokenly with the rising tide of Italian nationalism, agreed that he was welcomed to all church festivals "in like manner as diplomatic functionaries . . . a courtesy not extended to any other consul resident in Rome, [because an] American consul at Rome, in-as-much as we have no higher functionary, is here looked upon somewhat in the light of a sort of diplomatic agent."[89]

Nevertheless, until 1848 our relations with the Papal States were purely commercial and nondiplomatic. In 1848, however, a new—though shortlived—era in American-Vatican relations was inaugurated. Two years earlier Pius IX had been elected Pope, and both his election and the reforms he instituted at the beginning of his administration aroused widespread enthusiasm in America. Pius released political prisoners, granted greater freedom to the press, established a constitution, improved roads and railways, and even placed a box at the Vatican to receive complaints from his subjects. When a Council of State was formed, so enthusiastic was the response of the Americans residing in Rome that it was agreed to march in a body carrying a flag and with each American carrying a branch of laurel.[90]

The enthusiasm spread to this country. In New York the legislature formally praised the Pope's efforts to improve the condition of the Italian people and to "bestow upon them the incalculable blessings of national independence and constitutional freedom."[91] A demonstration was held at the Broadway Tabernacle in New York City in November 1847, at which an address of gratification and congratulation was made by Horace Greeley, and with appropriate resolutions was sent to Rome.[92] The New York *Herald,* competitor of Greeley's *Tribune,* suggested that "the United States, the greatest of all free countries in Christendom at this day [ought to] open diplomatic relations and express its sympathy with the illustrious Pontiff." The *Herald* suggested tactfully to President Polk that the million and a half Catholics in the country would especially appreciate such action by the President. Similar demonstrations, resolutions, and recommendations were made in other parts of the country.[93]

From the Americans living in Rome also came expressions of hope that the President would send a diplomatic representative to the Vatican. The Pope himself expressed to Brown the desire that diplomatic relations be established between the two states.[94] Responding to these entreaties, President Polk in his message to Congress in December 1847 sandwiched among a multitude of matters a small item reading:

> The Secretary of State has submitted an estimate to defray the expense of opening diplomatic relations with the Papal States. The interesting political events now in progress in these States, as well as just regard to our commercial interests, have, in my opinion, rendered such a measure highly expedient.[95]

The debate in Congress on the President's recommendation was bitter. The President was accused of trying to win Catholic votes; it was asserted that the matter was purely religious, and that our commercial relations with the Papal States did not warrant the appointment of a diplomatic representative. America at the time was afflicted with a strong Nativist movement which was bitterly anti-Catholic, and there is no doubt that the debate had overtones of Know-Nothing bigotry. But by the overwhelming votes of 137 to 15 in the House and 36 to 7 in the Senate the President was authorized to accredit a *chargé d'affaires* to the Papal States. This was in the nature of a compromise, since a number of Congressmen had urged the dispatch of a full minister.[96]

In accordance with the Congressional authorization, President Polk appointed as first *chargé* Jacob L. Martin, a devout Catholic who had been converted from Protestantism. The principles that were to guide his activities were laid down by James Buchanan, Secretary of State, in his letter of instruction:

> There is one consideration which you ought always to keep in view in your intercourse with the Papal authorities. Most, if not all the Governments which have Diplomatic Representatives at Rome are connected with the Pope as the head of the Catholic Church. In this respect the Government of the United States occupies an entirely different position. It possesses no power whatever over the question of religion. All denominations of Christians stand on the same footing in this country,—and every man enjoys the inestimable right of worshipping his God according to the dictates of his own conscience. Your efforts therefore, will be devoted exclusively to the cultivation of the most friendly civil relations with the Papal Government, and to the extension of the

commerce between the two countries. You will carefully avoid even the appearance of interfering in ecclesiastical questions, whether these relate to the United States or any other portion of the world. It might be proper, should you deem it advisable, to make these views known, on some suitable occasion, to the Papal Government; so that there may be no mistake or misunderstanding on this subject.[97]

It is important to note that at this time the Papal States covered an area of some 16,000 square miles, with a population subject to the Pope in excess of 3,000,000, and was in every sense a political state.[98]

Martin died a few months after his appointment. He was succeeded by Lewis Cass, Jr., who by an act of Congress in 1855 was elevated to minister resident. In the twenty years between Martin's appointment in 1848 and the discontinuance of relations in 1868, six persons served as diplomatic representatives. In these two decades the liberalism of Pius IX at the opening of his reign turned to extreme conservatism, with the result that the sympathy he had achieved in America was quickly dissipated. The extent of the changed attitude can be measured by the incident of the rejection by the Washington Monument Association of a block of marble for the monument sent by Pius IX in 1852, barely four years after the enthusiastic demonstration in the Broadway Tabernacle. When the Pope's representative, Monsignor Bedini, visited the United States in 1853, he was accorded official courtesy by the government but met with hostile demonstrations in many cities, some of them so violent as to endanger his life.[99]

Among the events that gave rise to this turnabout in attitude were the Papal order in 1850 to burn two thousand Protestant Bibles which were printed in Italian, the execution of which was averted only by the intervention of the American minister; the struggle for unification and independence on the part of the "Young Italy" movement under Mazzini; the Pope's invocation of French military resistance in his war with the Mazzini forces; the erroneous report that the Pope had officially recognized the Confederate government during the American Civil War; the Pope's promulgation of the *Syllabus of Errors* in 1864, with its condemnation of such American ideals as separation of church and state, religious liberty and public education, and the difficulties faced by Protestants seeking to participate in worship in Rome. (It was not until 1873, after the Pope had lost his temporal sovereignty, that for the first time a Protestant church was allowed to be built in Rome.)[100] The result of these events was that without formal action the ministry at the Vatican ended in 1868 by reason of the refusal of Congress in the preceding year to appropriate any further funds for its operation.[101]

Thus the situation stood until 1939. On December 23 of that year, after war had broken out in Europe, President Roosevelt addressed identical letters to Dr. George A. Buttrick, president of the Federal Council of Churches of Christ, and Dr. Cyrus Adler, president of the Jewish Theological Seminary, each reading:

> It would give me great satisfaction if you would, from time to time, come to Washington to discuss the problems which all of us have on our minds, in order that our parallel endeavors for peace and the alleviation of suffering may be assisted.

The letters appeared innocent enough, and both Dr. Buttrick and Dr. Adler accepted with cordiality.[102] When, however, the text of these letters was released to the press, it was disclosed that the President had also sent a Christmas letter to the Pope in which he expressed the view that "it is well that we encourage a closer association between those in every part of the world — those in religion and those in government — who have a common purpose." The letter further stated that "I am, therefore, suggesting to Your Holiness that it would give me great satisfaction to send to you my personal representative in order that our parallel endeavors for peace and the alleviation of suffering may be assisted."[103] Simultaneously the State Department disclosed that the President's representative would be Myron C. Taylor, an Episcopalian; that he would have the title "Personal Representative of the President of the United States of America to his Holiness, Pope Pius XII"; that he would have the rank of envoy extraordinary, but that the appointment did "not constitute the inauguration of formal diplomatic relations with the Vatican," and that he would serve without compensation.[104]

This announcement by the State Department did not entirely assure the Federal Council. In January 1940 its executive committee warned:

> If the appointment should unfortunately prove a steppingstone to a permament diplomatic relationship, we should feel obliged in good conscience to oppose it, as a violation of the principle of separation of governmental function and religious function, which is a basic American policy and which both history and conscience approve, and as an ultimate injury to all faiths.

Again, the following month, the Federal Council wrote to the President calling attention to its increased misgivings. The President replied that

> This appointment does not constitute the inauguration of formal

diplomatic relations with the Vatican. . . . Mr. Taylor was sent to Rome to assist parallel endeavors for peace and the alleviation of suffering.[105]

*The Christian Century* was more outspoken in its misgivings. Commenting editorially, it said:

To strip away all camouflage, the President has, in reality, established diplomatic relations with the Vatican without legal authority. He has done so, we believe, not as a peace move, but as a political move. Roman Catholics will be greatly pleased and can be counted on to remember it at the polls. Protestants and Jews are expected to be diverted by the sop of the invitations to Dr. Buttrick and Dr. Adler, and to forget it long before November. In that expectation we predict that the President will be disappointed. The American majority does not want to see relations established between this government and any religious body, and it will hold Mr. Roosevelt responsible for having tried to do this under the nearly sacrosanct cover of a campaign for peace.[106]

After President Roosevelt's death, Mr. Taylor was continued as the personal representative of President Truman. In June 1946 a delegation representing the Federal Council and nine major Protestant denominations called on the President to express their concern at Mr. Taylor's continued presence at the Vatican. The President assured them that the appointment was "a temporary expedient to give the President the fullest opportunity to make his contribution to the peace, that it might terminate at an early date but would certainly terminate with the signing of the peace treaties." A year and a half later, in November 1947, another delegation under the chairmanship of Bishop G. Bromley Oxnam again met with the President and proposed that instead of having a personal representative with "rank of ambassador" to the Pope, the President might have a representative, without any implication of diplomatic status, who would from time to time consult with the leaders of all religious bodies on the same basis. To this suggestion the President replied in March 1948 that "I cannot bring myself at this time and in the midst of world confusion, either to terminate the mission or to change its essential character." But in August 1948 the President announced through his secretary "that the mission of Myron C. Taylor, Personal Representative of the President of the United States of America to His Holiness the Pope, would be terminated when peace is made. . . . Moreover, that will remain the President's policy and will be strictly adhered to so long as he is in office."

In January 1950 Mr. Taylor resigned, and the executive committee of the Federal Council took the occasion to issue a statement

1. Reaffirming unalterable opposition to the appointment of either

an American Ambassador to the Vatican or a personal representative of the President to the Holy See;

2. Restating the conviction that the American principle of the separation of Church and State requires a policy of equal treatment of all religious bodies by our government; and

3. Expressing the judgment that the temporary departure from this principle by the President of the United States has had the unhappy effect of creating needless religious tension.

In September President Truman first disclosed that he was contemplating sending an official ambassador to the Vatican. The Federal Council prepared a document entitled "A Brief in Support of Maintaining a Valuable American Tradition" which it sent to the President.[107] The President countered by offering the post to Charles P. Taft of Cincinnati, brother of Senator Robert A. Taft, a former president of the Federal Council and a board member of the National Council of Churches. Mr. Taft declined the offer and urged the President to give up the idea.[108] But the President was in no mood to abandon the project. On October 20, 1951, a few hours before the scheduled adjournment of Congress, the President submitted to the Senate the name of General Mark W. Clark as the first full-fledged ambassador to the Vatican. Simultaneously a bill was introduced in Congress exempting General Clark from the operation of the law prohibiting officers of the armed forces from holding a civil post in government. The statement which the President released to the press read:

> The President has decided that it is in the national interest for the United States to maintain diplomatic representation at the Vatican.
>
> He has therefore nominated General Mark W. Clark to be Ambassador to the State of Vatican City.
>
> During the war, the late President Roosevelt appointed Mr. Myron Taylor as the personal representative of the President to His Holiness the Pope.
>
> During and after the war the Taylor mission performed an extremely useful service not only in the field of diplomacy but in the amelioration of human suffering. That service is set forth in official correspondence published from time to time.
>
> The President feels that the purposes of diplomacy and humanitarianism will be served by this appointment.
>
> It is well known that the Vatican is vigorously engaged in the struggle against communism. Direct diplomatic relations will assist in coordinating the effort to combat the Communist menace.
>
> Thirty-seven other nations have for a great many years maintained at the Vatican diplomatic representatives.[109]

It was obvious that General Clark's appointment could not be confirmed before the adjournment of the Senate, and that he could not serve as a recess appointee because of the lack of time to pass the exemption bill. The announcement of the appointment at that particular time appeared to many to be an act of pure politics. Certainly it aroused a storm of controversy, without any immediate practical results. Even some of the organizations and publications that supported the President's action were critical of his timing.[110]

With the exception of one small organ of Anglo-Catholicism, *The Living Church*, hardly a Protestant organization or publication in the country failed to express its extreme disapproval of the appointment. Leadership in the campaign against confirmation was taken by the National Council of Churches, which appointed a special committee under the chairmanship of Dr. Franklin Clark Fry, president of the United Lutheran Churches in America, to mobilize public opinion. Protestants and Other Americans United launched a nationwide campaign against the appointment, and Protestant ministers throughout the country preached sermons against it. With the exception of the American Jewish Congress, which urged the President to "recall the proposed appointment of an Ambassador to the Vatican in the interests of fundamental American democratic principles and of inter-religious harmony and accord within this country,"[111] Jewish groups maintained a discreet silence, although by and large American Jewry was opposed to the appointment.

The Protestants' campaign was effective. The White House was flooded with communications running six to one against the appointment. Senators and Representatives gave private assurance that the appointment would never reach the floor for ratification, nor would Congress ever be called on to vote on the exemption bill. Moreover, many of the Congressmen assured Protestant organizational representatives that the measures would never pass even if they did reach the floor. The result was that after a decent interval General Clark announced that he had requested the President to withdraw the nomination. The President "reluctantly" did so, but insisted that he had not given up the idea and would submit another nomination. Notwithstanding this reservation, President Truman left the White House at the end of his term without making another appointment.

During the administration of President Dwight D. Eisenhower, the issue of an ambassador to the Vatican remained dormant. No effort was made during the eight years of his Presidency to revive the question and the controversy it had engendered. In 1960, Senator John F. Kennedy, a Roman Catholic, became a leading candidate for the Democratic nomination for the Presidency, and this fact threatened to revive the controversy. The threatened controversy, however, never eventuated because very early in his campaign, Senator Kennedy declared that he favored strict separation of church and state and was "flatly opposed" to an exchange of ambassadors between this country and the Holy See.[112] Thus, the issue remained dormant.

Dormant, but by no means dead. The initiation of diplomatic representation came about, as we have seen, by the accession to the throne of Peter of a liberal, pro-democratic pope who won the respect and affection of the American people. The accession of John XXIII and his successor Paul VI, the efforts of the Church towards *aggiornamento*, the adjustment of the Church to the needs and demands of the mid-twentieth century and towards improved relations with non-Catholics, have likewise given rise to a less hostile attitude to the church on the part of American Protestantism and other non-Catholic forces. With it have come suggestions that the question of exchange of diplomatic representatives with the Vatican should be considered afresh. It is therefore safe to predict that it is only a matter of time before the nation will again be faced with the task of deciding between the *pros* and *cons* on the question.

## The Arguments Pro

In his statement announcing the appointment of General Clark, President Truman assigned as his reasons for the appointment "purposes of diplomacy and humanitarianism." The "purposes of humanitarianism" were not particularized, but by "diplomatic purposes" the President made it clear that he meant "coordinating the effort to combat the Communist menace." He also pointed out that "thirty-seven other nations have for a great many years maintained at the Vatican diplomatic representatives." More specifically and in detail, the following reasons have been assigned to support the appointment:

1. Extending diplomatic recognition is not unprecedented. For twenty years the United States maintained a *chargé d'affaires* and minister resident at the Vatican. Relations were discontinued, though never formally broken off, because of misunderstandings and the loss of sympathy and admiration for the Pope, but not for any reasons of basic national policy or constitutional principles. No difference, except in degree, exists between sending a minister resident and an ambassador to the Vatican.

2. Diplomatic relations with the Vatican is the regular, accepted practice in international relations. Many nations maintain such rela-

tions. Of the major powers outside the United States, only Communist Russia and Communist China do not maintain a diplomatic mission at the Vatican. Moreover, the countries that maintain such missions include Great Britain, which is at least as Protestant as the United States, and France, in which the separation of church and state prevails as it does in the United States.

3. The burden of proof rests on the opponents of relations; there is no apparent valid reason why we should not have a diplomatic mission at the Vatican. The Vatican is a sovereign, independent state to the same extent as all other countries with which the United States maintains diplomatic relations. It has all the aspects of statehood and sovereignty recognized in international law: territory, government, citizens or subjects, an army, a flag, currency, postage stamps and facilities, etc. Whatever may have been its status during the period between 1870 and 1929 when the Pope was a "prisoner" in the Vatican, the Lateran agreement of 1929, which is now part of the Italian constitution, restored to the Vatican its status in international law as a sovereign, independent state. The fact that its territory is small is irrelevant; we maintain a diplomatic mission in Luxemburg, and that state is extremely small. Nor is it relevant that the head of the Vatican state is also the head of the Catholic Church; the head of Great Britain is also the head of the Anglican Church, and, at the same time, of the Presbyterian Church of Scotland. The same situation prevails in the Scandinavian and Moslem countries, and that fact has never interfered with our policy of maintaining normal diplomatic relations with these sovereign states.

4. The Vatican is strategically located in the heart of Europe. It has intimate contact with most of the peoples of the world, including millions behind the "iron curtain." It receives reports of events and conditions in every corner of the globe; it is practically the sole or at least the best source for information not tainted with official propaganda concerning conditions in Communist-dominated countries. In short, it is the best "listening post" in the world. During the war with Germany and Japan, the presence of the President's personal representative enabled us to obtain valuable information regarding conditions in those countries. Today, in our "cold war" with Russia and her allies, we can, by keeping a diplomatic mission at the Vatican, obtain valuable information regarding conditions in these countries.

5. The United States and the Vatican are the two chief defenders of Christian civilization against the menace of Communism. The best way to coordinate the effort against this menace is by maintaining an embassy at the Vatican. Informal or unofficial relations

will not accomplish this purpose. It is too much to expect that the Pope can cooperate on completely friendly terms with a government that refuses to set up the machinery for friendly cooperation as have other nations. Moreover, as Professor Corwin stated,

> there exist at least two sound reasons of a broader nature which amply justify it as a timely move in the diplomatic game being presently played on the European chessboard. The first of these is the necessity of securing Catholic support for our cause on the Continent, since without it—and especially is this true as regards Italy and France—our policy promises to be dashed to bits against a combination of Communists and Neutralists. Secondly, the strong line being taken by the Papacy in the ideological war against communism is a further circumstance fortifying the intrinsic reasonableness of the President's action.[113]

6. A new spirit is coming to the fore within the Roman Catholic Church, a spirit of modernism and of reconciliation with the non-Catholic world. Diplomatic recognition of the Vatican would strengthen this spirit and encourage its advocates. Moreover, the effect of the new spirit within the Church is to minimize if not entirely eradicate the suspicions of the non-Catholic world with respect to the aims and purposes of the Church, and the fear that diplomatic recognition would promote the efforts of the Church to make the United States a Catholic country.

### The Arguments Con

In opposition to the appointment, the following arguments are presented:

1. The appointment is unprecedented. As stated by the National Council of the Churches of Christ:

> Obviously the civil and commercial interests of the Papal States in the middle of the nineteenth century have no counterpart in Vatican City today. Before 1870 the Pope was both Supreme Pontiff of the Roman Catholic Church and the sovereign of the Papal States, at that time a substantial territorial power. From 1870 to 1929, when a new settlement was reached with Italy in the Lateran Treaty and the Concordat, he had no temporal power. In the latter year he was recognized by Italy as sovereign of Vatican City. Vatican City has an area of one-sixth of a square mile and a population of about 1,000. In 1859 the area of the Papal States was 16,000 square miles; in 1853 their population was 3,124,758.[114]

2. Extending diplomatic recognition to the Holy See is inconsistent with the American principle of the separation of church and state. It would

give one church a preferential status in relation to the American government [and would thereby] set aside the principle of according all religious bodies the same status in the eyes of our government. Such a departure from our historic past might even lead—though not intended—to an ultimate acquiescence in the doctrine enunciated by the encyclical of Pope Leo XIII on "The Christian Constitution of States" which bluntly declared that "It is not lawful for the State to hold in equal favor different kinds of religion." What this encyclical condemns is what the United States has practiced.[115]

Nor would the objection be met by a proposal to establish similar diplomatic relations with other religious bodies. In the first place, this would not be practicable. In the second place, it would merely extend the scope of a wrong policy, but would not thereby make it a right policy.

3. The fact that other countries maintain a mission at the Vatican is not controlling. In the first place, some, like Denmark, Norway, and Sweden, do not and never have maintained a mission. Almost all those who do are predominantly Catholic in their population. In any event, none of them operates under the American Constitution and the American tradition of separation.

4. The analogy of Great Britain, where the Queen is head of the state church, is fallacious. Our ambassador to England is sent to the head of the government, not to the head of the church. There would not be the slightest difference in our relations if tomorrow the church of England were disestablished and the Queen no longer its head. On the other hand, the Pope's influence is not derived from his status as head of a state but as head of the Roman Catholic Church.

His representatives overseas derive their status from their authority in that church rather than from the civil or commercial power of Vatican City. Diplomatic relations with the Pope, or technically with the Vatican, are therefore, in effect diplomatic relations with the head of a church, with the Roman Catholic Church itself.[116]

5. The appointment would have grave domestic consequences. Whatever benefits might be derived from it externally would be far outweighed by the interreligious disharmony and acrimony it would evoke internally.

6. The "listening post" argument is not supported by the facts. The Vatican is a poor source for information of events behind the "iron curtain." According to *Time:*

The efficiency of the Vatican's "worldwide information service" has probably been exaggerated for many years. In recent years, its information channels from Eastern Europe have been effectively clogged by

313

Communist restrictions. The Vatican (and the rest of the Western world) undoubtedly gets a true general picture of what goes on behind the Iron Curtain, but the Vatican's information about specific events in Eastern Europe often arrives in Rome too late to be of use.

Vatican officials were completely baffled last year when the communized Warsaw government announced the signing of an agreement with Polish Catholic bishops. At first, they expressed doubt that any such document had been signed; two weeks later, they confirmed much of what Warsaw announced. When the Communist government in Czechoslovakia banished Archbishop Beran from Prague this year, again the Vatican did not know what was happening. When Archbishop Grosz was tried and sentenced by the Communists in Hungary, Rome had to depend for its information on regular press reports.

Moreover, the efficacy of this argument assumes that every bishop, priest, or member of a religious order throughout the world is in effect a spy reporting to his temporal superior, the Pope, on the internal political, military, and economic conditions of the country in which he resides and to which he owes civil allegiance. Furthermore, if a priest in Warsaw or Bucharest is an espionage agent of the Holy See, the priest in Washington, who owes the same duties to the Pope, is likewise an espionage agent, potential if not actual, of the Holy See.

7. The argument that relations are necessary to enlist the Pope's cooperation in the war against Communism assumes that the cooperation sought for is worth while, and that it would be withheld if diplomatic recognition were not accorded. Both assumptions are fallacious. The Catholic Church has been singularly unsuccessful in the struggle against Communism. Communism has made the greatest headway, outside Soviet Russia and China, in Catholic countries like Poland and Hungary, and has had no success at all in Protestant countries like Norway, Sweden, Great Britain, and the United States. Even on this side of the "iron curtain" there are more Communists in Italy than in any other West Europe country, and more Communists in Rome, in the shadow of the Pope's palace, than in any other city west of the Elbe. Nor can it be assumed that whatever aid the Vatican can offer in the war against Communism would be refused unless an ambassador were appointed. The Catholic Church has as much at stake in the struggle against Communism as does the United States, and it is inconceivable that it would prejudice the struggle by denying such aid merely because of its displeasure at America's refusal to send an ambassador to the Pope.

### The Constitutional Issue

Shortly after President Truman announced the appointment of

General Clark as ambassador to the Vatican, Dr. F. Ernest Johnson, then director of the Central Department of Research and Survey of the National Council of the Churches of Christ, sent a letter to a number of authorities in the field of constitutional law setting forth three specific inquiries:

1. Is there good ground for maintaining that the First Amendment to the Constitution prohibits diplomatic relations between our government and that of the Vatican state?

2. Would such an extension of the prohibition contained in the First Amendment be likely to carry with it the prohibition of other practices which involve some incidental benefit to religious bodies, separately or collectively?

3. By what procedure could the constitutional question be brought before the Supreme Court?

With one exception (the present writer) the correspondents answered the first query in the negative. They appeared to have agreed that, in the words of one correspondent, "the establishment of diplomatic relations with the Vatican could not be attacked unless it could be shown that such establishment interfered with the freedom of our people at home to maintain their religious beliefs and institutions in such way as they see fit," and it seems unlikely that "any such interference could be shown." Another correspondent remarked that "the prohibition would have to be read into the amendment by construction," and he could "not see the appointment of an ambassador to the Vatican as one step in the direction of the establishment of a United States Church. The connection seems . . . to be too remote, more remote, for example, than the maintenance of chaplains in the Services, which has been provided for by the Congress since the Constitution was adopted."

Those correspondents who expressed an opinion on the second question saw a likelihood that pushing the constitutional requirement of separation far enough to ban diplomatic relations with the Holy See would logically open the way to a curtailment of privileges that most religious bodies take for granted. Cited examples of such privileges were the exemption of church property from taxation and the furnishing of chaplains to the armed forces and to public institutions at government expense.

In answer to the third query all the respondents agreed that there was no practicable procedure for bringing the issue before the Supreme Court for adjudication.[117] As we have seen,[118] a taxpayer has no status as such to sue in the Federal courts to enjoin unconstitutional action on the part of the President or Congress. Conceivably, the issue might be brought into the courts if the United States Comptroller General would refuse to pay the ambassador's salary, the latter might then sue for his salary, and the issue would thus get into the courts.[119] This event is of course so unlikely as not to require further consideration. Moreover, even if the issue reached the Supreme Court, it might well hold the issue to be political rather than legal and therefore not justiciable.

One of the correspondents, Professor Corwin, published his reply in full in the "Letters to the Editor" column of the New York Times,[120] and a more complete examination is therefore possible of the reasoning which at least he employed to arrive at his conclusion. Professor Corwin said, in part:

> The Supreme Court has said that in the international field "the right and power of the United States . . . are equal to the right and power of the other members of the international family"; and that the lion's share of this power is vested by the Constitution in the President is not disputed. He alone may receive the diplomatic representatives of other Governments; he alone may choose persons, subject to the consent of the Senate, to represent the United States abroad; he alone may "recognize" foreign states and Governments.
>
> Thomas Jefferson and John Marshall did not see eye to eye in many things, but they did in this. "The transaction of business with foreign nations is executive altogether," said Jefferson. "The President," said Marshall, "is the sole organ of the nation in its external relations, and its sole representative with foreign nations." This being the case, however, any act performed by the President in the exercise of his diplomatic powers is presumably within his constitutional discretion; and, by the same token, it is entitled to be regarded, until the contrary is shown, as having been done in good faith for the benefit of the country.
>
> As to the principle of separation of Church and State — so far as it has constitutional basis it is a kind of "invisible radiation" from Amendment I, which says that "Congress shall make no law respecting an establishment of religion." But the nomination of an Ambassador is not lawmaking. Mr Truman has not attempted, in this instance, to usurp the legislative power of Congress. No rule of conduct has been imposed by the President upon the people of the United States touching the relation of Church and State, or touching anything else. He has performed an act of state of the most commonplace sort. . . .
>
> It is true, to be sure, that this action furnishes American Catholics an excuse to swell out their chests a bit, just as it has afforded some American Protestants an excuse to assail the Papacy as the foe of democracy. But these easily foreseeable repercussions do not affect the validity of the President's course. If, as the Supreme Court has held, a state is entitled to pay for the public transportation of children attending parochial schools in order to assure their safety on the highway, notwithstanding the fact that in doing so it aids such schools, then certainly the Pres-

ident is entitled to bolster our precarious European diplomacy by sending an Ambassador to the Vatican, notwithstanding the fact that the separation principle is not considered by some of our citizenry as forbidding them to mix religion with their politics.

Professor Corwin concluded his letter by expressing the view that there was no practicable way of bringing the issue to the Supreme Court, and that even if there were the Court "would almost certainly refuse to pass on its merits, on the ground that it was 'political' in character and hence not 'justiciable.' "

With the exception of the lone dissenter, all the correspondents polled by Dr. Johnson were professors of constitutional law at leading universities, and it is hard to escape the conclusion that their view on the constitutionality of the President's act was to a large extent influenced by the unanimous belief that it could not and would not be declared unconstitutional by the Supreme Court. It must, however, not be assumed that the courts are the exclusive forum in our democracy for the determination of constitutional issues. The right and duty to determine what is consistent with the Constitution and to act accordingly is shared as well by the executive and legislative branches of the government. The Senate, asked to confirm a nomination, would have to decide for itself whether the Constitution permits an American ambassador to the Holy See, and the whole of Congress would have to make the same determination before it might appropriate the funds to finance the embassy.

Professor Mark De Wolfe Howe of Harvard, apparently not included among the authorities polled by Dr. Johnson, described the danger of the approach that equates constitutionality with justiciability:

> Quite possibly Professor Corwin did not intend to leave in his reader's mind the impression that action may be characterized as unconstitutional only when the Supreme Court is empowered to condemn it. It is, however, dangerously easy to read his argument as if it supported that proposition. If "unconstitutional" is so defined for purposes of the current debate, and if Professor Corwin's argument that there is no means by which judicial review could be assured is also accepted, then the Presidential appointment and legislative appropriations in aid of it would be constitutional. Any such narrow definition of terms, however, would have most unfortunate consequences, for it would go far to justify the President and Congress in abdicating their responsibility to observe constitutional limits on their power. If it is important that those limits be seriously considered by the Congress and the President in normal circumstances, when the safeguard of judicial review is at hand, it is doubly important that the responsibility be thoroughly recognized

317

when no procedure exists whereby the issue of constitutional law may be brought to the judiciary for final solution.[121]

We have already dealt with the implication of Professor Corwin that the First Amendment does not restrict Presidential action since its wording refers only to "Congress."[122] The premise on which this thesis rests is that the First Amendment's prohibition of laws respecting an establishment of religion was intended to restrict an existing Federal power, and that since only Congress' power was restricted, the President remains free to act. This premise, as we have seen, is historically incorrect. There was complete unanimity among the framers of the Constitution that the Federal government, in its legislative, executive, and judicial divisions, had no power to intervene in matters of religion. Moreover, even if Professor Corwin's thesis were accepted, the act of Congress in appropriating funds for the embassy would clearly appear to be a "law" within the meaning of the First Amendment.

The constitutional objections to the appointment are not based on the fact—as Professor Corwin seemed to believe—that the Catholic Church is indirectly aided because the President's "action furnishes American Catholics an excuse to swell out their chests a bit." Nor is the objection based, as many Protestants seem to believe, on the contention that the action prefers the Catholic Church over all other religions. The objection lies in the belief that the embassy constitutes in fact either an alliance with a church, or at least a participation by the Federal government in the affairs of a religious organization—conduct that has at least four times been declared unconstitutional by the Supreme Court.[123]

There is, of course, no doubt that the President has power under the Constitution to send ambassadors to foreign countries. If the Vatican is a state, as Luxemburg or Saudi Arabia is, no constitutional obstacle exists to the appointment, even though the state is minute in area and absolutist in government. Nor is the constitutionality of the appointment affected by the fact that the person who is the head of the state is also head of the state church, any more than the ambassadorship to Britain or Sweden is invalidated by the fact that the heads of those countries are also the heads of the national churches.

On the other hand, suppose General Clark had been appointed solely as emissary to the Roman Catholic Church, or suppose that the appointment had been made during the period between 1870 and 1929, when the Pope was "prisoner" in the Vatican, and had no land, army, or government, but was frankly and exclusively the head of a world church. It would hardly be doubted that an appointment at that time would have violated the spirit if not the letter of the Constitution. Madison, who vetoed a bill to incorporate a church because he believed it violative of the First Amendment, would hardly have concurred in such an appointment. Nor, it would seem, would William Howard Taft, the only person who ever served as both President and Chief Justice. After the Spanish-American War, with its transfer of the Philippine Islands to American control, he wrote to Pope Leo XIII:

> The transfer of sovereignty and all governmental property rights and interests from the crown of Spain to the United States in the Philippine Islands contained in the Treaty of Paris was a transfer from a government between which and the Church of Rome there had been in those islands the closest association in property, religion, and politics, to a government which by the law of its being is absolutely prevented from having such associations with any church. To make the transfer effectual . . . all union of civil and clerical agencies for performance of political functions must end.[124]

The constitutional difficulty would not be avoided by designating the emissary to the Catholic Church as an "ambassador," notwithstanding the President's express constitutional power to appoint ambassadors. It would seem that the President's lack of constitutional power to make alliances with churches could not be evaded by designating his emissary an "ambassador."

Therein lies the constitutional issue: Has the Lateran Treaty of 1929 between Pope Pius XI and Mussolini made a constitutionally significant difference? Was General Clark's appointment merely the performance by the President of "an act of state of the most commonplace kind," as Professor Corwin designated it, or was it an act of "participation in the affairs of a religious organization"? In short: Was General Clark sent to the ruler of 100 acres of land—more or less—governed by a ruler of some thousand subjects, or was he sent to the head of an international church with 400,000,000 communicants?

That the Vatican itself had no doubts as to what the ambassadorship should be seems clear from the column from Rome of Anne O'Hare McCormick appearing in the New York *Times* of December 24, 1951. Evidently reflecting the Vatican's views, Mrs. McCormick wrote:

> Advocates who argue that the appointment is not to a religious leader but to the ruler of the scrap of real estate called Vatican City do not get much support here. The mission is either to the Pope as the

319

head of a worldwide church or it is nothing, it is pointed out; to pretend anything else is to make the appointment useless or reduce it to absurdity. All other countries sending representatives to the Vatican accredit them to the Holy See, and if the United States decides to send one at all it will follow the regular formula.

A reasonable argument can be made that equating an emissary to the Holy See with an ambassador to London or Paris is to elevate fiction over fact. The fiction does not rest primarily on the geographic minuteness of Vatican City, but rather on the expressed justification of the appointment. An ambassador is necessary, it is argued, because we need the Vatican as an ally in the war against Communism. Obviously, not much of military value is to be expected from the Pope's Swiss Guards, who, unlike members of the armed forces of the usual political state, are not subjects of the Pope but merely employees; in fact, they have struck for higher pay and better working conditions. The value of our proposed Vatican ambassador lies in his ability to obtain important information through the Vatican from behind the "iron curtain." But the Vatican obtains this information not because it is or pretends to be a political state, but because it is headed by Christ's vicar on earth, to whom thousands of priests and bishops in Communist-dominated Europe and Asia have sworn fealty and obedience, and to whom they report the information we want to obtain. As Mrs. McCormick clearly showed, it is a cooperation of a world church that we seek to enlist, not that of a city-state.

We have seen throughout this volume how important a role in the constitutional law of church and state is played by fictions. It may well be that whatever tribunal, judicial or legislative, called on to determine the constitutionality of a Presidential appointment of an ambassador to the Vatican will do what has so frequently been done, accept fiction for fact and uphold the appointment as an "act of state of the most commonplace kind." Yet if it does so it may well be — to use Roger Williams' phrase — "confounding the Civil and Religious"; certainly it will be using religion "as an engine for state purposes." Perhaps the appointment does not violate the strict letter of the Constitution; nevertheless, there are many who believe that it does violence to the spirit of the First Amendment and the American tradition of the mutual independence and freedom of church and state.

### CHAPTER NINE

# The Public School and Religious Education

## EVOLUTION OF THE AMERICAN PUBLIC SCHOOL
### *Colonial Backgrounds*

THERE ARE MANY who believe that the American public school, free, secular, and open to all, is the supreme achievement of American democracy. The evolution of that institution is a fascinating story, meriting much fuller treatment than is possible in this volume.[1] Here our treatment must be limited to that aspect of the development that deals with its secularization.

As is well known, the American secular school of today is founded on the religious schools of the colonial period. Its development parallels and is indeed part of the evolution of the principle of separation and freedom in religion from the theocracy of New England and the Erastianism of Virginia. The concept of public education divorced of denominational control was foreign to the colonial mind. As the Beards put it:

> The idea of elementary schools supported by taxation, freed from clerical control and offering instruction to children of all classes, found no expression in colonial America. Indeed it was foreign to the experience of the Greeks, Romans, and Europeans of the Middle Ages, whose psychology still dominated the West.[2]

Justice Frankfurter expressed the same thought in his concurring opinion in the McCollum case:

> . . . Traditionally, organized education in the Western world was Church education. It could hardly be otherwise when the education of children was primarily study of the Word and the ways of God. Even in the Protestant countries, where there was a less close identification of Church and State, the basis of education was largely the Bible, and its chief purpose inculcation of piety. To the extent that the State intervened, it used its authority to further aims of the Church.
>
> The emigrants who came to these shores brought this view of education with them. Colonial schools certainly started with a religious orientation. . . .[3]

The extent to which the sociology and economics of the Old World were reflected in the education practices of the New can be observed from the differences in the rate of the development of public education in the different sections of America. Virginia and the South were settled by the royalists of England; Southern society was laid out on aristocratic lines, and the plantation type of farming became established. Southern plantation owners had little interest in education for the common people. Governor Berkeley of Virginia is reported to have declared: "I thank God there are no free schools nor printing presses, and I hope we shall not have them these hundred years."[4] This philosophy pervaded Southern thinking for a long time, as is evidenced by the fact that no real system of public education of any consequence developed in the South until the 19th century.[5]

The lack of interest in the education of the poor was furthered by the fact that practically no middle class existed in Virginia in the colonial period. The children of the aristocratic land-owning class received their elementary education from private tutors and their higher education in England. Schooling was virtually restricted to the upper classes. Occasionally one might find a charity school giving a few poor children the opportunity to learn reading, writing, some arithmetic, and the catechism and religious observances of the Church of England.[6] By and large, however, the lower classes were not deemed worthy of more training than was required for the carrying on of their occupations. Accordingly apprentice schools for the children of the poor were established by law in 1672, where reading and writing were taught only as an incident to the learning of a useful trade.[7]

The tardiness of the South in developing a system of common education may be explained on social and economic grounds; yet the religious factor may also reasonably be assigned as an effective cause. The Anglican Church was dominant in the South, and Anglicanism was the major religion during the colonial period. Of all Protestant denominations, Anglicanism was closest to Roman Catholicism; it was the most episcopal, ritualistic, and least Bible-centered of all Protestant sects. For the lay communicant reliance on priests and rites was more important than reliance on the Bible. Hence there was no great religious compulsion in colonial Virginia for widespread literacy. When, however, the Great Awakening reached the South in the middle of the 18th century and the Anglicans were displaced by the Baptists and Methodists as the dominant sects, these Bible-centered, personalized, and democratic denominations laid great stress on individual communion with God through the Bible; and for this a widespread literacy was indispensable.

Religion was likewise an important factor in the leadership

taken by New England in the development of public education; though of course also significant were the socioeconomic elements (the proximity of residences as compared to the great distances between plantation centers in the South, the dominant middle class, the rise of trade and commerce, etc.). Government in New England was based on Congregational Church polity, the democratic town meeting, the freehold tenure of land, the Bible as the basis of a theocratic commonwealth, and a special emphasis on the right and importance of the individual in morals and in civic government.

What appears to be the first public school in America was established by the Boston Town Meeting in 1635. This school—like similar ones started in other parts of Massachusetts for the teaching and nurture of children—was largely financed out of the public treasury. These schools were open to all on equal terms, with the poor receiving free instruction.[8] The first compulsory education law in America was a Massachusetts act of 1642, whereby the selectmen of all towns were charged with seeing to it that all parents and masters provided for the education of their children. Though this was primarily an apprenticeship law for the training of children in some suitable employment, it also required that the parents of children be assured "especially of their ability to read and understand the principles of religion."[9]

The religious base of public education in colonial New England is evident from the preamble to the famous Massachusetts law of 1647, which established the American pattern of local or municipal responsibility in public elementary education. The law read:

> It being one chief project of that old deluder, Satan to keep men from the knowledge of the Scriptures, as in former times by keeping them in an unknown tongue, so in these later times by persuading from the use of tongues, that so at least the true sense and meaning of the original might be clouded by false glosses of saint-seeming deceivers, that learning may not be buried in the graves of our fathers in the church and commonwealth, the Lord assisting our endeavors,—
>
> It is therefore ordered, that every township within this jurisdiction, after the Lord hath increased them to the number of fifty householders, shall then forthwith appoint one within their town to teach all such children as shall resort to him, to read and write, whose wages shall be paid, either by the parents or masters of such children, or by the inhabitants in general, by way of supply, as the major part of those who order the prudentials of the town shall appoint. And it is further ordered that where any town shall increase to the number of one hundred families, or householders, they shall set up a grammar school, the master thereof being able to instruct youths so far as they shall be fitted for the university. Provided that if any town neglect the performance

hereof above one year, that every such town shall pay five pounds to the next school until they shall perform this order.[10]

When township schools were established in accordance with this law, town and church were identical, and there was no church-state problem in education. The schools so established were financed out of the same public treasury that financed all other township activities. When disestablishment and separation secularized the New England township, it was inevitable that the same forces should operate to secularize the township schools. This was the pattern that American education has adopted.

Professor Cubberley describes the New England townships and their relationship to the public education as follows:

> . . . The governing authorities for church and civil affairs were much the same. When acting as church officers they were known as Elders and Deacons; when acting as civil or town officers they were known as Selectmen. The State, as represented in the colony legislature or the town meeting, was clearly the servant of the Church, and existed in large part for religious ends. It was the State acting as the servant of the Church which enacted the laws of 1642 and 1647, requiring the towns to maintain schools for religious purposes. Now, so close was the connection between the religious town which controlled church affairs, and the civil town which looked after roads, fences, taxes, and defense — the constituency of both being one and the same, and the meetings of both being held at first in the Meeting-House — that when the schools were established the colony legislature placed them under the civil, as involving taxes and being a public service, rather than under the religious town. The interests of one were the interests of both, and, being the same in constituency and territorial boundaries, there seemed no occasion for friction or fear. From this religious beginning the civil school, and the civil school town and township, with all our elaborate school administrative machinery, were later evolved.
>
> The erection of a town hall, separate from the meeting-house, was the first step in the process. School affairs were now discussed at the town hall, instead of in the church. Town taxes, instead of church taxes, were voted for buildings and maintenance. The minister continued to certificate the grammar-school master until the close of the colonial period, but the power to certificate the elementary school teachers passed to the town authorities early in the eighteenth century. By the close of this century all that the minister, as the surviving representative of church control, had left to him was the right to accompany the town authorities in the visitation of the schools. Thus gradually but certainly did the earlier religious school pass out from under the control of the Church and become a state school. When our national government and the different state governments were established, the States were ready to accept, in principle at least, the theory gradually worked out in New England that schools are state institutions and should be under the control of the State.[11]

Although the New England free, tax-supported public school ultimately prevailed, it was not the sole educational system in colonial America. As has been seen, an entirely different system existed in the South. In the middle colonies, too, a school system developed different from the New England township school; there was not there the same identity of church and state as in New England and Virginia. Hence such schools as were founded communally would have to be either state-established or church-established. Following the model the colonists brought with them from the Old World, the schools which were founded in the middle colonies were generally religious schools of the parochial type, *i.e.,* founded, financed, and operated by the local church and clergy.[12] After the British seized New Amsterdam in 1664, when the Royalists were in control in England, there did spring up, as a consequence, a private school movement alongside the Dutch system with its parochial dominated institutions. But this mixture of types of schools in New York did not substantially alter the parochial system of schools in the middle colonies.[13]

The religious character of colonial elementary education is indicated by the curriculum used in the schools. In most cases it consisted largely of the Bible and moralizings based on the Bible. In fact, all the subjects in the curriculum were there because they made the Bible more understandable. The textbooks clearly showed that Christianity and the Bible were indispensable to the pupil's welfare and teaching. The books used were little more than adaptations from the Bible.

The chief book—indeed, practically the only one—used for the education of younger children in New England toward the end of the 17th century was the *New England Primer*. The *Primer* taught the alphabet with letters and pictures in the following manner:

A—In *Adam's* Fall     J —*Job* feels the Rod
     We sinned all        Yet blesses God
B—This *Book* attend    P—*Peter* denies
                       His Lord and cries

The *Primer* taught the alphabet also by sentences from the Bible. Numerals were taught with reference to Bible chapters, verses, and Psalms. Also included was the story of John Rogers, an English minister who was the first martyr of Queen Mary's reign, with special emphasis on his exhortation to his children before his death. The *Primer* closed with the Westminster Shorter Catechism.

Summarizing, it may be said that in the three areas of the original thirteen colonies during the 18th century there were three distinct types of control and support of education. In the South responsibility for education rested primarily with the family, and only the children of the wealthy plantation owners could obtain education other than apprentice training. In the middle colonies parochial-controlled education was stressed; whereas in New England there was established a town-sponsored school that was the foundation of the free, secular, and universal education that now pervades America.[14]

### The States Assume Responsibility

So the situation stood at the time of the Revolution and the founding of our nation. During the Revolutionary War there was no time to consider the problems of public education; but with the return of peace the importance the Continental Congress attached to common education is indicated by the provision in the Northwest Ordinance of 1787 that required that there "shall be reserved the lot No. 16, of every township, for the maintenance of public schools within the said township; also one-third part of all gold, silver, lead and copper mines, to be sold, or otherwise disposed of as Congress shall hereafter direct. . . ."[15] Daniel Webster, in his usual hyperbolic manner, doubted whether "one single law of any lawgiver, ancient or modern, has produced effects of more distant, marked and lasting character than the Ordinance of 1787. . . . It set forth and declared it to be a high and binding duty of Government to support schools and advance the means of education."[16]

The members of the Constitutional Convention, however, apparently felt that though the support of schools and education might be a high and binding duty of government, it was to be, under the system they were establishing, a duty of state rather than Federal government. In any event, they omitted any reference to education among the powers conferred on the national government, and thereby left the subject to the states under the Tenth Amendment, which reserved to the States the "powers not delegated to the United States by the Constitution nor prohibited by it to the States."

The states accepted the responsibility left with them. Even in the South they recognized this responsibility—to a large extent as a result of the writings of Thomas Jefferson, who urged universal education for utilitarian purposes controlled by civic authorities and free from sectarian control.[17] In 1779 Jefferson submitted to the Virginia legislature a bill for the More General Diffusion of Knowledge, which provided for the division of the state into districts, with an elementary school in each district to teach arithmetic, reading, and writing. The most promising pupil in each school would receive an academy or grammar school education, which would include classical and modern languages, English grammar, geography, and higher mathematics. The schools were to be financed by direct taxation, and were to be subject to local control; but "no religious reading, instruction or exercise shall be prescribed or practiced, inconsistent with the tenets of any religious sect or denomination."[18]

Though the bill itself failed to pass, the Virginia legislature in 1796 adopted the main features of the plan. This bill, along with Jefferson's other writings on education, had a profound effect on the development of public education in America. His optimistic view of the beneficial effects of universal education has since pervaded American educational philosophy. He was the first American to emphasize public education as an instrument for the realization of democracy and the furthering of social reform.[19] According to him, "If the condition of man is to be progressively ameliorated, as we fondly hope and believe, education is to be the chief instrument in effecting it." Freedom, too, could be secured only by widespread education: "Enlighten the people generally, and tyranny and oppression of body and mind will vanish like evil spirits at the dawn of day."[20]

Public education in the United States rests on three fundamental assumptions: First, that the legislature has the power to tax all— even the childless and those whose children attend private schools— in order to provide free public education for all; second, that the legislature has the power to require every parent to provide for his children a basic education in secular subjects; third, that the education provided by the state in the free schools must be secular. None of these assumptions was accepted without a struggle. Many persons found it difficult to accept the proposition that education is a function of the state (the Catholic Church still denies it); and found it entirely unreasonable that they should be taxed to educate other people's children.

This principle of universal responsibility for universal education was dramatically vindicated in 1835 by Thaddeus Stevens, one of the greatest and most maligned figures in American history. In that year a proposal was introduced in the Pennsylvania legislature to repeal a law enacted the previous year that permitted school districts to levy taxes for the support of public schools. Stevens spoke in opposition to the repealer, and his address not only caused its defeat but was printed and distributed throughout the country, serving for many years to further free public education. To the claim that it was unjust to tax people to educate others' children, Stevens replied:

> It is for their own benefit, inasmuch as it perpetuates the government and ensures the due administration of the laws under which they live, and by which their lives and property are protected. Why do they not urge the same objection against all other taxes? The industrious, thrifty, rich farmer pays a heavy county tax to support criminal courts, build jails, and pay sheriffs and jail keepers, and yet probably he never has had and probably never will have any direct personal use for them. . . . He cheerfully pays the burdensome taxes which are necessarily levied to support and punish convicts, but loudly complains of that which goes to prevent his fellowbeing from becoming a criminal and to obviate the necessity of those humiliating institutions.

To those who conceived of education as exclusively a private obligation, Stevens emphasized the importance of civic intelligence in an elective republic, and the function of the school in educating for citizenship, saying:

> If an elective republic is to endure for any great length of time, every elector must have sufficient information, not only to accumulate wealth and take care of his pecuniary concerns, but to direct wisely the Legislature, the Ambassadors, and the Executive of the Nation; for some part of all these things, some agency in approving or disapproving of them, falls to every freeman.[21]

So conclusive was the victory of Jefferson and Stevens, that the constitutions of all fifty states today provide in one way or another for free, tax-supported public education. Typical of the state constitutional provisions is the following from the constitution of Indiana:

> Knowledge and learning, generally diffused throughout a community, being essential to the preservation of a free government; it shall be the duty of the General Assembly to encourage, by all suitable means, moral, intellectual, scientific, and agricultural improvement; and to provide, by law, for a general and uniform system of common schools, wherein tuition shall be without charge, and equally open to all.

This victory was in harmony with the American spirit. As the Beards said:

> For a nation of farmers and mechanics, bent on self-government and possessed of the ballot, there was only one kind of an educational program in keeping with self-respect, namely, a free and open public school system supported by taxation and nonsectarian in its control.[22]

The validity under Federal and state constitutions of laws taxing nonparents and corporations for public education has been firmly established for a long time.[23] The Supreme Court put it simply in the Everson case: "It is much too late to argue that legislation intended to facilitate the opportunity to get a secular education serves no public purpose" which can constitutionally be financed out of tax-raised funds.

The second assumption—that the state can compel all parents to provide their children with a minimum secular education—will be discussed more fully later in this volume.[24] Here it may be sufficient to point out that this assumption also has been accepted by all the states, and its validity under Federal and state constitutions is now well settled. It is to the third assumption—that state education must be secular—that we now address ourselves.

### Mann's Struggle against Sectarianism

It is a widespread belief that the elimination of sectarianism from the American public schools resulted chiefly if indeed not exclusively from the efforts of Horace Mann in Massachusetts. The monumental contribution made to American public education by Mann is of course hardly open to doubt. And this contribution was not confined to the struggle against sectarianism. He opposed rote learning and urged education through pleasure; he strove for uniform textbooks, adequate school libraries, better school architecture, and more comfortable furnishings. Yet though he is probably best known for his successful campaign to eliminate sectarianism from public education, the victory was inevitable, and had largely been won before Mann became secretary of the first state education board in 1837. Mann's victory, stupendous as it was, was chiefly a defensive victory, securing a principle that had already been substantially achieved.

The factors that made the secularization of the public schools inevitable were to a large extent the same factors that resulted in the secularization of government secured by the First Amendment. These included the multiplicity of competing and jealous sects, the expansion of trade and commerce, and the rise of nationalism that resulted in the gradual change of the position of education as a medium for the promotion of religion to an agency for training for economic living and civic responsibility, and the rationalism, humanism, and Unitarianism that pervaded American life at the end of the 18th century. It was a combination of these and other factors that made possible Mann's successful defense of nonsectarianism in the Massachusetts schools.

The schools established in Massachusetts under the law of 1647 were pervaded by Calvinist pietism, but by 1789 other influences were more prominent in the State's public schools. A 1789 law described the objective of education as not merely to frustrate that old deluder Satan, but, in much broader terms, to inculcate "principles of piety and justice and a sacred regard for truth, love of country, humanity, and universal benevolence, industry and frugality; chastity, moderation and temperance, and those other virtues which are the ornament of society and the basis upon which the republican Constitution is founded. . . ." Under this law the Westminster Catechism was still recited in some schools, but the custom was breaking down under the onslaught of Unitarians, Universalists, Episcopalians, Baptists, and Methodists, whose children invaded the public schools to disturb the Congregationalists' monopoly.[25]

By 1826 there were almost five times as many children in the public schools of Massachusetts as there were in the private schools, and their religious heterogeneity made inevitable the enactment of the law of 1827, which, superseding the law of 1789, conferred on school committees the right to select textbooks for the public schools, "provided . . . that said committee shall never direct any school books to be purchased or used, in any of the schools under their superintendence, which are calculated to favor any religious sect or tenet."[26]

This law was enacted while Mann was a member of the Massachusetts Senate, and with his support. Ten years later the legislature established a state board of education, and Mann gave up a promising career as a lawyer and politician to heed the unanimous demand that he become its first secretary. In that capacity he found widespread disregard of the 1827 law, and he set about to enforce its provisions with a ruthless impartiality. As was to be expected, this program of strict enforcement brought down on him a torrent of sectarian wrath and abuse. Many charged him with atheism and hostility to religion; the more charitable declared only that he was motivated by a Unitarian bias. Mann was an avowed Unitarian, who rejected the concept of a Trinity in the Godhead, believed in the innate goodness of man and his ability to develop morally and spiritually, and regarded Jesus as a great and good man, divine only in the sense that he recognized his oneness with God better than any other man.[27] Whether his strict enforcement of the 1827 law was motivated by a Unitarian bias is another matter; Mann was an educator, and as such he needed no religious bias to motivate his passionate defense and enforcement of the law, as can be seen from his controversy with Frederick A. Packard.

(Before we consider the Mann-Packard dispute, a parenthetical observation is in order. It will be observed throughout this volume how often promoters of religion and religious education express their wrath against public officials who take seriously their oaths of office and enforce laws and judicial decisions against religious intrusions on the public school. Churchmen have frequently—expressly or implicitly—countenanced the disregard of laws and decisions that they deemed prejudicial to the rightful place of religion in the public schools. Aside from the questionable morality of such action by those whose special mission in life is to preserve and promote morality, such action contradicts the basic justification for bringing religion into the public schools—that religious education is necessary for citizenship training; for obedience even to distasteful laws is the first obligation of good citizenship.)

Packard, as agent of the American Sunday School Union, submitted to the Massachusetts educational authorities a list of the Union's books for use in the public schools. Mann, together with the governor of Massachusetts, examined the list, and judging it to be sectarian, rejected it. Packard chose Abbott's *Child at Home* as the best book on which to draw the issue, and wrote to friends in Massachusetts urging them to have the book placed in the schools. The nature of the book can be gauged from the following selection from the chapter on "Deception":

> But we must not forget that there is a day of most solemn judgment near at hand. . . . Oh, how dreadful must be the confusion and shame with which the deceitful child will then be overwhelmed! The angels will all see your sin and your disgrace. And do you think they will wish to have a liar enter heaven, to be associated with them? No! They must turn from you with disgust. The Savior will look upon you in his displeasure. Conscience will rend your soul. And you must hear the awful sentence, "Depart from me, into everlasting fire, prepared for the devil and his angels." Oh, it is a dreadful thing to practice deceit. It will shut you from heaven. It will confine you in eternal woe. Though you should escape detection as long as you live; though you should die and your falsehood not be discovered, the time will soon come when it will all be brought to light, and then the whole universe of men and of angels will be witnesses of your shame. If any child who reads this feels condemned for past deceptions, oh, beware, and do not postpone repentance till the day of judgment shall arrive.[28]

Since *Child at Home* was chosen by Packard to establish his contention that the books in the Sunday School Union's list were not sectarian, one can imagine what was contained in the other books. Mann described how such literature affected him:

> Like all children, I believed what I was taught. To my vivid imagination, a physical hell was a living reality, as much so as though I could have heard the shrieks of the tormented, or stretched out my hand to grasp their burning souls, in a vain endeavor for their rescue. Such a faith spreads a pall of blackness over the whole heavens, shutting out every beautiful and glorious thing; while beyond that curtain of blackness I could see the bottomless and seething lake filled with torments, and hear the wailing and agony of its victims. . . . Had there been any possibility of escape, could penance, fasting, self-inflicted wounds, or the pains of a thousand martyr-deaths, have averted the fate, my agony of apprehension would have been alleviated; but there, beyond effort, beyond virtue, beyond hope, was this irreversible decree of Jehovah, immutable, from everlasting to everlasting. . . . The consequences upon my mind and happiness were disastrous in the extreme. Often, on going to bed at night, did the objects of the day and the faces of friends give place to a victim of the awful throne, the inexorable judge, and the hapless myriads, among whom I often seemed to see those whom I loved best; and there I wept and sobbed until Nature found that counterfeit repose in exhaustion whose genuine reality she should have found in freedom from care and spontaneous happiness of childhood.[29]

Packard loosed on Mann a long campaign of vilification, even carrying the issue to the state board and the legislature in an effort to oust Mann from his position. He charged Mann not only with Unitarian bias but with an intent to drive God and religion out of the schools. The controversy spread throughout the state and even extended to various parts of the nation. Both the school board and the legislature stood firm behind Mann, until he resigned in 1848 and entered Congress to fill the vacancy caused by the death of John Quincy Adams.[30]

It is generally said that Mann's struggle was not against religion in the public schools but solely against sectarianism. Mann himself so interpreted his position. In a letter to a clergyman who accused him of heresy, Mann wrote:

> Every one who has availed himself of the means of arriving at the truth on this point, knows that I am in favor of religious instruction in our schools to the extremest verge to which it can be carried without invading those rights of conscience which are established by the laws of God and guaranteed to us by the Constitution of the State.[31]

In his final report in 1848 Mann set forth his credo. Referring to the time of his appointment in 1837, he said:

> . . . I believed then, as now, that religious instruction in our schools, to the extent which the Constitution and the laws of the State allowed

and prescribed, was indispensable to their highest welfare, and essential to the vitality of moral education. Then, as now, I believed that sectarian books and sectarian instruction, if their encroachment were not resisted, would prove the overthrow of the schools. . . . And I avail myself of this, the last opportunity which I may ever have, to say in regard to all affirmations or intimations that I have ever attempted to exclude religious instruction from the schools, or to exclude the Bible from the schools, or to impair the force of that volume, that they are now, and always have been, without substance or semblance of truth. . . .

. . . That our public schools are not theological seminaries, is admitted. That they are debarred by law from inculcating the peculiar and distinctive doctrines of any one religious denomination amongst us, is claimed; that they are also prohibited from even teaching that what they do teach is the whole of religion, or all that is essential to religion, is equally certain. But our system earnestly inculcates all Christian morals; it founds its morals on the basis of religion; it welcomes the religion of the Bible; and in receiving the Bible, it allows it to do what it is allowed to do in no other system, to speak for itself.

To Mann the purpose of religious education in the schools was to enable the child

to judge for himself according to the dictates of his own reason and conscience, what his religious obligations are and whither they lead. But if a man is taxed to support a school where religious doctrines are inculcated which he believes to be false, and which he believes that God condemns, then he is excluded from the school by the divine law, at the same time that he is compelled to support it by the human law. This is a double wrong.[32]

Mann's last report, as well as much else of his writing, makes it clear that he envisaged a distinction between religion and sectarianism, and that the dividing line was the Bible. As long as the Bible was permitted "to speak for itself" its reading constituted permissible religious education; once the teacher sought to explain, interpret, or comment on the written word, she engaged in impermissible sectarian instruction. The question of Bible reading in the public school will be discussed later in this volume, but some comment may be made here.

Mann was undoubtedly sincere in believing the validity of his distinction. "Had the Board," he said, "required me to exclude either the Bible or religious instruction, I certainly should have given the earliest opportunity to appoint my successor."[33] As an enlightened and progressive educator whose methods and principles were many years ahead of his time, Mann could not have had much confidence in the pedagogical value of a bare reading of the Bible, or of the ability of a child "to judge for himself" on the basis of such reading "what his religious obligations are and whither they lead." His frequent use of the term "religious instruction" along with "the Bible" indicates clearly that he approved at least expository comment by the teachers, as long as it was limited to the text of the Bible and was nonsectarian in its tenor. Yet it is difficult to believe that Mann could accept the practicability of nonsectarian comment—even limited to the exposition of the text. Is it likely that a Unitarian and a fundamentalist Baptist would teach the Gospel according to Matthew in even approximately the same way? To get an idea of the difficulties facing a teacher trying to teach the Bible "nonsectarianly," one can do no better than read the chapter "Can the Bible Return to the Classroom?" in Conrad Moehlman's *School and Church: The American Way.*

Actually, the distinction between "religious" and "sectarian" is only another of the fictions that are so prominent in the field of church-state relations in the United States. The term "nonsectarian" is frequently used to mean doctrine or practices generally acceptable to all Protestant sects; sometimes it means doctrine or practices that Protestants believe are generally acceptable to all Christians. Lately it has frequently been used to connote doctrine or practices that Protestants believe are generally acceptable to all Christians and Jews, *e.g.,* Christmas celebration and Lord's Prayer recitation. Moreover, as is well known, the Catholic child believes that the reading even without comment of the Protestant Bible is something "that God condemns"; and the Jewish child "believes to be false" that part of the Christian Bible that ascribes divinity to Jesus or to any other human being.

What Mann considered nonsectarianism was Christianity—and indeed less even than that; only as much of Christianity as was generally acceptable to all Protestant denominations. Mann seemingly recognized this: "If the Bible," he said in his last report, "is the exponent of Christianity . . . how can it be said that the school-system which adopts and uses the Bible is anti-Christian or an un-Christian system? . . . If the Old Testament were in the schools, could a Jew complain that Judaism was excluded from them? If the Koran were read regularly and reverently in the schools, could a Mahometan say that Mahometanism was excluded? Or, if the Mormon Bible were in the schools, could it be said that Mormonism was excluded from them?"[34]

### The Triumph of Secularization

Mann's solution proved quite acceptable to Protestants, when each sect realized that it could not expect to obtain control of the schools for the propagation of its own tenets. As long as Catholics and Jews were tiny, inconspicuous minorities their rights and their rare protests could be largely disregarded. When, however, Catholic immigration into this country increased and Catholics concentrated in cities, particularly along the Atlantic seaboard, where they became an organized and highly articulate segment of the population, their rights and protests could not be so easily ignored, and it became increasingly clear that Mann's simple dichotomy of religion vs. sectarianism was not quite adequate to solve all problems. Incidents in New York, Philadelphia, and elsewhere in the United States[35] made it clear that the rapidly growing Catholic population was not content with a solution that satisfied Protestant sects at the expense of non-Protestants.

Those to whom the American secular public school is one of the supreme achievements of our democracy should never forget the debt they owe to the Catholic Church and Catholic parents. The triumph of the secularization of the public school was in no small measure ·due to the persistence of the Church and the courage of Catholic parents in refusing to sacrifice their claims of conscience by yielding to a settlement that was entirely satisfactory to the Protestant majority. The provincial council of the Roman Catholic Church in Baltimore in 1840 imposed on priests the responsibility of seeing to it that Catholic children attending the public schools did not participate in Protestant instruction and practices, and directed them to use their influence to prevent the introduction of these practices into public schools.[36] Many Catholic parents, at the urging of their pastors, protested, and even resorted to court action, to prevent the subjecting of their children to Protestant teachings in violation of their conscience, and as a result suffered abuse and even physical harm.

The role of the Catholic Church in the secularization of American public Education has been recognized in a study of inter-religious relations sponsored by the National Conference of Christians and Jews, which says:

> In the early years of the expressed opposition of the Roman Catholic Church to the "public-school system," the leaders of that opposition repeatedly objected to the inclusion of any religious matter at all in the curriculum, any bible reading or prayers or hymns, even any references in the histories which might be interpreted as a reflection on their church. With the devastating logic characteristic of Latin thinkers, and always irritating to the pragmatic Anglo-Saxons, they insisted that if the schools were not to be under the direction of the churches but at the same time tax-supported, all material, conceivably religious, should be eliminated from the curriculum. However the Protestant population

might differ among themselves in theological theory and in their deductions from the Scriptures, they were agreed that the Bible in itself ought to be familiar to every citizen as it was "the charter of their liberties." Even the Deists of the period felt that observances which made a child conscious of his responsibility to his Maker were a necessary part of education. Catholic opposition to anything that smacked of religious instruction, direct or indirect, while it did not wholly succeed in determining the quality of public-school instruction, did, however, inevitably point to secularization.[37]

Of course the Catholic Church and Catholic parents were not motivated by a yearning for secularism in education—Catholicism does not recognize the possibility of isolating religious teaching from temporal knowledge. Its great complaint against the public schools today is that they are "godless." What the Catholic Church wanted was either the right to bring its own dogma into the public schools for the teaching of Catholic children, or a share of the public school funds for the support of Catholic parochial schools. American Protestantism—whether because of its devotion to the principle of the separation of church and state (as many Protestants say), or because of its antagonism to Catholicism (as many Catholics believe)—would not yield to either demand, and preferred rather to see even Protestant religion taken out of the schools. The result was the secularization of public education in America.

The American public school is a secular school, and not merely a nonsectarian school—even if a distinction could be drawn between the two. The Catholic Church, and many of the Protestant churches as well, undoubtedly do not approve of its secularity. Yet secular it is, in curriculum, method, and spirit. There are exceptions, of course. In many rural schools in the deep South or "Bible belt" some sessions are indistinguishable from those in Baptist Sunday schools. These are not merely not secular—they are obviously sectarian. In some parts of the North vestigial remains—such as a lifeless reading of a few verses from the Bible—can still be found, notwithstanding Supreme Court decisions declaring them unconstitutional. But basically the American public school is a secular school.

The public school today is on the defensive. Its secularity—frequently called "godlessness"—is attacked by many church spokesmen.[38] Statements regarding the secularity of the public schools are being leveled as charges or accusations—as if it were something to be denied or excused. But if we do not have a secular public school we cannot have a secular state: for the separation of church and state means the separation of church and state schools. It is true that the First Amendment became part of the Constitution before

336

the secularization of the schools was accomplished. The reason for that is that the Federal Constitution left the subject of education entirely to the states. As Justice Jackson said in his dissent in the Everson case:

> The Constitution says nothing of education. It lays no obligation on the states to provide schools and does not undertake to regulate state systems of education if they see fit to maintain them.

And that region of the country, New England, that set the pattern for public education in America, was the last to accept the principle of separation. If Virginia had adopted Jefferson's plan for public education, as it adopted his Bill for Establishing Religious Freedom, and if that plan, rather than the Massachusetts system, had set the pattern for common education in the United States, it is at least possible that the secularization of American public education would have been achieved a half century earlier than it was.

As it is, in the words of Justice Frankfurter, "by 1875 the separation of public education from Church entanglements, of the State from the teaching of religion, was firmly established in the consciousness of the nation."[39] President Grant was expressing the national will when in that year he made his famous remarks to the Grand Army of the Tennessee:

> Encourage free schools and resolve that not one dollar appropriated for their support shall be appropriated for the support of any sectarian schools. Resolve that neither the state nor the nation, nor both combined, shall support institutions of learning other than those sufficient to afford every child growing up in the land the opportunity of a good common school education, unmixed with sectarian, pagan, or atheistical dogmas. Leave the matter of religion to the family altar, the church, and the private school, supported entirely by private contributions. Keep the church and state forever separated.[40]

The devotion of America to the secular public school was so strong that Congress sought to protect its secularity by an express rather than an implicit constitutional provision. With but seven dissenters out of 187, the House of Representatives in 1876 proposed a constitutional amendment that would have prohibited the teaching of "the particular creed or tenets of any religion, or anti-religious sect, organization or denomination [other than] the reading of the Bible."[41] The reasons for the failure of the passage of the Senate counterpart of this amendment by the required two-thirds vote have already been discussed;[42] this failure was clearly not caused by any substantial disagreement with its substance. Today, either by constitutional provision or by statute, practically every state in the union prohibits religious teaching in the public schools, with the occasional exception of the reading of the Bible without comment.[43]

A secular state requires a secular state school; but the secularization of the state does not mean the secularization of society. Only by accepting a totalitarian philosophy, either in religion or politics or both, can the state be equated with society. We are a religious people even though our government is secular. Our democratic state must be secular, for it does not purport or seek to pre-empt all of societal life. Similarly the public school need not and should not be the totality of the educative process. Justice Jackson said in his dissent in the Everson case:

> Our public school . . . is organized on the premise that secular education can be isolated from all religious teaching so that the school can inculcate all needed temporal knowledge and also maintain a strict and lofty neutrality as to religion.

The Constitution, which precludes the use of the public schools for religious indoctrination, precludes as well the pre-empting of the whole of the child's time so as to leave no adequate part for religion. And to those who cannot accept the premise on which the public school rests, and believe that religious indoctrination cannot be effected independent of other education, the same Constitution guarantees the right to maintain private schools in which religion and education are inextricably integrated.

Many of those who attack the godlessness of the public schools reflect an attitude of defeatism toward the capacity of religion to win and hold its communicants on its own and are willing to endanger the integrity of the public school system in an attempt to utilize its machinery to succor religion. A cynic might suggest that if religion has reached the point where it is required to look to princes for salvation, it will not find it there.

## THE RELIGIOUS GROUPS AND THE PUBLIC SCHOOLS

### Protestant

There is probably no single Protestant position on any issue; there is even some Protestant dissent on the opposition to the appointment of an ambassador to the Vatican, or to direct Federal aid to parochial schools. Nevertheless, some generalizations may reasonably be made concerning Protestant attitudes toward the public school. These generalizations are probably valid in respect to most Protestant church groups and clergymen.

American Protestantism considers itself the parent and protector of the public school system in America. Protestants generally believe that it was under Protestant auspices that the public school system in America began. One Protestant layman expressed the thought with a naïve yet revealing simplicity: "The Catholics have their parochial schools and the Protestants have the public schools."[44] The pride Protestantism takes in the American public school system is fairly unanimous; but there unanimity ends. When it comes to the secularity of the public schools, sharp division is to be found. Two main emphases can be discerned. On the one hand is the group in which principal emphasis is on the preservation of the concept of the separation of church and state. This group does not disregard or minimize the importance of religious education, but recognizes that the use of the public school system to promote religious education would compromise the principle of separation and would thus impair religious freedom. This approach was well expressed by Erwin Griswold, Dean of Harvard Law School, and a layman prominent in the affairs of the Congregational Church (who, however, has since taken a considerably more conservative position on the question):[45]

> As I see it, the only sure protection for those who believe deeply in religious freedom is to maintain rigidly the line of separation between church and state. This does not mean that persons who are interested in the separation of church and state are irreligious or antireligious. It merely means that they are free to have whatever religious belief they are led to by their consciences. The right to have that belief should be protected by the state, but the belief and its teaching and its support should not only not be a function of the state, but the state should be wholly debarred from taking any action with respect to it, except the basic one of protecting freedom of religious belief. The moment that the state goes beyond that, the risk that the state will be supporting a particular religious belief or sect, and thus not giving equal religious freedom to all, becomes very great. . . . The only sure way to protect against the very serious risk that encroachments will get out of hand is, as I see it, to hold steadfast against encroachments at all.[46]

Many of this group are affiliated with Protestants and Other Americans United or sympathetic to its purposes. They realize that the integrity of their defense of the principle of separation against Roman Catholic encroachment would be seriously compromised by advocacy of the use of the public school system to promote religious education.

How widespread among Protestants are the views of this group is difficult to estimate. Their views find expression in what are probably two of the most highly influential Protestant publications, *The Christian Century* and *The Churchman*. Their views reflect the position of the liberal Protestant denominations, the Universalists and the Unitarians, and liberal wings within other Protestant denominations — Episcopalian, Congregational, and Methodist. They reflect the position of many Baptist ministers, like Joseph M. Dawson, formerly Executive Secretary of the Baptist Joint Conference Committee on Public Affairs,[47] who remain faithful to the tradition expressed by those Baptists who fought against the Virginia Assessment Bill and for Jefferson's Statute for Religious Liberty. They also reflect the position of the Seventh Day Adventists, whose publication *Liberty* has for many years been in the forefront of the struggle for the strict separation of church and state.

Prior to the Supreme Court's decisions in Engel vs. Vitale and the Schempp case, the major Protestant denominations, particularly those affiliated with the National Council of Churches, did not accept the view of separation above all else.[48] To them the Protestants United or *Christian Century* approach refused to recognize the importance of religion in a child's education and the proper place of religious instruction in the school system, and it sacrificed these values — indispensable to the survival of Protestant Christianity — to the one goal of "separation." To the cry of the "separationists" within Protestantism that the "educationalists" were playing "the Catholics' game," the latter replied that the "separationists" were playing the secularists' game. The "separationists" considered the Roman Catholic Church as the greatest menace to Protestantism, while the "educationalists" viewed secularism and irreligion as the prime menace. As one Protestant writer stated:

> Certainly the pressure from the Roman Catholic hierarchy will drive us to take a more definite position on the relation of church and state to education. Let us seek to make it pro-Protestant rather than anti-Catholic. . . . Secularism, like the dominance of an authoritarian sect, is an extreme to be avoided, a danger to be considered in forming a Protestant policy toward education. The problem is to combat secularism without succumbing to sectarianism.[49]

The position of the "educationalists" was forcefully expressed by one of its most articulate spokesmen, Luther A. Weigle, formerly dean of Yale Divinity School, who testified in favor of Bible reading in the Schempp case:

> We must keep sectarianism out of our public schools. But that does not necessitate stripping the schools of religion. To exclude religion from the public schools would be to surrender these schools to the sectarianism of atheism or irreligion. President Butler of Columbia University says, in his report for 1934: "So far as tax-supported schools

are concerned, an odd situation has been permitted to arise. The separation of church and state is fundamental in our American political order, but so far as religious instruction is concerned, this principle has been so far departed from as to put the whole force and influence of the tax-supported school on the side of one element of the population, namely, that which is pagan and believes in no religion whatsoever."

The principle of religious freedom is designed to protect religious belief, not to hinder or destroy it. It is meant to insure the free exercise of religion according to the dictates of conscience, not to limit that exercise by forcing secularism upon American citizens. For the State even tacitly to deny religion in its schools would be to impair the religious liberty of that vast majority of American citizens who believe in God and desire that the education of their children give proper place to religious belief.[50]

It seems clear that before the Engel and Schempp cases a large, possibly a major, segment of the American Protestant church was not content with the bargain made in the 19th century—the secularization of the public school rather than the public financing of Catholic education within or without the public schools. This segment of Protestantism approved the elimination of sectarianism from the schools, but believed that the elimination of religion was an unnecessary wrong that should be remedied quickly before our youth succumbed completely to secularism and irreligion. How religion was to be brought back into the schools without bringing sectarianism along with it was a matter on which these Protestants disagreed. But they did agree that religion must be brought back into the public schools, and they agreed with most other Protestants that public education must remain unified and not be split up into separate sectarian systems.

The decisions of the Supreme Court in the Engel and Schempp cases appear to have effected a significant change in Protestant thinking. As will be seen later, it was largely Protestant support of these decisions that defeated efforts to amend the Constitution to overrule them. To what extent these official organizational statements actually reflected the views of the rank and file of the Protestant clergy and of Protestant laymen cannot be gauged with any degree of accuracy. Supporters of the proposed amendments asserted that the official organizational statements were contrary to the feelings of the rank and file of Protestantism, particularly among the lay members of Protestant congregations. It may well be that this evaluation of Protestant thinking is correct, but it should be noted that there is really no practicable way of ascertaining the views of the members of a particular group, secular as well as religious, other than through the official utterances of the organizations which are generally accepted as spokesmen for their members.

In summary, it may be said that practically all Protestants are devoted to the principle of universal, common, nonsectarian education and to the American public school system. Many, however, believe the system is deficient in excluding religion, and that the deficiency can practicably be remedied without reverting to the sectarianism of the American colonial schools. On the other hand, many other Protestants believe that an attempt to reintroduce religion into the public schools will impair the principle of the separation of church and state, and inevitably bring with it increased encroachment by the Roman Catholic Church.

## The Catholic Church

Catholics have suffered much at the hands of the public school system during its period of transition from Protestantism to secularism, and there is therefore good reason to explain the historic hostility of the Catholic Church to the public school system. For it cannot be denied that in the past there have been clear manifestations of hostility to the public school system by spokesmen of the Catholic Church. The popularity of Paul Blanshard's *American Freedom and Catholic Power* has made many Americans familiar with the quotation from Father Paul J. Blakely's pamphlet, *May an American Oppose the Public School,* that "Our first duty to the public school is not to pay taxes for its maintenance." Blanshard also quotes Father William McManus, assistant director of the Department of Education of the National Catholic Welfare Conference, who, in testifying before a Senate Committee in 1947 said:

> In the totalitarian nation, the government is the teacher; the Government controls all the schools which it uses for the mental enslavement of the people. In the free nation, the government refrains from direct educational activities.[51]

Testifying before the House committee that was considering the same legislation, Elmer E. Rogers of the Scottish Rite Masons, Southern Jurisdiction, and a member of the executive committee of Protestants and Other Americans United, took delight in quoting a number of other statements from Catholic Church sources that showed bitter hostility to the American public school system.[52]

During recent years the Catholic Church has modified its expressed hostility to the public school system. Church spokesmen now deny that the church is opposed to the public school system; this, they argue, cannot be so, inasmuch as half the Catholic children in the country attend public schools. The enemy is not the public school, but its godlessness. The title of Bishop John F. Noll's pamphlet is descriptive: *Our National Enemy No. 1 — Education Without Religion.* Today the Catholic Church is by far the most vigorous and consistent opponent of the secularity of our public schools, although the intensity of the opposition has been somewhat lessened since the Schempp decision.

Nevertheless, it is not the absence of religion, nor even the absence of the Catholic religion along with all other religions, that is sufficient to explain the attitude of the Catholic Church toward the public school system. It must be remembered that Catholicism does not have that urgency toward universal literacy that is implicit in Protestantism and Judaism. These religions are Bible-centered, and consider the universal reading of the Bible highly desirable if not mandatory. Catholicism, on the other hand, is priest-centered, and considers attendance at rites, and the recitation of easily memorized prayers, as more important than the reading of the Bible. It is well known that during the Middle Ages literacy was practically limited to the priests and monks; only comparatively recently has the church made any substantial expression of the desirability of the lay reading of the Bible. It is perhaps this difference that explains the fact that public responsibility for universal education, which existed in Judea before the rise of the Catholic Church, is not again to be found until the 1647 statute of Calvinist Massachusetts. Even in recent years, doubts of the desirability of universal education — at least above the elementary level — have been occasionally expressed by organs of the Church. As recently as 1948 *America,* the country's leading Jesuit weekly, expressed the view that

> few will grant that the results of [the] experiment [of providing] free education in public high schools [have] as yet justified the cost to the public treasury.[53]

In the second place, the Catholic Church frequently finds itself an ally of the taxpayers' associations in a desire to reduce funds — or at least prevent their increase — for public schools. The present writer has heard from a number of public educational administrators that often the most effective opponents to increased funds for public schools — even more effective than the real estate lobbies — are legislators and public officials generally believed to be most subject to Catholic Church influence. The motivation, of course, is different. The Church, being tax exempt, is not directly concerned about increased real estate taxes; but it is concerned with the competition of the publicly financed schools with the privately supported parochial schools. Added funds for public schools mean increased and better facilities, making the public schools more attractive to Catholic children, who, according to the church, should be in the parochial schools. At least this is the explanation many public educators have given for the frequent church opposition to increased funds or facilities for public schools. That this interpretation has at least some basis can be seen from the following extract from an address by Reverend Thomas J. Quigley, superintendent of Catholic Schools in Pittsburgh, at the 1948 meeting of the Religious Education Association:

> Legislation which tends to handicap private schools strikes at another basic American principle which such organizations as the National Association of Manufacturers have recently been rushing to defend, namely the right of private enterprise. Certain elements of our citizenry have been screaming to high heaven about how government subsidization has created unfair competition with private industry, or private housing, and has thereby tended to destroy private enterprise. American Catholics stand on their right to private enterprise in education. Freedom of education is essential to freedom of thought without which all other freedoms become void and empty. *If the government subsidizes public education to the extent that it creates unfair competition with private schools and forces them out of existence, a basic American principle will be lost and we will have taken a long step in the direction of socialism.* Public and private schools are all part of American education. They should not be competitors but partners. No action of the government should serve to make them competitors, nor to subsidize one and handicap the other.[54]

In the third place—and most important—common education is dogmatically impermissible, even if the Catholic religion is taught on an equal basis with other religions. According to Catholic dogma, and in the words of Pope Pius XI in his 1930 encyclical, *Christian Education of Youth,* "education belongs pre-eminently to the Church."[55] Catholic dogma categorically denies the premise of the public school that "secular education can be isolated from all religious teaching"; on the contrary, secular education—according to Catholic teaching—is a contradiction in terms. In the same encyclical, Pius XI stated that the

> only school approved by the Church is one where . . . the Catholic religion permeates the entire atmosphere [and where] all teaching and the whole organization of the school and its teachers, syllabus and textbooks in every branch [is] regulated by the Christian [*i.e.,* Catholic] spirit.[56]

Or, as stated by the former educational director of the National Catholic Welfare Conference:

344

In the Catholic school, religion is not regarded as just one branch in the curriculum. It is not confined to mere religious instruction. It is the foundation, the heart and soul of all other disciplines.[57]

In his dissent in the Everson case, Justice Jackson cited the Canon Law to show the attitude of the Catholic Church toward education and the responsibilities of Catholic children and parents with respect to education. It may be worth while to set forth these canons here as they were quoted by Justice Jackson:

1215. Catholic children are to be educated in schools where not only nothing contrary to Catholic faith and morals is taught, but rather in schools where religious and moral training occupy the first place. . . . (Canon 1372).

1216. In every elementary school the children must, according to their age, be instructed in Christian doctrine.

The young people who attend the higher schools are to receive a deeper religious knowledge, and the bishops shall appoint priests qualified for such work by their learning and piety. (Canon 1373).

1217. Catholic children shall not attend non-Catholic, indifferent schools that are mixed, that is to say, schools open to Catholics and non-Catholics alike. The bishop of the diocese only has the right, in harmony with the instructions of the Holy See, to decide under what circumstances, and with what safeguards to prevent loss of faith, it may be tolerated that Catholic children go to such schools. (Canon 1374).

1224. The religious teaching of youth in any schools is subject to the authority and inspection of the Church.

The local Ordinaries have the right and duty to watch that nothing is taught contrary to faith or good morals, in any of the schools of their territory.

They, moreover, have the right to approve the books of Christian doctrine and the teachers of religion, and to demand, for the sake of safeguarding religion and morals, the removal of teachers and books (Canon 1381). Woywod, Rev. Stanislaus, The New Canon Law, under imprimatur of Most Rev. Francis J. Spellman, Archbishop of New York and others (1940).

Obviously no system of public education acceptable to Protestant "educationalists" would be considered satisfactory by the Catholic Church. This was made clear more than a century ago by Bishop Hughes during the New York controversy:

But it is asked, "then, what system would be deemed just by the Catholics?" I answer, any system that will leave the various denominations each in the full possession of its religious rights over the minds of its children. If the children are to be educated promiscuously as at present, let religion in every shape and form be excluded. Let not the Protestant version of the Scriptures, Protestant forms of prayers, Protestant hymns, be forced on the children of Catholics, Jews, and others, as at present, in the schools for the support of which their parents pay taxes as well as Presbyterians.[58]

It was also made clear in the discussion period at the Religious Education Association meeting in 1948 at which the Reverend Mr. Quigley spoke, when the following question and answer were expressed:

> *Question:* Is it possible to bring religion into the public schools?
> *Father John B. Casey* (Superintendent of Schools, Archdiocese of Indianapolis): From the Catholic standpoint, No. We stand for the integration of religion with every subject in the curriculum.[59]

The aim of the Church, frequently expressed, is "every Catholic child in a Catholic school." The function of the state in Catholic educational theory is primarily financial, *i.e.*, the support of religious schools. The Church believes that in a non-Catholic country like the United States the ideal solution is the one arrived at in Quebec, where there are no secular but only confessional schools, all of which are tax-supported; or at least a system like that in the Netherlands, where government and confessional schools are equally state-supported. Though the Church is sufficiently realistic to realize that neither of these systems is likely to be adopted in the United States in the foreseeable future, it continues its unceasing campaign against the secularism of the public schools.

### The Jewish Groups

Judaism is not a heirarchal religion, and there is no single person or body with inherent power to speak for all Jewry on any issue; hence there is no single position on the question of public school and religion that encompasses the views of all Jews or even all rabbis. There are some extreme Orthodox rabbis and congregations whose attitude toward secular education is more hostile than that of the Catholic Church. There are more who, while not hostile to the public school or even desirous of sharing in tax-raised funds appropriated for public education, nevertheless believe that a full Jewish religious education is obtainable only in a school in which secular as well as sacred subjects are taught under Jewish religious auspices. Thirty years ago the *yeshiva*, or Jewish parochial school, in which the school day was divided between religious and secular studies with the former occupying the major part, was limited to extremely religious, recent immigrants. Today many second and third generation Americans — including many who are themselves not observant of religious practices — are sending their children to the modern Jewish day school, where religious and secular education is integrated by the use of the techniques of modern, progressive education.

The number of Jewish children attending *yeshivas* and day

schools, however, still are but a small percentage of the Jewish children of America; and while the percentage has increased in recent years, it still remains small. One factor that might affect the situation and cause a substantial trend to the private schools would be a serious, imminent threat to the secularity of the public schools. In the absence of such a threat, American Jewish parents generally prefer to keep their children in the public schools, even if it were practicable—as in most cases it is not—to send them to the all-day religious schools.

Organizational Jewry, lay and religious, is practically unanimous in it defense of the public school and its secularity. The earliest protagonist was the Central Conference of American Rabbis, the organization of the Reform rabbinate. As early as 1904 the Conference adopted a resolution recognizing "the absolute necessity of separation of church and state," condemned the introduction and retention of sectarianism in the public school, and authorized the establishment of a committee on church and state to take the necessary steps to preserve the nonsectarianism of the public schools.[60] In the course of the years the lead of the Central Conference has been followed by all major Jewish organizations interested in religious or civic affairs.

The unanimity with which American Jewry opposes sectarianism in the public school is indicated by the filing of briefs *amicus curiae* in the McCollum case in 1947, the Engel case in 1962, and the Schempp case in 1963 by the Synagogue Council of America and the National Community Relations Advisory Council. The former is a coordinating body consisting of six organizations, three rabbinic and three congregational, representing the three divisions of Jewish religious life: Orthodox, Conservative, and Reform. The latter is a coordinating body, consisting of the major Jewish lay organizations—the American Jewish Congress, the American Jewish Committee, B'nai B'rith, the Jewish Labor Committee, and the Jewish War Veterans—as well as Jewish community councils in all the major cities of the country. These organizations, according to a statement in their motion to the Supreme Court for permission to file the brief in the McCollum case, "include in their membership more than eighty percent of Americans affiliated with Jewish organizations."

In their brief, the organizations set forth the reasons that impelled them to intervene in the case:

> . . . We regard the principle of separation of church and state as one of the foundations of American democracy. Both political liberty and freedom of religious worship and belief, we are firmly convinced, can remain inviolate only when there exists no intrusion of secular author-

ity in religious affairs or of religious authority in secular affairs. As Americans and as spokesmen for religious bodies, lay and clerical, we therefore deem any breach in the wall separating church and state as jeopardizing the political and religious freedoms that wall was intended to protect. We believe, further, that our public school system is one of the most precious products of our American democracy. We are, therefore, impelled to voice our opposition whenever attempts are made to compromise its integrity. . . .[61]

In an attempt to ward off charges of friendliness to secularism and irreligion, the brief stated:

Our opposition to religious instruction within the public school must in no way be interpreted as hostility to religious instruction as such. In Jewish history and tradition religious instruction has always been regarded as a most sacred responsibility. The overwhelming majority of Jewish children voluntarily attend after-hour and Sunday schools conducted by the local Jewish communities where they receive their religious education wholly independent of the public school system. We believe that the responsibility for religious education may not and should not be shared by the public school system. American Jewry are not prepared to concede the spiritual insolvency implicit in such a division of responsibility.

There is some difference of opinion among the Jewish organizations as to what separation of church and state in education entails in specific instances; but there is no difference of positions as to the basic principles as they were expressed in the concluding paragraph of the brief:

Since the adoption of the First Amendment, the United States has escaped much of the bitter religious conflict and sectarian strife which have risen in other parts of the world and driven men to violence and bloodshed. That good fortune has been due largely to two of the truly great contributions the American people has made to western civilization: the concept of the separation of church and state and the free public school system. The first, by protecting religion against the intrusion of civil authority and by making it impossible for the state to become a battleground for sectarian preference and favor, has preserved both our political freedom and our religious freedom. The second, by providing for the education of our children on terms of complete equality and without cognizance of their differences in religious beliefs or disbeliefs, has been the cornerstone of our American democracy. The intrusion of sectarianism upon the public school system . . . both threatens the separation of church and state and challenges the traditional integrity of the public schools. That intrusion, if permitted and sanctioned . . . will destroy the institutions which have preserved religious and political freedom in the United States and which have prevented religious warfare in this nation. . . .

348

## Others

The short word "others" used here encompasses almost half the population of the country—that half not affiliated with any church group. In discussions of the problem of religion and the public school, the rights and feelings of these "others" are pretty much ignored. These "others" occasionally make their views known, as at the 1950 Midcentury White House Conference on Children and Youth. The Conference consisted of 4,620 delegates, outstanding local leaders from every section of the country in the fields of religion, education, health, and welfare; of women's and service clubs; of labor unions, fraternal organizations, and other major groups. By and large it represented a clear cross section of American life.

For many months before the Conference religious groups engaged in arduous preparation for the Conference. At the Conference the committee on religion—in complete control of the church groups—submitted a report of four paragraphs that described government responsibility for religious education, including public aid to religious education and the operation of released-time programs. The debate was long and bitter. Finally the report was rejected, and instead, by a vote of two to one, the Conference adopted the following resolution:

> Recognizing knowledge and understanding of religious and ethical concepts as essential to the development of spiritual values and that nothing is of greater importance to the moral and spiritual health of our nation than the works of religious education in our homes and families and in our institutions of organized religion, we nevertheless strongly affirm the principle of separation of church and state which has been the keystone of our American democracy and declare ourselves unalterably opposed to the use of the public schools directly or indirectly for religious educational purposes.[62]

The Conference did not represent merely the unchurched; religious groups were liberally represented. It is significant that the resolution in support of separation and in opposition to public school sponsorship of religious education was offered by a noted Jewish religious educator. (In 1960 another White House Conference on Children and Youth was held, but no action was taken on the question of religion in public education.)

That those most directly concerned with the American public school system, the educators, agreed with the position taken at the White House Conference is indicated by a careful survey undertaken by the National Education Association in 1948. Superintendents of public schools in 2,160 communities responded to a questionnaire which asked them to report what they believed to be the prevailing view of the community on the following propositions:

(a) Formal religious instruction has no place in the public schools because the present public-school emphasis on spiritual and moral values, integrated with all instruction, is sufficient for school purposes.
(b) Some formal type of religious instruction should be worked out for public-school use, because the present curriculum is not adequate.

Better than 70% (1,561) of the superintendents reported that their communities felt that no formal religious instruction in connection with the public school was necessary, whereas less than 30% (599) reported community feeling that such programs were necessary. Nor did the reports indicate any discernible differences between large and small communities. Moreover, even in the 480 communities in which some form of religious instruction in connection with the public schools, either during school time or on school premises, was then in operation, fully 40% (192) of the superintendents reported that the prevailing view in their communities was that the program was unnecessary.[63]

Neither the Engel nor the Schempp case directly involved religious instruction in the public schools, and the amendments proposed to overrule these decisions seem to have been limited to Bible reading and prayer recitation. The fact, therefore, that, notwithstanding the adverse reaction in many quarters particularly to the Engel decision, no amendment to allow religious instruction in the public schools appears to have been seriously considered, is some indication that on the whole the American people are committed to the basic secularity of our public educational system.

This does not mean that there is universal satisfaction even among nonsectarian sources, with the complete absence of religion from the public school curriculum. As will be seen shortly, there are many proposals seeking some recognition of religion in public school teaching. In the main, however, these proposals are urged as being consistent with the basic secularity of public education, and with the premise that it is not the function of the public school to inculcate religious beliefs.

### THE CASE FOR PUBLIC SCHOOL RESPONSIBILITY FOR RELIGIOUS EDUCATION

Among the arguments for public school acceptance of responsibility for religious education, the following are the most frequently and forcefully urged:

(1) We are a religious people. In the words of Dean Weigle:

> The religious faith of America has inspired our history as a people
> and is embodied in our most characteristic institutions. America has no
> state church; but the American government is not godless. The Ameri-
> can government favors no sect and fosters no sectarianism, but is found-
> ed upon faith in God and it protects religion.... The religious faith
> of the American people is expressed in various public acts and customs
> of the federal, state and municipal governments—the annual proclama-
> tion and observance of a day of thanksgiving to God, the setting aside
> of Sundays and certain religious festivals as legal holidays, the opening
> of the sessions of legislative assemblies with prayer, the form of oaths
> used in courts of law and in the inauguration of public officials, the
> appointment of chaplains for the Army and Navy, and so forth.[64]

Hence, if religious education is excluded from the scope of public
school responsibilities we are false to our religious tradition.

(2) Religious education is necessary for the development of
character. This argument was expressed in perhaps extreme terms
by Dr. Fleming when he stated that if religion is excluded from the
public schools

> children will grow up with no knowledge of God and His rules of con-
> duct—practically pagans, potentially dangerous citizens, candidates for
> the prison cell, without hope in time or eternity. And the nation suf-
> fers. Crime is rampant. No home is exempt. Our property and lives are
> in danger. Our mothers, wives, and daughters may suffer and die at
> the hands of rapists.[65]

Others have presented the argument in somewhat more moderate
terms, but they insist that the grave condition of crime, juvenile delinquency, and low moral standards that faces America today can
only or at least most effectively be overcome by religious education,
and that religious education through the public school system is necessary if we would regain our previous high moral standards.[66] The
argument was well expressed in a letter to the New York *Times*:

> A good Catholic can never be a bad citizen. Likewise neither can a
> good Protestant or a good Jew fail in his civic or moral obligation. If, as
> one authority has said, there are hundreds of thousands of "spiritually
> hungry and spiritually naked" children in New York City alone, then a
> challenge exists that must be met promptly and fully. These children,
> to be good citizens, are in desperate need of religious orientation.[67]

Nor is the answer moral education without religious content.
"Religion," says the American Council on Education, "has always
supplied moral sanctions for men's actions."[68] According to a professor of religious education,

351

Public school leaders . . . are increasingly perturbed over the obvious fact that spiritual immaturity and religious illiteracy are widespread and they are beginning to suspect that the two may have some kind of positive correlation. Crime and delinquency are on the increase. The consumption of liquor has reached an all time high. Gambling has become a national scandal. American home life, once lauded as the bulwark of character and morality is in a deplorably unhealthy condition. . . . The feeling that the omission of religion from the total education of American children may have contributed to our present embarrassing predicament is no longer peculiar to churchmen.[69]

(3) Religion is the most important thing in human life. Western civilization is based on the spiritual teachings of Judeo-Christian religion. The contributions made by religion to our culture are writ large in the pages of history. Public school education stultifies itself if it ignores religion, the basis of the whole of civilization and perhaps the most potent motivating force in human life.

(4) The omission of religion from the curriculum is completely condemnatory. The principle of separation of church and state, no matter how broadly interpreted, does not require the state to be hostile to religion. If all subjects but religion are included in the curriculum but religion is conspicuously omitted, the inevitable result is that the child will be led to believe that religion is undesirable or at best unimportant. Dean Weigle expressed this thought forcefully:

> . . . But to omit religion from the public schools is to convey to children a negative suggestion. Such a policy is bound to discredit religion in their minds. It would lead them to conclude that religion is negligible, or unimportant, or irrelevant to the real business of life.
> The danger involved in such a negative policy is greater today than ever before just because the public schools are greater today than ever before. For the old-time public school to omit religion would have been a matter of little consequence for it omitted a great many things. But the public schools of today have the dimensions of life itself. . . . They provide for the education of children in practically every sound human interest—except religion. The omission and ignoring of religion by such schools convey a powerful and condemnatory suggestion.[70]

The same thought was expressed in 1884 by the Third Plenary Council of the Roman Catholic Church, when its committee on schools, convinced that the public school system was responsible for the religious indifference so prevalent in America, stated that:

> To shut religion out of the school, and to keep it for the home and the church, is, logically, to train up a generation that will consider religion good for home and church, but not for the practical business of life.[71]

(5) Children, even if they have an adequate basis of education

in their own faith, are woefully ignorant of the religious beliefs and practices of their classmates and neighbors. The results are interreligious tension, suspicion, and even fear. Only in the public school, where children of all faiths meet and spend so much of their time together, can this ignorance be dispelled. This argument, on which the concept of intercultural education is founded,.will be discussed more fully in the section dealing with joint religious holiday celebrations.

These are the principal arguments in favor of public school assumption of some responsibility for religious education. It is not suggested that even approximate justice has been done them; in this volume it is impracticable to do more than outline them, and that is all that has been attempted here. Students wishing a fuller discussion may consult some of the material listed in the footnotes.[72]

## THE CASE AGAINST PUBLIC SCHOOL RESPONSIBILITY

(1) Among the arguments against public school assumption of responsibility for religious education the one chiefly urged is that such assumption of responsibility is barred by the constitutional principle of the separation of church and state. This argument underlies the entire issue of the constitutionality and legality of religious education in connection with the public school, and will be discussed in the section dealing with that issue. Here it may suffice to quote a short extract from an opinion by an Iowa court, which states the position as forcefully and succinctly as can be found anywhere:

> If there is any one thing which is well settled in the policies and purposes of the American people as a whole, it is the fixed and unalterable determination that there shall be an absolute and unequivocal separation of church and state, and that our public school system, supported by the taxation of the property of all alike—Catholic, Protestant, Jew, Gentile, believer, and infidel—shall not be used directly or indirectly for religious instruction, and above all that it shall not be made an instrumentality of proselyting influence in favor of any religious organization, sect, creed, or belief.[73]

(2) Religion is a private matter. Whether or not we are a religious people—and this is open to question in view of the fact that almost half our population is unaffiliated with any organized religious group—we are also committed to the tradition that religion is not the concern of the government or any of its agencies, including state schools.

(3) The intrusion of religion on the public school system has always had and inevitably will have a divisive rather than an irenic

effect on intergroup relations. Conflict, disharmony, and bitterness always accompany attempts by the public school system to involve itself in religious affairs. The bitter controversies evoked by Bible reading and prayer recitation in the public schools, the released-time program, religious holiday observances in the public schools, and Federal aid to education, among many others, give proof of this sad but undeniable fact.

(4) There is no adequate proof that the public schools are not now doing an adequate job in character training and the inculcation of morals. There is no adequate proof that moral and ethical standards are lower today than they were in the past. Nor is there any adequate proof that religious education—at least as it is now practiced—is necessary or even helpful to training in character or morals; the frequent statements that they are necessary are pure assumptions never successfully established. Indeed, whatever scientific tests have been made indicate that the assumption is unfounded in fact.[74]

(5) The school day is insufficient to provide for religious education. In many communities the lack of adequate school facilities and teachers requires the shortening of the school day and the introduction of double and even triple sessions. There is adequate time after school hours and over the week ends for religious education, without further encroachments on the little time left for secular education.

(6) Invoking the aid of the public school implies lack of ability of the churches to hold their communicants. As a writer in *The Churchman*[75] put it:

> The only construction that can be placed upon Protestant advocacy of sectarianism in public school education is an admission of weakness. Are Protestant parents unable to lead their children toward religion in their own homes? And what of the churches? If Sunday school attendance has fallen off to an alarming extent, what is the reason for it? Why can we not emulate our Jewish friends, many of whose children receive intensive religious instruction after school hours?

## PROPOSED SOLUTIONS

Those who are dissatisfied with the present situation have proposed a number of solutions:

### Teaching Protestantism and Excusing Non-Protestants

Few proponents of religious instruction within the public school advocate the return to the pattern of sectarian education that prevailed in the pre-Mann period. That of course is what is involved basically in the teaching of Protestantism in the public schools — either by public school teachers or by Protestant clergymen — and excusing non-Protestants. Nevertheless, though few propose it, not a few schools in the southern "Bible belt" practice it. How this system and the privilege of nonparticipation affects non-Protestants has been described in the following words by a competent observer of Jewish life in the South:[76]

> There are established periods of Christian Bible study in all the elementary schools (in high schools it is now optional). The Jewish community maintains a respectful silence, primarily because of the tremendous preponderance of the Protestant population. The Jewish children have the option of leaving the room; but it's a difficult decision to make. Some believe it is better to remain seated than to have forty-three children watch one or two others shuffle out. Neither side, of course, can be expected to understand what it's all about. The Christian children wonder why one or two of their number "do not want to hear about God," and the Jewish child is also heartsick as well as bewildered. In some schools they maintain separate rooms for the daily devotionals, which is little better, because it involves only two or three Jewish children and their absence can be as conspicuous as their walking out. (The Roman Catholics have more or less solved this problem, below the high school level, by the great expansion of their parochial school system in recent years.)

Such sectarian teaching in the public school is undoubtedly illegal and unconstitutional under both state and Federal law. "Government," said the Supreme Court in the Zorach case, "may not undertake religious instruction nor blend secular and sectarian education. . . ." The fact that the practice is still fairly widespread in some parts of the country, notwithstanding the clear mandate of the Supreme Court in the Zorach, McCollum, Engel, and Schempp cases and the express prohibitions of sectarian teaching in the public school contained in the constitutions or statutes of every state, indicates clearly that practices are a poor guide to constitutionality. It also indicates the wide gulf that separates the preachings of some churchmen regarding the necessity of religious education to train our children to grow up to be law-abiding citizens from the practices of the same churchmen.

### Separate Teaching of Each Faith

Perhaps the most popular of all proposals is to allow each major religious denomination to teach its creed to the public school children of its communicants during a period set aside for that purpose during the public school day. If attendance is mandatory, the unconstitutionality of the program is hardly open to question. If attendance is voluntary, but the instruction is given within the public school building with participation by the public school authorities (although the actual teaching may be done by instructors offering their services voluntarily or receiving their compensation from sources other than the public school system), the system is essentially that which prevailed in Champaign, Illinois, and was involved in the McCollum case. Though it would be preferable to restrict the term "released time" to those plans under which participation by the public school system is limited to releasing the participating children for a specified period during the school day, the Champaign system is generally considered a released-time program, and therefore will be discussed in the next chapter, which is devoted to the released-time experiment.

### School Credit for Outside Religious Teaching

In a number of communities the public school—generally at the high school level—will give credit toward graduation for religious instruction obtained after public school hours or during week ends under the auspices of the child's church. This proposal has many advantages in the eyes of its proponents. It involves no expense to the public school system. There is no problem of divisiveness or conflict. It is fair to the children of minority faiths, and imposes no hardship on the nonreligious. Moreover, proponents of the plan urge, the plan does not and need not involve the public school in religious teaching itself. Dean Weigle urged that

> If the public schools cooperate . . . with the churches and synagogues . . . by the giving of credit . . . the school administrator should be careful not to assume responsibility for the content of the religious instruction given in the church and synagogue. Of plans for the giving of credit, therefore, those which depend upon the standardization of teaching conditions in the church school, are sounder than those which tempt the public school superintendent to assume responsibility for syllabi or examinations.[77]

It would seem, however, that the public school authorities would be abandoning their responsibility if they automatically accepted the certification of a church that a child has satisfied the educational requirements that warrant giving him credit toward graduation—at least, many public school authorities take that position. Johnson and Yost describe a West Virginia plan under which high school pupils may receive credit for Bible study as a substitute for an elective subject in the regular curriculum. To qualify for credit the pupil must have engaged in Bible study under a teacher who meets the academic and professional requirements of the public school. Each class must be held in a separate room "equipped with tables, maps, charts, blackboards, cases for books, and a reference library of at least six volumes, one of which must be a good Bible dictionary." Periods of at least forty-five minutes are prescribed; the syllabus is prepared by the public school authorities; and the pupils must pass an examination conducted by the high school authorities.[78]

Many other communities in which credit is given for outside religious instruction have similar provisions for public school supervision. In New York City a proposal was made in 1931 to introduce the plan in the city high schools. The plan was dropped after the American Association for the Advancement of Atheism petitioned for the same privilege to be accorded to children taking instruction in atheism under the Association's auspices. It is likely, however, that the abandonment of the plan resulted not from the Association's petition but from the opposition of the teachers' union and other groups.[79] Nevertheless, the practice is authorized by the New York State Board of Regents, and in some communities high school credit is given for religious instruction outside of school auspices.[80]

The legality of the plan of granting public school credit has been considered by only one court. In State ex rel. Dearle vs. Frazier[81] the Supreme Court of the state of Washington was called upon to pass on a resolution of the State Board of Education which provided that:

> Since the board looks with favor upon allowing credits for Bible study done outside of school, it is moved that a committee be appointed to consider a plan for allowing such credits, one-half credit to be given for Old Testament and one-half credit for New Testament on the basis of thirty to thirty-two credits for high school graduation, and that a syllabus of Bible study be issued under the auspices of the state department of education with rules and regulations for the distribution of examination questions at least once a year.

Accordingly, provision was made for the examination of pupils desiring to participate, on "the historical, biographical, narrative, and literary features" of the Bible, pursuant to a syllabus outline furnished by the department of education, which also provided that all instruction and interpretation should be given at home or by the religious organization with which the students were affiliated.

The constitution of Washington, like that of practically every other state in the union, prohibits the use of public funds or property for "any religious worship, exercise, or instruction, or the support of any religious establishment." It also provides that "all schools maintained or supported wholly or in part by the public funds shall forever be free from sectarian control or influence." In a unanimous decision the Supreme Court of Washington held that the plan violated both provisions of the constitution. With respect to the latter provision, the court held that the prohibition is "sweeping and comprehensive" and bars not only religious exercises and instruction, "but their natural consequences—religious discussion and controversy." These, the court said, would be the inevitable consequences of the plan, since not all citizens are agreed that the King James translation of the Bible is a true version of the Scriptures. Nor is there agreement as to the narrative and historical worth of the Bible, or whether many of the events narrated therein are historical or allegorical. Moreover, the court said:

> What guarantee has the citizen that the board, having a contrary faith, will not inject those passages upon which its own sect rests its claim to be the true church under the guise of "narrative or literary features"; and if they did so, where would the remedy be found? Surely the courts could not control their discretion, for judges are made of the same stuff as other men. . . .

In one of the instances in the law of church and state when fictions are not accepted as substitute for fact, the court said, with respect to the constitutional prohibition of the use of public funds in support of sectarian education:

> It is no more than a subterfuge to urge that the public moneys will not be applied for religious instruction because the teaching is done outside the school by a preacher or priest, or in the home of the pupil, or by a religious organization with which the student may be affiliated, for the time of the teachers, as well as their technical skill, will be consumed while under the pay of the state in furnishing the syllabus or outline, the conducting of examinations, the rating of papers, and the determining of proper credits.

### Teaching the "Common Core" of the Major Faiths

Another proposal offered is predicated on that interpretation of the First Amendment that holds that only preferential aid to religion is barred, and not equal aid to all religions. Briefly, the proposal is this: Though we do not have in the United States an ecumenical church or a universal religion, and we worship God in different ways, we all do—or should—worship God, and the same God. Moreover, we all believe—or should believe—in the immortality of the soul, the efficacy of prayer, and the adherence to moral obligations imposed by God. Since the basic elements of religion are therefore

358

common to all religions in the United States, we can, consistently with this interpretation of the First Amendment, extract these common elements and introduce them into the public school. Put simply, the advocates of this approach urge that there is such a thing as nonsectarian religion, and that it has a rightful place in all institutions of American political society, including the public schools.

Dean Weigle well expressed the "common core" solution in the following words:

> Underlying all our differences, America has a common religious faith—common not in the sense that everybody shares it, for there are some among us who deny or ignore God; but in the sense that it is common to the three great religious groups—Protestant, Catholic, and Jewish—to which the great majority of American citizens profess to belong. These citizens—Protestant, Catholic, and Jew—worship one God, Creator of all things and Father of men. They believe that His will has been revealed in the life and literature of the Hebrew people as this is recorded in the Bible, and that it is discernible in nature about us and in conscience within. They acknowledge the principle of human duty set forth in the Ten Commandments, in the teachings of the Hebrew prophets, in the Golden Rule, and in the law of love to God and to fellow men. They sing hymns and psalms that transcend differences of creed. They can all unite in the Lord's Prayer: "Our Father who art in heaven . . . Thy kingdom come. Thy will be done. . . ."
>
> There is nothing in the status of the public school as an institution of the state, therefore, to render it godless. There is nothing in the principle of religious freedom or the separation of church and state to hinder the schools' acknowledgement of the power and goodness of God. The common religious faith of the American people, as distinguished from the sectarian forms in which it is organized, may rightfully be assumed and find appropriate expression in the life and work of the public schools.[82]

The "common core" approach assumes the existence of such a thing as nonsectarian religion. This is much open to question. The "common core" of religious belief generally comes to mean the common core of orthodox Protestant belief, and "nonsectarian" comes to mean what a substantial majority—not of all, but of the believing—agree upon. When Dean Weigle said that "all can unite in the Lord's Prayer," he meant—though he may not have realized it—all believing Protestants. He could not have meant believing Jews, for most of them cannot in conscience join in a prayer from the New Testament and attributed to a person called "the Lord." (This is substantiated by his testimony as an expert witness in the Schempp case where, according to the court records, he stated that the Bible was nonsectarian, but later stated that the phrase "nonsectarian" meant to him nonsectarian within the Christian faith.) He could not even have meant believing Catholics, who commit a grave sin if they recite the version of the Lord's Prayer commonly recited in the public schools. Nor can the conscience of Catholics and Jews be so easily disposed of as indicated by Virgil Henry in his suggestion that

> Simple exercises of worship in assembly programs might be justified on the grounds that certain forms of worship—for example, saying the Lord's Prayer or the Twenty-third Psalm—are a part of our culture and that persons unaccustomed to such common experiences are not properly educated.[83]

What may be "culture" to Protestants may be forbidden sectarianism to Catholics and Jews. William Clayton Bower, too, proposed "that non-sectarian religion as a phase of culture should be included as an integral part of public education."[84] Dr. Bower vigorously opposed sectarianism in the public schools; yet he too found Christmas and Easter celebrations to be nonsectarian, and therefore as much entitled to a place in the public school as Thanksgiving celebrations. If "nonsectarian" has any real meaning at all, it means acceptable to all sects; and therefore it must mean that each faith decides for itself whether a particular act is nonsectarian, *i.e.,* acceptable to it. It is doubtful at least that a majority of rabbis—even Reform rabbis, much less Orthodox or Conservative rabbis—would consider Christmas and Easter celebrations to be nonsectarian.[85]

The American Council on Education has criticized the "common core" proposal on religious grounds, saying:

> . . . we think it objectionable from the religious point of view. Catholics, in particular, will object because of their traditional position that Christ established one true church to which all men are called. The notion of a common core suggests a watering-down of the several faiths to the point where common essentials appear. This might easily lead to a new sect—a public school sect—which would take its place alongside the existing faiths and compete with them. The great religious bodies in America hold their respective faiths too seriously to admit of such a procedure on the part of the public schools.[86]

In a policy statement entitled "The Churches and the Public Schools," adopted on June 7, 1963, by the General Board of National Council of Churches with only the representative of the Greek Orthodox Church dissenting, the "common core" proposal was disapproved in the following language:

> While both our tradition and the present temper of our nation reflect a preponderant belief in God as our Source and our Destiny, nevertheless attempts to establish a "common core" of religious beliefs to be taught in public schools have usually proven unrealistic and unwise. Major faith groups have not agreed on a formulation of religious

beliefs common to all. Even if they had done so, such a body of religious doctrine would tend to become a substitute for the more demanding commitments of historic faiths.

## Objective Teaching "about" Religion

An increasingly popular proposal to meet the problem of religious illiteracy without impairing the nonsectarianism of the public school or the principle of the separation of church and state, is to introduce objective teaching "about" religion, rather than teaching religion itself. The purpose of teaching "about" religion would not be—at least directly—to inculcate religious beliefs, but to enable the student to obtain an understanding and appreciation of religion and the part it plays in history and life. This proposal has come—among others—from such diverse sources as *The Christian Century,* the National Education Association, and the American Council on Education.

The Educational Policies Commission of the National Education Association has described the proposal as follows:

> The public school can teach objectively about religion without advocating or teaching any religious creed. To omit from the classroom all reference to religion and the institutions of religion is to neglect an important part of American life. Knowledge about religion is essential for a full understanding of our culture, literature, art, history, and current affairs. . . .
>
> Although the public schools can not teach denominational beliefs, they can and should teach much useful information about the religious faiths, the important part they have played in establishing the moral and spiritual values of American life, and their role in the story of mankind. The very fact of the variety of religions represented in this country increases the relevance of this suggestion. How many adults could state with reasonable clarity, regardless of agreement or disagreement, what the chief tenets of the various great religious faiths are? How many non-Catholics know what a Catholic believes? How many Catholics really know where Protestant views differ from their own? What are the essential elements of the faith of Islam or of the other major creeds held by the inhabitants of this shrinking world? The unity of our own country, our understanding of the other nations of the world, and respect for the rich religious traditions of all humanity would be enhanced by instruction about religion in the public schools. Like any other teaching in which deep personal emotions are involved, such instruction should, of course, give due consideration to the varying degrees of maturity of the students.[87]

The constitutionality of such a program is hardly open to doubt. The Constitution bars indoctrination but does not require ignorance. Teaching that, for example, assumes the divinity of Christ is barred

361

from institutions of public eduation; but teaching that explores the meaning ascribed to the divinity of Christ, and explains that many people believe in that divinity as a historic truth and that many others do not, is constitutionally permissible.

The difference was well explained in an editorial, "Public Schools Can Teach Religion," appearing in *The Christian Century* for April 28, 1948:

> . . . "teaching religion" . . . may mean two different things. It may mean (1) the inculcation of religious attitudes and devotion, together with the indoctrination of particular belief; in this sense religion is taught in the parochial schools; in this sense also it was taught under released time. Such teaching of religion is generally known by the more thoroughgoing phrase "religious education." Obviously, such religious teaching is constitutionally prohibited in the public schools and we are grateful that it is. The political community of which the school is an instrument must keep its hands off the religious devotion of the people. This is a function of the home and the church—a church independent of the state and voluntarily supported by its members.
>
> Or teaching religion may mean (2) the imparting of knowledge concerning religion. Perhaps this can be more clearly stated from the point of view of the pupil instead of the teacher. "Teaching religion" would then be the *study* of religion. It would be absurd as well as entirely beyond constitutional bounds to prohibit the study of religion in the public schools. . . .

The Committee on Religion and Education of the American Council on Education, which disapproved of teaching "common core" religion because Catholics would object to it, nevertheless approved objective teaching about religion even though it is obvious that Catholics would object to it. In New York, objections by the Catholic Church caused the removal from the public school approved reading list of Florence Mary Fitch's *One God—The Ways We Worship Him,* which in simple terms and illustrations depict Protestant, Catholic, and Jewish worship customs, The Council recognizes that the Church was not likely to allow its children to participate in such courses, and provided for it by saying that "the right of nonparticipation must be held inviolate." But if the inviolate right of nonparticipation makes "about" teaching practicable, why does it not make "common core" teaching equally practicable? Actually the objective teaching of religion is likely to be unacceptable to most churches, not the Catholic Church alone. It is unrealistic to believe that many public school teachers would long be permitted to discuss objectively the Biblical accounts of the creation, the flood, and the birth and resurrection of Jesus.

The Supreme Court has recognized that there is a constitutional difference between the two types of teaching. In the Schempp case the Court stated that:

> ... it might well be said that one's education is not complete without a study of comparative religion or the history of religion and its relationship to the advancement of civilization. It certainly may be said that the Bible is worthy of study for its literary and historic qualities. Nothing we have said here indicates that such study of the Bible or of religion, when presented objectively as part of a secular program of education may not be effected consistent with the First Amendment.[88]

This extract from the Schempp decision, coupled with the Court's ruling in that case that devotional reading of the Bible is constitutionally not permissible, has evoked a renewed interest in programs for the objective teaching "about" religion. Even before the Schempp decision, a survey conducted by Professor Richard B. Dierenfeld of the University of Minnesota in 1961 showed that of the public educational administrators responding, 76 percent answered yes to the question of whether their public school systems provided materials to classrroom teachers to help in "teaching about religion.[89]

It is interesting to note that the record in the McCollum case illustrates both the constitutionally barred "religious education" teaching and the constitutionally permissible "about" teaching. One teacher testified that she taught as follows:

> ... I teach children that Jesus Christ really lived. I teach that he was a divine person. ... I teach that he rose from the dead. ...
>
> We teach that God caused the big flood upon the earth. ...
>
> ... that Adam and Eve were the first man and woman. ... They were the last of His creations. God created the earth and he created life. ...
>
> ... I taught that God has qualities of love and guidance. ... I teach them at certain ages persons lived called prophets, that they could foretell future events. I taught them that Isaiah foretold the coming of Jesus. ... I teach that Jesus raised up people or restored people to life. I teach them that others have done that since that time; the Bible stories tell that Peter did. I teach that there are many heroes in the Bible; the main hero in the Bible is Jesus Christ. I teach them the main theme of the Bible is salvation. ...
>
> I teach the children to respect and reverence God. Occasionally I teach them to say prayers. ...
>
> I did not teach them about Brigham Young, the founder of Mormonism. When asked about Robert Ingersoll I probably mentioned only that he was a writer. ... I do not know the religious views of Thomas Edison. I never told them anything about the religious views of Luther Burbank. The children were too young to understand the religious views of Voltaire. We did not discuss the religious views of Darwin.[90]

This is obviously "religious education" of the impermissible type. On the other hand, the McCollum record discloses the following testimony:

> ... the children are taught the various religions, ideas and theories insofar as we are able to, taking into account a good many of them, from many periods, and the various cultures, and they also are taught the modern theories in this same respect. They are taught there are people who believe spirits exist and that there are people who believe spirits don't exist. Insofar as I am able to on these controversial questions I teach the positive and the negative: I try to teach a number of varied opinions, and try to cover the entire gamut, insofar as I am able to. Insofar as teaching the Bible stories, that is difficult because I am not so sure that they are always from the Bible. I read them from other written literature, literature written for children, publications from regular publishing houses; and we also follow them in the Bible, in the Koran, and other scripture of various cultures. In these lessons we refer to the alleged existence of Christ, to the creation of the earth as they are in the Bible. Right now we are teaching with reference to the creation of the earth, as they are in the Bible, and we are going into many different stories which are read to the children for the context, and we go into all of those stories that we are able to, and we get the children's opinions, asking their understanding, and they tell some they have read.... The literature in that class for the most part is based upon Biblical stories and stories from the scriptures of various cultures.... They do not learn the Lord's Prayer. They learn the Ten Commandments only insofar as we expect them to know what they are, or doxologies, or other sections of law from various cults. We study the Ten Commandments.[91]

This second extract indicates fairly clearly that teaching "about" religion is not impossible. Nevertheless, it is doubtful that objective teaching about religion is practicable in the public schools, at least at the elementary school level. The second extract of the testimony from the McCollum record did not refer to teaching in a public school; paradoxically, it described teaching in a church school—the church school of the Unitarian church of Urbana, Illinois. The first extract described teaching in the Champaign public schools.

The desirability of objective teaching "about" religion in the public schools is conceded by most students; the difficulty lies in establishing with reasonable probability that it is practicable. The impracticability and doubtful constitutionality of even such carefully planned programs as outlined by Virgil Henry is indicated by his view that "any provision to excuse from services of Worship," which he reluctantly accepts, "would not apply to the regular classes in which only a purely objective study of religion would occur."[92] Here, perhaps, is an excellent area for experimentation in private schools, secular or church, where obviously no constitutional difficulty arises. If widespread experimentation in private schools establishes that the plan is practicable, it might be then introduced experimentally in selected public schools. For the time being, this writer is inclined to agree with the statement of Professor John L. Childs:

> Whenever and wherever the leaders and adherents of the various churches agree that the creeds and the rival claims and practices of religion can be studied by the ordinary, empirical procedures characteristic of the other work of the public school, little difficulty will be experienced in making a study of these aspects of religion also a part of the program of public education. Until that more ideal situation is reached in the religious life of the country, the present working arrangement is likely to be continued.[93]

### Teaching "Moral and Spiritual Values"

Increasingly popular, too, is the proposal that the public schools undertake the teaching of moral and spiritual values. To some extent this popularity is probably attributable to the fact that the term "moral and spiritual values" is so impressive and undefined as to mean all things to all men. The term appears to have been originated by William Clayton Bower in 1944 in his book, *Church and State in Education*, but achieved popularity with the publication, in 1951, by the Education Policies Commission of the National Education Association of its report entitled, *Moral and Spiritual Values in the Public Schools*. The popularity of the idea was furthered by reports of a workshop on Moral and Spiritual Values in Education, established at the University of Kentucky.[94]

The vagueness of the term and its consequent popularity is evidenced by the survey of Professor Dierenfeld referred to above. In his questionnaire he explained "moral values" as referring to "such qualities as honesty, courage, loyalty, etc.," and "spiritual values" as referring to "such qualities as love, faith, reverence for a Supreme Being." It is hardly surprising, therefore, that 99.44% of his respondents answered yes to the question whether the aims and objectives of their school systems include the teaching of moral values, and 78.71% answered yes to the question whether the aims and objectives of their school systems include the teaching of spiritual values.

In New York City, in 1955, the Board of Superintendents adopted "A Guiding Statement for Supervisors and Teachers on Moral and Spiritual Values and the Schools." The proposal was vigorously attacked by the Protestant Council of Greater New York, the New

York Board of Rabbis, the United Parents Association, the Public Education Association, the New York Civil Liberties Union, and the American Jewish Congress as a device to introduce religious teachings into the public school. It was, however, warmly defended by the Roman Catholic Archdiocese of New York.[95] Bowing to the adverse criticism, the Board of Superintendents revised the program, and, although the revised program won over only the Protestant Council, this was sufficient and it was formally adopted by the city's Board of Education.[96] Differences between the two versions are indicated by the following extract from the New York *Herald Tribune* of July 30, 1956:

1955 — The American people are, characteristically, a religious people who derive their accepted moral and spiritual values from religion. These values are inherent in the Hebraic-Christian tradition. They presuppose the existence of a Supreme Being.

To the public schools, as to the home and church, the full life is, in the final analysis, the objective of all education for all children. . . . It implies the program of the public schools must reinforce the program of the home and church in strengthening belief in God.

Beyond doubt the teacher, as a person, has a most profound influence in building the character of children. . . . He is in a position to exemplify such values as love, kindness, humility, idealism and belief in God.

In industrial arts, as in the sciences and in mathematics, the observation of the wonders or the composition of metals, the grain and beauty of woods, the ways of electricity and the characteristic properties of the materials used invariably give rise to speculation about the planning and the orderliness of the natural world and the marvelous working of a Supreme Power.

1956 — Although religious pluralism characterizes American life, the great majority of Americans believe that God is the Author of the moral code in Whom each individual is ultimately responsible. Most people find in religion the basic and fundamental sanction for right conduct, justice and decency.

The school, as an agency of society, plays its part in the development of moral and spiritual ideals. One of the commonly accepted objectives of the public school is building and strengthening the moral character of our children.

The teacher is in a position to exemplify such qualities as justice, love, kindness, idealism, humility, reverence and a sincere respect for the religious and moral beliefs and the practices of all children.

In industrial arts, as in science and in mathematics, the observation of the wonders of the composition of metals, the grain and beauty of woods, the ways of electricity and the characteristic properties of the materials used in the laboratory frequently give rise to serious thinking about the wonders of the natural world.

Perhaps the best commentary on proposals for the teaching of moral and spiritual values in the public schools is contained in the pamphlet, *Safeguarding Religious Liberty,* containing the Statements of Policy and Position on Religion and Public Education jointly adopted by the Synagogue Council of America and the National Community Relations Advisory Council:

Insofar as the teaching of "spiritual values" may be understood to signify religious teaching, this must remain as it has been the responsibility of the home, the church and the synagogue. Insofar as it is understood to signify the teaching of morality, ethics and good citizenship, a deep commitment to such values has been successfully inculcated by our public schools in successive generations of Americans. The public schools must continue to share responsibility for fostering a commitment to these moral values, without presenting or teaching any sectarian or theological sources or sanctions for such values.

### CHAPTER TEN

# Released Time

## THE BACKGROUND

THE DIVORCE OF CHURCH AND STATE in education, resulting in the secularization of the public school, coupled with the practical disappearance of the Protestant denominational school, raised serious education problems for church groups. Since neither the Catholics nor the Jews had ever relied on state educational laws or facilities for the religious training of their children, the secularization of the public school created no additional problems for them. With the Protestants, however, the situation was different. The disappearance of the denominational institution as a primary factor in education necessitated the devising of some method to provide religious education for children of school age.

At first it was thought that the Sunday school would supply what the public school had previously provided; but in time it became evident to Protestant educators that Sunday schools were not an adequate substitute for religious education under public school auspices.[1] In 1932 a survey conducted by the United States Office of Education found "that a negligible amount of a child's time comes under the influence of the church and that only a small proportion of the children throughout the country have even brief contact with church influence." The survey also noted "changes in family life wherein parents tend to disregard religious education or to throw upon the churches or the community, the chief responsibility for youth's religious training." The 1940 White House Conference on Children in a Democracy stated that

> Despite the various efforts made by church groups to educate children in religion, the religious needs of many children are imperfectly met at the present time. It has been estimated that approximately one-half of the children and youth in the United States receive no religious instruction outside the home.[2]

There were several reasons for dissatisfaction with the Sunday school. One of them was, as stated by Justice Frankfurter in the McCollum case, "that by appearing to make religion a one-day-a-week matter, the Sunday school, which acquired national acceptance, tended to relegate the child's religious education, and thereby his religion, to a minor role not unlike the enforced piano lesson." Another, and possibly more telling reason, was the rise of the family car as an institution in American social life, with the result that Sunday became the day in which the family was likely to go on a picnic or visit relatives, with consequent irregularity of attendance, if any, at Sunday school.

In any event, Protestant educators became convinced that the weekday would have to be used for religious education. Hence attempts were made to establish a weekday church school, held one or more afternoons a week after the close of public school. This plan had been adopted by many Jewish communities with some degree of success; the congregational after-hours religious school is today still a major part of the Jewish educational system. The Protestants, however, were disappointed with the results they obtained. Again quoting Justice Frankfurter, they found that

> children continued to be children; they wanted to play when school was out, particularly when other children were free to do so. Church leaders decided that if the week-day church school was to succeed, a way had to be found to give the child his religious education during what the child conceived to be his "business hours."

Apparently the secularization of education in France created the same problem for church educators as it did in the United States. In 1882 the Third Republic enacted a law which provided that

> Public elementary schools will be closed one day a week in addition to Sunday in order to permit parents, if they so desire, to have their children given religious instruction outside of school buildings.[3]

This law does not appear to have been in effect long, for three alternative plans were later proposed in the upper house of the French Parliament, all of which were ultimately rejected. The plans were as follows:

> 1. Upon request of the parents, the ministers of different creeds or persons deputed by them shall be allowed to impart religious instruction on the school premises and outside of class hours, taking care to conform to the rules which shall be established, if necessary, by the department boards.
> 2. Religious instruction shall be given on Sundays and Thursdays and on one class day, every week, in the main hall of the mayoralty, or in the case of hamlets, in the school itself.
> 3. The public school teacher may, if he chooses, give religious instruction inside the school building, but not during school hours, to those children whose parents shall have asked for it.[4]

It is interesting to note that during World War II the Vichy regime in France sought to introduce a program of religious instruction within the public school system, similar to that in effect in Champaign and involved in the McCollum case. The proposal was defeated by intense opposition, which—significantly—included the protest of the French clergy, who apparently feared state control of the church.

Citing the French law of 1882 as precedent, Dr. George U. Wenner proposed to the Interfaith Conference on Federation, held in New York City in 1905, that the schools should "release" to the churches some of the child's time that the public school unduly monopolized. The Federation, accepting Dr. Wenner's proposal, urged that on the request of their parents, children should be excused from public school Wednesday afternoons, so that the churches could provide "Sunday school on Wednesday." This was to be carried out on church premises under church authority. Those children not desiring to attend church schools would continue their normal classes—though the school authorities were requested not to schedule particularly important or attractive activities during the hour in which other children were released for religious education. Although the proposal aroused considerable opposition and was not put into effect, it may be said to have marked the birth of the released-time movement.[5]

(At this point a definition of terms may be useful. Neither "released time" nor "dismissed time" has a defined meaning agreed upon by all. Each term is frequently used in different senses—sometimes by the same writer. For our purposes "released time" will be used to designate a system of religious education in connection with the public school under which those children desiring to participate in religious instruction are excused from their secular studies for a specified period weekly, while those children not participating in religious instruction remain under the jurisdiction and supervision of the public school for the usual period of secular instruction. No distinction is made in the use of the term between religious instruction classes held within or without the public school building; nor between classes held at the first or last period of the school day and those held sometime between these two periods. The term "dismissed time" is used to designate the system under which, on one or more days, the public school is closed earlier than usual, and all children are dismissed, with the expectation—but not the requirement—that some will use the dismissed period for participation in religious instruction. The term "free time" is sometimes used to designate what is here called "dismissed time"; if used at all, "free time" should be limited to mean the time after regular public school hours and on week ends in which the children are free of the regular obligations of the secular school system.)[6]

The actual practice of released time began in this country in 1913, when Dr. William Wirt, superintendent of schools in Gary, Indiana, suggested that, in view of the strain on communal facilities resulting from the industrial expansion of the city, a fuller use should be made of public school buildings.

> Building on theories which had become more or less current, he also urged that education was more than instruction in a classroom. The school was only one of several educational agencies. The library, the playground, the home, the church, all have their function in the child's proper unfolding. Accordingly, Wirt's plan sought to rotate the schedules of the children during the school-day so that some were in class, others were in the library, still others in the playground. And some, he suggested to the leading ministers of the City, might be released to attend religious classes if the churches of the City co-operated and provided them. They did, in 1914, and thus was "released time" begun. The religious teaching was held on church premises and the public schools had no hand in the conduct of these church schools. They did not supervise the choice of instructors or the subject matter taught. Nor did they assume responsibility for the attendance, conduct or achievement of the child in a church school; and he received no credit for it. The period of attendance in the religious schools would otherwise have been a play period for the child, with the result that the arrangment did not cut into public school instruction or truly affect the activities or feeling of the children who did not attend the church schools.[7]

By the end of 1915, 619 pupils were being excused in Gary to attend church school during one period a week. Attempts to introduce the program elsewhere met with varying success, but all in all progress was slow. In New York City an attempt was made to establish the "Gary Plan," as it was then known. The proposal was opposed by both Catholics and Jews; and the controversy was so heated that the public hearings were actually marked by riots, which brought an end to the whole attempt.[8] More often, however, the stumbling block proved to be apathy and inertia, rather than outright opposition. In 1923, after the Protestants were able to persuade the Catholic Church to drop its opposition, an interfaith committee of nine was formed to press for the introduction of the plan in New York City, but it met with no great success. The committee remained in existence for ten years, but accomplished little — notwithstanding a decision by the state's highest court in 1927 (in one of Joseph Lewis's many suits) that the White Plains board of education had violated neither constitution nor statute in putting the plan in operation in that city's public schools.[9]

It was not until 1941 that the program got started in New York City. During the previous year the state legislature had enacted the Coudert-McLaughlin bill, which expressly authorized the release of children for religious education. In view of the 1927 decision in the White Plains case, it was clear that the absence of a specific statute was not itself an obstacle. Nevertheless, the enactment of the law seemed to have a potent effect. The statute had been enacted in large part through the efforts of the Greater New York Interfaith Committee, a group of nine business men from the three major faiths. These laymen had been meeting for some time; and though their first contemplated project was to attack subversive activities, they decided to drop that project in favor of obtaining religious education for public school children.[10]

The Coudert-McLaughlin bill was passed by an almost unanimous vote. In signing the measure, Governor Herbert H. Lehman remarked that "a few people have given voice to fears that the bill violates principles of our Government." These fears, in his opinion, were groundless, since the "bill does not introduce anything new into our public school system nor does it violate the principles of our public educational system."[11]

In one respect the bill did introduce something new; and this something new turned out to be one of the two decisive factors that made the difference between success and failure. For when the New York City board of education again held hearings on the introduction of the released-time program, it again met the opposition that previously had succeded in defeating similar proposals. But the board now held that under the statute it had no discretion. Before the Coudert-McLaughlin bill had been enacted, the law of the state under the White Plains decision was that a local school board had the power, but was not obligated to introduce the released-time program. Under the new statute, the board ruled, its hands were tied; it was required to provide released-time religious education if any duly constituted religious body in the community requested it.

The second telling factor was the change in attitude on the part of the Catholic Church. When the plan was first proposed in New York the church was opposed; thereafter it withdrew its opposition, but exhibited no great interest. By 1941, however, the turnabout was complete, and the church became an ardent advocate and the chief beneficiary of the released-time program in New York. When the program first went into full operation in 1941, 101,633 children registered. Since then the figure has remained substantially constant (notwithstanding the increase in the public school population); varying from a low of 99,764 in 1943 to a high of 110,000 in 1948.[12] (Enrollees in 1964 numbered 109,572.[13]) Moreover, the distribution among the faiths has likewise remained constant; some 80 per cent of the children released each year have been Catholic.

Outside New York, too, the plan was slow in getting started. During the period between 1914 and 1920 the program made slight progress, principally in the Protestant Midwest. The combination of religious revival — which is a frequent concomitant of a war and post-war period — and the general prosperity of the American people and their churches, resulted in a spurt in the spread of the movement in the '20's. Conversely, the depression of the '30's had the twofold effect of drying up substantial sources of church funds and at the same time shifting the national consciousness to economic and political issues, thereby slowing down the growth of the movement. The return of prosperity and the religious revival that accompanied World War II again operated to revive interest in the program and give impetus to its further expansion.

## EXTENT OF THE PLAN

It is almost impossible to estimate with any degree of accuracy the number of states or communities in which the plan is now in operation or the number of school children participating; no two independent estimates as to any of these items correspond with any degree of closeness. This much is probably true: estimates by fervent or professional advocates of the program must be discounted; when compared with estimates based on studies by disinterested or opposing or even mildly sympathetic groups or students, they appear to be greatly exaggerated.

Let us first consider the number of states in which the program is in operation. Reverend Father Franer, a Catholic student of the subject, estimated that in 1937 the plan was in operation in 45 states.[14] Dr. Erwin L. Shaver of the International Council of Religious Education, chief promoter of the plan, reported in 1944 that it was in operation in at least 44 states; and reported again in 1946 that all but two of the 48 states had released-time classes.[15] On the other hand, a survey by the United States Office of Education in 1932 indicated that the plan was in operation in 35 states;[16] and a follow-up survey in 1940 showed that the number had increased to 38.[17] A study by the National Education Association published in February 1946 indicated that the program was in operation in 33 states;[18] while a questionnaire circulated by the American Civil Liberties Union in the same year resulted in 27 affirmative replies from the

42 states that replied to the questionnaire.[19] A follow-up survey by the National Education Association in 1949 showed that 43 states included systems that reported some type of released-time religious instruction.[20] A survey made by Professor Dierenfeld in 1961 indicated that some 30% of the nation's school districts cooperated in released-time programs.[21]

These figures indicate little except that the program is geographically widespread. The inconsistency in the estimates may be explained by the probability that the proponents of the program include in their listing any state from which they receive a report that a community or even a school has instituted the plan, whereas the disinterested students base their estimates on replies received from state departments of education; and an affirmative reply is generally received only if the plan is of sufficient extent and permanence to be noted by the state departments of education.

More important than the number of states in which the program operates is the number of communities involved. Here too is a wide variance among the estimates. The United States Office of Education survey in 1940 showed the plan in operaton in 488 public school systems, consisting of approximately 1,800 public schools. Reverend Father Franer estimated in 1947 that there were 2,000 communities using the plan; and in 1946 Dr. Shaver used the same figure. Today 3,000 is a frequent estimate.[22] On the other hand, in the National Education Association 1949 survey, of the 2,639 school superintendents who replied to a questionnaire sent to 5,100 local school systems, only 708 reported that they had any type of religious instruction program in connection with the public school system. Here too the disparity may be explained by the probability that the promoters of released time are less likely to receive reports of communities discontinuing released-time programs than of communities introducing such programs. Such programs have a distressingly high mortality rate.

Nor is there agreement as to the number of children participating in the program. Father Franer, who estimated that in 1937 the plan was in operation in 2,000 centers in 45 states, also estimated that the enrollment was only about 265,000. At the other extreme, there have been estimates as high as 2,500,000 enrollments.[23] Indeed, in February 1952 Dr. Shaver reported that Protestant children alone enrolled in released-time classes numbered 1,890,000.[24] Even disregarding Jewish enrollment — which is concededly small — Catholic enrollment on this basis must amount to at least 1,000,000, in view of the fact that in such large cities as New York, Chicago, and

Boston, which contribute substantial numbers to the program, at least three out of every four enrollees are Catholic. As a matter of fact, in 1947, when Dr. Shaver reported that 2,000,000 children of all faiths were participating in released-time classes, the official Catholic Directory reported that 905,386 Catholic children, or almost half the total, were enrolled in Catholic released-time classes.[25] The official Catholic Directory for 1948 reported that the number of Catholic children participating in released-time classes had increased to 1,078,436. The official Catholic Directory for 1952 reported that 1,545,220 public school children attend released-time classes, religious vacation schools, and other special classes. (There is no breakdown of these three categories.) Hence, if we accept the estimates of the proponents of the program, it would appear that some 3,000,000 children were enrolled.

On the other hand, the 1940 study of the Office of Education disclosed that of the 488 school systems reporting operation of the plan, 357 gave a combined average daily attendance of 164,013. The number of enrollments was unquestionably larger than the average attendance, for even in respect to actual attendance the reports were in many cases concededly incomplete. Nevertheless, after making generous allowances for such incompletness and for the school systems that failed to report, and considering also the accretions since 1940 (the most substantial one—some 110,000 enrollees—resulting from the introduction of the program in the New York City public school system in 1941), it is probable that the average released-time attendance in all public elementary and secondary schools in the country in 1950 was not much in excess of 1,250,000 school children.

Support for this estimate may be found in the 1949 survey of the National Education Association. That survey estimated that some 700,000 pupils were in attendance at religious classes in the 2,639 communities that replied to the questionnaire, and that these communities had an approximate enrollment of 13,000,000 pupils. The 700,000 would be about 5% of the total public school enrollment, and the figure may therefore be accepted as approximately the percentage of released-time enrollees in the public schools throughout the nation. (It is reasonable to assume that communities using the program were at least as likely to respond as those not having it.) The 1950 Statistical Abstract of the United States[26] estimated that in 1947 there were 23,659,158 pupils enrolled in the nation's public schools. If we adopt the 5% approximation, we obtain the figure 1,182,958, which cannot be too far off for the year 1950.

During the past decade there have been considerably fewer statistics published on the released-time program than in the preceding years. Professor Dierenfeld's survey of religion and the public schools, which included a question on released time, is about the only substantial statistical survey on released time made during this period; and this dealt only with the number of school districts cooperating with the program and not with the number of children participating. Whatever the reason for the dearth of statistical studies, there is little ground for belief that there has been any substantial increase in the number of children participating in the program.

Evidence supporting this conclusion is found in the records of the New York City Board of Education. In 1941 the number of enrollees was 110,000; in 1964, notwithstanding a substantial increase in the number of children in the City's public schools,[27] the number of released-time enrollees was only 109,572.[28]

## DISTRIBUTION AMONG THE FAITHS

Unfortunately, neither the United States Office of Education nor the National Education Association sought to ascertain how participation in the released-time program is distributed among the three faiths. Dr. Shaver's estimate of 1,890,000 Protestant enrollments seems to exceed by a substantial amount the total enrollment of all faiths. The 1947 Catholic estimate of 905,386 appears to be more reasonable, though this too is probably more than generous.

Despite these estimates by ardent protagonists of the released-time program, it remains true that there appear to be no accurate figures regarding the extent to which the three principal religious groups in the United States — Protestant, Catholic, and Jewish — have participated in the plan. Reports from observers are generally unanimous that there is little participation by the Jewish communities — principally because of opposition to the plan by the overwhelming majority of Jewish religious, professional, and lay leaders, but also partly because of the practical difficulties of operation where the Jewish pupils constitute a small fraction of the school enrollment.

Catholic participation apparently is determined by the attitude to the plan of Catholic Church leadership in a particular diocese. In the early days of the plan's development, Catholic Church leadership was opposed or apathetic; lately — particularly during the last decade — the Catholic Church has shown increasing interest in its potentialities, and Catholic participation has accordingly substantially increased. In those communities where the Catholic Church has taken an active interest in the plan, participation by Catholic children is substantial—in many cases from 80% to 100% of the Catholic children who attend public schools participate in the released-time classes.

No objective estimates of Protestant participation are available on a national scale. But more than three out of four children in American public schools are from families that are Protestant by profession or descent; and since the total attendance at released-time classes probably does not exceed one and a half million out of the more than forty-one million children enrolled in American public schools, it is obvious that released-time religious instruction reaches only a very small fraction of Protestant children.

In New York City the Public Education Association made studies of the operation of the released-time program in 1943, 1945, and 1949. Only in the first two surveys were figures on participation by the various faiths obtained. These figures (substantially the same in both years) indicate that in the 88 schools studied, 81 out of every 100 children released were Catholic, 14 were Protestant, and 5 were Jewish. The investigators in the 1949 study were of the opinion that if any change had taken place since 1945 it was to increase rather than decrease the disparity between Catholic enrollment on the one hand and Protestant and Jewish enrollment on the other, and the conclusion is probably valid today.

The same disparity exists in Chicago. A study made there in 1948 showed that while 18,000 Catholic children were released during that year, the number of Protestant children released was only 4,500.[29]

The National Education Association survey of 1949, though containing no questions concerning the religious affiliations of pupils participating in released-time classes, nevertheless substantiates the conclusion that in proportionate—and possibly even in absolute—figures the Catholic religion has become the chief supplier of children for released-time classes; and that Protestant participation is small in relation to the total Protestant population. The report of this study showed that out of the 2,639 school systems reporting, 45.9% of cities of over 100,000 that replied had religious education programs in operation; while in the five smaller population groups reporting, the percentage of participation steadily decreased until—in the group under 2,500 population—only 17.1% reported such programs in operation. When it is remembered that most Catholics live in large cities, it is clear that the Catholic Church is the mainstay of the released-time program in the United States. In view of this fact, and of the almost negligible extent of participation by Protestant children, it is ironic that American Protestantism has had almost desperate faith in the released-time experiment as the answer to the twin threats of irreligion and Catholic competition.

<h2>INTRODUCING THE PROGRAM</h2>

The introduction of the program in the public schools of a community is generally preceded by an intensive campaign conducted by an interested church group or groups. The International Council of Religious Education recommends a preparatory campaign of six months to a year, including publicity in sermons, mass meetings, newspapers, church bulletins, school papers, circular letters, and radio announcements.[30] In actual practice, however, observers report that the campaign is generally much quieter, and is limited to ministers and lay church leaders. Where there is a sizable Catholic and Jewish community, an interfaith committee is frequently organized, and this procedure is strongly recommended by the International Council.

In view of the present attitude of the Catholic Church toward the released-time plan in an increasing number of communities, obtaining Catholic cooperation presents in most cases no serious problem. Where the church does not desire to participate in the program, that generally marks the end of the project—at least in the larger communities. If the Church agrees to join, an attempt is usually made to obtain the cooperation of the local rabbi or rabbinic group.

The rabbi of a town or small city approached by ministers with a request to join an interfaith committee for released time is usually faced with a difficult choice. The overwhelming majority of American rabbis are opposed to the plan; but a rabbi faced with an urgent request by his Christian colleagues to join in an interfaith committee frequently finds it impossible to refuse. Ministers faced with dwindling Sunday school attendance are likely to look to released time as the only source of salvation, and are often unable to understand—much less sympathize with—the Jewish community's reluctance to participate. In the event the rabbi declines to join, the promoters of the plan must then decide whether they will seek to introduce it without Jewish participation. Should they decide to do so, they will occasionally find that the public school board—possibly motivated by a lack of sympathy for the program—will refuse to introduce it unless all three faiths agree. This of course results in even greater pressure on the rabbi, and an even greater strain on interfaith relations.

Occasionally the disclosure of plans to introduce released-time instruction gives rise to active opposition, which usually takes the form of a demand for a public hearing. The hearing is not infrequently permeated with bitterness, tension, and complete failure on the part of the opposing forces to understand or sympathize with each other's motives. In his Memorial against the Virginia Assessment Bill, Madison remonstrated that

> The very appearance of the Bill has transformed that "Christian forbearance, love and charity" which of late mutually prevailed, into animosities and jealousies, which may not soon be appeased.[31]

It is unfortunately true that a proposal to introduce the released-time program in a community too often has like consequences.

If a hearing takes place, and substantial and respectable opposition is marshalled at the hearing, the school board may decide not to institute the program, or may decide to refer the matter to the state attorney general for a legal opinion. Even where articulate opposition induces the school board not to act, the result frequently is merely postponement; after a period of several months the board may put the program into effect without prior publicity or hearing or even notice.

## How the Program Operates

There is wide diversity in released-time practices—not only in different communities, but frequently in the same community. Even in New York City, where the program operates under the detailed regulations of the state commissioner of education and the city board of education, the Public Education Association found "wide variations in the operation of the program."[32] Hence an exact picture of how the plan operates is impossible. It is, however, possible to set forth the salient features of the operation of the program in most communities.

(1) *Announcing the program.* It is a frequent if not usual practice to announce the inauguration or operation of the program at the opening assembly each school year. Frequently a local minister representing the sponsoring interfaith committee or church addresses the children, and explains to them the operation and benefits of the program.

(2) *Written requests.* It is the usual practice to require those children who desire to participate in released-time instruction to bring request cards signed by their parents. These cards are usually prepared by the interfaith committee that sponsor the program, or—if it is sponsored by a single parish—by the church. Occasionally they

are prepared by the public school authorities, although the use of public school supplies for that purpose has been declared illegal.[33]

(3) *The period of released-time instruction.* The usual period of release is one hour weekly—though it varies from as little as a half-hour weekly to as much as two hours weekly. If the religious instruction is given in church centers or elsewhere than in the school building, the released period is frequently the last period in the afternoon—since otherwise time must be allowed not merely to reach the center but to return to school. Even if the instruction is given during the last period in the afternoon, the time it takes the children to get to the center is lost—and this lost time may be considerable. It is a conservative estimate that on the average fifteen minutes of a one-hour weekly period is spent in moving from the public school classroom to the church center.

(4) *The place of instruction.* The 1940 Office of Education survey revealed that about 40% of released-time classes were conducted in public school buildings. This survey was of course conducted before the Supreme Court ruled in the McCollum case that public school premises could not constitutionally be used for religious instruction. Since that decision many school boards have undoubtedly required the released-time classes to move out of the school building, but it is nevertheless probably true that in many communities the classes still are conducted within the public school building. (Responses to the Dierenfeld questionnaire indicated that in about 13% of the cases, mostly in the South, the classes are conducted in the public school buildings.) In these cases the teacher in religious education, supplied by the interested church group, conducts the class either in the same classroom in which regular instruction is given or in another in the building—depending generally on whether the majority of the children in the class are enrolled for religious instruction. In many instances the secular teacher remains in the classroom with the religious teacher, though she is usually forbidden to participate. If Catholic or Jewish classes are also held, these children accompany their religious teacher to another classroom.

In most cases, however, it is fair to assume that released-time classes today are held in church centers away from the public school. The distances between school and church centers vary from community to community. In New York City, with its multitude of churches, the Public Education Association found that almost half the church centers were at least ten city blocks or half a mile distant from the school; and in one instance it was as far as sixty blocks or five subway stops.

(5) *Getting the children to the church centers.* In those communities that conduct the released-time programs outside the public school building, the school and church authorities are faced with the problem of getting the children to the church centers. The most frequent method of dismissing the released children is to form them into lines in the classroom or the hall according to their faiths; then they leave for the church centers, sometimes accompanied by a church representative and sometimes unescorted. If they are unescorted, principals and teachers are frequently troubled about the safety of the smaller children thus released. Occasionally the teacher in charge will refuse to allow the children to go without an escort. In other instances older pupils are assigned the responsibility of escorting the children; or a public school teacher will act as escort at least part of the way.

Failure on the part of the church centers to provide escorts for the released children raises other problems, less serious than traffic hazards, but nevertheless troublesome. In the first place, experience seems to indicate that the time between leaving the school and arriving at the center is longer, and the time available for religious instruction shorter, than when they are escorted. In the second place, a goodly proportion of the unescorted children do not arrive at the church center at all. All three Public Education Association surveys disclosed the seriousness of the truancy problem. Estimates of the percentage of truants vary. In some instances as much as 50% truancy has been reported; it is probable that the average truancy in released-time classes is well over 10%.

When the classes are held in church centers, the regulations generally require the church authorities to report the attendance and absences to the public school authorities. Regulations frequently forbid the public school principal or teacher from questioning the absent child or commenting on his absence. Theoretically the responsibility is exclusively on the church to see to it that the children get to the center after they are dismissed from the schools, and the only sanction for repeated truancy is depriving the truant child of the privilege of further participation. Actually the rule against teacher comment is honored at least as much in the breach as in the observance; for a conscientious teacher must exercise almost angelic self-restraint in not questioning a child who regularly leaves at 2 each Wednesday afternoon to attend religious classes and as regularly is reported by the church not to have shown up.

The comment of the Public Education Association's 1945 report is interesting:

The attitudes of the principals range from great concern about these absentees to cynicism. Several principals suspect, and with considerable grounds, that parents are signing the cards and taking advantage of this hour for shopping tours with their children, music and dancing lessons and, in some cases, having the child home early "to mind the baby." One principal cheerfully told the visitor [interviewer] that she hoped the truants were using the time to good advantage. Another principal who liked the idea of additional religious instruction is dissatisfied because there can be no check-up on attendance as he feels that this leads to truancy. There is now 10% more classroom truancy in his school than heretofore since some children finding it easy to escape during this released time hour, continue to do so at other times. One principal, in discussing the reactions of pupils to the program said, "the truants are definitely enthusiastic."

(6) *The program for the unreleased children.* The problem of what to do with the unreleased children is a difficult one for the public school authorities. Even if only a small percentage of children are released, it would seem unfair that the usual educational activity should be pursued, since the released children should not be penalized by missing necessary instruction. On the other hand, it is unfair to the majority to keep them occupied solely with "busy" work. As reported by the Public Education Association:

> Principals raised the question as to how they could schedule work that would be valuable for those who remain and at the same time would not be missed by those who are released.[34]

The United States Office of Education in its 1940 study showed that the three programs most frequently conducted for the nonreleased pupils were study periods, continuation of regular classes, and remedial work, occasionally with individual assistance for special problems. The National Education Association 1949 report showed that in at least half the schools regular classes were continued, while in 30% the time was used as a study period; and in a few schools courses were given in citizenship or character education. Although no similar study appears to have been made since 1949, it is probable that the situation has not changed significantly.

(7) *The programs for the released children.* The programs offered to the children in the religious instruction classes vary widely. Occasionally a program is offered in Protestant centers that stresses interfaith understanding rather than sectarian knowledge. A program of this type is the one reported in the United States Office of Education 1940 study from Madison, New Jersey:

Fourth Grade —
Exploring the Churches in Our Community.
> Purposes: To help fourth-grade boys and girls come to under-
> stand and appreciate the religious beliefs and practices of Protes-
> tant, Catholic churches, and Jewish synagogues.
>> To help prevent and eliminate misunderstandings, misconcep-
>> tions, and prejudice.
> Textbook: *Exploring Our Neighborhood*, Eakin.
> Workbook: *Under the Church Flag.*

Fifth Grade —
The Problems which Industrialized America Makes for the Worker.
The resulting task for religion and the church.
> Aim: To help children discover the situations, the causes for the
> conditions, and some attempted solutions.
>> To guide them in finding out how religion should function in
>> such situations.
> Textbook: *Living and Working in Our Country.*

Sixth Grade —
Religious Influence in Making some Civilizations What They Are.
> Purpose: To help children discover the interrelatedness of reli-
> gion to life.

Many source materials.
No single textbook.

More often, however, the program in the Protestant centers is typified by the following:

Cycle I
*If We Had Lived in Bible Times*
(Third and Fourth Grades)
A. Wandering Peoples. Old Testament. Fall 1943. A unit on shepherd life in early Bible times.
B. Dwellers in Cities. New Testament. Spring 1944. A study of Jerusalem in the time of Jesus and the implications of his teachings for life in New York today.
C. City of Zion. Old Testament. Fall 1942. A unit on life in Jerusalem in Old Testament times, with a study of some of the proverbs which grew out of the life of the people in those days.
D. Boyhood of Jesus. New Testament. Spring 1943. A unit on the village of Nazareth with particular emphasis on the boyhood of Jesus, and concluding with a study of Jesus' trip to Jerusalem at the age of twelve.

Sources:
*Child Life in Bible Times*, Taylor.
Mimeographed materials.[35]

A typical Catholic program is the following:

Course of Instruction

| Grade | Subject | Emphasis on: |
|-------|---------|--------------|
| I | Prayer | First Prayers, Sacred Stories |
| II | First Communion | Preparation for Confession and Communion |
| III | Apostles' Creed | The Life of Our Lord |
| IV | The Commandments | Commandments of God |
| V | The Sacraments | Grace; Sacramentals |
| VI | Apostles' Creed and Life of Christ | New Testament |
| VII | Commandments | The Commandments, Precepts of the Church |
| VIII | Sacraments | Sacrifice of the Mass, Church History[36] |

In most of the Jewish schools that avail themselves of released time, the considerations of financial expense and available manpower necessitate using the assembly form of instruction. The assembly method is believed to be the most expedient and most inexpensive method of giving religious instruction to large numbers of children within the limited time of one hour a week. It is also believed to have the additional advantage of not creating the impression in the minds of the children or their parents that released-time instruction is the equivalent of the daily after-hours or even Sunday religious school. The curriculum consists of ritual services, singing, reading selections from the Biblical "portion of the week," and stories from Jewish history and the Bible. During the holiday seasons the instruction centers on the holiday. The instruction given in classrooms is more systematic, and a more or less formal curriculum is developed. Released-time instruction is often viewed principally as a means of attracting children to the regular religious classes held after public school hours or on Sundays.

## THE CASE FOR RELEASED TIME

The arguments in support of the released-time program are basically those discussed in a preceding chapter, which support public school responsibility for religious education. As applied to released time they are:

(1) *The traditional arguments.* These have been outlined by Dr. Shaver as follows:

1. Times like these demand more and better religious education for children and youth. [Presumably this means that "times like these" are particularly critical because of the low state of morals and the prevalence of crime and delinquency, and that moral behavior and ethical

conduct can be assured only—or at least most effectively—by means of religious education.]

2. The short session of the Sunday church school does not give enough time.

3. Religion must be identified in the child's mind with weekday as well as Sunday life.

4. To give every child a truly complete "education for life," which society owes him, he needs education in religion as well as in other subjects of his weekly study program.

5. The church has a right to a fair proportion of the child's weekday time.

6. Weekday church schools enroll large numbers of children not reached by any other agency of religious education.[37]

Dr. Shaver summarized the case for released time in these words:

The fifty per cent of our children who are not now receiving any training in religion because of parental neglect or other reasons should not be denied this most important element in their complete social heritage. When parental indifference or other circumstances have failed to give a child a healthy body society has stepped in by means of private or public health agencies—to see that he has soundness of health. The same principle has been applied in giving every child his mental training, regardless of whether parents cared or could afford it. This has been done because the welfare of society is at stake. Social welfare is jeopardized as much or even more if any child is denied his right to know and to make use of all that society has learned in the area of religion. Whenever a cooperative weekday church school has been in operation, it has succeeded in reaching on the average one third of the neglected half of our children and youth, a remarkable evangelistic record.[38]

(2) *The interfaith argument.* Another argument for the program is that it promotes interfaith and intercultural harmony and understanding. With the plan in operation, children of one faith frequently begin to realize that their classmates too may be religious, even though they are not seen in church on Sunday. On the adult level, cooperative planning among members of different faiths to put the plan in operation also helps promote interfaith understanding and harmony.

(3) *The religious liberty claim.* Another argument for the program—one that has been asserted with some frequency—might be called the religious liberty argument in reverse. Opponents of public school involvement in religious education have always contended that the result of such involvement is an infringement on religious liberty. The released-time proponents now argue, on the contrary, that refusal to release children for religious education violates their

religious liberty. This argument has been stressed by Catholic supporters of the program, and is based on the decision of the United States Supreme Court in the Oregon parochial school case.[39] Under this decision parents have a constitutional right to send their children to private or parochial schools rather than to public schools. Financial considerations make it impossible for many parents to avail themselves of the right—particularly since the states refuse to support the parochial schools as they support the public schools. But if the state were to refuse to release a child for religious education in the church centers for one hour a week it would be abridging his religious liberty to an extent differing only in degree from its refusal to allow him to attend parochial schools at all. As sometimes put by the proponents: the whole is greater than any of its parts, and if it is a denial of religious liberty to refuse to allow children to attend religious schools for thirty-five hours a week, it certainly is a denial of religious liberty to refuse to allow them to attend those schools one hour a week—as much a denial of religious liberty as would be the refusal by public school authorities to release Jewish children wishing to attend synagogue service on Yom Kippur.[40]

(4) *The cultural pluralism argument.* The Yom Kippur analogy is also frequently used to meet the charge that the released-time program is divisive in effect because it points up religious differences among public school children. So, argue the released-time advocates, does excusing Jewish children on Yom Kippur, or Catholic children on a day of Catholic obligation. But the whole concept of cultural pluralism, which is so popular, particularly among Jewish educators, is predicated on the recognition of religious differences, and the acceptance of these differences as a necessary and desirable aspect of the American social scene.

(5) *The secularism-Communism argument.* The world today is engaged in a struggle between the forces of God-fearing democracy and atheistic Communism. The American public school, as an organ of democracy and godliness, must do all it can within the limits of our Constitution to meet the threat of secularism and Communism. According to Justice Anthony J. DiGiovanna in the Zorach case,[41] refusal to allow released-time religious instruction "would be a step in the direction of and be consonant with totalitarian and communist philosophies existing in jurisdictions where atheism and suppression of all religions are preferred to the freedom of the individual to seek religious instruction and worship." In a statement issued in November 1949 the Catholic Bishops in America denounced "secularism" as the "fertile soil in which such social monstrosities as fascism, nazism and

386

communism could grow. It is doing more than anything else to blight our heritage of Christian culture. . . ." And, said the Bishops, "in no field has secularism done more damage than in education."[42]

## THE CASE AGAINST RELEASED TIME

The released-time plan has been opposed on varied and numerous grounds, principally the following:

(1) *Separation of church and state.* The plan constitutes a violation of the principle of the separation of church and state—this is the most frequently advanced argument. Its force has been largely but not entirely vitiated by the decision of the Supreme Court in the Zorach case. Opponents argue that the Zorach case was decided by a sharply divided Court which may well reverse itself at a future time, particularly in view of its separationist decisions in the Engel and Schempp cases; that all the Court decided was that the plan as reflected in the regulations promulgated by the New York City board of education did not violate the Constitution, but that in practice released-time programs do not comply with these or similar regulations; and finally, that the Court decided on the law, not on the policy of separation.

(2) *The opening wedge.* Even if the released-time program is not in itself a threat to the nonsectarian public school, it constitutes an opening wedge that may lead to further encroachments, and ultimately to the return of the public schools to church control. Released time itself, the opponents feel, will prove ineffective, and demands will be made for further public school involvement in religious education. They point to the frank statements of such protagonists as W. S. Fleming, whose *God in Our Public Schools* criticized the released-time plan as ineffective, and proposed the reintroduction of Christian instruction in the public schools; and to the following statement by Harrison S. Elliot, general secretary of the Religious Education Association:[43]

> The difficulty with weekday religious education is that it introduces another atomistic element into the already broken up experience of children. Weekday religious education is integrally related neither to their life in the school nor to their life in the church. The experience with weekday religious education during the last thirty-five years has made this evident. . . . Weekday religious education results in the church's not facing its fundamental problem with children, but attempting to solve it by putting them into classes one day a week under public school coercion. . . . Weekday religious education . . . will not solve the problem. *It can be solved only by bringing the teaching of religion*

387

*back into the school* and by building up a life for children in church and at home which is educationally sound and definitely Christian.

(3) *Divisiveness.* The released-time plan emphasizes religious differences and therefore is a divisive influence. In their brief in the McCollum case the Jewish organizations stated that though they "base their opposition to the released time program on many grounds . . . no consideration bulks larger in that opposition than the divisive effects of the program." The brief quoted the following from Conrad Moehlman's *The Church as Educator:*[44]

> When procedure to line up the youngsters for their "religion" classes segregates Americans as Catholics, Lutherans, other Protestants, Jews, cultists, smaller sects, non-churchgoing pupils, a consciousness of religious cleavage is inevitable and it is baneful. . . . The religious disunity of the proponents of dismissed time plans is one of the principal arguments against released time. Released time not only divides public school students into four major groups, Catholics, Protestants, Jews and the majority or minority that remains behind in the classrooms, but it also breaks up Protestant withdrawers into separate "armies of the Lord," Liberal Protestant against fundamentalist Protestant, cultist against sectarian enthusiast, Lutheran against Baptist. When weekday church school sessions are held in the schoolrooms, they often become catechism against catechism.

(4) *Ineffectuality.* The time allotted under the plan is inadequate and must remain so unless a substantial portion of the little time devoted to secular education is sacrificed. The religious education that can be imparted under the conditions of released time must also be inadequate and pedagogically ineffective. Catholic educators before the church's reversal of its position on released time, and Jewish educators today, have frequently commented on the ineffectuality of released-time religious education. Moreover, released pupils may discontinue regular after-hours or Sunday school attendance in the belief of their parents that their spiritual needs are adequately provided for by the released-time instruction.

(5) *Proselytizing.* There is an ever-present danger of proselytizing. This concerns Jewish leaders especially, because of the minority position of the Jewish children, and their consequent vulnerability to intentional or unintentional proselytizing by their Christian schoolmates.

(6) *The effect on the public school program.* There is too little time provided for secular studies to afford time for religious instruction. In many communities even the time generally allotted must be cut down an hour or more daily because of the necessity of conducting school in double sessions by reason of the lack of adequate facilities

and teachers. Rarely, however, is the released-time period sacrificed for the institution of double sessions. Moreover, the plan—besides entailing substantial cost to the city and administrative difficulties to public school authorities—is unfair to the nonreleased children if the time is used merely for "busy" or similar work, or is unfair to the released children if the time is used for positive educational activity.

(7) *Hostile sectarian teachings.* Many people believe that there is much in present-day religious instruction that encourages religious prejudice, and particularly contributes to anti-Semitism. Though the state may not constitutionally prohibit such instruction, it should not facilitate the children's being subject to it. The record in the McCollum case illustrates this type of teaching, as does a study by the National Conference of Christians and Jews.[45]

## THE POSITIONS OF THE FAITHS

### *The Protestants*

Historically the released-time movement is a Protestant experiment, and—at least until the McCollum decision—Protestant church groups were its most energetic defenders and promoters. Even today there can be little doubt that the overwhelming majority of Protestant bodies support released time. Evidence of this can be seen in the unanimous vote authorizing a motion to file a brief *amicus curiae* in the Zorach case in behalf of the National Council of the Churches of Christ. Even Protestants and Other Americans United refused to oppose officially the released-time plan.

The publicly stated reasons for the Protestant support of the released-time experiment have been already set forth. Protestant church leaders say simply that it is the most effective answer to the alarming growth of irreligion among American youth. Privately, however, many of them acknowledge that they fear not only secularism, but Catholicism as well. To them the program is a necessary measure in the struggle of American Protestantism to hold its own against the ever-increasing influence of the Catholic Church on the American social, religious, political, and educational scene.

It would be a mistake, however, to assume that Protestantism is unanimous in its support of the released-time experiment. Aside from those who criticize the program because it does not go far enough in introducing religious education into the public school system, there are many influential Protestant leaders and groups who oppose it because it goes too far. Two leading Protestant national periodicals, *The Christian Century* and *The Churchman,* have expressed strong editorial opposition, as has *Zions Herald,* a liberal Methodist publication.

In the McCollum case briefs *amicus curiae* in opposition to released-time instruction were submitted by the American Unitarian Association, the General Conference of Seventh Day Adventists, and the Joint Committee on Public Relations of the Southern, Northern, and National Baptist Conventions. The leadership of Protestants and Other Americans United is unquestionably likewise in opposition. In the September 1951 issue of its *Church and State Newsletter* appeared a cartoon on "Tax Funds Diverted to Sectarian Uses," which depicted a number of moths in a clothes closet, labeled "Bus Transportation," "Textbooks," "Federal Aid," etc. One of the moths was labeled "Released Time," and this invoked a letter of protest by Dr. Henry Smith Leiper. Replying to this letter on October 4, 1951, Glenn Archer, executive director of Protestants and Other Americans United, said in part:

> Something more is involved in all of this than a question of legality. No court decision can positively determine public policy. Suppose that, for the sake of argument, we assume that the United States Supreme Court finds the New York system of "released time" constitutional. That would still not of itself make the system a desirable one from the point of view of the public welfare. I would still be opposed to the practice because I regard it as a divisive influence, an unfair use of the public school machinery for the recruitment of pupils for the religious classes, and a means of applying public pressures to non-conformists so as to make them "give in." I accept majority rule in matters of politics, but not in matters of religion. Our whole theory of religious liberty is predicated upon the idea that the dissenter, the minority, the non-conformers have rights that shall not be invaded by either government or ecclesiastical pressures. Nor can I agree that such a system advances the causes of true religion in the slightest. I make this statement as one who was trained for the church, having spent eight years in Methodist institutions. I have served the church in every conceivable capacity from janitor to minister. I come of a long background of ministers. At least twelve Methodist ministers bear my name and are related to me. I have an unusual sensitivity concerning the welfare of religion in this nation. . . .
>
> The movement of "released time" of course, dates back some two or three decades. The leaders of the movement have always frankly said that the "released time" device was needed because of parental lethargy and the ineffectiveness of religious education as conducted by the churches alone. Therefore, the prestige of the government with its compulsory public school machinery must be utilized to strengthen the hand of the churches. I think that the clergymen who advance these arguments must be unacquainted with the principles of religious liberty as formulated by such men as Roger Williams, Thomas Jefferson and

James Madison! Freedom of religion is perverted when it is taken to mean freedom only for churchgoers and not for the unchurched, and those who say that "freedom of religion does not mean freedom from religion" are merely playing with words. (See story headed "Right of Disbelief Upheld by Baptists" in *Church and State Newsletter,* September, 1951.)

Perhaps the most significant piece of evidence of the lack of unanimity among Protestants on the question of released time is the action of the Rhode Island Council of Churches, which in 1949 allied itself with that state's rabbinical bodies in a successful opposition to the passage of a bill, introduced and strongly supported by the Catholic Church, which would have permitted released-time religious instruction off school premises.[46]

On the whole, however, organized Protestantism today overwhelmingly supports the released-time plan, at least in principle. This support has been intensified rather than, as might be supposed, weakened by the Supreme Court's decisions in the prayer and Bible reading cases. While supporting these decisions and opposing efforts to nullify them by constitutional amendment, Protestantism looks to the released-time program as presenting one constitutional way for public school recognition of religious values.

### The Catholic Church

Before the McCollum decision there was no Catholic position on released time. Actually for a considerable period most church leaders were either opposed to the program or apathetic to it. The official Catholic position in respect to education is summed up in the slogan "Every Catholic child in a Catholic school," and many Catholic leaders looked at released-time instruction as a weak palliative. The Catholic position was stated by Father Richard Gabel in 1937:

> . . . Catholics desire all children in a Catholic school under Catholic teachers. Mere religious instruction does not suffice for it is necessary "also that every other subject taught, be permeated with Christian piety" and "that Religion may be in very truth the foundation and crown of the youth's entire training" in elementary, intermediate and higher institutions, as the Encyclical on *Christian Education of Youth* puts it.[47]

Whether or not the Church participated in a released-time program in any particular community was a matter for determination by the local bishop, and practices varied from diocese to diocese. This is still the situation today; the archdiocese of New York has cooperated in the New York released-time system since 1941; but neither the archdiocese of Philadelphia nor of Baltimore nor of Detroit has made any effort to introduce released-time practices in those cities. It is probably still true that church leaders prefer to expend their energies toward expanding the parochial school system in their dioceses rather than divert even part of it toward the operation of released-time programs.

But while participation in released time is still a matter of local option, the defense of the program apparently has ceased to be since the McCollum decision. It is not too much to say that the Catholic Church today is the most vigorous and passionate defender of the released-time principle. In view of the rather meager practical benefits — measured by Catholic educational standards — accruing from the program, it would seem that such passionate defense is subject to explanation only in terms of higher strategy. Similar considerations are probably also the explanation for the even more dramatic reversal of its position by the Catholic Church on the issue of Bible reading and prayer recitation in the public schools.[48]

As has been previously indicated, in those communities where the Catholic Church does participate in the program, it frequently is able to insure almost 100% enrollment by Catholic children in the public schools. It is quite likely that if Catholic participation were withdrawn in such cities as New York, Boston, Chicago, and Los Angeles, the released-time programs there would collapse.

### The Jewish Position

American Jewry is overwhelmingly opposed to the released-time program. Jewish community leaders in the United States believe that the responsibility for religious education must rest with the family, the church, and the synagogue. They feel that the use of public school influence for the purpose of obtaining attendance for religious instruction constitutes a dangerous compromise of the integrity of the separation of church and state, which is the only guarantee of true religious liberty. They feel also that the operation of the plan has harmful effects on interfaith understanding and relationships. For the Jewish children in a community, released time is frequently neither advantageous nor necessary; in most American communities the after-hours and Sunday Jewish religious schools are usually able to enroll, without the use of released time, the overwhelming majority of the Jewish children in the community. It is probable that at least three out of every four Jewish children in this country receive religious education at some time or other.[49]

The opposition of the Jewish community to the released-time

plan has manifested itself in resolutions adopted by the major Jewish organizations—rabbinic, congregational, and secular. This unanimous opposition, however, like the Catholic defense, is of rather recent vintage. In the early days some Jewish educators also thought that the program might be a useful supplement to the existing Jewish educational system. But, following the leadership of the Central Conference of American Rabbis and the American Jewish Congress, the Jewish organizations came to the conclusion that whatever benefits, if any, could be obtained from the program were outweighed by its disadvantages and dangers.[50]

In recent years, actual support for released-time religious instruction has been expressed by the extreme Orthodox wing of American Judaism. This wing, however, represents only a small fraction of American Jewry.

## RESULTS OF THE RELEASED-TIME PROGRAM

### *Erasing Religious Illiteracy*

It is now more than half a century since Superintendent Wirt instituted a program of dismissing children who desired to participate in religious instruction; and during this period sufficient experiential data have been accumulated to warrant a number of at least tentative conclusions regarding the results of the released-time experiment. (Practically all of the data in this section—and in fact in much of this chapter—dates from 1952 and earlier. Numerous studies of released time were made during that period. Once, however, the Supreme Court upheld the constitutionality of the program in 1952, scholarly interest in it seems to have evaporated. For whatever reason, there have been since 1952 no substantial reported studies of released time in the United States.)

In the first place, the promoters of released-time instruction profess to be satisfied with the results. Though they recognize its limitations and admit that it is not the total solution, they maintain that their hopes have been realized beyond expectation. Dr. Shaver estimated that the "cooperative" weekday church schools have succeeded in reaching on the average one-third of the children in the community who otherwise would not receive religious instruction, a "remarkable evangelistic record."[51] His predecessor as director of the Department of Weekday Religious Education of the International Council of Religious Education, Dr. W. Dyer Blair, was no less enthusiastic. Writing in 1940, he said:[52]

Another claim in the early days of the weekday church school movement, and continues to be, is that the weekday schools of religion would solve the problem of reaching the unreached, the unchurched. The results in this respect have been significant. These schools reach with a program of Christian education a much larger number of children and youth of a given community than any other agency of Christian education that the Protestant churches have ever used. Neither the Sunday School, the Vacation Church School, nor the Young People's Societies — nor all three combined — reaches as high a percentage for the grade levels served of the total children and youth groups in the community as does the weekday church school. This is true for nine-tenths of all towns and cities where the released time plan is operating. It is no unheard-of thing to have every single child in the school grades served in regular attendance in the religious classes. The enrollment of 90 to 99 percent of the public school constituency in the weekday church school is quite common. To reach less than 80 percent is the exception.

On the other hand, observers less professionally involved in the released-time program have been considerably more restrained in their estimates of the results of the experiment. According to one Protestant writer,

the record of over thirty-five years makes it seem unlikely that the released-time program is in any active way bridging the chasm between the religiously illiterate portion of our population and those under religious instruction. . . . The record shows that 75% of those enrolled in such schools have been duplications of Sunday School enrollments, leaving only 25% of the estimated enrollment of weekday church schools as actual additions to the total number of our population under religious instruction.[53]

Even if duplication is disregarded, the number of children reached by the released-time program is still extremely small. The figures on attendance at released-time instruction given earlier in this chapter reveal that after fifty years released-time instruction still reaches only a fractional part of American youth. The benefits to Protestant religious education have been exceedingly small. In Chicago released-time religious instruction reached only 4,500 Protestant children, whereas Sunday church schools in the same area reached 150,000 children.[54] In all of New York City it is unlikely that more than 15,000 Protestant children receive religious instruction through the released-time program. If the program is reaching unchurched children, it is fair to say that it is primarily unchurched Catholic children who are being reached.

The extent to which the program has effectively met or failed to meet the problem of religious illiteracy is also indicated by the short life expectancy of released-time programs as revealed by surveys of the United States Office of Education in 1940 and the National Education Association in 1949. According to the Office of Education report, approximately one-third of the school systems did not carry the released-time program more than one year. The median of years during which pupils were released was only two years.[55] The National Education Association report showed that of the 1,018 school systems reporting that they ever had a program of religious education in connection with the public school system, 310 or better than 30% had discontinued their programs.[56]

In the National Education Association survey half of the communities that had discontinued their programs gave the McCollum decision as the reason for the discontinuance. Yet, in view of the equally high rate of discontinuance reported in the Office of Education survey eight years before that case, it is not unlikely that in many cases the McCollum ruling was assigned to explain a decision that would have been taken anyway. The other reasons assigned for discontinuance were a shortage of good teachers (12.6%); a general lack of interest (11.0%); and a lack of sufficient pupil enrollment (8.1%).

The Office of Education survey reported that two major reasons were given for discontinuing released-time programs:

> First, decisions of the sponsoring agencies to discontinue the program; and second, dissatisfaction with the program due to a lack of suitably prepared teachers, inadequately planned programs, and unsatisfactory results. Comments explaining action taken by the churches included the burden placed upon the ministers and church members for both time and money; a waning interest on the part of the community, the teachers, and the pupils; and the factor of church denominations which became a problem in some communities. Dissatisfaction with the program centered chiefly in the teachers' inability to meet the public-school's standards of teaching and to maintain discipline among the pupils. Waning interest of the community and the pupils was largely attributed to inadequate teaching. Other difficulties connected with the conduct of weekday classes included lack of curriculum; too great a distance between schools and weekday centers; inadequate heating of centers; inadequate attendance records; small numbers of children released, which complicated the school program, and need for general church supervision.[57]

### Improving Interfaith Relations

There is little objective evidence to support the argument that the released-time program tends to promote interfaith understanding. One thing is hardly open to question: promotion of the plan and attempts to introduce it in specific communities have had a patently deleterious effect on intergroup relations, particularly between Christians and Jews, but also between Protestants and Catholics. As Justice Frankfurter pointed out in the McCollum case,

> the divergent views expressed in the briefs submitted here in behalf of various religious organizations, as *amici curiae,* in themselves suggest that the movement has been a divisive and not an irenic influence in the community.

Of course proponents of the program may justly reply that the program itself should not be charged with the consequences of opposition to its introduction; the fair test of its effectiveness as an influence in bettering interreligious understanding is in its operation after its introduction. There are many individual instances of harmonious intergroup relationship in the operation of the program. In 1949 the Public Education Association reported as one such instance the cooperation of a Catholic and a Lutheran church in using the same escort.[58] In its 1943 study the Association also reported an instance in which "the Catholic priest picks up Protestant as well as Catholic children and drops the Protestants at their church continuing on with his own flock." (This may or may not be the same incident reported in 1949). "In another school, the Parents Association is on record as being opposed to the program. However, Catholic children are being released and the church is not providing escorts. The Parents Association has taken on the job of escorting these children to the church and all the parents participating are Jewish."

On the other hand, incidents indicating an opposite effect on intergroup relations are not lacking. In the same 1943 study the Public Education Association reported that in one school, where— though the population was about one-third colored—the race issue had raised no problem in the school until it was raised at the religious center, where parents objected to the attendance of colored children at religious instruction. The Association also reported that in another school the principal had worked unceasingly to bring about understanding and cooperation between Irish Catholics and Jews who had been feuding for years, but introduction of the released-time program accentuated religious differences and again brought dissension into the school.

In the 1949 study, eighty out of the one hundred principals questioned found no difference one way or the other in intergroup relations as a result of the operation of the program. The other twenty differed sharply as to its effect. The conclusion reached by the Association observers was that

> several factors like the dismissal procedure may make for a conscious-

ness of difference. It is not to be assumed, however, that consciousness of difference and disrespect of difference are synonymous. The report found no evidence in the overt behavior of the children observed, that the released time program, as it operates here, makes for disrespect.

The National Conference of Christians and Jews has sponsored one study on the effect of the released-time program on interfaith relations in a number of communities. With respect to the textbooks used in the released-time classes, the report said:

> In comparison to the number of texts examined, passages of an antagonistic or derogatory nature in Catholic books were numerous . . . many of the examples used in the catechetical study materials make comparisons to show the truth of the Catholic faith and the falsehood of other faiths, and the superiority of Catholic ways and customs to those of other religious groups. This is basic Catholic doctrine but it often results in placing individuals of other groups in a seemingly inferior position as persons.
>
> Most Protestant material contained no reference to the inter-religious problem. . . . Material prepared by conservative Protestant groups sometimes speaks of the Jews as being inferior because they are outside the Christian family. There is a surprising absence of reference to the Jew as a contemporary person. Old Testament references tend to show him in a much more favorable light than New Testament references. Most appreciative reference to both Jews and Catholics are very brief although there are a few well developed units on inter-religious problems.
>
> Jewish textbooks examined are singularly free from derogatory and antagonistic remarks. On the other hand, they make little reference toward appreciation of members of other religious groups. They were as a group without any reference to inter-religious problems.

On the whole, the study found that "the contribution of the weekday religious program, in the six communities studied, to positive interreligious relationships was very limited," although there appeared to be "a slight but consistent tendency on the part of 'released-time' students to show a more positive attitude toward members of other religious groups." The study also revealed in the communities studied a strong sense of being the object of "Jewish antagonism, the unwillingness of significant minorities in all communities to enter into common social relationships with Jews, and the presence of substantial misunderstanding and misinformation about all faiths, and that of the Jews in particular."[59]

It must be noted that in recent years the three major religious groups have been re-examining the texts used in their religious schools with a view toward improving interfaith understanding and appreciation. The Declaration on Religious Liberty of Vatican II is almost certain to intensify this effort. Nevertheless, though one may agree with the National Conference study that "a weekday program of religious education can make an important contribution to positive inter-religious relationship if leaders of all the religious groups in any particular community cooperate wholeheartedly to utilize its potentialities," it remains true that there is no evidence that the practice of released time has made any appreciable contributions to interfaith relationships.

### The Community's Moral Standards

It is unlikely that even the most ardent protagonist of the released-time experiment will assert that it has had an appreciable effect on the moral standards of contemporary America. On the contrary, it is vigorously declared that moral standards among teenagers are lower and crime and delinquency far more prevalent than five decades ago, when the experiment was launched, and that released-time religious instruction is therefore much more needed today than it was then.

Of course it is unfair to attribute to the program the failure to keep moral standards high in America since 1913. In this period we have had two world and two lesser wars and an unprecedented depression. Protagonists of the experiment may well aver that but for the fact that hundreds of thousands if not millions of American youth had received some foundation in ethics and morals through the released-time instruction, the situation might be considerably worse than it is. This is not susceptible of proof one way or the other, and must be accepted more or less on faith. Nevertheless it remains true that there is no objective evidence to substantiate the assertion that released-time instruction has appreciably raised moral standards or helped diminish crime and delinquency.

### THE LAW AND THE CONSTITUTION

Released-time religious education is specifically authorized by statute in thirteen states: California, Indiana, Iowa, Kentucky, Maine, Massachusetts, Michigan, Minnesota, New York, Oregon, Pennsylvania, South Dakota, and West Virginia.[60] Since many more than these thirteen have the system in operation in some communities, it is obvious that the absence of a specific statutory authorization is no great handicap to the establishment of a released-time program. It is generally assumed, and has been so held by the courts, that the local boards of education have implicit power to institute the program even without a specific statute.[61]

Before the McCollum decision four courts had passed on the constitutionality of released-time programs, and all but one upheld its constitutional validity. The one exception was a New York lower court decision[62] which in 1925 invalidated the released-time system in Mount Vernon partly on the ground that the consent cards signed by parents were printed by pupils on public school presses. The court said:

> The fact that no particular denomination was favored or intended so to be by this action of the board of education does not affect the question. The fact is that the property of the board was permitted to be used directly in aid of such schools of religious instruction whose members saw fit to avail themselves of the action taken by the defendants. It seems perfectly clear that it was illegal for the defendants to permit the printing of the cards to be done on its presses.

This aspect of the decision is probably still sound law — at least it has never been overruled. The court, however, went on to hold that aside from the use of the public school presses, institution of the released-time program was beyond the statutory and constitutional power of the Mount Vernon board of education. That part of the court's holding was overruled by the 1927 decision of the state's highest court validating the White Plains released-time program, which — except for the fact that public school presses were not used — was in all respects the same as the Mount Vernon program. In this decision the Court of Appeals said:[63]

> A child otherwise regular in attendance may be excused for a portion of the entire time during which the schools are in session, to the extent at least of half an hour in each week, to take outside instruction in music or dancing without violating the provisions of the Compulsory Education Law, either in letter or in spirit. Otherwise the word "regularly" as used in the statute would be superfluous. Practical administration of the public schools calls for some elasticity in this regard and vests some discretion in the school authorities. Neither the Constitution nor the law discriminates against religion. Denominational religion is merely put in its proper place outside of public aid or support. . . .
> The separation of the public school system from religious denominational instruction is thus complete. Jealous sectarians may view with alarm the introduction in the schools of religious teaching which to the unobservant eye is but faintly tinted with denominationalism. Eternal vigilance is the price of constitutional rights. But it is impossible to say, as a matter of law, that the slightest infringement of constitutional right or abuse of statutory requirement has been shown in this case.

The decision of the New York court in the White Plains case was followed in 1946 by the Supreme Court of Illinois,[64] and in 1947 by the District Court of Appeals of Los Angeles, California.[65] In the Los

Angeles case the court did not trouble to conceal its sympathy with the released-time program:

> No one who keeps pace with the trends of modern society can deny that instruction of the youth of the state in faith and morality is of utmost necessity and importance. All too regretfully it must be said that in present-day American life the family as a unit has not done its part in this vital field of education of our boys and girls. Else juvenile courts would not be groaning under an avalanche of cases of derelictions of children. What more logical advance could be made in the science of sociology than the unification of religious leaders in a coordinated effort to teach children faith and morality—and for that purpose to excuse them from schools for one hour a week to go to the church or tabernacle or synagogue of their parents' choice.

The concurring opinion of Justice White is interesting and significant because it expresses the philosophy that the dissenting United States Supreme Court Justices in the Zorach case contended was implicit in the majority opinion:

> Throughout her entire argument, appellant misconceives the American principle of religious freedom. What she contends for is freedom *from* religion rather than freedom *of* religion. Appellant's argument leads one to the conclusion that the doctrine of separation of church and state looks upon religion as something intrinsically evil, and against which there should be a rigid quarantine. Nothing is farther from the true concept of the American philosophy of government than such an argument. In the constitution of every state of the union is to be found language which either directly, or by clear implication, recognizes a profound reverence for religion and an assumption that its influence in all human affairs is essential to the well being of the community. . . .

It may respectfully be suggested that it is Justice White and not the appellant who "misconceives the American principle of religious freedom." If the debates in the state conventions and legislatures on the clause in the Constitution forbidding religious tests for Federal office show anything, they show pretty clearly that it was the deliberate intention of the Constitutional fathers to guarantee freedom "*from*" religion no less than freedom "*of*" religion. Indeed, they were pretty well convinced that only by assuring freedom "from" religion would freedom "of" religion be secured; or, in the words of Justice Jackson in his dissent in the Zorach case, "The day this country ceases to be free for irreligion it will cease to be free for religion. . . ." In any event, however one interprets the majority opinion in the Zorach case, the unanimous opinion of the Supreme Court in the "Miracle" and notary public test oath cases would seem to make it clear that our Constitution still guarantees freedom "from" religion as well as freedom "of" religion.

It should be noted that though the California court relied on the New York court's decision in the White Plains case, the Los Angeles program was different from the one in White Plains. In White Plains public school participation was limited to excusing those children whose parents signed consent cards for attendance at religious instruction. But in Los Angeles the board of education distributed literature describing the released-time program, paid the expense of preparing, printing, and distributing the literature and the consent cards, and directed the teachers and superintendents of schools to keep attendance records and to oversee the working of the plan. It is at least doubtful that the New York Court of Appeals would have upheld a released-time program involving such public school participation.

## THE McCOLLUM CASE

### *The Facts*

In all the cases discussed in the preceding section, the released-time classes were held in church centers off public school premises. Moreover, none of these cases was brought to the United States Supreme Court; and though the California case was decided a month after the Everson case, not even that case gave real consideration to the interpretation of the First Amendment contained in the Everson case. In the McCollum case for the first time the Supreme Court applied the broad principles announced in the Everson case to the troublesome problem of public school intervention in the field of religious education.

The facts of the McCollum case as stated by the Supreme Court were substantially as follows: In 1940 interested members of the Jewish, Roman Catholic, and some of the Protestant faiths formed a voluntary association, called the Champaign Council on Religious Education, and obtained permission from the board of education to offer classes in religious instruction to public school pupils during regular school hours. The instructors in religion were engaged by the Champaign Council subject to the approval and supervision of the superintendent of public schools. At the beginning of each term the public school teachers distributed to the children cards on which parents could indicate their consent to the enrollment of their children in the religious instruction classes. Children who obtained such consent were released by the school authorities from the secular work for a period of thirty minutes each week in the elementary schools and forty-five minutes in the junior high school. If the majority of children in a particular class participated in the religious instruction they remained in their regular classroom; the children who did not participate were sent to other parts of the school building, sometimes accompanied by their regular teachers and sometimes not. Only the Protestant instruction was conducted within the regular classroom; where children were released for Catholic or Jewish instruction they left their classroom with their religious teacher for instruction in some other part of the building. (There had been no Jewish classes for several years before the suit was brought.) When the religious instruction was conducted in the regular classroom—which was apparently the usual place—the regular teacher frequently, if not always, remained in the room during the instruction period. At the end of the session the religious instructor left the classroom, the children who had participated in Catholic or Jewish instruction or who had not participated in any religious instruction returned, and regular class work was resumed.[66]

These were the facts that the Court found to be sufficient to invalidate the program. But there was much more to the case than these bare facts. What this bare recital does not reveal is the human element—Terry McCollum, the ten-year-old victim of a bitter conflict between a determined atheist mother and an equally determined God-fearing public school board.

That Vashti McCollum was an atheist was made clear almost from the first words of her petition. In her second paragraph she alleged that she

> adheres to the school of thought known as "Rationalism" including atheism, is not a believer in any religious creed or doctrine and accepts no part of any bible as true where such part is not in accord with reason. Her views and understanding concerning religion are further set forth as those in the publication entitled "Rationalism vs. Religious Education in the Public Schools," written by her father, Arthur G. Cromwell, and a copy of which is hereto attached, marked "Exhibit A" and made a part hereof.[67]

The tenor and intellectual level of "Exhibit A" can be gauged from the following brief extracts:

> Religious worship is a chronic disease of the imagination contracted in childhood. Religionists know this; hence their determination to force religious training in the public schools while the plastic minds of our youth absorb readily and have no means of self-determination. . . .
> Religion is born of fear, ignorance and superstition. . . . .
> From the first day that the first crook realized he could hoodwink a few credulous beings into believing he had some personal tie-up with an unknown deity, religion and its unscrupulous preachers have fought

to perpetuate the racket that permitted them to prey upon the innocence and credulity of the masses. . . .

Why Mrs. McCollum and her attorney saw fit to use her petition as a propaganda medium for atheism is not clear; at best it was not likely to be of help in obtaining a favorable court decision on the merits. Certain it is, however, that propaganda was their intent. How else does one explain the inclusion in the petition of "Exhibit A"; or of the following random paragraphs from Mrs. McCollum's petition:

One of said instructors in religious education teaches a doctrine that there is a supernatural and divine being, person or thing, called "God"; that there is a relationship between mankind and said alleged God, whereby all earthly persons are dependent upon and responsible to said God. She also establishes in the minds of pupils a certain sectarian theory that said God is of masculine gender (by use of pronouns) and that said God and a female person named "Mary" (also known as the wife of Joseph) were the father and mother of a male child, called "Jesus Christ"; that thereafter the parents (then referred to as Joseph and Mary) fled with said child into Egypt until after the death of Herod; that said male child grew to manhood, and by reason of his relationship to and favoritism on the part of said God, he was endowed with miraculous, personal proclivities, but was ultimately killed by Jews, on Good Friday; that thereafter, on Easter Sunday, life was revived in his body, and he met personally with some of his disciples, and he departed from them still living in said post mortem life.

Said instructor sometimes refers to said God by other names, such as "Lord" and "Jehovah." She teaches that said God once caused a great flood upon the earth, and thereby drowned many people and other dry-land animals but preserved couples of species by placing them in an ark which weathered the storm; that said God, pursuant to a covenant, favored certain persons, such as Abraham, Jacob and Joseph; that Jacob had a struggle with an angel of God, which struggle said instructor interprets as a religious experience; that Adam and Eve were respectively, the first man and woman; that the Old Testament teaches of the "calling" of the Jewish nation; that Jacob had two wives, and that the offspring of such polygamy became God's chosen and preferred people; that Moses was associated with Jehovah; that God revealed himself to Moses through the medium of a burning bush; that God has the qualities of love and guidance; that God has performed supernatural and miraculous achievements in Egypt, and has shown signs and miracles to Pharaoh. . . .

She also teaches the sectarian religious views that Jesus could be loved; that some angels gave a Christmas message to some shepherds; that Jesus was baptized in a river; that Jesus healed the sick (without teaching that he used drugs or surgery); that he raised the dead by reviving life in deceased persons. . . .

Determined as Vashti McCollum was that her son was not to be instructed that Jesus healed the sick without the use of drugs or surgery, equally determined were the public school authorities of the small university town, Champaign, that Terry would receive such instruction; at least, circumstances so combined as to make him pay dearly for his and his mother's obstinate refusal to allow him to participate in such instruction.

Terry McCollum's regular teacher was Mrs. Bessie Taylor, and the instructor who came in Thursday mornings to teach religion was Miss Mae Chapin, who was designated by the Champaign Council on Religious Education to teach the Protestant classes. In the first semester of the fifth year, Terry and one other boy were the only ones not participating in religious education, but in the second semester the other boy enrolled and Terry remained the solitary dissenter. The nature of Miss Chapin's teachings has already been indicated; it was interdenominational Protestantism, acceptable to the major Protestant denominations in Champaign with the exception of the Lutherans[68] — but not, of course, in accordance with Catholic or Jewish religious teachings. It does not appear in the record what the exact religious composition of Terry McCollum's class was, or whether there were in it any Catholic, Jewish, or Lutheran children. But the trial court did find that the Protestant classes taught by Miss Chapin and her colleague Mrs. Sarah Jorgensen were attended by "children of some twenty-one sects, including Catholic, Jewish and Protestant, as well as many children without any particular religious preference. . . ."

In view of the presence of Jewish children in the Protestant classes it is relevant to consider one aspect of the teaching to which the Jewish children were subjected. The following is from the testimony of Miss Chapin:

THE WITNESS (*continuing*): I do not think I spoke ever of the Jews as enemies; that was several years ago and I do not remember.
Q. Will you tell just what you did teach with reference to who his enemies were?

. . .

A. I think if you read the Bible you will know them.
Q. I want to know what you teach. Don't you teach that the Jews were the enemies of Christ?
A. They were hostile to Jesus in many ways.

. . .

Q. Did you teach the children that the Jews were afraid of Jesus?
A. Some of them were.
Q. How about the others?
A. Some of them were not.

. . .

Q. Have you during the last three years at any time been teaching that the Jews had anything to do with the crucifixion of Jesus Christ?

. . .

THE WITNESS (*continuing*): Individual Jews did participate. I did not tell the children so, I did not mention it. In connection with the crucifixion of Christ, in my teaching during the last three years I mentioned that Jews were present at his trial and perhaps testified. I do not teach those doctrinal things. I just teach the Bible story and the paper you talk about, I have not used since several years ago. I have had such an outline. I have taught that some of the Jews accepted Jesus and that some of them rejected him. I do not teach the pupils that the Jews were accepted or rejected but I may have stated that, but remember that those things are explained. If you use an outline an explanation is given to the pupils. An outline does not include everything.

Line 13 on page 3 of the exhibit says, "The Jews rejected Jesus." It does not mean as a people. It means individuals.[69]

This testimony by Miss Chapin was given on cross examination and obviously reluctantly. It is at least likely that on occasions the teaching on Jewish participation in the crucifixion was even more direct.[70] But even in the form in which it appears in the record, it is not difficult to imagine the mental operations and feelings of a ten-year-old Jewish child listening to such teaching in what is to most children the citadel of truth, and in the unobjecting presence of his regular public school teacher to whom the child looks for truth and knowledge. It is hardly surprising that rabbis and Jewish parents are not infrequently faced by a Jewish child's statement that "We Jews killed Christ; I learned it in school."

All the children in Mrs. Taylor's class participated in Miss Chapin's instruction except Terry; and his obduracy raised for Mrs. Taylor the difficult problem of what to do with him during the weekly half hour when Miss Chapin took over the class. Mrs. Taylor usually remained in the classroom and "observed" while the religious instruction was given, but she could do this only if she found some way of disposing of Terry. According to Terry, she tried to solve the problem by urging him to enroll so that the class would have "100%." Terry was willing, but his mother capriciously and unreasonably refused to consent.

Mrs. Taylor obviously did not quite know what to do with Terry during the religious instruction period. She could not devote her time to him, for that would interfere with her joining in the religious instruction, and she was reluctant to miss that. Searching for a solution, she placed the boy at a desk in the hall outside the classroom, a procedure sometimes employed as a method of punishment. Passing schoolmates teased him, believing he was being punished for being an atheist and for not participating in religious instruction—a misconception which, it may be said, is pregnant with significance.

Mrs. Taylor found nothing wrong with this arrangement and probably would have continued it — at least while the music room was being used. Terry, however, went home crying as a result of the experience, and his mother protested to the school authorities, thereby bringing an end to this practice. When the music room (which was next to the teachers' washroom) was unoccupied, Mrs. Taylor placed him there alone, making certain that the door remained closed. Protests from Mrs. McCollum brought a stop to this practice too; whereupon Mrs. Taylor finally arrived at what was undoubtedly to her the happy solution of depositing him with the other fifth grade teacher during the period of religious instruction, with the result that the latter's pupils also could observe the consequences of heterodoxy.

During the Colonial period in the United States history, three of the penalties commonly inflicted for heterodoxy were imprisonment, the pillory, and banishment. We have progressed far since colonial times, and Terry McCollum could not be imprisoned for refusing to enroll for religious instruction. But he could be confined alone in a closed room on the far side of the school building. He could not be placed in an actual pillory; but he could be subjected to the public obloquy and ridicule which was the object of the pillory, by being placed at a desk in the public corridor to be jeered at and scorned by his schoolmates. He could not be banished from Champaign or even from the public school because of his refusal to conform, but he could be "dumped" into another class for the period of religious instruction.

## Justice Black's Opinion

These were the facts presented to the United States Supreme Court in December 1947. All the Illinois judges who had passed on Mrs. McCollum's complaint agreed that neither her rights nor her son's rights had been infringed on, and that the Champaign released-time program did not violate either the Illinois or the Federal constitution. But between January 1947, when the Illinois Supreme Court upheld the constitutionality of the Champaign program, and December of that year, when the case was argued in Washington, the United States Supreme Court had decided the Everson case, in which it had broadly interpreted the First Amendment as prohibiting all government aid to religion even on a nonpreferential basis, and held that the limitations of the First Amendment were applicable to the States.

It was therefore fairly obvious that the Champaign system could not stand unless the Court were to repudiate the principles of the Everson case. Counsel for the Champaign board of education quite candidly urged the Court to do exactly that, and argued that historically the First Amendment was intended to forbid only government preference of one religion over another—not an impartial government assistance of all religions—and that the Fourteenth Amendment did not make the "establishment of religion" clause of the First Amendment applicable as a prohibition against the states.

Parenthetically it may be remarked that even if the Court had reversed itself and allowed nonpreferential state aid to religion, it could sustain the validity of released-time practices only by sanctioning the fiction that the released-time program—in Champaign (or elsewhere)—was nonpreferential. That this assumption would be fictional is indicated in the first place by the fact that Protestant religious instruction was conducted in the same classroom in which the regular classes were held, whereas the Catholic children were required to go to a basement room. But far more important, participation in the released-time program was not open to all sects. In Champaign the public school authorities required applicant groups to work through the interfaith Council on Religious Education. This requirement not only eliminated participation by Jehovah's Witnesses, but by so orthodox a religious sect as the Lutherans. This situation was not unique in Champaign. It is not an accidental but an inevitable consequence of the released-time plan that there appears to be no record of participation anywhere in the United States by Jehovah's Witnesses, or by religious groups other than those teaching traditional Protestantism, Catholicism, and—infrequently—Judaism.

Moreover, to dismiss Mrs. McCollum's petition the Supreme Court would have had to swallow a second fiction—that attendance in Miss Chapin's classes were entirely voluntary, notwithstanding the pressures exerted on Terry McCollum and notwithstanding the "100%" less one attendance at religious instruction as contrasted with the less than 10% attendance in nearby Chicago.

Justice Black, speaking for six of the nine Justices, found it unnecessary to accept or reject either of these fictions. He acknowledged the contentions of Mrs. McCollum that:

(1) In actual practice certain Protestant groups have obtained an overshadowing advantage in the propagation of their faiths over other Protestant sects; (2) the religious education program was voluntary in name only because in fact subtle pressures were brought to bear on the

students to force them to participate in it; and (3) the power given the school superintendent to reject teachers selected by religious groups and the power given the local Council on Religious Education to determine which religious faiths should participate in the program was a prior censorship of religion.

He did not, however, deem it necessary for his decision to pass on these contentions. Expressly reiterating the principles of the Everson case that the state may not pass laws that "aid all religions," he declared the Champaign system of released time unconstitutional because the operation of the state's compulsory education system assisted and was integrated with the program of religious instruction carried on by separate religious sects; and that the state might not consistently with the First and Fourteenth Amendments utilize its public school system to aid any or all religious faiths or sects in the dissemination of their doctrines or ideals.

> Pupils compelled by law [the Court said] to go to school for secular education are released in part from their legal duty upon the condition that they attend the religious classes. This is beyond all question a utilization of the tax-established and tax-supported public school system to aid religious groups to spread their faiths. And it falls squarely under the ban of the First Amendment (made applicable to the States by the Fourteenth) as we interpreted it in *Everson vs. Board of Education.*
> . . . Here not only are state's tax-supported public school buildings used for the dissemination of religious doctrines. The State also affords sectarian groups an invaluable aid in that it helps to provide pupils for their religious classes through use of the state's compulsory public school machinery. This is not separation of Church and State.

### Justice Frankfurter's Concurring Opinion

Six of the nine Justices joined in the opinion of Justice Black. These were, besides Justice Black, Chief Justice Vinson and Justices Murphy, Douglas, Rutledge, and Burton. The latter two justices, together with Justice Jackson, also joined in a concurring opinion written by Justice Frankfurter. These four Justices had dissented in the Everson case because they believed that the principles there announced by the Court required the invalidation of the law that provided for state payment of the expense of transporting children to parochial schools.

In his concurring opinion, Justice Frankfurter set forth in detail the history of the released-time experiment, the extent of its practice, and the variations of these practices, stating:

> Respects in which programs differ include, for example, the amount of supervision by the public school of attendance and performance in

the religious class, of the course of study, of the selection of teachers, methods of enrollment and dismissal from the secular classes, the amount of school time devoted to operation of the program; the extent to which school property and administrative machinery are involved; the effect on the public school program of the introduction of "released time"; the proportion of students who seek to be excused; the effect of the program on non-participants; the amount and nature of the publicity for the program in the public school.

Then, after describing the general operation of the program in Champaign, he recognized the realities of the situation and swept aside its fictions, stating:

Religious education so conducted on school time and property is patently woven into the working scheme of the school. The Champaign arrangement thus presents powerful elements of inherent pressure by the school system in the interest of religious sects. The fact that this power has not been used to discriminate is beside the point. Separation is a requirement to abstain from fusing functions of Government and of religious sects, not merely to treat them all equally. That a child is offered an alternative may reduce the constraint; it does not eliminate the operation of influence by the school in matters sacred to conscience and outside the school's domain. The law of imitation operates, and non-conformity is not an outstanding characteristic of children. The result is an obvious pressure upon children to attend. Again, while the Champaign school population represents only a fraction of the more than two hundred and fifty sects of the nation, not even all the practicing sects in Champaign are willing or able to provide religious instruction. The children belonging to these non-participating sects will thus have inculcated in them a feeling of separatism when the school should be the training ground for habits of community, or they will have religious instruction in a faith which is not that of their parents. As a result, the public school system of Champaign actively furthers inculcation in the religious tenets of some faiths, and in the process sharpens the consciousness of religious differences at least among some of the children committed to its care. These are consequences not amenable to statistics. But they are precisely the consequences against which the Constitution was directed when it prohibited the Government common to all from becoming embroiled, however innocently, in the destructive religious conflicts of which the history of even this country records some dark pages.

Toward the end of Justice Frankfurter's concurring opinion is found a sentence that was destined to cause much trouble and confusion:

We do not consider, as indeed we could not, school programs not before us which, though colloquially characterized as "released time," present situations differing in aspects that may well be constitutionally crucial.

## *Justice Jackson's Concurring Opinion*

If there was not enough confusion resulting from the fact that though there are only nine Justices in the Court, the two opinions referred to were apparently concurred in by ten justices, added confusion was evoked by Justice Jackson's determination to write his own separate concurring opinion (in which no one else joined) besides concurring in Justice Frankfurter's concurring opinion. Moreover, Justice Jackson's opinion was intrinsically confusing. In the Everson case Justice Jackson complained that the Court's holding (that the statute involved was constitutional) was inconsistent with the whole tenor of the Court's opinion. In the McCollum case Justice Jackson appears to have been guilty of the same fault. The entire tenor of his opinion would seem to lead to the conclusion that Mrs. McCollum had no standing to sue and had not shown any real injury which the Court could redress. Nevertheless he agreed with the Court's determination that the Champaign released-time program went beyond the permissible constitutional limitations. Apparently the purpose of his concurrence was to indicate his view that religion cannot altogether be eliminated from the public school curriculum, and that if the Court were "to eliminate everything that is objectionable to any of these [256] warring sects or inconsistent with any of their doctrines [it would] leave public education in shreds." He continued:

> Perhaps subjects such as mathematics, physics or chemistry are, or can be, completely secularized. But it would not seem practical to teach either practice or appreciation of the arts if we are to forbid exposure of youth to any religious influences. Music without sacred music, architecture minus the Cathedral, or painting without the scriptural themes would be eccentric and incomplete, even from a secular point of view. Yet the inspirational appeal of religion in these guises is often stronger than in forthright sermon. Even such a "science" as biology raises the issue between evolution and creation as an explanation of our presence on this planet. Certainly a course in English literature that omitted the Bible and other powerful uses of our mother tongue for religious ends would be pretty barren. And I should suppose it is a proper, if not an indispensable, part of preparation for a worldly life to know the roles that religion and religions have played in the tragic story of mankind. The fact is that, for good or for ill, nearly everything in our culture worth transmitting, everything which gives meaning to life, is saturated with religious influences, derived from paganism, Judaism, Christianity—both Catholic and Protestant,—and other faiths accepted by a large part of the world's peoples. One can hardly respect a system of education that would leave the student wholly ignorant of the currents of religious thought that move the world society for a part in which he is being prepared.

## Justice Reed's Dissent

Even Justice Reed's dissent was not a model of complete clarity. On the one hand, he seemed to regret the bargain made in the Everson case, in which parochial bus transportation was declared valid in exchange for a broad interpretation of the First Amendment. (Justice Reed's dissent set forth the standard list of government aids to religion that are invariably used to discredit the Everson principle.) On the other hand, he did not expressly reject the Everson principle, but said only that it should not have been held to invalidate the Champaign released-time program any more than it invalidated the New Jersey bus transportation system. Apparently, Justice Reed was willing to accept broad principles as long as they did not affect actual practices. In any event, what is clear is that Justice Reed felt that the Champaign released-time program was perfectly constitutional, and that neither the troublesome Mrs. McCollum nor her equally troublesome son Terry had any legitimate grievance that the Court could or should redress.

## THE FOUR-YEAR CONFUSION

This, then, was the McCollum decision. But what did it mean? Did it outlaw all released-time — as distinguished from dismissed-time — programs, or only those similar to the Champaign system? And if the latter, when was a system sufficiently like that prevailing in Champaign to be deemed within the ban of the McCollum decision? Specifically, did the McCollum decision outlaw an off-the-premises released-time program such as was conducted in New York?

Justice Black's decision seemed clear enough; its language could hardly be read otherwise than as intending to invalidate any released-time program that involved the use of the tax-established and tax-supported compulsory public school machinery as an aid in recruiting children for religious instruction — regardless of the use of school buildings or other specific aspects of the Champaign situation. The state compelled all children to attend school for a specified number of hours weekly for secular instruction. It then, in effect, entered into an agreement with the willing parents to release their children in part from that obligation if they used the released time to participate in religious instruction. This release, Justice Black held, was an aid to religion in violation of the First Amendment.

Justice Black and the other justices were familiar with all the details of the New York system and its operation off the school premises. The Protestant Council of New York City had filed a brief

411

*amicus curiae* setting forth in full the nature of the New York released-time system, pointing out its differences from the Champaign system and specifically requesting the Court to limit its decision so as not to include the New York system. The New York plan was discussed in detail in Justice Reed's dissenting opinion, which also set forth in full the New York statute and regulations.

With knowledge of all these facts, Justice Black cast his opinion in language clearly broad enough to outlaw both the Champaign and the New York released-time programs. Justice Reed recognized this in his dissent, and stated that under the "Court's judgment . . . children cannot be released or dismissed from school to attend classes in religion while other children must remain to pursue secular education, [and] religious instruction of public school children during public school hours is prohibited."

Justice Black's opinion was clear enough; and since it represented the views of six of the nine justices, there seemed to be no substantial basis for all the real or simulated confusion which followed. The Champaign Circuit Court was under no doubt as to what the Supreme Court meant. The final order of mandamus that it granted to Mrs. McCollum prohibited within the city of Champaign "the use of the state's public school machinery to help enroll pupils in the several religious classes of sectarian groups." The Champaign Board of Education and the Champaign Council of Religious Education accordingly discontinued all religious instruction during public school hours and substituted after-school-hours instruction.[71]

The basis of the resulting confusion was the sentence in Justice Frankfurter's concurring opinion that

> We do not consider, as indeed we could not, school programs not before us which, though colloquially characterized as "released time," present situations differing in aspects that may well be constitutionally crucial.

Paradoxically—as it later turned out—Justice Frankfurter, who wrote this sentence, did not construe it as limiting the broad sweep of Justice Black's decision, although Justice Douglas—who did not concur in the sentence but joined only in Justice Black's broad opinion—did so construe it. But we are getting ahead of our story.

In any event what followed was a great deal of discussion as to what was meant by Justice Frankfurter's concurring opinion; it evoked as much discussion as did the majority opinion. Indeed, in his opinion validating the New York City system in the Zorach case, Justice DiGiovanna went into great detail as to the meaning of Justice Frankfurter's concurring opinion, without once even mentioning Justice Black's majority opinion.

Justice Frankfurter's quoted sentence, coupled with an understandable desire to preserve the churches' substantial investment in religious education in cooperation with the public school, engendered a widespread confusion as to the exact holding in the McCollum decision. State attorneys general and municipal corporation counsels called on by local school boards for advice came up with varying interpretations, though in most cases substantially satisfactory to the group operating released-time classes.[72] It is not surprising that more than four months after the decision was handed down the International Council of Religious Education could announce proudly that 90% of state and local released-time systems were "determined to continue their programs."[73]

The general line was that the decision in the McCollum case must be limited to the facts before the Court in that case, and did not invalidate all released-time programs. This was sometimes accomplished by a neat bit of arithmetic. Since four justices concurred in the opinion of Justice Frankfurter, and Justice Reed believed that all released-time programs are constitutional, it followed that five—a majority—of the nine justices agreed that not all released-time programs are unconstitutional, and that the McCollum decision must be limited to the particular facts.

The most obvious difference between the Champaign plan and many other released-time programs is that the latter, particularly in large cities, are conducted in church centers off the public school premises. This—alone or in conjunction with other asserted differences—was seized upon by state and municipal authorities as justification for continuing local released-time programs off public school premises.

Before the Zorach case reached the New York courts, only two lower courts passed on released-time cases on the basis of the McCollum decision; and they reached opposite conclusions. In one case[74] the court enjoined the continuance of the St. Louis system of released time, which differed from the Champaign system in that classes in religious instruction were not held in school buildings, school authorities neither exercised supervision over the teachers nor required them to keep attendance records and the school kept none, and there was no limitation on the sects entitled to participate in this program.

These differences [the court held] are inconsequential. The controlling fact in both cases is that the public schools are used to aid sectarian groups to disseminate their doctrines. Whether these sectarian classes are conducted in the school buildings or elsewhere can make no difference, since attendance upon them during compulsory school hours is deemed attendance at school. Failure to exercise supervision over the instructors of religion and to require the keeping of proper attendance records does not make the school program legal; it merely indicates laxity on the part of the school authorities. The fact that any sect may participate in this program is immaterial; the public schools cannot be used to aid one religion or to aid all religions.

The other case was brought in New York by the ubiquitous missionary of militant atheism, Joseph Lewis. The decision, upholding the New York City released-time system, does not require any further discussion, since Lewis withdrew his appeal before it was argued, leaving the ultimate decision of the issues for the Supreme Court in the Zorach case.[75]

## The Zorach Case

### The Protagonists

Unlike the plaintiff in the McCollum case, the petitioners in the Zorach case were not atheists but church-affiliated citizens. Tessim Zorach was a parishioner of the Holy Trinity Episcopal Church and an active supporter of the Melishes. Esta Gluck, the other petitioner, was an active member of the American Jewish Congress and president of the parent-teachers' association of her local school district. The children of Zorach and Gluck attended public schools in New York City in which the released-time program was in operation, and also regularly attended Protestant and Jewish religious schools at times other than during the public school day.

The suit of Zorach and Gluck to test the legality of the New York released-time program was supported by a group of organizations including the American Civil Liberties Union, the United Parents Association, the Public Education Association, the New York Board of Rabbis, the American Jewish Congress, B'nai B'rith, and the American Jewish Committee. The defendants in the suit were the State Commissioner of Education and the New York City Board of Education. After the suit was begun, the Greater New York Coordinating Committee on Released Time (formerly the Interfaith Committee) intervened. Thereafter its counsel, Charles H. Tuttle, attorney for the Protestant Council of New York, and Porter Chandler, attorney for the Roman Catholic Archdiocese of New York, were most active and energetic in the defense of the suit.

## *The Facts in the Record*

In 1940, after the state of New York had enacted a statute permitting released-time religious education, the State Commissioner of Education promulgated the following rules and regulations to govern the operation of released time throughout the state:

1. Absence of a pupil from school during school hours for religious observance and education to be had outside the school building and grounds will be excused upon the request in writing signed by the parent or guardian of the pupil.
2. The courses in religious observance and education must be maintained and operated by or under the control of a duly constituted religious body or of duly constituted religious bodies.
3. Pupils must be registered for the courses and a copy of the registration filed with the local public school authorities.
4. Reports of attendance of pupils upon such courses shall be filed with the principal or teacher at the end of each week.
5. Such absence shall be for not more than one hour each week at the close of a session at a time to be fixed by the local school authorities.
6. In the event that more than one school for religious observance and education is maintained in any district, the hour for absence for each particular public school in such district shall be the same for all such religious schools.[76]

It should be noted that paragraph 2 limits release to children enrolling for instruction by "a duly constituted religious body." When the case was argued before the United States Supreme Court, the justices sharply questioned the counsel for the board of education concerning this regulation, indicating clearly that they considered it discriminatory against parents and children not connected with a "duly constituted religious body." Under this questioning, the counsel for the board stated that the regulation would be construed broadly, and that the board of education would allow the release of children to receive religious instruction even from their parents at home.

Shortly after the state commissioner promulgated the above regulations, the New York City Board of Education established the following additional regulations to govern released-time procedure in the city's public schools:

1. A program for religious instruction may be initiated by any religious organization, in cooperation with the parents of pupils concerned. There will be no announcement of any kind in the public schools relative to the program.
2. When a religious organization is prepared to initiate a program for religious instruction, the said organization will notify parents to enroll their children with the religious organization, and will issue to

each enrolled pupil a card countersigned by the parent and addressed to the principal of the public school, requesting the release of the pupil from school for the purpose of religious instruction at a specific location. The said cards will be filed in the office of the public school as a record of pupils entitled to be excused, and will not be available or used for any other purpose.

3. Religious organizations in cooperation with parents, will assume full responsibility for attendance at the religious center and will file with the school principal weekly, a card attendance record and in cases of absence from religious instruction, a statement of the reason therefor.

4. Upon the presentation of a proper request as above prescribed, pupils of any grade will be dismissed from school for the last hour of the day's session on one day of each week to be designated by the Superintendent of Schools. A different day may be designated for each borough.

5. Pupils released for religious instruction will be dismissed from school in the usual way and the school authorities have no responsibility beyond that assumed in regular dismissals.

6. There shall be no comment by any principal or teacher on the attendance or non-attendance of any pupil upon religious instruction.[77]

The petition of Zorach and Gluck alleged that: (1) "the administration of the system necessarily entails use of the public school machinery and time of public school principals, teachers and administrative staff;" (2) the state's "compulsory educational system . . . assists and is integrated with the program of sectarian religious instruction;" (3) the "operation of the released time program has resulted and inevitably results in the exercise of pressure and coercion upon parents and children to secure attendance," (4) is "a utilization of the State's tax-established and tax-supported public school system to aid religious groups to spread their faith," and (5) "has resulted and inevitably will result in divisiveness because of difference in religious beliefs and disbeliefs." For these reasons the petition alleged that the New York released time was unconstitutional and demanded that it be discontinued.

### The Facts Not Disclosed in the Record

During the course of the litigation a number of affidavits were filed in court to show the actual operation of the released-time program, and to establish that in practice the regulations were not complied with. These affidavits referred to schools in different sections of the city over a period of several years. For technical reasons that need not be gone into here, these affidavits were not included in the record considered by the appellate courts in New York or by the United States Supreme Court; but because of the insight they give on the realities of released-time religious instruction they will be set forth here.

It is true that the persons making these affidavits were never subject to cross-examination on trial. It is also true that the situations described in these affidavits might have been atypical and exceptional, and that in the other schools in the city the regulations of the state commissioner of education and the city board of education were strictly adhered to. On the other hand, the persons filing the affidavits undertook in their affidavits to appear at the trial and testify in person subject to cross-examination. It was only because of the strenuous opposition of the board of education that no trial was ever held, notwithstanding the insistent urging of counsel for Zorach and Gluck. Moreover, in filing these affidavits, counsel for Zorach and Gluck stated that the affidavits reflected conditions typical throughout the city, and averred that sufficient additional witnesses would be produced on trial to prove that assertion. Strenuous opposition by the counsel for the city board of education prevented the holding of a trial at which such witnesses could be produced. It is therefore entirely fair to set forth the substance of these affidavits here.[78]

Leah Cunn, who had been a pupil in a public school in Brooklyn, swore in her affidavit that

When the released time students departed at 2:00 P.M. on Wednesdays, I felt left behind. The released children made remarks about my being Jewish and I was made very much aware of the fact that I did not participate with them in the released time program. I endured a great deal of anguish as a result of this and decided that I would like to go along with the other children to the church center rather than continue to expose myself to such harassment. I asked my mother for permission to participate in the released time program and to accompany my Catholic classmates to their religious center, but she forbade it.

The divisiveness created by the released time program among the public school children became a part of our after-school play. Following the introduction of released time at P.S. 163, Brooklyn, I began to notice that I was ostracized by the other children in after-school activities. I was not permitted to share in their play and they made unflattering remarks about my not going to the church center because I was Jewish. As a result of arguments about my non-participation in released time, my classmates called me such names as "Christ killer" and "dirty Jew."

I still live in the same neighborhood and to this day I do not talk to many of the girls with whom I went to school because of the arguments and fights which developed among us as a result of our differences which developed from the released time program.

The priest of St. Finbar's Church frequently visited P.S. 163, Brooklyn, and I have heard him speak to children in the public school about their participation in the released time program. Several times a month I would see the priest of St. Finbar's Church walking around the halls of the school, stopping and talking to children, and complimenting those children who participated in the released time program.

After the participating children had left the public school for released time religious education on Wednesdays, the few remaining children did not continue their regular classroom work. No new work was taken up during the hour from 2 to 3. When I tried to do my homework, the classroom teachers prohibited it, saying homework must be done at home. We were, however, permitted to read a book while the classroom teachers busied themselves with their clerical work at the front of the room. Occasionally the remaining students from my class were doubled up with remaining students from another class so that one teacher would have a free hour.[79]

### The mother of Leah Cunn filed an affidavit stating:

My children complained bitterly to me about this hour in school. They complained that the teachers would not permit them to do their homework and that the hour was in the nature of punishment since nothing was taught to them and they were not permitted to do educationally significant work.

The released time program made my children much more aware of the fact that they were different and not members of a dominant religious group in the community. Soon after the released time program commenced at P.S. 163, Brooklyn, my children asked me why they could not become Catholics and go to released time for religious instruction with their classmates. They were insistent in their demands and emotionally upset when I explained to them that they could not participate with the Catholic children in their released time religious instruction.

My children were very unhappy and moody on Wednesdays because of the released time program, to the extent that I dreaded the day because of its effect upon the happiness and contentment of my children.

### Anne Stewart, a former pupil, swore that

Before the released time program went into effect I was almost unaware of the religious differences of my public school classmates. The released time dismissal procedure, however, made religion a much more important element in class friendships than it had ever been before. The Jewish students in the class did not participate in released time and the released students assumed that anyone remaining in the school during the released time hour was Jewish, which was not true in my case since I am an Episcopalian.

The procedure, by which children lined up according to the church they attended, intensified hostility between the Italian Catholic and the Irish Catholic students who attended different churches. I could sense the hostility between these two groups.

My sixth grade teacher, Miss Croft, urged the children in the class to participate in the released time program and she stated that those students who did not participate would be required to do long division arithmetic problems during every released time hour, whereas those children who did participate in the released time program were to be excused from this exercise. While I was in Miss Croft's class, the students who remained in the public school after 2 o'clock on Thursdays were given long division arithmetic problems beyond the level of the normal expectation of the sixth grade.

When I was in the seventh grade, my teacher, Miss Loeber, publicly asked the children in my class whether they attended a church which was participating in the released-time program. When some children said that they did attend such a church, Miss Loeber asked them why they were not participating in the released time program for religious education.

Except for the sixth grade when the children had difficult arithmetic problems assigned to them if they did not participate in the released time program, no regular classroom work was done by the remaining children. The classroom teachers did their clerical work while the unreleased students were left to entertain themselves. This hour was always extremely dull for me. I felt as if I were being penalized even when I just sat and read, for not participating in the released time program. I, too, would have liked to be excused from school during that hour.

Charles Stewart, father of Anne Stewart, filed an affidavit in which he stated:

I reside at 65 University Place, Borough of Manhattan, City and State of New York, and am the father of three daughters, Anne age 17 1/2, Katherine age 16, and Josephine age 12, who secured part or all of their elementary school education at Public School 3, Manhattan. I was a member of the local School Board of the First District of Manhattan until 1944 and at one time I was head of the Roger Ascham School in White Plains, N.Y. I am ready and willing to be a witness in the above entitled proceeding, and I have given my consent to have my daughters, Anne and Katherine, be witnesses in this proceeding.

All three of my children have been brought up in a religious background and have attended Sunday School. I have always been zealous in my efforts, however, to make them disregard religious differences in their social and educational life. Shortly after the released time program went into effect at P.S. 3, Manhattan, I noticed a marked change in the attitude of my oldest daughter who was at that time attending the public school. She became painfully conscious of the religious differences among her classmates and always referred to her classmates' respective religions, something she had never done before. I soon noticed that my middle daughter, Katherine, acquired similar habits.

P.S. 3, Manhattan, is located in a predominantly Catholic neighborhood, and my daughters asked that I give them permission to participate in the released time program with their Catholic classmates. This I refused to do, and my daughters were deeply hurt by that refusal. They told me that they felt that they were being left out of things by remaining in school during the released time hour.

419

My youngest child, Josephine, has become painfully conscious of the differences between Catholicism and Protestantism because she is one of the few children to remain in her public school class during the released time hour. She feels that she is a Protestant martyr from 2 to 3 o'clock on every Thursday when her classmates depart for religious instruction.

My three children have complained to me about the dullness of the released time hour. They have all stated that no work of any consequence is taken up and that the unreleased children are left to their own devices. I have confirmed this fact by numerous visits to P.S. 3, Manhattan, in connection with my activity as a member of the Parents Association and Chairman of the Welfare Committee of that organization.

I have had occasion to be on the public school premises several times when children were being dismissed for released time. I have personally observed the lack of routine activity in my daughters' classrooms during the released time hour. I have also seen children filing into the school auditorium, where they were divided into groups, according to their respective religions. Nuns and priests came into the school auditorium to meet the children and to escort them out of the school building to the religious centers.

Wendy Gluck, daughter of Esta Cluck, stated in her affidavit that

When I was in the second and third grades at P.S. 130, Brooklyn, my teacher was Miss Jeffries who was also in charge of the released time program at the school. Miss Jeffries distributed blank consent cards to the children in her class and asked the children publicly for a show of hands of those who were going to participate in the released time program. This was a regular procedure at Public School 130. All of my teachers, except Miss Russo whom I had in the fifth and sixth grades, used to ask for a show of hands in the beginning of the term to see how many children were going to participate in the released time program. Miss Jeffries scolded those students who had participated in the released time program the term before but who did not raise their hands to show that they were continuing.

Miss Jeffries sent a student messenger from her classroom to fetch children who were reported absent from released time instruction. On at least one occasion I was the messenger sent by Miss Jeffries to bring such released time absentees to her classroom. When the children appeared in the classroom, Miss Jeffries would scold them before our class because they had been dismissed at 2 o'clock but had failed to appear at the religious center. She would then turn around and talk to our class about truancy from released time. This was done in the presence of the child who was ridiculed and used as an example. Miss Jeffries said that there were more students in each class who should participate in released time program but who were not doing so. This frequently occurred on the Thursday following the Wednesday released time day.

In 1948 Miss Sullivan was my teacher of mathematics. She frequently urged children in the class to participate in the released time program. Miss Sullivan said to our class that she had once been a teacher in a parochial school, that it was the best type of school because religion was taught as a daily subject and made part of the regular school work and that it was important for students who attend public schools to get religious instruction through the released time program. When the children in Miss Sullivan's class left for released time religious instruction on Wednesday, she occasionally asked them to say a prayer for her.

Before Mr. Lubell became Principal of P.S. 130, Brooklyn, Miss Doughty was principal. I recall one occasion on which Miss Doughty urged the children at a school assembly to participate in the released time program. On another occasion I recall that she directed her remarks about released time to the teachers. She said that the teachers should be sure to dismiss those children who were supposed to be excused for religious education under the released time program.

I recall one occasion when our entire class was asked to get permission from our parents to go to the Immaculate Heart of Mary Parochial School to see moving pictures. The students secured their parent's consent on mimeographed slips of paper and the entire class, accompanied by the public school teacher, went to the parochial school where we were shown a series of cartoons. Arrangements for the movies were made by Miss Jeffries. While I was in the lower grades after the visit to the parochial school, I was under the impression that the children released on Wednesdays for religious instruction were being shown movies.

Children who participated in the released time program would frequently study their catechism books in the public school classrooms on Wednesdays to prepare for their released time class.

After the children who were participating in the released time program left the public school the program for the remaining children depended upon the individual teacher and the number of children remaining in the classroom. Sometimes we continued our regular classroom work; sometimes we had a study period; and sometimes we were permitted to play games or talk while the teacher did her clerical work at her desk.

## Esta Gluck herself swore that

Miss Jeffries, a second and third grade teacher at P.S. 130 in Brooklyn, was very active in soliciting student participation in released time for religious instruction. Such activities were carried on by Miss Jeffries both on and off the school premises and both during and after school hours. She visited parents for the purpose of recruiting Catholic students for released time and her activity in this respect is common neighborhood knowledge.

During the Spring 1950 semester I called to the attention of Mr. Lubell (the principal) another incident in which Miss Jeffries had participated. A student in her class became ill and vomited in the classroom. Miss Jeffries said to the sick student that she did not object to looking at the vomit as much as she objected to looking at the student's face because he did not participate in the released time program. Mr. Lubell was shocked and told me that he would speak to Miss Jeffries about the incident.

Mr. Lubell told me on several occasions of the pressures to which he had been subjected by a minister in the neighborhood who had complained to the Board of Education because the school planned student field trips during the released time hour. As a result of these complaints, field trips generally have been discontinued at P.S. 130 for the period from 2 to 3 o'clock on Wednesdays. Recently, I met the minister, Rev. Harold Sweezey, in connection with some unrelated neighborhood problem and he complained to me about Mr. Lubell's lack of cooperation in the released time program. He told me that Mr. Lubell was not as cooperative as the prior principal, Miss Doughty, had been.

Minnie Sutro, formerly a teacher and assistant principal, stated in her affidavit:

When I taught at P.S. 54, Brooklyn, it was customary for the students to bring consent cards, signed by the clergyman and parent, to the grade teacher each September. These cards were used by the classroom teacher to prepare a list of students in her class who were authorized to be dismissed for released time. Thereafter these cards were sent to and filed in the school office. Every February, when there were half-year promotions, each classroom teacher would indicate on the child's personality and testing record card which was forwarded to the next classroom teacher, whether the child had participated in the released time program during the preceding term. After I agreed to become a witness in the above entitled proceeding, I secured from P.S. 54, Brooklyn, a copy of a record card which, although differing in some aspects from the personality and testing cards in use at the school while I taught there, is currently in use at that school. A photostatic copy of that record card is attached hereto and made a part hereof. The last column headed "R.I." is used to indicate whether or not the student participated in the released time program for religious instruction.

Each individual classroom teacher was required to watch the time so that she would dismiss at 2 o'clock on Wednesdays those children in her class who participated in the released time program. At 2 o'clock on Wednesdays it was customary for me to interrupt my class instruction to inform the participating students that it was time for them to get their wraps and leave for religious instruction. I would check the departing students against the daily attendance and my list of students who were scheduled for released time. There was usually a great deal of noise and confusion in the classroom and in the school corridors, since the dismissal procedure disrupted the entire school discipline and routine.

After my resignation I had occasion during the spring of 1949 to visit P.S. 54, Brooklyn one Wednesday at about 2 p.m. I observed a nun from a local church lining up her released time students in the school vestibule preparatory to escorting them to the church center for religious instruction.

It was extremely difficult to carry on a normal teaching program during the afternoon on released time days. I occasionally found that some of my students scheduled for released time would be studying their catechism instead of paying attention to the classroom lesson. Several times I took catechisms away from these children until 2 o'clock, when I returned their religious books to them as they left the classroom.

The released time program interrupted the group work planned for the public school class. It broke up the various groups and all new and meaningful activities had to cease. It was extremely difficult to teach anything which would not penalize those children who remained or which, on the other hand, would not make the released students feel that they were missing something valuable. Remedial activities were not practical because I observed, in my classes, that the students who needed the remedial work most were those who participated in the released time program.

Leona Abrams, another former teacher, filed an affidavit in which she averred:

For approximately four years, from 1943 to 1947, I was designated by my principal as the teacher responsible for administering the released time program at P.S. 179, Manhattan. I found that my duties in connection with the released time program were very burdensome and entailed constant interruption of my teaching program, to the detriment of my own class. The detailed work involved in administering the released time program was particularly burdensome at the beginning of each term when I frequently lost a considerable amount of time from my teaching responsibilities. I asked the children to bring their signed consent cards to me between 8:30 a.m. and 9:00 a.m. but the students disregarded my instructions and brought the cards to me in my classroom at any time during the school day. These constant interruptions in my classroom work made it difficult for me to teach. They became a source of irritation which necessarily affected my work as a teacher and my own classes bore the brunt of the burden. These interruptions continued throughout the school term, although to a lesser degree after the first few weeks, when only transferrers or children wishing to drop or to enroll for released time instruction would interrupt my classes.

At P.S. 179, Manhattan, students were allowed to be dismissed for the first released time period during each semester even though they had not filed properly executed consent cards. Thereafter, children were released only if their names appeared on a list which I prepared of all children who had filed consent cards with my office. These lists where forwarded to the appropriate teachers so that they could determine which children had permission to be released for religious instruction.

Each classroom teacher was responsible for watching the time on released time days, so that she would know when to dismiss the children for religious education. This required the teacher in charge of the dismissal on each floor to leave her own classroom unattended while she or a student messenger entered the other classrooms on the floor in order to notify each teacher that time for religious education had arrived. The teacher in charge of the dismissal procedure on each floor escorted all of the released children from that floor to the outer yard or exit of the school building.

The released time program also disrupted the classroom work while those children who were authorized to leave obtained their coats, hats, and books, and departed.

The teachers on each floor arranged among themselves that a different teacher would assume the responsibility each week for supervising the dismissal and escorting the children downstairs to the exits. When religious education programs were occasionally cancelled by the church centers, I had to prepare notes for the various teachers of children who attended those centers and send such notes with student messengers to each such class to advise the teacher of the cancellation.

Lists of absentees from released time religious classes were always received from the church centers. These lists were usually lengthy. The principal was anxious for me to check the list thoroughly since he believed this necessary to prevent habits of truancy from developing as a result of the released time program. It was impossible for me to comply with the principal's request with respect to checking absentee lists, and also to give adequate attention to my teaching responsibilities to my class. I therefore checked only those students who appeared to have a record of continued absence. I was obliged to take time out from my own teaching in order to question those children concerning their continued absences from the religious center after they were released from the public school for the purpose of securing religious education at such centers. Some children said that they had stayed in school instead of leaving for religious education. If the parents of such children wanted them to discontinue participation in the released time program, I told the children that their parents should write to the church center to that effect. In cases of truancy, I communicated with the student's classroom teacher and suggested that she communicate with the parents because the child was learning habits of truancy.

On one occasion during 1945 a local priest came to P.S. 179, Manhattan, to discuss the released time program with the principal. The priest was brought to my classroom, while my class was in session, and asked that I circulate an announcement to the school, stating that the released time program was beginning and specifying the day of the week and the time of the day when that program was to be in operation. The priest also asked me how he could assist in facilitating the record keeping incidental to the program. During the following years a priest would come to the school at the beginning of each year to remind me that the released time program was in operation.

It was customary for the nuns or other persons responsible for escorting the children to the religious centers to wait near the school exit. These escorts frequently arrived early. Often they came to my classroom several minutes before dismissal time and requested that certain children be excused from my class. Occasionally, after the group of children had been dismissed, a student messenger would come to my room to inquire why a certain child had not been dismissed. It was then necessary for me to check my records to determine whether the particular child was authorized to be dismissed and to locate the room in which that child was being taught. I would then send a student messenger from my class to the classroom of the teacher to inquire why such children had not been dismissed.

The classroom activity for the unreleased children during the released time hour was left entirely to the discretion of the individual classroom teacher. Some teachers devoted the hour to art, while other teachers gave their students a study period which the teachers used to catch up on their own clerical work. The activity for the remaining children depended on the conscientiousness of the individual teacher and the number of children remaining in her class.

From my own experience it was not always practical to comply with the Superintendent's instruction to teach remedial work to the remaining children during the released time hour because the larger percentage of children who needed such remedial work were the ones who participated in the released time program.

### Henrietta Birman, a retired teacher-clerk, deposed that

Released time dismissal occurred at 2.00 p.m. on Tuesdays in the Borough of the Bronx. At Public School 78, the teacher in charge of administering the released time program, Miss Wallace, would send a student monitor to every classroom. This monitor would open the classroom door and announce in a loud voice "Church time, church time." At this signal the students who participated in the released time program would get their hats and coats, race out of the classrooms, and run through the public school halls to the school yard. They created such bedlam that the principal threatened, on a number of occasions, to withdraw the privilege of participating in the released time program unless the students left more quietly. This noisy dismissal procedure interrupted the entire public school teaching program and no work was possible until after the dismissed students had left the building.

It was customary for Miss Wallace to stand in the public school yard to supervise the released time children as they left the school building. Under her supervision three separate lines were formed, according to the different religions, Catholic, Protestant and Jewish.

Miss Wallace did not permit the released time students to leave the public school yard until an authorized escort from the church or temple arrived to escort the children to the religious center.

If an escort failed to arrive on time, Miss Wallace would detain that particular line of children in the school yard until the escort arrived. If no escort arrived after a lapse of twenty minutes, Miss Wallace would send the students back to their regular classrooms from which they were not dismissed until the end of the regular school day. During this period of time when Miss Wallace was supervising the dismissal in the public school yard, her class remained uncovered and unsupervised.

On Wednesdays after released time classes had been held, lists of absentees were received at the school office from all religious centers to

425

which children from Public School 78 had gone. It was the custom for either the principal or the classroom teacher to discuss truancy cases with the individual student. If a student had been absent twice without cause from released time instruction, the privilege of participating in the released time program was withdrawn. I recall a number of occasions on which, after a student had been denied permission for further participation in the program, a clergyman called in person or phoned the principal to plead for "clemency" for the child. Although Miss McKay, the principal, usually adhered to her original decision, she occasionally relented and allowed the truant to resume participation in the released time program, after such calls or visits from clergymen.

When the released time program was originally introduced at Public School 78, the Bronx, the Jewish groups in the community did not participate. However, later in the term, a number of parents of Jewish children told me that they were going to organize a released time program for their children since the Jewish students felt left out of things and inferior because they were not participating in the released time program. As a result, the Jewish temple in the community began to conduct religious classes at 2 o'clock on Tuesdays and to participate in the released time program.

Maurice A. Dawkins made the following affidavit:

I am Minister of Education at the Community Church, 40 East 35th Street, in the Borough of Manhattan, City and State of New York. I taught at Public School 184, Manhattan, from 1947 to 1948 and prior thereto, I was the Director of Religious Education at the Walker Memorial Baptist Church, in the Borough of Manhattan. I am ready and willing to be a witness in the above entitled proceeding.

Although Public School 184, Manhattan, had no official policy concerning checking the attendance of students released for religious education under the released time program, I felt morally obligated, as a result of the high truancy rate, to speak to my pupils concerning their truancy from the religious centers to which they were sent under the released time program. The day following released time, pupils in my class would come to me and proudly report that certain of their classmates had "played hookey" from their religious instruction. I felt that unless I spoke to those children, I would create serious problems in overall class morale and discipline.

Furthermore, as a religious teacher I could not divorce myself from the problems of released time instruction and the attitudes of my students toward it. I did not want my students to feel that released time for religious instruction was a lark and an excuse to get out of the public school. One of the basic functions of religious education, I believe, is to teach a child honesty. Truancy, however, teaches dishonesty and thereby undermines all religious concepts. A truant from released time instruction learns to lie to his minister, to his parents and to his public school teacher. I could not, therefore, as a public school teacher, allow attendance at released time classes to go unchecked and permit this hour, which was set aside for religious instruction, to become one in which children learned dishonesty.

At the beginning of each new term, and occasionally during the school semester, I was obliged to go to the office of Public School 184, Manhattan, to compile a list of all those students in my class who had filed consent cards authorizing them to be dismissed for religious instruction. This was necessary so that only those students would be dismissed who were authorized to be dismissed.

It was necessary for me to plan my classroom work so that those students who left for released time instruction would miss no valuable work. In order to do this I had to shorten the amount of time which I would normally have devoted to each classroom subject. In this way, the day's work on released time days was finished by 2:00 p.m., instead of 3:00 p.m., as I would normally have planned it. Scheduling classroom work during the released time hour was extremely difficult. If I planned some minor subject, such as Art, many students scheduled for released time would ask to remain in school during that hour. If, on the other hand, I scheduled uninteresting work, those children who remained in the public school felt that they were being cheated and they resented not being able to attend released time instruction.

Frequently a released time student would plead to remain in school during the released time hour because he had heard from his classmates that the students who remained the previous week had had an interesting lesson, such as wood carving, something this particular child did not want to miss. This dilemma upset me greatly and was impossible to solve. As a teacher, I felt that students who remained in school were entitled to a meaningful hour of classroom instruction and guidance and, on the other hand, I wanted those children who were released for religious instruction to feel that their activity during that hour was important and that they were not going to miss anything essential by leaving the classroom.

On several occasions I overheard students, as they left the public school classroom for religious instruction, say to one boy who never participated in the released time program because his parents preferred for him to remain in school, "Don't you ever go to church?" I could see the unreleased child's face turn solemn and unhappy because he felt rejected and not part of "the group." When that occurred I spoke to the unreleased child for the purpose of making him feel more comfortable and less rejected.

Prior to my becoming a public school teacher, I was a supervisor of religious education at the Walker Memorial Baptist Church in Manhattan and I was responsible for administering the church's released time program. I found that the church was faced with difficult truancy and discipline problems which did not exist in our regular Sunday School courses of instruction. It was impossible for the church to cope with this problem without the aid of the public school machinery. It was necessary for us to check with the public school authorities to determine which children were bona fide absentees before we could deal with these children who were actually our truancy problems. We did not have the funds, personnel, or time to verify a child's absence from released time instruction by communicating with his parents. I, therefore, communicated with the individual public school teachers at the close of each released time session to determine which students absent from church, were also absent from the public school. Occasionally I enlisted the aid of the public school teacher in dealing with a child who was absent without cause from his released time instruction. This problem, however, became increasingly burdensome and I was forced to rely, more and more, upon the individual public school teacher to deal with these truancy cases. This procedure necessitated frequent visits to the public school teachers during school hours or during lunch hours and the public school teachers spoke to the students about their truancy from released time during the course of the normal public school day.

The majority of the children who elected to participate in the released time program of the Walker Memorial Baptist Church were not enrolled in our regular Sunday School classes, nor did they so enroll after attending released time instruction. They seemed to be the problem children of the public school. They gave me the impression of coming for released time religious instruction as a device to escape an additional hour of school. Therefore, we were plagued with truancy and discipline problems with which our religious teaching staff was unable to cope. The first half hour of the released time hour was devoted almost exclusively to discipline. Many of the children would race through the church building to the gymnasium, swimming pool, roof or other rooms. Usually, by the time they were finally gathered together and quieted down, about twenty minutes of instruction time remained. The attitude in the classroom was tense and the children were hostile. It was almost an impossibility to teach anything, especially the principles of religion, against a background of this type. The teachers who participated in the religious instruction program considered it a detriment to the total religious programs instruction of the churches.

### The Proceedings in the New York Courts

These lengthy affidavits have been set forth here because they show, better than survey and statistics, how the released-time program affects at least some of the persons most directly concerned — children, parents, teachers, and clergymen. They were filed in court to support the second aspect of the petitioners' claim. The first aspect was that under the McCollum case all released-time — as distinguished from dismissed-time — programs were *per se* unconstitutional. The second aspect was that even if a released-time program is not of itself unconstitutional, the New York City program as actually operated was unconstitutional. The petitioners asserted that it was inherent in the program and inevitable that the regulations prescribed by the state commissioner of education and the city board of education should be disregarded and violated in practice.

To support this second argument the affidavits were filed in court. (Only affidavits of children already graduated from the school involved and teachers and principals retired from the school system were filed in court and thus became a public record; therefore only these affidavits have been set forth here.) In further support of their assertion, the petitioners cited the findings of the Public Education Association. Illustrative of this point was the practice of questioning children or parents of children who absented themselves from released-time classes. The regulations prohibit this practice; but a Public Education Association survey conducted in 1942 found that in 16 out of 82 schools visited this regulation was admittedly not followed. The results of this survey were made public, and unquestionably came to the attention of the public school authorities. Nevertheless in the follow-up survey made in 1943 the number of schools admittedly not following the regulation had increased to 25 out of 89. Again the results were made public, and again a follow-up survey was made in 1945. By this time the number of schools not following the regulation had increased to 33 out of 88.

Justice DiGiovanna dismissed all this evidence as presenting merely "administrative difficulties."[80] For technical reasons the affidavits did not become part of the record of appeal from Justice DiGiovanna's decision, and were not considered by the upper New York courts or by the United States Supreme Court. All these courts considered and passed on only the first aspect of the petitioners' case: the assertion that the New York City released-time program, as authorized by the statute and regulations, was unconstitutional on the ground that all released-time programs were outlawed by the McCollum decision.

Justice DiGiovanna's decision[81] was affirmed by a divided court in the Appellate Division,[82] and by a divided court in the Court of Appeals.[83] An appeal was then taken to the United States Supreme Court.

### Justice Douglas's Opinion

By a vote of six to three the Supreme Court upheld the constitutionality of the New York released-time program as authorized by the statute and regulations.[84] Justice Douglas said:

New York City has a program which permits its public schools to release students during the school day so that they may leave the school buildings and school grounds and go to religious centers for religious instruction or devotional exercises. A student is released on written request of his parents. Those not released stay in the classrooms. The

429

churches make weekly reports to the schools, sending a list of children who have been released from public school but who have not reported for religious instruction.

This "released time" program involves neither religious instruction in public school classrooms nor the expenditure of public funds. All costs, including the application blanks, are paid by the religious organization. The case is therefore unlike *McCollum v Board of Education*, 333 U.S. 203, which involved a "released time" program from Illinois. In that case the classrooms were turned over to religious instructors. We accordingly held that the program violated the First Amendment which (by reason of the Fourteenth Amendment) prohibits the states from establishing religion or prohibiting its free exercise.

Appellants, who are taxpayers and residents of New York City and whose children attend its public schools, challenge the present law, contending it is in essence not different from the one involved in the *McCollum* case. Their argument, stated elaborately in various ways, reduces itself to this: the weight and influence of the school is put behind a program for religious instruction; public school teachers police it, keeping tab on students who are released; the classroom activities come to a halt while the students who are released for religious instruction are on leave; the school is a crutch on which the churches are leaning for support in their religious training; without the cooperation of the schools this "released time" program, like the one in the McCollum case, would be futile and ineffective. . . .

The briefs and arguments are replete with data bearing on the merits of this type of "released time" program. Views *pro* and *con* are expressed, based on practical experience with these programs and with their implications. We do not stop to summarize these materials nor to burden the opinion with an analysis of them. For they involve considerations not germane to the narrow constitutional issue presented. They largely concern the wisdom of the system, its efficiency from an educational point of view, and the political considerations which have motivated its adoption or rejection in some communities. Those matters are of no concern here, since our problem reduces itself to whether New York by this system has either prohibited the "free exercise" of religion or has made a law "respecting an establishment of religion" within the meaning of the First Amendment.

It takes obtuse reasoning to inject any issue of the "free exercise" of religion into the present case. No one is forced to go to the religious classroom and no religious exercise or instruction is brought to the classrooms of the public schools. A student need not take religious instruction. He is left to his own desires as to the manner or time of his religious devotions, if any.

There is a suggestion that the system involves the use of coercion to get public school students into religious classrooms. There is no evidence in the record before us that supports that conclusion. The present record indeed tells us that the school authorities are neutral in this regard and do no more than release students whose parents so request. If in fact coercion were used, if it were established that any one or more teachers were using their office to persuade or force students to take the religious instruction, a wholly different case would be presented. Hence we put aside that claim of coercion both as respects the "free exercise" of religion and "an establishment of religion" within the meaning of the First Amendment. . . .

We would have to press the concept of separation of Church and State to . . . extremes to condemn the present law on constitutional grounds. The nullification of this law would have wide and profound effects. A Catholic student applies to his teacher for permission to leave the school during hours on a Holy Day of Obligation to attend a mass. A Jewish student asks his teacher for permission to be excused for Yom Kippur. A Protestant wants the afternoon off for a family baptismal ceremony. In each case the teacher requires parental consent in writing. In each case the teacher, in order to make sure the student is not a truant, goes further and requires a report from the priest, the rabbi, or the minister. The teacher in other words cooperates in a religious program to the extent of making it possible for her students to participate in it. Whether she does it occasionally for a few students, regularly for one, or pursuant to a systematized program designed to further the religious needs of all the students does not alter the character of the act.

. . . Government may not finance religious groups nor undertake religious instruction nor blend secular and sectarian education nor use secular institutions to force one or some religion on any person. But we find no constitutional requirement which makes it necessary for government to be hostile to religion and to throw its weight against efforts to widen the effective scope of religious influence. The government must be neutral when it comes to competition between sects. It may not thrust any sect on any person. It may not make a religious observance compulsory. It may not coerce anyone to attend church, to observe a religious holiday, or to take religious instruction. But it can close its doors or suspend its operations as to those who want to repair to their religious sanctuary for worship or instruction. No more than that is undertaken here.

This program may be unwise and improvident from an educational or a community viewpoint. That appeal is made to us on a theory, previously advanced, that each case must be decided on the basis of "our own prepossessions." Our individual preferences, however, are not the constitutional standard. The constitutional standard is the separation of Church and State. The problem, like many problems in constitutional law, is one of degree.

In the *McCollum* case the classrooms were used for religious instruction, and the force of the public school was used to promote that instruction. Here, as we have said, the public schools do no more than accommodate their schedules to a program of outside religious instruction. We follow the *McCollum* case. But we cannot expand it to cover the present released time program unless separation of Church and State means that public institutions can make no adjustments of their schedules to accommodate the religious needs of the people. We cannot read into the Bill of Rights such a philosophy of hostility to religion.

## Justice Black's Dissent

In his dissenting opinion, Justice Black, who wrote the majority opinion in the McCollum case, said:

*Illinois ex rel. McCollum v Board of Education* held invalid as an "establishment of religion" an Illinois system under which school children, compelled by law to go to public schools, were freed from some hours of required school work on condition that they attend special religious classes held in the school buildings. Although the classes were taught by sectarian teachers neither employed nor paid by the state, the state did use its power to further the program by releasing some of the children from regular class work, insisting that those released attend the religious classes, and requiring that those who remained behind do some kind of academic work while the others received their religious training. We said this about the Illinois system:

"Pupils compelled by law to go to school for secular education are released in part from their legal duty upon the condition that they attend the religious classes. This is beyond all question a utilization of the tax-established and tax-supported public school system to aid religious groups to spread their faiths. And it falls squarely under the ban of the First Amendment. . . ."

I see no significant difference between the invalid Illinois system and that of New York here sustained. Except for the use of the school buildings in Illinois, there is no difference between the systems which I consider even worthy of mention. In the New York program, as in that of Illinois, the school authorities release some of the children on the condition that they attend the religious classes, get reports on whether they attend, and hold the other children in the school building until the religious hour is over. As we attempted to make categorically clear, the *McCollum* decision would have been the same if the religious classes had not been held in the school buildings. We said:

"Here *not only* are the State's tax-supported public school buildings used for the dissemination of religious doctrines. The State *also* affords sectarian groups an invaluable aid in that it helps to provide pupils for their religious classes through the use of the State's compulsory school machinery. *This* is not separation of Church and State." (Emphasis supplied.)

*McCollum* thus held that Illinois could not constitutionally manipulate the compelled classroom hours of its compulsory school machinery so as to channel children into sectarian classes. Yet that is exactly what the Court holds New York can do. . . . Here the sole question is whether New York can use its compulsory education laws to help religious sects get attendants presumably too unenthusiastic to go unless moved to do so by the pressure of this state machinery. That this is the plan, purpose, design and consequence of the New York program cannot be denied. The state thus makes religious sects beneficiaries of its power to compel children to attend secular schools. Any use of such coercive power by the state to help or hinder some religious sects or to prefer all religious sects over nonbelievers or vice versa is just what I think the First Amendment forbids. In considering whether a state has entered this forbidden field the question is not whether it has entered too far but whether it has entered at all. New York is manipulating its compulsory education laws to help religious sects get pupils. This is not separation but combination of Church and State.

## Justice Frankfurter's Dissent

Justice Frankfurter, also dissenting, said in part:

The Court tells us that in the maintenance of its public schools, "[the state government] can close its doors or suspend its operations" so that its citizens may be free for religious devotions or instruction. If that were the issue, it would not rise to the dignity of a constitutional controversy. Of course a State may provide that the classes in its schools shall be dismissed, for any reason, or no reason, on fixed days, or for special occasions. The essence of this case is that the school system did not "close its doors" and did not "suspend its operations." There is all the difference in the world between letting the children out of school and letting some of them out of school into religious classes. If everyone is free to make what use he will of time wholly unconnected from schooling required by law, those who wish sectarian instruction devoting it to that purpose, those who have ethical instruction at home, to that, those who study music, to that—then of course there is no conflict with the Fourteenth Amendment.

The pith of the case is that formalized religious instruction is substituted for other school activity which those who do not participate in the released-time program are compelled to attend. The school system is very much in operation during this kind of released time. If its doors are closed, they are closed upon those students who do not attend the religious instruction in order to keep them within the school. This is the very thing which raises the constitutional issue. It is not met by disregarding it. Failure to discuss this issue does not take it out of the case. . . .

The result in the *McCollum* case was based on principles that received unanimous acceptance by this Court, barring only a single vote. I agree with Mr. Justice Black that those principles are disregarded in reaching the result in this case. Happily they are not disavowed by the Court. From this I draw the hope that in future variations of the problem which are bound to come here, these principles may again be honored in the observance.

The deeply divisive controversy aroused by the attempt to secure public school pupils for sectarian instruction would promptly end if the advocates of such instruction were content to have the school "close its doors or suspend operations"—that is, dismiss classes in their entirety, without discrimination—instead of seeking to use the public schools as the instrument for securing attendance at denominational classes. The unwillingness of the promoters of this movement to dispense with such

433

use of the public schools betrays a surprising want of confidence in the inherent power of the various faiths to draw children to outside sectarian classes — an attitude that hardly reflects the faith of the greatest religious spirits.

## Justice Jackson's Dissent

Justice Jackson, in his dissenting opion, said in part:

This released time program is founded upon the use of the State's power of coercion, which, for me, determines its unconstitutionality. Stripped of its essentials, the plan has two stages, first, that the State compel each student to yield a large part of his time for public secular education and, second, that some of it be "released" to him on condition that he devote it to sectarian religious purposes.

No one suggests that the Constitution would permit the State directly to require this "released" time to be spend "under the control of a duly constituted religious body." This program accomplishes that forbidden result by indirection. If public education were taking so much of the pupils' time as to injure the public or the student's welfare by encroaching upon their religious opportunity, simply shortening everyone's school day would facilitate voluntary and optional attendance at Church classes. But that suggestion is rejected upon the ground that if they are made free many students will not go to the Church. Hence, they must be deprived of freedom for this period, with Church attendance put to them as one of the two permissible ways of using it.

The greater effectiveness of this system over voluntary attendance after school hours is due to the truant officier, who, if the youngster fails to go to the Church school, dogs him back to the public schoolroom. Here schooling is more or less suspended during the "released time" so that the nonreligious attendants will not forge ahead of the churchgoing absentees. But it serves as a temporary jail for a pupil who will not go to church. It takes more subtlety of mind than I possess to deny that this is governmental constraint in support of religion. It is as unconstitutional, in my view, when exerted by indirection as when exercised forthrightly. . . .

A number of Justices just short of a majority of the majority that promulgates today's passionate dialectics joined in answering them in *Illinois ex rel. McCollum v Board of Education*. The distinction attempted between that case and this is trivial, almost to the point of cynicism, magnifying its nonessential details and disparaging compulsion which was the underlying reason for invalidity. A reading of the Court's opinion in that case along with its opinion in this case will show such difference of overtones and undertones as to make clear that the *McCollum* case has passed like a storm in a teacup. The wall which the Court was professing to erect between Church and State has become even more warped and twisted than I expected. Today's judgment will be more interesting to students of psychology and of the judicial processes than to students of constitutional law.

*What the Zorach Case Holds*

It is clear that the majority opinion in the Zorach case validates the New York City released-time system only to the extent that the system complies with the statute and regulations. It holds that a released-time program under which the school does no more than "close its doors or suspend its operations as to those who want to repair to their religious sanctuary for religious instruction" does not violate the requirement of the separation of church and state in the First Amendment. On the other hand, if the program "involves religious instruction in public classrooms [or] the expenditure of public funds [or] action by teachers to persuade or force students to take religious instruction [or is one in which the public school authorities are not] neutral in this regard, [or] enforce attendance at religious schools by punishing absentees from the released time program for truancy," it would seem that the program would be unconstitutional.

In conclusion, it may be suggested that the majority opinion is predicated on a fiction — the fiction that the released-time program involves no more than that the public school "closes its doors or suspends operations as to those who want to repair to their religious sanctuary for worship or instruction." In reality, released time does not mean releasing time for religious instruction; it means releasing children for religious instruction and *not releasing those who do not want to partake in religious instruction.* The refusal of the promoters of the program to accept a dismissed-time system under which all children are released indicates quite clearly that they depend on the nonrelease of the other children as the factor inducing enrollment for released-time religious instruction. It may also be suggested that the singular lack of success that the released-time program has achieved in fifty years would indicate that to the overwhelming majority of children continued participation in secular instruction does not appear so unpleasant as to induce them to choose the alternative of religious instruction.

### CHAPTER ELEVEN

# Bible and Prayer
# in the Public School

## BIBLE READING
### The Background

HORACE MANN'S MISSIONARY ENDEAVORS to exclude sectarianism from the public schools of Massachusetts did not include the elimination of simple Bible reading. Massachusetts had but recently emerged from its Congregationalist establishment, and Catholicism had not yet spread to New England to any appreciable extent. Since the Bible was acceptable to all Protestant sects, and had been the foundation of public education for two centuries, the continuation of Bible reading as part of the curriculum was more or less accepted as a matter of course.

The Mann compromise—the Bible but not sectarianism—was only a temporary solution even in New England. In communities where Catholics constituted a substantial segment of the population, its inherent unworkability became obvious even earlier. In November 1843 Bishop Francis Kenrick of Philadelphia—then a hotbed of Nativism—petitioned the school board of that city to allow Catholic children to use the Catholic version of the Bible where Bible reading was required. The board either granted the request,[1] or directed that a child whose parents objected to Bible reading should not be obliged to be present at Bible exercises[2]—it is not clear which. Whichever it was, the Nativist element raised the cry that the Catholics were seeking to eject the Bible from the public schools. From that day on, public school Bible reading became a rallying cry for Nativism and Know-Nothingism.

It may be that American Catholicism—unlike American Judaism—would in any circumstance never have accepted and accommodated itself to the American nonsectarian public school system. It is possible that if the objections of the Catholics to Protestant Bible reading had been respected—as simple justice and fair play clearly dictated that they should—the Catholic Church would nevertheless have not contented itself with after-hours or Sunday religious instruction; and would in any event have built up a competing system of parochial education for Catholic children. But it is by no means certain that American Catholic parenthood would have gone along

436

with the church in its plans, and would not have preferred to educate their children in the public schools if their children had been accepted with friendliness and sympathy rather than with enmity and suspicion, and if the elementary religious rights of their children had been respected. All this is speculative. What is fairly certain is that the disgraceful chain of events set off by Bishop Kenrick's request left the Catholic Church with little choice but to embark on a campaign to have every Catholic child educated in a Catholic school and left Catholic parents with little choice but to go along. Nor is it speculative that the long-standing animosity of the Catholic Church to the American public school can in large measure be traced to the ensuing half-century conflict around Bible reading.

The immediate effects of the Bishop's petition were both dramatic and tragic. For several months the controversy simmered, and then suddenly erupted in riots. Catholic churches were attacked; two in the Philadelphia suburb of Kensington were reduced to ashes. A convent was completely destroyed. Bishop Kenrick ordered all Catholic worship suspended and every Catholic church in the city closed; but this action did not avert the more serious consequences that the Bishop hoped it would. Many houses in the Irish section were destroyed by fire, some of the residents were shot down as they ran out, and a number of non-Catholic bystanders likewise lost their lives.[3]

In New York, reports of the Philadelphia riots caused Bishop Hughes to place large groups of armed men around each Catholic church, with instructions to defend the building by force if necessary. Fortunately it did not prove necessary. Bishop Hughes also led the Catholic Church in a dual campaign to seek the division of public education funds between public and church schools, and for laws against the required reading of the "Protestant Bible" in the public schools. Catholic votes threatened to defeat at the polls those legislators who refused to accept these demands. Protestantism, speaking through the American and Foreign Christian Union, replied by declaring that the Bible would not be expelled from public school classrooms "so long as a piece of Plymouth Rock remained big enough to make a gun flint out of."[4]

In Massachusetts the Know-Nothing party succeeded in capturing the state legislature in 1855, and passed a number of laws specifically aimed at the newly arrived Catholics. These laws restricted office-holding to native-born citizens, required twenty-one years' residence for the right to vote, and appointed a "Nunnery Committee" to investigate conditions in convents, parochial schools, and seminar-

CHURCH, STATE, AND FREEDOM

ies; it also enacted a statute requiring Bible reading in the public schools.[5] The other laws were repealed after the Nativists lost control of the legislature, but the Bible-reading statute remained on the books—the only state statute requiring public school Bible reading until the 20th century.[6]

Where the local board of education, notwithstanding the absence of a specific mandatory statute, instituted or approved Bible reading, the Catholic Church, acting through parents of Catholic children in the public schools, frequently invoked the intervention of the courts. Some of the resulting decisions will be discussed later in this section, but the earliest of these cases, Donahoe vs. Richards[7] and its background, merit recounting here.

In 1854 a Jesuit priest, John Bapst, formerly president of Holy Cross College, was engaged in missionary work among the Indians in Maine. Among the parishes he served was the town of Ellsworth, near Bangor. The school committee of the town adopted a regulation requiring all children to read the King James Bible. Father Bapst advised his parishioners to defy the committee and take the issue to the courts for judicial determination. Acting on his urging, the father of Bridget Donahoe directed his daughter to refuse to read from the Protestant Bible as directed by her teacher. When the rebellious Bridget was expelled, her father brought suit to compel her reinstatement.

Father Bapst's action became known to the residents of the town, who indignantly called a town meeting, at which a resolution was adopted to the effect that if Father Bapst ever entered Ellsworth again he would be tarred and feathered and ridden out of town on a rail. A few months later Father Bapst returned to Ellsworth, and while hearing confessions on Saturday night, a mob broke into his house, dragged him out, tore off his clothing, tarred and feathered him, and after two hours of cruel treatment, finally released him. Although the ringleaders were known and the grand jury was in session, no one was indicted or even arrested in connection with the incident.[8]

When the controversy finally reached the Supreme Court of Maine for determination, that court declared blandly that the law regards "the Pagan and the Mormon, the Brahmin and the Jew, the Swedenborgian and the Buddhist, the Catholic and the Quaker, as all possessing equal rights." But, the court held, Bridget's rights had not been infringed, for "reading the Bible is no more an interference with religious belief, than would reading the mythology of Greece or Rome be regarded as interfering with religious belief or

438

an affirmance of the pagan creeds." The fact, the court held, that the Ellsworth school committee designated the King James Version as the text to be used did not warrant judicial interference or violate Bridget's rights, for the selection of books was exclusively within the discretion of the committee, and its selection of a particular version did not place a sanction of "purity" on the version selected.[9]

Five years later a Massachusetts court was faced with a problem arising from the stubborn rebellion of another Catholic child. Tom Wall was an eleven-year-old pupil in a Boston public school where the Bible was read daily and the Ten Commandments recited weekly. The evidence showed that Tom's "father had told him for his life not to say them [the Commandments], and that his priest had also told him not to say them, and that on the Sunday previous to March 14th, the priest [Father Wiget] while addressing nine hundred children of St. Mary's Church, of whom Wall was one, told them not to be cowards to their religion, and not to read or repeat the Commandments in school, and that if they did he would read their names from the altar."

The next day Tom Wall came to school, "with the determination not to read or repeat" the Commandments. (For this, it appears, he later received a blessed medal from Father Wiget.) Moreover, some sixty others of his Catholic schoolmates, comprising about two-thirds of the children of the school, likewise announced that they would not repeat the Commandments. Here was rebellion on a large scale, and it was clear to McLaurin F. Cooke, the teacher, that Tom Wall was the ringleader. With the approval of the principal, the teacher urged Tom to obey, "but Wall, still refusing, was punished . . . with a rattan stick, some three feet in length and three-eights of an inch thick, by whipping upon his hands. From the time the punishment commenced to the time when it ended, repeated inquiries were made of Wall if he would comply with the requirements of the school. Some thirty minutes time was occupied in the whole," but the conclusion was obvious from the beginning. Eleven-year-old Tom Wall could hardly hold out forever against the majesty and power of the Commonwealth of Massachusetts. After thirty minutes of chastisement "Wall submitted to the requirement of the school," and the "master ceased to punish."

Two days later Tom Wall's father caused the teacher to be arrested for assault; but the court discharged him on the ground that the punishment inflicted was not in violation of the pupil's constitutional rights. If, said the court, a Catholic pupil may legally refuse for conscientious reasons to read from a version of the Bible that his father and priest do not approve, it is clear that he may also not be compelled to hear it read. And if a Catholic child may refuse, so too may the Jew and indeed the Protestant, who may say, "I am a conscientious believer in the doctrine of universal salvation. There are portions of the Bible read in school which it is claimed by others tend to prove a different doctrine; my conscience will not allow me to hear it read, or to read it. Another objects as a believer in baptism by sprinkling. . . . Still another objects as a believer in one God. . . . And so, every denomination may object for conscience sake, and war upon the Bible and its use in common schools."

The provision in the state constitution guaranteeing religious liberty presented no difficulty:

> Those who drafted and adopted our constitution, could never have intended it to meet such narrow and sectarian views. That section of the constitution was clearly intended for higher and nobler purposes. It was for the protection of all religions—The Buddhist and the Brahman, the Pagan and the Jew, the Christian and the Turk, that all might enjoy an unrestricted liberty in their religion, and feel an assurance that for their religion alone, they should never, by legislative enactments, be subjected to fines, cast into prisons, starved in dungeons, burned at the stake, or made to feel the power of the inquisition.
>
> It was intended to prevent persecution by punishing for religious opinions. The Bible has long been in our common schools. It was placed there by our fathers, not for the purpose of teaching sectarian religion, but a knowledge of God and of his will, whose practice is religion. It was placed there as the book best adapted from which to "teach children and youth the principles of piety, justice, and a sacred regard for truth, love to their country, humanity, and a universal benevolence, sobriety, moderation and temperance, and those other virtues which are the ornaments of human society, and the basis upon which a republic constitution is founded."
>
> But, in doing this, no scholar is requested to believe it, none to receive it as the only true version of the laws of God. The teacher enters into no argument to prove its correctness, and gives no instructions in theology from it. To read the Bible in school for these and like purposes, or to require it to be read without sectarian explanations, is no interference with religious liberty.

The most interesting part of the decision is the court's invocation of the principle of the separation of church and state:

> That most wonderful specimen of human skill and human invention, the Suspension Bridge, that spans the dark, deep waters at Niagara, with strength to support the heaviest engines with cars laden with their freight, and defying the whirlwind and the tempest, is but the perfection of strength from the most feeble beginning. A tiny thread was but safely secured across the abyss, and final success became certain. Thread after thread were interchanged, until iron cables bound oppo-

site shores together. May not the innocent pleading of a little child for its religion in school, if granted, be used like a silken thread, to first pass that heretofore impassable gulf which lies between Church and State, and when once secured, may not stronger cords be passed over it, until cables, which human hands cannot sever, shall have bound Church and State together forever?[10]

It should not be supposed that the cases of Bridget Donahoe and Tom Wall were unique. About the same time that Tom Wall was flogged for his rebellious refusal to participate in reading from the Protestant Bible, some one hundred other Catholic children were expelled for the same reason.[11] In Indiana in the 1880's a Catholic girl who refused to learn a chapter from the Protestant Bible as required, recited "Maud Muller" instead. Here again was rebellion, but this time the rod was spared; instead the child was kept after school day after day in an attempt to break her stubborn will. Apparently only physical force is adequate to break religious conscience, for unlike Tom Wall the Indiana girl never did yield.[12]

It would be equally erroneous to assume that all school committees and officials adopted the strong arm procedure. The Cincinnati "Bible War" of 1869 presents an entirely different picture.[13] The practice of daily readings from the King James Bible had been in effect since the establishment of the Cincinnati public school system in 1829. Neither note nor comment on the text of the Scriptures was made by the teachers. The practice went unchallenged until 1842, when the Catholic Bishop (later Archbishop) John Purcell, serving as a city school examiner, caused a modification to be enacted "that no pupil should be required to read the Testament or Bible against the wishes of parents or guardians." When in 1852 the board of education codified its procedure and declared that "the opening exercises in every department shall commence by reading a portion of the Bible," the pupils were permitted to "read such version of the sacred scriptures as their parents or guardians may prefer."

Notwithstanding the liberal action of the school board since 1842, the Catholic Church developed a separate parochial school system in Cincinnati which by 1869 had between twelve and fifteen thousand enrolled children. Catholic parents were not pleased with the dual system, and were anxious for a consolidation that would bring their children back into the public schools. At first they received some encouragement—or at least no strenuous objection— from Archbishop Purcell. Accordingly two resolutions were introduced in the board of education, one providing for the appointment of a committee to negotiate with the church authorities for consolidation, and the other repealing the regulation that provided for Bible-reading exercises, and specifically prohibiting all religious instruction in the schools, including Bible reading.

It was not long before the hopes of the Catholic parents were dashed by the publication of a letter to the negotiating committee from Bishop Purcell, in which he said:

> The entire government of public schools in which Catholic youth are educated can not be given over to the civil power.
> We, as Catholics, can not approve of that system of education for youth which is apart from instruction in the Catholic faith and the teaching of the Church.
> If the School Board can offer anything in conformity with these principles, as has been done in England, France, Canada, Prussia, and other countries where the rights of conscience in the matter of education have been fully recognized, I am prepared to give it respectful consideration.

This put an abrupt end to the proposed negotiations, for it was clear that under the constitution and laws of Ohio the school board could not if it wished divide public school funds with church schools, as "in England, France, Canada, Prussia, and other countries."

Bishop Purcell's disregard of the second (Bible) resolution made it quite clear that the church no longer had an interest in it. Indeed, he seemed to indicate that the defeat of the proposal would not be entirely unwelcome to him, and he "denounced" one Catholic member of the school board who persisted in seeking the adoption of the Bible resolution and settlement of the school question. But though the negotiating committee was discharged from further action on the consolidation proposal, the Bible resolution remained to be acted on.

The debates around this resolution were heated. The anti-Catholic cartoons of Thomas Nast were reproduced in the newspapers. The papers also quoted the statement in the New York *Freeman's Journal* of Bishop Hughes, "Let the public school system go where it came from—the devil," as well as the prophecy from the Cincinnati *Catholic Telegraph*: "It will be a glorious day for Catholics in this country when our school system will be shivered to pieces." One prominent Protestant minister called the resolution an attempt on the part of "the black brigade of the Catholic priesthood [to] form an ecclesiastical kingdom of God within the Republic." Another minister member of the board passionately asked, "If we raise the flag on the school house, shall the Star Spangled Banner be entwined with the black flag of atheism?" (This linking of Catholicism to atheism sounds strange today, yet it was by no means uncommon during the period of the secularization of the American public school system.) But the combination of the "black brigade of priesthood" and the "black flag of atheism" proved too much for the defenders of God and the Bible. By a vote of 22 to 15 the board of education passed the Bible resolution and brought an end to Bible reading in the public schools of Cincinnati. But a group of staunch defenders of the faith immediately brought suit in the Cincinnati court to declare the resolution illegal. At the ensuing trial, which lasted five days, both sides were represented by nationally prominent counsel. The board's counsel consisted of one person who was later to become a justice of the United States Supreme Court, one later to become governor of Ohio, and a third, United States minister to Italy; nevertheless they were charged by one clergyman with being consorts of the "irreligious, profane, licentious, drunken, disorderly and criminal portions of our population."

In a two to one decision the Cincinnati court declared the resolution void, and held that the board's action had trespassed on the sacred character of the Scriptures, and that the exclusion of religious instruction from the public schools was contrary to the constitutional recognition of Christianity as an essential element of good government. The dissent, written by Alphonso Taft—the father of President and Chief Justice William Howard Taft—saw in the board's action no violation of the rights of conscience nor any abuse, profanation, or degradation of the Bible.

The board appealed to the State Supreme Court, which reversed the lower court and upheld the board's authority to exclude the Bible.[14] The Supreme Court's decision did not hold that Bible reading in the public schools violated the constitution and therefore *must* be excluded; it held only that the board *could* exclude it. Yet the language of the court's opinion is so broad and its interpretation of the meaning of separation so comprehensive as logically to require a holding that Bible reading in the public schools is inconsistent with the principle of separation. The Court said in part:

> Legal Christianity is a solecism, a contradiction of terms. When Christianity asks the aid of government beyond mere impartial protection, it denies itself. Its laws are divine, and not human. Its essential interests lie beyond the reach and range of human governments. United with government, religion never rises above the merest superstition; united with religion, government never rises above the merest despotism; and all history shows us that the more widely and completely they are separated, the better it is for both. . . .

If it be true that our law enjoins the teaching of the Christian religion in the schools, surely, then, all its teachers should be Christians. Were I such a teacher, while I should instruct the pupils that the Christian religion was true and all other religions false, I should tell them that the law itself was an unchristian law. One of my first lessons to the pupils would show it to be unchristian. That lesson would be: "Whatsoever ye would that men should do to you, do ye even so to them; for this is the law and the prophets." I could not look the veriest infidel or heathen in the face, and say that such a law was just, or that it was a fair specimen of Christian republicanism. I should have to tell him that it was an outgrowth of false Christianity, and not one of the "lights" which Christians are commanded to shed upon an unbelieving world. I should feel bound to acknowledge to him, moreover, that it violates the spirit of our constitutional guaranties, and is a state religion in embryo; that if we have no right to tax him to support "worship," we have no right to tax him to support religious instructions; that to tax a man to put down his own religion is of the very essence of tyranny; that however small the tax, it is a first step in the direction of an "establishment of religion;" and I should add, that the first step in that direction is the fatal step, because it logically involves the last step. . . .

Counsel say that to withdraw all religious instruction from the schools would be to put them under the control of "infidel sects." This is by no means so. To teach the doctrines of infidelity, and thereby teach that Christianity is false, is one thing; and to give no instructions on the subject is quite another thing. The only fair and impartial method, where serious objection is made, is to let each sect give its own instructions, elsewhere than in the state schools, where of necessity all are to meet; and to put disputed doctrines of religion among other subjects of instruction, for there are many others which can more conveniently, satisfactorily, and safely be taught elsewhere. . . .

The principles here expressed . . . are as old as Madison, and were his favorite opinions. Madison, who had more to do with framing the constitution of the United States than any other man, and whose purity of life and orthodoxy of religious belief no one questions, himself says:

"Religion is not within the purview of human government." And again he says: "Religion is essentially distinct from human government, and exempt from its cognizance. A connection between them is injurious to both. There are causes in the human breast which insure the perpetuity of religion without the aid of law."

In his letter to Governor Livingston, July 10, 1822, he says: "I observe with particular pleasure the view you have taken of the immunity of religion from civil government, in every case where it does not trespass on private rights or the public peace. This has always been a favorite doctrine with me."

### Extent and Nature of the Practice

The extent of Bible reading in the public schools in 1963 when the Schempp decision was handed down cannot be estimated with any degree of certainty. Undoubtedly the practice was widespread.

According to the survey made by the National Education Association in 1946 only eight state superintendents of schools answered no to a question whether Bible reading was permitted in the state. Even this small estimate was probably excessive. New York, for instance, is listed as one of the states in which Bible reading was not practiced, yet a by-law of the New York City board of education provided that "the regular assemblies of all schools shall be opened by reading to the pupils a portion of the Bible without comment."[15] The survey reported that twenty-four states permitted the practice, and it may be assumed that in most of the other states the practice was in force in at least some communities. This conclusion is supported by Professor Dierenfeld's 1961 survey in which 41.74% of the respondents answered in the affirmative to the question whether Bible reading was conducted in their public school systems.[16]

The National Education Association survey indicated that in twelve states and the District of Columbia Bible reading in the public schools was specifically required by statute. With the exception of the Massachusetts law, these statutes were of recent vintage; all had been enacted since 1913. This is the same period in which the released-time experiment was launched and has developed; and since both practices are basically Protestant enterprises, the coincidence of the two movements would seem to mark the period beginning with World War I as the era of Protestant dissatisfaction with the bargain made in 1791 — at least insofar as the bargain implied the secularization of state-controlled schools.

In those states in which Bible reading was either required or permitted, the condition was imposed — as it was in the New York City by-law quoted above — that the teacher could not comment on the passages read.[17] The theory underlying this condition is that the Bible itself is nonsectarian, and the danger of sectarian comment by the teacher would be met by prohibiting all comment. This is illustrated by the North Dakota statute, which read:

> The Bible shall not be deemed a sectarian book. It shall not be excluded from any public school. It may at the option of the teacher be read in school without sectarian comment, not to exceed ten minutes daily. No pupil shall be required to read it nor be present in the schoolroom during the reading thereof contrary to the wishes of his parents or guardian or other person having him in charge.[18]

The bar on comment also shows the general Protestant assumption that the Scriptures are self-revealing and require no interpretation by any ecclesiastical intermediary. Occasionally, too, in communities where there was a substantial Jewish population, the statute or by-law might limit the reading to the Old Testament;[19] except that even in those communities the recitation of the Lord's Prayer was permitted.[20] Provision was also made in many statutes and school board rules for the excuse of any pupils whose parents objected to their participation.[21]

The state laws did not usually specify which version of the Bible was to be used. Frequently, however, the local school board specified that the King James Version should be used; but whether or not specified by statute or school board regulation, the practice was almost invariably to use the King James Version. All the reported court cases on Bible reading in which the version of the Bible used is identified involved the King James Version.[22]

## The Case for Bible Reading

(1) *Public school responsibility for religious education.* All the arguments in support of government responsibility for religious education are, of course, applicable to Bible reading. These have been discussed[23] and need not be repeated here.

(2) *Tradition.* The Bible is the foundation of the American public school system; it has always been part of the public school. It is a traditional and indispensable part of the American educational and cultural scene.

(3) *Symbol.* The reading of a few verses of the Bible may not leave any deep religious significance or impression upon the children, but it should remain as a symbol of our allegiance to God.

(4) *Nonsectarianism.* The Bible is nonsectarian; it can be accepted by all, and its reading in the schools can give offense to no one. The differences between the King James and Douay versions are so slight as to be inconsequential.[24] It will be remembered that when in 1876 the House of Representatives overwhelmingly passed a resolution for a constitutional amendment prohibiting the use of public funds for any school in which the "creed or tenets of any religious sect is taught," the proposed amendment specifically provided that it should "not be construed to prohibit the reading of the Bible in any school or institution."

(5) *Literature.* The Bible is the greatest work of literature western civilization possesses. We read the *Odyssey* and Shakespeare's plays in the schools; why exclude the Bible?

(6) *Voluntariness.* In any event, it has been the universal practice to excuse objecting children from participating in Bible reading or even being present; hence no one could justifiably object to a practice in which other children wish to participate. That a child electing

446

not to participate may suffer embarrassment is no reason for depriving the other children of the opportunity to participate. Jehovah's Witnesses children who refuse to salute the flag in school may not be compelled to do so,[25] but the embarrassment suffered by them for exercising their right to abstain is not ground for eliminating flag salutes from the school. As Justice Jackson said in the McCollum case:

> . . . it may be doubted whether the Constitution which, of course, protects the right to dissent, can be construed also to protect one from the embarrassment that always attends nonconformity, whether in religion, politics, behavior or dress.

## The Case against Bible Reading

(1) *Sectarianism.* The nonsectarianism of the Bible is a fiction. To the Jewish child devoted to the religion of his fathers, the New Testament in its entirety is blasphemous for attributing divinity to a human being. Characterizing the King James Version as "nonsectarian" is an affront to Catholics, for the translators' dedicatory preface states that the purpose of the translation was to give "such a blow unto that Man of Sin (the Pope) as will not be healed [and] to make God's holy truth to be yet more and more known to the people whom they ('Papist persons at home or abroad') desire still to be kept in ignorance." Moreover, a Catholic child commits a grave sin if he knowingly owns or reads from the King James or other unauthorized version of the Bible. Protestants have no competence to judge insignificant the differences between the King James and Douay versions; only Catholics may make such a determination, and they refuse to do so. To Bridget Donahoe and Tom Wall and the girl who recited "Maud Muller" and hundreds of other Catholic children the differences were not insignificant.

(2) *Involuntariness.* Equally fictional is the asserted voluntariness of Bible reading. It is true that instances of the use of naked force have pretty much disappeared; but compulsion and pressure more subtle and circumstantial have not disappeared. A number of years ago, for instance, a Jewish child was kept in a closed wardrobe while the rest of the class engaged in Bible instruction.[26] Several courts have recognized the compulsion of circumstances. Justice Frankfurter, in his concurrence in the McCollum case, said:

> That a child is offered an alternative may reduce the constraint; it does not eliminate the operation of influence by the school in matters sacred to conscience and outside the school's domain. The law of imitation operates, and non-conformity is not an outstanding characteristic

447

of children. The result is an obvious pressure upon children to attend. . . .

An Illinois court noted that

the exclusion of a pupil from this part of the school exercises in which the rest of the school joins, separates him from his fellows, puts him in a class by himself, deprives him of his equality with the other pupils, subjects him to religious stigma and places him at a disadvantage in the school, which the law never contemplated.[27]

A similar observation was made by the Supreme Court of Wisconsin:

When . . . a small minority of the pupils in the public school is excluded, for any cause, from a stated school exercise, particularly where such cause is apparent hostility to the Bible which a majority of the other pupils have been taught to revere, from that moment the excluded pupil loses caste with his fellows, and is liable to be regarded with aversion and subjected to reproach and insult.[28]

In the Engel case[29] the United States Supreme Court made the same point:

When the power, prestige and financial support of government is placed behind a particular religious belief the indirect coercive pressure upon religious minorities to conform to the prevailing officially approved religion is plain.

(3) *The literature fiction.* The analogy of the Bible to the *Odyssey* and other works of literature is another fiction. Obviously, if the Bible were read as a work of literature as is the *Odyssey* there would be no constitutional objection. As the Supreme Court said in the Schempp case:[30]

It certainly may be said that the Bible is worthy of study in its literary and historical qualities.

But the Bible is not read as a work of literature; it is read as an act of devotion. In the argument of the Doremus case before the United States Supreme Court, the attorney general of New Jersey was questioned on this point, particularly by Justice Jackson, and he frankly asserted that he would be less than honest if he did not admit that the Bible reading provided for by the New Jersey statute was a religious, not a literary act; and the same admission was made in the Schempp case. The very existence of statutes requiring public school reading of the Bible manifests the unreality of the "literature" claim; as far as is known, no statute requires the public school reading of Homer or Shakespeare, nor does any prohibit a teacher from commenting on Homer or Shakespeare, nor provide for the excusing of children whose parents object to Homer or Shakespeare.

(4) *Ineffectuality.* If the daily reading of a few verses from the Bible is a symbol, it is little more, and a pretty ineffectual symbol at that. The reading is almost always hurried, perfunctory, and completely devoid of religious meaning except to those whose convictions do not allow them to accept even a perfunctory reading of the Protestant Bible. The effect of public school Bible reading on one schoolboy was related to this writer by a rabbi asked by the boy to identify the "good Mrs. Murphy" who was going to follow him the rest of his life. It took some questioning by the rabbi to ascertain that the boy was referring to the "goodness and mercy" of the 23rd Psalm. Equally revealing was the confusion of the suburban commuter's school child who allegedly recited daily, "Lead us not into Penn Station."

## The Positions of the Faiths

The Protestants were for a long time the principal if not the sole advocates of Bible reading in the public schools. Before 1963 Protestant groups overwhelmingly favored the practice; even Protestants and Other Americans United had not expressed itself in opposition. This Protestant position was not, however, unanimous; the Unitarians, Universalists, and Seventh Day Adventists, as well as some Lutheran and Southern Baptist groups, opposed it. These, however, undoubtedly represented but a comparatively small minority among organized Protestants.

The Supreme Court's decisions in the Engel and Schempp cases have had a profound effect upon American Protestantism. Today the Protestant churches overwhelmingly do not favor devotional Bible reading in the public schools. Even before the Schempp case the General Board of the National Council of Churches, in June 1963, adopted a policy statement on the Churches and the Public Schools (with only the Greek Orthodox Church dissenting) in which it had this to say:

> The full treatment of some regular school subjects requires the use of the Bible as a source book. In such studies — including those related to character development — the use of the Bible has a valid educational purpose. But neither true religion nor good education is dependent upon the devotional use of the Bible in the public school programs.

The United Presbyterian Church was even more forthright in its opposition. In a Statement of Policy entitled "Relations Between

449

Church and State" adopted by the 175th General Assembly in May 1963, it said: "Bible reading and prayers as devotional acts tend toward indoctrination or meaningless ritual and should be omitted for both reasons."

For more than a century the Catholic Church and Catholic parents were the chief opponents of public school Bible reading. But as with the released-time plan, the McCollum decision effected on the part of the Church a complete change of position in respect to Bible reading. Of course the Church would prefer that the Douay version be used — at least by Catholic children. But in the Doremus case it was — as usual — the King James Version that was involved; and in an important article in *Catholic Action* George E. Reed of the legal staff of the National Council of Catholic Men expressed the view strongly that Bible reading in the public school should be sustained by the Supreme Court.[32] This article was the first indication of what before long manifested itself as a complete reversal of position on the question. The intensity of the Catholic Church's defense of Bible reading and prayer recitation in the public schools was shown by its reaction to the Engel and Schempp cases, as will be recounted shortly.

The organized Jewish community is overwhelmingly opposed in principle to the practice of Bible reading in the public schools. Although only the American Jewish Congress filed a brief *amicus curiae* in the Doremus case, all the organizations affiliated with the Synagogue Council of America expressed their opposition, and all filed a brief *amicus curiae* in both the Engel and Schempp cases.

Among the nonreligious organizations, the chief opponent has been the American Civil Liberties Union, which filed a brief *amicus curiae* in the Doremus case and sponsored the Engel and Schempp cases.

### The Constitutional Issue

Before 1963 the United States Supreme Court had never determined the constitutionality of Bible reading in the public schools; but it had, in effect, decided that *exclusion* of the Bible does not violate any constitutional right. In Clithero vs. Showalter[33] the Court dismissed for lack of a substantial Federal question an appeal from a decision of the Supreme Court of the state of Washington[34] that refused to direct the state superintendent of schools to institute Bible reading in the public schools.

In the Doremus case[35] the Court was presented with an opportunity to determine the converse of the Clithero case — whether the *inclusion* of Bible reading violated a constitutional right. The Court

450

dismissed the appeal on the ground that the only plaintiff who could complain, the mother of a pupil, had lost her standing because the pupil had graduated from school before the appeal was brought.[36] The decision in the Zorach case was carefully limited to religious instruction outside the public school building, and gave no hint as to how the Court would decide a Bible-reading case.

The decisions of the state courts were in conflict. It should be noted that, with the exception of the New Jersey court's decision in the Doremus case and a Tennessee case in 1956[37] all the decisions were handed down before the McCollum case was decided. None of them — other than these two — involved an attack on the basis of the First Amendment. The issue in the other cases was whether the practice of Bible reading violated state constitutional provisions, which generally prohibit "sectarian" teaching in the public schools. The issue in most of the state cases, therefore, was whether the Bible was a sectarian book, and whether its reading constituted teaching.[38]

The majority of the state decisions sustained the validity of Bible reading.[39] As cogent a justification for the majority view of constitutionality as can be found was expressed by the Kentucky court in Hackett vs. Brooksville Graded School District[40] in the following words:

> The main question we conceive to be, is the King James translation of the Bible, — or, for that matter, any edition of the Bible, — a sectarian book? There is, perhaps, no book that is so widely used and so highly respected as the Bible; no other that has been translated into as many tongues; no other that has had such marked influence upon the habits and life of the world. It is not the least of its marvelous attributes that it is so catholic that every seeming phase of belief finds comfort in its comprehensive precepts. Many translations of it, and of parts of it, have been made from time to time. . . . There is controversy over the authenticity of some parts of some of the editions, and there are some people who do not believe that any of it is the inspired or revealed word of God; yet it remains that civilized mankind generally accord to it a reverential regard, while all who study its sublime sentiments and consider its great moral influence must admit that it is, from any point of view, one of the most important of books. . . .
>
> That the Bible, or any particular edition, has been adopted by one or more denominations as authentic or by them asserted to be inspired cannot make it a sectarian book. The book itself, to be sectarian, must show that it teaches the peculiar dogmas of a sect as such, and not alone that it is so comprehensive as to include them by the partial interpretation of its adherents. Nor is a book sectarian merely because it was edited or compiled by those of a particular sect. It is not the authorship nor mechanical composition of the book, nor the use of it, but its contents, that give it its character. . . .

If the legislature or the constitutional convention had intended that the Bible should be proscribed they would simply have said so. The word "Bible" is shorter and better understood than the word "sectarian." It is not conceivable that if it had been intended to exclude the Bible from public schools that purpose would have been obscured within the controversial word.

Nor can we conceive that under the American system of providing thorough education of all the youth, to fit them for good citizenship in every sense, the legislature or the constitutional convention could have intended to exclude from their course of instruction any consideration of such a work, whose historical and literary value, aside from its theological aspects would seem to entitle it to a high place in any well-ordered course of general instruction. The history of a religion, including its teachings and claim of authority, — as, for example, the writings of Confucius or Mahomet, — might be profitably studied; why may not also the wisdom of Solomon and the life of Christ? If the same things were in any other book than the Bible, it would not be doubted that it was within the discretion of the school boards and teachers whether it was expedient to include them in the common school course of study without violating the impartiality of the law concerning religious beliefs.

The opposing view, accepted by a minority of courts,[41] was best expressed in an eloquent opinion by the Supreme Court of Illinois handed down in 1910. The case, People ex rel. Ring vs. Board of Education,[42] was bitterly contested, and lengthy opinions were written by both the majority and the minority of the court. The plaintiffs were Catholic parents of children in the public school, who alleged that the Catholic Church "believes the King James version of the Bible to be an incorrect and incomplete translation and that it disapproves of it being read as a devotional exercise; . . . that during the reading from the Bible and the reciting of the Lord's prayer the pupils are required to rise in their seats, fold their hands and bow their heads; . . . that there is no parochial or private school in the county . . . to which the relators could send their children for instruction; that the laws of Illinois make it compulsory upon them to send their children to school. . . ."

The majority of the court held that the plaintiff's constitutional rights had been violated. Its opinion first outlined the development of religious liberty, the separation of church and state, and secular public schools. The following paragraphs conclude this aspect of the opinion:

The Puritan in New England and the Cavalier in Virginia each established his own church and taxed the people for its support. Nonconformists were discriminated against and in some cases were oppressed and persecuted or driven out. The Pilgrims, who fled from the

452

oppression of the majority at home, made their religion a part of their civil government,—not religion, but *their* religion. In the new country, being themselves in the majority, they became oppressors of the minority, which refused to conform to the religion preferred by the laws which they enacted. Quakers were banished from Massachusetts, and Roger Williams was driven out of the colony to found the new colony of Providence, whose government should have authority, "only in civil things." By this express limitation of the authority of the magistrate to civil things was the fundamental principle of the separation of Church and State then and there for the first time definitely declared.

The ordinance of 1787 for the government of the Northwest Territory declared that "religion, morality and knowledge being necessary to good government and the happiness of mankind, schools and the means of education shall forever be encouraged." . . . The ordinance did not, however, by any means as originally adopted, impose upon the States the duty of religious instruction in the schools which were to be encouraged. It recognized education as a means promotive of religion and morality by the increase of knowledge. The recital or preamble recognized religion, morality and knowledge as three things essential to good government and the happiness of the people, and to secure those three things it enacted, not that religious instruction (which is not within the province of civil government) should be given by the States, but that the means of education should be encouraged and thus the essentials of good government should be promoted.

The court then considered whether the Bible was a sectarian book. It set forth the history of the King James and Douay versions and the differences between the two versions. Then the court continued:

Christianity is a religion. The Catholic church and the various Protestant churches are sects of that religion. These two versions of the Scriptures are the bases of the religion of the respective sects. Protestants will not accept the Douay Bible as representing the inspired word of God. As to them it is a sectarian book containing errors, and matter which is not entitled to their respect as a part of the Scriptures. It is consistent with the Catholic faith, but not the Protestant. Conversely, Catholics will not accept the King James' version. As to them it is a sectarian book inconsistent in many particulars with their faith, teaching what they do not believe. The differences may seem to many so slight as to be immaterial, yet Protestants are not found to be more willing to have the Douay Bible read as a regular exercise in the schools to which they are required to send their children, than are Catholics to have the King James' version read in schools which their children must attend. Differences of religious doctrine may seem immaterial to some, while to others they seem vitally important. Sectarian aversions, bitter animosities and religious persecutions have had their origin in apparently slender distinctions. . . . The importance of men's religious opinions and differences is for their own, and not for a court's determination. With such differences, whether important or unimportant, courts or governments have no right to interfere. It is not a question to be determined by a court in a country of religious freedom what religion or what sect is right. That is not a judicial question. All stand equal before the law— the Protestant, the Catholic, the Mohammedan, the Jew, the Mormon, the free-thinker, the atheist. Whatever may be the view of the majority of the people, the court has no right, and the majority has no right, to force that view upon the minority, however small. It is precisely for the protection of the minority that constitutional limitations exist. Majorities need no such protection,—they can take care of themselves.

Having determined that the Bible is a sectarian book, the court then considered whether the reading of the Bible constitutes instruction:

The reading of the Bible in school is instruction. Religious instruction is the object of such reading, but whether it is or not, religious instruction is accomplished by it. The Bible has its place in the school, if it is read there at all, as the living word of God, entitled to honor and reverence. Its words are entitled to be received as authoritative and final. The reading or hearing of such words cannot fail to impress deeply the pupils' minds. It is intended and ought to do so. They cannot hear the Scriptures read without being instructed as to the divinity of Jesus Christ, the Trinity, the resurrection, baptism, predestination, a future state of punishments and rewards, the authority of the priesthood, the obligation and effect of the sacraments, and many other doctrines about which the various sects do not agree. Granting that instruction on these subjects is desirable, yet the sects do not agree on what instruction shall be given. Any instruction on any one of the subjects is necessarily sectarian, because, while it may be consistent with the doctrines of one or many of the sects, it will be inconsistent with the doctrine of one or more of them. The petitioners are Catholic. They are compelled by law to contribute to the maintenance of this school and are compelled to send their children to it, or, besides contributing to its maintenance, to pay the additional expense of sending their children to another school. What right have the teachers of the school to teach those children religious doctrines different from that which they are taught by their parents? Why should the State compel them to unlearn the Lord's Prayer as taught in their homes and by their church and use the Lord's Prayer as taught by another sect? If Catholic children may be compelled to read the King James' version of the Bible in schools taught by Protestant teachers, the same law will authorize Catholic teachers to compel Protestant children to read the Catholic version. The same law which subjects Catholic children to Protestant domination in school districts which are controlled by Protestant influences will subject the children of Protestants to Catholic control where the Catholics predominate. In one part of the State the King James' version of the Bible may be read in the public schools, in another the Douay Bible, while in school districts where the sects are somewhat evenly divided, a religious contest may be expected at each election of a school director to determine which sect shall prevail in the school. Our constitution has wisely provided against any such contest by excluding sectarian instruction altogether from the school.

The court then discussed the power of the state to engage in religious education:

> . . . The State is not, and under our constitution cannot be, a teacher of religion. All sects, religious or even anti-religious, stand on an equal footing. They have the same rights of citizenship, without discrimination. The public school is supported by the taxes which each citizen, regardless of his religion or his lack of it, is compelled to pay. The school, like the government, is simply a civil institution. It is secular, and not religious, in its purposes. The truths of the Bible are the truths of religion, which do not come within the province of the public school. No one denies their importance. No one denies that they should be taught to the youth of the state. The constitution and the law do not interfere with such teaching, but they do banish theological polemics from the schools and the school districts. This is done, not from any hostility to religion, but because it is not part of the duty of the State to teach religion, — to take the money of all and apply it to teaching the children of all the religion of a part, only. Instruction in religion must be voluntary. Abundant means are at hand for all who seek such instruction for themselves or their children. Organizations whose purpose is the spreading of religious knowledge and instruction exist, and many individuals, in connection with such organizations and independently, are devoted to that work. Religion is taught, and should be taught in the churches, Sunday schools, parochial and other church schools and religious meetings. Parents should teach it to their children at home, where its truths can be most effectively enforced. Religion does not need an alliance with the State to encourage its growth. The law does not attempt to enforce Christianity. Christianity had its beginning and grew under oppression. Where it has depended upon the sword of civil authority for its enforcement it has been weakest. Its weapons are moral and spiritual and its power is not dependent upon the force of a majority. It asks from the civil government only impartial protection and concedes to every other sect and religion the same impartial civil right. . . .

Finally, the court held (in an extract from the opinion we have previously quoted), that the fact that the plaintiffs' children could request to be excused from participation did not make the program voluntary or remove from it the taint of unconstitutionality.

Thus the situation stood in 1963 when the Schempp case was decided by the Supreme Court. But before this occurred the Court was called upon to consider the constitutionality of Bible distribution and prayer recitation in the public schools. These two developments will therefore be recounted before we return to the latest chapter in the chronicle of Bible reading in the public schools.

## BIBLE DISTRIBUTION

Keeping copies of the Bible in the school library for use by those children wishing to do so is obviously no violation of any constitutional prohibition.[43] It would indeed be a sorry school library that did not possess a copy of the Bible. A more difficult question, however, is presented by the efforts of the Gideons Society to place a copy of the New Testament and Psalms in the hands of every public school child in the country.

The Gideons Society was organized in Illinois in 1910 under the name Gideons, International. Its purpose was frankly missionary. Its declared object was "to recognize the Christian commercial traveling men of the world with cordial fellowship to encourage one another in the Master's work; to improve every opportunity for the betterment of the lives of our fellow travelers, business men and others with whom we may come in contact, scattering seeds all along the pathway for Christ." In 1937 this statement was revised so as to state the objectives more broadly: "to associate Christian business men for service, and to carry to the world the Gospel of the Lord Jesus Christ." Its constitution makes it clear that its object of achieving conversion to Christianity is to be accomplished by widespread distribution of the Bible:

> Article 2. — Object.
> Section 1. The object of the Gideons is to win men and women for the Lord Jesus Christ, through . . . (c) placing the Bible, God's Holy Word — or portions thereof in hotels, hospitals, schools, institutions, and also through the distribution of same for personal use.

For many years the society had limited its activities primarily to placing copies of the Bible in hotel and hospital rooms. In 1950, however, it published a small paper-covered volume consisting of all of the New Testament, the Psalms, and Proverbs, and launched a nationwide campaign (which is still continuing notwithstanding the Schempp decision) to distribute these volumes to public school children. The procedure employed by the Gideons in distributing the abridged Bible in the school system is more or less standardized. After receiving permission from the local board of education or school principal, the Gideons representative is given an opportunity to appear before the student body during classes or at a student assembly, frequently convened for that purpose; in either case attendance is generally compulsory. During the course of these meetings the Gideons colporteur is introduced by the school principal or by a teacher, and is permitted to deliver an address outlining the purposes and advantages of Bible distribution and instruction. He advises the students that they are to be given a copy of the New Testament as a gift if they obtain their parents' consent. The speech, frequently evangelical in tone, encourages the students to persuade a parent to record his consent by signing a printed form that is distributed to each student at the conclusion of the meeting. The form itself is often prepared and printed by the school. When the signed form is returned, it is exchanged by the designated school authority—usually a teacher—for a copy of the Gideons Bible. Included on the flyleaf of each Bible is a pledge to be signed by the recipient requiring him to promise to read the book as condition to the gift.

The initiation of the program aroused a storm of protest in many communities—generally from Catholics and Jews. In Connecticut the Catholic Men's and Women's Club protested to the state board of education against the proposal.[44] In Sandwich and Bourne, Massachusetts, the Catholic Church—speaking through the Chancery Office of the Fall River diocese—likewise protested on the ground that the Gideons Bible is sectarian.[45] Father L.J. Daby, a local priest, stated emphatically,

> The issuing of the Gideon Bible, a sectarian Bible, in our public schools recently, I take strong exception to. This is not Russia where children are being regimented, and we don't want such actions in this country.[46]

In the Boston Area, on the instructions of the Archdiocesan Superintendent of Parochial Schools, all Catholic public school children who had received the Gideons Bibles in the public schools were directed by their priests to return them.[47]

In other communities the rabbis took the lead, and in some they made joint protests with the priests; in a few communities even Protestant ministers indicated their disapproval. In Reno, Nevada, for example, the county ministerial association approved the action of the school trustees in forbidding the distribution of the Gideons Bible in the public schools.[48]

In Detroit the board of education rejected the Gideons offer on the ground that "the version offered is acceptable only to some religious groups and its distribution would violate Supreme Court decisions. It would lead to unfortunate controversy which would disturb the harmonious atmosphere of the community."[49] Commenting editorially on the Gideons offer, *The Christian Century* said:[50]

> An offer by the Gideons to distribute Bibles to 117,000 public school children in Detroit seems to have been turned down by the board of education in that city. As this is written, the board has declined to accept or reject the offer, after spending an evening in heated discussion.

457

We believe that the offer should be rejected and we hope that is the final outcome of the discussion in the automobile city. Protestants have no more right to use the public schools for sectarian purposes than have Jews, Catholics or atheists. The version of the Bible which would be distributed by the Gideons would probably be the King James, which Catholics do not accept. Jews of course reject both the King James and Douay versions, and people holding no religion want neither the Old nor the New Testament. We believe that widespread and determined efforts should be made not only to place the Bible in the hands of every child and every person but to instruct them in its riches for Christian living. But the public schools are not the place for these efforts, and we doubt that the Gideons are the people best equipped to carry it on. This is the task of the evangelical churches. Those churches did not raise the issue of religious liberty in the public schools of Detroit. Instead the issue was raised by an organization whose objectives are chiefly confined to the distribution of Bibles, and generally these Bibles contain extraneous matter inserted inside the front or back covers reflecting views which are not universally accepted even among Protestants. The agitation in Detroit ought to serve as a reminder to the churches that they have a duty not only to respect separation of church and state in relation to the schools but also to pursue their own calling with greater zeal.

In most communities, as in Detroit, this has been recognized; and where objection has been raised permission has generally been refused or the Gideons have withdrawn their offer. In Rutherford, New Jersey, however, the joint protests of the Catholic and Jewish communities were unsuccessful in inducing the public school authorities to refuse consent or the Gideons to withdraw their offer. As a result, the local priest and rabbi joined in sponsoring a test case brought by the parents of Catholic and Jewish children in the public schools.

At the trial evidence was presented to show that the Gideon Bible was not a nonsectarian book, that the assertion of voluntariness in accepting or rejecting the book was not realistic, and that the distribution was harmful to the aims and purposes of public school education. This testimony was accepted by the Supreme Court of New Jersey which, in a unanimous decision (Tudor vs. Board of Education of Rutherford[51]) handed down in 1953, held the practice unconstitutional.

On the issue of sectarianism the New Jersey Supreme Court said:

A review of the testimony at the trial convinces us that the King James version or Gideon Bible is unacceptable to those of the Jewish faith. In this regard Rabbi Joachim Prinz testified:
"The New Testament is in profound conflict with the basic principles

of Judaism. It is not accepted by the Jewish people as a sacred book. The Bible of the Jewish people is the Old Testament. The New Testament is not recognized as part of the Bible. The teachings of the New Testament are in complete and profound conflict with what Judaism teaches. It presupposes the concept of Jesus of Nazareth as a divinity, a concept which we do not accept.

"They are in complete and utter conflict with what we teach, for we teach the oneness of God, which to our—and in accordance with our belief, excludes the existence of a Son of God. We accept Jesus of Nazareth as one of the figures of Jewish history, a Jew, born a Jew, died as a Jew, but we do not accept Jesus of Nazareth as the Christ. . . .

"No, it is certainly not a nonsectarian book. It is a book that is—expresses the view of one denomination among the many religious denominations of the world."

In rejecting the argument of voluntariness, the court's opinion said:

The defendant contends that the distribution of the Gideon Bible in no way injects any issue of the "free exercise" of religion, that "no one is forced to take a New Testament and no religious exercise or instrument is brought to the classrooms of the public schools." In other words, it asserts the arguments of *Zorach* v. *Clauson,* that the "accommodation" of religion is permissible. This argument, however, ignores the realities of life. . . . Prof. Isidore Chein, Supervisor of Psychology and Acting Director of the Research Center for Mental Health at New York University, testified on behalf of the plaintiff:

". . . I would expect that a slip of this kind, distributed under the authority of the school, would create a subtle pressure on the child which would leave him with a sense that he is not quite as free as the statement on that slip says; in other words, that he will be something of an outcast and a pariah if he does not go along with this procedure.

". . . I think that they would be in a situation where they have to play along with this or else feel themselves to be putting themselves in a public position where they are different, where they are not the same as other people, and the whole pressure would exist on them to conform."

Dr. Dan Dodson, professor in the School of Education of New York University and director of curriculum and research in the Center for Human Relations Studies, when questioned as to the divisive effect of the distribution of the Gideon Bible stated:

"I would say that any instance of this kind in which the—a document that has the importance that this has to certain religious groups, including my own, would be distributed or used as a means of propaganda or indoctrination by official channels, such as the school system, would create tensions among the religious groups; there would be a controversial problem.

"I would say that it would raise questions among the children as to who is and who isn't, in terms of receiving the Bible. It would also create problems as to why some accepted it and others didn't. That would be divisive." . . .

We cannot accept the argument that here, as in the *Zorach Case*, the State is merely "accommodating" religion. It matters little whether the teachers themselves will distribute the Bibles or whether that will be done by members of the Gideons International. The same vice exists, that of preference of one religion over another. This is all the more obvious when we realize the motive of the Gideons. Its purpose is "to win men and women for the Lord Jesus Christ, through . . . (e) placing the Bible—God's Holy Word . . . or portions thereof in hotels, hospitals, schools, institutions, and also through distribution of same for personal use." The society is engaged in missionary work, accomplished in part by placing the King James version of the Bible in the hands of public school children throughout the United States. To achieve this end it employs the public school system as the medium of distribution. It is at the school that the pupil receives the request slip to take to his parents for signature. It is at the school that the pupil actually receives his Gideon Bible. In other words, the public school machinery is used to bring about the distribution of these Bibles to the children of Rutherford. In the eyes of the pupils and their parents the Board of Education has placed its stamp of approval upon this distribution and, in fact, upon the Gideon Bible itself. Dr. Dodson further testified:

"I would say it would leave a lefthanded implication that the school thought this was preferential in terms of what is the divine word, and that the backing of the State would inevitably be interpreted as being behind it."

Dr. William Heard Kilpatrick stated:

"The Protestants would feel that the school is getting behind this thing; the Catholics would feel that the school is getting behind a Protestant affair; the Jews would feel that the school is getting behind the Protestant religion as opposed to their religion; and the people who don't accept any religion would feel that the school is actually trying to teach religion through this means."

This is more than mere "accommodation" of religion permitted in the *Zorach Case*. The school's part in this distribution is an active one and cannot be sustained on the basis of a mere assistance to religion.

The decision in the Tudor case, which the United States Supreme Court refused to review, was followed by the Supreme Court of Florida[52] and in rulings by attorneys-general in practically every state in which the issue has arisen.[53]

### PRAYERS

Many of the state court cases concerning Bible reading in the public schools also involved the singing of religious hymns and the recitation of prayers.[54] The usual procedure had been to read several verses from the Bible as part of a daily morning devotional exercise that included the singing of hymns and the recitation of prayer; and though the courts concentrated their opinions on the Bible reading, the constitutionality of the program should be considered as a whole. Perhaps the courts' emphasis on the Bible-reading aspect may be explained by the fact that the characterization of "nonsectarian" was less easily applied where hymns and prayers accompany the Bible reading. Nor was it easy to sustain the "literature" claim by drawing analogies to Homer, reading from whom is not known to be accompanied by any prayers to Zeus or Hera.

Occasionally even this fiction of the nonreligiosity of prayer was accepted unblushingly by the courts. In Spiller vs. Inhabitants of Woburn[55] the Supreme Court of Massachusetts held that a school regulation requiring the opening of sessions with Bible reading and prayer, during which the pupils were required to bow their heads, did not constitute a devotional or religious ceremony, since the purpose of the requirement of bowed heads was merely to insure quiet and decorum. Hence a stubborn little girl who refused to bow her head was properly expelled from the school. And in Billard vs. Board of Education of Topeka,[56] the court accepted a teacher's explanation that she caused the class to recite the Lord's Prayer every morning not as a religious exercise but merely to quiet them and prepare them for their regular studies. Under these circumstances the court found no violation of any constitutional prohibition.

The prayer frequently prescribed to accompany Bible reading is the Lord's Prayer.[57] The courts that had held the Bible to be nonsectarian had no difficulty in so holding the Lord's Prayer.[58] Aside from the differences between the Protestant and Catholic versions of the Lord's Prayer, it would seem that characterizing the Lord's Prayer as nonsectarian constitutes a cavalier disregard of the conviction of adherents of the Jewish faith. As far as is known, no recognized Jewish religious authority agrees with that characterization. The prayer itself is preceded by the injunction—hardly acceptable to pious Jews whose religion requires them to pray in synagogues—that

> And when thou prayest, thou shalt not be as the hypocrites are: for they love to pray standing in the synagogues and in the corners of the streets, that they may be seen of men [Matthew 6:5].

Even more important, designating as the "Lord" any human being violates a basic article of Jewish faith.

In November 1951 the New York State Board of Regents proposed what it considered a truly nonsectarian prayer for daily recitation in the public schools of the state. It issued a "policy statement" which asserted that the American people have always been religious, that a program of religious inspiration in the schools would assure that the children would acquire "respect for lawful authority and obedience to law [and that] each of them will be properly prepared to follow the faith of his or her father, as he or she receives the same at mother's knee or father's side and as such faith is expounded and strengthened by his or her religious leaders."[59]

The "policy statement" then said: "We believe that at the commencement of each school day the act of allegiance to the flag might well be joined with this act of reverence to God: 'Almighty God, we acknowledge our dependence upon Thee, and we beg Thy blessings upon us, our parents, our teachers and our country.' "[60]

The announcement aroused a storm of controversy. The proposal was opposed by the leading Protestant weekly, *The Christian Century*, which deemed the practice ineffectual, and the prayer "likely to deteriorate quickly into an empty formality with little, if any, spiritual significance."[61] The leaders of the Lutheran Church of Our Redeemer in Peekskill, New York, charged that Christ's name had "deliberately been omitted to mollify non-Christian elements," and that the prayer "therefore is a denial of Christ and His prescription for a proper prayer. As such it is not a prayer but an abomination and a blasphemy."[62]

Opposition, but for different reasons, was also voiced by all the major Jewish organizations, including the American Jewish Congress, the Synagogue Council of America and the New York Board of Rabbis,[63] as well as such nonsectarian organizations as the American Civil Liberties Union, the New York Teachers Guild, the United Parents Association, and the Citizens Union.[64]

On the other hand, strong support came from many Protestant and Catholic church leaders, such as the Reverend Norman Vincent Peale, Dr. Ralph Sockman, Charles H. Tuttle, Bishop William Scully of Albany, and Msgr. John S. Middleton, secretary for education of the Archdiocese of New York.[65] *The Tablet,* official organ of the Brooklyn Catholic Diocese, quickly became the most passionate defender of the proposal; and John F. Brosnan, a member of the Board of Regents, speaking before the Friendly Sons of St. Patrick, charged that "the only criticism came from those who do not believe in God."[66]

The Regents' proposal was not mandatory; it was merely a recommendation which local school boards were free to adopt or not. In New York City, after a stormy public hearing, the Board of Education decided not to institute recitation of the prayer in the public schools of the city, but instead compromised by providing for the daily recitation of the fourth stanza of the patriotic hymn, *America.* ("Our fathers' God, to Thee, Author of liberty, to Thee we sing.

Long may our land be bright with freedom's holy light, protect us by Thy might, great God our King.")

No survey appears to have been taken to determine how many school boards did adopt the Regents' prayer. A reasonable estimate is that not more than ten percent of them did so. However, among those that did was the school board in New Hyde Park, a Long Island suburb of New York. With the aid of the New York Civil Liberties Union, a group of parents of children in the public schools of that community brought suit in the state courts to declare the practice unconstitutional.

The New York Supreme Court, in a lengthy and scholarly decision,[67] upheld the action of the New Hyde Park School Board, although it required the school authorities to promulgate regulations to assure that participation by the children would be entirely voluntary and that nonparticipation would not be penalized; suggesting, for example, a regulation which would permit nonparticipating pupils to arrive at school after the exercises.

The decision was upheld by the appellate courts in New York,[68] although a number of opinions were written in the courts, some of them not entirely consistent with each other.

As best as can be judged from the various opinions, the school board's action was sustained on four separate but somewhat related grounds:

(1) The prayer formulated by the Board of Regents is "nonsectarian," *i.e.*, it is acceptable to all faiths and is preferential to none. Its recitation in concert by the children may constitutionally be made part of the daily public school program since the purpose of the First Amendment is only to preclude preferential treatment of some religions over others.

(2) Since provision is made in the lower court's decision to assure complete freedom of nonparticipation on the part of any child, there is no infringement on the First Amendment.

(3) The First Amendment is made applicable to the states by virtue of the due process clause of the Fourteenth. Public school recitation of prayer is a long-standing practice. A practice which has continued so long in time cannot be held to be wanting in due process.

(4) We are a religious people. Those who wrote our Constitution were friends of religion. Exclusion of prayer from the public school curriculum manifests a hostility to religion, and such motivation cannot reasonably be ascribed to the framers of our Constitution.

The decision was appealed to the United States Supreme Court and thus the landmark decision of Engel vs. Vitale[69] was handed down by the Court in June 1962.

By a vote of six to one (Justice Frankfurter was ill and there was one vacancy on the bench when the case was argued), the Supreme Court overruled the New York courts and held the practice unconstitutional as violative of the First Amendment's ban on establishment of religion. The majority opinion was written by Justice Black, who had written the majority opinions in the Everson, McCollum, and Torcaso cases and who had dissented in Zorach vs. Clauson.

"We think," said Justice Black, "that by using its public school system to encourage recitation of the Regents' prayer, the State of New York has adopted a practice wholly inconsistent with the Establishment Clause. There can, of course, be no doubt that New York's program of daily classroom invocation of God's blessings as prescribed in the Regents' prayer is a religious activity. It is a solemn avowal of divine faith and supplication for the blessings of the Almighty."

The state laws requiring or permitting use of the prayer, he continued, must be struck down because "the constitutional prohibition against laws respecting an establishment of religion must at least mean that in this country it is no part of the business of government to compose official prayers for any group of the American people to recite as part of a religious program carried on by the government."

The history of government-sponsored prayer both in the Old World and the New has been a history of oppression, coercion, and conflict. When our Constitution was written, Justice Black stated:

> [The] people knew, some of them from bitter personal experience, that one of the greatest dangers to freedom of the individual to worship in his own way lay in the Government's placing its official stamp of approval upon one particular kind of prayer or one particular form of religious services. . . . The first Amendment was added to the Constitution to stand as a guarantee that neither the power nor the prestige of the Federal Government would be used to control, support or influence the kinds of prayer the American people can say. . . . Under that Amendment's prohibition against governmental establishment of religion, as reinforced by the provisions of the Fourteenth Amendment, government in this country, be it state or federal, is without power to prescribe by law any particular form of prayer which is to be used as an official prayer in carrying on any program of governmentally-sponsored religious activity.

The Court rejected the argument that since the prayer was

"nondenominational" and since pupils could remain silent or be excused from the room if they requested, there was no constitutional violation. The opinion stated:

> Neither the fact that the prayer may be denominationally neutral, nor the fact that its observance on the part of the students is voluntary can serve to free it from the limitations of the Establishment Clause, as it might from the Free Exercise Clause of the First Amendment, both of which are operative against the States by virtue of the Fourteenth Amendment. . . . The Establishment Clause, unlike the Free Exercise Clause, does not depend upon any showing of direct governmental compulsion and is violated by the enactment of laws which establish an official religion whether those laws operate directly to coerce non-observing individuals or not. . . . The Establishment Clause . . . stands as an expression of principle on the part of the Founders of our Constitution that religion is too personal, too sacred, too holy, to permit its "unhallowed perversion" by a civil magistrate. Another purpose of the Establishment Clause rested upon an awareness of the historical fact that governmentally-established religions and religious persecutions go hand in hand. . . . The New York laws officially prescribing the Regents' prayer are inconsistent with both the purposes of the Establishment Clause and with the Establishment Clause itself.

Nothing, according to Justice Black, could be more wrong than the argument that to apply the Constitution in such a way as to prohibit state laws respecting an establishment of religious services in public schools is to indicate a hostility toward religion or toward prayer. Men who had faith in the power of prayer were the leaders of the fight for the adoption of our Constitution and Bill of Rights. "It is," he said, "neither sacrilegious nor anti-religious to say that each separate government in this country should stay out of the business of writing or sanctioning official prayers and leave that purely religious function to the people themselves and to those the people choose to look to for religious guidance."

Justice Black concluded the opinion by disposing of the assertion that the recitation of the Regents' prayer constituted at most a minor infringement on the separation of church and state:

> It is true, that New York's establishment of its Regents' prayer as an officially approved religious doctrine of that state does not amount to a total establishment of one particular religious sect to the exclusion of all others — that, indeed, the governmental endorsement of that prayer seems relatively insignificant when compared to the governmental encroachments upon religion which were commonplace 200 years ago. To those who may subscribe to the view that because the Regents' official prayer is so brief and general there can be no danger to religious freedom in its governmental establishment, however, it may be appropriate

465

to say in the words of James Madison, the author of the First Amendment:

"It is proper to take alarm at the first experiment on our liberties. . . . Who does not see that the same authority which can establish Christianity in exclusion of all other religions may establish with the same ease any particular sect of Christians, in exclusion of all other sects? That the same authority which can force a citizen to contribute three pence only of his property for the support of any one establishment, may force him to conform to any other establishment in all cases whatsoever?"

## The Reaction to Engel vs. Vitale

Supreme Court decisions that arouse furor are hardly unprecedented. Throughout its history, the Court has witnessed reactions of outrage to this or that decision, often accompanied by demands to amend the Constitution, impeach the Justices, or restrict the powers of the jurisdiction of the Court. The furor, however, which greeted the decision in Engel vs. Vitale was probably unusual in its intensity. Southern Senators and Congressmen, already embittered at the Court because of its decision outlawing racial segregation in the public schools, were particularly emphatic in their reaction. The remark of Representative George W. Andrews of Alabama was typical: "They put the Negroes in the schools," he said, "and now they've driven God out."[70]

Senator Robert C. Byrd of West Virginia asked: "Can it be that we, too, are ready to embrace the foul concept of atheism? . . . Somebody is tampering with America's soul. I leave it to you who that somebody is."[71] Representative L. Mendel Rivers of South Carolina declared that "The Court has now officially stated its disbelief in God Almighty." And Senator Sam Ervin of North Carolina asserted that "The Supreme Court has made God unconstitutional."[72]

It should, however, not be supposed that this strong adverse reaction was limited to Southern Congressmen. The Governors' Conference, which happened to be holding its annual meeting when the decision came down, adopted a resolution with only the governor of New York abstaining, deploring the decision and calling for a constitutional amendment to overrule it.[73] Former President Herbert Hoover called the decision "a disintegration of one of the most sacred of American heritages." The Reverend Dr. Billy Graham, the noted evangelist, asserted: "This is another step towards the secularization of the United States . . . the framers of our Constitution meant we were to have freedom of religion, not freedom from religion."[74]

466

The reaction of Catholicism was particularly forceful. Cardinal Spellman declared: "I am shocked and frightened that the Supreme Court has declared unconstitutional a simple and voluntary declaration of belief in God by public school children. The decision strikes at the very heart of the Godly tradition in which America's children have for so long been raised."[75] On September 1, 1962, *America*, the national Jesuit weekly, published an editorial entitled "To Our Jewish Friends" in which it remarked that following the decision "there have been disturbing hints of heightened anti-Semitic feeling," and that "all necessary steps should be taken to prevent an outbreak of anti-Semitism." It then continued: ". . . we should recognize that full responsibility for the decision in *Engel vs. Vitale* is not to be pinned on the Jewish community. Along with that well-publicized Jewish spokesman, Leo Pfeffer, and such organizations as the American Jewish Congress, responsibility for the concerted opposition to the New York prayer—and to other forms of religious practice in the public schools and public life—belongs to the American Civil Liberties Union, the Ethical Culture Society, the Humanist associations, some Unitarians, many atheists and certain other groups with doctrinaire views on the meaning and application of the principle of separation of Church and State."

The editorial charged further that "one long-range objective" of this "sector of the Jewish Community" is to "create a 'climate of opinion' in which the [Supreme] Court can more readily continue to make decisions in consonance with the principle of separation of church and state as that principle has been interpreted in absolutistic terms by Leo Pfeffer, by the American Jewish Congress, and by the Supreme Court in the *McCollum* case of 1948."

"It would be most unfortunate," the editorial continued, "if the entire Jewish community were to be blamed for the unrelenting pressure tactics of a small but overly vocal segment within it. . . . Conceivably with help from some important Jewish groups, the recitation of the Lord's Prayer, as well as the reading of passages from the Bible in the public schools, can and may, in the near future be declared unconstitutional. We wonder, therefore, whether it is not time for provident leaders of American Judaism to ask their more militant colleagues whether what is gained through the courts by some victories is worth the breakdown of community relations which will inevitably follow them. What will have been accomplished if our Jewish friends win all the legal immunities they seek, but thereby paint themselves into a corner of social and cultural alienation? The time has come for these fellow citizens to decide among themselves precisely what they conceive to be the final objective of the Jewish community in the United States—in a word, what bargain they are willing to strike as one of the minorities in a pluralistic society. When victories produce only a harvest of fear and distrust, will it all have been worth-while?"

*The Christian Century*, reacted sharply. In an editorial entitled, "Is *America* Trying to Bully the Jews?" *The Christian Century* called the *America* editorial "a thinly veiled threat" whose purpose "seems to be to frighten Jews into deserting Protestants and other Americans who support the Supreme Court's ruling." The editorial then continued: "Along with 'certain other groups with doctrinaire views on the meaning and application of the principle of separation of church and state,' the American Jewish Congress and its general counsel, Leo Pfeffer, are cited by *America* as responsible for the court's decision. . . . Do the editors of *America* mean to imply that the only way Jews will be able to forestall anti-Semitic attacks is to maintain silence on issues involving the constitutional liberties of all citizens, including Jews? If so, they are guilty of an attempt to bully a segment of our population as part of a general assault on the liberties of all Americans. . . . We hope and believe that the American Jewish Congress and its distinguished counsel will persist in using all legal means to uphold liberties which they will continue to share with all Americans so long as the repressive spirit that informs the *America* editorial is resisted with courage."

Two weeks after the initial editorial appeared, *America* published a second editorial on the subject. In this editorial, entitled, "The Main Issue," the editors said: "This fall the Supreme Court will rule on a number of cases relative to religious practices in the schools. If, as they are now bending every effort to do, Leo Pfeffer and his fellow campaigners succeed in winning Supreme Court decisions that strike down the Lord's Prayer and Bible reading in school classrooms, there will be once again—as there was at the time of the Engel decision, only more so—an intensely unfavorable public reaction. When and if such decisions are handed down, then unless it has been made clear that Dr. Pfeffer and the American Jewish Congress do not speak for the whole of American Jewry, Jews in general will be unfairly blamed for what in fact will have been accomplished by a mere handful of militants, allied with an assortment of humanist groups, ethical culturists, Unitarians, secularists and atheists."

It should not, however, be assumed that *The Christian Century* was the only non-Jewish voice raised in support of the decision. The Reverend Dr. Martin Luther King, revered Negro leader who was later to win the Nobel Peace Prize, called it "a sound and good decision reaffirming something that is basic in our Constitution, namely, separation of church and state." A group of Protestant leaders, including the dean of Harvard Divinity School, joined in a statement supporting the decision. Support, too, came from the Joint Baptist Committee on Public Affairs and from the United Church of Christ. The reaction of American Jewry was, as could be expected, wholly favorable to the decision.

## THE SCHEMPP-MURRAY CASES

Thus the situation stood when the Schempp and Murray cases reached the Supreme Court. In the former case, the Unitarian parents of children in the public schools of Abington Township, a suburb of Philadelphia, brought suit in a Federal court to declare unconstitutional a Pennsylvania statute requiring the reading without comment of ten verses from the Holy Bible on the opening of public school each day. The statute provided for the excuse from participation or attendance of any child at the written request of his parent or guardian.

At the trial it was shown that each morning, in the particular high school attended by the plaintiff's children, the Bible reading exercises were broadcast into each homeroom through an intercommunication system. This was followed by recitation of the Lord's Prayer, in which the students were asked to join. The exercises were closed with the flag salute and announcements of various kinds relating to school activities. The evidence showed that, although the school furnished only the King James (Protestant) version of the Bible, the student selected to do the reading could use a different version, and at times the Douay (Catholic) and Jewish versions were used. There were no prefatory statements, no questions asked or solicited, no comments or explanations made, and no interpretation given at or during the exercises. The students and parents were advised that the students might absent themselves from the classroom if they so elected. The plaintiff testified that the literal reading of the Bible was contrary to his religious beliefs and teachings, but that he did not seek to have his children excused because he felt their relationships with their teachers and classmates would be adversely affected.

Expert testimony was introduced at the trial by both sides. On behalf of the plaintiff, Dr. Solomon Grayzel, editor of the Jewish Publication Society which published the Jewish translations of the Bible, testified that there were marked differences between the

469

Jewish Holy Scriptures and the Christian Holy Bible, and that the latter was deemed sectarian and unacceptable to Jews. For the defendants, testimony was given by Dr. Luther A. Weigle, formerly dean of Yale Divinity College, to the effect that the Bible was "nonsectarian" within the Christian faith.

The trial court, consisting of three judges, unanimously held that the reading of the verses, even without comment, possessed a devotional and religious character, and constituted in effect a religious observance. The practice was therefore held unconstitutional and its discontinuance decreed.

In the Murray case no statute was involved. The suit, brought by Mrs. Madalyn Murray, an avowed atheist, challenged the daily Bible reading and Lord's Prayer recitation which had been practiced in the Baltimore public schools pursuant to a rule promulgated in 1905 by the city board of school commissioners. No trial was held in the Murray case; the Maryland trial court dismissed the complaint and the state's highest court, by a vote of four to three, upheld the dismissal. The two cases, Abington School District vs. Schempp and Murray vs. Curlett, were presented to the Supreme Court together and a single opinion[76] was handed down in June 1963. The opinion was written by Justice Clark, and was concurred in by all the other members of the Court except Justice Stewart.

It is true, said Justice Clark, that religion has been closely identified with our history and government. The fact that the Founding Fathers believed devotedly that there was a God and that the inalienable rights of man were rooted in Him is clearly evidenced in their writings, from the Mayflower Compact to the Constitution itself. Today our oaths of office, from the President's to an alderman's, end with the supplication "So help me God." Congress opens with a prayer, and the crier of the Supreme Court itself invokes the grace of God in declaring the sessions of the Court open. Some 64% of Americans have church membership and only 3% profess no religion whatever.

However, the opinion continued, it is equally true that religious freedom is imbedded in our public and private life. Freedom to worship was indispensable in a country whose people came from the four quarters of the earth and brought with them a diversity of religious opinions. Under this ideal of religious freedom it has long been recognized that government must be neutral and, while protecting all, must prefer none and disparage none.

The Court's opinion then examined the various earlier decisions interpreting the provision in the First Amendment that "Congress shall make no law respecting an establishment of religion or prohibiting the free exercise thereof." As early as 1940 the Court had stated in the case of Cantwell vs. Connecticut that the "fundamental concept of liberty" protected against state infringement by the Fourteenth Amendment embraces the liberties guaranteed by the First Amendment, including the provision against establishment or prohibition of the free exercise of religion. A large number of cases since then repeatedly held that the ban against establishment is applicable against the states as it is against the Federal government, and this principle was again reaffirmed in this case.

Reaffirmed too was the Court's rejection of the contention that the Establishment Clause forbids only governmental preference of one religion over another. Ever since the Everson case of 1947, it has been the law that under the First Amendment "neither a state nor the Federal government can pass laws which aid one religion, aid all religions, or prefer one religion over another." In the light of the Court's consistent interpretation of the clause, the opinion said, the contentions of those who question their history, logic, and efficacy, "seem entirely untenable and of value only as academic exercises."

There is, the Court's opinion continued, an overlapping between the nonestablishment and Free Exercise clauses of the Amendment.

> ... The Establishment Clause has been directly considered by this Court eight times in the past score of years and, with only one Justice dissenting on the point, it has consistently held that the clause withdrew all legislative power respecting religious belief or the expression thereof. The test may be stated as follows: what are the purpose and the primary effect of the enactment? If either is the advancement or inhibition of religion then the enactment exceeds the scope of legislative power as circumscribed by the Constitution. That is to say that to withstand the strictures of the Establishment Clause there must be a secular legislative purpose and a primary effect that neither advances nor inhibits religion. ... The Free Exercise Clause, likewise considered many times there, withdraws from legislative power, state and federal, the exertion of any restraint on the free exercise of religion. Its purpose is to secure religious liberty in the individual by prohibiting any invasions thereof by civil authority. Hence it is necessary in a free exercise case for one to show the coercive effect of the enactment as it operates against him in the practice of his religion. The distinction between the two clauses is apparent—a violation of the Free Exercise Clause is predicated on coercion while the Establishment Clause violation need not be so attended.

Applying these principles to the cases before it, the Court found that, since the challenged exercises were of a religious character,

471

they were unconstitutional as was the statute that required them. Religious exercises that are prescribed as part of the curricular activities of students who are required by law to attend school violate the First Amendment's ban on laws respecting an establishment of religion.

In the Maryland case it was argued by the school authorities that (unlike the finding of the trial court in the Pennsylvania case) the purpose of the morning program was not religious but secular, in that it sought to promote moral values, contradict the materialistic trends of our times, perpetutate our institutions, and teach literature. But, Justice Clark said, "even if its purpose is not strictly religious, it is sought to be accomplished through readings, without comment, from the Bible. Surely the place of the Bible as an instrument of religion cannot be gainsaid, and the State's recognition of the pervading religious character of the ceremony is evident from the rule's specific permission of the alternative use of the Catholic Douay version as well as the recent amendment permitting nonattendance at the exercises. None of these factors is consistent with the contention that the Bible is here used either an an instrument for non-religious moral inspiration or as a reference for the teaching of secular subjects."

The invalidity of the practices was not mitigated by the fact that individual students might absent themselves upon parental request, for that fact is no defense to a challenge under the Establishment Clause. Nor was it a defense that the religious practices here might be relatively minor encroachments on the First Amendment. "The breach of neutrality that is today a trickling stream may all too soon become a raging torrent and, in the words of Madison, 'it is proper to take alarm at the first experiment on our liberties.'"

The banning of religious exercises did not establish a "religion of secularism," nor did it manifest a hostility to religion. Nor did this decision mean that the study of the Bible for its literary and historic qualities, or the study of religion presented objectively as part of a secular program of education, would necessarily violate the First Amendment. What were banned by this decision were only "religious exercises, required by the States in violation of the command of the First Amendment that the Government maintain strict neutrality, neither aiding nor opposing religion."

Finally, the Court's opinion rejected the contention that the concept of neutrality, which did not permit a state to require a religious exercise even with the consent of the majority of those affected, collided with the majority's right to the free exercise of religion. The

Free Exercise Clause has never meant that a majority could use the machinery of the state to practice its beliefs. Freedom of worship is not dependent upon the outcome of any election.

"The place of religion in our society," the opinion concluded, "is an exalted one, achieved through a long tradition of reliance on the home, the church and the inviolable citadel of the individual heart and mind. We have come to recognize through bitter experience that it is not within the power of government to invade that citadel, whether its purpose or effect be to aid or oppose, to advance or retard. In the relationship between man and religion, the State is firmly committed to a position of neutrality."

## THE REACTION TO SCHEMPP-MURRAY

What is perhaps most significant about the reaction to the Schempp-Murray decision was its relative mildness, that is, relative when compared with the response that greeted the Regents' prayer decision a year earlier. Considering the fact that unlike the Regents' prayer decision, which dealt with a practice that existed in only ten percent of the schools in one state (New York), the Schempp-Murray decision affected practices in perhaps half the public schools of the nation, the critical reaction it evoked was remarkably moderate, characterized more by sorrowful resignation than outraged defiance.

Few significant sociopolitical phenomena can be adequately explained by one cause, and undoubtedly many factors were responsible for the mildness of the reaction. One of these was the circumstance that at the time the decision was handed down the nation was engulfed in the civil rights crisis, in respect to which church-state issues were of secondary importance. A second was the fact that in view of the earlier Regents' prayer decision, the Schempp-Murray ruling was, if not inevitable, certainly universally expected and came almost as an anticlimax. Third, and by no means least in importance, was the fact that the pro-separation forces had used to good purpose the twelve months intervening between the two decisions. During this period the American people had the benefit of a concentrated education in the meaning of the First Amendment's guaranty of religious freedom and church-state separation and its relationship to public education unprecedented in the history of our country.

The reaction to the decision can in a sense be said to have begun even before the decision was handed down. For a number of statements from important opinion moulders were issued prior to the

473

decision on the assumption that the decision would be what it in fact turned out to be—an out-and-out invalidation of devotional Bible reading and Lord's Prayer recitation in the public schools. Three months before the decision was announced, Dr. C. Emanuel Carlson, executive director of the Baptist Joint Committee on Public Affairs, with which are affiliated more than 17 million Baptists, declared that the Baptists oppose the use of the Bible for devotional purposes in the public schools.[77] Equally important was the adoption in May of an overall statement on church and state by the General Assembly of the United Presbyterian Church. The statement, an uncompromising affirmance of the principle of church-state separation with all its implications and consequences, stated unequivocally that: "Religious observances [should] never be held in a public school or introduced into the program of the public school. Bible reading (except in connection with courses in literature, history or related subjects) and public prayers tend toward indoctrination or meaningless ritual and should be omitted for both reasons."[78]

Not quite as forthright, yet far more important because of its source, was the policy statement, "The Churches and the Public Schools," adopted by the General Board of the National Council of Churches on June 7, exactly ten days before the decision in Schempp-Murray was handed down. On the use of the Bible in the public schools, the statement had the following to say:

> The full treatment of some regular school subjects requires the use of the Bible as a source book. In such studies—including those related to character development—the use of the Bible has a valid educational purpose. But neither true religion nor good education is dependent upon the devotional use of the Bible in the public school program.[79]

The significance of this pronouncement was not negated by the fact that the non-Protestant constituent of the National Council, the Greek Orthodox Church, disclaimed and disassociated itself from it.

But perhaps most significant of all was the action of the Jesuit national weekly, *America*. Its condemnation of the Regents' prayer decision had been among the most bitter, and before the Schempp-Murray decision was handed down, it published an editorial indicating its expectation (with so many others) that Bible reading and Lord's Prayer recitation would be declared unconstitutional. While it was (mildly) critical of this expected ruling, it asserted forcefully its opposition to any effort to amend the Constitution to overrule it. The First Amendment, it said, should for all practical purposes be deemed unamendable.[80]

Thus, when the decision was announced, it did not appear surprising that there was considerable support for it, not merely from Jewish sources (which was to be expected) but from Protestants as well. However, it should by no means be assumed that there was no hostile Protestant reaction. Bishop Fred Pierce Corson, president of the World Methodist Council, expressed the belief that the ruling "penalized religious people who are very definitely in the majority in the United States."[81] Episcopal Bishop James A. Pike of California claimed that the decision imposed "secularism by default" on the public school system.[82] Dr. Robert A. Cooke, president of the fundamentalist National Association of Evangelicals, called the decision a "sad departure from the nation's heritage under God" which "opens the door for the full establishment of secularism as a negative form of religion."[83] The evangelist, Rev. Billy Graham, said that he was shocked by the decision, which he called a penalty for the "eighty percent" of Americans who "want Bible reading and prayer in the school." These voices, influential as they were, were nevertheless in the minority, and when it is realized that American Protestantism had been committed to Bible reading in the public schools from the day that the first public school was opened, it can be seen that this dramatic change of position on the part of Protestantism was remarkable indeed.

Catholic reaction was on the whole hostile. On the day that the Schempp-Murray decision was announced, the five American Cardinals were in Rome preparing to participate in the election of a successor to Pope John XXIII. Before entering the consistory, three of the five commented on the decision. Cardinal McIntyre of Los Angeles stated that it could "only mean that our American heritage of philosophy, of religion and of freedom are being abandoned in imitation of Soviet philosophy, of Soviet materialism and of Soviet-regimented liberty."[84] Cardinal Cushing of Boston declared that "the Communists are enjoying this day," and that he deemed it to be "a great tragedy that the greatest book that was ever published cannot be read in the public system of education."[85] (This, of course, the decision did *not* hold; it outlawed only *devotional* reading of the Bible.) Cardinal Spellman of New York, after deploring the decision as a victory for secularism and setback for the national welfare, asserted that "no one who believes in God can approve such a decision."[86] None of these statements was surprising, either in content or in tenor. What was more significant was that the other two American Cardinals, Albert Meyer of Chicago and Joseph Ritter of St. Louis, refused to comment on the decision, although requested to do so by the same newspapermen who interviewed the other three Cardinals.[87] In fact, Cardinal Ritter had earlier joined the president of the St. Louis Church Federation and the president of the city's rabbinical association in a statement that all persons committed to law "must support the United States Supreme Court and obey its decisions whether they will meet with our approval or not."[88]

On the whole, however, the reaction of American Catholics was closer to that of the three Cardinals than of Cardinal Ritter, although the general tone was somewhat softer than theirs or than that which had greeted the Regents' prayer decision. Archbishop Patrick A. O'Boyle, chairman of the administrative board of the National Catholic Welfare Conference, called the decision "disappointing." Picking up a theme that had been prominent a year earlier, he added that "In democratic life the tyranny of the few is always a temporary victory; it may be uncomfortable, but its fortunes will be ultimately reversed."[89] The Reverend Thurston N. Davis, S. J., editor-in-chief of *America,* said that most American Catholics consider that a grave injury was done to public education by the decision, "an injury which will affect an overwhelming majority of those Americans who choose to entrust the education of the children to the public schools." Editorially, *America* struck a note that was to be repeated often from Catholic sources: "Now that the decision is made, we insist on its clear and logical corollary: equal aid to all schools."[90]

As in the case of the Regents' prayer decision, the major opinion-moulders in the general press reacted favorably to the Schempp-Murray ruling. Typical of these was the New York *Times* editorial, which concluded that "Far from interfering with freedom of religion, the Supreme Court decision helps to guarantee it."[91] Among the less prominent local newspapers, opinion was divided as it had been a year earlier; but whereas the majority opinion throughout the nation appeared to have been unfavorable to the Regents' prayer decision, the situation was now reversed and the majority seemed favorable to Schempp-Murray. And this too testified to a change which was quite remarkable.

## THE BECKER AMENDMENT[92]

It is not unusual for controversial Supreme Court decisions to evoke demands for constitutional amendment. Quite often bills are introduced into Congress for that purpose. But in most cases these are recognized as being purely for public relations back home. They are not taken too seriously and are soon forgotten. It was therefore not surprising that after the Supreme Court's ruling in 1962 in Engel vs. Vitale, and again after its ruling a year later in the Schempp-

Murray decision, 111 Congressmen in all introduced 150 separate measures to amend the Constitution so as to permit prayer recitation, Bible reading, or both in the public schools.[93] But for the singular persistence of Congressman Frank Becker of New York, it is quite likely that these many proposals and the entire effort would have quickly been forgotten.

Becker, however, undertook a one-man crusade to assure that the effort would succeed. First, he prevailed upon the Congressmen who had introduced separate measures to join on one single bill.[94] After this new measure was referred to the House Judiciary Committee, Becker began rounding up signatures to a petition for its discharge so that it might be voted on by the House. Ironically, Becker himself had before always refused to sign discharge petitions, including those for civil rights bills aimed at achieving equality for Negroes and other racial minorities. The reason for the difference, Becker explained, was that all other discharge petitions "dealt with material things and material benefits. This one deals only with the spiritual. The urgency of this matter leaves no alternative if we are to prevent the advocates of a godless society to accomplish in the United States that which the Communists have accomplished in Soviet Russia."

The proposed amendment (H.J. Res. 693, 88th Congress) agreed to by the various Congressmen read as follows:

SECTION 1. Nothing in this Constitution shall be deemed to prohibit the offering, reading from or listening to prayers or Biblical Scriptures, if participation therein is on a voluntary basis, in any governmental or public school, institution, or place.

SECTION 2. Nothing in this Constitution shall be deemed to prohibit making reference to belief in, reliance upon, or invoking the aid of God or a Supreme Being, in any governmental or public document, proceeding, activity, ceremony, school, institution, or place or upon any coinage, currency, or obligation of the United States.

SECTION 3. Nothing in this Article shall constitute an establishment of religion.

Becker was able to obtain about 160 of the needed 218 signatures, and the chairman of the House Judiciary Committee, Congressman Emanuel Celler of New York, though personally opposed to the measure, found it expedient to open public hearings on the Becker and similar proposals. It was this that turned the tide, for at these hearings the overwhelming testimony by the leaders of all faiths and by constitutional lawyers strongly opposed any change in the First Amendment. The result was that the Judiciary Committee took no action on the Becker Amendment which passed into the limbo of numberless unsuccessful efforts to amend the Constitution to overrule a particular Supreme Court decision.

## COMPLIANCE WITH THE DECISION[95]

Compliance with the decision in Schempp-Murray outlawing devotional Bible reading and Lord's Prayer recitation appears at the present time to be universal along the Atlantic Coast north of the Mason-Dixon line and along the Pacific Coast. Undoubtedly, long-standing practices are being continued in some rural districts and even in individual schools in large cities, but there seems to be no open defiance of the decision on the part of any official of a state or a major city. Moreover, where defiance by local school authorities is brought to the attention of the state authorities, the latter appear to take prompt and generally effective action (including the institution of legal proceedings as in New Jersey and Massachusetts) to effect compliance with the Supreme Court's decision. On the whole, the attitude of state and local authorities in these states where Bible reading and prayer recitation were long-standing practices was summarized by Gov. John H. Chafee of Rhode Island in stating that though "unfortunate" the Supreme Court's ban must be obeyed.

In the midwest, too, compliance with the Schempp decision has been the rule rather than the exception. Open defiance by state officials or public school authorities in large cities is rare. On the other hand, noncompliance (rather than announced defiance) with the ban may be fairly widespread among small towns and villages in rural districts in the midwest, or in any event considerably more widespread than along the Atlantic and Pacific Coasts.

In the south, the pattern appears to be one not merely of noncompliance, but often of open defiance. The reason for this is partly the fact that religious practices such as Bible reading and prayer recitation have been far more widespread in the south than in any other part of the country, and partly the south's hostility to and defiance of the Supreme Court's decision in the School Segregation Case. But even here, reluctant compliance is slowly becoming manifest, at least in the large cities, such as Miami and Atlanta. All in all, it appears to be only a question of time before nationwide compliance will be achieved, and the practice of public school sponsored Bible reading and prayer recitation will no longer be a current practice but a matter of history.

### CHAPTER TWELVE

# Religious Practices in the Public School

## HOLY DAY CELEBRATIONS

FEW ACTIVITES in the public school are as widespread and long-standing as the annual Christmas celebration. The spirit of joy and good cheer that pervades the home, church, and department store at the approach of December 25th enters the public school classroom with all its spirit and enthusiasm. The children prepare costumes for the Christmas play, dress up the Christmas tree, and rehearse "Silent Night" and "O Little Town of Bethlehem." Forgotten now are the petty quarrels and the occasional bitterness and misunderstanding arising out of incidents in the operation of the released-time program, or the opening of a large new parochial school opposite the rather dilapidated public school building, or the passing by a public school bus of a Catholic child going to parochial school. Everywhere there is gladness, peace on earth, and good will toward all.

Into this atmosphere of joy and serenity Isaac Bildersee, assistant superintendent of schools in Brooklyn, threw a bombshell. On November 24, 1947, he sent a letter to the twenty-three principals in his district—a district from 75 to 90% Jewish in population—that read in part:

> 1. The use of Christmas trees or other inflammable decorations in the class rooms and in any part of the building is prohibited by order of Superintendent Jansen and the Fire Department.
> 2. Christmas and other similar occasions may be celebrated only as seasonal, pre-vacation occurrences. There must not be any references, any dramatization, song or other aspects of the occasion to any religious significance involved. Christmas carols with reference to the nativity may not be sung, nor may decorations include religious symbols of any faith.

When the contents of this letter became public, the heavens fell. Voices of protest came from the National Apostleship of Prayer, the Catholic War Veterans of New York, and the National Conference of Christians and Jews. Episcopal Bishop Charles K. Gilbert called the banning of Christmas carols "distressing," although he admitted that the question was "difficult" and that "naturally, freedom of religion should be observed."[1]

Others found no difficulty in the question. Rev. J. Henry Carpenter, executive secretary of the Brooklyn Division of the Protestant Council of the City of New York, the largest general Protestant organization in the city, and a local leader of the National Conference of Christians and Jews, expressed the view that

> Christmas has been celebrated in the schools of our nation ever since the founding of our great public educational system. It is no time now, when we are fighting materialism and irreligion in the world, to eliminate such celebration from our public educational system.[2]

The Commission on Moral and Civil Affairs of the New York City Protestant Council called Bildersee's order "an anti-religious act."

Rev. Norman Vincent Peale, of the Marble Collegiate Church and later president of the Protestant Council of New York, called the ban "one of the most severe blows interfaith amity has yet received." Kate Smith, nationally known popular singer, denounced Bildersee's order in a nationwide, noontime radio editorial that included such language as:

> .. disgust . . . right from the Moscow book . . . Never in my memory have approximately 135 million Christians of this country been so insulted . . . utterly stupid. . . . If [Bildersee] is still being permitted to occupy his office . . . it is a further insult. . . . He should be barred from any further educational activities until this incident receives a thorough airing.[3]

Dorothy Thompson, prominent columnist, wondered "whether some measures demanded by minorities are not heading toward a dictatorship over the majority." Mayor William O'Dwyer stated that the order "ought to be revoked at once." The New York State Council of the Knights of Columbus called the order "an insult to all Christians," and demanded an immediate investigation.[4]

In the crescendo of fury, a few voices on the other side could be heard—and they came from the expected sources. The American Civil Liberties Union approved Dr. Bildersee's order because its "stand has always been against religious observances in the public schools." The American Jewish Congress expressed itself as "heartily in accord" with the directive because it believed "that the public schools should be free of any celebrations or activities which may embarrass persons of any race or religion and that the principle of the separation of church and state, which is one of the basic concepts of American democracy, must be preserved in the public school system." Rabbi Israel Goldstein, of Congregation B'nai Jeshurun, was of the view that "the public schools should not be a place for any kind of sectarianism."[5] Others who agreed with Bildersee were the United Parents Association, the Teachers Guild, and the New York Board of Rabbis.[6]

These, however, were but voices in the wilderness; the forces on the side of God and Christmas won a quick and conclusive victory. Bildersee's letter became public on December 5. On December 8 it was revoked by Superintendent of Schools William Jansen in a letter, sent to all principals and district superintendents, which sought to calm the storm and restore the serenity that generally accompanies the Yule season:

> We are approaching that happy season of the year when the minds of all men are filled with thoughts of brotherhood and peace, of peace within themselves, peace within their homes, peace within their community, their nation, and the world. As teacher of the young, we are again privileged to place before our children this joyous message and to bring through our daily work brightness and hope into the lives of the school children of New York City. . . .
>
> In the observance of Christmas this year, our schools will, as in the past, present such appropriate programs and exercises as are, in the good judgment of the principal, the teachers, and the participants, suited to the occasion. It is expected, as always, that the principles of freedom of religious worship will be respected.
>
> In the past, people of all faiths have joined in this time of good will and comradeship. That is why there has been a general joining together in the lighting of Christmas trees in public places. . . .
>
> With appreciation of the contribution that all of you have made in the past year to the welfare and happiness of children, I extend to you my best wishes for a Merry Christmas and a hope for a happier year ahead.

It should be noted that Dr. Bildersee's original letter called attention to the fact (not reported in any of the newspaper accounts) that the ban on Christmas trees came from Superintendent Jansen and the Fire Department. Dr. Jansen's reference to "general joining together in the lighting of Christmas trees in public places" did not expressly revoke the ban, yet it is likely that at least some principals construed it as an implicit invitation to bring Christmas trees into the schools.

Dr. Jansen's letter closed the incident. After it was made public and the children in the twenty-three schools under Dr. Bildersee's jurisdiction returned to rehearsing the carols, Dr. Bildersee sought to explain the motives that impelled him to issue his directive. The explanatory statement was made in a letter to Father Genova, the priest of an important Catholic church in the district, who made it public. The letter read:

> Christmas has been established as a national holiday—worldwide among the civilized nations of the Western world—and I should be the last one to ask that the Christmas spirit of good will be in the least abated, or that by the slightest implication its essential spiritual meaning should be denied to children of those faiths who accept it as such.
>
> I had hoped to avoid the hurt to children's feelings that I know has ensued in some instances because they were required to join in the singing of songs that were directly contradictory of their established faiths. I do not believe that any of us would seek to hurt "even the least of these." Similarly, the display of symbols and decorations directly connected with one religion or another has given offense in the past.
>
> I hope that all our principals will afford to all their pupils an opportunity to participate in a festival of good feeling and good will in such a manner as to give happiness to all and offense to none.

Father Genova expressed gratification that the "unfortunate incident" was closed, and declared that Dr. Bildersee and the local school principals had always been "cordially cooperative" with his church.

The incident in Brooklyn involved a school official; two years later an explosive incident occurred in Chelsea, Massachusetts, in which the wrath of the community was visited on two mothers. Chelsea is a suburb of Boston. The population then was about 45% Jewish, 45% Catholic, and the rest Protestant. On December 5, 1949, Mrs. Abraham Wolper presented to the Chelsea School Committee a petition signed by her and another resident of Chelsea, Mrs. Goldie Roller, stating: "This is to respectfully request undersigned to appear before its committee to present our views in reference to the singing of Christmas carols and the presentation of religious pageants." Three years earlier, according to Mrs. Wolper, her seven-year-old son had refused to sing Christmas carols at a Chelsea public school and was consequently put out of the room.[7] Why she waited three years before taking action is not clear; nor is it clear what motivated Mrs. Roller in joining in the petition. Nevertheless it should be noted that the petition did not request the banning of carols or religious pageants; all that was requested was an opportunity to be heard.

When Mrs. Wolper first brought her petition to the office of the superintendent of schools, he asked her (according to Mrs. Wolper) if she really wanted to go through with the petition, observing that the children "don't have to sing if they don't want to," and that he had a problem with his own child in that the Lord's Prayer recited in his school was not the Catholic version, that the law "could not be changed"; that he observed Jewish children hanging around the streets on Jewish high holy days instead of attending services; and that he was considering ordering Saturday public school sessions in view of the precedent for this in thirteen other Massachusetts communities.

Mrs. Wolper persisted; and when her husband brought the petition to the school committee he suggested that the hearing might be held in private, but a member of the committee insisted that the hearing, set for December 15, be open to the public, and the mayor of Chelsea moved that the hearing be advertised in the press. (As it turned out, the hearing was never held; but in view of the publicity the request received not only in the Chelsea and Boston press but even in New York, it would have been a waste of public funds to pay for advertisements.) When reporters questioned Mrs. Wolper, she said that "Jingle Bells" and similar seasonal songs were unobjectionable but that she objected to Christological carols. "This is a happy season for children," she said. "It is wrong for them to have songs which some children feel they cannot sing. It makes my son unhappy when his classmates ask him why he doesn't sing the songs. There are pageants also of a religious nature. Such things should not be in the public schools."

The press immediately took up the issue. The Chelsea *Record* printed a banner headline, "Seek to Ban Singing of Carols in Public School." Boston papers carried similar headlines and slogans. Feelings ran high in Chelsea and Boston. The Wolpers and the Rollers received scores of threatening letters (many from Jews) and anonymous telephone calls. An indignant citizen clipped the Chelsea *Record's* account of the petition and forwarded it to the House Committee on Un-American Activities in Washington. Many letters to the newspapers were written—not a few from leading Jewish citizens, who protested that they were in complete disagreement with the petitioner. A former Congressman and president of the local B'nai B'rith lodge told the press that the Wolpers "do not represent me, my family or any other Jewish person in the city of Chelsea. Their viewpoint is their own and I know hundreds of Jewish persons who deeply regret their attitude." A Jewish alderman wrote to the school board that "as a graduate of the Chelsea schools I have never found the singing of Christmas carols to be in any way objectionable to my religious beliefs."

On December 10 *The Pilot*, official organ of the Catholic archdiocese of Boston—where Tom Wall was beaten into submission a century earlier—published an editorial on the Chelsea affair entitled "Christmas in Chelsea." The editorial so well reflects the tenor of the reaction of the more responsible elements of the community that it merits being set forth here in full:

> "Children, between midnight on Saturday, December 24 and the first moments of December 26 a twenty-four hour period will elapse. This can be figured out from astronomy or from any trustworthy clock if you care to sit and watch it. I am not allowed to suggest that most of the civilized world will observe this period as a special holiday. This is Chelsea, 1949 version, although I am not permitted to tell you from what this 1949 year period is computed."
>
> The above paragraph, we feel, will probably satisfy Mr. and Mrs. Abraham Wolper of 56 Cook Ave., Chelsea, as a suitable classroom reference to the great feast which the rest of the world will celebrate on December 25. These people and some others have petitioned the school board in that city to abandon the singing of Christmas carols and the like in public schools. Most of the Jewish people in that community are properly horrified at this affront to their Christian neighbors, a gesture particularly ill-advised at a moment when religious bigotry in other quarters is having a heyday.
>
> It is hard to believe that the traditional singing of Christmas songs will make many Jewish children "unhappy." It is unlikely that their parents, occupying honored places in American life, would wish to wall them up in an ostrich-like ghetto without recognition of the way of life followed by the majority of those with whom they live.
>
> This disagreeable incident in itself is of no great importance. But its implications are highly unpleasant. If Jewish pressure, for example, were brought to bear on the Jewish merchants of Chelsea and elsewhere to overlook the holiday and refuse to carry Christmas merchandise, with the accompanying decorations and usual promotion, a very real damage might ensue to a friendly and cooperative group of our fellow citizens.

It is highly probable that the not too subtle hint of a boycott of Jewish merchants contained in the last paragraph of the editorial was expressed often and much more directly in Chelsea. It was this consideration that caused the Chelsea *Record* to write on December 8 that

> In fairness to one of Chelsea's finest and most respected citizens *and to his business*, the Chelsea *Record* wishes to make known to all residents of Chelsea that Morris Wolper is in no way identified with the petition which seeks to ban the singing of Christmas carols and the presentation of religious pageants in the public schools.

Morris Wolper himself quickly announced through the press that he was "definitely not in accord with the action of Abraham Wolper, who is no relation and whom [he does] not even know." As a matter of fact—according to one report—he even threatened to sue Abraham Wolper for $10,000 damages.

The intensity of community feeling and the threats of violence caused the Wolpers to leave Chelsea and go into hiding in a neighboring community. Mrs. Roller, the cosigner of the petition, was reported to have become almost hysterical as a result of the numerous telephone calls she received. She protested that she had not examined the petition carefully when she signed it, that she was not even acquainted with the Wolpers, that her rabbi had advised her that she had a moral responsibility to sign it, and that it was her understanding that the petition would bear a thousand names. Finally, on December 10, she wrote to the Chelsea *Record* that she had been "misled and innocently involved in this issue," and announced that she was withdrawing from the petition and from the entire matter.

The Wolpers quickly followed suit. On December 12 they wrote to the superintendent of schools that their objectives had been misinterpreted and that they therefore withdrew their petition. The next day a special meeting of the school committee was called; the Wolper and Roller letters were read, and the public hearing was canceled.

So ended the Chelsea affair. Two weeks later the children in the public schools of the city were singing Christmas carols and hymns lustily; probably the Wolper and Roller children were singing even more lustily than their classmates. But whether they were singing out of love or out of fear is a question no one can answer.

The Bildersee and Chelsea incidents were unfortunately not unique. In Camden, New Jersey, an agreement between the local Jewish Community Council and the public school authorities was entered into under which a directive was issued to all principals of the city public schools permitting Jewish children to abstain without penalty from participating in Christmas pageants and carol singing. One of the schoolteachers read the letter to her class, with sarcastic comments about "American democracy," and refused to permit the singing of Christmas carols in her classes because of the effort involved in dismissing the Jewish pupils before the singing got under way. One teacher asked the Jewish children to go to another room while the non-Jewish children went to the auditorium for carol singing. In another school a Jewish child—a member of the choir singing Christmas carols—refused to utter the words "Jesus Christ," but the teacher requested her to leave the choir if she did not utter every word.[8] Some opposition came from enraged Jewish parents, who protested that they felt that no harm had come to their children during the many years of Christmas celebrations in classroom; that the action of the Jewish Community Council had served only to set Jewish children apart from their non-Jewish classmates; and that it added fuel to anti-Semitism.[9]

In Toronto in December 1950 a sermon by Rabbi A. L. Feinberg, in which he expressed the view that Christological holiday observances had no place in a public school attended by children of all faiths, evoked a host of acrimonious editorials in the Canadian press—almost all to the effect that Canada is a Christian country. A number of other rabbis in Toronto hastened to disassociate themselves from the statement; and Rabbi Feinberg himself issued an explanatory statement amounting in effect to a retraction.[10] A similar incident occurred the following year in Westbury, Connecticut. In Suffern, New York, bitterness was evoked in December 1950 by an objection on the part of the local rabbi to religious carols.[11] In Lynbrook, Long Island, in 1951 the local school superintendent directed the discontinuance of such carols; but the board of education overruled him after protests from a group of parents led by the pastor of the Lutheran Church, who stated that "Things have not changed so in our country that we must change the tradition of Christianity."[12]

In White Plains, New York, 1,200 persons gathered at the December 1950 monthly meeting of the board of education—rarely attended by more than 50—and vociferously demanded the revocation of a decision by the superintendent of schools that dropped Nativity plays from the Christmas programs in the public schools. The meeting followed a resolution by the local Holy Name societies condemning the action, and the circulation of a petition that began "The undersigned Christian students . . . demand the return of the Nativity play." An open meeting of the board on the question was held, because the Catholic monsignor refused to attend a closed meeting of religious leaders requested by the superintendent. (The Protestant and Jewish clergymen expressed their willingness to attend.) It was also reported that on the Sunday before the board meeting, at all Catholic masses in the city, the parishioners were instructed that it was their duty to present their views to the school board. Observers who attended the meeting could not help sensing an undercurrent of almost hysterical bitterness against the Jewish community who were held responsible for the ban—even though many of the speakers attested to their great admiration and affection for their Jewish neighbors, and concentrated their attack on the school board and the superintendent (all of whom were Protestant), with frequent criticisms of "progressive education" and an occasional sneer at the entire concept of public education. There were only two non-Catholic speakers at the meeting, both Protestants, and both appealed for moderation, suggesting that the problem needed consideration. At the end of the meeting the board voted unanimously to revoke the ban and permit Nativity plays as in the past. (Shortly after the meeting, the term of one member of the board expired. For the first time in many years, a Catholic candidate was named to oppose him. After a campaign marked by Protestant-Catholic bitterness, the Catholic candidate won.)[13]

These incidents have all concerned Christmas celebrations, principally because Easter celebrations in the public schools—where they are held—are largely of the "bunny" and "Easter egg" type. There is, however, a discernible movement to desecularize these celebrations and infuse them with a real religious content. In view of the association of Easter with the crucifixion, the explosive potentialities of such celebrations in neighborhoods with substantial Jewish school populations give much cause for concern.

One case history will be sufficient to illustrate this. It concerned Dade County, consisting of the cities of Miami and Miami Beach in Florida.[14] Miami is a large southern city, overwhelmingly Protestant and in many respects still something of the typical "Bible belt" community. Miami Beach, on the other hand, is considerably smaller and newer, whose population is largely middle class Jewish.

The two cities share a single county and educational system. As Jewish families from northern cities, particularly New York, moved to Miami Beach in increasing numbers, they found the public schools permeated with typical Protestant practices, such as Bible reading, Lord's Prayer recitation, and morning devotionals. As the Jewish residents grew more numerous they became increasingly restive and many complaints were made to the school authorities, all to no avail.

One specific incident in 1958 was particularly disturbing to the Jewish community. The usual practice in the schools was to open each day with a morning devotional. This consisted of reading several verses from the Bible, recitation of the Lord's Prayer and of the Pledge of Allegiance to the flag, and a short "inspirational message." The last was usually prepared and delivered by a student under the supervision of his teacher. On occasions, however, a local or visiting clergyman would be invited to deliver the "message."

On one morning in 1958, the students in one predominantly

Jewish public school in Miami Beach were startled to hear over the public address system, which piped the devotionals into the various homerooms, a fundamentalist sermon by a visiting clergyman warning them that they would suffer eternal damnation in a fiery hell unless they confessed Christ. This incident convinced a number of Jewish parents that litigation was the only resource available to meet the situation.

At about the same time, Harlow Chamberlin, an avowed atheist and parent of a child in the Dade County school system, reached the same conclusion, and, with the aid of the American Civil Liberties Union, instituted a suit to bring a halt to the religious practices. The Jewish parents, joined by a Unitarian, brought a similar suit with the aid of the American Jewish Congress. The two suits were joined and presented together.

The plaintiffs challenged a number of practices, including Bible reading, prayer recitation, Christmas, Hanukah, and Easter celebrations, use of religious films in public school instruction, religious baccalaureate programs, and religious tests for qualification and promotion of teachers. After a long trial, the court upheld the practice of Bible reading and prayer recitation, dismissed for technical reasons some of the other objections, and declared unconstitutional the holy day celebrations, the exhibition of religious films, and free use of public school premises for after-hour Bible classes.

The practice which aroused the most objection was the annual Easter program, conducted in a number of junior and senior high schools on the Thursday immediately preceding Good Friday. The high point of the program was the performance of what (for reasons which will shortly become apparent) was known among teachers as the "ketchup" play.

The evidence as to this was presented by former pupils at the schools. (Counsel for the plaintiffs avoided calling as witnesses children who were still attending school in the county.) The accuracy of the testimony was challenged by the defendants only in respect to one fact. The pupils testified that attendance at the program was compulsory; the school officials testified that if any child presented a written request by his parent that he be excused from attending, it would have been respected, but no child brought such a request.

The testimony showed that some time early in the morning session, the regular teaching was suspended and the children were marched down to the school auditorium. There they were seated, and the school chorus, dressed in choir robes, marched slowly down the two side aisles carrying lighted candles and singing hymns appropriate to Easter. The candles and the auditorium lights were then extinguished, and a spotlight from the rear shone at the center of the stage. To the accompaniment of solemn music, the curtains then parted to reveal a stage completely bare except for one object in the center at which the spotlight was focused. This was a large wooden cross and on it was the body of a boy, naked except for some sheeting around his loin. He was an extremely lean boy, so lean—according to the testimony of one pupil—that the spotlight focusing on him enabled the audience to see his bones, as in an X ray. The boy's hair was long, almost to his shoulders, and his wrists were tied to the arms of the cross. From his palms and one side of his body there flowed what appeared to be blood, but was later identified by school authorities as ketchup.

The music died down; the auditorium was silent; and then, from one side of the stage the voice of a boy was heard reading from a Bible on a lamplighted lectern a verse from the New Testament account of the trial, passion, and crucifixion of Jesus. (The witnesses were unable to identify which of the four Gospels was used.) As the boy finished reading, a girl's voice was heard from the other side of the stage, reading the next verse, and thus they alternated verse for verse.

As each verse was read, the boy on the cross acted it out in pantomime. For example, when the verse describing the placing of a crown of thorns on the head of Jesus was read, the boy on the cross writhed as if in pain and discomfort, seeking to throw off the thorns from his head.

During the entire reading, the boy on the cross made no sound. Finally, the verse was read in which Jesus gave up the ghost and died. At this point, the boy on the cross broke his silence, emitted a deep moan as of the agony of death, and let his head drop to one side—arms still outstretched, with wrists tied to the cross, in the classic depiction of Jesus on the cross.

Then—as one pupil testified—"the curtain came down, we were marched back to our class and went back to our mathematics lessons."

It must be added that the Dade County school superintendent had no knowledge of the "ketchup play" program. As soon as the testimony was presented in court, and without waiting for any decision by the judge, he ordered the program to be dropped immediately. Nevertheless, the program had been going on for a number of years, had spread from school to school, and, though repulsive to many students—non-Jewish as well as Jewish—was not considered in the least objectionable by the teachers. But for the institution of the lawsuit, the program would in all probability have been continued to the present time.

On the basis of the Holy Day incidents summarized here, this writer offers the following observations:

(1) No non-Jew has the moral right to act on the assertion that it will not harm the Jewish child to sing Christological carols or participate in Nativity or Crucifixion plays. No non-Jew can rightfully assume that no Jewish child, no matter what his religious background is, will suffer psychological hurt from singing "Come, let us adore Him, Christ the Lord," or "Born is the King of Israel." Nor can any non-Jew rightfully assert that such singing will not violate the Jewish child's religious conscience, any more than the school principals in the 19th century could rightfully assert that the Catholic child's religious conscience would not be violated by reading from the King James Bible. Such a decision can be made only by the child, his parents, and his spiritual adviser.

(2) It is not a sufficient answer to say that the Jewish child need not join in the singing or the pageant if he does not want to. It is unfair and unconscionable to place on the child the burden of isolating himself from his classmates, to stand alone during the festivities and the preparations for them—which in many schools occupy practically all the school time in December.

Nor is it a sufficient answer to say that the minority must yield to the desires of the majority. In the first place, in Dr. Bildersee's district, in Chelsea, where many of the Catholic children attended parochial schools, and in Miami Beach the Jewish children were in the majority. In the second place—and far more important—unless we abandon the idea of a nonsectarian common school open on equal terms to children of all faiths, the terms "majority" and "minority" have no relevance in matters of religion.

(3) It would be fatuous to believe that Christmas can be banished from the public school. It is as much part of the American school culture as Thanksgiving and graduation day. Nor has anyone seriously proposed that it should be banished. All that has been urged is that the deeply Christological elements of the celebration be kept for the church and the home and not brought into the public school. The letter sent to all principals by the superintendent of schools of Cleveland Heights, Ohio, in November 1951 illustrates this point:

## Observance of the Christmas Holiday Season

The primary purpose of the school program of intercultural education is to provide activities and a school environment designed to foster understanding and appreciation of the worth and dignity of the individual of whatever religion or creed, and to lessen tensions and prejudice. Observance of the Holiday season should contribute to this purpose, while maintaining the firmly established American principle of separation of church and state.

The following broad statement of policy is presented as a general guide to principals in planning Christmas programs and activities sponsored by the school.

1. The emphasis should be centered on the cultural aspects of the season.

2. Material for classroom projects and assembly programs should be selected with understanding consideration of the culture, religious background, and training of the pupils involved.

3. All activities should make a positive contribution to a total school environment that respects the traditions and religious teachings of all pupils, and that develops appreciation of the cultural background of all groups.

4. The choice of activities and of material for programs may vary in different schools within the system; however, the activities in each school should be in good taste such that they can be accepted by all without embarrassment; thus the program will contribute to democratic living.

(4) Such a program is subject to the oft-voiced criticism that it takes Christ out of Christmas and secularizes the day most holy to all Christians. Christian religious leaders—Protestant almost as much as Catholic—are deeply concerned about the secularization of Christmas. Jews are particularly vulnerable on this score. A large part of the retail trade that flourishes in the pre-Christmas period is Jewish-owned, and these Jewish merchants have an economic stake in a Christmas whose concentration is on the exchange of gifts. Nevertheless, Christian leaders cannot logically have it both ways. They cannot assert—as so many do—that Christmas belongs in the public school because it has become a national or cultural holiday, and at the same time deplore its national and cultural character and urge its greater religiosity.

(5) The above-related incidents, interreligious "dialogues," and the Supreme Court decisions on religion in the public schools have combined to make Christian clergymen and public educators conscious that a problem does exist, and have modified the views of both groups on the question. Typical of the trend, although undoubtedly still ahead of the present Protestant consensus, is the following from the statement "Relations Between Church and State in

the United States," adopted by the 175th General Assembly of the United Presbyterian Church in the United States:

> The Special Committee on Church and State *recommends* that:
> a. Churches recognize the administration of religious training and observance as the domain of church and family.
> b. United Presbyterians actively strive to recapture from popular custom the observance of religious holidays in order to restore their deepest religious meaning.
> c. Since the association of seasonal activities with religious holidays in the public schools tends to pervert their religious significance, such association be discouraged as foreign to the purpose of the public school.
> d. Religious holidays be acknowledged and explained, but never celebrated religiously, by public schools or their administrators when acting in an official capacity.
> e. Whenever possible, students of various religious faiths should be allowed sufficient time to permit the celebration of their religious observances away from public school property.
> f. Religious observances should never be held in a public school or introduced into the public school as part of tis program.

Illustrative of the views of public educators is the following from the Report "Religion in the Public Schools," issued June 30, 1964, by the Commission on Religion in the Public Schools of the American Association of School Administrators:

> The Commission recommends the policy that encourages reasonable recognition of Christmas in the schools in the spirit of exposition of the differing rites and customs of families, cultures, and creeds—each with deep meaning for its adherents, and in sum revealing the many different religious, philosophical, and cultural practices and beliefs held by Americans.
> The public schools are and of a right should be responsive to their communities, within constitutional and other relevant limits. But they also have uniquely the commitment to teach the meaning, the obligations, and the rights of citizenship, including the necessity for protection against the establishment of religion and against intrusion on the religious freedoms of any and all citizens in the United States. In such a context, the Christmas in the schools becomes a manageable problem and a potential asset.

(6) Above all, there is a crying need for understanding on all sides and a dispassionate approach to the problem. Christian and Jewish clergymen and parents can work together in numerous civic endeavors all year with harmony and friendliness, but when the problem of holy day celebrations in the public school arises, Madison's phrase again becomes appropriate:

> The very appearance ... has transformed that Christian forbearance, love and charity which of late naturally prevailed, into animosities and jealousies which may not soon be appeased.[15]

## JOINT HOLIDAY CELEBRATIONS

In the past two decades a new approach has been proposed to the solution of the problem of Jewish children and Christmas in the public schools. Perhaps by fortunate coincidence, the month of December in which Christmas occurs is also the month in which is celebrated the Jewish Hanukah, the holiday celebrating the successful revolt of the Maccabeans against the Syrians. It was therefore natural to propose that in districts with substantial Jewish populations Hanukah be brought into the public schools to be celebrated jointly with Christmas. Later the calendar coincidence of Easter and Passover gave rise to the proposal that these two holidays should likewise be celebrated jointly in the public schools. This latter proposal, however, has not yet been urged as strenuously and extensively as the former.

It is not fair to say that the introduction of the proposal for joint Christmas-Hanukah celebrations was motivated by the feeling that since Christmas cannot be taken out of the schools, the Jews are at least entitled to bring Hanukah in. It is nevertheless true that the proposal is strictly Jewish in origin, and that its popularity among Jewish parents is undoubtedly due in large measure to the conviction that Christmas in the schools is here to stay.

The joint holiday celebration proposal is largely the idea of B'nai B'rith, the largest Jewish fraternal organization. Its declared value lies in its nonsectarian nature, and its potentialities for intercultural education. Thus, according to B'nai B'rith:

> A Christmas pageant, with the singing of Christmas carols, is a sectarian observance; it is monist in approach and in a school of ethnically and religiously diversified composition, it cannot fail to make certain groups feel deprived and excluded. But a festival celebration during late December with the singing of Hanukkah *and* Christmas songs — and even better, a Hanukkah-Christmas — and other Festivals that are observed at this time of year celebration — is an intercultural observance; it is universal in approach and in harmony, as no sectarian ceremony could be, with the pluralistic temper of our society.[16]

The Jewish Community Council of Cleveland, which for a number of years promoted joint celebrations, set forth as well as anyone else the philosophy of joint holiday celebrations in the public schools.

> Goodwill does not grow in a vacuum, and no amount of exhortation will prove effective to young people unless concrete symbols and shared experiences are also utilized. The many similar themes of the Hanukkah and Christmas holidays seem to provide a splendid opportunity for building mutual respect among Jewish and Christian students by stressing the common factors in their heritages. Both holidays are

493

times of great joy and goodwill, of sending gifts, of lighting candles; both celebrate the beginning of an era of spiritual cleansing and religious freedom.

This holiday season, therefore, seems to offer a natural opportunity to promote intergroup education. The values of such celebrations — particularly in schools with a significant Jewish enrollment — seem obvious. At their best, they give students a sense of belongingness in their own tradition and a respectful understanding for the other fellow's. What more natural to build on the children's interests, particularly when the holidays have so much in common — merrymaking, lights and candles, excellent stories and songs, strong accent on children's fun? Certainly here is a wonderful opportunity to help children to feel comfortable about cultural differences — the essence of intergroup understanding.[17]

For a while the joint holiday observance proposal was popular among Jewish organizations. More recently, however, practically all the major Jewish organizations have changed their views and today oppose such programs. This position is expressed in a statement of principles entitled "Safeguarding Religious Liberty" issued by the Synagogue Council of America and the National Community Relations Council in the following words:

> Joint religious observances, such as Christmas-Hanukah and Easter-Passover, are in our opinion no less a breach of the principle of separation of church and state and violate the conscience of many religious persons, Jews and Christians alike.

There seems to be no discernible consensus of Protestant church opinion on joint holiday celebrations. Many individual ministers undoubtedly look on the experiment with sympathy — possibly in part because it removes any embarrassment arising out of the singing of Christmas carols and the presentation of Nativity pageants. On the other hand, many other Protestant ministers, particularly Lutherans, are undoubtedly opposed to the experiment.

There is no doubt about the position of the Catholic Church on joint holiday celebrations, at least up to the present. It was expressed in an editorial in the December 17, 1949, issue of the Boston *Pilot*, which said that

> Inter-faith relations gain nothing at all by hodge-podge mixtures of very different observances; the result is not harmony but confusion.

It was expressed in an article in *Information*,[18] published by the Missionary Society of St. Paul the Apostle. The title of the article, "Whose Birthday Is This?" gives a fairly good idea of its tenor.[19] But the most authoritative and detailed statement of the Catholic position on joint holiday celebrations is contained in the January 1946 issue of *The American Ecclesiastical Review*,[20] in an article by a member of the faculty of Catholic University. The article discusses a book called *The Story of the Springfield Plan*,[21] which popularized the intercultural education program. The article discusses in full the aspects in which the Springfield Plan is inconsistent with Catholic religious teachings. It then says:

> There is another reservation we feel must be made regarding the religious aspect of the Springfield Plan as it has been worked out in practice according to the book we are discussing. Pp. 44–47 describe "The Festival of Lights" celebrated in one of the Springfield elementary schools. "As committees met to plan the school Christmas program three years ago," [the authors write], "the point was made that nearly half the children would be left out, since it was not their holy day that was to be celebrated. In view of the fact that the Jewish Channukah also falls in December, the decision was made to combine the observance of the two religious festivals in one program having two parts symbolized by the two lights: Channukah, the candle, and Nativity, the star." In another book about the Springfield Plan[22] there is a photograph of children working on a large poster: "Festival of Lights" runs across the top, while the lower part of the poster is divided into two sections, with (printed in small letters) "Hanukkah the Candle," and "Nativity the Star," each occupying one side. (p. 97) Now we do not for a moment doubt either the good faith or the good intentions of the adults and children who planned this pageant. We are sure that it was effectively and reverently performed by the children who took part in it. But surely it is impossible, on a little reflection, not to have grave doubts about the propriety of such a joint celebration. On Christmas we celebrate the Nativity of the Son of God. Can we really believe that Jesus Christ is divine, God Himself, and at the same time subordinate the observance of His earthly birth-date under a general title "Festival of Lights" so as to make room for the observance, on *exactly equal terms*, of the story of Channukah? The October issue of *Common Sense,* commenting approvingly on this celebration, remarks: "The students see for themselves the resemblances between the Christian story of the child, and the Jewish tale of Hannah and her sons." The danger is that a Catholic child would be led to regard the two celebrations as equally important from a religious standpoint, as being on exactly the same religious level. Surely the respect and the love we owe to our fellow-citizens of the Jewish faith (and no Catholic following the teachings of the Church can be "anti-Semitic" to the slightest degree) do not demand a joint celebration of Christmas and Channukah—a celebration which might, in the eyes of Catholic children, rob the feast of Christmas of its *absolutely unique* importance in the history of God's Providence to men.[23]

In view of such opposition from official Catholic and Jewish sources, it is not surprising that, after a brief flurry, joint holiday celebrations began to lose favor, and are probably not widespread at the present time. However, the ascension to the papacy of John

XXIII in 1958 and the declarations of the Second Vatican Council initiated a strong and continuing effort toward ecumenicism, one consequence of which has been the liberalization of restrictions on relationships between Catholics and non-Catholics, even in areas of worship. If this trend continues, as appears likely, there may well be a revival of interest in joint holiday celebrations in the public schools.

## GARBED NUNS AS PUBLIC SCHOOL TEACHERS

There has been considerable controversy, and not a little litigation, around the employment of garbed nuns as public school teachers. There are two aspects to the issue: first, the right of teacher nuns to wear distinctive garb while teaching in the public school, and second, the eligibility of nuns—distinctively garbed or not—to teach in the public schools. Usually the controversy over the wearing of distinctive garb is merely an incident around the incorporation of parochial schools into the public school system—a subject to be discussed later. The shortage of teaching nuns in the parochial schools is so critical that few nuns would be allowed to teach in those public schools that are not at least partly parochial schools. The issue is often pointed at the wearing of distinctive garb because that aspect is so conspicuous and not subject to dispute as to the factual truth—as is, for instance, the charge of religious indoctrination by the nun teachers in the course of their instruction.

In the absence of specific statute it appears to be the law in most states that the mere wearing of the distinctive garb of her order by a nun otherwise fully qualified and licensed to teach in the public school does not violate Federal or state constitutional prohibitions concerning sectarian teaching in the public schools. There is some language in a New York case[24] that might be construed as indicating that the mere wearing of the distinctive costume of a religious order brings into the school "sectarian influence" inconsistent with the state's constitutionally declared policy against sectarianism in the public schools; but the case itself held only that a regulation of the state superintendent of public instruction that prohibited the wearing of religious garb by teachers was a reasonable and valid exercise of the powers conferred on him. It must be conceded, the court said, that

> some control over the habiliments of teachers is essential to the proper conduct [of public schools]. Thus, grotesque vagaries in costume could not be permitted without being destructive of good order and discipline. So, also, it would be manifestly proper to prohibit the wearing of badges calculated on particular occasions to constitute cause of offense

to a considerable number of pupils, as, for example, the display of orange ribbons in a public school in a Roman Catholic community on the 12th of July. . . .

The New York case was followed in New Mexico,[25] where, however, the state Supreme Court went further and ruled that even if the regulation of the state board of education were to be rescinded, religious garb might not be worn in view of its "propagandizing effect."

In the absence of such regulation or statute, however, most of the decided cases hold that no constitutional prohibition is violated.[26] In upholding the right of nun teachers to wear the religious habit of their order while teaching, a North Dakota court said:

> We are all agreed that the wearing of the religious habit . . . does not convert the school into a sectarian school, or create sectarian control within the purview of the constitution. Such habit, it is true, proclaimed that the wearers were members of a certain denominational organization, but so would the wearing of the emblem of the Christian Endeavor Society or the Epworth League. The laws of the state do not prescribe the fashion of dress of the teachers in our schools. . . .[27]

On the other hand, if a statute is enacted prohibiting the wearing of such garb by teachers in the public schools, there seems little doubt of the constitutionality of the statute as against an argument that it infringes on the religious liberty of the teacher. In New York, as we have just seen, a regulation by the state's highest educational officer was held valid even in the absence of a specific statute; and the same result was reached in New Mexico. In Pennsylvania, after the courts had ruled that a teacher's wearing of religious garb did not violate the state constitution,[28] the legislature quickly passed a law prohibiting public school teachers from wearing religious garb. The supreme court of the state held that the statute did not unconstitutionally prescribe a religious test for public school teachers, but was merely a valid exercise of the legislature's power to regulate the administration of the state schools; and that the statute's declared purpose that it was "important that all appearances of sectarianism should be avoided in the administration of the public schools of this Commonwealth" was a valid legislative object.[29]

Most states have statutes[30] or regulations that prohibit the wearing of religious garb by public school teachers; apparently only twelve states permit the practice, according to the National Education Association survey of 1946.[31] In North Dakota the court decision allowing public school teachers to wear nun's garb was abrogated at a popular plebescite, which after a bitter campaign voted to prohibit the practice. The referendum did not prohibit the employment of nuns as public school teachers, but merely their wearing of distinctive garb while they were performing their duties. The Catholic bishops of the state announced that the nun teachers would be permitted to wear "modest dress" while they were teaching in lieu of the garb of their order; and since then they have continued in their employment.

The attack on the employment of nuns as public school teachers has also been based on the fact that, since they have taken vows of poverty, their earnings are either paid directly to the religious order of which they are members or are turned over to the order by the teachers directly on receipt. The courts have uniformly held that this fact is not ground for disqualifying the employment of nuns as teachers.[32] As the North Dakota court said:

> The fact that the teachers contributed a material portion of their earnings to the religious order of which they are members is not violative of the constitution. A person in the employ of the state or any of its subdivisions is not inhibited from contributing money, which he or she has earned by service so performed, for the support of some religious body of which he or she is a member. To deny the right to make such contribution would in itself constitute a denial of that right of religious liberty which the constitution guarantees.[33]

What these cases (necessarily) leave unanswered is the problem of the taxability under Federal and state income tax laws of the salaries so paid or turned over to the religious orders.

Except in Missouri no court has held that entirely aside from garb and payments of salaries, nuns are ineligible to teach in the public schools. On the contrary, the courts have held that refusal to employ a duly licensed and qualified teacher merely because she is a nun would violate either the general constitutional guaranty of religious liberty contained in all state constitutions, or the specific prohibition contained in many state constitutions and statutes against religious tests or qualifications for public school teachers. Thus, for example, the New York court that upheld a regulation barring the wearing of religious garb by school teachers expressly said:

> There is no reason either in morals or in law why they [nuns] or any other qualified persons should not be allowed to teach, whatever may be their religious convictions, provided they do not by their acts as teachers promote any denominational doctrine or tenet.[34]

The view that a nun may not *per se* be excluded from employment as a teacher in the public school system has been espoused by the American Civil Liberties Union, which filed a brief *amicus curiae* in the Dixon, New Mexico, case.[35] In that case the plaintiffs sought —

among other relief—that all members of Catholic religious orders be declared ineligible and forever barred from teaching in the public schools. The basis of this demand was the assertion that the oath taken by nuns on joining a religious order, coupled with the doctrinal teachings of the Catholic Church regarding education, would make it impossible for a nun conscientiously and completely to perform the duties of her office. The Civil Liberties Union, which has taken the same position with respect to public school teachers who are members of the Communist Party, is of the view that qualification to hold public office or employment must be judged exclusively by acts and not by beliefs. If a nun (or a Communist) employed as a public school teacher is shown to have abused her position by seeking to indoctrinate her pupils in her own sectarian tenets, she should be disciplined, and, if necessary, dismissed; but to disqualify her in advance would be to punish her for thoughts and beliefs, in violation of the whole spirit of the First Amendment.

The contrary view appears to have been taken in Missouri. In the New Mexico case the court refused to disqualify all nun teachers, though it did disqualify those who on the evidence were found to have engaged in religious teaching in their public school classrooms. In Harfst vs. Hoegen,[36] one of the many cases involving the incorporation of a parochial school into the public school system, the Missouri Supreme Court went further: it disqualified all members of the order involved in the litigation—apparently including those who had not yet even taught in the public schools. The court said:

> . . . In the instant case it is true that the Sisters followed the course of secular instruction prescribed for public schools but in addition they also instructed in the faith of their religious belief as their obligation required them to do. The Sister Superior testified that the members of her order have dedicated their lives to teaching and to the Catholic faith; to both the religious training and education of children; to teach no other faith but that of their religion; to devote themselves to a religious life. She also testified that before coming to the St. Cecelia school she had taught in parochial schools and that the teaching was the same in them as in the St. Cecelia school except that in the parochial schools there was even more time devoted to instruction in religion. "I couldn't teach any differently," she stated. She then told of the religious instruction she was giving to her pupils in the St. Cecelia public school using the Catholic catechism and the child's Catholic Bible as texts.
>
> From her testimony we must conclude that the members of her religious order, their lives dedicated to the training of children both in religion and education, come within this constitutional interdiction as teachers of religion and payment to them from public school funds is forbidden. . . .

499

What the court said in that case—though limited to the particular order involved—would seem to be applicable to all teaching nuns; and in 1952 the next logical step was taken. In that year a lower court in Missouri held that the dogmatic teachings of the Catholic Church in education and the duties of Catholic teachers, within as well as without the public school system, coupled with the oath of discipline taken by nuns, disqualified them from employment as public school teachers.

The 1952 case involved two teaching orders of nuns, one of which was the same one involved in the previous case. The court quoted the law of the Third Plenary Council of Baltimore, a pastoral letter of the hierarchy, and the sections of the Canon Law dealing with the duties of members of religious orders and with education.[37] On the basis of these teachings, the court said:

> The Court further finds that upon admission to the respective orders the nuns who become members thereof, take stringent vows of obedience, poverty and chastity; that said nuns and each of them by virtue of their oaths of obedience place exclusive control over their personal actions in the hands of Church authorities and their superiors in their religious orders; that by virtue of their oaths of poverty said nuns and each of them renounce their civil, economic and secular beings; that by the very nature of the obligations of their oaths of obedience said nuns, and each of them, place themselves beyond the control of civil authorities (except where agreeable to their superiors) . . . that said nuns and each of them by their oaths cease to exist as free citizens and as individual economic units, and during their service execute contracts, receive and pay out money in taxes only in a nominal perfunctory and formal sense, while in reality, acting as instruments and agents of their religious orders, engage in executing the policies of the Roman Catholic Church; that by the very nature of their obligations and of the control to which they submit themselves, the final and absolute control of the secular or sectarian existence and personal actions of the nuns of the orders of the Poor School Sisters of Notre Dame and the Sisters of the Adoration of the Most Precious Blood of O'Fallon is vested in the Church authorities; that because of the character of their obligations said nuns are disqualified from teaching in any public school in the State of Missouri.
>
> The Court further finds that in case of conflict between the directions and orders of the defendant school directors of Reorganized School District Number 8, Franklin County, Missouri, with the obligations, orders and directions of the superiors in their respective religious orders of the Roman Catholic Hierarchy the nuns and each of them by virtue of their oaths of obedience would be required to ignore the orders of the secular school authorities and obey the orders of the religious superior and Church Hierarchy.
>
> The Court further finds that the devotion of said nuns to their reli-

gious beliefs and obligations render it improbable that any of them, if permitted to teach in free public schools, would be able to or would feel obligated to subordinate the dedication of their life and efforts to the effectuation of the Roman Catholic Church policy to the civil policy of the State of Missouri; therefore, the Court finds that, regardless of the garb which said nuns may wear, that the sisters of the highly esteemed, benevolent and charitable religious orders may not lawfully be employed as teachers in any free public schools.[38]

This reasoning, logically applied, would bar not only nuns but all Catholics—at least, all practicing Catholics—not only from employment as public school teachers but from almost any public employment. For example, a believing Catholic might be barred from serving in the legislature because his vote in a measure to legalize the dissemination of birth control information might be dictated by ecclesiastical dogma rather than by the needs and will of the community. So, too, a believing Catholic might be disqualified from serving as a judge in view of the papal dictate forbidding Catholic judges to grant divorces.

Moreover, the logic of this reasoning is not limited to Catholics. It would, for example, disqualify a Quaker from serving as President of the United States, since the President is also commander-in-chief of the armed forces.[39] Yet we know that Herbert Hoover served as President for four years, and that no one charged that his religious affiliations and beliefs ever prejudiced the full performance of his official duties. We know, too, that Catholic judges throughout the country grant divorces freely—not only to Protestant and Jewish petitioners, but even to Catholics who establish the legal requirements. Catholic health, hospital, and welfare officials carry out statutes and regulations providing for the supplying of information and devices for contraception to welfare patients and clients.

The problem is not a simple one, and the issue by no means clear. The employment of nuns as teachers may—and no doubt frequently does—lead to the situation described by one judge:

> . . . With faces averted from the world they have renounced; wearing their peculiar robes, which tell of their church, their order, and their subordination to the guidance of their ecclesiastical superiors; using their religious names, and addressed by the designation, "Sister," —they direct the studies and the deportment of the children under their care, as ecclesiastical persons. They cannot, or they will not, attend teachers' institutes. They have no touch with those engaged in the same pursuit about them. They do not attend public examinations; but, examined in the seclusion of the "Mother House" of their order, after having been selected by the "Sister Superior" in compliance with the written request

of the directors, they come to their work as a religious duty, and their wages pass, under the operation of their vows, into the treasury of the order. . . .[40]

Nevertheless, it would appear that it would be more consistent with the spirit of the Constitution and the American tradition of civil liberties if we should follow the principle stated by Jefferson in the Virginia Statute for Establishing Religious Freedom,

> That it is time enough for the rightful purposes of civil government for its officers to interfere when principles break out into overt acts. . . .

If a nun or any other teacher abuses her position by seeking to indoctrinate her pupils in the tenets of her faith, she should be dismissed. It is true that what a teacher does in the classroom, unobserved by any adult, is generally difficult of proof; and it is quite likely that many abuses will go undetected. But civil and religious liberties necessarily mean that no person shall be punished in advance of the commission of an offense; or be deprived of the right to earn a livelihood in public employment because of his religious beliefs. These liberties are precious; and if an occasional undetected abuse is the price we have to pay for them, it is a bargain price we should gladly pay.

## BACCALAUREATE SERVICES

During recent years considerable objection has been raised by representatives of the Catholic Church to services with a religious motif as a ceremonial marking of graduation from public high schools. The issue has arisen in communities all over the nation.[41]

Typical was an incident in Pittsfield, Maine, where in June 1959 sixteen Roman Catholic students were barred from attending a high school commencement because, following an order by their bishop, they refused to attend the school's baccalaureate services.[42]

Similarly in June 1950 the local priest in Fairhaven, Massachusetts, criticized the long-established custom of holding the baccalaureate exercise of the town high school in the Unitarian Church. He called the custom a slight against other religious groups—including the Catholic, Baptist, Congregational, and Jewish. He requested the school committee to transfer the exercises to one of the town's public buildings; and pointed out also that the planned program included the reading of the Bible and the singing of hymns, and that Catholics are not permitted to participate in such services. The priest's objections caused the school committee to cancel the service.[43]

At about the same time the priest of a parish in Westchester

County, New York, protested the "annual religious baccalaureate service for the Catholic, Protestant and Jewish students, [because] Catholics are forbidden by Canon 1258 of the Code of Canon Law of our church to actively participate in the religious services of non-Catholics." The planned program included Bible readings, the singing of hymns, an invocation, and a benediction.

When the local school board received the protest it requested a ruling from the state commissioner of education. The commissioner's counsel replied by letter that "baccalaureate services are religious services and consequently under the State constitution may not be held in schools."[44] The school board accordingly revised its program so that a student instead of a clergyman would recite the Twenty-third Psalm, and the patriotic hymns "America" and "America the Beautiful" would replace the religious hymn, "O God, Our Help in Ages Past." The priest accepted the revision and agreed to participate and give the benediction.[45]

The next year, however, when it appeared that the school board was again planning to revert to the form and content of previous years, the priest made a formal complaint to the state commissioner of education. In his petition to set aside the order of the school board, he said:

> From an examination and analysis of the officially proposed program it is immediately evident that it is a religious service in both content and form. The very title of the program is "Order of Service." The program contains all the elements and form of a certain type of non-Catholic religious service. It moves along from the opening Procession and processional hymn to an invocation prayer, by a clergyman, to a choral hymn, to a Scripture reading, from the King James version of the Bible, to a Baccalaureate address, by some clergyman, on the ethical topic of "Courage," to a choral selection of a "Negro Spiritual" hymn, to a Benediction prayer by a clergyman and finally to the concluding Recessional.

In a formal decision, the state commissioner of education upheld the petition, stating:

> A Baccalaureate Service is generally a religious service. The program before me indicates that the proposed service follows the general pattern and is a religious service. The fact that more than one religious denomination were represented on the program would not change its religious character. (*Everson v Board of Education.* 330 U.S. 1): "Neither a state nor the Federal Government can set up a church. Neither can pass laws which aid one religion, aid all religions, or prefer one religion over another. . . ."
>
> The courts have said many times that the holding that public property may not be so utilized indicates no hostility to religion on the

part of government but rather the complete separation so that the free exercise of religion is in no way hampered by governmental interference. It should be noted, however, that it is not intended to hold that opening and closing of school functions with customary invocation and benediction is prohibited. These customs are followed in the Legislature as well as many other public functions and do not violate the Constitution. . . .

The issue before me in this case is not whether the Baccalaureate Service should or should not be held but whether it may legally and properly be held in the school building. It is my view, as indicated heretofore, that the utilization of the type of service represented in this appeal constitutes the teaching of a religious tenet, and the use of the school for such purpose would violate the State Constitution.[46]

In his opinion the commissioner suggested that the services might be held in churches rather than in school buildings; when the services are initiated and conducted by the denominations in the churches independent of the public school authorities, no constitutional issue arises. Those denominations which are willing to conduct interfaith services are free to do so for such of the graduating students as are willing to attend. Those whose religious convictions preclude interfaith service are free to hold separate services for the graduates of their faith. The suggestion of holding baccalaureate services in churches, however, aggravates rather than solves the problem where a single program for all graduates is arranged by the school authorities; if a baccalaureate service with religious overtones may not constitutionally be held in a public school building, its unconstitutionality is not remedied by its being held under public school auspices in a church building.

Nevertheless, the Supreme Court of New Mexico, in the only case that appears to have reached a State supreme court, held that the constitutional rights of Catholic students were not violated by the holding of baccalaureate and commencement exercises in Protestant churches—at least "Where there is no other suitable auditorium or place available." The court said:

> The churches were the only buildings in the Lindrith community with sufficient seating capacity to accommodate the pupils and the people of the community who desired to attend these functions. The Legion Hall was large enough to accommodate those who desired to attend but it did not have sufficient seating capacity.
>
> These functions are of great interest to the pupils and their relatives, and like other communities throughout the state the churches are the only buildings which could comfortably accommodate those present. We are firmly committed to the doctrine of separation of Church and State, both by our constitutional provisions and statutes, as well as our

decision in Zellers v Huff, 55 N.M. 501, 236 P. 2d 949; but we do not feel they require us to prohibit the holding of these time honored programs in a building where all who desire to attend may be accommodated. Neither are we fearful that those conducting the services or exercises will fail to observe the proprieties of the occasion and thus give offense to anyone attending.

The trial court correctly refused to enjoin the holding of such services or exercises in a church where there was no other suitable auditorium or place available.[47]

It may be suggested that if these functions "are of great interest" to Protestant pupils and their relatives, they are also of great interest to Catholic pupils and their relatives — particularly where the absence from baccalaureate services subjects the pupils to disciplinary action, as in Monongahela, Pennsylvania. In that community three Catholic graduates refused to attend baccalaureate services because a Protestant minister helped conduct the service and participation under such circumstances was forbidden to Catholics. When the absentees appeared in cap and gown at the later commencement services at which diplomas were distributed, they received envelopes containing some torn newspapers. The superintendent of schools explained that the withholding of the diplomas was "merely disciplinary and has nothing to do with religion, [since] everyone's religion is respected in our school system."[48] Fortunately saner minds prevailed, and at the next meeting of the school board it was unanimously voted that the three absentees should receive their diplomas by mail.[49]

Sometimes the lack of other suitable buildings that necessitate the holding of baccalaureate services in churches works the other way. Rev. Liston Pope, formerly dean of Yale Divinity School, related how he "unwittingly became involved in one of those touchy situations [when he was] invited to address a group of students in a nearby Connecticut town. It turned out that the tax-supported school in question was holding its assemblies temporarily in the basement of the Catholic church across the street. Catholic officials successfully insisted that the school cancel [his] talk, on the ground that the entire building had been blessed and a Protestant clergyman therefore could not speak there."[50]

It may be that the current trend towards ecumenicism with its more liberal approach to Catholic participation in interfaith programs may modify Catholic opposition, although there is no substantial evidence of this at the present writing. Jewish opposition, encouraged by the prayer and Bible-reading decisions, is likely to continue and probably become even more articulate and determined.

## Religion in State Universities[51]

In recent years there has been a strong movement for the establishment of schools or departments of religion in state and municipal universities. The leadership in this area was taken by the University of Iowa, which in 1923 established a School of Religion. Although a separate corporation, it is fully integrated into the university structure. Its director is paid by the university, but its three professors, a Protestant, a Catholic, and a Jew, are selected and paid by their respective denominations. Today some 60 out of slightly over 100 state universities and land-grant colleges offer instruction in religion on an academic credit basis. Seventeen of these have chairs in religion financed by state universities. Fifteen universities have independent schools of religion more or less closely affiliated with the university.[52]

Jefferson's views on religion in state universities are of interest, among other reasons, because they have been cited to support the positions of both the proponents and opponents of a broad interpretation of the First Amendment and its restrictions on religion in public education. Justice Reed, in his dissent in the McCollum case, pointed out that Jefferson, as one of the founders of the state-controlled University of Virginia, was faced with the problem of constitutional limitation of religious education in public schools. As we have noted — though not mentioned by Justice Reed — Jefferson's plan for universal common elementary education specifically excluded all religion. At Jefferson's suggestion, however, the regulations of the University of Virginia provided that

> Should the religious sects of this State, or any of them, according to the invitation held out to them, establish within or adjacent to, the precincts of the University, schools for instruction in the religion of their sect, the students of the University will be free, and expected to attend religious worship at the establishment of their respective sects, in the morning, and in time to meet their school in the University at its stated hour.[53]

Professor Butts has shown with much cogence that neither this regulation nor any direct writings of Jefferson lends much support to the assertion that he looked with sympathy on any involvement by the state university in religion.[54] He points out that the regulation, unlike the released-time plan (in defense of which Justice Reed cited it), required the students to "meet their school in the University at its stated hour" notwithstanding the time at religious worship or instruction at the establishment of their respective sects. In the second place, at a time when, in most colleges and universities in the country, ministers were presidents and commonly members of boards of control, daily chapel attendance was compulsory, courses in religion were required, and professors of theology and doctors of divinity had prominent places on the faculty, the University of Virginia had none of these. While Jefferson was rector it had no chaplain, no courses or professors of theology, and no chapel or other place for religious worship. An early proposal to set aside a room for religious worship was dropped, and a specific request to hold religious services in university buildings on Sunday was denied.

There appears to be only one case to reach a highest state court involving an attack on the constitutionality of a state university's involvement in religious affairs. In 1951 one W.W. Sholes brought suit against the University of Minnesota, charging that its program of religious activities, including the employment of a coordinator of student religious activities, its cooperation with religious foundations operating on the campus, and its permitted use of university rooms and buildings "for the holding of ecclesiastical rituals, liturgical observances and studies, evangelical programs to win others to the Faith and public services of religious worship," all constituted violations of the charter of the university, the Minnesota constitution, and the First Amendment of the Federal Constitution.

The Supreme Court of Minnesota in 1952 dismissed the action on the sole ground that the plaintiff should first have made demand on the regents of the university to eliminate the objectionable practices before invoking the aid of the courts. "It is only a matter of fairness and a requirement of orderly procedure," the court said, "that a citizen be required to seek relief from the board of regents before proceeding in court."[55]

The absence of authoritative judicial determination allows freer rein for one's own conclusions. As has been previously suggested, no constitutional mandate is violated by the objective teaching of religion in the public schools. It has also been suggested that such objective teaching is today not practicable at the elementary school level, and that violation of the Constitution can safely be avoided only by excluding the content of religion from the public school curriculum. This, however, is not necessarily true of colleges or universities. The constitutional principles are the same at both levels, but the dangers of violation at the higher level can probably be reduced to a point where they constitute an acceptable calculated risk. The college student has received his basic religious training in his home or church and is thus ready for exploration of other religious or even nonreligious beliefs. Moreover—unlike the elementary school child—he no longer accepts as incontrovertible truths all he hears from his teacher or reads in a textbook. Finally, unlike the elementary school child, he does not lack opportunity to hear a nonreligious approach to ultimate reality — as any member of the usual college science or philosophy class can attest.

It would seem, therefore, that tax-supported colleges may constitutionally provide for the objective study of religious institutions, practices, and principles. Such study must obviously be multisectarian and nondevotional; and since the doctrine of some religions prohibits examination into the content of other religions without special ecclesiastical authorization, it must be noncompulsory.

In summary, the following propositions concerning religion and state universities may be offered as reasonably tenable:

(1) Courses in comparative religion, the philosophy of religions, and similar studies are constitutionally permissible if the end sought is understanding rather than belief — although of course belief may well result from understanding.

(2) Compulsory religious chapel attendance, whether sectarian or nonsectarian, and whether on or off the campus, is unconstitutional. Even if it is not compulsory, college credit may not be accorded such attendance.

(3) Whether college credit may be granted for courses attended at a theological or denominational institution would depend on whether the courses attended could constitutionally have been given at the state university.

(4) College administrators may not take the responsibility for religious initiative and action; religious organizations should assume this responsibility, and should maintain privately owned chapels and religious centers adjacent to the campus. The religious activities of these organizations may be publicized, as a public service, within the college, but the college administration and faculty should refrain from encouraging or discouraging attendance.

### CHAPTER THIRTEEN

# State Aid to Religious Education

## THE PAROCHIAL SCHOOL SYSTEM

### Extent of the System

THE ISSUE OF STATE AID to religious education in the United States is almost entirely the issue of state aid to Catholic parochial schools.[1] Parochial schools or their equivalent are conducted to a limited extent by Protestants and Jews; but, aside from tax exemption, there has been no discernible demand from Protestants or, except among the Orthodox, from Jews for financial aid from government in sustaining their school systems. Indeed, the Seventh Day Adventists— who probably have a larger percentage of their faith enrolled in parochial schools than any other denomination, including even the Catholics[2]—are among the most vigorous of all denominations in their opposition to state aid.[3] Certainly there has been no demand for state aid on the part of nonpublic secular schools, which are generally either private schools for wealthy children or model schools connected with a teachers' college. Hence, while the Catholic Church and its supporters usually employ the term "private schools" in their campaigns and arguments for state aid, it should be understood that for all practical purposes what is meant is the Catholic parochial school system.

The extent of parochial elementary and secondary schools among Protestants is not known with any degree of certainty. Dr. Stokes estimated that in 1947 there were about 150,000 Protestant children attending some 2,500 parochial elementary and secondary schools.[4] Professor Rian estimated for the same year that the number of children attending Protestant parochial schools did not exceed 200,000, with a possible additional 100,000 in church-related preparatory schools.[5] United States Office of Education estimates place about four percent of the nonpublic school children in Protestant parochial schools. The Office estimated that in 1960 there were about 7,780,000 children in nonpublic schools, which would place approximately 310,000 in Protestant parochial schools. Half to two-thirds of these children are in Lutheran schools. Other Protestant denominations conducting parochial schools to any substantial extent are the Seventh Day Adventists, the Reformed Churches, and the Mennonites.[6]

The exact extent of parochial or day schools among Jews is likewise not known. A careful study made in 1927 indicated that in that year there were only twelve Jewish parochial schools in all the United States, and these were located in three large cities.[7] In 1937 it was estimated that some 3,000 Jewish children were being educated in all-day Jewish parochial schools.[8] Since then the number of children attending Jewish day schools (a name preferred by Jewish educators to parochial schools) has increased at a rate higher probably than any other denomination. Today, more than 50,000 children attend Jewish day schools.[9]

The number of children attending Catholic parochial schools has likewise been increasing at a substantial rate from year to year, although perhaps at no greater rate than the increase in Catholic population. Today between five and a half and six million children are enrolled in some thirteen thousand Catholic elementary and secondary schools in the United States.[10] The percentage of Catholic children of school age attending Catholic schools is generally put by Catholic authorities at 50%, although a survey conducted by the New York *Times* in 1952 estimated that at that time as much as 60% of the Catholic children of elementary and secondary school age attended parochial schools.[11]

## Philosophy of the Parochial School

The Catholic parochial school system is predicated on the sections of the Canon Law set forth in Justice Jackson's dissent in the Everson case which have already been quoted.[12] The encyclical of Pope Pius XI *On the Christian Education of Youth* states that the "only school approved by the Church is one where . . . the Catholic religion permeates the entire atmosphere [and where] all teaching and the whole organization of the school and its teachers, syllabus and textbooks in every branch [is] regulated by the Christian spirit."[13]

These words of Pius XI epitomize the whole Catholic philosophy of education and the educational foundation of the Catholic parochial school system. Catholic doctrine does not conceive of religion as a subject which, like history or music, can be taught more or less independently of other subjects a specified number of school hours weekly; in the Catholic school religion is not merely a branch in the curriculum, nor is it confined to mere instruction. The ultimate goal of education is the praise, reverence, and service of God; and everything else in education must be subordinated and directed toward this ultimate end.[14] Hence there is no place for purely secular instruction in the Catholic school; indeed, the term "secular education" is almost a self-contradiction. Everything taught in the Catholic school is to be taught with the ultimate goal of education in mind — everything must be impregnated with God and religion. As stated by the Reverend Joseph H. Fichter, S.J., in an authoritative book published in 1958:

> It is a commonplace observation that in the parochial school religion permeates the whole curriculum and is not confined to a single half-hour period of the day. Even arithmetic can be used as an instrument of pious thoughts, as in the case of the teacher who gave this problem to her class: "If it takes forty thousand priests and a hundred forty thousand sisters to care for forty million Catholics in the United States, how many more priests and sisters will be needed to convert and care for the hundred million non-Catholics in the United States?"[15]

## *The Development of the System*

Obviously with such a philosophy the Church could not adjust Catholic education to the American secular school system; and the development of an independent Church-controlled school system may well have been inevitable. If it was not, it was made inevitable by the treatment accorded Catholic children in the Protestant public schools.

The model for Catholic schools in America was founded in Maryland by the end of the 18th century. In 1808 the diocese of Baltimore, which up to that time had the whole of the United States in its jurisdiction, was divided into an additional four dioceses — New York, Philadelphia, Boston, and Bardstown (covering Kentucky, Tennessee, and the Northwest Territory). As a result, the Baltimore type of school was copied and expanded in these new dioceses as well as in the other dioceses later created.

In 1829 the First Provincial Council of Baltimore enacted the first Catholic general school law in the country. The canon provided that

> We judge it absolutely necessary that schools should be established, in which the young may be taught the principles of faith and morality, while being instructed in letters.[16]

The Second Provincial Council in 1833 appointed a committee to prepare suitable textbooks for Catholic schools.

Several years after this Council came the unsuccessful effort on the part of the Catholic Church in New York to establish the right to share in the funds raised for public education which will be described later. This campaign convinced the New York hierarchy that the development of a strong school system was even more important than the building of new churches.[17]

The concern for education was shared by other dioceses. The First Plenary Council held in Baltimore in 1852 ordered that pastors themselves should teach Christian doctrine to the young, and bishops were exhorted to establish a Catholic school in every parish and to pay the teachers from parochial funds. The Second Plenary Council in 1864 reiterated this exhortation; but the definitive position of the church on parochial education in America was stated by the Third Plenary Council in 1884.

Probably to a large extent the action of the Third Council was influenced by elaborate instructions sent in 1875 by the Holy Office in Rome to the American hierarchy in reply to certain questions. The conclusion of the reply is emphatic, and left no room for doubt as to the Vatican's views on parochial education in the United States:

> Likewise, if any parents neglect to provide this necessary Christian training and education for their children or permit them to attend schools in which the ruin of their souls cannot be avoided; or if, when a suitable Catholic school is located in the place, well-built and equipped, or an opportunity is provided for them to educate their children along Catholic lines in some other district, they send their children, despite all this, to the public schools without adequate reason and without those necessary precautions which might remove the danger of the perversion of their faith, then, if they continue to do so defiantly, they can not, in accordance with the clear teaching of Catholicism, receive absolution in the sacrament of Holy Penance.[18]

In line with these instructions, the Third Plenary Council set forth the following four basic principles on which the Catholic parochial school system in the United States rests:

> 1. Near each church, where it does not yet exist, a parochial school is to be erected within two years from the promulgation of this Council, and is to be maintained *in perpetuum*, unless the bishop, on account of grave difficulties, judge that a postponement be allowed.
>
> 2. A priest who, by his grave negligence, prevents the erection of a school within this time, or its maintenance, or who, after repeated admonitions of the bishop, does not attend to the matter, deserves removal from that church.
>
> 3. A mission or a parish which so neglects to assist a priest in erecting or maintaining a school, that by reason of this supine negligence the school is rendered impossible, should be reprehended by the bishop and, by the most efficacious and prudent means possible, induced to contribute the necessary support.
>
> 4. All Catholic parents are bound to send their children to the parochial schools, unless either at home or in other Catholic schools they may sufficiently and evidently provide for the Christian education of

their children, or unless it be lawful to send them to other schools on account of a sufficient cause, approved by the bishop, and with opportune cautions and remedies. As to what is a Catholic school, it is left to the judgment of the Ordinary to define.[19]

The Third Plenary Council's edict marks the real beginning of the parochial school system in the United States. Since 1884 the system has grown to the point where it includes more than 13,000 schools, serving over 5,500,000 children, taught by more than 150,000 teachers.[20] In 1948 only about 5% of these were laymen, the rest being members of religious orders, largely nuns. By 1960, however, 25.8% were lay teachers, and the percentage is still rising.[21]

## The Case for Parochial Schools

The arguments presented in favor of the parochial school system include:[22]

(1) They represent the conscientious wishes of a large element of the population to advance at much personal sacrifice the cause of religion and education in ways they think best. Aside from all other considerations, the wishes of so important a segment of the population should be respected.

(2) They provide a welcome change from the deadening sameness of public school education. America is a country of many cultures and many faiths. This diversity should be reflected in education, and the parochial schools help to achieve this.

(3) They save taxpayers large sums of money that would otherwise have to be spent for additional accommodations in public schools. This argument is most frequently presented to support the Catholic case for a share of tax-raised funds for education.

(4) Many modern religious educators, non-Catholic as well as Catholic, agree that religion is too important to be taught simply as another subject like geography or music. The parochial schools are the logical consummation of this conclusion by providing education which, while assuring the acquisition of the necessary secular instruction, at the same time assures that religion is accorded the position in the educational scheme to which it is entitled.

(5) In view of their concentration on moral training, parochial schools offer the most promising counterinfluence to the low ethical standards prevailing today and the most effective safeguard against crime and juvenile delinquency.

## The Case against Parochial Schools

The arguments against the system include:[23]

(1) Educational equipment, personnel, and standards are low in comparison with the public schools. Classes are overcrowded; most of the teaching nuns do not have the education and training required of public school teachers; equipment is frequently inferior. Theoretically, the state education authorities have the responsibility of inspection and requiring equivalence to public schools; but in most states inspection is little more than perfunctory, and in many is completely neglected.

(2) The product is accordingly inevitably inferior. Parochial school children entering secular institutions of higher learning find the competition severe. Moreover, parochial school pupils furnish more than their proportionate quota of juvenile delinquents. This discrepancy is especially significant in view of the frequent practice of transferring to the public schools the most serious discipline problem students from the parochial schools.

(3) The saving of taxpayers' money is an unwanted and false economy. Even more money could be saved by lowering the standards and the graduating ages in the public schools. This is not done because we operate on the premise that universal education on a high standard is a profitable investment for a democratic state. Hence, supplying inferior education at a reduced price is no bargain.

(4) Education under authoritarian influences is not best for life in a democracy. The principal emphasis is on obedience and respect for authority, rather than the obligations of the individual conscience.

(5) Too much time is devoted to religion, which further handicaps the parochial school child in comparison with his public school neighbor.

(6) The parochial school is divisive. It creates a cultural ghetto, isolating a large segment of American children from everyday contact and co-living with their fellow Americans. This is by far the most frequent and most emphasized argument against the parochial school system.

## CONSTITUTIONAL PROTECTION OF PAROCHIAL SCHOOLS

The constitutional security of the parochial school system in the United States rests on several decisions of the United States Supreme Court. These decisions have secured parochial schools not only against complete abolition by hostile state legislatures, but also against arbitrary and unreasonable restrictions on their operations.

Of these cases, by far the most important—though not the first in time—is the so-called Oregon Parochial School Case—Pierce vs.

Society of Sisters.[24] In 1922 the people of Oregon were largely under the influence of Ku Klux Klan elements, and were motivated by the ultranationalistic "100% Americanism" that was so prevalent in the period during and immediately after World War I. By popular petition and referendum they enacted a Compulsory Education Act that required all children, with limited exceptions, to attend only public schools.[25] The purpose of the act—the effective date of which was postponed until 1926—was concededly to eliminate parochial and private schools.

The constitutionality of the act was attacked in two actions brought by the Society of Sisters, an order of teaching nuns that operated a number of parochial schools in the state, and the Hill Military Academy, a private, secular elementary and preparatory school. It should be noted that one decision was written in both cases; and obviously no religious liberty issue was involved in the suit by Hill Military Academy.[26] Moreover, when the Sisters' suit was brought it was not yet clear that the Fourteenth Amendment incorporated—as a restraint on state action—the First Amendment's guaranty of religious liberty against Federal infringement. What was well recognized was the Supreme Court's vigilance in protecting business and property interests against undue state interference. It was for these reasons that no suit was brought by parents of children in parochial schools, even though it would seem clear that the parents were the persons most directly affected by the statute. For the same reasons, the Sisters' complaint stressed not the religious issue involved but the large financial investment they had in the buildings and equipment of the schools, and the financially profitable character of the business of operating parochial schools.

The United States Supreme Court recognized the plaintiffs' business interests and the interference therewith by the statute, which—though not expressly restricting the operations of parochial and private schools—in effect prevented their operation by making it illegal for their patrons or customers to patronize them. Injunctions, the Court said, have frequently been issued "to protect business enterprises against interference with the freedom of patrons or customers." It is unfortunate that in vindicating the fundamental right to educate religiously, the parties and the Court were required to employ the fiction that instructing children in the faith of their fathers is a profit-making business like mining coal or manufacturing steel.[27]

The court sustained the complaint of the Sisters and the Hill Academy. The court said:

The inevitable practical result of enforcing the Act under consideration would be destruction of appellees' primary schools, and perhaps all other private primary schools for normal children within the State of Oregon. [These parties] are engaged in a kind of undertaking not inherently harmful, but long regarded as useful and meritorious. Certainly there is nothing in the present records to indicate that they have failed to discharge their obligations to patrons, students or the State. And there are no peculiar circumstances or present emergencies which demand extraordinary measures relative to primary education.

In so holding the court overruled the arguments presented by the state of Oregon to support its claim that the law was not unreasonable or arbitrary. It is worthwhile to set forth here an extract from the argument of the state's attorneys to the court:

The voters of Oregon who adopted this law had the right to act on the belief that the fact that the great increase in juvenile crime in the United States followed so closely after the great increase in the number of children in the United States who were not attending public schools, was more than a coincidence. The voters in Oregon might also have based their action in adopting this law upon the alarm which they felt at the rising tide of religious suspicions in this country, and upon their belief that the basic cause of such religious feelings was the separation of children along religious lines during the most susceptible years of their lives, with the inevitable awakening of a consciousness of separation, and a distrust and suspicion of those from whom they were so carefully guarded. The voters of Oregon might have felt that the mingling together, during a portion of their education, of the children of all races and sects, might be the best safeguard against future internal dissentions and consequent weakening of the community against foreign dangers. . . .

The subject of immigration is one which is exclusively under the control of the Central Government. The States have nothing to say as to the number or class of the immigrants who may be permitted to settle within their limits. It would therefore appear to be both unjust and unreasonable to prevent them from taking the steps which each may deem necessary and proper for Americanizing its new immigrants and developing them into patriotic and law-abiding citizens. At present, the vast majority of the private schools in the country are conducted by members of some particular religious belief. They may be followed, however, by those organized and controlled by believers in certain economic doctrines entirely destructive of the fundamentals of our government. Can it be contended that there is no way in which a State can prevent the entire education of a considerable portion of its future citizens being controlled and conducted by bolshevists, syndicalists and communists?

We shall discuss in Part III of this volume the extent to which a state may restrict religious liberty to ward off the threatened dangers that induced the people of Oregon to enact the antiparochial school law.

Here it is sufficient to note that the arguments so frequently offered to defend the parochial school system—widespread criminality and delinquency, religious bigotry, Communism—were used by the attorney general of Oregon in a vain effort to defend a law that in effect sought to outlaw parochial schools.

In its opinion in the Pierce case the Supreme Court cited and relied on the case of Meyer vs. Nebraska[28] which it had decided two years earlier. The Meyer case and its companion cases, Bartels vs. Iowa and Bohning vs. Ohio,[29] involved Lutheran schools. The same social and political milieu that gave rise to the Oregon act was responsible for the Nebraska, Iowa, and Ohio statutes. These laws, however, did not outlaw parochial schools, but merely required that English be the language of instruction in all schools, and that no child be taught a foreign language until he had completed eight grades of elementary schools.

The defendants in these cases were teachers of German in parochial schools who were convicted of violating the statute by teaching German to children—in the Meyer case by the use of a collection of Biblical stories. The courts, in reversing the convictions, relied not only on the constitutional right of German teachers to pursue a gainful occupation not inherently evil or dangerous to the welfare of the community, but also on the right of parents to have their children taught "Martin Luther's language" so that they might better understand "Martin Luther's dogma." The latter aspect of the decision will be discussed in that part of this volume which treats religious liberty. The former aspect is relevant here, for it indicates that not only is the state constitutionally inhibited from totally outlawing parochial schools, but also from arbitrarily and unreasonably restricting their curriculum.

The wall of the constitutional protection of parochial schools was completed in 1927 by the decision of the Supreme Court in Farrington vs. Tokushige.[30] In that case the court sustained an injunction restraining the governor of Hawaii from enforcing a law that placed the privately controlled foreign language schools in the territory under strict and detailed government control. For example, one of the regulations imposed under the law was that "no subjects of study shall be taught, nor courses of study shall be followed, nor entrance, nor attendance qualifications required, nor textbooks used, other than as prescribed by the department [of public instruction]." The court held that no facts were presented to warrant such extreme regulations, that "give affirmative direction concerning the intimate and essential details of such schools, intrust their control to public officers, and deny both owners and patrons reasonable choice and discretion in respect of teachers, curriculum and textbooks."

The Farrington case, it should be noted, did not on its face involve religious schools, and no religious liberty issue was specifically raised; on the contrary, the Hawaii law expressly exempted "Sabbath schools" from its operation. It was aimed primarily at the Japanese language schools, which it was felt hindered the cultural assimilation and Americanization of Hawaiian American children of Japanese ancestry. It is clear, however, that the effect of the decision is to extend strong constitutional protection against possible state legislative or executive action hostile to parochial schools.

Mention should also be made of the St. Johns University case. Four Catholic students of that college, conducted by the Vincentian Fathers in Brooklyn, N.Y., were expelled for violating eccesiastical law—two by engaging in a civil marriage and the other two by acting as witnesses to it. The New York courts, in 1962, upheld the expulsion,[31] and while the ground for the decision, stated to be applicable to secular as well as religious schools, was the broad jurisdiction which colleges have to regulate their internal affairs, the decision constitutes another legal safeguard for the parochial schools system.

### INSPECTION AND REGULATION OF PAROCHIAL SCHOOLS

The Pierce, Meyer, and Farrington cases do not prohibit state inspection or the reasonable nondiscriminatory regulation of parochial schools. There would be little doubt, for example, that the state can require all schools to maintain fire escapes or other equipment to guard the safety of children. Nor would the constitutionality of the law be affected by the fact that in some cases it might put a parochial school out of operation because of its financial inability to install fire escapes. Moreover, the state's power undoubtedly extends beyond prescribing physical requirements for building and equipment. In the Meyer case the court noted that the "power of the State ... to make reasonable regulations for all schools, including a requirement that they shall give instructions in English, is not questioned." And in the Pierce case the court said:

> No question is raised concerning the power of the State reasonably to regulate all schools, to inspect, supervise and examine them, their teachers and pupils, to require that all children of proper age attend some school, that teachers shall be of good moral character and patriotic disposition, that certain studies plainly essential to good citizenship must be taught, and that nothing be taught which is manifestly inimical to the public welfare.

It is of course true that the court said only that "no question" has been "raised" concerning the state's power—not that the state has such power. But in the Everson case the court cited the Pierce case for the proposition that "the State has power to impose secular educational requirements"; and this—coupled with the court's dismissal of the appeal in Donner vs. New York[32]—would seem to indicate fairly clearly that the negative language in the Pierce case implies an affirmative recognition of the state's inherent constitutional power reasonably and nondiscriminatorily to inspect and regulate parochial schools in respect to their secular aspects.

Though there is little doubt of the state's power to inspect and regulate parochial schools, it is also true that in most states the power is more frequently honored in its nonexercise than in its exercise. Careful inspection is generally limited to attendance records and the giving of certain required courses. The possible reasons for this neglect are partly inadequate budgets for an educational inspection force, and partly the political danger in the vigorous enforcement of the law against parochial schools.[33]

Whatever the reasons are, they are not, in most cases, the lack of adequate laws on the statute books. Three-fourths of the states provide by law that the education in parochial schools shall be equivalent to the education given in public schools—though these statutes are usually general rather than specific.[34] One of the simplest types of supervision is the registration of private schools with the state department of education. Some states[35] accept only those private schools that meet the approval of the state departments; attendance at schools not so approved does not satisfy the state's compulsory attendance law.

A few states have fairly specific statutes; the Rhode Island law is typical of these. It provides in part:

> For the purpose of this Chapter the school committee shall approve a private school or private instruction only when it complies with the following requirements, namely: That the period of attendance of the pupils in such school or on such private instruction is substantially equal to that required by law in public schools; that registers are kept and returns to the school committee, the superintendent of schools, truant officers and the director of education in relation to the attendance of pupils, are made the same as by the public schools; that reading, writing, geography, arithmetic, the history of the United States, the history of Rhode Island, and the principles of American government shall be taught in the English language substantially to the same extent as such subjects are required to be taught in the public schools, and that the teaching of the English language and of other subjects indicated herein shall be thorough and efficient; . . .

Equivalent education is sought in some states[36] by requiring private schools to remain open for the same length of time as the public schools of the same locality; other states[33] require the same course of study. Private schools are generally required to use English as the medium of instruction, though New Hampshire expressly permits devotional exercises to be conducted in any language other than English; and several other states[38] impliedly do the same by providing that state supervision shall not be interpreted to interfere with a school's program of religious education.

State laws frequently require instruction in the Constitution of the United States and of the particular state, in history, in government, and in patriotism. Physical training, accident prevention, traffic regulation, and fire prevention are required studies in some states. Occasionally[39] a state law requires teachers in parochial schools to be certified by the state department as qualified for public school teaching; but most states have no such requirement. (In view of the large reliance of the parochial schools on teaching nuns, the widespread prevalence and enforcement of such a law might be fatal to the parochial school system.)

To summarize the actual practice, it may be said in the words of the National Education Association study of 1946 (still valid today):

> Supervision of private schools is far from complete in all features of the program; nor is it widespread in any one feature. In general, it may be said that supervision is conspicuous by its absence rather then by its presence.

## THE PROBLEM OF FINANCES

The financial burden of maintaining the vast private educational system which is the Catholic parochial school system is obviously gigantic. The Catholic school system absorbs between 12% and 15% of the total American population of school age.[40] The extent of the cost to the Catholic community of educating these children can be imagined when it is realized that in New York City alone — according to estimates made by Cardinal Francis Spellman in 1952 — it would have cost the public school system $425,000,000 merely to erect the buildings necessary to educate the children who were then in the city parochial schools, and $110,000,000 annually to operate and maintain them,[41] figures which would be substantially higher today. According to the National Catholic Welfare Conference, Catholic expenditures for education in 1960 saved taxpayers $1.8 billion.[42]

Moreover, the Catholic school system in the United States has for the past two decades or more been engaged in a tremendous program of expansion. In the decade after 1941 — 1942 the enrollment in Catholic elementary schools increased by 35% and in secondary schools by 42%. In the decade from 1952 to 1962 Catholic school enrollment increased from about three and a quarter to almost five and a half million.[43]

What this means is that the new buildings and new pupils will require additional teachers, supplies, and all other items of operation, maintenance, and upkeep. The major education expense in the public schools is the salaries of teachers. In the Catholic schools teachers' salaries have for a long time been a comparatively minor expense, since some 90% of the teachers were members of religious orders whose only expense was the cost of their subsistence. Without the practically free services of these teaching nuns and brothers, the parochial school system could never have been established and maintained. But the source of supply of teaching nuns and brothers has about reached its limit; the percentage has already dropped to 75% and new pupils will in large part have to be served by lay teachers who must be paid salaries like other teachers.

This picture makes it fairly clear that the financial problem of the Catholic parochial school system is serious, and is likely to become increasingly so. With the exception of the aid resulting from tax exemption — without which the system could not long survive — this burden is carried almost entirely by the Catholic community. Whether American Catholics can sustain this gigantic burden, in addition to the upkeep of other activities of the church at home and abroad, is far from certain. What is fairly certain is that Catholic demands to share in tax-raised funds for education are going to be increasingly articulate and insistent.

Until now Catholic attempts to obtain government financial support for parochial education have manifested themselves in four principal areas: outright grants of public funds, incorporation of parochial schools into the public school system, indirect or auxiliary aid from public funds, and the sharing by parochial schools in Federal aid to education. Each of these efforts has aroused considerable controversy and acrimony, particularly along religious lines. Each will be considered in detail; but before we do so, something should be said of the arguments for and against state aid and the positions of the faiths on this issue.

## THE CASE FOR STATE AID[44]

The following arguments have been most vigorously urged in

support of state financial aid to parochial school education.

(1) *Our religious tradition.* American democracy is based on a strong religious tradition. Our Declaration of Independence declares the dependence of human rights on God. The many proclamations of the Presidents, the declarations of Congress, the invocations to God in state constitutions, the appointment of government chaplains, and a host of other similar official acts give irrefutable evidence of the religiosity of American life and tradition. Adherence to this tradition requires that government aid religion to fulfill its mission. The multiplicity of denominations in the United States makes it impracticable for the government to limit its aid to the one true faith; but giving impartial and nondiscriminatory aid to all religious groups would be an act of loyalty to the religious tradition of our life without violating the principle of the separation of church and state as that principle has been understood by all until its meaning was distorted by the Supreme Court in the Everson and McCollum decisions.

(2) *The civil function of parochial schools.* Aside from its essential role in the field of religion, the parochial school system performs a vital civic function: it provides millions of children the same instruction in secular subjects that is given in the public schools. Even if the principle of separation of church and state is construed to bar nonpreferential aid to religion, it does not prohibit the state from paying for what it receives. If there were no parochial schools the state would have to pay for the secular instruction that Catholic children now receive in parochial schools. State financial support of this secular aspect of parochial school education can hardly be called aid; it is merely paying what it would in any event have to pay. Whatever may be the case theoretically, in actual practice secular subjects are taught the same way in parochial and in public schools; arithmetic is arithmetic wherever it is taught. Moreover, in view of the fact that the major item in the educational budget, teachers' salaries, is largely absent in parochial schools because of the generosity of the teaching nuns, the cost to the state would be much less than if the Catholic children were educated in the public schools, even if it were assumed that the state were to pay the entire cost of parochial education—which of course no one demands. Fairness requires that the state pay at least a part of the tremendous cost of secular instruction in parochial schools.

(3) *Double taxation.* Catholic parents whose religious convictions require them to send their children to parochial schools are subject to the unfair burden of double taxation. On the one hand, they are

required to pay for the godless public school education that they may not in conscience give their children; on the other hand, under the compulsory school attendance laws they are required to provide their children with an education in basic secular subjects at their own expense. Moreover, in the Pierce case the United States Supreme Court held that Catholic parents have a constitutional right to send their children to parochial schools; but this right is purely illusory if the parents do not have the economic means to pay for parochial school education, and if the state is unwilling to make it possible for the parochial school to provide that constitutionally guaranteed education without cost or at nominal cost to these parents.

(4) *The precedents.* Governmental aid to religious education is by no means unprecedented. On the contrary, the grant of public funds to religious schools would be no more than a logical and rational extension of long-standing practices. The exemption religious institutions receive under the Federal and state tax laws is an instance of substantial government aid. Under the National Youth Administration program established in 1935 private educational institutions were accorded the same benefits as public schools, and religious schools along with secular schools received the benefit of the part-time service performed by students and paid for by the Federal government. Under the Federal School-Lunch Act of 1946, too, children in parochial schools were treated exactly the same as in public schools. Under the Legislative Reorganization Act of 1946, in its provision for the education of Senate and Congress pages at the expense of the Federal government, it was expressly stated that the pages might attend private or parochial schools if they so chose, provided that "such private or parochial school shall be reimbursed by the Senate and House of Representatives only in the same amount as would be if the page or pages were attending a public school." Government aid is provided, directly or indirectly, under the G.I. Bill of Rights, the National Defense Education Act, the College Aid Act, the Anti-Poverty Act, and under the Elementary and Secondary Education Act of 1965.[45] It is clear, therefore, that the granting of government funds to help parochial schools in their work would be no more than following well-established precedents.

(5) *The solutions in other countries.* The United States is practically alone among all the nations of the world in that it does not recognize in a material way the function of parochial schools in the educational system.[46] Even France — where the principle of the separation of church and state is revered as much if not more than in the United States — provision has been made to aid financially in the education

523

of children in confessional schools.[47] Can it be that all these countries are wrong and only the United States is right? Is it not more likely that we are mistaken as to what is fair and just and consistent with democratic principles?

(6) *The welfare of children.* In any event, no reasonable person can take exception to the inclusion of children attending parochial schools in state-financed benefits that are intended to better the welfare of children. To discriminate against Catholic children in providing hot lunches or medical or dental services would be an act of pure discrimination on religious grounds — without even the spurious justification of the so-called principle of the absolute separation of church and state. Transporting children to school in buses is also a welfare benefit aimed at protecting children from the perils of the road in a fast-moving vehicular civilization and the dangers of inclement weather. Textbooks, remedial instruction, guidance counseling, preschool training and other auxiliary services, particularly to underprivileged children, can be placed in the same category.[48]

## The Case against State Aid[49]

The following arguments have been presented most vigorously against state aid:

(1) *Separation of church and state.* This, by all odds, is the most frequently and most vigorously asserted argument against state aid to religious education. Those who interpret the separation principle as barring even nonpreferential aid to religion have no intellectual difficulty in opposing state aid to religious schools. Those (particularly Protestants) who do not relish the concept of state neutrality as between belief and nonbelief sometimes argue that state aid to parochial schools is in fact preferential, inasmuch as it is only or principally in the Catholic religion that parochial schools are a major factor. Hence, to choose as the beneficiary of state aid that aspect of religion that is more or less peculiar to one faith, rather than those aspects (*e.g.,* church buildings, clergymen's salaries, etc.) which are general, is in fact if not in theory preferential and discriminatory. More often, however, it is argued that the nonpreferential state aid contemplated by the First Amendment does not include outright monetary aid, but merely such recognition of religion as is manifested by Presidential proclamations of thanksgiving and opening legislative sessions with prayer.

(2) *Divisiveness.* Parochial schools divide American children along religious lines, and are therefore a hindrance to true cultural unity. Though under the Pierce decision the Catholic Church and

Catholic parents have the constitutional right to effect this result, the result must be recognized as undesirable—even though unavoidable—and it certainly should not be facilitated by the grant of public funds. Moreover (this argument is most frequently urged by Jews), the religious instruction given in parochial schools—particularly concerning the crucifixion—frequently increases if it does not actually create anti-Semitism among Catholic children.[50] While, as a consequence of the liberal spirit within Catholicism under John XXIII and Paul VI and the actions of the Second Vatican Council, an effort is being made to modify the teachings regarding Jews in texts used in Catholic schools, the extent of such modification can be only modest, unless the Church is prepared to deny the veracity of the Gospels—which, of course, it is not. Although under the Constitution the state may not interfere with teachings in religious schools notwithstanding their harmful effect, certainly the state may not underwrite these teachings to make them financially possible.

(3) *No double taxation.* The double taxation argument is fallaciously based on the premise that the public school education of children is a benefit only to their parents, of which the parents may or may not avail themselves. But this is not the theory of the American program of universal education; if it were, the childless and corporations could not be taxed for education. We operate on the theory that all the public is benefited by the secular education of children and all the public must pay for it—whether or not they have children, and whether or not they want to send them to the public schools.

(4) *Fragmentization of the school system.* If Catholics may establish parochial schools out of public school funds, so too may Lutherans, Baptists, Episcopalians, Jews, and all other sects. The inevitable result will be the fragmentization and destruction of the public school system.

(5) *Interreligious rivalries.* Once it is admitted that public funds may be used for religious schools, there will inevitably follow conflict and rivalry among the sects as to how the funds are to be divided. The public officials responsible for the division will be subjected to unceasing pressure from religious groups, and these will exert every effort to elect to those offices members of their faith on whom they can rely for generous treatment. We may then have in this country a Catholic Party, a Jewish Party, and an Episcopalian Party. That this is not a fantastic impossibility is proved by the fact that—as will be seen shortly—for a brief period we had in this country a Catholic Party organized expressly and exclusively for the purpose of electing

legislators favorable to allocating public funds to Catholic schools.

(6) *The opening wedge.* No one objects to the inclusion of Catholic children in a program of hot lunches or medical care or any other public welfare benefits; but these welfare benefits should be distributed by and through public agencies. The danger in allowing their distribution through the parochial schools is that the program will constitute an opening wedge and serve as a precedent for wider benefits. If hot lunches, then why not bus transportation? If bus transportation, why not secular textbooks? If secular textbooks, why not nonreligious supplies and equipment (desks, chairs, blackboards, etc.) and why not the salaries of lay instructors teaching secular subjects?

## THE POSITIONS OF THE FAITHS AND OTHERS

### *Protestants*[51]

Notwithstanding their support of the Elementary and Secondary Education Act of 1965, Protestant church groups are still almost unanimously opposed to direct state aid to religious schools. Protestant opposition is no recent phenomenon—it is as old as the public school system. Indeed, its opposition to state aid to religious schools was one of the principal factors in eliminating sectarianism from the common schools; for the Protestants preferred to see Protestantism removed from the public schools rather than allow public funds to be used to support schools in which Catholicism was taught to the children of that faith.

Today there is probably no major Protestant group of any prominence in the country that favors direct government financial aid to confessional schools; and this includes such Protestant denominations as the Lutherans and Seventh Day Adventists, which maintain such schools. The pages of *The Christian Century* and *The Churchman* are replete with editorials and articles opposing the use of public funds for parochial school education. The General Board of the National Council of Churches in 1961 adopted with but one dissenting vote a statement saying, in part:

> We oppose grants from federal, state or local tax funds for non-public elementary and secondary schools.

On welfare benefits the situation is not so clear. The consensus of organized Protestantism is probably reflected in the statement of the 175th General Assembly of the United Presbyterian Church, adopted in May 1963, recommending that:

The policy of supplying welfare services to all children, whatever school they may be attending, be supported provided such services are identifiable by recipients as public services and the expenditures are administered by public authorities responsible to the electorate.

The consensus here is perhaps less certain. Yet it is probable that a consensus does exist. For example, even Protestants and Other Americans United is likely to agree with the position of the United Presbyterian Church (and taken earlier by the Federal Council of Churches[52]) that true welfare services—such as medical and dental services—should be made available nondiscriminately to all children, provided that they are treated as health and not educational measures, *i.e.*, that provision therefore is contained in legislation other than that whose purpose is to provide funds for education; and further that such services are administered or supervised by a public agency. Conversely, it is unlikely that any substantial Protestant church body would consider the grant (as distinguished from the loan) of free secular textbooks as anything but an educational service that should not be extended to parochial schools. There might be some difference among Protestants as to which category transportation belongs in; but it is probable that the majority of Protestant church leaders today would consider it a prohibited educational service rather than a permitted welfare one.

## The Catholic Church

The position of the Catholic Church on government aid to parochial schools is clear: the Church views the parochial school system as an equal partner with the public schools in the nation's educational pattern, and believes that as such an equal partner it is morally and legally entitled to share public funds with the public schools. Rev. George Johnson clearly and succinctly stated the Catholic Church position in an article in *The Atlantic Monthly*.[53]

The Catholic argument is that, since the states possess laws compelling all children to go to school, it is the duty of the state to provide schools that [are in] accord with the dictates of the parents' conscience.

The position of the Church was set forth in more detail in a statement that was submitted by the National Catholic Welfare Conference to a subcommittee of the House of Representatives considering Federal aid to education. In this statement the Conference set forth five basic principles that should govern the relationship between nonpublic schools and the government in a democracy.[54] The substance of these five principles is as follows:

PRINCIPLE I. Parents have the primary and principal right in the education of their children. This right carries with it the corresponding duty to arrange for the formal education of their children in a school which will prepare the child for the responsibilities of adulthood and of citizenship. In exercising this right and in performing this duty parents may select either a public or a nonpublic school for the education of their children. . . .

PRINCIPLE II. In our democracy the establishment, maintenance and general control of schools are responsibilities of the people in a community. The people fulfill these responsibilities generally in three ways:

1. Through a school board which controls a public school.
2. Through a church which controls a parochial school.
3. Through an association which controls a private school.

It has been characteristic of American education that the people, like the various schools in a community, have worked together in a common effort to train good citizens for the community and the Nation. . . .

PRINCIPLE III. Unlike a totalitarian state, the government in a democracy has of itself nothing to teach. It does not attempt to impose itself upon the citizens.

In a democracy the functions of the government in education are restricted to:

1. Financing schools which meet standards set in terms of citizenship.
2. Enforcing compulsory education laws.
3. Engaging in direct educational activities in such fields as military science and government service.

PRINCIPLE IV. Education is not to be regarded as a governmental service similar to police or fire protection. . . . Education does not belong to the Government in the same way as do other activities that need public support and control; its purposes and processes are to be determined not by governmental dictation and political power, but by those people, particularly the parents, whose interests the schools are intended to serve.

PRINCIPLE V. The financing of schools through public taxation is a responsibility of government, especially of local and State governments. This responsibility entails an obligation to observe the norms of distributive justice in distributing tax funds among the schools within the community. Since government itself has nothing to teach, and because government receives a full return from its educational investment when a school produces well-trained citizens, therefore every school to which parents may send their children in compliance with the compulsory education laws of the State is entitled to a fair share of tax funds. Local and State governments which refuse to support schools not under the control of the local school board are guilty of an injustice against other qualified schools within the community.

It should be noted that under these principles the ideal system is one in which there are no state schools at all, except specialized schools that train for military or government service. Otherwise the government's function is limited to enforcing compulsory education laws and financing nongovernmental schools. Under these principles the ideal educational system is the one prevailing in the Province of Quebec, where there are no public schools in the American sense of the term, but only government-financed confessional schools. There is little doubt that the Catholic Church in the United States would consider the Quebec solution ideal for our country. It would undoubtedly likewise accept the solution in the Netherlands, where Catholic, Protestant, and public schools are all considered equal partners in the educational system and all share proportionately in tax-raised funds for education.

The Church however, is realistic enough to recognize the unlikelihood of achieving either of these ideal solutions in this country in the near future. Hence, while insisting on the justice of its demands for a partner's share in tax-raised funds for education, the Church is willing for the present to accept a solution under which auxiliary or welfare benefits are granted on an equal basis to children attending parochial schools. By "auxiliary benefits" the church means principally transportation, textbooks and library resources, nonreligious instructional supplies, remedial instruction, preschool training, counseling, testing and guidance, and health and welfare services. This, the church believes, is the minimum it can in good conscience accept.

## The Jews and Others

The position of organized Jewish groups is by and large the same as that of the Protestant groups. With the exception of a comparatively small minority, principally among the Orthodox, they oppose government aid to religious schools, but approve the inclusion of all children in programs for the distribution of the noneducational welfare benefits. They do not generally consider transportation and instructional supplies to be welfare benefits, but limit that term to hot lunches and medical and dental services.

Among the nonreligious groups, strongest opposition to direct aid to parochial schools has come from major educational organizations, such as the National Education Association, the Council of Chief State Officers, the National Congress of Parents and Teachers, the American Association of School Administrators, and the National School Boards Association, and from the American Civil Liberties Union. The American Federation of Labor-Congress of Industrial Organizations, on the other hand, has expressed sympathy for the Catholic position and seeks to find some compromise solution.

## DIRECT GRANTS OF STATE FUNDS TO PAROCHIAL SCHOOLS

### The Struggle in New York

Today practically every state in the union prohibits the appropriation of public money to schools controlled by religious organizations.[55] How this came about is best indicated by a summary of the struggle in New York — in the main typical of the struggle in many other states; and the solution evolved in New York served as a pattern followed in many other states.

In 1838 John Hughes became bishop of New York. It was about this time that New England, under the leadership of Horace Mann, abolished the denominational character of its schools. In New York tax-raised moneys were turned over to the Public School Society for distribution among nonsectarian schools. In a number of communities some public support was given to religious schools of different denominations, including Catholic; but in New York City by 1824 the Public School Society succeeded in gaining absolute control of the funds for education. Thereafter the Society refused to allot any funds for denominational education except in denominational orphan asylums. The validity of these payments to Catholic orphan asylums for the education of the children was later upheld by New York's highest court, notwithstanding a state constitutional provision prohibiting the payment of public funds to any denominational school or institution of learning. The court held that an orphan asylum is not an educational institution within the purview of the constitutional prohibition..[56]

Dissatisfied with the refusal of the Society to allot any funds for denominational schools, a number of Protestant and Catholic schools appealed to the state legislature. A committee of the legislature, after a full hearing at which all sides were heard, ruled that "the school fund of the state [was] purely of a civil character, and that the entrusting of it to religious or ecclesiastical bodies was a violation of an elementary principle in the policies of the state and country." The ruling was not accepted by the Catholics, particularly not by Bishop Hughes, who contended that though the schools under the jurisdiction of the Public School Society were presumably nonsectarian, they were in effect Protestant in their teaching staffs, textbooks, Bible instruction, and in the general atmosphere of the classrooms. All this, Bishop Hughes protested, constituted a menace to the faith of Catholic children; the only just thing to do, he contended, was to allot to the Catholic schools a fair share of the Public School Fund.[57]

William H. Seward, governor of the state, was impressed with the Catholic case. In his message to the legislature in January 1840 he noted that many children of Catholic immigrants were in effect excluded from the public schools because of their permeation with Protestantism. He therefore recommended to the legislature that it enact legislation that would help finance the establishment of schools in which these children might be instructed by teachers professing the same faith as the children.[58] When word of the governor's action reached New York City, the Church immediately drew up a petition to the common council of the city asking for a share of the school fund. The petition was concurred in by a Scotch Presbyterian church and a Hebrew congregation; but it was opposed by the Public School Society, a large number of Protestant churches, and many individual citizens, and it failed to obtain approval by the council.

The city's rejection of the petition only served to spur the Church on to more intensive activities. A series of public meetings were held to arouse public support. Speaking at one of these meetings, Bishop Hughes set forth the Church's opposition to the public schools, and the basis of its right to share in the public funds for education. Morality, he argued, could not be taught without religion; religion itself would disappear and be replaced by infidelity or indifference. Moreover, the public school, as it was then conducted, tended to draw the pupil away from his religion. The Catholic parochial schools, on the other hand, made an effective contribution to the public welfare by combining religious instruction with the same secular education given in the public schools. Therefore they should be given "a fair and just proportion of the funds appropriated for the common schools, provided Catholics will do with it the same thing that is done in the common schools, and leave no reason to complain that the system is not followed." Since Catholics could not conscientiously attend public schools, particularly in view of the anti-Catholic bias in the textbooks, they had a right to educate their children in schools and by teachers of their own selection at public expense, provided that no part of the public money was diverted to the teaching of the Catholic faith.[59]

The controversy induced the city board of aldermen to reopen the issue and conduct a public hearing, at which Bishop Hughes presented the Church position forcefully and eloquently, but to no avail. By a vote of 15 to 1 the request was rejected.[60] Undaunted, Bishop Hughes then petitioned the state superintendent of schools, who issued a report favorable to the Church's plea and recommending that the state legislature change the law to allow appropriations for Catholic schools and to curb the powers of the Public School Society.

This action intensified the acrimony surrounding the issue. The Catholics accused the Protestants of injecting prejudice and bigotry into the discussions, and the Protestants charged that Bishop Hughes and his followers were seeking to undermine religious liberty and the separation of church and state.[61]

The legislature adjourned without taking action. Before it convened again in 1841 a new election took place. For the first and—as far as is known—the last time in American history there appeared on the ballot a Catholic Party, consisting of candidates pledged to support the position of the Church. In comparative figures the Catholic Party received a small number of votes, and soon disappeared as a separate party; but from November 1841 the Catholic Church was in politics to stay.

When the legislature reconvened in January 1842, it again turned down Governor Seward's request that parochial schools receive public financial support; and it also ended the role of the Public School Society in distributing tax money for school purposes. A board of education was established in New York City that had the sole right to use tax funds for educational purposes.[62] Two years later the state legislature made the prohibition even more specific and comprehensive. It enacted a law directing that

> no school shall be entitled to a portion of the school moneys in which the religious sectarian doctrine or tenet of any particular Christian or other religious sect shall be taught, inculcated or practiced, or in which any book or books containing compositions favorable or prejudicial to the particular doctrine or tenets of any Christian sect shall be used, or which shall teach the doctrine or tenets of any other religious sect, or which shall refuse to permit the visits and examinations provided for in this act.[63]

During the half-century following the enactment of these laws sporadic attempts were made to undo the legislation and obtain support for parochial schools from public funds.[64] Seeking to put an end to such attempts, the state constitutional convention of 1894 adopted a provision (Article 9, Section 4) reading:

> Neither the state nor any subdivision thereof shall use its property or credit or any public money, or authorize or permit either to be used, directly or indirectly, in aid or maintenance, other than for examination or inspection, of any school or institution of learning wholly or in part under the control or direction of any religious denomination, or in which any denominational tenet or doctrine is taught.

The convention committee on education, in reporting the provision, stated:

The first sentence of the last section of the proposed article needs no explanation or defense. In the opinion of the committee there is no demand from the people of the State upon this convention so unmistakable, widespread and urgent; none, moreover, so well grounded in right and reason, as that the public school system of the State will be forever protected by constitutional safeguards from all sectarian influence or interference, and that public money shall not be used, directly or indirectly, to propagate denominational tenets or doctrines.[65]

A proposal to limit the section so that it should "not apply to schools in institutions subject to the visitation and inspection of the State Board of Charities," was defeated on the ground that it "is in flagrant derogation of a sound and universal principle, that none but public schools shall receive the support of public moneys, and that the people of this State, or any section of this State, shall not be taxed for the support of education of a sectarian nature in any schools whatever."[66]

In opposition to Section 4 it was argued that it was discriminatory, that it was contrary to the requirements of public welfare, and that support of religious schools was in fact given to the children rather than to the schools involved. In support of the provision, Elihu Root urged:

It is not a question of religion, or of creed, or of party; it is a question of declaring the great American principle of eternal separation between Church and State.[67]

This provision of the state constitution was adopted; and — except for an amendment in 1938 to permit transportation to parochial schools — remained unchanged in all subsequent revisions of the constitution. It should be noted that not only does the provision bar public financial aid to parochial schools but also prohibits the teaching of "any denominational tenet" in the public schools.

## The Constitutions and the Laws

The struggle in New York that culminated in the adoption of a constitutional bar of government support of parochial schools was duplicated in many other states. By 1875 it was a generally accepted proposition throughout the nation that tax-raised funds should be used only for schools publicly controlled and free of sectarian influence or control. In that year President Grant urged the Army of the Tennessee:

Resolve that neither the state nor the nation, nor both combined, shall support institutions of learning other than those sufficient to afford every child growing up in the land the opportunity of good common school education, unmixed with sectarian, pagan or atheistical dogmas.

The next year Congress sought to write into the Federal Constitution an express provision barring the use of state funds in support of denominational schools. Although the proposed amendment failed to receive the necessary two-thirds vote in the Senate, the principle was firmly founded in the American political system. Every state admitted to the union since 1876 was compelled by Congress to write into its constitution a requirement that it maintain a school system "free from sectarian control."[68] Today practically every state in the nation has a constitutional provision that either expressly or impliedly prohibits the appropriation of public money to schools controlled by religious organizations.[69]

By and large, the state legislatures have been faithful to these constitutional provisions, and direct appropriations of public funds to religious schools have been uncommon. In the relatively few cases in which the constitutional prohibition was violated, the state courts in the main have upheld the constitution and enjoined the illegal payment.[70] Occasionally state courts have permitted violations of the spirit of the constitutional provision; and sometimes have acquiesced in the violation even of the letter. Instances of the former are cases in which appropriations of public funds were made to orphan asylums or institutions for dependent children under sectarian control;[71] although even here other state courts have refused to distinguish between sectarian education in asylums or institutions for dependent children and sectarian education in schools.[72] An instance of judicial acquiescence in a violation of the plain letter of the constitution is the case—already discussed—in which the New York courts held that an outright grant of public funds to Canisius College in Buffalo was not subject to judicial attack by a mere taxpayer.

Until recently, little doubt was expressed that the First Amendment of the Federal Constitution bars the appropriation of Federal funds to sectarian schools. It will be remembered that in Bradfield vs. Roberts[73] the United States Supreme Court upheld a grant of Federal funds for the benefit of a hospital controlled by a corporation organized by an order of nuns. The court ruled that both the corporation and the services rendered by the hospital were nonsectarian, and therefore the grant was not violative of the Constitution. Implicit in this decision is the holding that the Constitution would be violated by a grant of Federal money for sectarian purposes, or to an institution controlled by a sectarian organization.

The same holding is implicit too in the case of Quick Bear vs.

Leupp.[74] In that case the Supreme Court ruled that treaty funds held by the Federal government as trustee for Indians who were in fact its real owners could be disbursed to private, religious schools at the designation of the Indians to pay the cost of their tuition. It is true that the court at first summarily disposed of the constitutional issue with the statement:

> Some reference is made to the Constitution in respect to this contract with the Bureau of Catholic Indian Missions. It is not contended that it is unconstitutional, and it could not be.

The actual decision in the case, however, was based on the holding that the moneys expended belonged not to the government but to the Indians. That the decision would have been different if the moneys had in fact come from the Treasury appears clear from the following statement of the court:

> But it is contended that the spirit of the Constitution requires that the declaration of policy that the Government "shall make no appropriation whatever for education in any sectarian schools"[75] should be treated as applicable, on the ground that the actions of the United States were always to be undenominational, and that, therefore, the Government can never act in a sectarian capacity, either in the use of its own funds or in that of the funds of others, in respect of which it is a trustee; hence that even the Sioux trust fund cannot be applied for education in Catholic schools, even though the owners of the fund so desire it. But we cannot concede the proposition that Indians cannot be allowed to use their own money to educate their children in the schools of their own choice *because the Government is necessarily undenominational, as it cannot make any law respecting an establishment of religion or prohibiting the free exercise thereof.*

In any event, under the Everson, McCollum, and Zorach cases it is clear that the First Amendment bars the appropriation of government funds to sectarian schools. In the Everson case the court ruled that the payment out of public funds of the expense of transporting children to parochial schools did not violate the First Amendment; but made it clear that a payment of public funds to the school itself for its sectarian purposes would violate the Constitution. In the McCollum case the court held that the use of public school property for religious education violated the First Amendment. In the Zorach case the court expressly stated that "Government may not finance religious groups."

This is the view taken by the Federal government, in respect to elementary and secondary schools. Thus, in the publication *The State and Nonpublic Schools* issued in 1958 by the Department of Health, Education, and Welfare, the statement is made[76] that "Direct aid for sectarian purposes is prohibited ... by the 1st and 14th Amendments to the Constitution of the United States." A legal memorandum issued in 1961 by the Health, Education, and Welfare general counsel states that, "Across-the-board grants to church schools may not be made."[77]

That this view has been widely held is indicated by the following statement made in 1949 by Cardinal Spellman:

> In the State of New York, as in practically every other state, the State constitution prohibits the use of public funds for the support of sectarian schools. The Supreme Court of the United States has interpreted the Federal Constitution in the same sense.[78]

More recently, however, the view has been expressed, particularly but by no means exclusively in Catholic Church sources, that secular and religious subjects in parochial schools can be separated and that it would not violate the Constitution for government to support financially the teaching of the secular subjects. As stated in a legal memorandum issued by the National Catholic Welfare Conference,

> There exists no constitutional bar to aid to education in church-related schools in a degree proportionate to the value of the public function it performs. Such aid to the secular functions may take the form of matching grants, or long-term loans to institutions, or of scholarships, tuition payments or tax benefits.

Despite this, it is difficult to escape the conclusion that the First Amendment, as construed in the Everson and McCollum cases, forbids use of Federal funds to support parochial schools even in respect to its secular subjects. The Everson and McCollum cases also settled the issue of the applicability of the First Amendment to the states. It is now no longer open to question that the states are precluded to the same extent as the Federal government from making any law respecting an establishment of religion; indeed, both these cases and the Zorach, Engel, and Schempp cases all involved action by states rather than by the Federal government. It is therefore clear that a state grant of public funds for the support of sectarian schools would violate the Federal Constitution as well as its own. (In Almond vs. Day[79] and Swart vs. South Burlington School District,[80] the highest courts of Virginia and Vermont respectively ruled unconstitutional under both state and Federal constitutions the use of public funds to pay tuition to sectarian schools.) In June 1966, Maryland's highest court ruled in the case of Horace Mann League vs. Board of Public Works that the Federal Constitution bars granting of state funds to sectarian colleges to construct classroom, science, dormitory, and other college buildings. Whether a taxpayer could seek relief in the Federal courts if the state does not allow a taxpayer to sue—or even if it does—has already been discussed. Of course, even if a taxpayer could not sue to enjoin the appropriation, that fact would not affect its unconstitutionality.

## INCORPORATING PAROCHIAL SCHOOLS
### INTO THE PUBLIC SCHOOL SYSTEM

### *The Background*

Litigation involving the outright appropriation of public funds to sectarian schools is rare; the Canisius College case is almost unique since 1900.[81] But this paucity is more than made up by the abundance of litigation on attempts to incorporate Catholic parochial schools into the public school system. Moreover, this litigation invariably brings with it interreligious bitterness and conflict as intense as evoked by any issue in church-state relationships—not excluding the ambassadorship to the Vatican and Jewish objections to religious Christmas observances in the public schools.

The Baltimore Plenary Councils of the Catholic Church—particularly the Third—had exhorted if not commanded the establishment of a church school in every parish. Many parishes faithfully complied, only to find out sooner or later that the economic burden of maintaining the school was too heavy for the Catholic community to bear. The first possible solution that presented itself was to obtain aid by sharing in the moneys raised by taxation for public education. This effort proved almost invariably unsuccessful; and it evoked a countereffort on the part of Protestantism that succeeded in writing a prohibition of such sharing in practically every state constitution in the union.

The second possible solution was to incorporate the parochial school into the public school system, and thus indirectly obtain the desired share of tax-raised funds for education that, because of Protestant resistance, could not be obtained directly. There was adequate and respectable precedent for this solution; most of the Protestant parochial schools of the middle states had been simply transferred into the states' public school systems. In many communities a century later this procedure was attempted with respect to Catholic parochial schools. In some it was effected after the local school board had acquired a majority of Catholic members; in others—as we shall see—it was effected with the cordial approval and cooperation of many non-Catholic taxpayers who welcomed the additional state aid that came to their community as a result of such a substantial increase in the public school population.

The attempted incorporation of the Catholic parochial schools into the public school system was of course vastly different in its outcome and consequences from the public school's absorption of the Protestant church schools. Professor Zollmann, in his standard volume, *American Church Law*, explained the difference thus:

> The Protestant denominations, being generally in the majority, naturally were somewhat favored, and quite frequently succeeded in having their particular religious instruction continued in the public school which succeeded their parochial school. In consequence, the shift of Protestant parochial schools into the public school system was rapid and unimpeded. The same cannot be said of the Catholic schools. The Catholics, being in the minority in most communities, naturally received a less liberal treatment. Hence they quite generally retained their parochial schools and have them to the present day.

This explanation appears to be an oversimplification and historically inaccurate. In the first place, it ignores completely Horace Mann's struggle in Massachusetts. In the second place, the Protestant church school preceded the public school system which grew out of it; whereas the Catholic parochial school system came into being on a substantial scale after the public school system had been well established. Finally, the transfer of the Protestant church schools to the public authorities resulted in their secularization. True, this transformation was frequently bitterly contested, and often required judicial intervention to effect it. But when a choice could not be avoided, American Protestantism accepted secularization. This the Catholic church never did, and this is the basic reason for the difference in the outcome. Nevertheless, Professor Zollmann's explanation for the continued existence today of the Catholic parochial school system has this much possible truth in it: it may be that if Catholic children received a more cordial welcome and acceptance in the ex-Protestant parochial schools, their parents might have resisted the demands of the Church for the establishment of a separate Catholic school system.

That the Catholic Church would not accept secularization as the price for tax support is evidenced by the fact that whereas clerical teachers in ex-Protestant public schools are a rarity, every Catholic parochial school incorporated into the public school system retains its staff of nuns and brothers. It is evidenced further by Cardinal James Gibbons' description of how the incorporation worked in the town of Faribault, Minnesota, which has given its name to this compromise plan:

> The schools are leased to the State authority for one year, the contract being renewable at the pleasure of the two parties. The same

teachers (Religious of St. Dominic) are retained. After hearing mass in the parish church, the children are marched to school. At 3:30 P.M., at the close of the school hours, the pupils are instructed in their cate-chism for an hour, and then dismissed. No textbooks to which the Archbishop objects are retained. Instead of receiving a precarious and small compensation from the parents, the teachers now receive a salary of $50 a month each from the school authorities. The teachers as well as the pupils are subject to an examination by the school board, and this arrangement has benefited both teachers and pupils. The schools are now more numerously attended than before.

The Faribault plan obviously does not contemplate the seculari-zation of parochial schools so incorporated into the public school sys-tem. Yet it must not be supposed that it was welcomed by the Cath-olic Church. It was clearly a compromise; and there was always the danger that ultimately the jurisdiction of the public school authori-ties would be extended at the expense of church control. Moreover, it represented a retreat not only from the promulgations of the Bal-timore Plenary Councils but also from the Canon Law and the papal encyclicals. Hence many American bishops and other church leaders strenuously opposed the Faribault plan.

The controversy within the American Catholic community was taken to the Congregation of the Propaganda in Rome, which in April 1892 issued something of a compromise decision that

The Decrees of the Baltimore Councils in respect to parochial schools remaining in full force, the agreement entered into by Archbish-op Ireland relative to the schools of Faribault and Stillwater, in view of all the circumstances, may be tolerated.

The anti-Faribaultists refused to accept this grudging approval of the plan. When Cardinal Francesco Satolli came to this country the next year as apostolic delegate, they laid the controversy before him, but he too refused to back the councils in full; instead, he left it to the local bishop in each case to decide whether or not the main-tenance of a parochial school in a particular parish was practicable; and if it was not, whether Catholic children might safely be permit-ted to attend the public schools. The controversy appeared to be fi-nally settled in 1893 in favor of the anti-Faribaultists by a direct let-ter from Pope Leo XIII to Cardinal Gibbons declaring that "the decrees which the Baltimore Councils, agreeably to the directions of the Holy See, have enacted concerning parochial schools, and what-ever else has been prescribed by the Roman Pontiffs, whether di-rectly or through the Sacred Congregations, concerning the same matter are to be steadfastly observed."[52]

Notwithstanding this implicit repudiation, the Faribault compromise did not disappear; in one form or another it is in effect in many predominantly Catholic communities—particularly in the midwest.[83] By 1937 there were at least 340 Catholic schools operating more or less under the Faribault plan.[84] One of the principal projects of Protestants and Other Americans United is to seek out these schools and by legal action terminate the partnership between church and state on which these schools operate.

The incorporation of Catholic parochial schools into the public school system has evoked much bitter controversy—not only between Catholic and Protestant communities, but even within Catholic communities. Much of this controversy has reached the courts for final determination. Before the decisions are discussed, it may be worth while to consider as case histories a few instances in which the controversies were so intense as to receive national attention.

### North College Hill[85]

North College Hill is a small Cincinnati suburb with a population in 1945 of some 7,500 persons. Before 1940 it was a pleasant, peaceful community, largely residential, and divided about evenly between Catholics and Protestants. In 1940 North College Hill had four public schools, two of which were on the elementary level and two were for high school and junior high school students. It also had on Grace Avenue a parochial school known as the St. Margaret Mary School. In 1940 the city school board, consisting of three Protestants and two Catholics, adopted a proposal under which the parochial school was incorporated into the public school system on the Faribault pattern. The parochial school building was rented to the public school authorities for an annual rental of $3,500, and the teaching nuns, Sisters of the Congregation of Precious Blood, were retained as teachers at a salary of $100 monthly—substantially less than that paid to regular teachers in the city public schools.

During the following year the new school, officially designated as Public School Number 3 but popularly called the Grace Avenue School, operated as a public school with the same curriculum and personnel as it had when it was officially a parochial school. But after a while non-Catholic elements in the community began to object to the arrangement, and started to organize for the 1941 board election.

The Cincinnati archdiocese, in a formal statement issued at the time the controversy was finally on the verge of settlement, asserted that the Church had not taken any initiative in the incorporation of the parochial school into the public school system, and that the church authorities "were never enthusiastic about it; they merely tolerated it." Moreover, the statement continued, the "parish of St. Margaret Mary and the Sisters benefited very little financially by the arrangement."

It is difficult to reconcile this statement with the action of the priest of the St. Margaret Mary parish during the election campaign. The campaign was fought almost exclusively on the issue whether the Grace Avenue School should be continued in the public school system or returned to the Church. Five candidates committed to its return ran against five candidates opposed. During the course of the campaign the parish priest addressed a letter to his parishioners naming the candidates opposed to returning the school to the Church, and then saying:

> If we do not elect the above five [named] candidates we will lose the money paid by the Board of Education to the Sisters as salary; we will lose what can be made on the $3,500 as rental for the school; we will lose the $500 paid to the parish by the Sisters as rental for the cottages in which they live; we will lose the privilege of free text books; (formerly you paid four times more than you pay now for work books plus 25¢ for the religion course.) *The pupils of our schools have lost none of the benefits they enjoyed in the previous years but have been given additional ones.* Children now pay 5 cents to see movies given at the school, whereas they used to pay 10 cents—a saving of 50%. To prevent all these heavy losses, please vote for the above candidates.

The campaign ended in the election of a new board consisting of four Protestants and one Catholic. The result may have been influenced by the board's action in increasing the annual rental paid for the building from $3,600 to $6,000, and the fact that the basement was retained for parish use, which included the playing of bingo games for money. The new board notified the parish that the existing arrangements, due to expire in June 1942, would not be renewed. This decision was accepted by the community, which in 1943 elected Protestants to the two vacancies to be filled. In July 1943 Dr. William A. Cook was appointed to the position of superintendent of schools.

In the fall of 1945 a regular biennial election was held to fill the places of three members whose terms were to expire January 1, 1946. Again the candidates campaigned primarily on the parochial school issue, and again the community split largely along sectarian lines. It is clear, however, that a number of Catholics were opposed to the incorporation of the parochial school into the public school system; and it is likewise clear that a number of non-Catholics supported the incorporation. These were persuaded in part at least by the argument that the added children classified as public school pupils would substantially increase the amount of state aid the school system would receive. The election brought three Catholics into the board, giving them a majority of the five members.

The new members met with Superintendent Cook, who agreed to cooperate with them to bring about reincorporation. This he did by nominating the teaching nuns to be members of the public school system. He made this contingent on two conditions—both of which were fulfilled: that the nuns hold the required teaching certificates, and that the board's counsel affirm the legality of the action. Thereafter the building was again relet to the public school authorities for $6,000 annually, and the nuns were placed on the regular payroll of the board of education, though at substandard salaries. (The payment of substandard salaries to the nuns was insisted on by the Catholic majority members of the board.)

At first the relations between Dr. Cook and the majority of the board were amicable; but this period of harmonious cooperation lasted less than three months. The first incident was the attempt of the majority to reinstate one of the city's principals who had been demoted to teacher for cause by the previous board at the recommendation of Dr. Cook. Under Ohio law, the superintendent is the only one who may nominate a principal or teacher for appointment; and Dr. Cook's refusal to nominate the demoted principal aroused the bitter hostility of the majority of the board. Indeed, for a while the president of the board—the majority's leader—stated that the board would make no appointments of any principals or teachers on Dr. Cook's recommendations until he nominated the demoted principal.

This position threatened the whole public school system, since a substantial number of vacancies occur each year that must be filled before the fall term begins. Moreover, the majority took the position that they would approve no nominations until all applications were submitted to them for review. It was evident that the intent of the majority was—in the words of the president—that the "recommendations of Dr. Cook will not be accepted until the person we desire is recommended." Finally, in August 1946, just three weeks before the fall term was about to begin, the majority relented and approved eleven of the thirteen recommendations made by Dr. Cook to fill vacancies.

That the controversy between Dr. Cook and the majority was basically a religious controversy was indicated by the fact that every proposal by Dr. Cook was rejected by a vote of the three Catholic members in opposition and the two Protestants in its favor. It was also evident when, in April 1946, the president of the board attended, without invitation, a meeting of the local parent-teachers association and became involved in a heated argument in which he referred to "your school" and "our school"—an apparent admission that he considered the Grace Avenue School as only nominally a part of the public school system.

Other incidents, including a request by teachers supported by Dr. Cook for a cost-of-living bonus, served to aggravate the tension between Dr. Cook and the majority of the board. By the fall of 1946 it became evident to all that the majority would not renew Dr. Cook's contract on its expiration, July 31, 1947. The final break came at the regular monthly meeting of the board in February 1947, when by a vote of three to two the office of superintendent was declared vacant as of July 31, 1947, on the ground that Dr. Cook had been guilty of insubordination.

The reaction of the community was immediate and cumulative. Within twenty-four hours 28 of the 31 teachers in three schools signed a petition to the board protesting Dr. Cook's dismissal. At the same time a delegation of high school students called on Dr. Cook to say that they wished to go on strike; but Dr. Cook succeeded in dissuading them—though, as it turned out, only temporarily. Petitions in support of Dr. Cook were signed by three-fourths of the high school students, and by all but a few of the students in the seventh and eighth grades.

At the March meeting of the board the majority refused to reconsider. The tension in the community mounted to a point where an explosion sooner or later became inevitable. Immediately after the March meeting more than 90% of the 750 students in three schools failed to report for classes. The strike, accompanied by daily mass picketing, was not called off until two months later, and then only on the urging of a representative of the National Education Association. A petition of protest was circulated among the residents of North College Hill and was signed by more than 1,100 citizens, mostly parents of children in the public school system. A mother of a student in the school system started a legal action to enjoin all payments to the parish church and the teaching nuns on the ground that the Grace Avenue School remained, for all practical purposes, a parochial school, and that the payments violated the Ohio and Federal constitutions.

The explosion came in the April meeting of the board. More

than a thousand persons attended, crowding a school gymnasium. First an attempt was made by one of the Protestant members of the board to present more petitions in support of Dr. Cook. When this failed the secretary of the board read, one by one, letters of resignation from 29 of the 30 teachers in three of the city's five public schools. (One of the other two schools was the Grace Avenue School, and the other was a school attended exclusively by Negro children. The teachers of this school did not take sides in the controversy.)

Many members of the audience, parents and children, began to cry. The majority members remained adamant. A number of citizens became infuriated. They rushed to the platform and struck a majority member of the board, who suffered a discolored eye and torn clothes. Other members of the board got under the table. The police, who were present during the entire meeting, had difficulty in ending the fracas. Finally they succeeded in getting the Catholic members out, and the meeting broke up without formal adjournment. Five persons, including the husband of the woman who had started the suit to stop payments, were arrested and jailed until bail could be raised—though it does not appear that any of them was ever actually brought to trial.

In May the Ohio Education Association issued a statement declaring the North College Hill system an unprofessional place in which to work; and this statement was endorsed by the National Education Association. In June the two organizations issued jointly a detailed, formal statement, in which they condemned the three majority members on ten counts. The statement concluded by urging all members of the teaching profession to refuse employment in North College Hill, and requesting school administrators to give preference in filling vacancies to the teachers who resigned.

This action by the education associations resulted in the final settlement of the controversy. The majority members found it impossible to fill the vacancies caused by the dismissal of Dr. Cook and the resignation of the bulk of the system's teaching staff. Having no alternative, they finally accepted the offer of the minority member that all five resign. The resignation of the whole board on June 17, 1947, brought the public school system under the control of the Probate Court. One of the first acts of the Probate judge was to renew Dr. Cook's contract for a three-year period; he also appointed a new board consisting of four Protestants and one Catholic. The new board confirmed Dr. Cook's contract; the teachers were rehired and the strike was called off. In November an election resulted in an all-

Protestant board. The arrangement between the parish and the public school system was discontinued, and the Grace Avenue School again became the St. Margaret Mary parochial school.

After the Probate judge stepped in and the ultimate settlement of the controversy became clear, the chancellor of the Cincinnati archdiocese of the Catholic Church issued a long statement presenting the Church's side of the controversy. Briefly, its position was that the arrangement between the parish and the school system was entirely legal; that it was profitable to the public school system — much more so than to the Church, which merely tolerated but was not enthusiastic about it; that the controversy between Dr. Cook and the majority of the board was unrelated to any religious differences, but that the religious issue was artificially brought in by Protestant clergymen who were guilty of anti-Catholic prejudice; that religion was not taught in the Grace Avenue School during school hours, but only before school began or after school hours; that the teaching nuns had regular teaching certificates; that the three Cincinnati daily papers were unfair in reporting the controversy; that the Probate judge was unfair in rehiring Dr. Cook for three years and in appointing only one Catholic to the school board.

One conclusion stands out from the North College Hill incident: an attempt to invoke state machinery in the aid of religion always carries with it the danger of acrimony and strife dividing the people along religious lines, and of bringing with it the very evils which the fathers of the Constitution sought to avoid by declaring the government to be without constitutional power to assume the responsibilities that belong to the church.

### *Dixon, New Mexico*[86]

The incident that became known as the Dixon School case involved not merely that remote community of 1,200 souls, but a large number of similar communities with similar school systems throughout the state of New Mexico. The controversy erupted in Dixon, and that hamlet gave its name to the ensuing litigation, which, however, concerned the educational system of the entire state.

In one important respect the Dixon situation was different from that in North College Hill and in most of the other communities where Catholic parochial schools have been incorporated into the public school system. In the latter the public schools were established first, and incorporation was later effected to relieve the parish of some or all of the financial burden of maintaining a parochial school that was formed because of the decrees of the Baltimore Councils and the declarations of the Vatican. In New Mexico it was the church which, through its missionary schools to the Indians, first brought education and Christian culture into the remote wilderness.

Even today the poverty, remoteness, severe winters, and absence of modern facilities make it difficult to obtain secular teachers for mountainous and rural communities, to which, however, devoted members of the Catholic religious orders willingly go. Many of these communities, with their Mexican and Indian ancestry, have been predominantly Catholic for centuries; the Protestant and other non-Catholic residents are comparatively recent arrivals. In a number of poverty-stricken communities there have been no public school buildings at all, and in not a few the Church allowed the public school authorities to use its property gratuitously or at a nominal rental.

On the other hand, it is no less true that efforts on the part of non-Catholic residents to alter the situation have been strenuously opposed and frequently frustrated by the Church—undoubtedly jealous of its dominant position in education and reluctant to relinquish it. In Dixon, for example, a new public school had been built with the aid of WPA funds; and it was to this school that the Protestants—constituting about half the population—sent their children. That is, they sent their children until one day it was closed, without notice, and all the children transferred to the Catholic school taught by the Sisters of St. Francis. The public school building was abandoned and allowed to rot and decay. In view of the dominance of the Church in determining educational policy, there can be little doubt as to the source of responsibility for this condition.

One incident, cited by the Supreme Court of New Mexico, is sufficient to indicate the power of the Church there. The religious (members of Catholic orders, usually nuns but occasionally brothers) who taught in the public schools were selected and assigned to various schools by the heads of their respective orders, and were accepted by the school boards without question. In addition, transfers and substitutions were made at will by the same authority, and these were likewise accepted by the boards. Indeed, in the many schools in different counties involved in the subsequent litigation, there was only one instance where a county board of education attempted to assert its authority in the selection of a teacher. In one county the board asked the Mother Superior of the order not to send back the principal of the local school for the coming school year, but requested two other Sisters be retained there as teachers. The request went unanswered for months by the Mother Superior, who finally appeared, questioned the local president of the board, said the complaint against the principal was trivial, that she would not have her Sisters shoved around, and if there were any more complaints about her Sisters she would take all of them out of the school. The Sister to whom the board had objected was returned to the school for the following year, and the Sisters the board had desired to retain were transferred.

The situation in Dixon in 1948 was more or less typical of that in other communities. The transfer of the public school to the church building was not accompanied by any physical change in the buildings or classrooms. Crucifixes, holy fonts, pictures, statues, and a host of other subjects and symbols peculiar to the Catholic faith abounded in the building and the classrooms. The religious in Dixon were members of the Franciscan Order, which is a working rather than a teaching order. As a result, many of the teachers had no real training in education; indeed, some of them were recent German arrivals who could hardly speak intelligible English.

Public school classes began officially at nine in the morning; but the school buses arrived regularly in time for mass at half past eight. Protestant children who came by bus — as most did — were required either to attend mass or stay outside the building — even in the winter and in inclement weather — until the building officially opened at nine for public school purposes. Children were required to recite "Hail Mary" several times each day. According to one affidavit, a Protestant youngster who refused to go to confession was locked in a room until nine o'clock at night, when he jumped out through a window and went home; his parents then took him out of school. There was an affidavit showing that Protestant children were urged by their teachers to go to confession, and acquired the habit of crossing themselves; that the children were enlisted by the teachers to sell raffles for a fund to erect a new church building; that a Protestant child received a poor grade in deportment for refusing to attend mass.

Further it was charged — and the courts found it to be a fact — that in another community commencement exercises were held in the Catholic church, to which the graduating class was marched to receive their diplomas. They came into the church with their hands folded in the gesture of prayer, passed the altar, and bowed to two statues of the Virgin Mary. The diplomas were handed out by the archbishop of Sante Fe, whose ring each child kissed as he received his diploma. Children who did not wish to participate in this ceremony could receive their diplomas by mail.[87]

A showdown finally came between the Protestant parents and the school authorities. The Protestants objected to the holding of public school in the church buildings, but were advised by the county board of education that funds were not available to erect a public school building. The Protestants then donated money and labor, put up a school building, gave it to the county and asked that it be opened and staffed with lay teachers. This request was denied; the new school was placed under a nun as principal, and the teaching of sectarian religion continued. Later a committee of Protestants appeared before the county board of education and demanded, among other things, that it stop the teaching of sectarian religion in the Dixon schools. The board held it did not have jurisdiction and declined to act, referring the protestors to the state board of education. They then appeared before the state board, and were told it was exclusively an appellate board, and since it had no written appeal from the county board it could do nothing. The meeting evidently waxed warm; and for the first time the members of the state board became really exercised over the matter. After the protestors had been dismissed, and the board had been in practically closed session for a time, the state superintendent of public instruction — who was also a member ex-officio of the state board — called on the archbiship of the diocese of Sante Fe and solicited his help. Another meeting of the board was held, and finally a directive relating to the operation of the school at Dixon was adopted, reading in part as follows:

> In an earnest effort to solve the community school problems of Dixon, the State Board of Education recommends and insists that the following plan be carried out:
> 1. That the new school recently completed at Dixon teach the first six grades, including the pre-first.
> 2. That this new school have all qualified lay teachers, with a lay principal.
> 3. That the public school, taught by Catholic Sisters, teach the 7 — 12 grades.
> 4. That school buses bringing children to Dixon run on a schedule that would bring the children to school on time, but not necessarily earlier.
> 5. That no religious instruction be given in either school by the teachers on school days. . . .

The archbishop directed a letter to all religious teaching within the public schools of the Archdiocese that read as follows:

> In view of the present agitation against Sisters in Public Schools and to avert grave future difficulties that could prove disastrous to the continuation of Sisters in public schools in the State of New Mexico, I request that no religious instructions be given in public school buildings by the teachers on school days. Catechism should be taught on Saturdays and Sundays.
>
> School buses bringing children to school will run on a schedule that will bring the children to school in time, but not necessarily earlier, and will leave immediately after school.

A special letter accompanied the copy of this letter sent to the religious at Dixon, in which the archbishop advised the religious to remove all religious emblems from public school rooms, forbade the saying of prayers or giving of religious instruction in the school on school days, and stated further that if any Sister did not obey these orders she would be removed from the Dixon public schools.

The archbishop's directive, notwithstanding its strict language, was not completely effective even in Dixon. In any event, it did not prevent the bringing of a suit for an injunction by a group of Protestant parents in many communities in the state (including Dixon) where the Dixon pattern was in effect.

A long trial followed, at which some 2,200 pages of testimony were taken. Thereafter a decision was handed down sustaining most of the charges. Both parties appealed to the state supreme court, which in 1951 sustained the lower court, but went further in one respect—it barred the wearing of religious garb by all public school teachers—even though the trial court had refused to issue such a blanket injunction. On the other hand it refused to bar all nuns from teaching in the public schools—refusing in that respect to follow the Missouri case of Harfst vs. Hoegen.[88] It did bar the future employment of those nuns and brothers who were found to have been guilty of sectarian teaching. (This debarment was required by New Mexico law.) All in all, the court made the following rulings:[89]

1. That 139 of the defendants [Religious] be forever barred from receiving any school moneys and employment in the public schools of New Mexico.

2. That school students are subject to the supervision of school authorities and teachers from the time that they arrive at the school in the morning until they leave in the afternoon.

3. That the constitution of New Mexico requires that the State board of education adopt a uniform system of textbooks.

4. That the adopting of sectarian indoctrinated textbooks and furnishing them to the tax supported schools violates the constitution

of New Mexico and the First Amendment to the Constitution of the United States.

5. That the furnishing of free textbooks to schools other than tax supported schools violates the Constitution of New Mexico.[90]

6. That the furnishing by the State of sectarian indoctrinated textbooks to private parochial schools is in violation of the First Amendment to the Constitution of the United States.

7. That the furnishing by the State of free school bus transportation to pupils of parochial schools is in violation of the constitution of New Mexico and the First Amendment to the Constitution of the United States.[91]

8. That the teaching of sectarian doctrine in the tax supported schools violates the constitution of New Mexico and the First Amendment to the Constitution of the United States.

9. That the holding of tax supported school classes in buildings which have religious emblems such as crosses, grottos, religious statuary and religious pictures, all peculiar to a certain denomination, violates the First Amendment to the Constitution of the United States.

10. That the holding of tax supported school classes in a building owned by the Roman Catholic Church or an Order thereof or an official thereof, part of said building being retained by said Order, Church or Official for use as a private or parochial school is in violation of the First Amendment to the Constitution of the United States.

11. That there is no separation between Church and State as contemplated and required by the First and Fourteenth Amendments to the Constitution of the United States in 27 named schools in New Mexico.

It was argued in behalf of the Church that the entire controversy was academic, inasmuch as the divorce of the parochial schools from the public schools had been completely effected by the joint action of the archbishop and the state board of education before the appeal was argued. The state supreme court, however, issued its decision and its injunction to prevent a possible repetition of the situation at some future time.

### Other Cases

The North College Hill and Dixon controversies are unfortunately not unique, but are typical of what happens when members of a community decide to revolt against the kind of education imposed on their children when a parochial school is incorporated into the public school. These controversies frequently find their way into the courts — usually on suit by irate Protestant parents. The effect on Protestant-Catholic relations in the community is invariably disastrous. The conflicts among warring sects that our constitutional fathers strove so valiantly to keep from these shores are reproduced in miniature in small midwestern towns. Political campaigns are fought along religious lines, with a slate of candidates supported by the Catholic Church opposed by a slate supported by Protestant ministers and parishioners.

It would be a mistake, however, to assume that the Catholic community is always united behind the Church in the controversies arising out of the incorporation of parochial schools into the public school system. In North College Hill — and in many other cases — not a few Catholic parents sided with those opposed to the incorporation. Moreover, in some instances the controversy is entirely among Catholics. One of the leading cases in this area, a Missouri case decided in 1941,[92] was begun by a group of Catholic parents who objected to a consolidation of school districts that resulted in the abandonment of a public school and the transfer of the children to an incorporated parochial school. In Pierz, Minnesota, where — according to a report of the state department of education — public and parochial schools were so intermingled as to be indistinguishable, a Catholic parent was excommunicated for conducting a poll of church members that resulted in a vote in favor of the erection of a public rather than a parochial high school.[93]

Excommunication, of course, is not available against dissident Protestant parents; but where the Church and its adherents have strong control over the public school machinery — as is usually the case where incorporation is effected — other means are occasionally available. In Lima, Wisconsin, the school of the Holy Rosary Catholic parish was accredited as a public school in 1936. In the ensuing fifteen years it absorbed most of the other rural public schools around it through consolidation. Most of these communities were predominantly Catholic in population; and when a Protestant parent objected strenuously, his child was educated in the nearest public school, and the Catholic-controlled public school authorities in the district where he lived paid for the child's transportation and tuition (which, under Wisconsin law, must be paid if a child attends a school outside his own district). This happy solution, however, was abruptly terminated in 1951, when a court ruled that such payments were illegal.

Thereafter parents who preferred nonsectarian education for their children had no alternative but either to pay the transportation and tuition themselves or send their children to the local public-parochial school. Since most of the parents were proverbially unwealthy farmers, they were compelled to choose the latter alternative. One obdurate Protestant farmer, William G. Fox, refused to accept either alternative; he simply refused to send his two children to the Lima school or pay the $2,000 due for tuition and transportation to the secular public school in Durand. Accordingly Fox was charged with violation of the state's compulsory school attendance law, although he was never brought to trial. In July 1952, after the state board of education decided to cut off all further state aid to the Lima district on the ground that the school had become "too closely identified" with the Catholic Church, the taxpayers voted to discontinue it as a public school, and to return it to its pre-1936 status as a parochial school.[94]

### The Law and the Constitution

The illegality of incorporating parochial schools into the public school system under the Faribault plan would seem to be too clear to require discussion. Aside from the requirements of the First Amendment as interpreted in the Everson, McCollum, Zorach, Engel, and Schempp cases, the Faribault arrangement would seem to be in clear violation of state constitutional prohibitions of the use of tax-raised funds for sectarian education. Yet a number of courts faced with the situation have found ways to avoid a ruling against its legality. They have accomplished this by the use of all the devices (discussed earlier in this volume) for avoiding judicial determinations against powerful religious bodies.

For example, the dissenting parent may be thrown out of court for — in effect — the technical fault of choosing the wrong form of action: as by choosing mandamus rather than injunction,[95] or injunction rather than mandamus.[96] Or relief may be barred by reason of delay in bringing the suit and the fact that the community has long tolerated the arrangement.[97] In other cases, a generous use of fictions achieves the same result.[98]

Possibly the most flagrant example of the use of fictions to sustain a Faribault situation was the decision of the Supreme Court of Indiana that in 1940 sustained the validity of the incorporation of the parochial schools of Vincennes into the public school system.[99] The court did this by ignoring the forest and passing on the separate trees, each of which was found faultless. Thus the fact that all the children attending the school were Catholics obviously did not make the school less a public school. Neither was there anything illegal in employing only nuns as teachers, since it was not disputed that they possessed the necessary teaching certification. In the absence of any statute or regulation by the state department of education, it was not illegal for the teachers to wear clerical garb while teaching. Nor was it illegal for the public school board to rent part of the parochial school building from the church; and since the building was still owned by the church, it had the right to maintain in each room crucifixes, holy water fonts, and pictures of the Holy Family. Finally, it was not material that the nuns also taught the children catechism, since this instruction took place each morning a half hour before the school day officially opened. The court simply ignored two trees which might have given it trouble: first, the fact that the arrangement was entered into only after the church informed the public school authorities that lack of finances would compel the closing of the parochial school in the community, and secondly, that the control of the schools remained in the bishop.

Most courts, however — particularly in the recent cases — have considered these situations for what they actually are, and have ruled them violative of state constitutional prohibitions.[100] Under the Everson, McCollum, Zorach, Engel, and Schempp decisions these public-parochial school arrangements would likewise violate the First Amendment.[101]

How many communities today maintain parochial schools as part of the public school system is not known. It has been estimated that in 1937 at least 340 communities had the Faribault plan in operation.[102] Today there are probably more; and this notwithstanding the patent illegality of the plan. In many communities the church and the school board apparently operate on the assumption that as long as no one feels strongly enough about the situation to resort to court action, there is no reason why the plan should not be put in operation. Possibly Catholic churchmen feel that since morally church schools are entitled to support out of tax-raised funds, it is morally permissible for them to connive with public school authorities (who take an oath of office to uphold the constitution) to obtain such funds by incorporating the parochial school into the public school system. Ten years after a clear and comprehensive decision of the Supreme Court of Missouri outlawing such public-parochial school systems,[103] school districts in Franklin[104] and Cole[105] countries in Missouri unconcernedly continued such systems — like probably many other counties that have not yet come to light.

The danger to the public school system in the Faribault plan is not merely in the use of public school funds to support sectarian schools; far more important is the frequent if not the usual consequence of the abandonment of the public school after the incorporation of the parochial school. This is a natural, almost inevitable result. Incorporation takes place in communities where the population and the school board are predominantly Catholic. As Catholics they find it difficult or impossible to maintain a parochial school, while as taxpayers they are required to maintain a public school; hence they transfer the parochial school to the public school system, and thus obtain state aid for that school. But this only partly alleviates the situation, since state aid provides but a portion of the cost of maintenance, and the balance must come out of their pockets as taxpayers. It is natural, therefore, that after a while they should find little use for two schools where one would do; and since the community is predominantly Catholic, fairness would seem to dictate that the Catholic public school be retained, and the secular public school be abandoned. That is what happened in Missouri and New Mexico and Minnesota and probably many other states.

These arrangements are too profitable and convenient to be dropped voluntarily. Rarely are they discontinued except under the compulsion of a court order or a state education board's decision to withhold further state aid (which, of course, destroys the whole profit in the plan). The burden of defending the public school rests on the individual, courageous parent—the Foxes in Lima, and the Zellers in Dixon, and the striking high school pupils in North College Hill. Here above everywhere else is eternal vigilance the price of a free and independent public school.

# Indirect and Federal Aid

## INDIRECT AID

THE STRUGGLE TO OBTAIN direct financial grants of public funds for parochial education was lost early in the history of our public educational system. The decisive campaign was waged in New York in the 1840's; and though more or less similar battles were fought in other states, the conclusion was foregone. The direct grant of public funds to parochial schools as parochial schools required affirmative action on the part of the state legislatures, and in no legislature did the Catholics have a majority. On the contrary, during the middle of the 19th century anti-Catholic Know-Nothingism was strong in a number of legislatures, and there were not a few legislators who would have much preferred to abolish parochial schools altogether. The reason for their inability to accomplish this was the fact that the influence of Know-Nothingism was sporadic and temporary; America generally was free of the bigotry and prejudice that permeated the Nativist and Know-Nothing parties.

But though Protestant America was not much attracted by anti-Catholicism, it was no more sympathetic to Catholic plans to share in tax-raised funds for common schools. Every attempt to enact legislation allowing parochial schools to share in public school funds was defeated; and to prevent possible weakening by later legislatures, the states one after the other enacted constitutional prohibitions against such grants of public funds.

Defeated in this direction, the Catholic Church sought to accomplish its purpose by the incorporation of parochial schools into the public school system. This method had a number of advantages. It was practicable, since it required only the control of the local board of education—which could be acquired in predominantly Catholic communities. Moreover, it was attractive to many thrifty non-Catholic taxpayers, who saw in it an opportunity to obtain further state aid. It did not arouse widespread controversy—as would the introduction of specific aid measures in the state legislature—but could be put in effect quietly and without publicity. Finally, calling the parochial institution a "public" school made proper obeisance to the state constitutional prohibitions against the grant of public funds to private schools.

On the other hand, the incorporation plan had a number of serious drawbacks, which indicated that it was not likely to be the ultimate solution of the financial problem of Catholic education in America. In the first place, it was a compromise. As long as the community's secular public school was retained, it was usually practicable to keep the public-parochial school exclusively for Catholic children; but before long the temptation to abandon the secular school frequently proved too strong, and required the transfer to the ex-parochial school of the non-Catholic children—which in turn required some modification of the purely Catholic teaching theretofore possible. This compromise was not acceptable to many members of the hierarchy, who insisted on strict adherence to the dictates of the Baltimore Plenary Councils. Moreover, the Faribault plan was practicable only in a relatively small number of communities with predominant Catholic populations; it obviously could not be effected in larger cities, or in towns in which the Catholics constituted a minority of the population. Finally, the present-day efforts of such organizations as Protestants and Other Americans United indicate that the Faribault plan faces a good deal of litigation.

Almost by accident, a third method of obtaining public funds for parochial education was discovered—the indirect or child-benefit approach. The potentialities of this approach are tremendous; they are only now beginning to be recognized by the Catholic Church, which—though continuing to assert in principle its claim that the parochial school is an equal partner in the educational system—is pressing its demands more and more in terms of fairness to children. In addition, this approach avoids the disadvantages and drawbacks of the Faribault compromise; if it is fully exploited, it can be made as profitable as the direct grants of public funds to parochial schools, without violating state or Federal constitutional mandate. Finally, it has an appearance of justice and fairness that appeals to many non-Catholics who would never approve direct grants.

Before we consider the potentialities and consequences of the indirect benefits approach, let us consider first its constitutional development.

## SECULAR TEXTBOOKS

According to the National Education Association survey of 1946, in five states (Louisiana, Mississippi, New Mexico, Oregon, and West Virginia) secular textbooks paid for out of tax-raised funds were furnished for the free use of children attending parochial schools.[1] Since that time the supreme courts of two of these states (New Mexico and Oregon)[2] have ruled that this practice violated the state constitutions, and it may be assumed that it has since been discontinued. On the other hand, since that time two other states (Rhode Island and New York)[3] have enacted laws providing for the loan of secular textbooks to children attending nonpublic schools. It would appear therefore that five states now provide free textbooks for use by parochial school pupils.

The major stimulus to free textbook use in parochial schools comes from Title II of the Elementary and Secondary Education Act of 1965. This authorizes the expenditure of $100,000,000 annually for "the acquisition of school library resources and printed and published instructional materials for the use of children and teachers in public and private elementary and secondary schools." The grants are in the first instance to be made to the states, but recognizing that in many states use of tax-raised state funds for this purpose would violate the state constitutions, the Act provides that in such cases, the United States Commissioner of Education shall himself arrange for provision of the materials to the private schools, deducting their cost from the allocation to the state.

The sum, divided among all the public and private schools in the fifty states of the Union, is not much more than nominal. The legislation may perhaps stimulate states to enact similar laws appropriating state funds for the same purpose; New York has already done so notwithstanding a clear state constitutional provision prohibiting such laws.[4] Nevertheless, the furnishing of free textbooks does not of itself today represent a serious threat to public schools funds. The danger lies in the theory invoked by the courts to sustain the practice notwithstanding constitutional prohibitions against the use of tax-raised funds in support of sectarian education, and the action of Congress in endorsing that theory, at least in part.

The first attempt to distinguish between direct aid to sectarian schools, and indirect aid that aids the parochial school children directly and the school itself only indirectly, appears to have been made in a New York case in 1922.[5] There the court was required to decide the constitutionality of the action by the state department of education in furnishing textbooks for use in parochial schools. To sustain this action it was urged that permitting the use of publicly owned textbooks by parochial school children was a benefit to the pupils and not an aid to the school. The court disposed of the argument in the following words:

557

The school is not the building and its equipment; it is the organization, the union of all the elements in the organization, to furnish education in some branch of learning—the arts or sciences or literature. It is the institution and the teachers and the scholars together that make it up. The pupils are a part of the school. . . . It seems to us to be giving a strained and unusual meaning to words if we hold that the books and the ordinary school supplies, when furnished for the use of pupils, is a furnishing to the pupils, and not a furnishing in aid or maintenance of a school of learning. It seems very plain that such furnishing is at least indirectly in aid of the institution and that, if not in actual violation of the words, it is in violation of the true intent and meaning of the Constitution and in consequence equally unconstitutional.

The court, it should be noted, found no constitutional difference between direct and indirect aid to sectarian schools—both types were deemed equally prohibited. Seven years later the Louisiana Supreme Court, in Borden vs. Louisiana State Board of Education,[6] took a contrary view. There too it was argued that the inclusion of parochial schools in the state program of the free distribution of secular textbooks benefited the children rather than the schools. This time, however, the child-benefit argument was received more sympathetically. The court upheld the applicability of the free textbook statute to parochial school children, saying:

One may scan the acts in vain to ascertain where any money is appropriated for the purchase of school books for the use of any church, private, sectarian, or even public school. The appropriations were made for the specific purpose of purchasing schoolbooks for the use of the school children of the state, free of cost to them. It was for their benefit and the resulting benefit to the state that the appropriations were made. True, these children attend some school, public or private, the latter sectarian or non-sectarian, and that the books are to be furnished them for their use, free of cost, whichever they attend. The schools, however, are not the beneficiaries of these appropriations. They obtain nothing from them, nor are they relieved of a single obligation because of them. The school children and the state alone are the beneficiaries.

It is also true that the sectarian schools, which some of the children attend, instruct their pupils in religion, and books are used for that purpose, but one may search diligently the acts, though without result, in an effort to find anything to the effect that it is the purpose of the state to furnish religious books for the use of such children. . . . What the statutes contemplate is that the same books that are furnished children attending public schools shall be furnished children attending private schools. . . . Among these books, naturally, none is to be expected adapted to religious instruction.

A companion case, Cochran vs. Louisiana,[7] was appealed to the United States Supreme Court. The appeal was argued 17 years before the Everson decision made it clear that under the First and Fourteenth Amendments the states, no less than the Federal government, may make no law respecting an establishment of religion. Hence the case was not argued on the assertion that the Louisiana statute was inconsistent with the principle of the separation of church and state. What was claimed was that the statute was a tax for a private rather than a public purpose, and therefore violated the prohibition of the Fourteenth Amendment against state laws depriving persons of property without due process of law.[8]

The United States Supreme Court, however, accepted the child-benefit theory. It quoted the extract from the Louisiana Supreme Court decision set forth above, and added:

> Viewing the statute as having the effect thus attributed to it, we can not doubt that the taxing power of the State is exerted for a public purpose. The legislation does not segregate private schools, or their pupils, as its beneficiaries or attempt to interfere with any matters of exclusively private concern. Its interest is education, broadly; its method, comprehensive. Individual interests are aided only as the common interest is safeguarded.[9]

The Supreme Court decision determined only validity under the Federal constitution; its decision was not binding on state courts interpreting their own constitutions. Most state courts have refused to follow the court's reasoning, or to adopt the child-benefit theory. In 1938 the New York Court of Appeals[10] specifically refused to follow the Louisiana court's decision and the United States Supreme Court's affirmance, but instead approved the 1922 decision of the Appellate Division that prohibited textbook distribution to parochial school children. The Supreme Court of New Mexico in 1951 simply ignored the Cochran decision when it ruled that textbooks might not be supplied to parochial schools.[11] The Supreme Court of Oregon went further and, in 1963, in invalidating a state law providing textbooks for parochial schools, expressed its disagreement with and refused to follow the Cochran decision.[12]

Only one state supreme court has followed the Louisiana court's decision. In 1941 the Supreme Court of Mississippi upheld the constitutionality of a state law that provided for the free use of textbooks by children in all qualified elementary schools, private and sectarian as well as public and secular.[13] The language of the Mississippi court is worth quoting, because it raises the interesting possibility that not only is it constitutional for the state to include parochial schools in its program of distributing free textbooks but that it might be unconstitutional to exclude such schools. The court said:

The religion to which children of school age adhere is not subject to control by the state; but the children themselves are subject to its control. If the pupil may fulfil its duty to the state by attending a parochial school it is difficult to see why the state may not fulfil its duty to the pupil by encouraging it "by all suitable means." The state is under a duty to ignore the child's creed, but not its need. It cannot control what one child may think, but it can and must do all it can to teach the child how to think. The state which allows the pupil to subscribe to any religious creed should not because of his exercise of this right, proscribe him from benefits common to all. . . . The narrow construction contended for by complainants would compel the pupil to surrender use of his books when and because he elected to transfer from a public school to a qualified parochial school. *Such would constitute a denial of equal privileges on sectarian grounds. . . .*

Obviously a state not only "should not" but constitutionally may not "proscribe" a child "from benefits common to all" because he "subscribe[s] to any religious creed." Nor may a state deny "equal privileges on sectarian grounds." It would follow logically that a state that supplies free textbooks to children in public schools must — not merely may — supply free textbooks to children in parochial schools.

This aspect of the child-benefit theory will be considered further in our discussion of the transportation cases. Here it is pertinent to point out the potentialities of the textbooks decision. Both the Louisiana court and the United States Supreme Court stressed the fact that the textbooks supplied were not sectarian. But there is nothing unique in the nonsectarianism of secular textbooks; pens, notebooks, blackboards, desks, and laboratory equipment are likewise nonsectarian, and their use likewise benefits the pupils primarily. If it is constitutional to provide free nonsectarian textbooks to parochial school children, why is it not equally constitutional to provide these other services? (Title II of the Elementary and Secondary Education Act includes not only books but "periodicals, documents, magnetic tapes, phonograph records and other related library materials" as well.) Further, why is it not equally constitutional to pay the salaries of lay instructors teaching nonreligious subjects in parochial schools — or indeed, even the proportionate part of the salary of teaching nuns, who, after all, devote most of their time to teaching arithmetic, reading, and spelling, and only a small part of the school day teaching catechism?

Actually, the logical application of the Cochran decision and the child-benefit theory would completely frustrate the state constitutional prohibitions against the allocation of public school funds to schools not under public control. For, as one court said, "practically every proper expenditure for school purposes aids the child."[14] Indeed, if a proposed expenditure does not benefit the child it is not proper for the public school to make it at all.

Perhaps it is because of these logical implications of the Borden and Cochran decisions and their effects on public school funds that the states have generally refused to follow these cases in textbook situations. But Congress has accepted in part (by providing that the books shall only be loaned to children and legal title shall remain in the state) and—as will be seen in the next section—many states have adopted the child-benefit theory in full in providing for transportation to parochial schools at public expense.

## TRANSPORTATION AT PUBLIC EXPENSE

### *The Background*

Formerly the problem of transporting children to school was generally one for each parent to solve for himself. In more recent times, however, there has been great emphasis in educational circles on the consolidation of rural schools so as to achieve more and better pedagogic facilities for the same dollar spent for education. Though the movement away from many little red schoolhouses to the single, modern, well-equipped, and well-staffed consolidated school has undoubtedly raised the standard of rural education, it has brought with it the problem of transporting to school the children who live in distant communities. It was therefore necessary to add transportation to the educational facilities provided by the consolidated school.

The same problem faced the parochial schools in rural areas; and they too found it necessary to provide transportation. Whether the transportation expenses were paid directly by the parent or by the parochial school was of little moment, since in either event the ultimate burden was on the parents who sustained the parochial school and all its facilities. It was quite natural therefore for Catholic parents to demand the same tax-paid transportation to parochial schools that other children received to public schools. In many cases the proximity of the parochial school to the public school meant that there would be little added expense to the taxpayer. In addition, to many it seemed a cruel injustice to some children to compel them to walk in inclement weather great distances to their school while their non-Catholic neighbors were transported to their schools in warm, safe buses. One of the most effective cartoons used in campaigns to obtain free transportation to parochial schools has been one entitled "The Non-Sectarian Bus," showing a bus passing by a forlorn little schoolboy standing on a rural road in bitter weather, while the bus driver calls out to him, "I can't take you, you're Catholic."

561

It is for these reasons that Catholics have had considerably more success in obtaining free transportation to parochial schools than free textbooks. At least 22 states today provide free transportation to parochial schools.[15]

## The State Cases

The courts also have had somewhat less difficulty in accepting the child-benefit theory in bus transportation cases than they have had in textbook cases — although here too the great majority of state courts have ruled against the constitutionality of statutes or regulations providing for free transportation to parochial schools.[16] A minority of state courts, however, have accepted the child-benefit theory in transportation cases.[17]

The New York Court of Appeals, in a decision which was later abrogated by an amendment to the state constitution that expressly permitted the expenditure of public funds for transportation to nonpublic schools, disposed of the child-benefit argument as follows:

> The argument is advanced that furnishing transportation to the pupils of private or parochial schools is not in aid or support of the school within the spirit or meaning of our organic law but, rather, is in aid of their pupils. That argument is utterly without substance. . . . Free transportation of pupils induces attendance at the school. The purpose of the transportation is to promote the interests of the private schools or religious or sectarian institution that controls and directs it. "It helps build up, strengthen, and make successful the schools as organizations." . . . Without pupils there could be no school. It is illogical to say that the furnishing of transportation is not an aid to the institution while the employment of teachers and furnishing of books, accommodations and other facilities are such an aid.[18]

Another state court used the following language in rejecting the child-benefit contention:

> It is urged that the present legislative act does not result in the use of public funds for the benefit or support of this sectarian institution or school "as such;" that such benefit as flows from these acts accrues to the benefit of the individual child or to a group of children as distinguished from the school as an organization. That argument is not impressive. A similar argument was said to be "utterly without substance" in Judd v Board of Education. It is true this use of public money and property aids the child, but it is no less true that practically every proper expenditure for school purposes aids the child. We are convinced that this expenditure, in its broad and true sense, and as commonly understood, is an expenditure in furtherance of the constitutional duty or function of maintaining schools as organizations or institutions. The State has no authority to maintain a sectarian school. Surely the expend-

iture of public funds for the erection of school buildings, the purchasing and equipping and the upkeep of same, the payment of teachers, and for other proper related purposes is expenditure made for schools as such. Yet the same argument is equally applicable to those expenditures as to the present one.

If the cost of the school bus and the maintenance and operation thereof was not in aid of the public schools, then expenditures therefor out of the school funds would be unauthorized and illegal. Yet, we assume it is now acquiesced in by all that such expenditures are properly in aid of the public schools and are authorized and legal expenditures. If the maintenance and operation of the bus and the transportation of pupils is in aid of the public schools, then it would seem necessarily to follow that when pupils of a parochial school are transported such service would likewise be in aid of that school.[19]

The rationale of the child-benefit theory in transportation cases was perhaps best expressed in the dissenting opinion in the New York case from which we have already quoted. The dissenting judges said:

> The statute in question does not have the effect of giving public money, property or credit in aid or maintenance of religious schools. The aid is given to the pupils who are legally attending such schools, to assist them to spend the required time in attendance upon instruction. In most cases those in parental relation choose the school at the beginning of the school year, and the arrangements for transportation cannot be initiated until the attendance figures show whether and to what extent such facilities may be needed. There is no benefit to the schools except, perhaps, as one may conceive an accidental benefit in the sense that some parents might place their children in religious schools when they anticipate transportation provision, though they might hesitate to do so if the children were compelled to make their own way. The constitutional provision is not designed to discourage or thwart the school where religious instruction is imparted. . . .[20]

### The Everson Case

The issue reached the United States Supreme Court in 1947 in the Everson case. The Cochran case had been argued on the sole ground that the expenditure of tax-raised funds to supply textbooks for use by parochial school children constituted an unconstitutional tax for private purposes. The same argument was presented to the Supreme Court in a taxpayer's attack on a resolution adopted by the board of education of the small township of Ewing, adjoining the city of Trenton, whose population of some 10,000 residents was unable to sustain its own high school. The children of Ewing attending high school were transported by public bus to Trenton, and the township's board of education reimbursed the parents for the fares advanced by them. Prior to 1941 only the parents of children attending public high schools received reimbursement, but in that year the state statute was amended to allow local boards of education to provide for transportation of pupils to all nonprofit schools. Acting in accordance with this statute, the Ewing board of education provided for the reimbursement of transportation expenses to the parents of children who attended the public and Catholic high schools in Trenton.

In attacking this resolution and the statute before the United States Supreme Court, the counsel for the taxpayer, Arch R. Everson, did not limit themselves to the argument unsuccessfully urged in the Cochran case. They argued also that the statute and resolution forced inhabitants to pay taxes to help support and maintain schools that were dedicated to and regularly taught the Catholic faith. This, they contended, was a use of state power to support church schools that was contrary to the prohibition of the First Amendment, which the Fourteenth Amendment made applicable to the states.

In a five to four decision the court upheld the validity of the statute and resolution.[21] The majority opinion was written by Justice Black, with Chief Justice Vinson and Justices Murphy, Reed, and Douglas concurring. The minority consisted of Justices Rutledge, Frankfurter, Jackson, and Burton.

In disposing of the public-tax-for-private-purposes argument, Justice Black conceded that the court had

> in rare instances, struck down state statutes on the ground that the purpose for which tax-raised funds were to be expended was not a public one, [but] this far-reaching authority must be exercised with the most extreme caution [else] a State's power to legislate for the public welfare might be seriously curtailed, a power which is a primary reason for the existence of states. . . . It is much too late to argue that legislation intended to facilitate the opportunity of children to get a secular education serves no public purpose.

Since the parochial schools involved here meet the state's requirements for secular education, it is as much a use of public funds for public purposes when it is expended to transport children to these parochial schools as it is to transport them to public schools.

As to the second argument, the court, after reviewing the history of the First Amendment, agreed that the Fourteenth Amendment made the First Amendment applicable to the states, and also that the First Amendment prohibited the government from making laws that aid all religions as much as laws that aid one religion. This aspect of the court decision has already been discussed, but one point should be noted here. Ironically enough, the regulation was open to constitutional attack even under the narrow interpretation of the First Amendment, for it expressly limited its applicability to public schools and *Catholic* parochial schools, and therefore was patently preferential. The court sought to meet this objection by stating that "if the inclusion clause had been properly challenged, we do not know whether New Jersey's highest court would construe its statutes as precluding payment of the school transportation of any group of pupils, even those of a private school run for profit," and that there is nothing in the record that would offer the slightest support to an allegation that there were any children in the township who attended or would have attended—but for want of transportation—any but public and Catholic schools. (To this Justice Rutledge replied in his dissent, "I cannot assume, as does the majority, that the New Jersey courts would write off this explicit limitation from the statute. Moreover, the resolution by which the statute was applied expressly limits its benefits to students of public and Catholic schools. There is no showing that there are no other private or religious schools in this populous district. I do not think it can be assumed there were none.")

Although, Justice Black continued, the statute and resolution approach "the verge" of the state's power under the First Amendment, they do not exceed that power. The purpose of the statute and resolution, he held, was to enable children to "ride in public buses to and from schools rather than run the risk of traffic and other hazards incident to walking or 'hitchhiking,' " and this obviously is within the state's constitutional power. Said Justice Black:

> It is undoubtedly true that children are helped to get to church schools. There is even a possibility that some of the children might not be sent to the church schools if the parents were compelled to pay their children's bus fares out of their own pockets when transportation to a public school would have been paid for by the State. . . . [But] state paid policemen detailed to protect children going to and from church schools from the very real hazards of traffic, would serve much the same purpose and accomplish much the same result as state provisions intended to guarantee free transportation of a kind which the state deems to be best for the school children's welfare. And parents might refuse to risk their children to the serious danger of traffic accidents going to and from parochial schools, the approaches to which were not protected by policemen. Similarly, parents might be reluctant to permit their children to attend schools which the state had cut off from such general government services as ordinary police and fire protection, connections for sewage disposal, public highways and sidewalks. Of course, cutting off church schools from these services, so separate and

so indisputably marked off from the religious function, would make it far more difficult for the schools to operate. But such is obviously not the purpose of the First Amendment. That Amendment requires the state to be a neutral in its relations with groups of religious believers and non-believers; it does not require the state to be their adversary. State power is no more to be used so as to handicap religions, than it is to favor them.

At the end of his opinion Justice Black returns to the point from which he started. The state has power to impose minimum secular standards on all schools. New Jersey's parochial schools have met these requirements. Therefore New Jersey has the constitutional power "to help parents get their children, regardless of their religion, safely and expeditiously to and from accredited schools" to enable them to obtain the secular education required by the state.

It can thus be seen that the court decision is justified on two more or less separate grounds: first, that the state may validly enact legislation to protect all children from the hazards of traffic; and second, that since the state may validly enact legislation to provide children with a secular education, it may validly enact legislation to transport children to a place where others than the state supply that secular education. These justifications, in turn, rest on two assumptions: first, that the purpose of the New Jersey statute and the Ewing resolution was to insure the safety of children from the risks of traffic; and second, that Catholic parochial schools provide that secular education which that state is constitutionally empowered to provide.

It is submitted that both these assumptions rest on fictions. As both dissenting opinions, by Justices Jackson and Rutledge, point out, the New Jersey statute and the Ewing resolution do not provide transportation for children on the streets; they provide transportation only for children going to school, either to a public school or to a Catholic parochial school. A child going to visit a neighbor or to a motion picture theatre is just as much subject to the hazards of the road as a child going to school. Yet New Jersey did not make any provision for the transportation of children going to any destination other than school—public or parochial. If New Jersey had so provided, none would dispute that the purpose of the legislation was to provide welfare benefits—indisputably within the state's police power. Since it was restricted to school transportation it would seem clear that the purpose of the legislation was to provide an educational service.

It would therefore seem fallacious to equate—as Justice Black did—bus transportation and police or fire protection. The purpose of supplying traffic police is to protect children from accidents; all children are protected, Catholics and Protestants, believers and non-believers. The purpose of supplying fire protection is to preserve society's economic assets, whether in the form of church buildings or burlesque theatres. But the purpose of supplying bus transportation is to get children to school, not (at least, primarily) to protect them from traffic hazards. Transportation to schools is generally provided in rural rather than urban areas, which indicates that distance rather than traffic hazards is the motivating consideration. It is not without significance that the New Jersey statute under attack did not mention traffic hazards, but provided only for transportation "whenever in any district there are children living *remote* from any school-house. . . ." If the purpose of supplying bus transportation is to protect children from traffic accidents, the state can constitutionally supply free transportation not merely to church schools but to churches as well—just as it can constitutionally supply traffic police protection on the streets leading to churches.

No less fictional is the second assumption of the court, that Catholic "church schools give their students in addition to secular education, regular religious instruction." Were this so, there would be no need for or purpose to separate parochial schools; Catholic children, as Jewish children do, would obtain their religious education after regular school hours. We have already set forth the extracts from the Canon Law quoted by Justice Jackson to show that Catholic parochial schools do not merely teach religion as another subject in a secular curriculum. We have also quoted other authoritative writings from Catholic sources showing that the very term "secular education" is deemed a contradiction in terms and is entirely unacceptable to the church. It is for that reason that the Faribault plan could not be accepted by the church as anything but a temporary compromise dictated by necessity. These authoritative church writings leave little doubt that the education received in Catholic parochial schools is not the secular education which a state may constitutionally provide or pay for.

Justice Rutledge, in his dissent, eloquently expressed the difficult necessity of denying states the power to provide for the transportation of children to parochial schools:

> No one conscious of religious values can be unsympathetic toward the burden which our constitutional separation puts on parents who desire religious instruction mixed with secular for their children. They pay taxes for others' children's education, at the same time the added cost of instruction for their own. Nor can one happily see benefits de-

nied to children which others receive, because in conscience they or their parents for them desire a different kind of training others do not demand.

But if those feelings should prevail, there would be an end to our historic constitutional policy and command. No more unjust or discriminatory in fact is it to deny attendants at religious schools the cost of their transportation than it is to deny them tuitions, sustenance for their teachers, or any other educational expense which others receive at public cost. Hardship in fact there is which none can blink. But, for assuring to those who undergo it the greater, the more comprehensive freedom, it is one written by design and firm intent into our basic law.

Of course discrimination in the legal sense does not exist. The child attending the religious school has the same right as any other to attend the public school. But he foregoes exercising it because the same guaranty which assures this freedom forbids the public school or any agency of the state to give or aid him in securing the religious instruction he seeks.

Were he to accept the common school, he would be the first to protest the teaching there of any creed or faith not his own. And it is precisely for the reason that their atmosphere is wholly secular that children are not sent to public schools under the *Pierce* doctrine. But that is a constitutional necessity, because we have staked the very existence of our country on the faith that complete separation between the state and religion is best for the state and best for religion.

As Justice Rutledge pointed out, the logical application of the court's approach would nullify the First Amendment guaranty of the separation of church and state. If transportation to church schools can be justified under the state's police power to provide for the welfare of children, so also can many other expenditures. Fire hazards are no less dangerous than traffic hazards. Why then may not the state provide for the fireproofing of all schools which children attend? Why too may it not pay for the repair of unsafe walls and ceilings—and where repair is impracticable, for their replacement? When the Everson decision is coupled with the Cochran decision, they lead logically to the conclusion that a state may, notwithstanding the First Amendment, finance practically every aspect of parochial education, with the exception of such comparatively minor items as the proportionate salaries of teachers while they teach the catechism and the cost of holy fonts and junior missals, a conclusion that no court, federal or state, is today prepared to accept.

It may well be because of its realization of the logical implications of the Cochran-Everson approach that the church is willing to compromise—at least temporarily—on the auxiliary or welfare-benefits line. The compromise is more one of theory than actuality. It is a compromise of theory because it does not accept the justice of the church's claim to be an equal partner in the nation's educational endeavor. It is not a compromise of actuality, for—properly exploited—it can get the church a partner's share in the finances of the endeavor.

That parochial schools are aided by the provision of bus transportation is recognized by the majority of the court in the Everson case. The majority also recognized that the state aid of religion is proscribed by the First Amendment. What in effect the court held was that where there is a clash between the prohibitions of the First Amendment and the welfare of children, the latter interest is superior. As we shall see later, the court had so held in respect to the First Amendment's guaranty of religious freedom.[22] Since the establishment aspect of the First Amendment is not superior to the free exercise aspect, there is no reason why a similar holding may not be made with respect to the former aspect. Government-paid chaplaincies in the armed forces, as we have seen, can be justified on the ground that the interest of national self-defense is superior to the ban on establishments; and the interest of child safety may likewise be superior.

But—as we shall see in the next chapter—a choice may constitutionally be made only if a choice must be made. If the superior interest can be protected without infringing on the First Amendment guaranty, it is unconstitutional to infringe on that guaranty merely because that is the way of least resistance or less likely to arouse political recriminations. And even if bus transportation is considered a safety device, it is possible for the state to assure the safety of children attending parochial schools without impairing the First Amendment guaranty of the separation of church and state. The state need only prescribe as a condition for the maintenance of private schools that where necessary the school shall provide for the transportation of the attending children. This is exactly what the state does when it requires private schools to comply with state fire, safety, and health regulations for buildings. It is because the state can practicably assure the health and safety of children by enforcing these regulations that it would be unconstitutional for the state to pay for the fireproofing of parochial schools or for the fuel necessary to keep them healthfully warm. For the same reason it should be unconstitutional for the state to provide transportation instead of requiring the parochial school to provide it.

This reasoning does not render it unconstitutional for a state to provide free medical and dental services or free hot lunches to children in parochial schools. These are not educational services but true welfare benefits. A child needs medical and dental care and hot lunches, whether he goes to a public school, to a parochial school, or to no school at all. But he does not need transportation to a school unless he receives instruction at that school; and only in that case is his safety and health protected if the school building is fireproof and the rooms warm and ventilated.

Another difficulty with the reasoning of the majority in the Everson case has already been alluded to in our discussion of the textbook cases. If transportation is a welfare service for the benefit of children, it is not enough to hold that it is constitutional for a state to provide free transportation to religious schools; we must logically go further, and hold that the state may not constitutionally exclude religious schools from its program of transportation for school children. Both the First Amendment, guaranteeing religious freedom, and the Fourteenth, banning laws denying to any person the equal protection of the laws, preclude a state from discriminating on religious grounds in its distribution of welfare benefits. Justice Black recognized this logical implication, and sought to guard against it by saying that "we do not mean to intimate that a state could not provide transportation only to children attending public schools." But it is difficult to see how such a holding can be avoided, in view of the immediately preceding statement that a state "cannot exclude individual Catholics, Lutherans, Mohammedans, Baptists, Jews, Methodists, Non-believers, Presbyterians, or members of any other faith, *because of their faith, or lack of it,* from receiving the benefits of public welfare legislation."

The Supreme Court almost had the opportunity to pass directly on this point. In 1947 the Supreme Court of Pennsylvania dismissed a suit by the father of a ten-year-old girl attending a parochial school that sought to compel the school board of Kennett Square to pay for the transportation of his child to the parochial school.[23] The parent appealed to the United States Supreme Court on the ground that the board's action in paying only for transportation to public schools denied him the freedom of religion and the equal protection of the laws.[24] Unfortunately, before the Supreme Court had an opportunity to pass upon the question, the parent withdrew the appeal for "personal reasons."[25] The issue therefore still remains to be decided by the court.

Just as the Cochran decision was not followed by many state courts in construing their own constitutions, so too the Everson case does not as yet appear to have had a substantial effect on the state courts. Since the decision was handed down, ten state supreme courts have had occasion to pass on the issue and of these, eight (Washington, New Mexico, Missouri, Alaska, Wisconsin, Iowa, Oklahoma, and Oregon)[26] have ruled bus transportation to parochial schools violative of their state constitutions, and only two (Connecticut and Maine)[27] have upheld it.

Moreover, in the Engel case,[28] Justice Douglas, whose vote with the majority in the Everson case was crucial, stated that he now considered that decision incorrect and that in his present opinion tax-supported bus transportation to parochial schools was unconstitutional. Nevertheless, when the Connecticut decision was appealed to the United States Supreme Court in 1961 the Court dismissed it for want of a substantial Federal question,[29] thus in effect reaffirming the Everson decision. It is clear, therefore, that today it is not a violation of the First Amendment for a state to finance bus transportation to parochial schools, although it would probably be adjudged a violation of state constitutions in most states.

## Shared Time[30]

### *The Background*

For a variety of reasons — primarily vulnerability to legal attack, reluctance of state legislatures, and inadequacy — neither the Faribault plan of incorporating parochial schools into the public school system nor indirect aid in the form of textbooks and bus transportation was able to meet the financial needs of the parochial school system or its demands for a share of tax-raised funds. The practical veto power held by the Catholic Church on any bill for Federal aid to education that did not include parochial schools acted as a strong incentive for continuance of the search to find some way to meet Catholic demands within the limitations of the First Amendment. Out of this search came the recent interest in the shared-time or dual enrollment (the terms are used interchangeably) plan.

Briefly, under the shared-time plan a child divides his school day between the parochial and a nearby or even adjacent public school, taking some of his courses in one and the remainder in the other. The idea is by no means a new one. As we have seen,[31] Jefferson had proposed that religious sects be invited to establish schools adjacent to the University of Virginia to enable those students who desired to do so to obtain religious instruction at the sectarian schools and secular instruction at the university. The same idea at the elementary and secondary school level is effectuated constitutionally in released-time religious instruction conducted off public school premises.

In both cases, however, the student is primarily an enrollee in the public institution, taking in the sectarian school only such instruction as the public institution is constitutionally forbidden to give. Shared-time education, on the other hand, envisages the child as primarily a parochial school enrollee, or at most a dual enrollee. But even this is not new. Apparently as long ago as 1923 the idea was put into practice in certain midwestern communities. A decision of the Supreme Court of Wisconsin, which in that year ruled unconstitutional the use of public funds to transport students to parochial schools, referred to three categories of pupils: those attending public schools full time, those attending parochial schools full time, and those attending both schools part time.[32]

How widespread the practice was cannot be estimated with any degree of accuracy. One ardent advocate of the plan asserted in 1963 that it had operated in some 21 states,[33] but this probably includes instances of the patently unconstitutional shared-facilities practice, under which parochial school classes enter into the public school to utilize its facilities as part of their own course of instruction.

Soviet Russia's success in orbiting a satellite intensified the search for a solution to the Federal aid deadlock, for it was widely recognized that such aid was indispensable if we were to compete successfully with the Russians in the brave new technological world. The shared-time idea was grasped upon, particularly in Protestant circles, as a means to break the Federal aid deadlock without basically impairing church-state separation. Since major opposition to Federal aid to parochial schools has come from Protestants, it was quite natural for the Administration, desperately seeking to obtain enactment of a Federal aid bill, to incorporate the shared-time plan in its proposed measure. Thus it came about that the Elementary and Secondary Education Act of 1965 — discussed more fully in the next section — endorses the plan by specifically including "dual enrollment" as one of the services for which the Federal funds allocated by the Act may be used.

### What It Is and How It Works

The shared-time proposal would divide the child's school time between public and parochial schools. For such religiously neutral subjects as languages, mathematics, physics, chemistry, gymnasium, vocational training, etc., the child would go to the public school. For subjects which the church feels must be taught with religious orientation — history, literature, social sciences, etc. — the child would go to the parochial school. The benefit the church would receive by this would come from its being relieved of the costly budget items of expensive equipment as well as the salaries of teachers teaching the religiously neutral subjects.

The plan is not limited to Catholic schools. Protestant church schools and Jewish all-day schools could likewise take advantage of it. However, 90% of the children attending nonpublic schools are Catholic children enrolled in parochial schools, so that for all practical purposes this is a plan for the indirect aid of the Catholic Church.

The plan would not work in elementary schools, since these do not generally have departmentalized instruction. It could work in high schools, but only about one out of every five children attending parochial schools attends Catholic high schools, so that the benefits to the Catholic school system would appear to be quite limited, and it is perhaps for this reason that the Catholic Church has shown little enthusiasm for the plan. On the other hand, if the plan were adopted it is likely that more Catholic parochial school children would continue in Catholic high schools on the shared-time basis. The plan also could be used in junior high schools, although the Catholic school system is not now set up on a junior high school basis.

In 1963, Congressman Adam Clayton Powell of New York introduced a bill in Congress for the appropriation of five million dollars annually for three years to finance experimental shared-time programs. Hearings were held on this bill in February 1964, at which the National Education Association presented the results of a preliminary study it had made, which showed that a total of 35 states had one or more school systems with a shared-time program in operation. The study showed that the overwhelming majority of these programs were in the midwest. In Michigan 42 school districts participated; in Ohio, 36; in Illinois, 26; and in Wisconsin, 25. The only nonmidwestern state with a substantial number of districts participating was Pennsylvania, with 31. The study also revealed the following significant information.

1. The typical (median) shared-time program had been in operation for eight years. The range was from one year in 18 districts to 40 or more years in Houghton, Michigan, and Ludington, Michigan.

2. The number of parochial-school pupils enrolled part time in the 135 public school systems totaled 7,237, and this was equal to 2.8 percent of the full-time enrollment of these public school systems.

3. The subjects most frequently offered to parochial-school pupils were those which were very expensive to offer, or for which qualified teachers were scarce. The subjects most frequently offered

in these shared-time arrangements of the 135 school systems were as follows:

Industrial arts, offered by 65%
Home economics, offered by 39%
Instrumental music, offered by 34%
Physical education, offered by 15%
Physics, offered by 12%
Advanced science and/or mathematics, offered by 10%
Modern foreign languages, offered by 10%

4. None of the following subjects was taught on a shared-time basis by more than two of the 135 reporting districts:

| | |
|---|---|
| World history | Social studies |
| Economics | Problems of democracy |
| Sociology | Dramatics |
| English | |

### The Case for Shared Time

The following arguments are most frequently presented in favor of the shared-time plan.

1. It will break the deadlock on Federal aid. The proof of this is that after three quarters of a century of frustration because of the sectarian issue, Congress included a provision for shared time in a bill for Federal aid to education, and the bill became law—the first Federal law for what is practically general aid to elementary and secondary education in American history.

2. It provides aid to the child, not to the parochial school, and therefore is consistent with church-state separation. Whatever aid accrues to the parochial school is indirect and therefore constitutionally permissible under the Cochran and Everson decisions.

3. It will meet in a modest way the justifiable grievance of the Catholic community that it is subject to double taxation and that Catholic children are discriminated against because their religious conscience requires them to take some of their schooling under church auspices. Even if this feeling is not valid, it is unhealthy in a democratic society for so large a part of the community to live in a belief of being victims of unjust discrimination by the majority.

4. The Catholic community and the church will acquire an interest in the public school system and will therefore accord greater support to it.

5. The public school should be open to all children; no child should be barred from it simply because his conscience requires him to take some subjects under church auspices.

6. It will help break down at least in part the wall isolating the Catholic parochial school children (about half the Catholic children in the country) from the rest of the American community. Jefferson justified his proposal, referred to above, on the ground that "by bringing the sects together, and mixing them with the mass of other students, we shall soften their asperities [and] liberalize and neutralize their prejudice."[34] The same result can be expected of the shared-time plan.

7. It works. Shared-time programs, though not so called, have been in operation in various parts of the country for up to 40 years and there is no evidence that they have been anything but completely satisfactory.

### *The Case Against Shared Time*

1. It will not solve the church-state dilemma in Federal aid. Inclusion of shared-time was not sufficient to assure enactment of the Elementary and Secondary Education Act of 1965; it was necessary to add other provisions which in practice could constitute direct Federal aid to parochial schools in violation of the Constitution.[35] Certainly, the Catholic Church has given no indication that it will accept shared-time programs as meeting its claim to participation in public support for its schools.[36]

2. Nor will the goal of breaking down the wall of segregation isolating parochial school students be likely to be achieved in practice. Convenience, economy, efficiency, and the desires of the parochial school authorities will make it almost inevitable that the parochial school students will enter the public school as a separate group, be taught there as a separate group, and leave as a separate group. This will accentuate the segregation and isolation rather than break it down.

3. Operating a school during part of the day for the whole student body and during the rest for only part of the student body will wreak havoc with the orderly administration of the school and its curriculum.

4. Not only would the added expense be prohibitive but the result would be wasteful. The influx of large numbers of new students would require extensive and costly expansion of facilities utilized at only a fraction of capacity for a good part of every school day. It would be incongruous yet unavoidable to find that after a heavy bond issue is approved in a community in order to build new classrooms the school itself will be half empty every afternoon or every morning.

5. The plan would necessarily blur the line which separates public from parochial education. In order for the plan to work the public and parochial school authorities would have to coordinate their operations. This could lead in many communities to joint operation of the public school system by public and church authorities. Such a consequence would be fatal to the integrity of our independent, secular public educational system.

6. Likely too would be efforts by church authorities not only to review but to censor even religiously "neutral" subjects in order to "protect" parochial school children in public schools.

7. Modern teaching methods seek integration rather than compartmentalization of school subjects. Shared time would reverse this trend and set back the course of progress in education.

8. Because a substantial percentage, and in many cases perhaps even a majority, of the total school population will be taking their humanities courses elsewhere, the public schools will lessen their interest in the humanities subjects and concentrate on such subjects as physical sciences, manual training, home economics, etc. Thus, what is most meaningful and significant in public education will become watered down.

9. Finally, it would fragmentize the public school system by encouraging proliferation of parochial schools. We might end up in many communities with a situation where all the important subjects needed for human relations are taught in a multiplicity of separate religious schools and the public school used as a common manual training institution, physical science laboratory, or gigantic gymnasium.

### The Positions of the Faiths and Educators

Strongest support for the shared-time plan is to be found in organized American Protestantism. Arthur S. Fleming, vice president of the National Council of Churches, testifying in its behalf at the hearings on the Elementary and Secondary Education Act of 1965, welcomed "the inclusion in the pending proposal of the concept of 'dual school enrollment' or 'shared time.'" He quoted from a statement of the National Council, which said:

> We believe that boys and girls now limited by the resources of some religious day schools will be benefited by the equipment and program offerings for the portion of the time they attend the public school. We believe that benefits will ensue for all children if those now enrolled in separate systems have the opportunity to associate with each other

576

through dual school enrollment. We believe that this association and intermingling of the children in the school will result in a broadened support for public education and will serve to unify our now partially divided communities.[37]

There is something of an ambivalence on shared time within the Catholic Church. On the one hand it is recognized that at best the plan is a compromise — even more so than the Faribault plan. It fails to recognize the Church's claim to a right to participate as an equal partner in the nation's educational system. It compromises the official Catholic teaching that no subject, not even physics, chemistry, home economics, or physical education, may be taught exclusively as a secular subject without Catholic orientation and supervision. Moreover, while the risk to the faith of the Catholic child participating in this instruction in the public schools is less than in courses such as history, social sciences, and the humanities, it is by no means absent. The mere daily intermingling of Catholic and non-Catholic children in a public school environment presents a risk.

On the other hand, the Church recognizes that at the present time it is unlikely to achieve non-Catholic acceptance of its claim to full partnership in education, and that it can reach this goal only in stages. Moreover, the prevailing ecumenical spirit within Catholicism tends to neutralize in part Catholic isolationism and makes less difficult Catholic participation in shared-time programs. Above all, the almost prohibitive cost of equipment needed in modern science courses and manual training leaves the church with little alternative but to accept the invitation to participate in shared-time programs. Hence, on the whole, it may be said that the Catholic Church favors shared time education, though with little enthusiasm.[38]

The organized Jewish community is practically unanimously opposed to participation in the shared-time plan. Even the groups within Orthodoxy which favor Federal and state aid to religious schools are not desirous of participating in the programs, although they do not oppose the program for non-Jews.[39]

Although the National Education Association warmly supported the Elementary and Secondary Education Act of 1965 with its provision for shared-time facilities, public school administrators are less than enthusiastic. More than two-thirds of those replying to a survey by *The Nation's Schools* opposed shared time.[40] They cited financial difficulties, the problem of class scheduling, and a belief that it violated the church-state separation principle as grounds for their opposition.

577

*Legality and Constitutionality*

State laws, as they now read, present a formidable obstacle to the widespread adoption of shared-time programs. In some states, laws require full time attendance on the part of all public school enrollees, other than those who are physically handicapped.[41] In others, the amount of state aid public schools receive is determined by full time attendance, so that acceptance of parochial school students for part time instruction would impose a probably prohibitive additional financial burden on local public school districts.

State laws, however, are easily amendable. A more difficult question is that of constitutionality, both under state and the Federal constitutions. Validity of shared-time programs under state constitutions depends on the particular constitution, and state attorneys general and legal advisers to departments of education have expressed differing viewpoints.[42] State constitutions, like state laws, are within the exclusive jurisdiction of state courts; and varying decisions are to be expected, as in the case of other indirect aids to parochial schools, such as textbooks and bus transportation.

There is also considerable difference of opinion as to constitutionality under the First Amendment to the Federal Constitution. It would seem, however, that the shared-time plan on its face is not unconstitutional. In the Pierce case[43] the Supreme Court ruled that children have a constitutional right to secure all their secular education in parochial schools. It is hard to see, therefore, how it would be unconstitutional to permit them to secure part of their secular education in parochial schools and the remainder in public schools. In Zorach vs. Clauson[44] the Court ruled it constitutional to excuse children from part of their regular secular studies to participate in religious instruction off public school premises. It is, therefore, difficult to see how it would be unconstitutional to release them to participate in secular instruction.

It has been argued that by relieving parochial schools of the necessity of purchasing expensive laboratory, gymnasium, home economics, and manual training equipment, the state is thereby according them substantial aid.[45] In a sense this is true, but in receiving this aid the parochial schools are surrendering their pupils to the public schools for part of the school day. By this logic, they would be receiving even more aid if they surrendered their pupils to the public schools for all instruction other than in religion. Nevertheless, in Zorach vs. Clauson this was held to be constitutional. All in all, it is difficult to see why a state may not constitutionally accept children for part rather than full time instruction if it elects to do so.

All this, however, is predicated on the assumption that the parochial school child enrolling in the public school for part time instruction is assimilated into the public school community and, during the time he is in the public school, treated exactly as every other public school child. Should the parochial school children be taught as a separate and segregated group, there would be grave questions as to the constitutionality of the program. So, too, would there be should any partnership arrangement eventuate between the public and parochial school authorities in respect to authority over the children while they are in the public school. There are many other aspects in which operation of shared time may result in constitutional violations. In sum, therefore, it is suggested that the constitutionality or unconstitutionality under the First Amendment of shared-time education would depend upon how it is carried out in practice.

## FEDERAL AID TO EDUCATION

### *The Background*[46]

Almost from its beginning the Federal government has shown great interest in education, though the problem of aid to religious and other private schools did not emerge until later. Before the adoption of the Constitution, the Northwest Ordinances of 1785 and 1787 established a policy of disposing of the public domain so as to encourage education. The 1785 Ordinance reserved lot number 16 "of every township, for the maintenance of public schools, within said township." The Ordinance of 1787 recited that "Religion, morality, and knowledge, being necessary to good government and the happiness of mankind, schools and the means of education shall forever be encouraged." The use of public lands in part for education helped to establish schools on a firm basis in many of the western states. Congress also on a number of occasions early in the history of the country granted land to public and private institutions.

But a nationwide system of publicly controlled, nonsectarian elementary schools and institutions of higher learning was at the time of framing of the Constitution only a distant hope of a few statesmen and reformers. Education was then almost universally regarded as a matter for church concern and control, and therefore one not within the functions and powers of the Federal government. It does appear that at one time during the Constitutional Convention control over education was included in a list of specific powers considered for assignment to the Federal government; but this item was later deleted from the list.

Notwithstanding this deletion, some of the delegates to the Convention were of the opinion that the responsibility for promoting education had been assigned to the Federal government under the "general welfare" clause. Alexander Hamilton, for example, expressed this opinion in 1791. To remove constitutional doubt, Jefferson in 1806 and Madison in 1817 urged an amendment to the Constitution specifically giving the Federal government control over education. Since such an amendment was never adopted, public education as it slowly developed during the 19th century came under the control of the states under the Tenth Amendment, which reserves to the states the powers not delegated to the Federal government. Thus the United States, instead of acquiring a single national system of education as in most other countries, acquired as many systems as there are states.

The creation of a national university was widely advocated during the early years of our nation. At the Constitutional Convention the draft of the Constitution prepared by Charles C. Pinckney of South Carolina specifically authorized Congress to establish a national university. Madison also favored the idea, but assumed that an express provision was not necessary in view of the exclusive jurisdiction of Congress over the capital district where the university was to be located. Every President from Washington through John Quincy Adams favored the proposal; and several of them made specific and repeated requests to Congress for its effectuation. These proposals came to nought through inertia rather than opposition; and by 1820 the idea of a national university was more or less a matter exclusively for historians.

Although the Federal government established neither a national school system nor a national university, it did from its earliest days aid in the establishment of schools and colleges by the states; indeed in most cases the states inherited public school systems originally established by the Federal government. For most of the states admitted since 1789 were first organized as territories, and in organizing each of these territories Congress established school systems that were later taken over by the states.

In 1802 Congress took definite action in continuation of the general policy in the support of education that was initiated by the 1785 Ordinance. With the admission of Ohio to the union in that year, Congress began setting aside lands for school support at the time of admission of a state. As other states formed from the public domain were admitted, the grants of sections in townships for schools were continued. New states also received lands for the endowment of academies and universities. Occasionally since 1802 Federal lands have been granted to specifically designated educational institutions.

During the first half of the 19th century Congress also provided certain monetary grants to states, which were frequently used to support education. These monetary grants were derived principally from the sale of public lands. Except for the few grants to specific institutions, the land and monetary grants were for education in general. Congress did not define the kind of education to be provided, nor attempt to influence the operation or curriculum of the school systems and educational institutions thus aided by the Federal government. The income from these grants is now mostly depleted, but is still considerable in a few of the states.

Though these direct grants for general education ended by the middle of the 19th century, the continuing concern of the Federal government in universal education is evidenced by the fact that every state admitted since 1876 was compelled to write into its constitution a provision—usually irrevocable without the consent of Congress—that required the state to maintain a nonsectarian public school system open to all children without charge.

The Morrill Act of 1862 marked a change in the policy of the Federal government in subsidizing education. Whereas earlier grants had been in the form of aid to general education, all permanent programs for a century after passage of the Morrill Act were for the purpose of supporting some specialized educational activity. In order to promote the establishment of "colleges for the benefit of agriculture and mechanic arts," the Morrill Act of 1862 distributed land to the states for conversion into income-bearing stock. Further Federal support was given the land-grant colleges by the second Morrill Act of 1890. Other acts of Congress providing Federal aid to special types of education included the Hatch Act of 1887, which established agricultural experiment stations, the Smith-Lever Act of 1914 to aid the study of agriculture and home economics, the Smith-Hughes Act of 1917, and the George-Barden Act of 1946, both of which aided vocational education.

During the depression of the '30's the Federal government gave financial support to education in a variety of ways. These depression activities, however, were secondary to the main considerations of relief—whether for the benefit of the teacher or the student. In the World War II and "cold war" periods Federal aid was given to help the erection of schools in areas where defense industries created new communities almost overnight without provision for public education.

A variety of programs of Federal aid for special types of educational activity were adopted by Congress in the post-Civil War century. These included nautical education, aeronautical education, nurse training, veterans' aid, and many grants for specific research projects. The success of efforts to obtain Federal aid for special educational activities contrasts sharply with the dismal failure for a century of repeated efforts to obtain Federal aid for general education. This marked difference between substantial success and dismal failure cannot be explained on the theory that Congress deemed it more important that the younger generation be educated in agricultural arts and home economics than in reading, writing, and arithmetic. This reason for the difference was in large measure the ability of the proponents of aid to special educational activities to avoid the bitter controversial issues that marked attempts to secure Federal aid for general primary and secondary education. Among the most bitter of these controversial issues, and one that still appears insoluble, is the place of religion and religious schools in a program of Federal aid.

The post-Civil War period brought on serious educational finance problems both in the North and the South. In the North a substantial expansion of school facilities was required for the great number of immigrants who were attracted to this country during the era of western expansion. In the South the problem was even more acute; the states in effect had to establish a public school system for the emancipated Negroes as well as for the white children. The economic wealth of the North made it possible for most of the states above the Mason-Dixon line to solve this financial problem more or less satisfactorily, but the improverished and segregation-obsessed South has still not been able to accomplish this.

The problem of including or excluding nonpublic schools did not become acute until later years, though charges of Catholic opposition to any program of Federal aid began to be made comparatively early in the long and tortuous history of the struggle for Federal aid to general education. In 1881 Senator Blair introduced the first of a series of bills, extending until 1890, which would have provided for Federal aid to general education. The Blair bills provided for the allocation of Federal funds among the states in accordance with the proportion of illiterate residents in each state. The later Blair bills provided that if in any state separate schools were maintained for white and colored children, the sum allocated to that state was to be apportioned between the two school systems on the basis of their respective ratios in the population of the state. The Blair bills also provided that the funds appropriated should be applied only to nonsectarian public schools.

Although the exclusion of nonpublic schools does not appear to have been the major cause for the failure of passage of the various Blair bills, in 1888 Senator Blair did attribute to "Jesuit" influence the growing sentiment against his measure. He charged that the change in the policy of leading newspapers in New York, Boston, and Chicago from support to opposition was due to the fact that "upon the staff of every great paper of this country today is a Jesuit, and the business of that man is to see that a blow is struck whenever there is an opportunity to strike at the common-school system in America. . . ."

In 1890 Senator Blair again bitterly charged the "Jesuits" with contributing substantially to the opposition; and maintained that if the South could be converted wholeheartedly to the public school system, it would serve as "the great bulwark of free institutions in all coming time." This followed from the fact that the South was overwhelmingly Protestant, and free from "the vast influx of immigration which has overflowed and transformed the Northern States, in whose school systems the Jesuit has as much power in all the great centers as the older element of our population and in many places much more." He hoped that by developing and strengthening its public school system the South would "by reflex action, hereafter, be enabled to aid to save us the public-school system of the North now so threatened and in many places already controlled by Jesuitical craft and power." He felt that opposition of the Catholic groups to the Blair bill was so "inveterate and influential" that it contributed more than anything else "to endanger its enactment into law."

The defeat of the last Blair bill in 1890 brought to an end for more than a quarter of a century any further attempts to obtain Federal aid for general education. During World War I, however, the great number of draftees rejected by the armed services for illiteracy dramatically brought to the country's attention not only the deplorable extent of illiteracy but the serious effects it might have on the national defense. At the same time it revealed to many the real interest that the nation as a whole has in the education of all its children. For the first time it showed that the responsibility for education rests on the Federal government as well as on the states.

This realization of the educational problem and the Federal interest in it gave rise to the Smith-Towner bill in 1918 and in the Sterling-Reed bills in 1923. These bills provided for the establishment of a Department of Education headed by a cabinet member. In order "to encourage the States in the promotion and support of education," the bills provided for the annual distribution of $100,000,000 among the states. Nothing came of these bills, nor of similar bills introduced in the late '20's.

With the possible exception of the United States Chamber of Commerce, no organized group was more intense and effective in its opposition to these bills than the Catholic Church. Besides Senator Blair, Senator Hoke Smith in 1919 attributed to certain Catholics "the only discordant note of opposition," and cited a resolution by the Federation of Catholic Societies of Louisiana that charged that the passage of the Smith-Towner bill would rob "state and family and individual of their God-given rights." He also quoted a baccalaureate sermon delivered at Georgetown University in which a faculty member of Loyola College labeled the bill as "the most dangerous and viciously audacious bill ever introduced into our halls of legislation, having lurking within it a most damnable plot to drive Jesus Christ out of the land" and as aiming "at banishing God from every schoolroom, whether public or private, in the United States." According to the speaker, the Smith-Towner "bill destroys all freedom of education, takes away the sacrosanct duty and right of parents to educate their own children and the right of the children to be so educated. It is a direct assault upon religion and it penalizes Jesus Christ, His faith and all who believe and teach it."

Senator Smith, in reply, stated that the charge that the bill would drive God from the school room could have been made only by one "who opposes public education . . . and all schools except denominational and parochial schools." Other Catholic spokesmen, though less intemperate in their language, were no less firm in their opposition. They maintained that the bill sought to establish Federal control over education, that it would throw education into politics, that it would standardize education, and destroy state and local initiative.

Like its predecessors, the Smith-Towner and companion bills went down in defeat. But the panic and depression of the '30's again highlighted the crisis in education, and again evoked proposed legislation to provide Federal aid. In 1937 Senators Pat Harrison and (later Justice) Hugo Black joined with Representative Fletcher of Ohio in introducing a bill that would have ultimately provided $300,000,000 of Federal funds annually to be appropriated to the states for their use in improving "their public schools in the manner prescribed by their respective legislatures."

The Harrison-Black-Fletcher bill was attacked by Catholic representatives with the same arguments used to defeat its predecessors—and with some new ones, not entirely consistent with the others. For example, the bill was opposed because it threatened to bring on Federal control of education, and sought to command the states as to how they were to operate their school systems. On the other hand, it was also opposed—even by the same spokesmen—[47] on the ground that it contained no measures to insure the proper expenditure of the funds by the states, which, under the phrase "for improvement of their public schools," could use the money for "golf courses, football stadia," or "almost anything." Catholic opposition resulted in the defeat of the Harrison-Black-Fletcher bill as it had defeated its predecessors.

The Harrison-Black-Fletcher bill marked a new turn in the position of the Catholic Church in relation to Federal aid to education; and this may be said to represent the beginning of the current controversy. During the half century between the Blair bills and the Harrison-Black-Fletcher bill, the position of the Church was one of uncompromising and unqualified opposition to all programs of Federal aid. It was charged by some that the real reason for the Church's opposition was its fear that added funds to public school education would enhance the competitive attraction of public schools for Catholic parents, whose children—according to Catholic teachings—belong exclusively in parochial schools. The financial aspect, however, was not the expressed reason for the Church's opposition; the principal ground was the fear of the centralized control of education in Washington—which, the Church argued, was an inevitable consequence of Federal financial support. Obviously, opposition predicated on that fear must be unqualified—and the Church's opposition was unqualified. No offers to amend the various bills could be accepted by the Church in exchange for its abandonment of its opposition; if Federal funds must mean Federal control, the only way to avoid the control would be to refuse the funds.

But in testifying before a Congressional committee in 1937 in opposition to the Harrison-Black-Fletcher bill, a responsible Church spokesman, Msgr. Michael J. Ready, General Secretary of the National Catholic Welfare Conference, for the first time indicated that Church opposition was not necessarily unchangeable. During the course of his testimony he demanded that the bill be amended so as to include parochial schools within its benefits.[48] Though the rest of his testimony — as well as that of Dr. George Johnson, then Secretary General of the National Catholic Educational Association — was apparently in unqualified opposition to all bills for Federal aid, it was not long before it became evident that Msgr. Ready's almost accidental interpolation would mark the new position of the Church; and that Federal aid, instead of being a threat to the Church, would be a possible source of badly needed financial assistance to parochial education. The turnabout was complete in 1949, when, in a formal statement presented to a Congressional committee, the National Catholic Welfare Conference said without qualification — and with a bland disregard of the Church's directly opposite position for 60 years:

> By authority of the general-welfare clause of the Constitution, the Federal Government has an obligation to secure for every American child, regardless of his place of residence, an opportunity for an adequate education.[49]

The Harrison-Black-Fletcher bill was succeeded by the Harrison-Thomas bill of 1939. In testifying on this bill, Dr. George Johnson, appearing for the National Catholic Welfare Conference, insisted that the bill permit the states to decide for themselves whether Federal money could be used for nonpublic schools. (This in effect became the so-called Taft compromise that the Church later refused to accept.) When, however, he testified on the Harrison-Thomas bill of 1941 he demanded that nonpublic schools in every state receive some part of any funds voted by Congress for education.

It was not until 1945 that the Church came out in active support of a specific bill for Federal aid. In that year the Thomas-Hill bill, successor to a host of measures dating back to the first Blair bill, was introduced, and like its predecessors provided Federal funds exclusively for public schools. In the same year the Mead-Aiken bill was introduced, and immediately won the warm support of the Church. This bill did not leave it to the states to decide for themselves whether any part of the Federal funds was to be used for nonpublic schools; it provided that such schools were to share in the funds even in those states whose constitutions barred the use of any tax-raised funds for religious schools. This was to be accomplished by a "trustee" device. The national board proposed to be set up by the Mead-Aiken bill was to select among three persons nominated by the governor of each state a trustee to receive and disburse the funds for nonpublic schools that were allotted to his state. In making the allotment the national board was directed to "take into consideration the extent to which the burden of the educational needs of the State are borne by nonpublic schools."

As one writer has pointed out:

> This [Mead-Aiken] measure would have guaranteed Federal funds for nonpublic schools even in those states which by law did not permit state support for these schools. Supposedly, a fundamental principle of the Catholic position had been opposition to Federal control of education. This point had been raised against bills on every other occasion by their representatives, no matter how the bills were drawn. Yet a proposal which would have meant the deepest penetration by the Federal government into the fundamental pattern of the educational system received Catholic support.[50]

The Thomas-Hill bill failed of passage because of opposition by the Catholic Church; and the Mead-Aiken bill failed of passage because of opposition by Protestant church groups and the National Education Association. In 1947 Senator Robert A. Taft introduced a compromise measure. The Taft bill was based on the principle that, except for financing, education and educational policy are exclusively for the states. Senator Taft explained his bill as follows:

> This bill is a State-aid bill, and the State should be authorized to use the Federal funds for the same educational purposes for which it uses its own State funds. If the State recognizes private and parochial schools as part of its State educational system, then the bill provides that it may use Federal funds in the same proportion in which its State funds are used for such schools. On the other hand, if the State educational policy is to operate only through public schools, Federal money can only be used for that purpose. . . . The question has nothing to do with the highly controversial problem whether States should appropriate public funds for parochial schools. One may feel strongly either way on that subject, but it is a matter for each State and the people of each State to determine.[51]

The Taft bill was not acceptable to the Catholic Church; but the Supreme Court 1947 decision in the Everson case gave it an opportunity to propose a compromise of its own. Reverend William E. McManus, testifying for the National Catholic Welfare Conference, introduced the Church's proposal by first appealing for Protestant tolerance, saying:

> Is it not a travesty of religious freedom to claim that this Government of the people cannot furnish bus service for all children because in the process somebody's religious feelings might be offended? Must the school bus be a non-sectarian vehicle? Suppose that a parochial school child has been put off the school bus and is crushed under the wheels of a truck. Can the civic officials—the mayor, the coroner, and sheriff—look at the mangled body, shrug their shoulders, and absolve

themselves of blame by saying, "The youngster was a non-public school child; if her parents had sent her to the public school, this would not have happened?"

Then Father McManus proposed a compromise bill that would set aside a small fraction of the Federal appropriation to be used to "provide funds so that the children attending all schools, public and nonpublic, would receive certain essential school services, such as transportation, non-religious textbooks and supplies, and health and welfare services. These funds would be distributed according to the pattern of the School Lunch Act." Having made his appeal to tolerance and justice, Father McManus concluded with an appeal to "political sagacity." He noted pointedly that "it is a fact for the record that the educational bills which have passed Congress, are those which provided for funds for the direct or indirect aid of both public and private educational institutions, and the bills which died, Congress after Congress, are those which were discriminatory and unjust in their failure to count the children in nonpublic schools among the beneficiaries of the Federal government's assistance."[52]

The proposal of the Church was incorporated in a bill introduced by Representative Fogarty which provided that 10% of each annual allocation of Federal funds should be set aside for nonreligious textbooks, health service, and transportation of pupils—for all schools, public and nonpublic. The Fogarty bill was opposed by practically all Protestant church groups and by the National Education Association, and passed neither house of Congress. The Taft bill and its successor the Thomas bill, however, represented an acceptable compromise both to the National Education Association and to a number of Protestant groups. The Federal Council of Churches, in a resolution adopted by its executive committee in 1947, approved the Taft-Thomas compromise by urging "that federal funds shall be used only for such schools as the constitution or statutes of the several states make eligible for state support."[53] The Taft and Thomas bills were opposed by the Protestant groups associated with Protestants and Other Americans United. Each bill passed the Senate, but neither passed the lower house.

The controversy around Federal aid reached the greatest intensity in the campaign on the Barden bill.[54] In May 1949 Representative Graham A. Barden of North Carolina, himself a former schoolteacher, introduced the first of a series of bills providing $315,000,000 annually to aid the states in equalizing their educational burdens. The bill provided that the funds were to be used for "public elementary and secondary schools," and defined this term as "tax supported grade schools and high schools which are under public supervision and control."[55] This, of course, was not the first Federal aid bill introduced into Congress that limited its benefits to public schools; until the Mead-Aiken bill was proposed in 1945 all important Federal aid bills were limited to public schools. The bitterness that the Barden bill aroused in the Catholic Church can be explained most plausibly by the express exclusion, in defining the term "current expenditures" for which the Federal funds might be used, of "expenditures for transportation . . . and health services." This express exclusion may well have been deemed by the Church as wholly gratuitous, motivated by anti-Catholic bigotry. (In the second Barden bill introduced in the next session of Congress,[56] this negative exclusionary provision was omitted, and the same result was effected by affirmatively defining "current expenditures" to include "only expenditures for salaries of teachers and of school supervisory, administrative and maintenance personnel, expenditures for school supplies, and expenditures for the maintenance of school buildings." By this time, however, the fat had long been in the fire.)

The opening gun in the Church's campaign against the Barden bill was fired by Cardinal Spellman on June 18, 1949. Addressing 15,000 Catholics on the campus of Fordham University, the Cardinal urged his audience to pray for the souls of Congressman Barden and his "disciples of discrimination," who, in venting "venom upon children," were committing "a sin shocking as it is incomprehensible," and were guilty of promoting an "irrational, un-American, discriminatory thesis that the public school is the only true American school."

On the Sunday after the Cardinal's address the Barden bill was denounced from the pulpit of St. Patrick's Cathedral at each of the seven masses held there that day; and the 10,000 worshipers were directed as a religious obligation to demand that it be killed in Congress. Posters displayed near every door of the cathedral and in the reception hall of the rectory assailed the bill as "unjust, un-American, and divisive." For the first time in the history of the cathedral, printed matter was distributed or exhibited condemning proposed legislation.

The cry was taken up with a distinctly impressive unanimity. Throughout the country, masses and other religious services in Catholic churches were used to arouse Catholic opposition to the Barden bill. The Catholic press echoed the charges in unvarying language. The bill was declared to be a "forerunner of statism" that imposed on children the obligation to "deny God" in order to share

589

in its benefits. "Unfair," "discriminatory," "un-American," and "hypocritical" were the charges most frequently hurled at the measure.

The political consequences became apparent immediately. Thousands of letters and telegrams from irate Catholic voters swept down on Washington. One Congressman was reported to have received more than 25,000 communications in opposition not only to the Barden bill but to the Thomas bill as well. The Catholic National Welfare Conference news service reported that the volume of mail matched that received during the Taft-Hartley campaign and President Franklin D. Roosevelt's attempt to reorganize the Supreme Court.

So far the incident was no more than another of the many instances of the church in politics, and not basically different from other instances of the Church—Protestant, Catholic, or Jewish—in politics. The volume of Catholic mail that poured into Washington in opposition to the Barden bill was probably exceeded by the volume of Protestant mail that reached Washington in opposition to General Clark's appointment as ambassador to the Vatican. The campaign around the Barden, Thomas, and Fogarty bills undoubtedly strained Protestant-Catholic relations in the United States; but by this time it should be clear that interreligious conflict and animosity is almost an inevitable consequence of church attempts to obtain material aid from government.

What made the Barden controversy unique in the intensity of the bitterness it aroused was the attack by Cardinal Spellman on Eleanor Roosevelt, the late President's widow. In her column "My Day" that appeared in the New York *World Telegram* of June 23, 1949, she commented on Cardinal Spellman's Fordham University address of a few days earlier, and expressed her opposition to Federal aid to church schools.

This column evoked many letters from Mrs. Roosevelt's readers; and in subsequent columns on July 8 and 15 she insisted that her position was not motivated by bias against the Catholic Church, and that she had not indicated approval or disapproval of the Barden bill, declared to be discriminatory against Negroes in the South, or any other particular bill.

Only the June 23 column mentioned Cardinal Spellman; and it seemed therefore somewhat surprising that the Cardinal did not reply until July 21—almost a month later. Moreover, the reference to the Cardinal was entirely casual, impersonal, and innocuous, serving only as an introduction to the discussion of the merits of the issue. It therefore seemed even more surprising that it should have evoked the violent if delayed reaction in the Cardinal's lengthy letter of July 21. The Cardinal's letter, released to the press,[57] charged Mrs. Roosevelt with having launched a personal attack upon him and with being guilty of anti-Catholic prejudice and of "discrimination unworthy of an American mother."

The public reaction to the Cardinal's letter was immediate, and—except among some Catholic Church spokesmen—was almost universally critical. Even newspapers—ever fearful of arousing the ire of the Catholic Church—editorially defended Mrs. Roosevelt and expressed regret at the tone of the Cardinal's letter.[58] Protestant leaders and publications, as was to be expected, sharply and unanimously attacked the Cardinal. The American Civil Liberties Union and the American Jewish Congress in separate resolutions deplored the Cardinal's charge of bias, which, they said, tended to prevent fair discussion of public issues on the merits. Former Governor Herbert H. Lehman issued a statement in which he said that he was "deeply shocked at the attack of Cardinal Spellman on Mrs. Roosevelt," and expressed the view that "in our American democracy every responsible citizen is entitled to express his or her views on public issues without being . . . vilified or accused of religious bias." He stated that he knew of no single act of Mrs. Roosevelt's "that would in the slightest degree indicate bias or prejudice against any religion or any race," but on the contrary that her "whole life has been dedicated to a constant fight for tolerance and brotherhood of men as children of one God."

This statement by Governor Lehman and his subsequent political career are significant. Within a few months Governor Lehman was nominated by the Democratic Party and elected to the Senate of the United States. His election was made possible by his commanding majorities in New York City and other urban areas in which the Catholic vote is strong; and this indicates quite clearly that the Catholic population of the state did not agree with Cardinal Spellman in his attack on Mrs. Roosevelt. Further than that, the fact that he was nominated by the state Democratic Party is fairly good evidence that the Church itself realized that it did not have public sympathy on its side in this controversy, for it is highly unlikely that the Democratic Party in New York would nominate for high office any person stated to be *non grata* by the Church.

Cardinal Spellman, too, appears to have recognized the line-up of public opinion. Mrs. Roosevelt replied to his letter with a letter[59] in which she sought to answer his charges one by one, reiterated her opposition to tax-paid transportation, textbooks, and school lunches for children attending nonpublic schools, and asserted that she had no bias against the Catholic Church, and had supported Governor Alfred E. Smith in his campaign for the Presidency, as well as many other Catholic candidates for public office.

Shortly after this letter was published in the press, Cardinal Spellman—who in his letter to Mrs. Roosevelt had said that he would "not again publicly acknowledge" her, called her, and asked her to "look over a statement" he intended to release to the press. In this statement—which Mrs. Roosevelt called "clarifying and fair"—the Cardinal averred that the Church does not "expect public funds to pay for the construction and repair of parochial school buildings or for the support of teachers, or for other maintenance costs," since this would be unconstitutional, but only for "auxiliary services" of transportation, nonreligious textbooks, and health aids. "We are asking Congress," he said, "to do no more than to continue, in its first general aid-to-education measure, the non-discriminatory policy it has followed in the School Lunch Act and other Federal laws dealing with schools and school children."[60] The modest Canossa in reverse begun by the Cardinal's clearance of his statement with Mrs. Roosevelt was completed some two weeks later, when, on his way to dedicate a chapel in Peekskill, he made a social call on the woman whom he said he would not "publicly acknowledge."[61]

For her part, Mrs. Roosevelt maintained her position steadfastly during the rest of her life. When, early in 1950 Representative (later President) John F. Kennedy of Massachusetts introduced a bill which would have set aside a percentage of Federal funds for the transportation of pupils to parochial schools, Mrs. Roosevelt quickly expressed her opposition to the bill[62]—although this time without incurring any attack by Cardinal Spellman or other Catholic spokesmen.

## The Road to the 1965 Education Act

The Spellman-Roosevelt-Barden controversy sharpened the lines and drove many important organizations away from compromise and toward opposition to the position of the Catholic Church. The Congress of Industrial Organizations continued to support the original Taft compromise of allowing each state to decide for itself whether or not parochial schools should share in Federal aid to education,[62] but it stood almost alone. The American Federation of Labor, which was the original sponsor of the Church-supported Mead-Aiken bill for the mandatory inclusion of parochial schools, changed its position and recommended separate bills to raise the salaries of public school teachers and aid in a public school construction program and a separate bill to provide "Federal funds to protect and promote the health and welfare of every child in the United States." (This proposal was unacceptable to the Church because it divorced welfare from education.) The National Education Association, which had deviated from its long-standing position of Federal aid to public schools only to sponsor and support the Taft compromise, returned to its original position and endorsed the Barden bill, and the principle of public aid of public schools only. A similar stand was made by the National Congress of Parents and Teachers, representing 35,000 local parent-teacher associations throughout the nation.[64] Many Protestant church groups veered to the position of Protestants and Other Americans United and to support of the Barden bill principle. The Synagogue Council of America and the American Jewish Congress, as well as many other Jewish organizations, likewise endorsed the Barden bill either specifically by name or in substance.

The controversy appeared to have killed for decades any hope of obtaining Federal aid for general education. The Thomas bill had passed the Senate before the "explosion" occurred; but neither it nor the Barden bill, nor the Fogarty or Kennedy bills or any other general aid bill, was ever brought to the floor of the House of Representatives for a vote—it was much too dangerous politically for legislators to take sides. Another chapter had been added to the tragic history of frustration that began with the first Blair bill.

Yet, less than fifteen years after the Spellman-Roosevelt-Barden controversy died down Congress passed what was in fact if not in name the first general elementary and secondary school aid bill in American history. Not only that, but the bill had the support of most Protestant churches, the Catholic Church, the National Education Association, the AFL and CIO, and practically every major newspaper in the nation. Jewish organizations were practically the only dissenters; and even their formerly united ranks had split, with the Orthodox wing expressing its support of the measure.

A number of elements combined to bring about this almost miraculous consumation so devoutly wished by so many. Among these were the following:

(1) The election and martyrdom of the first Catholic President in American history. Early in his campaign Kennedy mitigated much of the Protestant hostility to and suspicion of a Catholic President by expressing himself in favor of Federal aid to public education but against aid to parochial schools, which, he said, would be unconstitutional.[65] On February 20, 1961, a little more than a month after his

inauguration, he sent a message to Congress calling for enactment of legislation to provide Federal funds to aid the states in constructing public schools and paying teachers' salaries. The message contained the following sentence: "In accordance with the clear prohibition of the Constitution no elementary or secondary school funds are allocated for constructing church schools or paying church school teachers' salaries; and thus nonpublic school children are rightfully not counted in determining the funds each state will receive for its public schools." He obtained from the general counsel of the Department of Health, Education, and Welfare a legal opinion to the same effect.[66] These acts, followed by his assassination, went far to soften Protestant-Catholic tensions and served to create an atmosphere of friendliness which helped to make possible Protestant acceptance of a measure which it would probably not have accepted earlier.

(2) The ecumenical spirit. The accession to the throne of Peter by John XXIII in 1958 opened up a new chapter in Protestant-Catholic relations. The urge for Christian ecumenicism, which had long pervaded Protestantism at least on the higher levels, suddenly appeared to achieve a hope of reality, particularly in the light of the expressions at the second Vatican Council, and placed upon many Protestants an imperative to meet Catholicism at least halfway on such issues as Federal aid to education.

(3) The popularity and political astuteness of President Johnson. In the first two years in office, the President was able to induce Congress to enact a substantial number of controversial measures which it had refused to do for many years, such as medical care for the aged, a broad civil rights measure, a voting rights bill, as well as the aid to education measure.

(4) The moderateness of the Catholic position. As we have seen, Cardinal Spellman, in his controversy with Mrs. Roosevelt, disclaimed any demands for general financial aid to parochial schools, asserting only a claim for indirect or auxiliary aid such as bus transportation. However, in the early sixties the Catholic position hardened, and the church increasingly demanded full and equal participation (to the extent of its secular instruction) with public schools in any Federal aid to education legislation.

Nevertheless, the Church accepted and warmly endorsed the 1965 act even though, unlike the College Aid act of 1963, it authorized no direct grants to nonpublic institutions. Its purpose was to provide direct aid not to the institutions but to the pupils. As stated in identical language in the reports issued by the education committees of both Houses of Congress,[67]

The bill does not authorize funds for the payment of private school teachers, nor is it intended that this provision authorize the financing of instruction for nonpublic schools. Facilities are not to be constructed nor equipment procured which will be to the pecuniary advantage of any nonpublic institution. Rather it is intended that the local public educational agency, through its preserved autonomy over local school matters, will have wide latitude in fashioning programs of direct benefit and advantage to elementary and secondary school pupils regardless of whether they are enrolled in public schools.

There were undoubtedly many reasons for the moderateness of the Catholic position. One of them may have been Catholic response to the ecumenical spirit evidenced by the Protestants. Another may have been the recognition by the Church that the Protestant and public educational organizations would not accept any measure that went further than the one the administration proposed. But probably the major reason was discovery by the Church of the potentialities of even indirect aid. This is clearly indicated in a significant editorial in the April 24, 1965, issue of *America* entitled "Federal Aid at Last," which said in part:

> Now, the new Federal law does nothing at all to help private schools directly. It gives them no money; it vests no property in them. Every benefit conferred on their pupils comes to them through the public school system. Even the textbooks that will be put into their pupils' hands will remain the property of public school districts.
>
> But the new law at least recognizes that these schools exist and are educating children. In a variety of ways, it proposes to assist and improve the education of these children. The aid is, in every instance, directly to the child rather than to the school he attends. But it is aid, and it holds a promise for the future of a truly pluralistic school system.
>
> The "child benefit" principle is capable of being extended to every phase of education other than the directly religious. It could well justify tuition grants to the parents of children in any nonprofit school that the state recognizes as giving an acceptable general education. Here, as with Federal aid to public schools, the Elementary and Secondary Education Act is a beginning rather than an end.

(5) The technological competition with Soviet Russia. Russia's success in launching a satellite in 1958 sparked a widespread demand in the United States for educational expansion, particularly in the sciences. It was generally recognized that this could be accomplished only with substantial Federal financing, which, experience had shown, could not be obtained unless some accommodation were reached with the Catholic Church. Qualms regarding church-state separation, many people felt, must yield to the paramount demands of national defense.

(6) The appeal of impoverished childhood. To those, particularly within Protestantism, to whom the technological competitive requirements of the Cold War would have little appeal, President Johnson presented the more potent appeal of underprivileged children. The measure was drafted in terms of aid to disadvantaged children living in urban slums and rural low income areas. Protestantism could not easily reject such an appeal.

(7) The accumulation of precedents. By the time the 1965 measure was acted on by Congress there was already a sizable list of Federal laws which, rightly or wrongly, were asserted to justify at least the indirect aid to nonpublic schools contemplated by Congress in the 1965 Act.[68] Among the precedents most frequently mentioned were the G.I. Bill of Rights, the National School Lunch Act of 1946, the National Education Defense Act, the College Aid Act, and the Anti-Poverty Act. Each of these merits some consideration, before we examine the 1965 Education Act.

## Veterans Benefits

Known popularly asthe G.I. Bill of Rights, a law enacted in 1943[69] provided for tuition to be paid by the Government for training of veterans in the occupation or profession they would seek to earn their livelihood, including religious ministry. Under the original arrangement, tuition payment was made directly to the schools which the veterans attended, including divinity schools. In addition subsistence payments were made to veterans. Eight years later, after the Everson and McCollum decisions, the law was changed to provide for payment to the veterans, leaving it to them to take care of tuition,[70] and this pattern was followed in respect to Korean veterans.[71]

## The National School Lunch Act[72]

The purpose of the act is to improve the health and well-being of the nation's children by granting funds and goods to state agencies in order to provide nutritious lunches to children attending elementary and secondary schools. The act contains a section which was adopted in the 1965 act; it provides that in any state where public agencies are not permitted by law to disburse funds to nonpublic schools, they shall be disbursed directly to such schools for purposes of the lunch program. This section has been used by the Department of Agriculture, which administers the program, in more than half of the states.[73]

## *National Defense Education Act*[74]

Adopted in 1958 as America's response to the Soviet satellite success, the NDEA has been amended and expanded a number of times to provide ever-increasing Federal funds for education in the interests of national defense. Each amendment, too, expands the ways in which Federal funds are made available for the benefit, directly or indirectly, of sectarian educational institutions.

For example, the original act set up a fund to make loans to pay for college tuition and subsistence, and, in order to encourage teaching, provided that 50% of the loan would be cancelled if the borrower thereafter taught in a public elementary or secondary school for five years. In 1964, this was amended to confer the same privilege upon persons teaching in nonpublic schools. The original act provided grants to enable public elementary and secondary schools to purchase equipment for the teaching of science, mathematics, and foreign languages — presumably the subjects most closely related to national defense. The act also provided that 12% of the amount appropriated by Congress was to be set aside as a fund to make low cost loans to nonpublic elementary and secondary schools for the same purpose. (Twelve percent presumably represented the ratio of nonpublic to public schools.) In 1964 English, reading, history, geography, and civics were added so that today the NDEA loan provision extends to practically the whole of the secular curriculum at parochial secondary schools.

## *Higher Education Facilities Act of* 1963[75]

The debates in Congress attending the passage of the act, more popularly known as the College Aid Act, unlike those attending the G.I. Bill of Rights and the NDEA, thoroughly explored the church-state issue. There were serious doubts as to the constitutionality of including church-related educational institutions, and, as we have seen,[76] a provision was added by the Senate, but dropped in conference, which would have authorized a court test on the question of constitutionality.

The legal memorandum of the Department of Health, Education, and Welfare, which asserted the unconstitutionality of Federal grants or loans to parochial schools at the elementary or secondary level, drew a distinction between such schools and church-related institutions at the college or university level. As to the latter, government grants for the construction and expansion of academic facilities could be constitutional. The following factors, the memorandum stated, distinguish American higher education: the fact that the connection between religion and education is less apparent and that religious indoctrination is less pervasive in a sectarian college curriculum; the fact that free public education is not available to all qualified college students; the desirability of maintaining the widest possible choice of colleges in terms of student's educational needs in a situation no longer limited by the necessity of attending schools located close to home; the extent to which particular skills can be imparted by only a relatively few institutions; the disastrous national consequenses in terms of improving educational standards which could result from exclusion of, or discrimination against, certain private institutions on grounds of religious connection; and the fact that, unlike elementary and secondary schools, collegiate enrollment does not have the power of state compulsion supporting it.

A number of comments suggest themselves.

(1) The distinction between lower and higher education in respect to the church-state issue appears to be a novel one. Nothing in the language of any Supreme Court decision supports it; nor does it appear to have been made in any state court decision.

(2) The factors listed in the memorandum may well be relevant to a decision on the wisdom or desirability of according governmental aid at the higher level, but hardly to the question of constitutionality.

(3) It is particularly difficult to comprehend the relevancy of the argument—often made—that aid at the college level is constitutionally permissible because "collegiate enrollment does not have the power of state compulsion supporting it." If relevant at all, it would seem to point to a directly contrary conclusion. One of the arguments most often asserted by Catholic spokesmen in support of their claim to governmental funds for parochial schools is that unless the government makes it financially feasible for Catholic children to attend parochial schools their religious liberty is violated by being forced against their consciences to attend secular public schools pursuant to compulsory attendance laws. This argument is obviously absent where, as at the college level, there is no compulsion by law to attend.

In any event, both the administration and the Congress accepted the validity of the distinction and enacted the College Aid Bill. This authorized the grant of Federal funds for the construction or improvement of undergraduate academic facilities "especially designed for instruction or research in the natural and physical sciences, mathematics, modern foreign languages or engineering or for use as a library." The act also authorized Federal loans for the construction of other academic facilities at either the undergraduate or graduate level. Only facilities used "for sectarian instruction" or "for religious worship" or "primarily in connection with . . . a department of divinity" were excluded.

## *Economic Opportunity Act of* 1964[77]

This law, more commonly known as the Anti-Poverty Act, was the immediate forerunner of the 1965 education act. But more than that, it, rather than the NDEA or College Aid Act, provided the motif for the 1965 measure. The latter, as will be seen shortly, was justified not by the demands of national defense, but by the needs of the poor and underprivileged. The Anti-Poverty Act, which set the stage for the education act, sought to meet the problem of poverty in a variety of ways, but the major emphasis was on education and training to enable the poor to advance economically. Thus, substantial sums were authorized to finance work-training programs, work-study programs, and adult basic education programs. However, the part of the law most relevant to church-state relations was Title (or part) II. The purpose of this title was to provide stimulation and incentive, through substantial Federal grants, for communities to mobilize their resources to combat poverty through community action programs. The programs contemplated activities in such fields as employment, job training and counseling, and special remedial and other noncurricular education assistance for the benefit of low-income individuals and families. Under this title, there were launched many programs of preschool preparation for poor children under the general name "Operation Headstart."

The act provides that community action programs may be conducted or administered by public or private nonprofit agencies or a combination of both. The Office of Economic Opportunity (OEO), to which was assigned responsibility for allocating funds and otherwise administering the law, took the position that sectarian or church-related agencies were qualified to participate in the program and receive Federal funds.

There can be no doubt that this determination accords with the legislative intent of Congress, as reflected in the debate attending enactment of the measure. Nevertheless, so interpreted, the act raises serious church-state questions, particularly in the light of the legal memorandum of the Department of Health, Education, and Welfare. The opinion of the memorandum was that the Federal government could not constitutionally finance the teaching of reading in parochial schools, but in the opinion of the OEO it could finance the teaching of *remedial* reading to backward pupils, or preschool *preparation for reading* in parochial schools. The legal memorandum of the Department of Health, Education, and Welfare had taken the position that under the First Amendment the Federal government could finance *welfare* but not *educational* services for children in parochial schools. The OEO took the position that reading instruction for average children was an educational service, but remedial reading instruction for the backward or preschool child was a welfare service.

Yet, the OEO was sensitive to the church-state implications of the grant of Federal funds to religious organizations. Accordingly it issued a regulation that in such cases

> The grantee shall ensure, and shall provide in any contract or other arrangement with the church-related school, schools or school system, that: (1) None of the grant funds shall be used for the teaching of religion, for religious proselytization, or religious worship.
>
> (2) There shall be no religious instruction, proselytization or worship in connection with any program supported in whole or in part by this grant and conducted outside of normal school hours (such as after-school programs, summer-school programs) or conducted for persons who are not participating in the regular curriculum (such as pre-school, adult-education, or a program for dropouts).
>
> (3) In any of the programs described in (2) above, admission shall not be based directly or indirectly on religious affiliation or on attendance at a church-related school or other church-related institution. Affirmative steps shall be taken to make known the general availability of such programs in the area served.
>
> (4) Participation in programs supported in whole or in part by this grant shall not be used as a means of inducing participation in sectarian or religious activities or of recruitment for sectarian or religious institutions.
>
> (5) The textbooks and other materials used in programs supported in whole or in part by this grant shall be devoid of sectarian or religious content.
>
> (6) Facilities renovated or rented for programs financed in whole or in part by this grant shall be devoid of sectarian or religious symbols, decoration, or other sectarian identification. Other facilities used primarily for such programs shall, to the maximum feasible extent, be devoid of sectarian or religious symbols, decoration, or other sectarian identification.
>
> (7) Grant funds shall not be used in any manner to release funds regularly expended by the school, schools, or school system. For example, grant funds shall not be used to pay in any part costs which would otherwise be incurred by the school, schools, or school system in their regular operation.[78]

Whether even strict compliance with these conditions on the part of a parochial school would render a grant to it of Federal funds immune from successful legal attack under the First Amendment (if the barrier of status to sue could be overcome) is far from certain.

## *Elementary and Secondary Education Act of* 1965[79]

On January 12, 1965, President Johnson submitted to Congress a message calling for the enactment of legislation providing substantial Federal funds for elementary and secondary education. Three months later almost to the day (April 11, 1965) he signed into law what the National Education Association called "the greatest single commitment ever made by the Federal government for the improvement of education in the elementary and secondary schools of this Nation."[80] Rarely had so important a measure passed from introduction to enactment in so short a time, particularly after more than a half century of earlier frustration and defeat.

As has been indicated, the act adopted the approach of the Anti-Poverty Law—aid to the poor—and while this approach probably assured passage of the education bill, at the same time, as we shall shortly see, it almost proved a stumbling block.

The act authorizes the expenditure annually of approximately a billion and a quarter dollars for different educational purposes. The major authorization, of more than a billion dollars, is under Title I, and is in effect the type of Federal legislation that had so often before been defeated—a grant for general public education, almost unlimited as to the specific educational purposes for which the funds could lawfully be used, such as the construction of school facilities, the hiring of more teachers, or any other legitimate public educational purpose. The act imposes a number of specific conditions on the grants, two of which are relevant here. The first, in line with the basic approach of the law, requires that the funds be used to meet the needs of educationally deprived children of low-income families. This means, for example, that if a state agency wishes to use part of the funds to build a new school, it must be located in a low-income neighborhood.

It is the second condition, however, that, in its application, may raise serious church-state questions. Section 205 (a) of the act provides that for a public educational agency to receive a grant under Title I it must satisfy the United States Commissioner of Education "that, to the extent consistent with the number of educationally deprived children in the school district of the local educational agency who are enrolled in private elementary and secondary schools, such agency has made provision for including special educational services and arrangements (such as dual enrollment, educational radio and television, and mobile educational services and equipment) in which such children can participate."

What this means is that if, in a particular neighborhood 15% of the disadvantaged children, for example, attend nonpublic schools, then 15% of the Federal funds granted for that neighborhood must be used to provide "special educational services and arrangements" in which the nonpublic school children can participate.

Although the act specifically mentions only "dual enrollment (shared time), educational radio and television, and mobile educational services and equipment," a local public agency need adopt none of these but may choose any one of many other special educational services or arrangements approved by the Commissioner of Education.[81]

Title II authorizes the expenditure of $100 million for the purchase of school library resources, textbooks, and other instructional materials. Legal ownership of these materials must remain in public agencies but they would be available for use by children and teachers in nonpublic schools.

Title III authorizes $100 million annually for "supplementary educational centers and services." The purpose of this title was to provide for programs that would enrich educational experiences and opportunities through programs not ordinarily part of the regular school curriculum (*e.g.*, guidance, counseling, remedial instruction, foreign language instruction for elementary school children, visits to museums and concerts).

It is this title which most closely followed the pattern set by the Anti-Poverty Act. In the first place, the services contemplated were not unlike those authorized under that act. Secondly, they were to be available to nonpublic school as well as public school children. Third, the bill as originally drafted provided that no local agency could receive a grant under this title unless the Commissioner of Education was satisfied that "in the conduct of such program there will be representation of or participation by" not only the public school authorities but also "nonprofit private agencies, organizations or institutions."

The last mentioned provision (which became to be known as the "consortium" provision) was taken from the Anti-Poverty Act. There it aroused no controversy. Its incorporation into the education bill, however, raised serious church-state as well as policy questions. These were first called to the attention of Congress by the present writer, testifying, at its request, before the House Committee on

Education.[82] Protestant organizations, which supported the measure, had second thoughts as to this aspect, and began to express serious reservations and opposition. The objections were summarized by George R. LaNoue, consultant to the National Council of Churches, as follows:

> What sort of theory of Church-State relationships would such a partnership imply? Doesn't giving a church or a church agency direct administrative authority in a public program constitute an establishment of religion? Many local school boards and all state departments of education have authority to enforce standards on private schools, and in some cases to provide services for their students. Yet no one has seriously suggested that this entitled private schools to appoint members of a state or local school board.
>
> The reality of urban politics is such that if parochial school supporters controlled a share of the school board appointments, they would have even more veto power over local school expenditures than they now have over federal aid. This kind of exercise of political power by churches in behalf of their institutional self-interest was exactly what the First Amendment was designed to prevent. The public school coalition did not object to having persons knowledgeable about the problems of private schools on the boards of the proposed centers, but they insisted that they come as individuals and not as institutional representatives.[83]

These objections caused Congress to change the bill. Title III as enacted provides only that responsibility for carrying out programs for supplementary educational services shall belong to public agencies but that "in the establishing or carrying out of that program there will be participation of persons broadly representative of the cultural and educational resources of the area to be served."[84]

Even as amended, there was considerable challenge to the constitutionality of the act. Yet, on its face, there is nothing unconstitutional in it. There is no mention in it of parochial schools or church-related institutions. Just as in the Constitution, there is no reference to religion except in the last section, and as there the reference is negative and exclusionary. The section provides that "Nothing contained in this Act shall be construed to authorize the making of any payment under this Act, or under any Act amended by this Act, for religious worship or instruction."

Throughout, the act speaks of "private" schools, and theoretically there is nothing to prevent the Commissioner of Education from interpreting the law as limited to private *secular* schools. This, of course, he has not done; nor could he, without violating the clear intent of the Congressional leaders as expressed in the debates attendant upon enactment of the measure.

This suggestion, however, is not a mere academic exercise. In order to preserve its constitutionality, the act could well be interpreted by the Supreme Court as limited to public and secular private schools; such an interpretation would be no more at odds with the intent of Congress than the Court's interpretation of the statute exempting conscientious objectors from military service.[85]

The constitutionality of the Elementary and Secondary Education Act of 1965 may well depend upon its application. By steadfastly rejecting proposals to add a section permitting judicial review on constitutionality, Congress sought to ward off the threat of a court test. Yet, experience has shown that where the constitutionality of major laws is seriously questioned, sooner or later the question will be passed upon by the Supreme Court. It is not too rash to suggest that somehow or other the Court will accept jurisdiction of a suit challenging the constitutionality under the First Amendment of the administration of the Elementary and Secondary Education Act of 1965.

PART THREE

# "... OR PROHIBITING THE FREE EXERCISE THEREOF ..."

### CHAPTER FIFTEEN

# Freedom and the Common Defense

## THE MEANING OF "RELIGION"

IT IS PRETTY LATE in this volume to define our terms; standard operating procedure in expository works like this is to define one's terms at the beginning. We have disregarded this procedure, and have not sought to define any of our principal terms—"state," "church," or "religion." We have done this for two reasons. In the first place, we think the importance of definition has been overrated; as often as not it hinders rather than aids the communication of ideas. In the second place, it is difficult if not impossible to arrive at an adequate and acceptable definition of such a term as "religion." Every attempted definition carries with it the bias of the definer.

For example, the standard legal definition of the term "religion" is the one given by the United States Supreme Court in Davis vs. Beason:[1] "The term 'religion' has reference to one's views of his relations to his Creator, and to the obligations they impose of reverence for his being and character, and of obedience to his will." This would seem to have been a fairly workable definition for the time when it was formulated (*i.e.*, when religion assumed a belief in a deity); but in the same case the court said that to call the Mormons' advocacy of polygamy "a tenet of religion is to offend the common sense of mankind"; and the same court could not accept as "religion" the belief of the "Thugs of India" in assassination or the belief in "human sacrifices by our ancestors in Britain."[2] Yet each of these beliefs had reference to the believer's "views of his relations to his Creator, and to the obligations they impose." Madison characterized as an "arrogant pretension" the implication that "the civil magistrate is a competent judge of religious truths."[3] To a substantial extent, the same characterization is appropriate to an implication that the civil magistrate is a competent judge of what constitutes religion.

Arrogant or not, a judge who is required to determine whether a particular statute is a law prohibiting the free exercise of religion must decide—if the issue is controverted—whether the act whose free exercise has been prohibited is in fact an act of religion. Do laws that prohibit fortune telling, astrology, and spiritualism prohibit the free exercise of religion? State courts faced with the problem have held that the free exercise of religion—if it be religion—must yield to the state's power to prevent fraud.[4] This problem will be discussed further in the section dealing with the prevention of fraud. It is sufficient to note here that these holdings neatly evade rather than solve the problem; if the acts practiced were truly religious they were not fraudulent any more than communion, mass, or *bar mitzvah* is fraudulent. (The fact that the medium or spiritualist receives a fee for his services cannot be the distinguishing factor, for so does the priest officiating at mass or the rabbi officiating at *bar mitzvah*.) A judge's "fraud" may well be a defendant's "religion."

In his dissenting opinion in the Everson case Justice Rutledge asserted that

> "Religion" appears only once in the Amendment. But the word governs two prohibitions and governs them alike. It does not have two meanings, one narrow to forbid "an establishment" and another, much broader, for securing "the free exercise." "Thereof" brings down "religion" with its entire and exact content, no more and no less, from the first into the second guaranty, so that Congress and now the states are as broadly restricted concerning the one as they are regarding the other.

Undoubtedly this is historically correct, else the word "thereof" would not have been used. Nevertheless, court decisions have in the course of time given the word somewhat different connotations with substantially differing practical results. As used in the establishment clauses, it connotes what would be deemed religion in the generally accepted understanding of that term. The free exercise of religion, on the other hand, connotes the freedom of each individual to act or refrain from acting as his individual religious conscience dictates, even though generally the action would be deemed secular and without religious significance. Thus, since prayer and Bible reading are generally deemed acts of religion, the establishment clause forbids them in public schools. On the other hand, saluting the flag and vaccination are generally considered secular, and while the free exercise clause may entitle an individual not to be compelled to participate, the establishment clause does not forbid the state to sponsor the activity. In sum, the First Amendment might be paraphrased to read "Congress shall make no law respecting an establishment of religion or prohibiting the free exercise of religious conscience."

Congress has made one attempt at defining religion. In 1948 the draft law, which exempted persons whose objection to war was based on "religious training and belief," was amended to define that term as "an individual's belief in relation to a Supreme Being involving duties superior to those arising from any human relation, but [not including] essentially political, sociological, or philosophical views or a merely personal moral code." In United States vs. Seeger,[5] which will be further considered later in this chapter, the Supreme Court was called upon but did not find it necessary to pass on the constitutionality of this definition.

Despite this, the Court has indicated quite clearly that the term "religion" is not synonymous with theism, or belief in a supernatural deity. In Torcaso vs. Watkins,[6] the Court referred to "religions based on a belief in the existence of God" as distinguished from "those religions founded on different beliefs." In a footnote, the Court noted that "Among religions in this country which do not teach what would generally be considered a belief in the existence of God are Buddhism, Taoism, Ethical Culture, Secular Humanism and others." In the same opinion the Court cited a lower court decision[7] in which it was held that the Ethical Culture Society qualified for tax exemption as a religious organization.

It is reasonable to suggest that an earlier generation would have been surprised at a holding that the term religion as used in our Constitution and laws does not encompass belief in God. Yet, if the Court were bound by the meaning generally ascribed to religion in the 18th century, when our Constitution was written, with its requirement of a belief in God, it would likewise be bound by the meaning then generally ascribed to God as the anthropomorphic deity depicted in the Bible. America in the mid-twentieth century would hardly accept such a definition, and the only conclusion is that neither the term God nor religion can be given a precise or static definition.

The term religion may not be subject to precise definition, but there is little doubt that as it was used in the First Amendment it was intended to have and has been interpreted by the Supreme Court as having a broad and comprehensive meaning.[8] The free exercise of religion protected by the First Amendment extends far beyond the freedom of worship; it includes the right to believe, to practice, to preach, and to teach. Moreover, it includes the right of no religion, as well as the right of religion; nonbelievers no less than believers are protected by the First Amendment. The Constitution secures freedom from religion no less than freedom of religion. The constitutional fathers, as we have seen, deliberately chose to make nonbelievers eligible to hold even the high office of President. Certainly they could not have intended that nonbelievers should otherwise be held accountable for their nonbelief. Can there be any doubt of the unconstitutionality of a statute imposing a fine or special tax for failure to attend some house of worship or otherwise manifest belief in God, no matter how that term is defined?

The religion clause of the Amendment goes even further than protecting nonbelief; it protects disbelief as well. It might appear to be a distortion of terms to include the right to preach and teach not merely nontheism but also atheism in the phrase "free exercise of religion." The Supreme Court of Tennessee, in the Scopes case, held that teaching the theory of evolution was not part of any "religious establishment or mode of worship" within the protection of the state constitution;[9] and it may be that most other state courts would likewise rule that their own constitutional religious freedom guaranties would not include the right to teach irreligion. Yet the background of the religious clause of the First Amendment bears strong evidence that the clause was intended to protect the right to attack religion as well as to preach it.

The issue might appear academic, inasmuch as the Amendment also protects the freedom of speech and of the press; and as the "Miracle" decision established, the right to attack religion is undoubtedly protected by these guaranties.[10] Indeed, the first two Jehovah's Witnesses cases in which opinions were written by the United States Supreme Court[11] were decided by the Court on the speech and press guaranties rather than on the religious freedom guaranty. And in another Jehovah's Witnesses case, the Court "doubted" that the Amendment confers greater protection to the freedom of religion than to the freedom of nonreligious expression;[12] so, too, in a free speech case the Court said: "The First Amendment gives freedom of mind the same security as freedom of conscience."[13] There would thus seem to be little practical difference whichever clause of the First Amendment a missionary atheist chose to invoke.

Whether or not the issue is academic, historically the freedom of religion clause—at least in the minds of Jefferson and Madison—envisaged freedom to attack religion. Jefferson, it will be remembered, pleaded that "it does me no injury for my neighbor to say that there [is] . . . no God. It neither picks my pocket nor breaks my leg."[14] It was this right to say that there is no God that Jefferson secured in his Statute for Establishing Religious Freedom and its guaranty that "all men shall be free to profess, and by argument maintain, their opinions in matters of religion."[15] It was this right too which was vindicated by the Federal Communications Commission in sustaining the right of an atheist to radio broadcast time on the ground that "Freedom of religious belief necessarily carries with it freedom to disbelieve. . . ."[16]

If religious freedom includes freedom of disbelief, it obviously includes freedom of dissent; heterodoxy is protected no less than orthodoxy. "Freedom of religious belief," said the United States Supreme Court," "embraces the right to maintain theories of life and death and of the hereafter which are rank heresy to followers of the orthodox faiths." It includes views that "might seem incredible, if not preposterous, to most people."[17] There are today probably more than 300 different sects, with faithful adherents throughout the United States. The beliefs of all these, no matter how extreme or fantastic to the average citizen, are entitled under the First Amendment to equal protection. The state may constitutionally prohibit assassination, human sacrifice, and polygamy; but this is not because the belief of the Hindu Thug, the primitive Briton, or the 19th century Mormon does not constitute "religion" within the meaning of the First Amendment's free exercise clause, but only because the societal interest in the preservation of human life or of the monogamous family is deemed by the state to be paramount to the Thug's or Briton's or Mormon's right to exercise his religion.

## THE CLASH OF CONFLICTING INTERESTS

Therein lies the constitutional problem under the "free exercise" clause: how to resolve this clash of conflicting interests, this demand of the individual to practice his religion, and the demand of society through the state that he do or refrain from doing certain acts, thereby conducting himself inconsistently with the dictates of his religion. This problem is of course by no means unique to the religion clause of the Amendment; indeed, it is a substantial if not a major part of all constitutional law. According to its preamble, the Constitution was ordained and established "to form a more perfect union, establish justice, insure domestic tranquillity, provide for the common defense, promote the general welfare and secure the blessings of liberty." Constitutional law — at least insofar as it affects the individual (as distinguished from disputes between a state and another state or the Federal government) — is largely concerned with reconciling the last-named purpose — securing liberty — with each of the preceding specific purposes. How, for example, can the individual's liberty not to engage in warfare be reconciled with the purpose of providing for the common defense? How can an individual's liberty not to be taxed be reconciled with the purpose of promoting the general welfare—a very expensive undertaking—or his liberty to preach anarchism be reconciled with the purpose of insuring domestic tranquillity?

Religious liberty is of course included in the phrase "blessings of liberty"; and the constitutional law of religious liberty, to which this concluding part of this volume is devoted, is the reconciliation of religious liberty with the preceding specific purposes of government as stated in the preamble of the Constitution. The formation of a more perfect union generally involves issues and disputes among the states, or between the states and the Federal government, and does not concern us here. That aspect of the problem that involves the individual's obligation to help promote national unity will be discussed as part of the problem of common defense, to which it is related as part of the over-all problem of national security. Since in this country we do not have ecclesiastical courts, the purpose of establishing justice rarely conflicts with religious liberty. Exceptional conflicts between religious liberty and the establishment of justice arising out of the disqualification of atheists or nonswearing Quakers as court witnesses, and the Pope's warning to Catholic judges regarding judgments of divorce, have already been considered.

There has recently arisen one case which, exceptional as it is, shows that religious liberty can conflict with the establishment of justice. Our judicial system rests in large part on the jury, and this means that the law can compel even unwilling persons to serve on juries and administer justice. A woman in Minnesota summoned to serve refused to do so on the ground that the Bible commanded "Judge not that ye be not judged." The Minnesota courts refused to accept this as a valid excuse and adjudged her to be in contempt of court.[18] She appealed to the United States Supreme Court, which directed the Minnesota court to reconsider its decision.[19] The latter court did so and came to the conclusion that the assertion of this claim to religious liberty did not constitute a grave danger to the administration of justice in Minnesota and dismissed the charge against her.[20]

However, this clash between religious liberty and establishment of justice was a rare and exceptional case. The principal problems with which we shall be concerned deal with the reconciliation of religious liberty with "providing for the common defense" (this chapter), "insuring domestic tranquillity" (the next chapter), and "promoting the general welfare" (the last chapter).

Substantially the same problem of the reconciliation of conflicting interests in the free exercise of religion is involved in the attempted reconciliation of the other freedoms secured by the First Amendment. The right of free speech does not—to use a familiar illustration—bar government from prohibiting practical jokers from yelling "Fire!" in a crowded theatre. Nor does the right of a free press bar government from prohibiting the publication during war of the times of departure and the destinations of vessels. It is the resolution of these conflicting interests that is the responsibility of the legislative or executive to determine initially in its consideration of measures seeking to restrict a freedom guaranteed by the Amendment, and of the judiciary in passing on the correctness of the initial determination.

In seeking to resolve this problem the courts have evolved what has become known as the "clear and present danger" test. Actually, this so-called test is more of an approach to the problem than a satisfactory means of solving it. As an approach and a general frame of constitutional reference against which specific cases should be decided, it is useful and reflects a tradition of American democratic reluctance to restrain individual liberties where restraint can be avoided.

To a certain extent the "clear and present danger" approach is a compromise. On the one hand, the state could restrict any action or speech which, in the opinion of the legislature or executive, manifested a tendency, even remote, to bring on evils that the state deems it necessary to prevent for the protection of society. Under such an approach the government could constitutionally prohibit the publication of *War and Peace,* because it might lead a reader to pacifistic convictions and induce him to refuse to serve in the armed forces for the necessary defense of his country. Or it could ban the Bible on the possibility that reading Genesis might lead some fathers to believe that they too have received a godly command to sacrifice their only son.

At the other extreme is the approach suggested by Jefferson, who, in his Statute for Establishing Religious Freedom, said that

> to suffer the civil magistrate to intrude his powers into the field of opinion and to restrain the profession or propagation of principles, on the supposition of their ill tendency, is a dangerous fallacy, which at once destroys all religious liberty, because he being of course judge of that tendency, will make his opinions the rule of judgment, and approve or condemn the sentiments of others only as they shall square with or differ from his own; . . . It is time enough for the rightful purposes of civil government, for its officers to interfere when principles break out into overt acts against peace and good order.[21]

True it is that if the state waits until principles have broken out into overt acts against peace and good order, much of the danger that the magistrate may judge others' sentiments according to their agreement or disagreement with his own will be prevented. (The danger will not be completely eliminated, because the magistrate will still have to determine whether what broke out was actually against peace and good order, and, if so, whether it was in fact attributable to the preached principles.) But it is unreal to expect such patience on the part of the modern state. The state will punish overt acts of disorder after they are committed, but will also act to prevent their commission, even if it involves restricting the freedom of expression of those counseling the commission of the acts.

The "clear and present danger" approach lies somewhere between the ill tendency and overt-act standards — its proximity to the one or the other depending largely on the subjective evaluation of the civil magistrate applying it. It was first suggested by Supreme Court Justice Holmes in a World War I sedition case. In affirming a conviction under the Espionage Act of 1917 Justice Holmes said:

> The question in every case is whether the words used are used in such circumstances and are of such a nature as to create a clear and present danger that they will bring about the substantive evils that Congress has a right to prevent. It is a question of proximity and degree.[22]

The "clear and present danger" approach was generally disregarded by the Supreme Court in other sedition cases in the World War I era; the Court uniformly sustained convictions which it felt could reasonably be said to have a tendency to bring on the evils that Congress or the states had a right to prevent.[23] It was, however, revived and accorded almost dogmatic status by the "Roosevelt Court" in the late '30's and the '40's, and was shortly applied to religious freedom cases. Although the "clear and present danger" approach survived World War II practically intact, for a number of years the "cold war" sucked out of it all but ceremonial significance in political cases.[24] The demise of McCarthyism restored some vitality to the doctrine in political cases,[25] but it has maintained greater and more consistent vitality in religious freedom cases. It is perhaps not without significance that on the same day the Supreme Court sustained a conviction against a young radical who in a street speech used derogatory language against the President and the American Legion,[26] it reversed a conviction against a fiery Baptist street missionary who used far more inflammatory language against the Catholic Church.[27] The view expressed by the Court as recently as 1945 that "the First Amendment gives freedom of mind the same security as freedom of conscience"[28] is today open to doubt.

Applied to religious freedom, the "clear and present danger" approach constitutionally justifies a restriction on religious freedom only if it is clearly and immediately necessary to protect an interest more important to democratic society than the unrestricted exercise of religion. Three distinct value judgments must be exercised by a court passing on a claimed infringement of religious liberty: first, the importance of the threatened interest as against the infringed right; second, the clarity and immediacy of the danger to the threatened interest; and third, the practicability of avoiding the danger by an "alternative method," that is, one which does not require an infringement of the constitutional right.

In each case, judgment must be exercised in the light of the preferred position accorded by our constitutional democracy to the freedoms secured by the First Amendment. The legislative regulation of commercial interests is presumed to be constitutional; a statute imposing a tax on business enterprises or fixing the hours of labor or rates of pay will (or should) not be judicially invalidated unless its arbitrariness or unreasonableness is free from doubt. But no such presumption of constitutionality is enjoyed by legislative or executive restrictions on rights secured by the First Amendment. In fact, the presumption is almost reversed; the government restriction is subject to a more searching judicial scrutiny than other government acts. The courts are suspicious of restraints on the majestic freedom of religion; and the burden lies heavy on those seeking to justify such restraints.

Hence the superior importance of the protected interest must be clear. The community may have an interest in having all children spend part of their formative years in close school association with children of all other faiths or of no faith, so as—in Jefferson's words—to "liberalize and neutralize their prejudices." This interest, however, is not so important as to justify the restriction of the religious liberty of those whose convictions preclude participation in education divorced from religion.[29] So too the community may have an interest in protecting home owners from the annoyance of being required to answer doorbells rung by unsolicited handbill distributors; but this interest is not sufficiently important to justify the application of an ordinance prohibiting such unsolicited doorbell ringing to Jehovah's Witnesses, whose religious convictions compel them to circulate missionary handbills.[30]

Even if the communal interest sought to be protected is clearly of sufficient importance to warrant the restriction of religious freedom for its protection, it must be equally clear that the interest is actually in immediate danger as a result of the religious activity sought to be restrained. There can be little doubt of the importance to the community of preventing filicide; but that danger is not sufficiently clear and immediate to justify a law prohibiting the teaching of Abraham's offering of Isaac on the altar. So too the community has an indisputable vital interest that its citizens retain their jobs, earn livelihoods, and provide for themselves and their families. Yet that interest would not justify jailing the preacher who takes as his text that verse of the Sermon on the Mount that commands,

> Take no thought for your life, what ye shall eat, or what ye shall drink, nor yet for your body, what ye shall put on.

In the materialistic society in which we live, where the service of Mammon exceeds the service of God, there is no clear and present danger that the number of congregants who heed the preacher will be large enough to interfere substantially with our economic system.

The extent of the danger may depend on the number of persons exercising the right. An occasional "eccentric" refusing to serve on a jury may not constitute a significant threat to our judicial system,[31] but the result could be different if numerous citizens were converted to that viewpoint. Similarly, the claim to unemployment compensation by a small number of Seventh Day Adventists and Orthodox Jews who refuse to accept offered jobs requiring them to work on Saturdays[32] may not threaten the solvency of the state's unemployment compensation fund, but it might if a large number of workers were to be converted to Sabbatarianism.

It may seem strange that a person's constitutional right under the First Amendment may depend on how few other persons assert the same right. Yet, on further consideration it does not appear so unreasonable. The purpose of a Bill of Rights is to protect minorities; it needs no First Amendment to protect the majority that finds no violation of its conscience in serving on juries or working on Saturday. The smaller the minority, the more likely it is to need constitutional protection; the greater it is, the more likely it is to obtain the protection it needs through legislative exemption rather than judicial intervention. Christian Scientists have been able to obtain substantial legislation exempting their practitioners from laws requiring medical licenses to practice the art of healing or requiring their children to attend biology or physical hygiene classes teaching the germ theory of disease. Jews have been unsuccessful in the courts but quite successful in the legislatures in obtaining exemption from compulsory Sunday observance laws. On the other hand, the much smaller minority of Jehovah's Witnesses have been compelled to rely almost exclusively on the First Amendment (although in recent years Jehovah's Witnesses have been rising remarkably in both numbers and respectability, and it is possible that before long they too will be able to obtain their exemptions through legislation).

Finally, government restriction of religious liberty to protect a clearly and immediately threatened paramount communal interest is constitutionally justifiable only if it is clear that the interest cannot be safely protected except by restricting religious liberty. Thus the interest of the community in a secularly educated citizenry, though superior to the religious liberty of parents whose religious convictions preclude their allowing their children to obtain a secular education,[33] can nevertheless be adequately protected without requiring all children to attend public schools.[34] So also the community's interest in unlittered streets can be adequately protected by arresting litterers rather than prohibiting the distribution of religious handbills.[35]

The foregoing principles are a composite of Supreme Court decisions in many religious liberty cases, particularly involving Jehovah's Witnesses.[36] The remainder of this volume will be devoted to exploring the Supreme Court's application of these principles in specific instances of the clashing of communal interests and individual liberties. Before we do this, however, we should briefly note two expressed dissents to these principles: a qualified one by the late Justice Jackson, and an absolute one by the late Justice Frankfurter. Justice Jackson[37] would have used these criteria of judgment in cases involving restrictions on activities that concern only members of the faith. Where, however, a religious group enters the secular market—as where it sells books or pamphlets—it must compete on equal grounds with secular interests, and its activities are equally subject to state regulations; which are valid if not arbitrary and capricious, and not discriminatory against religiously motivated activities.

Justice Frankfurter's dissent was basic.[38] To him there were no preferred constitutional rights; restrictions on religious interests were entitled to neither more nor less judicial protection than restrictions on commercial interests; in both cases unconstitutionality may be adjudged only on a finding of the absence of rational justification for the legislation. The "clear and present danger" doctrine has no relevance to restrictions on religious freedom. Such restrictions, like all legislative action, are presumed to be valid. Only legislation that interferes with the effective means of inducing political change—like legislation restricting political discussion—warrants suspicious judicial scrutiny. In all other cases the value judgments required by the "clear and present danger" doctrine must—in a democracy—be exercised by the people's legislature, subject to revocation or revision by the people's action at the ballot box.

Aside from these dissents, the composite of holdings previously set forth is a reasonable approximation of the present status of the constitutional law of religious freedom. This approach is explicit in many of the religious freedom cases, and, it is submitted, implicit in all—even in those decided long before the "clear and present danger" doctrine was articulated, and even in those which have been decided without specific reference to religious freedom. Although this approach does not require the state to wait until an actual outbreak of disorder occurs, and therefore does not go as far as Jefferson would have wished, the requirements of the clarity, immediacy, and gravity of danger indicate a clear policy of allowing the freest possible scope to religious beliefs and practices.

## NATIONAL DEFENSE

Probably no interest of the state is deemed by it to be more important than defense against a foreign enemy. The Supreme Court has often recognized its paramountcy over other interests. Individual liberties secured by the Constitution must yield when the nation's safety is in peril. For example, the demands of national defense as interpreted by the military have been held by the Supreme Court to justify the uprooting of thousands of law-abiding American citizens of Japanese ancestry during World War II, and exluding them from their homes on the West Coast, for no other reason than the accident of their Japanese ancestry.[39] Similarly, the prohibition by the Thirteenth Amendment of involuntary servitude must yield to the nation's right to conscript an army of—if necessary—unwilling soldiers, without which even the most just and defensive war could not be successfully waged.[40]

Furthermore, the overriding demands of military defense obviously cannot be frustrated by the conscientious objection to military service entertained by some religious denominations or individuals. It may be that respecting the scruples of the relatively few religious objectors to bearing arms would not seriously prejudice the nation's war effort. Congress has, in effect, made just such a determination in the 1917 and successive Selective Service laws, which specifically exempt conscientious objectors from combatant services. But, in view of the gravity of the danger and the terrible consequences of a wrong guess, this is a decision that should be made by the people's representatives in Congress rather than by nine lifetime judges free from political responsibility. Therefore the exemption accorded to conscientious objectors—and also to ministers of religion—is exclusively a matter of Congressional judgment, subject to revocation or modification by Congress in its discretion. The Supreme Court rejected as "astonishing" the assertion that it is a "fixed principle of our Constitution, zealously guarded by our laws, that a citizen cannot be forced and need not bear arms in a war if he has conscientious religion scruples against doing so." Said the court:

> Of course, there is no such principle of the Constitution, fixed or otherwise. The conscientious objector is relieved from the obligation to bear arms in obedience to no constitutional provision, express or implied; but because, and only because, it has accorded with the policy of Congress thus to relieve him. . . . The privilege of the . . . conscientious objector to avoid bearing arms comes not from the Constitution but from the acts of Congress.[41]

The power to conscript an army in peacetime, or to impose universal military training in peacetime, would not appear to be as clearly paramount to the religious scruples of conscientious objectors. Yet here too the decision must be made by Congress and not the court, in view of the obvious necessity of immediately available mass armies of adequately trained soldiers to wage a modern war likely to break out without advance warning. If Congress and the people assume that the surest way to avoid a repetition of Pearl Harbor is by a militarily trained citizenry, it is not the function of the Supreme Court to evaluate the correctness of that assumption—even on the petition of a religious objector.

A state's power to raise a militia likewise appears to be paramount to the religious convictions of conscientious objectors. This is the basis of the holdings in two Supreme Court cases, Hamilton vs. Regents of the University of California[42] and In re Summers[43]—though both cases might be explained on other grounds. In the Hamilton case, decided in 1934, the Supreme Court was called on to review the action of the University of California in expelling a number of students who refused to enroll for a required course in military training. The students were young members of the Epworth League who declared themselves bound by their own consciences and the discipline and tenets of the Methodist Church, which, they alleged, required them to abstain from military training in peace no less than military service in war. The students alleged in their appeal to the Supreme Court that their constitutional right of religious freedom was unlawfully abridged by their expulsion from the university for adhering to their convictions.

The court rejected the students' claim as "untenable," saying:

> Government, Federal and State, each in its own sphere owes a duty to the people within its jurisdiction to preserve itself in adequate strength to maintain peace and order and to assure the just enforcement of law. And every citizen owes a reciprocal duty, according to his capacity, to support and defend government against all enemies.

The Hamilton case was followed in the Summers case in 1945. There the Supreme Court upheld the action of the Illinois courts in refusing to admit to the bar an otherwise duly qualified legal applicant who was a conscientious objector. The fact, the court held, that Congress has exempted conscientious objectors from combatant service in war does not compel the states to grant a similar exemption. If the state can constitutionally compel military service by religious objectors under the penalty of imprisonment, it can apply to lesser sanction of exclusion from the legal profession just as it could apply the lesser sanction of exclusion from a tuition-free state university.

These cases might be justified on the ground that admission to practice at the bar or to a free state university is a privilege and not a right, and as a privilege may be granted or withheld, or granted on such conditions as the state sees fit to impose.[44] But it is doubtful that the cases can be adequately explained in that manner. In the first place, the opinions themselves clearly indicate that the decisions were based on the state's constitutional power to compel military service. In the second place, even if it is admitted (which is by no means certain) that earning a livelihood by engaging in the legal profession is a privilege rather than a right, a state, unlike an individual, may not discriminate arbitrarily in the distribution of its privileges. California, for instance, could not condition the admission of Catholics to the university on their foregoing mass during the four years of attendance;[45] and Illinois could not require legal applicants of the Jewish faith to partake of a nonkosher meal served at a dinner tendered by the judges to newly admitted members of the bar. It is no answer to say that these are unreasonable conditions, whereas bearing arms is a reasonable condition—for that assumes the very point in issue; it is a reasonable condition only if a state has the constitutional power to impose it on conscientious objectors—otherwise it is not reasonable.

The Hamilton and Summers cases can be adequately explained only on their expressed holdings: that a state has the constitutional power to compel military service even by those whose religious convictions preclude participation in such service. But, so explained, they are open to some questioning. As we have said, the decision whether exempting conscientious objectors from serving in the national armed forces would present a clear and present danger to the national defense should be made by Congress rather than the courts. The decision so made, however, should be binding on the states no less than on the Supreme Court. The Congress has decided through two world wars that national defense would not be endangered by excusing religious objectors from combatant service. It is difficult to see how the states can make a contrary decision and thereby unnecessarily deprive some of their citizens of the freedom to adhere to their religious beliefs. It is not too great a burden to impose on the states not to conscript for the state militia those whose religious convictions against combatant service have been respected by the Congress — which, after all, has the initial responsibility for national defense.

The Summers case followed the Hamilton decision, but it also relied on United States vs. Schwimmer[46] and United States vs. Macintosh.[47] These cases held that an alien who refuses to pledge that he will bear arms may not be admitted to citizenship, even if his refusal is predicated on religious objections. This holding was overruled in Girouard vs. United States.[48] There the court held that Congress did not intend to disqualify from citizenship those aliens whose religious convictions barred them from combatant service.

This decision, it must be noted, was not based on constitutional power but on Congressional discretion; it held only that the naturalization laws did not indicate an intent by Congress to make the promise to bear arms an indispensable condition of acquiring citizenship. It was clearly recognized that Congress could constitutionally have imposed the condition if it had wished to do so. Moreover, the court refrained from expressly overruling either the Hamilton or the Summers case. We may therefore accept as the law today that both Congress and the states have the constitutional power to compel all to engage in armed combat, irrespective of individual religious contrary convictions; and to impose for refusal such lesser sanctions as exclusion from citizenship, publicly controlled educational institutions, and the practice of the law.

The constitutional power to conscript an army naturally brings with it the power to prevent or punish conduct that interferes with the exercise of that power. Hence Congress may make it a penal offense to counsel or advise resistance to conscription.[49] Here, however, the "clear and present danger" approach comes into full play —

in fact, it was in this type of case that the doctrine originated,[50] and it is almost exclusively to this type of case that Justice Frankfurter would limit it. It is here that the courts are called on to determine whether the words were spoken in such circumstances as to create a clear and present danger that the addressee would resist conscription. The problem is not primarily one of the freedom of religion, but of the freedom of speech,[51] and need not detain us here except to note that if the circumstances are such as to create the clear and present danger of resistance to conscription, the fact that the counselor is a minister of religion or a conscientious objector acting by reason of religious compulsion does not constitutionally excuse him.[52]

Since Congress and the states are not constitutionally required to accord any exemption to religious objectors, they obviously can grant less than a full exemption. For example, they can limit the exemption to actual wartime, and require all to engage in military training during peacetime.[53] Congress may require the conscientious objector to engage in noncombatant military service, and jail him if he refuses. It may require—and has required—conscientious objectors to register with their draft boards, and jail them if they refuse or counsel others to refuse.[54] (During World War II one out of every six persons in the Federal prisons had been incarcerated for violation of the Selective Service Act because of his religious convictions.[55])

If Congress may exempt religious objectors, may it condition the exemption on membership in some recognized denomination or sect, such as the Quakers or Seventh Day Adventists, whose doctrine and discipline declare military service sinful? This condition was imposed by the Selective Service Act of 1917. Here we come to a problem that concerns primarily the separation aspect of the First Amendment; for it may well be argued that such a condition prefers certain religions over others. (It will be remembered that in the argument of the Zorach case before the Supreme Court, the members of the court indicated their concern about the regulation of the state commissioner of education that limited participation in the released-time program to "duly constituted religious bodies." The same objection might be made to the broad exemption granted to ministers of religion as compared with the narrow exemption granted to lay conscientious objectors, who, unlike ministers and divinity students, are subject to induction for defense work under civilian direction.[56])

The 1940 Selective Service Act liberalized the requirements for exemption to include anyone who by "reason of religious training and belief" possessed conscientious scruples against "participation in war in any form"—thus making it unnecessary to prove membership in a particular pacifist denomination. This removed the preference of certain religious groups over others; and might thus be justified under that interpretation of the First Amendment that limits it to prohibiting preferential treatment among religions and sects. It does not, however, remove the objection under the Everson-McCollum interpretation of the Amendment; it still prefers religious believers to nonbelievers, for the 1940 act was held not to exempt those whose objection to participating in military service is based on a "political and social philosophy respecting the folly and futility of war."[57]

In 1948 the constitutional issue was sharpened even further when Congress amended the law not only to bar those whose objection to war is based on "essentially political, sociological or philosophical views or a merely personal code," but also to define religion as a belief in a Supreme Being. This would seem to be unconstitutional even under the narrow interpretation of the First Amendment which was held in Torcaso vs. Watkins[58] to forbid government from aiding "those religions based on a belief in the existence of God as against those religions founded on different beliefs."

The constitutional issue was presented to the Supreme Court in three cases involving three draftees each of whom was denied exemption by his local draft board because he did not believe in God or a Supreme Being within the common understanding of those terms. One of the draftees refused to answer "yes" or "no" to the question as to his belief in a Supreme Being but asserted that his "skepticism or disbelief in the existence of God" did "not necessarily mean lack of faith in anything whatsoever"; that his was a "belief in and devotion to goodness and virtues for their own sakes, and a religious faith in a purely ethical creed." He cited such personages as Plato, Aristotle, and Spinoza for support of his ethical belief in intellectual and moral integrity "without belief in God, except in the remotest sense."

Another of the draftees defined religion as the "sum and essence of one's basic attitudes to the fundamental problems of human existence"; he said that there was a relationship to Godness in two directions, "vertically towards Godness directly," and "horizontally towards Godness through Mankind and the World," and he accepted the latter.

The third draftee quoted with approval the Reverend John Haynes Holmes' definition of religion as "the consciousness of some power manifest in nature which helps man in the ordering of his life in harmony with its demands . . . [It] is the supreme expression of human nature; it is man thinking his highest, feeling his deepest, and living his best."

Unanimously the Supreme Court held that all three draftees did indeed believe in a "Supreme Being" in the sense intended by Congress. By using that term rather than "God" Congress indicated its intent not to limit the exemption to persons believing in an anthropomorphic deity but intended to include all who possess "a sincere and meaningful belief which occupies in the life of its possessor a place parallel to that filled by the God of those admittedly qualifying for the exemption."[59] Accordingly, all three draftees were entitled to exemption as religious objectors.

One can express some doubt that this was what Congress intended or that it wanted to exempt such young men as the three draftees involved in these cases. Nevertheless, the Supreme Court was able by its interpretation to avoid passing on the constitutionality of the 1948 exemption to the conscription law. But this avoidance is likely to be only temporary relief; sooner or later some rash draftee will assert that his objection to military service is not motivated by religion or by a belief in a Supreme Being no matter how defined, but solely on his belief that war is morally wrong. Faced with such a case, present decisions of the Court would seem to point to a holding that Congress can constitutionally exempt objectors motivated by religion while not exempting those motivated by moral, philosophic, or political considerations,[60] but that it may not require belief in God or a Supreme Being, however defined, as a condition of exemption.[61] This would require the Court to define religion without reference to God or a Supreme Being—no doubt a difficult task, but hardly more difficult than defining God.

The narrower exemption accorded by the Selective Service Act of 1917 was in fact attacked during World War I under the "establishment" clause of the First Amendment. The Supreme Court disposed of it summarily, commenting:

> We pass without anything but statement the proposition that an establishment of a religion or an interference with the free exercise thereof repugnant to the First Amendment resulted from the exemption clauses of the act to which we at the outset referred, because we think its unsoundness is too apparent to require us to do more.[62]

Although the contention would seem to have merited more respectful consideration, the preferential treatment in the exemption, as well as the exemption itself, are constitutionally justifiable under any interpretation of the "establishment" clause. We have seen that the overriding paramountcy of national defense empowers Congress to disregard religious objections to military service, notwithstanding the religious freedom clause of the First Amendment. The same national interest justifies restriction on speech, press, or assembly where such restriction is clearly and immediately necessary to avert a danger to that interest. But national defense is paramount to all individual liberties secured by the First Amendment — not excluding the liberty to be free from laws respecting an establishment of religion.

It is on this basis that the Federal government could constitutionally finance missionary activities among the Indians. It is on the same basis that paid chaplaincies in the armed forces can be justified. And it is on this basis that exemption limited to religious objectors can be justified. For Congress may well have decided that compelling persons to engage in war in violation of their religious convictions would hurt rather than help the war effort. Moses exempted from war duty the "fearful and fainthearted . . . lest his brethren's heart faint as well as his heart." (Deuteronomy 20:8). Congress has not seen fit to exempt the fainthearted; no doubt because — though the Mosaic exemption did not adversely affect the conquest of Canaan — modern warfare is likely to leave few without faint heart. But it has seen fit to exempt the religious objectors lest their resistance spread to their brethren. Since philosophic and political objections to war may not have the same contagious potentialities as religious objections, Congress limited the exemption to religious objectors. If the result is to compromise the separation of church and state, that is tragically not the only constitutionally secured liberty that is sacrificed to the demands of war.

Or the exemption of religious objectors may be justified by means of another constitutional approach: this approach can also justify the government employment of chaplains in the armed forces. The conscription of religious objectors is constitutionally permissible, not because it is not an infringement of the freedom of religion assured by the First Amendment, but because it is necessary to infringe the freedom in the interests of national safety. This infringement, however, is constitutionally permissible only to the extent that it is necessary; and Congress has determined that — subject to the condition it has imposed — coerced military service by religious objectors is not necessary for national defense.

## LOYALTY AND UNITY

### *Cultural Unity*

The nation's security requires not only an army, but — equally important — a loyal and united citizenry supporting the army and the defense effort. It therefore cannot be doubted that both Congress and the state legislatures may take necessary measures to assure loyalty and unity. Here, however, there is not that urgent immediacy that characterizes the power to conscript an army. Moreover, the consequences of a wrong guess are not likely to be as disastrous. Hence there is less reason here for the unquestioning judicial acceptance of the legislature's determination that a particular measure is necessary to insure loyalty or unity. It is for this reason that—as we shall see—the United States Supreme Court has scrutinized with suspicion and skepticism laws restricting religious freedom in the interests of national loyalty and unity.

The problem of resolving the conflicting demands of religious liberty and national loyalty and unity first came to the Supreme Court in 1923 in Meyer vs. Nebraska,[63] and later in several associated cases.[64] The issue involved in these cases was the validity of state statutes enacted in 1919 that prohibited "teachers in any private, denominational, parochial school [to] teach any subject to any person in any language other than the English language," and further prohibited the teaching of any foreign language until the pupil should have successfully passed the eighth grade. The defendants were teachers of German in Lutheran and Reformed parochial schools—in the Meyer case by the use of "a collection of Biblical stories."

The purpose of the statutes—according to the attorney general of Nebraska arguing in the Meyer case—"was to create an enlightened American citizenship in sympathy with the principles and ideals of this country, and to prevent children reared in America from being trained and educated in foreign languages before they had an opportunity to learn the English language and observe American ideals. It is a well known fact that the language first learned by a child remains his mother tongue and the language of the heart of the children reared in this country who will eventually become citizens of this country." It is within "the police power of the States," he continued, "to compel every resident . . . so to educate his children that the sunshine of American ideals will permeate the life of the future citizens of this Republic."

These statutes were but an incident in the long history of the many futile attempts to destroy a minority group's cultural pattern by forbidding the use of its language. They were reminiscent of the Prussian statutes outlawing French teaching in Alsace after 1870, immortalized in Alphonse Daudet's classical story, "The Last Lesson." The Germans prohibited the use of the French language not only in schools, but even on gravestones.[65] Both Prussia and Czarist Russia had vainly attempted to stamp out Polish by forbidding its teaching in the schools. The Austro-Hungarian government promulgated numerous decrees seeking to eliminate from the empire all languages other than German or Hungarian.[66] About the same time the Nebraska, Iowa, and Ohio statutes were enacted, Italy passed laws seeking to wipe out the German language in the territory acquired from Austria; and its partner in totalitarianism, Nazi Germany, later forbade the use of the local language in schools in areas incorporated into the Greater Reich.[67]

An eminent American historian used the following language to describe the background of the Nebraska, Ohio, and Iowa laws:

> Many have been the attempts to compel dissident nationalities to conform to the nationalism of the dominant majority. Germans between 1871 and 1914 pursued fairly systematically a policy of Germanising dissentient Poles, Danes and Alsatians; they forced the use of the German language in the schools and even in religious instruction. . . . This "Germanisation" or "Prussianisation" was paralleled in other countries by a "Russification," "Magyarisation," "Ottomanisation," etc.; and the "Americanisation" which has recently been much in evidence in the United States, if not employing all the methods of "Prussianisation," sets itself a familiar goal.[68]

It is important to note the political and social climate in which the Nebraska, Iowa, and Ohio statutes were passed. It was a period marked by intense nationalism and xenophobia. The statutes were not aimed at the German language alone — the armistice bringing the first World War to a close had been signed long before the laws were passed. They were aimed at all foreign languages, and were enacted at a time when many Americans believed that the welfare of our country demanded the elimination of cultural differences. Homogeneity was the goal to be attained, even if religious liberties were impaired in the process. People who boasted of being "100% American" were looked upon with favor, whereas "hyphenated Americans" were in disrepute.

The courts of Nebraska, Ohio, and Iowa upheld the validity of the statutes because of the felt necessity of securing unity and loyalty. In upholding the Nebraska law, the supreme court of that state explained that the

> . . . legislature had seen the baneful effects of permitting foreigners, who had taken residence in this country, to rear and educate their children in the language of their native land. The result of that condition was found to be inimical to our own safety. To allow the children of foreigners, who had emigrated here, to be taught from early childhood

the language of the country of their parents was to rear them with that language as their mother tongue. It was to educate them so that they must always think in that language, and, as a consequence, naturally inculcate in them the ideas and sentiments foreign to the best interests of this country.[69]

The United States Supreme Court reversed the state courts and invalidated the statutes in the first of a series of decisions in which the court has held that coerced unity and loyalty—assuming unity and loyalty can be attained through coercion—is not a goal that is constitutionally obtainable at the expense of religious liberty. Although the decision stressed the right of education rather than the right of religion, the case itself concerned religious no less than intellectual liberty, and the court's language was equally applicable to the religious liberty aspect of the case.

The court first held that the term "liberty" in the Fourteenth Amendment ban on state deprivation of "life, liberty or property without due process of law" included "not merely freedom from bodily restraint but also the right of the individual to contract, to engage in any of the common occupations of life, to acquire useful knowledge, to marry, establish a home and bring up children, to worship God according to the dictates of his own conscience, and generally to enjoy those privileges long recognized at common law as essential to the orderly pursuit of happiness by free men."

The court then held that though the ends sought to be achieved by the statute were commendable, they might not be effected by coercion in violation of the individual's "liberty" as thus defined. The court said:

That the State may do much, go very far, indeed, in order to improve the quality of its citizens, physically, mentally and morally, is clear; but the individual has certain fundamental rights which must be respected. The protection of the Constitution extends to all, to those who speak other languages as well as to those born with English on the tongue. Perhaps it would be highly advantageous if all had ready understanding of our ordinary speech, but this cannot be coerced by methods which conflict with the Constitution—a desirable end cannot be promoted by prohibited means. . . .

The desire of the legislature to foster a homogeneous people with American ideals prepared readily to understand current discussions of civic matters is easy to appreciate. Unfortunate experiences during the late war and aversion toward every characteristic of truculent adversaries were certainly enough to quicken that aspiration. But the means adopted, we think, exceed the limitations upon the power of the State and conflict with rights assured to plaintiff in error. The interference is plain enough and no adequate reason therefor in time of peace and domestic tranquillity has been shown.

The court did not use the language of the "clear and present danger" approach; yet a reading of the decision indicates clearly that that approach is implicit. In view of the prevailing "peace and domestic tranquillity" there was no such clear and immediate danger to the nation's safety and security as would warrant the abridgment of the defendant's constitutional rights. "No emergency," the court said, "has arisen which renders knowledge by a child of some language other than English so clearly harmful as to justify its inhibition with the consequent abridgment of rights so long freely enjoyed."

Interestingly—though the "clear and present danger" approach is implicit in the court's decision—a dissenting opinion was filed by Justice Holmes, the author of that approach, who used the approach later urged by Justice Frankfurter. It cannot be held, Justice Holmes said, that "considering the end in view, the statute passes the bounds of reason and assumes the character of a merely arbitrary fiat." Since "men reasonably might differ," he was "unable to say that the Constitution of the United States prevents the experiment being tried."

The next case to reach the Supreme Court that required the weighing of the conflicting interests of loyalty and unity as against religious liberty was Pierce vs. Society of Sisters,[70] which was decided in 1925. Here the religious-freedom aspect was explicit, and was argued by counsel not only for the parties but also in the briefs of the *amici curiae*—the American Jewish Committee, the North Pacific Union Conference of Seventh Day Adventists, and the Protestant Episcopal Church—who argued against the Oregon statute attacked in the suit. The Oregon statute required all parents to send to public schools their children between the ages of eight and sixteen. The effect—and purpose—of this statute was to outlaw private and parochial schools. We have already quoted some of the arguments of the attorney general of Oregon in support of the law. Those arguments urged that the increase in juvenile crime might be attributed to the lack of public school education by many children, that interreligious prejudice might result from religious segregation, and that subversive economic doctrines might be taught in nonpublic schools.

The aspect of national security is made explicit in the following further quotation from the attorney general's argument:

> . . . This law may also be sustained under the powers of the State in connection with its duties to aid the United States in time of war. The power and duty to be prepared for war is shared by the State government.
> The discretion of the States in the exercise of their powers is broad enough to justify a State in holding that a compulsory system of public

school education will encourage the patriotism of its citizens and train its younger citizens to become more willing and more efficient defenders of the United States in times of public danger. This is particularly true in view of the fact that if the Oregon School Law is declared unconstitutional there will be nothing to prevent the establishment of private schools, the main purpose of which will be to teach disloyalty to the United States, or at least the theory of the moral duty to refuse to aid the United States even in the case of a defensive war. . . .

The Supreme Court unanimously rejected this argument, and invalidated the Oregon statute. Justice Holmes did not dissent here, although he had dissented in Meyer vs. Nebraska. Also interesting is the fact that though the court had used the substance if not the words of the "clear and present danger" approach in the Meyer case, it here used the "reasonable relation" approach and came up with the same result—a fact that might cause some cynics to speculate how much of judicial opinions may be the rationalization of conclusions desired to be reached. The court said:

> Under the doctrine of *Meyer v Nebraska*, we think it entirely plain that the Act of 1922 unreasonably interferes with the liberty of parents and guardians to direct the upbringing and education of children under their control. As often heretofore pointed out, rights guaranteed by the Constitution may not be abridged by legislation which has no reasonable relation to some purpose within the competency of the State. The fundamental theory of liberty upon which all governments in this Union repose excludes any general power of the State to standardize its children by forcing them to accept instruction from public teachers only. The child is not the mere creature of the State; those who nurture him and direct his destiny have the right, coupled with the high duty, to recognize and prepare him for additional obligations.

It is difficult to justify the decision under the "reasonable relation" approach. It can hardly be denied—and it was not denied in the Meyer case—that fostering unity is a "purpose within the competency of the State." Nor is it easy to accept the court's statement that legislation requiring all children to attend public school "has no reasonable relation" to this purpose—certainly reasonable men might differ on this question; and under the Frankfurter approach that should be sufficient to declare the law valid. This is particularly so since the law did not—as the Court implies it did—prevent parents from preparing their children "for additional obligations," inasmuch as it did not prohibit attendance at religious schools in addition to attendance at public schools.

The decision can be adequately explained only by the use of the "clear and present danger" approach. The statute does infringe on the religious liberty of Catholics, for—as we have seen—Catholic doctrine requires all education for Catholic children to be given by Catholic teachers under Catholic auspices. Although the Oregon law cannot be said to be so patently unreasonable as to justify a holding that the people of Oregon acted arbitrarily, it can be said that the danger the law sought to avert was not so clear and present as to justify the infringement on Catholics' religious liberty.

The approach by which the court reached its decision is perhaps not important—what is important is the decision; and the Pierce decision may be said to be the Magna Charta of the parochial school system. It also reemphasized what had previously been stated in the Meyer case: that coerced unity—if constitutionally permissible at all—may not be purchased at the expense of religious liberty.

The basic issue underlying the Meyer and Pierce cases again came before the Supreme Court in 1927 in the case of Farrington vs. Tokushige.[71] The statute involved, enacted by the legislature of the Territory of Hawaii, was aimed at the numerous foreign language schools in the Territory. These were principally Japanese schools and—though the statute expressly exempted "Sabbath schools"—the Japanese schools at which it was aimed were "Buddhist schools" conducted on church property by church leaders.[72]

Unlike the Oregon statute involved in the Pierce case, the Hawaii law did not purport to outlaw private schools; what it did was to subject them to detailed and minute government regulation that would have made their operation difficult if not impossible. That its motivation was the same as that of the Oregon law—as well as the Nebraska, Ohio, and Iowa laws—is indicated by the "declared object of the Act," which was "to fully and effectively regulate the conducting of foreign language schools and the teaching of foreign languages in order that the Americanism of the pupils may be promoted. . . ." It is also indicated by the argument of the attorney general of Hawaii, who said:

> It would be a sad commentary on our system of government to hold that the Territory must stand by impotent, and watch its foreign-born guests conduct a vast system of schools of American pupils, teaching them loyalty to a foreign country and disloyalty to their own country, and hampering them during their tender years in the learning of the home language in the public schools. . . .

The Supreme Court invalidated the Hawaiian statute on the authority of the Meyer and Pierce cases. The court stated that it appreciated "the grave problems incident to the large alien population of the Hawaiian Islands, [but] the limitations of the Constitution must not be transcended."

In the World War II period another legislative attack was made in Hawaii on the foreign language schools. In 1943 the Territorial Legislature enacted a statute prohibiting the school teaching of any foreign language to any child who had not passed the fourth grade in public school and did not thereafter maintain an average score in English writing and reading in public school.

Suit was brought in Hawaii by a number of Chinese foreign language schools to declare the statute unconstitutional. The religious-liberty issue was even clearer in this case than in the Farrington and Meyer cases, for unlike the statute in the latter case, "ancient" languages were not exempted; hence the statute could prohibit a Catholic child preparing for the priesthood from learning the Latin necessary for the performance of his priestly functions until he reached the age of fifteen. The law also made illegal the teaching of the Bible or prayers in Hebrew to Jewish children in religious schools (although actually the law was never applied to any but the Chinese foreign language schools).

Guided no doubt by the Supreme Court decisions in the Meyer, Pierce, and Farrington cases, the legislators of Hawaii did not base the 1943 law on the necessity of achieving loyalty and unity; instead they based it on another societal interest, the welfare of children—with a possibly prophetic anticipation of the Supreme Court decision the following year that elevated to high constitutional status a legislature's power to protect the welfare of children.[73] The Hawaiian statute contained a legislative finding that

> ... the study and persistent use of foreign languages by children of average intelligence in their early and formative years definitely detract from their ability properly to understand and assimilate their normal studies in the English language, which are required by law to be pursued by all children of school age, and definitely retard their progress in understanding and assimilating such studies; that the study and persistent use of such foreign languages in such early and formative years may and do, in many cases, cause serious emotional disturbances, conflicts, and maladjustments; that the teaching of foreign languages compels and encourages the study and persistent use of such foreign language, to the detriment, as aforesaid, of ... the health and welfare, of children of tender age....

At the trial the attorney general of Hawaii introduced much expert evidence to show the undesirable educational and psychological effects of bilingualism on children;[74] nevertheless it is more than probable that the real motivation was cultural unity, as in the previous cases. The law was passed in 1943 in the middle of the war between our country and Japan. During the same period of anti-Japanese hysteria the state senate of California, where there was also a large Japanese minority, appointed a legislative committee on Japanese resettlement. The committee "vigorously opposed . . . the return of any Japanese to California until after the end of the war with Japan, and recommended the strengthening of the anti-Japanese Alien Land Laws,[75] the anti-Japanese Fishing Laws,[76] and the regulation of Japanese Language Schools."[77] There is little reason to believe that the motive underlying the action of the Hawaiian legislature was different from that underlying the California senate committee's recommendation to regulate Japanese language schools.

Nor does the fact that the ban was limited to children below ten years of age negate the probability that the dominant purpose of the legislation was to promote cultural uniformity and nationalist loyalty rather than prevent educational retardation. Antiforeign language statutes whose expressed purpose is to promote nationalism are generally limited to children in elementary schools. The Nebraska, Iowa, and Ohio statutes invalidated in the Meyer and Bartels cases prohibited foreign language instruction to children who had not yet attained the eighth grade in elementary school. The Hawaiian statute declared invalid in the Farrington case prohibited attendance by children who had not passed the second grade. The order concerning the use of the German language in Luxemburg, issued by the Nazi gauleiter, permitted the use of the French language in postelementary schools; under the 1943 Hawaiian statute the permissive point was the fourth grade for average children and the fifteenth year for the below-average children. The substance, however, was not different. Possibly the best proof of the intent of the 1943 law is the fruits thereof; its passage effectively and permanently closed all the Japanese foreign language schools. After the war only the Chinese schools sought to reopen.[78]

In any event, the three-judge District Court that passed on the case in Hawaii did not find any constitutional distinction between the 1943 statute and the earlier one. On the authority of the Farrington and Meyer cases the court declared the 1943 law unconstitutional under the Fifth Amendment. The government of Hawaii appealed to the United States Supreme Court, which without considering the substantive issue, reversed the judgment of the District Court and sent the case back for a new trial before a one-judge District Court.[79] The new trial was never held because the Hawaiian legislature repealed the 1943 law, and — after negotiation with the foreign language schools — passed a new law generally deemed satisfactory by all sides, thus bringing the controversy to a happy conclusion.[80]

## National Unity and Loyalty

In some ways the most dramatic legal incident in the struggle between national unity and religious freedom is the series of flag-salute cases that culminated in the decision in West Virginia State Board of Education vs. Barnette.[81] These cases illustrate how a proposition deemed by the United States Supreme Court so devoid of constitutional merit as not even to warrant consideration ultimately became the doctrine of the court; they also illustrate (as in another way did the Zorach case) the real, if unadmitted, effect that critical public opinion may have on Supreme Court decisions.

The flag-salute issue arose from the refusal of Jehovah's Witnesses children in the public schools to participate in the usual assembly ceremony of saluting and pledging allegiance to the American flag. We shall have more to say in the next chapter regarding the beliefs of Jehovah's Witnesses. Here it is pertinent to note that the members of this sect believed that

> To salute the flag would be a violation of Divine commandment stated in Exodus 20:3−5, to wit, "Thou shalt have no other Gods before me. Thou shalt not make unto thee any graven image or any likeness of anything that is in heaven above, or that is in the earth beneath, or that is in the water under the earth. Thou shalt not bow down thyself to them nor serve them." [Moreover, the] salute to the flag means in effect that the person saluting the flag ascribes salvation to it, whereas salvation is of Jehovah God.[82]

The Supreme Court was first called on to invalidate a compulsory flag salute resolution in 1937 in the case of Leoles vs. Landers;[83] in that year an appeal was taken to the court from a decision of the Supreme Court of Georgia that upheld the state's right to compel Jehovah's Witnesses children in the public schools to salute the flag. The United States Supreme Court summarily dismissed the appeal on the authority of Hamilton vs. Regents of the University of California, and held that there was no arguable constitutional issue. Undaunted, the counsel for Jehovah's Witnesses, Hayden C. Covington of Brooklyn (who in his way has probably contributed as much to the development of the constitutional law relating to civil liberties as any man in American history) tried again,[84] and again,[85] and yet again.[86] His perseverance was finally rewarded in 1940, when the Supreme Court agreed to consider at length an appeal in a flag-salute case. Perhaps it was not the perseverance of the counsel for Jehovah's Witnesses as much as the necessity of asserting its own supremacy that was responsible; for in the case in which the Supreme Court did take jurisdiction the lower courts had upheld the contention of Jehovah's Witnesses that the enforcement against them of flag-salute regulations violated their constitutional rights.

In 1937 the children of Walter Gobitis, a member of Jehovah's Witnesses, were expelled from the public schools of Minersville, Pennsylvania, for their stubborn refusal to salute the flag in compliance with a regulation to that effect duly adopted by the school board of Minersville. Walter Gobitis applied to the Federal District Court for an injunction against the enforcement of the order. In December 1937 Federal District (later Circuit Court) Judge Albert Maris denied the school district's motion to dismiss the suit.[87] He held that public officials were in no position to question the religious basis of a sincere refusal to engage in a ceremonial act such as saluting the flag where public safety, health, or morals, or personal or property rights were not prejudiced by the refusal, and that refusal to salute the flag did not threaten any danger that the state had an overriding interest to prevent. He noted pointedly that the effect of the school board's ruling was to make the flag—a symbol of religious liberty—a means of imposing a religious test as a condition of receiving the benefits of public education. In June 1938 Judge Maris granted an injunction against the enforcement of the school board's "salute or be expelled" order.[88] It should be noted that Judge Maris issued the injunction notwithstanding the Supreme Court's summary dismissal of the appeal in Leoles vs. Landers.

The Minersville school board appealed to the Circuit Court of Appeals, which—in the face of Leoles vs. Landers and its three successors—affirmed Judge Maris's decision.[89] The issue, according to the Circuit Court of Appeals, was whether the flag-salute requirement was so necessary to the safety and good morals of society as to take precedence over the liberty of conscience. The court noted that this was not a case where a school board prohibited action which the plaintiffs asserted their religious convictions compelled them to perform, but one in which they were commanded to perform an affirmative act in violation of their conscience. The court held that a ceremonial device to instill respect for country did not outweigh the freedom of religious conscience.

The school board appealed to the United States Supreme Court. The Committee on the Bill of Rights of the American Bar Association and the American Civil Liberties Union submitted briefs as friends of the court, in support of the injunction. In view, however, of the four preceding decisions it was to be expected that the Supreme Court would reverse and vacate the injunction; yet many were astonished when, in June 1940, the court, with one lone dissenting voice, did just that.[90] They were also astonished that the court's opinion should be written by Justice Frankfurter, long identified in the public mind as a "liberal."[91]

Justice Frankfurter began his opinion by paying his respects to the constitutional guaranty of religious freedom, calling it a "precious right," entitled to "every possible leeway" in resolving the conflict between individual freedom and national security. He continued:

> Certainly the affirmative pursuit of one's convictions about the ultimate mystery of the universe and man's relation to it is placed beyond the reach of law. Government may not interfere with organized or individual expression of belief or disbelief. Propagation of belief—or even of disbelief in the supernatural—is protected, whether in church or chapel, mosque or synagogue, tabernacle or meetinghouse. . . .

But "the freedom to follow conscience" is not unlimited; it must be reconciled with other freedoms and interests which make up our constitutional democracy.

> . . . The religious liberty which the Constitution protects has never excluded legislation of a general scope not directed against doctrinal loyalties of particular sects. . . . Conscientious scruples have not, in the course of the long struggle for religious toleration, relieved the individual from obedience to a general law not aimed at the promotion or restriction of religious beliefs. The mere possession of religious convictions which contradict the relevant concerns of a political society does not relieve the citizen from the discharge of political responsibilities. . . . National unity is the basis of national security. . . .

The last-quoted sentence is the key to the Court's opinion: "National unity is the basis of national security," and in the interest of national security, religious freedom must yield. The concept is then developed further:

> . . . The ultimate foundation of a free society is the binding tie of cohesive sentiment. Such a sentiment is fostered by all those agencies of the mind and spirit which may serve to gather up the traditions of a people, transmit them from generation to generation, and thereby create that continuity of treasured common life which constitutes a civilization. "We live by symbols." The flag is the symbol of our national unity, transcending all internal differences, however large, within the framework of the Constitution.

Justice Frankfurter was himself dubious as to the effectiveness of the Minersville school board's method of promoting national unity; but obviously it could not be held that its judgment was necessarily arbitrary and devoid of rationality. If reasonable men could differ on the issue, and "the remedial channels of the democratic process remain open and unobstructed" (*i.e.,* Jehovah's Witnesses are not hindered in their attempts to obtain repeal of the regulation), the court may not substitute its judgment for the board's; otherwise the court would become "the school board for the country," a function that was not given to the court and should not be assumed by it.

Justice (later Chief Justice) Stone alone dissented. He conceded that

> ... the constitutional guaranties of personal liberty are not always absolutes. Government has a right to survive and powers conferred upon it are not necessarily set at naught by the express prohibitions of the Bill of Rights. It may make war and raise armies. To that end it may compel citizens to give military service and subject them to training despite their religious objections. ... But it is a long step and one which I am unable to take, to the position that government may, as a supposed educational measure and as a means of disciplining the young, compel public affirmations which violate their religious conscience.

It was not enough, Justice Stone felt, that the end sought by the state was legitimate. Where means sought to achieve the end infringe on constitutional rights, they are constitutionally permissible only if no other means are available. This was not the case here:

> ... even if we believe that such compulsions will contribute to national unity, there are other ways to teach loyalty and patriotism which are the sources of national unity, than by compelling the pupil to affirm that which he does not believe and by commanding a form of affirmance which violates his religious convictions. Without recourse to such compulsion the state is free to compel attendance at school and require teaching by instruction and study of all in our history and in the structure and organization of our government, including the guaranties of civil liberty which tend to inspire patriotism and love of country. ...

The justification offered to support restrictions on religious freedom must be examined by the court with suspicious scrutiny.

> History teaches us that there have been but few infringements of personal liberty by the state which have not been justified, as they are here, in the name of righteousness and the public good, and few which have not been directed, as they are now, at politically helpless minorities. ... The Constitution may well elicit expressions of loyalty to it and to the government which it created, but it does not command such expressions or otherwise give any indication that compulsory expressions of loyalty play any such part in our scheme of government as to override the constitutional protection of freedom of speech and religion.

To the assertion that the remedy lies with the legislature rather than the Court, Justice Stone replied:

> ... I am not persuaded that we should refrain from passing upon the legislative judgment "as long as the remedial channels of the demo-

cratic process remain open and unobstructed." This seems to me no more than the surrender of the constitutional protection of the liberty of small minorities to the popular will.

The Gobitis decision elicited two completely opposite reactions. One was shown by the pungent comment of *The Christian Century* that "It is bitterly ironical that a free government should inflict a penalty for refusal to salute a symbol of freedom";[92] by the comment of Dean Christian Gauss of Princeton Theological Seminary, that "When liberal democratic nationalists, like Felix Frankfurter, write these decisions, we may well ask whether Americanism has not already progressed to an ungodly stage; . . ."[93] and by the numerous other similar critical comment in law reviews, liberal periodicals and organs of religious groups—not excluding organs of the Catholic Church, the chief target of Jehovah's Witnesses' diatribes.[94]

The opposite reaction was less intellectual but more emphatic.[95] The court's decision was announced on June 3, 1940. Between June 12 and June 20 hundreds of physical attacks upon the Jehovah's Witnesses were reported to the United States Department of Justice. At Kennebunk, Maine, their Kingdom Hall was burned. At Rockville, Maryland, the police assisted a mob in dispersing a Bible meeting. At Litchfield, Illinois, practically the entire town mobbed a company of some sixty Witnesses who were canvassing it. At Connersville, Indiana, several Witnesses were charged with riotous conspiracy, their attorney mobbed, beaten, and driven out of town. At Jackson, Mississippi, members of a veterans' organization forcibly removed a number of Witnesses and their trailer homes from the town. In Nebraska a Witness was lured from his house, abducted, and castrated. In Richwood, West Virginia, the chief of police and deputy sheriff forced a group of Witnesses to drink large doses of castor oil, and paraded the victims through the streets, tied together with police department rope. In the two years following the Gobitis decision there was an uninterrupted record of violence and persecution of the Witnesses. Almost without exception the flag and flag salute were the causes.

In his *Notes on Virginia*[96] Jefferson observed that:

> . . . By our own act of assembly of 1705 c. 30, if a person brought up in the Christian religion denies the being of a God, or the Trinity, or asserts there are more gods than one, or denies the Christian religion to be true, or the scriptures to be of divine authority, he is punishable . . . on the second [offense] . . . [by being judged unfit] to be guardian. . . . A father's right to the custody of his own children being founded in law on his right of guardianship, this being taken away, they

may of course be severed from him, and put by the authority of the court into more orthodox hands.

Almost two and a half centuries after the Virginia Act, a judge in Pontiac, Michigan, warned the Witnesses that if they would not accept the very gracious ruling of the school board and train their children better in Americanism, it would be the obligation of the court to take the children out of their homes long enough to give them environment and training to understand what Americanism is.[97]

In Oklahoma a group of Witness children, expelled from the public schools for refusal to salute the flag, were being tutored by a former schoolteacher in her home. The law descended on her and she was convicted of failing to require the flag salute in her private classes—although she had formulated a different exercise, consisting of a pledge of allegiance to God and country and expressing respect for the flag.

There were some bright spots in the dark picture of the two years following the Gobitis decision. The first was the critical response the decision evoked among enlightened religious and civic leaders and law school professors and review editors. The second was the sponsorship by the American Legion of a bill, enacted by Congress on June 22, 1942, as Public Law No. 623, which, after defining the pledge of allegiance and describing the flag salute, stated that "civilians will show full respect to the flag when the pledge is given by merely standing at attention, men removing the headdress."

A number of courts refused to follow the logical conclusion of the Gobitis decision. Though they recognized the right of the public schools to expel Witness children who refused to comply with the mandate of the Supreme Court in the Gobitis decision, they could not bring themselves to follow the act of the Virginia assembly of 1705 by committing the children to a state institution as delinquents.[98] The Supreme Court of New Hampshire explained the reasons for its decision:

> If the order appealed from is executed, these three children and their parents will be visited with the breaking up of the family, an institution of primary value in our social life. The reason . . . would be no more than the conscientious acts of the children, based upon the religious teachings of their parents . . .
> It would be one thing to say that the Legislature intended to permit school authorities to prescribe ceremonial forms for such teaching, and to exclude from public school privileges those children who decline, for whatever motive, to conform. But in view of the sacredness in which

the state has always held freedom of religious conscience, it is impossible for us to attribute to the Legislature an intent to authorize the breaking up of family life for no other reason than because some of its members have conscientious religious scruples not shared by the majority of the community. . . .[99]

This almost complete unanimity among enlightened opinion was bound to have its effect on the United States Supreme Court. When the court again considered the issue in 1943 it expressly noted the adverse criticism the Gobitis decision had evoked among law review editors. (Of the six law review articles cited by the court, two appeared in reviews published by law schools in Catholic universities.) The low esteem to which the Gobitis decision had fallen was indicated when in 1942 the Federal District Court in West Virginia refused to follow the decision, in the belief that it would be overruled, and granted an injunction to Witness Walter Barnette restraining the West Virginia State Board of Education from enforcing a compulsory flag salute regulation.[100]

The Board of Education appealed to the United States Supreme Court. As anticipated by the District Court, the Supreme Court in a six to three decision expressly overruled the Gobitis decision and sustained the injunction.[101] Of the eight justices who formed the majority in the Gobitis case, two were no longer on the bench, and had been succeeded by Justices Jackson and Rutledge, who took the opposite view. These were joined by Chief Justice Stone, the lone dissenter in the Gobitis case, and by Justices Black, Douglas, and Murphy, who acknowledged that they were in error in that case. Justices Frankfurter, Roberts, and Reed maintained the position they had expressed in the earlier case.

The majority opinion in the Barnette case, written by Justice Jackson, is an eloquent and epochal document in the history of the freedom of religion—although Justice Jackson expressly refused to base the decision on that freedom. To him compulsory flag salute regulations were unconstitutional because they restricted the freedom of speech—that guaranty being broad enough to include the freedom not to speak, and flag saluting is a form of speech or communication of ideas. A "Bill of Rights which guards the individual's right to speak his own mind" cannot be held to have "left it open to public authorities to compel him to utter what is not in his mind."

In reply to Justice Frankfurter's fear that passing judgment on the efficacy of flag salute regulations would make the court a board of education for the country, Justice Jackson stated:

The Fourteenth Amendment, as now applied to the States, protects the citizen against the State itself and all of its creatures — Boards of Education not excepted. . . . Such Boards are numerous and their territorial jurisdiction often small. But small and local authority may feel less sense of responsibility to the Constitution, and agencies of publicity may be less vigilant in calling it to account. The action of Congress in making flag observance voluntary[102] and respecting the conscience of the objector in a matter so vital as raising the Army contrasts sharply with these local regulations in matters relatively trivial to the welfare of the nation. There are village tyrants as well as village Hampdens, but none who acts under color of law is beyond reach of the Constitution.

Justice Jackson rejected the assertion that the ballot box is the place where the remedy for unwise flag salute regulations is to be sought:

The very purpose of the Bill of Rights was to withdraw certain subjects from the vicissitudes of political controversy, to place them beyond the reach of majorities and officials and to establish them as legal principles to be applied by the courts. One's right to life, liberty, and property, to free speech, a free press, freedom of worship and assembly, and other fundamental rights may not be submitted to vote; they depend on the outcome of no election.

He rejected also Justice Frankfurter's view that a state should have the same broad discretion in regulating personal liberties as it has in regulating property rights:

. . . The right of a State to regulate, for example, a public utility may well include, so far as the due process test is concerned, power to impose all of the restrictions which a legislature may have a "rational basis" for adopting. But freedoms of speech and of press, of assembly, and of worship may not be infringed on such slender grounds. They are susceptible of restriction only to prevent grave and immediate danger to interests which the state may lawfully protect. . . .

He then dealt with the real basis of the Gobitis decision and the real issue in the Barnette case.

Lastly, and this is the very heart of the Gobitis opinion, it reasons that "National unity is the basis of national security," that the authorities have "the right to select appropriate means for its attainment," and hence reaches the conclusion that such compulsory measures toward "national unity" are constitutional. Upon the verity of this assumption depends our answer in this case.

National unity as an end which officials may foster by persuasion and example is not in question. The problem is whether under our Constitution compulsion as here employed is a permissible means for its achievement.

Struggles to coerce uniformity of sentiment in support of some end thought essential to their time and country have been waged by many good as well as by evil men. Nationalism is a relatively recent phenomenon but at other times and places the ends have been racial or territorial security, support of a dynasty or regime, and particular plans for saving souls. As first and moderate methods to attain unity have failed, those bent on its accomplishment must resort to an ever-increasing severity.

As governmental pressure toward unity becomes greater, so strife becomes more bitter as to whose unity it shall be. Probably no deeper division of our people could proceed from any provocation than from finding it necessary to choose what doctrine and whose program public educational officials shall compel youth to unite in embracing. Ultimate futility of such attempts to compel coherence is the lesson of every such effort from the Roman drive to stamp out Christianity as a disturber of its pagan unity, the Inquisition, as a means to religious and dynastic unity, the Siberian exiles as a means to Russian unity, down to the fast failing efforts of our present totalitarian enemies. Those who begin coercive elimination of dissent soon find themselves exterminating dissenters. Compulsory unification of opinion achieves only the unanimity of the graveyard.

It seems trite but necessary to say that the First Amendment to our Constitution was designed to avoid these ends by avoiding these beginnings. . . .

Justice Jackson concluded:

If there is any fixed star in our constitutional constellation, it is that no official, high or petty, can prescribe what shall be orthodox in politics, nationalism, religion, or other matters of opinion, or force citizens to confess by word or act their faith therein. . . .

In their concurring opinion Justices Black and Douglas agreed that religious liberty was not absolute:

No well-ordered society can leave to the individuals an absolute right to make final decisions, unassailable by the State, as to everything they will or will not do. The First Amendment does not go so far. Religious faiths, honestly held, do not free individuals from responsibility to conduct themselves obediently to laws which are . . . imperatively necessary to protect society as a whole from grave and pressingly imminent dangers. . . . But we cannot say that a failure, because of religious scruples, to assume a particular physical position and to repeat the words of a patriotic formula creates a grave danger to the nation.

Like his concurring associates, Justice Murphy emphasized the futility of the means adopted to achieve the desirable end of national unity and loyalty:

I am unable to agree that the benefits that may accrue to society from the compulsory flag salute are sufficiently definite and tangible to justify the invasion of freedom and privacy that is entailed or to compensate for a restraint on the freedom of the individual to be vocal or silent according to his conscience or personal inclination. The trenchant words in the preamble to the Virginia Statute for Religious Freedom remain unanswerable: ". . . all attempts to influence [the mind] by temporal punishments or burthens, or by civil incapacitations, tend only to beget habits of hypocrisy and meanness. . . ." Any spark of love for country which may be generated in a child or his associates by forcing him to make what is to him an empty gesture and recite words wrung from him contrary to his religious beliefs is overshadowed by the desirability of preserving freedom of conscience to the full. It is in that freedom and the example of persuasion, not in force and compulsion, that the real unity of America lies.

In his dissenting opinion, Justice Frankfurter expanded the arguments he had set forth in the Gobitis decision, and emphasized again the dangers of judicial invalidation of the arguable and not patently unreasonable decisions of elected legislators and boards of education.

On the same day that the Court handed down the Barnette decision it announced its decision in Taylor vs. Mississippi.[103] This involved the validity of a statute that made it a felony to preach or teach anything designed to encourage violence, sabotage, or disloyalty to the United States and the state of Mississippi or "to create an attitude of stubborn refusal to salute . . . the flag." The evidence showed that the defendant, in the course of interviews with several women whose sons had been killed in combat, stated that it was wrong to fight our enemies and that "the quicker people here quit bowing down and worshipping and saluting our flag and government, the sooner we would have peace." A second defendant published a pamphlet suggesting that the Catholic Church was responsible for flag saluting. The third defendant (all were Witnesses) distributed a book replete with such sentences as: "Satan influences public officials and others to compel little children to indulge in idolatrous practices by bowing down to some image or thing, such as saluting flags and hailing them, and which is in direct violation of God's commandment (Exodus 20:1 – 5)."

In view of the Barnette decision, it was obvious that the convictions could not stand.

If [said the Supreme Court], the Fourteenth Amendment bans enforcement of the school [flag salute] regulation, *a fortiori* it prohibits the imposition of punishment for urging and advising that, on religious grounds, citizens refrain from saluting the flag. If the state cannot constrain one to violate his conscientious religious conviction by saluting the national emblem, then certainly it cannot punish him for imparting his views on the subject to his fellows and exhorting them to accept those views.

The Taylor case held in effect that the First Amendment

protects the preacher and teacher of religion no less than the practitioner. It and the other cases discussed in this chapter held that though national safety justifies the infringement of religious freedom where the danger is immediate and grave—as where such freedom would hamper raising an army to repel our national enemies—infringement is not justified where the danger is remote or uncertain, or where the means are not clearly appropriate to achieve a desirable end, like national loyalty and cultural unity.

### CHAPTER SIXTEEN

# Freedom and Domestic Tranquillity

## PROTECTING THE PUBLIC MORALS

THE PROTECTION of the moral standards of the community may conveniently be considered as part of the problem of reconciling religious freedom with domestic tranquillity. Fortunately there has been little conflict in the country between these interests.[1] On the contrary, religion considers the preservation of morals one of its prime responsibilities. The major difference between religion and government in this area — expressed in campaigns to prohibit intoxicating liquors or curb pornographic literature — lies in the complaint of religion that government does not go far enough in protecting public morals. The only substantial area in which the interests of religion and public morality have conflicted in this country is the Mormons' belief in plural marriages.

Actually, the conflict between the Mormon belief in polygamy and American sanctification of the monogamous family unit is not a conflict between morality and immorality, but between Christian and Biblical concepts of family life. It is both unfair and inaccurate to designate the Mormons as immoral; in many respects they were and are more Puritanical than almost any other element of our population. Moreover, as we shall see shortly, practical consequences flow from designating as immoral religiously practiced polygamy.

Christian marital concepts are so firmly embedded in American society and the monogamous family unit is so passionately defended, that violence and persecution were inevitable results of the Mormons' attempt to establish their Church of Jesus Christ of Latter Day Saints in strict compliance with the principles of faith promulgated by Joseph Smith and Brigham Young. It was equally inevitable that their claim of religious liberty, predicated on the belief that plural marriages are not merely permissible but obligatory, would evoke little sympathy among legislatures or courts. Bigamy and polygamy are crimes under the laws of every state in the union, and no state court has accepted as a defense the defendant's religious belief that his act was commanded by God.

The issue first reached the United States Supreme Court in 1878 in Reynolds vs. United States.[2] In that case the court sustained a conviction under an act of Congress that made it criminal to practice bigamy in any of the American territories. In its decision holding that the religious-freedom clause of the First Amendment did not constitute a defense to the prosecution, the court outlined the historical background and intent of the First Amendment.[3] It then continued by asserting that "polygamy has always been odious among the northern and western nations of Europe, and, until the establishment of the Mormon church, was almost exclusively a feature of the life of Asiatic and of African people." After relating the legal history of polygamy in England and America, the court said:

> . . . there never has been a time in any State of the Union when polygamy has not been an offence against society, cognizable by the civil courts and punishable with more or less severity. In the face of all this evidence, it is impossible to believe that the constitutional guaranty of religious freedom was intended to prohibit legislation in respect to this most important feature of social life. Marriage, while from its very nature a sacred obligation, is nevertheless, in most civilized nations, a civil contract, and usually regulated by law. Upon it society may be said to be built, and out of its fruits spring social relations and social obligations and duties, with which government is necessarily required to deal. . . . The only question which remains is, whether those who make polygamy a part of their religion are excepted from the operation of the statute. If they are, then those who do not make polygamy a part of their religious belief may be found guilty and punished, while those who do, must be acquitted and go free. This would be introducing a new element into criminal law. Laws are made for the government of actions, and while they cannot interfere with mere religious belief and opinions, they may with practices. Suppose one believed that human sacrifices were a necessary part of religious worship, would it be seriously contended that the civil government under which he lived could not interfere to prevent a sacrifice? Or if a wife religiously believed it was her duty to burn herself upon the funeral pile of her dead husband, would it be beyond the power of the civil government to prevent her carrying her belief into practice?
>
> So here, as a law of the organization of society under the exclusive dominion of the United States, it is provided that plural marriages shall not be allowed. Can a man excuse his practices to the contrary because of his religious belief? To permit this would be to make the professed doctrines of religious belief superior to the law of the land, and in effect to permit every citizen to become a law unto himself. Government could exist only in name under such circumstances.

In 1890 the Supreme Court was again called on to pass on the constitutionality of a law proscribing polygamy. In Davis vs. Beason[4] it upheld the conviction of a Mormon who registered and voted in the Territory of Idaho notwithstanding a Territorial statute disenfranchising practitioners or teachers of polygamy. The court said:

... Bigamy and polygamy are crimes by the laws of all civilized and Christian countries. They are crimes by the laws of the United States, and they are crimes by the laws of Idaho. They tend to destroy the purity of the marriage relations, to disturb the peace of families, to degrade woman and to debase man. Few crimes are more pernicious to the best interests of society and receive more general or more deserved punishment.... To call their advocacy a tenet of religion is to offend the common sense of mankind. If they are crimes, then to teach, advise and counsel their practice is to aid in their commission, and such teaching and counselling are themselves criminal and proper subjects of punishment, as aiding and abetting crime are in all other cases.

... It was never intended or supposed that the [First] amendment could be evoked as a protection against legislation for the punishment of acts inimical to the peace, good order and morals of society. With man's relations to his Maker and the obligations he may think they impose, and the manner in which an expression shall be made by him of his belief on those subjects, no interference can be permitted, provided always the laws of society, designed to secure its peace and prosperity, and the morals of its people, are not interfered with. However free the exercise of religion may be, it must be subordinate to the criminal laws of the country, passed with reference to actions regarded by general consent as properly the subjects of punitive legislation. There have been sects which denied as a part of their religious tenets that there should be any marriage tie, and advocated promiscuous intercourse of the sexes as prompted by the passions of its members. And history discloses the fact that the necessity of human sacrifices, on special occasions, has been a tenet of many sects. Should a sect of either of these kinds ever find its way into this country swift punishment would follow the carrying into effect of its doctrines, and no heed would be given to the pretence that, as religious beliefs, their supporters could be protected in their exercise by the Constitution of the United States. Probably never before in the history of this country has it been seriously contended that the whole punitive power of the government for acts, recognized by the general consent of the Christian world in modern times as proper matters for prohibitory legislation, must be suspended in order that the tenets of a religious sect encouraging crime may be carried out without hindrance.

The effect of this decision was to allow a person to be punished merely for being a Mormon as long as the tenets of the church required plural marriages. For it was not charged that the defendant had himself either practiced or preached polygamy; it was charged only that he was a member of the Church of Jesus Christ of Latter Day Saints, which, he knew, taught and counseled polygamy. This meant that no one could be a Mormon unless he believed in polygamy. It meant further that no one could be a Mormon without either practicing or counseling polygamy, and therefore no one could be a Mormon without *ipso facto* committing a crime. This was guilt by association with a vengeance. Analogously, the decision meant that no one can be a member of the Catholic Church who believes that divorce or contraceptive birth control might be permissible in some circumstances even if he himself practiced neither—a proposition which a sect believing in the irrevocability of baptism could never accept.

Moreover, it is difficult to reconcile the court's statement that the Constitution protects beliefs but not actions, with its affirmance of a conviction based exclusively on membership in the church. In this respect the case is entirely different from the conviction of the Communist Party leaders upheld by the Supreme Court in Dennis vs. United States.[5] In the latter case the indictment and conviction were based not on membership in the Communist Party but on conspiracy to teach its doctrines. In Davis vs. Beason there was no charge other than that the defendant was a member of the Mormon Church.

Finally it may be suggested that the Supreme Court had no constitutional jurisdiction or competence to cast out of the religion of Christianity a denomination calling itself a Church of Jesus Christ. It is not for a civil court under the American system of the separation of church and state to adjudicate what Christ did or did not command. Nor was it within the court's constitutional competence to be shocked at the Mormon assertion that the practice of polygamy is "a tenet of religion." The approach in the Reynolds case was more consistent with the constitutional principles envisaged by Jefferson and Madison. It did not deny that the practice of polygamy may be a tenet of religion; nor did it imply that it is the function of civil courts to protect orthodox Christianity from less conventional sects. It was based on the fact that marriage is a relationship created, regulated, and protected by civil authority, and that the preservation of the monogamous family unit is more important to American society than the unrestrained religious liberty of believers in polygamy.

The logic implicit in Davis vs. Beason was made explicit in another case decided by the Supreme Court in the same year. In Church of Latter Day Saints vs. United States[6] the Court sustained the constitutionality of an act of Congress that voided the charter of the Mormon Church and declared its property forfeited. Since polygamy had been prohibited, but notwithstanding that fact the church had used its funds to propagate its religion, of which polygamy was an integral part, Congress, the court held, had the power to confiscate the funds so as to prevent their use for this illegal and immoral purpose.

The late Canon Stokes[7] related an incident that casts an interesting and ironic light on the passion with which America treated Mormonism. In 1879 the Federal government sent a circular letter to the American foreign ministers in Europe, asking them to call to the attention of the governments to which they were accredited the American laws against polygamy, and requesting that they prevent the preaching of Mormonism and the emigration of professed Mormons to the United States. The governments of the European countries to which the request was made replied to the country that gave the world the concept of religious freedom that they could not undertake to inquire into the religious beliefs of emigrants.

The uneven battle was given up in 1890. In that year the Church of Jesus Christ of Latter Day Saints formally adopted a declaration of submission to Federal law. This declaration became part of the church's Articles of Faith, and merits quotation here:

> . . . This practice [plural marriage] was established as a result of direct revelation, and many of those who followed the same felt that they were divinely commanded so to do. For ten years after plural marriage had been introduced into Utah as a Church observance, no law was enacted in opposition to the practice. Beginning with 1862, however, Federal statutes were framed declaring the practice unlawful and providing penalties therefor. The Church claimed that these enactments were unconstitutional, and therefore void, inasmuch as they violated the provision in the national Constitution forbidding the government making laws respecting any establishment of religion or prohibiting the free exercise thereof. Many appeals were taken to the national court of final resort, and at last a decision was rendered sustaining the laws as constitutional and therefore binding. The Church, through its President, thereupon discontinued the practice of plural marriage, and announced its action to the world, solemnly placing the responsibility for the change upon the nation by whose laws the renunciation had been forced. This action has been approved and confirmed by the official vote of the Church in conference assembled.[8]

Notwithstanding this solemn proclamation, polygamy has not entirely disappeared in the Mormon Church. Fundamentalists in the Church of Latter Day Saints — as in all other churches — retain a stubborn regard of the law of the prophets as being superior to the law of the government. In 1955 the United States Supreme Court refused to disturb a state court decision depriving Mormons of the custody of their children because the parents persisted in teaching them the orthodox Mormon tenets respecting polygamy.[9] In 1945 several Mormon fundamentalists were convicted of violating the Mann Act,[10] which makes it a crime to transport in interstate commerce "any woman or girl for the purpose of prostitution or debauchery, or for any other *immoral* purpose." The Mann Act had been passed—primarily at least—to curb the white slave traffic (its official title is the White Slave Traffic Act), but the Supreme Court held that the statute was applicable to a Mormon fundamentalist who travelled across state lines with his plural wives.[11] The court disposed of the religious issue by citing the Reynolds, Davis vs. Beason, and Church of Latter Day Saints cases. But these decisions held only that polygamy could constitutionally be made criminal notwithstanding its religious motivation. It would seem to be an extreme interpretation of the statute and the intent of Congress to classify in the same category as commercial prostitution and to designate as immoral a Mormon's adherence to his religious convictions.

## JEHOVAH'S WITNESSES

To a large extent the problem of adjusting the conflicting interests of domestic tranquillity and religious liberty revolved around the Jehovah's Witnesses cases. Probably no sect since the early days of the Mormon Church has been as much a thorn in the communal side and as much a victim of communal hate and persecution as Jehovah's Witnesses. The Mormons' difficulty lay in their unconventional approach to marriage; except for that one eccentricity they were quite respectable; and once that problem was solved the Church of Latter Day Saints was accepted as an honored member of the community of faiths.

The Witnesses too appear to be rapidly on the road to respectability, if indeed they have not already achieved it. But unlike the Mormons they have not been required to pay the price of diluting their dogma, although in recent years their tactics appear to have become somewhat less aggressive than formerly.

Nevertheless, during the nineteen thirties and forties, they were the principal victims of religious bigotry and persecution in the United States. Perhaps the chief difficulty during this period was their refusal to salute the flag (we have already discussed this aspect of their activities and it need not detain us further); but it was far from the only cause of their unpopularity. Aside from their views on the flag salute, their teachings are not such as are likely to win many friends among the Gentiles. Their aggressive missionary tactics are reminiscent of those employed by the early Christians, and the reception accorded them by the nonbelievers is likewise reminiscent of that visited on the early Christians.

The Jehovah's Witnesses are followers of Charles T. Russell, who started out as a Presbyterian but ended as the founder of a new and militant religious sect. In 1868 Russell decided that all existing schools of religion were wrong, and he built up a religion of his own, centered in calculations as to the second coming of Christ and the battle of Armageddon. His followers were first known as "Russellites," but under Russell's successor as leader, Joseph F. Rutherford, the group adopted the name "Jehovah's Witnesses."

To accomplish their purpose of disseminating their interpretations of the Bible and their religious beliefs, the "Russellites" in 1884 formed a corporation now known as the Watchtower Bible and Tract Society. The Society owns printing plants in Brooklyn, Berne, and other cities, which are devoted to the printing of books, magazines, and pamphlets embodying the Witnesses' beliefs. The Society also supplies Witnesses with phonographs, sound trucks, and records carrying the Witnesses' missionary message. Armed with books, pamphlets, and portable phonographs, the Witnesses spread the gospel by street corner meetings, by street accostation, and by door-to-door preaching and distribution of their literature.[12]

The mission of the Witnesses as seen by themselves can be understood from the following paragraph in a resolution adopted at their 1931 convention:

As Jehovah's Witnesses our sole and only purpose is to be entirely obedient to his commandments; to make known that he is the only true and almighty God; that his Word is true and that his name is entitled to all honor and glory; that Christ is God's King, whom he has placed upon his throne of authority; that his kingdom is now come, and in obedience to the Lord's commandments we must now declare this good news as a testimony or witness to the nations and to inform the rulers and the people of and concerning Satan's cruel and oppressive organization, and particularly with reference to Christendom, which is the most wicked part of that visible organization; and of and concerning God's purpose to shortly destroy Satan's organization, which great act will be quickly followed by Christ the King's bringing to the obedient peoples of earth peace and prosperity, liberty and health, happiness and everlasting life; that God's kingdom is the hope of the world and there is no other, and that this message must be delivered by those who are identified as Jehovah's Witnesses.[13]

How the Witnesses operated in a typical community was described by Justice Jackson in his dissent in one of the Witnesses' cases.[14] Jeannette, Pennsylvania, is an industrial city that in 1940 had an estimated population of 16,000 inhabitants. In 1939 the Witnesses instituted a "Watchtower Campaign" in the city. Each house in the city was visited, the bell was rung or the door knocked on, and the householder advised that the Witness had important information. If the householder would listen, a record was played on a portable phonograph. Its subject was "Snare and Racket," and the following is representative of its contents:

> Religion is wrong and a snare because it deceives the people, but that does not mean that all who follow religion are willingly bad. Religion is a racket because it has long been used and is still used to extract money from the people upon the theory and promise that the paying over of money to a priest will serve to relieve the party paying from punishment after death and further insure his salvation.

This line of attack was taken by the Witnesses generally on all denominations, but particular emphasis was placed on Catholicism.

On Palm Sunday of 1939 more than 100 Witnesses, strangers to the city, arrived in upward of 25 automobiles. The cars were parked outside the city limits, and headquarters were set up in a gasoline station with telephone facilities, through which the director of the campaign could be notified when trouble occurred and would rush down to the police court to furnish bond for any Witness arrested for disturbing the peace or otherwise violating the law. The Witnesses went from door to door, playing their records, distributing their literature, and soliciting contributions.

Typical of the literature the Witnesses sold or distributed without charge was the book *Enemies* written by Russell's successor, Rutherford. In it Rutherford states that "the greatest racket ever invented and practiced is that of religion. The most cruel and seductive public enemy is that which employs religion to carry on the racket, and by which means the people are deceived and the name of Almighty God is reproached. There are numerous systems of religion but the most subtle, fraudulent and injurious to humankind is that which is generally labelled the 'Christian' religion; because it has the appearance of a worshipful devotion to the Supreme Being and thereby misleads many honest and sincere persons." The Roman Catholic religion is, according to Rutherford, "the great racket, a racket that is greater than all other rackets combined." Under the chapter heading "Song of the Harlot," the book says: "Referring now to the foregoing Scriptural definition of harlot, What religious system exactly fits the prophesies recorded in God's Word? There is but one answer, and that is, The Roman Catholic Church organization."

The spirit and temper of the Witnesses' campaign is set forth in Rutherford's book *Religion* as follows:

> God's faithful servants go from house to house to bring the message of the kingdom to those who reside there, omitting none, not even the houses of the Roman Catholic Hierarchy, and there they give witness to

the kingdom because they are commanded by the Most High to do so. "They shall enter in at the windows like a thief." They do not loot nor break into the houses, but they set up their phonographs before the doors and windows and send the message of the kingdom right into the houses into the ears of those who might wish to hear; and while those desiring to hear are hearing, some of the "sourpusses" are compelled to hear. Locusts invade the homes of the people and even eat the varnish off the wood and eat the wood to some extent. Likewise God's faithful witnesses, likened unto locusts, get the kingdom message right into the house and they take the veneer off the religious things that are in that house, including candles and "holy water," remove the superstition from the minds of the people, and show them that the doctrines that have been taught to them are wood, hay and stubble, destructible by fire, and they cannot withstand the heat. The people are enabled to learn that "purgatory" is a bogeyman, set up by the agents of Satan to frighten the people into the religious organizations, where they may be fleeced of their hard-earned money. Thus the kingdom message plagues the religionists, and the clergy find that they are unable to prevent it. Therefore, as described by the prophet, the message comes to them like a thief that enters in at the windows, and this message is a warning to those who are on the inside that Jesus Christ has come, and they remember his warning words, to wit: "Behold, I come as a thief." (Revelation 16:15). The day of Armageddon is very close, and that day comes upon the world in general like a thief in the night.

It is hardly surprising that communities—particularly those with a substantial Catholic population—were not likely to look with favor on the coming of the Witnesses; and the reception accorded them was generally less than cordial. In many communities the outraged citizenry took the law into their own hands and resorted to force and violence. In others the Witnesses were met by the legal arm of the community; new laws were enacted and old laws resurrected to supply the weapons necessary to curb the Witnesses. All kinds of laws were used or attempted to be used for this purpose; laws against disturbing the peace, antipeddling ordinances, laws against the use of sound trucks, traffic regulations, revenue laws—these and many others have been invoked in one way or another against the Witnesses.

To counter this legal attack, the Witnesses had nothing to offer except their own courage or foolhardiness—depending on one's point of view—and the Constitution. For whenever a Witness was haled before a court of law he invariably invoked his constitutional right of religious freedom. Out of this repeated invoking of the First Amendment and the frequent appeals to the Supreme Court evolved much of the present-day constitutional law of religious freedom. In all these Jehovah's Witnesses cases the task facing the court was to weigh the conflicting interests of religious liberty against the specific communal interest sought to be protected—such as preserving communal peace, regulating street traffic, protecting private property, insuring the citizens' quiet and privacy, and raising needed revenue. Of course not all the cases in which these issues were brought to the Supreme Court during the past three decades involved Jehovah's Witnesses, and our discussion of the Supreme Court decisions will concern some non-Witness cases. The Witnesses were nevertheless the principal religious disturbers of the peace, and their cases were most frequently appealed to the Supreme Court. It is for that reason that we have set forth in some detail the background of Jehovah's Witnesses, the method of their operations, and the content of their teachings.

### Preserving the Public Peace

That the state has the power and the duty to prevent and punish disturbances of the peace is of course not disputed by anyone. Nor can it be reasonably disputed that the preservation of substantial domestic tranquillity is more important to organized society than the unrestricted exercise of religion. Of course the danger of disturbances of the peace does not justify a ban on the discussion of all controversial subjects or all missionary activities—even though such an absolute ban might contribute substantially to the maintenance of communal peace. Here as elsewhere conflicting interests must be weighed; and in the weighing due consideration must be given to the preferred position in the democratic scheme of things enjoyed by the freedom of expression and of religion—only a clear immediacy of a serious breach of the peace warrants restriction of these freedoms. Hence, although throwing obnoxious Jehovah's Witnesses into jail for disturbing the peace might have appeared to many constables and police justices as an effective and attractive solution to an otherwise difficult problem, it presented constitutional difficulties—so, in any event, the public authorities of New Haven, Connecticut, discovered.

In April of 1938 Jesse Cantwell, a Witness, accosted two pedestrians on the sidewalk in New Haven and courteously requested and received their permission to play to them a phonograph record. The sound of the record did not, as far as the evidence revealed, disturb residents of the street, attract a crowd, or impede traffic; but its contents were likely to arouse the ire of the listeners—particularly if they were Catholics. Indeed, one of the two listeners testified that he felt like hitting Cantwell, and the other that he was tempted to throw him into the street. The record contained the usual message of the Witnesses: a general attack on all organized religious as instruments of Satan, and a specific attack on the Catholic Church, with an offer to sell a book containing "conclusive proof that for more than fifteen hundred years a great religious system, operating out of Rome, has by means of fraud and deception brought untold sorrow and suffering upon the people."

The listeners resisted the temptation to resort to violence, but warned Cantwell to move on before something serious happened to him. Cantwell picked up his phonograph and books and walked up the street, only to be arrested and convicted of the common law offense of inciting a breach of the peace.

The United States Supreme Court reversed the conviction on the basis of the First Amendment's guaranties of the freedom of religion and of speech.[15] The Court agreed that the "State of Connecticut has an obvious interest in the preservation of peace and good order within her borders," and suggested that a narrowly drawn statute regulating street discussions of religious affairs or the playing of phonographs on public streets might present a more difficult constitutional problem, but a conviction under the "general and undefined" common law concept of breach of peace could not be sustained.

"No one," the Court said, "would have the hardihood to suggest that the principle of freedom of speech sanctions incitement to riot or that religious liberty connotes the privilege to exhort others to physical attack upon those belonging to another sect. When clear and present danger of riot, disorder, interference with traffic upon the public streets or other immediate threat to public safety, peace or order appears, the power of the state to prevent or punish is obvious." On the other hand, the Court continued, it is equally obvious "that a State may not unduly suppress free communication of views, religious or other, under the guise of conserving desirable conditions."

The latter was the effect of the conviction; for there was "no assault, or threatening of bodily harm, no truculent bearing, no intentional discourtesy, no personal abuse." On the contrary, there was "only an effort to persuade a willing listener to buy a book or to contribute money in the interest of what Cantwell, however misguided others may think him, conceived to be true religion."

In the realm of religious faith [the Court continued] and in that of political belief, sharp differences arise. In both fields, the tenets of one man may seem the rankest error to his neighbor. To persuade others to his own point of view, the pleader, as we know, at times, resorts to exaggeration, to vilification of men who have been, or are, prominent in church or state, and even to false statement. But the people of this nation have ordained in the light of history, that, in spite of the probability of excesses and abuses, these liberties are, in the long view, essential to enlightened opinion and right conduct on the part of the citizens of a democracy.

The court concluded that, although "the contents of the record not unnaturally aroused animosity," nevertheless, Cantwell's conduct "raised no such clear and present menace to public peace and order as to render him liable to conviction of the common law offense" of inciting breach of the peace.

On the other hand, the freedoms secured by the First Amendment do not immunize what the Supreme Court has characterized as "verbal acts." In Chaplinsky vs. New Hampshire[16] the court affirmed the conviction of a Witness under a state statute making it a crime to "address any offensive, derisive or annoying word to any other person who is lawfully in any street or other public place, or call him by any offensive or derisive names." The evidence showed that the Witness, while being brought to a police station after citizens complained to a traffic officer of his tactics in distributing his literature, was met by the city marshal, to whom he said, "You are a God damned racketeer, [and] a damned Fascist and the whole government of Rochester are Fascists or agents of Fascists."

To the assertion that the conviction violated the defendant's freedom of religion, the court expressed doubt "that cursing a public officer is the exercise of religion in any sense of the term." But even if the defendant's activities were religious, "they would not cloak him with immunity from the legal consequences for concomitant acts committed in violation of a valid criminal statute." The statute is not invalid as an unconstitutional abridgment of free speech, for "resort to epithets or to personal abuse is not in any proper sense communication of information or opinion safeguarded by the Constitution, and its punishment as a criminal act" raises no constitutional question.

Allowing [the Court said] the broadest scope to the language and purpose of the . . . Amendment, it is well understood that the right of free speech is not absolute at all times and under all circumstances. There are certain well-defined and narrowly limited classes of speech, the prevention and punishment of which has never been thought to raise any Constitutional problem. These include the lewd and obscene, the profane, the libelous, and the insulting or "fighting" words—those

656

which by their very utterance inflict injury or tend to incite an immediate breach of the peace. It has been well observed that such utterances are no essential part of any exposition of ideas, and are of such slight social value as a step to truth that any benefit that may be derived from them is clearly outweighed by the social interest in order and morality.

Disturbances of the peace growing out of the missionary activities of Jehovah's Witnesses and similar aggressive sects or missionaries could be avoided by punishing the Witnesses even where no disturbance actually results. This procedure, as the Cantwell case showed, was subject to constitutional difficulties. Equally effective but no less subject to constitutional difficulties was the simple procedure of denying the Witnesses permission to engage in their missionary activities in public streets or parks.

In substance this was the expedient attempted in Havre de Grace, Maryland. There Daniel Niemotko and other Witnesses applied for and were denied permission to hold a Bible talk in the public park, although no permit had been requested by any other organization for any of the three Sundays sought by the Witnesses and the park was therefore available for use. When, after the denial of the application, the Witnesses nevertheless attempted to conduct their meeting, they were immediately arrested, tried, and convicted of disorderly conduct.

As we shall see later, a municipality has the constitutional power to regulate the use of streets, parks, and other places in order to accommodate the varying uses to which those places are put by the public. But, the Supreme Court held in reversing the conviction,[17] a community has no right to deny such use to a religious sect merely because it dislikes the sect or disagrees with its views.

Any statute that gives a municipal official absolute discretion to allow or disallow religious or political meetings in streets and parks violates the First Amendment. As the action of the Havre de Grace official indicated, under such a statute permission is likely to be granted or refused in accordance with the official's agreement or disagreement with the views expressed at the meeting. Streets and parks have immemorially been used for purposes of assembly, communicating thoughts among citizens, and discussing political and religious questions;[18] and though statutes may be enacted for the purpose of preventing serious interference with the normal use of streets and parks, a statute that confers on a public official broad powers to grant or withhold licenses makes him a censor of the views sought to be expressed.

657

A similar case was decided by the Supreme Court in 1955.[19] The city of Pawtucket, Rhode Island, had an ordinance forbidding political or religious meetings in any public park, but the ordinance had been interpreted by the authorities as not forbidding church services in the parks. Catholics had held mass in a park and Protestants could conduct church services there without violating the ordinance. However, when Jehovah's Witnesses held a public meeting there, the minister who addressed the assemblage was arrested for violating the ordinance.

The Supreme Court reversed the conviction on the ground that by treating the religious services of Jehovah's Witnesses differently from those of other faiths, the city was discriminating against them. The services of Jehovah's Witnesses are different from and undoubtedly less ritualistic than those of other religious groups. But it is not the business of the state to say that what is a religious practice or activity for one group is not religion under the protection of the First Amendment. Nor is it within the competence of government to approve, disapprove, classify, regulate, or in any manner control sermons delivered at religious meetings. To call the words which one minister speaks to his congregation a sermon, immune from regulation, and the words of another minister an address, subject to regulation, is an indirect way of preferring one religion over another and is barred by the Constitution.

The fact that a speaker has previously attacked religious groups and even caused some disorder is not of itself sufficient to validate a statute granting a public official a restraining control over the right to speak on religious subjects. In Kunz vs. New York[20] the Supreme Court held unconstitutional a New York City ordinance making it unlawful to hold public worship without first obtaining a permit from the city police commissioner.

One Carl Jacob Kunz, an ordained Baptist minister (not a Jehovah's Witness), had been preaching in the public streets for some six years under the auspices of the "Outdoor Gospel Work," of which he was director. It was his conviction, and, he felt, his duty to "go out on the highways and byways and preach the word of God." In 1946 he applied for and received a permit under the ordinance; but his meetings brought many complaints to city authorities that he was engaged in scurrilous attacks on Catholics and Jews. At his meetings Kunz preached, among other things of like tenor, that "the Catholic Church makes merchandise out of souls," that Catholicism is "a religion of the devil," and the Pope is "the anti-Christ." He denounced the Jews as "Christ-killers" and said of them, "All the garbage that didn't believe in Christ should have been burnt in incinerators. It's a shame they all weren't."

On the basis of this evidence his permit was revoked and his applications for permits in 1947 and 1948 were refused. Notwithstanding his inability to obtain a permit, he continued to hold meetings in Columbus Circle, where in 1948 he was arrested for violation of the ordinance, convicted, and fined $10. He was defended by the American Civil Liberties Union, which appealed in his behalf to the United States Supreme Court.

The court reversed the conviction on the ground that

> an ordinance which gives an administrative official discretionary power to control in advance the right of citizens to speak on religious matters on the streets of New York . . . is clearly invalid as a prior restraint on the exercise of First Amendment rights.

The fact that Kunz's earlier meetings had caused disorder was immaterial; there are appropriate public remedies to protect the peace and order of the community if speeches should result in disorder or violence, but these remedies do not include advance suppression.

Justice Jackson entered a vigorous dissent. He conceded that:

> A hostile reception of his subject certainly does not alone destroy one's right to speak. A temperate and reasoned criticism of Roman Catholicism or Judaism might and probably would, cause some resentment and protest. But in a free society all sects and factions, as the price of their own freedom to preach their views, must suffer that freedom in others. Tolerance of unwelcome, unorthodox ideas or information is a constitutionally protected policy not to be defeated by persons who would break up meetings they do not relish.

But he argued that the state has both the power and the duty to preserve the peace and prevent riots. If the speaker's remarks are such that because of their content or the circumstances in which they are uttered "the situation threatens to get out of hand for the force present," the policemen on the spot "may require the speaker, even if within his rights, to yield temporarily to the greater interests of peace." This unquestionably interferes with the speaker's freedom of religion or speech, yet, because necessary and unavoidable, is not unconstitutional. Why then should the prevention of this outbreak be unconstitutional when it is effected by denying the speaker a license or permit to incite the outbreak by use of "insulting or fighting words"?

Referring to the Chaplinsky case, Justice Jackson said:

> There held to be "insulting or 'fighting' words" were calling one a "god damned racketeer" and a "damned Fascist." Equally inciting and

more clearly "fighting words," when thrown at Catholics and Jews who are rightfully on the streets of New York, are statements that "The Pope is the anti-Christ" and the Jews are "Christ-killers." These terse epithets come down to our generation weighted with hatreds accumulated through centuries of bloodshed. They are recognized words of art in the profession of defamation. They are not the kind of insult that men bandy and laugh off when the spirits are high and the flagons are low. They are not in that class of epithets whose literal sting will be drawn if the speaker smiles when he uses them. They are always, and in every context, insults which do not spring from reason and can be answered by none. Their historical associations with violence are well understood, both by those who hurl and those who are struck by these missiles. Jews, many of whose families perished in extermination furnaces of Dachau and Auschwitz, are more than tolerant if they pass off lightly the suggestion that unbelievers in Christ should all have been burned. Of course, people might pass this speaker by as a mental case, and so they might file out of a theatre in good order at the cry of "fire." But in both cases there is genuine likelihood that someone will get hurt.

There are two possible objections to Justice Jackson's position. In the first place, there is a fundamental distinction between the language used by Chaplinsky and that used by Kunz. Chaplinsky was not seeking to convert or convince anyone; when he called the city marshal "a God damned racketeer and a damned Fascist" he was striking a verbal blow. He was not seeking to convert or convince the marshal; nor was he engaged in the communication of ideas. Hence his verbal act could well be excluded from the protection of the First Amendment because of its own evil nature, and not because of the danger that it might bring on some other evil. On the other hand, Kunz—like Jehovah's Witnesses—was sincerely seeking to convert his listeners to Christ. His references to the Pope as "the anti-Christ" and to the Jews as "Christ-killers" were part of his missionary message, and were made for the purpose of converting Catholics and Jews to the religion of Christ as he understood it. A constitutional distinction may be made between expletive and argument; but it is not as certain that such a distinction may be made between temperate and intemperate argument. Few religious reformers, from Isaiah and Jesus to Luther and Billy Sunday, have been considered temperate in their preachings by any but their disciples.

In the second place, even assuming (what is by no means certain) that in an emergency the Constitution permits the police to prevent an outbreak of violence against a speaker by temporarily silencing him rather than restraining the would-be assailants, it must be recognized that such action is permissible only because the danger is immediate and no alternative method is practicable. If an alternative is available — as for example calling more policemen — the justifying emergency no longer exists and suppression is no longer permissible. The constitutional method of avoiding an outbreak the next time the missionary seeks to preach is not to deny him the right to preach but to have a sufficient number of policemen present. If this is a more expensive method, it must be remembered that constitutional democracy is not necessarily the most economical form of government; it would be much cheaper, for instance, for a President to designate his successor than to engage in expensive national elections every four years.

Moreover, the immediacy of a violent outbreak can generally be sensed with some degree of accuracy. The subjective judgment of the policeman cannot of course be avoided; but if he does make a mistake of judgment in suppressing a street preacher, the only consequence is that the preacher must come back the next day and start over again. It is far more difficult to predict with any degree of accuracy, before he has started to speak or even reached the scene of his meeting, but when he is merely seeking a license, that a preacher's meeting will cause an outbreak. In such a case the police official's judgment is more likely to be colored by his agreement or disagreement with the preacher's views, and he is likely to underestimate the public's tolerance. It should be noted that Kunz's 1946 permit was revoked not because of any disorder attending his meetings, but because he "ridiculed and denounced religion." In the two years that Kunz spoke without a permit no serious incident occurred, and when he was finally arrested and convicted it was not for causing a disturbance but for speaking without a permit. Finally, it should be noted that the consequence of the official's mistake of judgment is not merely the inconvenience of coming back again the next day, but the perpetual silencing of the preacher.

On the basis of the Cantwell, Chaplinsky, Niemotko, Fowler, and Kunz cases the following conclusions may reasonably be drawn:

(1) The First Amendment guarantees the right to preach and teach religion in the public streets and parks.

(2) The states have the constitutional power to restrict street preaching where such action is clearly and immediately necessary to preserve the public peace.

(3) This constitutional power includes the power to punish "verbal acts," such as expletives and "fighting words."

(4) It does not include the power to prohibit street meetings by sects or individuals whose preachings may incite an outbreak of

disorder because of their attacks on other religions or because of their intemperate language.

(5) Nor does it include the power to confer on a public official unbridled or broad discretion to grant or withhold as he sees fit the permits necessary for street or park meetings.

## BLACK MUSLIMS

A group that appears to have inherited the communal animosity formerly visited upon the Mormons and Jehovah's Witnesses are the Black Muslims.[21] These are Negroes who challenge the goal of integration and assert the supremacy of the black race and undying enmity between black and white. They also profess to adhere to the faith of Islam, and maintain temples for Islamic worship, although they are not accepted by the recognized Moslem churches.

Because of their racial views and their reported resort to violence (the assassination of a schismatic leader, Malcolm X, was widely attributed to followers of the orthodox leader, Muhammad Elijah), there has been some claim that the Black Muslims are not a bona fide religious group but racial extremists acting under the guise of religion. However, the courts faced with passing upon their grievances against the constituted authorities have generally recognized their status as a religious group.[22]

Most of their grievances arise out of the restrictions upon their members who are inmates of prisons. In many cases they claim that they are not permitted to practice their religion to the same extent as members of the more conventional faiths, that they are deprived of opportunity to read the Koran, to hold religious meetings, to obtain pork-free meals, and to obtain the services of Black Muslim religious advisors.

In most cases prison wardens have been making every effort to accommodate Black Muslims in their beliefs as far as can be done without unduly interfering with prison discipline. Where the Muslims have found it necessary to bring legal proceedings, the majority of state and lower Federal courts faced with the issue have held that Muslims could not legally be accorded less opportunity to practice their religion than other prisoners unless their demands present a clear and present danger to the functioning of the prison.[23] Where restrictions imposed on the Black Muslim prisoners are reasonably necessary to assure effective prison administration, the courts have held that their constitutional rights are not violated thereby.[24]

The United States Supreme Court has not yet passed fully upon the issue, but it is probably only a question of time before it will do so. When this occurs, it is submitted that consistency with the Court's broad interpretation of religious liberty[25] and of the constitutional requirement of equal treatment among sects[26] would seem to require a determination that a person does not lose all claim to religious liberty on his incarceration in a prison[27] (else how justify state employment of prison chaplains?), and that while wide discretion will be accorded to prison officials in performance of their duties, they will still be required to establish any clear and present danger to the functioning of the prisons to justify restriction on the religious rights of Black Muslims.

## BLASPHEMY AND SACRILEGE

### Blasphemy

It may appear surprising, yet 14 states today still have statutes providing for the punishment of blasphemy as a civil crime.[28] That these statutes are not necessarily dead letters is indicated by the fact that as late as 1928 a warrant was issued (though never served) under the Massachusetts blasphemy statute for the arrest of the noted educator and scholar Horace M. Kallen, who was charged with having said: "If Sacco and Vanzetti were anarchists, so also were Socrates and Jesus Christ."[29] In the same year a missionary atheist who distributed antireligious literature in Arkansas was convicted of "ridiculing the Christian religion."[30]

Since such statements have been judicially condemned as civil crimes on the ground that blasphemy has "a tendency to disturb the public peace,"[31] blasphemy is appropriately considered in this chapter dealing with the balancing of the demands of religious liberty and public order. Blasphemy has been defined as "maliciously reviling God or religion"[32] — although, as we shall see, the word "religion" is used in this sense to connote only the Christian religion. Blasphemy has also been defined as "exposing [God or the Holy Scriptures as contained in the Old and New Testaments] to contempt and ridicule."[33] Thus one who declared that the Holy Scriptures are a mere fable and that they contain a great many lies was convicted under a blasphemy statute.[34]

The courts that have sustained blasphemy statutes have done so on the ground that blasphemy was a civil offense at English common law, and therefore could properly be made a civil offense under American state statutes.[35] But, like Sunday laws — which we have already discussed — blasphemy laws were religious and ecclesiastical in origin; and the sole reason for intervention by the English secular

663

courts was the desire to protect and sustain an established church as a part of the apparatus of government. This is clearly shown by Lord Hale's decision in Taylor's case,[36] which involved John Taylor, a religious maniac, charged with having publicly uttered violently antireligious remarks. The judgment of the court, handed down in 1676, is illuminating:

> And Hale said, that such kind of wicked blasphemous words were not only an offense to God and Religion, but a crime against the Laws, State and Government, and therefore punishable in this Court. For to say Religion is a Cheat is to absolve all those obligations whereby civil societies are preserved, and that *Christianity is a parcel of the laws of England;* and therefore to reproach the Christian Religion is to speak in subversion of the law.

The political context that evoked this decision is summed up by Professor Holdsworth in his definitive treatise on the history of English law:

> During the Tudor period, as in the medieval period, Church and State were regarded from many points of view as a single society which had many common objects, and the two members of that single society were still regarded as bound to give one another assistance in carrying out those common objects. The Church must help the State to maintain its authority and the State must help the Church to punish nonconformists and infidels. The Church was the Church of the State, and membership of it was therefore a condition precedent for full rights in the State. The King was the supreme governor of the Church and the law of the Church was the King's ecclesiastical law.[37]

English common law emphasis on the regulation of blasphemy as ancillary to the establishment of religion has persisted even to relatively recent cases. English courts have been forthright in describing blasphemy as a desecration or a showing of disrespect for that religion that is sanctioned by the state and is integrated into the structure of government. It was therefore natural that attacks on non-Christian or even non-Anglican religions would not be punishable under blasphemy laws. In Gathercole's Case[38] in 1838 the English court recognized this, declaring:

> A person may, without being liable to prosecution for it, attack Judaism, or Mohammedanism, or even any sect of the Christian religion (save the established religion of the country); and the only reason why the latter is in a different situation from the others is because it is the form established by law, and is therefore a part of the constitution of the country. In like manner, and for the same reason, any general attack on Christianity is the subject of criminal prosecution, because *Christianity is the established religion of the country.*

What is surprising is that the same concept should be echoed in a leading New York case. In People vs. Ruggles[39] the defendant was convicted of the common law crime of blasphemy for stating, "Jesus Christ was a bastard and his mother was a whore." In affirming the conviction in 1811, Chancellor Kent stated:

> The reviling is still an offense because it tends to corrupt the morals of the people, and to destroy good order. . . . The people of this State, in common with the people of this country, profess the general doctrines of Christianity . . . and to scandalize the author of these doctrines is not only in a religious point of view, extremely impious, but even in respect of the obligations due to society, in gross violation of decency and good order. . . . Though the constitution has discarded religious establishments, it does not forbid judicial cognizance of those offenses against religion and morality, which have no reference to any such establishments. . . . This [constitutional] declaration, (noble and magnanimous as it is), never meant to withdraw religion in general and with it the best sanctions of moral and social obligation from all consideration and notice of the law. . . .

Although Chancellor Kent spoke of "judicial cognizance of . . . offenses against religion and morality which have no reference to . . . establishment," he also indicated that the protection afforded by blasphemy laws was primarily intended for Christianity as the prevailing national religion, professed by the people of the country. In a subsequent portion of his opinion he made this even clearer:

> The free, equal and undisturbed enjoyment of religious opinion, whatever it may be, and free and decent discussion on any religious subject, is granted and secured; but to revile with malicious and blasphemous contempt the religion professed by almost the whole community, is an abuse of that right. Nor are we bound, by any expressions in the constitution, as some have strangely supposed, either not to punish at all, or to punish indiscriminately the like attacks upon the religion of Mahomet or of the Grand Lama, and for this plain reason, that the case assumes that *we are a Christian people, and the morality of the country is deeply ingrafted upon Christianity and not upon the doctrines or worship of those imposters.*

It would seem clear that under the American principle of the separation of church and state as interpreted by the United States Supreme Court in the Everson, McCollum, Engel, and Schempp cases—even as qualified by the Zorach decision, and even as construed by those claiming that the First Amendment was intended to bar only the preferential treatment of religion—a law that prefers the religion of Christ to "the religion of *Mahomet* or of the *Grand Lama*" is inconsistent with the establishment clause of the First Amendment.

Even before the Everson decision at least one court recognized that the Ruggles case and its concept of blasphemy are inconsistent with the principle of separation. In July 1894 the grand jury of Lexington, Kentucky, indicted one C. M. Moore for blasphemy because he printed in a newspaper the following:

> When I say that Jesus Christ was a man exactly like I am, and had a human father and mother like I had, some of the pious call it blasphemy. When they say that Jesus Christ was born as the result of a sort of Breckinridge-Pollard hyphenation between God and a Jewish woman, I call it blasphemy, so you see there is a stand-off.

Judge Parker, in dismissing the indictment, expressly refused to follow the Ruggles decision, and said:

> The leading case in this country in which the crime of blasphemy was discussed was that of the People v Ruggles decided by the Supreme Court of New York in 1810, Chief Justice Kent delivering the opinion. . . .
> Whilst this opinion did not declare that Christianity was part of the law of the State of New York, but expressly disclaimed that there was an established religion in that state; yet the closeness with which it adhered to the definition of blasphemy as laid down by Blackstone, and the great reliance placed upon the English decisions, make us hesitate to walk in the path trod by Chief Justice Kent himself. For in England there was an established church.
> In this country, where the divorce between church and state is complete and final, we should examine with care and accept with caution any law framed and intended for a country where church and state are one. The difficulties in reconciling religious freedom with the right to punish for an offense against any given religion are manifest. From the opinion given in The People v Ruggles, we may deduce as conclusions of the court that the people generally in this country are Christians; that Christianity is engrafted upon the morality of the country; . . . that to revile the Christian religion is an offense, but that to revile other religions is not an offense punishable by law. . . .
> Under this Constitution no form of religion can claim to be under the special guardianship of the law. The common law of England, whence our law of blasphemy is derived, did have a certain religion under its guardianship, and this religion was part of the law. . . . The essence of the law against blasphemy was that the offense, like apostasy and heresy, was against religion, and it was to uphold the established church, and not in any sense to maintain good order. . . .
> Blasphemy is a crime growing from the same parent stem as apostasy and heresy. It is one of a class of offenses designed for the same general purpose, the fostering and protecting of a religion accepted by the state as the true religion, whose precepts and tenets it was thought all good subjects should observe. In the code of laws of a country enjoying absolute religious freedom there is no place for the common law crime of blasphemy.[40]

Aside from the establishment clause, blasphemy statutes would seem to violate the free exercise of religion clause, which—as we have seen—protects the freedom of irreligion as well as of religion. Moreover, they would also seem to violate the free speech and free press clauses of the First Amendment. Under these clauses speech— spoken or printed—may not be punished for their "tendency to disturb the public peace." If language used in a particular case caused a breach of the peace or presented a clear and present danger of a breach of the peace, it might be constitutionally permissible to impose punishment. In such a case, however, the fact that the language reviled religion or Christianity would not be material one way or the other; the only crime for which the defendant could be prosecuted would be breach of the peace—not blasphemy.

Moreover, even if the offense were called breach of the peace, it would seem, under the cases discussed earlier in this chapter, that prosecution would be constitutional only if the language could be described as verbal acts, *i.e.*, "fighting" or "insulting words." If the language that reviled religion or Christianity were used as part of the communication of ideas—whether temperately or intemperately—it could not constitutionally be the basis of a prosecution for breach of the peace. It will be remembered that during the Revolutionary War period Baptist preachers were jailed in Virginia not for heresy or blasphemy but for disturbing the peace,[41] and it was that infringement of religious liberty that gave rise to the Virginia Statute for Religious Freedom and its successor, the First Amendment.

However regrettable the reviling of the religious tenets of a faith may be, ridicule has always been employed by the adherents of competing faiths. When Elijah debated the prophets of Baal at Mount Carmel and challenged them to make their God manifest, he "mocked them, and said, Cry aloud; for he is a god: either he is talking, or he is pursuing, or he is in a journey, or peradventure he sleepeth and must be awaked" (I Kings 18:27). In like vein, the authors of the King James version of the Holy Bible found it necessary to refer to the Pope in the preface to their work as "that man of Sin"—a remark that ever since has made the King James Bible abhorrent to members of the Roman Catholic Church. Satire and ridicule are often found in religious argument. A vital part of one's freedom to practice one's religion is the freedom to combat any religious error, and, indeed, to reveal opposing religious views as ridiculous and absurd.

### Sacrilege and "The Miracle"

The foregoing discussion of the constitutionality of blasphemy statutes has been necessary because the United States Supreme Court has never specifically passed on the question. The case of the motion picture "The Miracle" involved what was actually blasphemy—though termed "sacrilege"; but the statute was not a criminal statute penalizing blasphemous or sacrilegious films, but a licensing or censorship law, and therefore not necessarily determinative of the issue whether blasphemy may be punished as a civil crime.

A full understanding of the decision of the Supreme Court in "The Miracle" case requires some familiarity with the plot of the motion picture, and the incidents that finally led to the Court's decision. "The Miracle" was a short, 40-minute Italian language picture with English subtitles. The director, script writer, and entire cast were all devout Catholics. Its plot briefly was this: The opening scene depicts a simple-minded peasant girl tending a herd of goats on a mountainside in Italy when a bearded stranger approaches. The garb worn by the girl and the stranger appear to have been important issues in the controversy. The New York Board of Regents, in its report banning the film, described the stranger and his costume as "similar to the traditional images of the Saint [Joseph] . . . [with] garments such as were used in the Holy Land in the time of Christ." It describes the girl as "dressed in clothes caricaturing those worn in church processions honoring the Virgin Mary." Actually the stranger's garments consisted of a U.S. Army field jacket, U.S. Army olive drab trousers, a U.S. Army fatigue cap swung over his shoulders, and U.S. government issue shoes. The girl wore a cotton house dress, a woolen plaid shawl, cotton stockings, and old leather shoes.

In any event, the girl imagines the stranger to be St. Joseph, spouse of the Virgin Mary, who has come to take her to heaven, where she will be happy and free. She pleads with him to transport her to heaven, murmuring—according to the English subtitles:

> I'm not well . . . and taking a loaf of bread He broke it . . . And an Angel of the Lord appeared in his dream and said . . . Joseph . . . Son of David . . . Have no fear to take Mary as your bride . . . for what has been conceived here . . . St. Joseph . . . cast aside my body and my soul . . . I'd feel so happy without this weight . . . St. Joseph has come to me . . . What Heaven . . . Heaven on earth . . . The mad woman has received grace.

While the girl is pleading with him the bearded stranger says nothing, but plies her with wine; then, while the girl is under the combined influence of her fantasies and the wine, the stranger apparently seduces her (this is not expressly stated but is discreetly implied). When the girl later awakens she finds the stranger gone;

she climbs down the mountainside, not knowing whether the incident was real or a dream. She meets two priests, and asks them, "Saints do appear, don't they?" The older priest answers, "If the Lord wills it." The younger priest scoffs, saying: "I'm a monk twenty years and I've never seen a miracle." The old priest dismisses him with the remark: "He's a materialist."

Months later, while tending the village children as their mothers work in the vineyards, the girl faints and the women discover that she is pregnant. "It is the grace of God," she murmurs, and excitedly runs into the church to prostrate herself in front of the statue of St. Joseph. Thereafter she refuses to do any menial work, because, she says, "Even if I were to die of hunger . . . I must respect the child." Although the housewives humor her, the younger people are not so kind; in a scene of brutal torment they mock her, exclaiming: "What honor! You've descended among us mortals!" They cruelly shove and beat her, and clamp a basin on her head as a halo. Abused even by the beggars, she gathers her pitiful rags and leaves the village, to live alone in a cave.

When her time to give birth arrives, the girl starts back to the village. But when she sees the crowds in the streets, her fears cause her to turn toward a church on a high hill. She struggles toward it, crying desperately. A goat is her sole companion. She drinks water that is dripping from a rock. When she finds the front door of the church locked, the goat attracts her to a small side door; she struggles into the church basement. The final scene shows the girl's face, in a close-up, full of tenderness; the cry of an unseen baby is heard. The girl reaches toward it and murmurs, "My son! My love! My flesh!"

This, in brief, is the story of "The Miracle." It should be noted that it casts doubt on the veracity of the virgin birth of Christ as set forth in the New Testament, only to the extent that the recounting of any admitted hallucination casts doubt on the veracity of the alleged historic incident that is the basis of the hallucination. Nothing in the film itself — with the possible exception of its title — directly suggests disbelief in the New Testament version of Christ's birth.

"The Miracle" had been publicly exhibited in Rome under a permit directly issued by the government censor. The Lateran agreements, which — according to the Constitution of the Italian Republic — govern the relations between the Catholic Church and the Italian government, require the government to suppress any public story, play, or film that offends the Catholic religion. No objection to "The Miracle" was made by any representative of the Catholic

Church in Italy. Nor was any objection voiced by the Vatican's representatives on the screening committee when the film was entered in the Venice Film Festival of 1948. Even the Vatican newspaper, *L'Osservatore Romano,* in reviewing "The Miracle" did not criticize it on religious grounds. Nothing occurred in Catholic Italy to give any indication of the vehement attacks to which the picture was to be subjected in New York.

"The Miracle" was passed without objection by the United States Customs authorities when it was brought into this country. In March 1949 it was licensed for exibition with Italian dialogue by the Motion Picture Division of the New York State Department of Education, the official censor of motion pictures. In November 1950 it was again licensed by the Division for exhibition, with English subtitles, as part of the film trilogy, "Ways of Love," with "A Day in the Country," and "Jofroi." (No objection was ever raised to either of the latter two pictures.)

Thus armed, the trilogy opened a month later in the small Paris Theater in New York City that specialized in foreign language and "art" pictures, and was patronized by a select, fairly intellectual audience. The reaction was quick and violent. No sooner had the film opened than the Church's Legion of Decency, which publishes a weekly index of forbidden pictures, prepared a report condemning it and commanding the faithful to refrain from seeing it. This in itself would have meant little, for few religious Catholics patronized art theaters, and the Legion's "condemned" ratings for foreign films rarely had an appreciable effect on their success.

More effective was the action of the city commissioner of licenses, Edward T. McCaffrey, a devout Catholic, and a former State Commander of the Catholic War Veterans. Two days before Christmas Commissioner McCaffrey informed the management of the theater that he found the picture "officially and personally to be a blasphemous affront to a great many of the citizens of our City." He stated that unless the picture were withdrawn he would close the Paris Theater by revoking its license.

To avoid the closing of the theater, Joseph Burstyn, the distributor of "The Miracle," withdrew the film; but—with courage and devotion to principle rare in the motion picture field—decided to contest the issue with the Church. He went to court and obtained an injunction against Commissioner McCaffrey. In issuing the injunction, New York Supreme Court Justice Aron Steuer ruled that the commissioner's jurisdiction to issue and revoke theater licenses did not confer on him the power to censor the films exhibited in the theaters.

The exhibition of the film was resumed on December 29, 1950. But on Sunday, January 7, 1951, a statement by Cardinal Spellman was read at all masses in St. Patrick's Cathedral in New York City. The Cardinal called on all Catholics in the United States to boycott "The Miracle" and any theater showing it. He described the picture as a "despicable affront to every Christian," a mocking of "our faith," and an example of "art at its lowest." He criticized the Motion Picture Division for approving the picture, declaring that its members should be "censured" for offending and insulting "millions of people." Finally he called on all "right-thinking citizens" to unite in changing and strengthening Federal and state laws so as to make it "impossible for anyone to profit financially by blasphemy, immorality and sacrilege."

That afternoon picketing began at the theater. Representing the Catholic War Veterans and other Catholic organizations, the pickets carried signs reading: "This picture is an insult to every decent woman and her mother," "This picture is blasphemous," "This picture is a desecration of faith." The marching pickets' shouting was less dignified; it included such exhortations as: "Don't enter that cesspool!" "Don't look at that filth!" "This is a Communist picture!" and "Buy American!"

On the other hand, a number of Protestant clergymen expressed themselves publicly to the effect that the film was not "sacrilegious," but on the contrary pious and reverent. Ironically enough, Amtorg, purchasing agent for Communist-controlled countries, rejected the film as "pro-Catholic propaganda." Nor was Catholic opinion unanimous. Otto Spaeth, distinguished Catholic layman, an official delegate to the First International Congress of Catholic Artists, and a former president of the Liturgical Arts Society, wrote:

> At the outbreak of the controversy, I immediately arranged for a private showing of the film. I invited a group of Catholics, competent and respected for their writings on both religious and cultural subjects. The essential approval of the film was unanimous.
> There was indeed "blasphemy" in the picture, but it was the blasphemy of the villagers, who stopped at nothing, not even the mock singing of a hymn to the Virgin, in their brutal badgering of the tragic woman. The scathing indictment of their evil behavior, implicit in the film, was seemingly overlooked by its critics.

Neither the picketing, the two occasions on which the police emptied the theater because of anonymous threats to bomb it, nor the summons served on the manager by the Fire Department for allowing people to stand in the aisles and in the back, succeeded in causing Joseph Burstyn to withdraw "The Miracle." What ultimately did succeed was the action of the State Board of Regents in rescinding the license that had been granted by its Motion Picture Division.

Under New York law, the Motion Picture Division of the Department of Education is required to "cause to be examined every motion picture submitted to them . . . and unless such film or part thereof is obscene, indecent, immoral, inhuman, *sacrilegious* or is of such a character that its exhibition would tend to corrupt morals or incite to crime, [the Division] shall issue a license therefor." The Board of Regents on its own initiative appointed three of its members—a Protestant, a Catholic and a Jew—as a subcommittee to view the picture and report. The committee returned with a report that the picture was in fact "sacrilegious." The Board then ordered a private showing of the picture, and after seeing it agreed with its committee, and on February 16, 1951, revoked the license—thus bringing to a temporary end the short but eventful career of "The Miracle" in New York. The Regent's ruling is interesting, particularly in its rather surprising reference to religious freedom:

> In this country where we enjoy the priceless heritage of religious freedom the law recognizes that men and women of all faiths respect the religious beliefs held by others. The mockery or profaning of those beliefs that are sacred to any portion of our citizenship is abhorrent to the laws of this great State. To millions of our people the Bible has been held sacred and by them taught, read, studied and held in reverence and respect. Generation after generation have been influenced by its teachings. This picture takes the concept so sacred to them set forth in both the Protestant and Catholic versions of the Bible (St. Matthew, King James and Douay Versions, Chapter I, verses 18—25) and associates it with drunkenness, seduction, mockery, and lewdness.

Burstyn appealed to the New York courts, but both the Appellate Division[43] and the Court of Appeals[44] upheld the action of the Board of Regents. In disposing of the constitutional issues the courts relied on a 1915 decision of the United States Supreme Court[45] (in the early days of films), which held "that the exhibition of moving pictures is a business pure and simple, originated and conducted for profit, like other spectacles, not to be regarded . . . as part of the press of the country or as organs of public opinion," and therefore not entitled to the protection of the First Amendment.

Ephraim S. London, attorney for Burstyn—and sharing his courage and determination—appealed to the United States Supreme Court. In arguing the appeal he urged the Court to overrule its 1915

decision, and to establish the principle that "sacrilegious" or blasphemous films are entitled to the protection of the First Amendment. A
brief *amicus curiae* in support of the appeal was submitted jointly by
the American Civil Liberties Union, the American Jewish Congress,
the Metropolitan Committee for Religious Liberty (the New York
City chapter of Protestants and Other Americans United), and the
International Motion Picture Organization. A brief in opposition to
the appeal was submitted by the New York State Catholic Welfare
Committee.

In May 1952 the Supreme Court handed down its decision,[46] in
which it unanimously reversed the New York courts. It specifically
overruled the 1915 decision, and held that "expression by means of
motion pictures is included within the free speech and free press
guaranty of the First and Fourteenth Amendments." The court
continued:

> The statute involved here does not seek to punish, as a past offense,
> speech or writing falling within the permissible scope of subsequent
> punishment. On the contrary, New York requires that permission to
> communicate ideas be obtained in advance from state officials who
> judge the content of the words and pictures sought to be communi-
> cated. This Court recognized many years ago that such a previous re-
> straint is a form of infringement upon freedom of expression to be es-
> pecially condemned. The Court there recounted the history which indi-
> cates that a major purpose of the First Amendment guaranty of a free
> press was to prevent prior restraint upon publication, although it was
> carefully pointed out that the liberty of the press is not limited to that
> protection. . . .
>
> New York's highest court says there is "nothing mysterious" about
> the statutory provision applied in this case: "It is simply this: that no
> religion, as that word is understood by the ordinary, reasonable person,
> shall be treated with contempt, mockery, scorn and ridicule. . . ." This
> is far from the kind of narrow exception to freedom of expression
> which a state may carve out to satisfy the adverse demands of other
> interests of society. In seeking to apply the broad and all-inclusive defi-
> nition of "sacrilegious" given by the New York courts, the censor is set
> adrift upon a boundless sea amid a myriad of conflicting currents of
> religious views, with no charts but those provided by the most vocal and
> powerful orthodoxies. New York cannot vest such unlimited restrain-
> ing control over motion pictures in a censor. Under such a standard the
> most careful and tolerant censor would find it virtually impossible to
> avoid favoring one religion over another, and he would be subject to an
> inevitable tendency to ban the expression of unpopular sentiments
> sacred to a religious minority. Application of the "sacrilegious" test, in
> these or other respects, might raise substantial questions under the
> First Amendment's guaranty of separate church and state with freedom
> of worship for all. However, from the standpoint of freedom of speech
> and of the press, it is enough to point out that the state has no legiti-

mate interest in protecting any or all religions from views distasteful to them which is sufficient to justify prior restraints upon the expression of those views. It is not the business of government in our nation to suppress real or imagined attacks upon a particular religious doctrine, whether they appear in publications, speeches, or motion pictures.

It is important to note that though the New York courts' definition of "sacrilege" as treating religion with "mockery" or "scorn" makes it substantially synonymous with blasphemy, the Supreme Court's decision does not hold that a statute penalizing "sacrilege" so defined would be unconstitutional; it holds only that a prior restraint or censorship of a film or other publication for "sacrilege" is unconstitutional. Yet the court's reference to "the First Amendment's guaranty of separate church and state," and the last sentence in the extract from the court's opinion quoted above, would seem to make it clear that the result would have been the same even if the statute had made it a crime to exhibit "sacrilegious" films — at least in the absence of convincing evidence of a clear and present danger of an outbreak disturbing the peace as a result of the exhibition of such a film.

That such evidence would have been difficult to produce is indicated by the subsequent history of "The Miracle." After the Supreme Court decision was announced, the State Board of Regents restored the license for the film. The picture reopened at the same theater at which it had previously been shown. It remained there for at least the normal run of a foreign film, unmarked by picketing, rioting, or any disturbance of the peace — though few other theaters braved the expressed threat of boycott by exhibiting it.[47]

Justice Frankfurter wrote a concurring opinion in which he set forth a detailed history of the meaning of the word "sacrilege," and showed that the term was universally used to mean the physical violating or profaning of sacred articles, and not the ridiculing of concepts or dogma. Justice Frankfurter then continued:

> If "sacrilegious" bans more than the physical abuse of sacred persons, places or things, if it permits censorship of religious opinions, which is the effect of the holding below, the term will include what may be found to be "blasphemous." England's experience with that treacherous word should give us pause, *apart from our requirements for the separation of Church and State*. The crime of blasphemy in Seventeenth Century England was the crime of dissenting from whatever was the current religious dogma. King James I's "Book of Sports" was first required reading in the churches; later all copies were consigned to the flames. To attack the mass was once blasphemous; to perform it became so. At different times during that century, with the shifts in the

attitude of government towards particular religious views, persons who doubted the doctrine of the Trinity (*e.g.*, Unitarians, Universalists, etc.) or the divinity of Christ, observed the Sabbath on Saturday, denied the possibility of witchcraft, repudiated child baptism or urged methods of baptism other than sprinkling, were charged as blasphemers, or their books were burned or banned as blasphemous. Blasphemy was the chameleon phrase which meant the criticism of whatever the ruling authority of the moment established as orthodox religious doctrine. . . .

This language seems to express clearly a position that the concept of blasphemy is inconsistent with the guaranties of the First Amendment, and that it is not material whether the particular statute provides for pre-expression censorship or post-expression punishment. It is therefore reasonable to predict that if the issue should come to the Supreme Court for decision, it would hold all blasphemy statutes unconstitutional.

## REGULATING THE USE OF PUBLIC PROPERTY

### *Streets and Parks*

One of the duties of the state is to regulate the use of publicly owned property. Streets and parks must be policed and kept clean, traffic must be regulated, congestion must be avoided, reasonable quiet must be assured, and in general such supervision must be provided as will assure equal use by all members of the public. Not infrequently the function of the state in regulating the use of public property conflicts with the desire of some sect or individual to use the property in the exercise of his religion. If such a conflict reaches the court, it must weigh the competing interests and resolve the contest in the light of the principles and criteria that have been set forth at the beginning of Part Three of this volume.

Certain principles appear to be clearly established. Religious meetings on the streets undoubtedly interfere with the smooth flow of traffic; moreover, they occasionally break out in violence or other breaches of the peace. Even if no abnormal disturbance occurs, the preacher's loud shouting—particularly if he should avail himself of that modern device of the devil, the voice-amplifying system—is likely to annoy those seeking to enjoy quiet rest or meditation on the green of a public park. These concededly undesirable concomitants of religious meetings can undoubtedly be effectively avoided by the simple expedient of prohibiting all religious meetings in public streets and parks. Unfortunately for perplexed public officials, there can be little doubt that the resort to this simple and effective expedient is unconstitutional.[48]

675

The fact that the state or city may own the streets and parks does not empower it to bar religious meetings. Even the rights of private ownership are not absolute, and may occasionally have to yield to the superior interest of religious liberty.[49] Moreover, although a private owner has the right in most instances to act even arbitrarily in respect to his own property, the state must act within the limits of the Constitution when it deals with its property. It is true that the Supreme Court of Tennessee in 1927 ruled that the state had the power to prohibit the teaching of evolution in public schools, since — like any private employer — it can impose whatever conditions it sees fit on teachers seeking to work for it.[50] Also — as we have seen — there has been some attempt to explain the decision in Hamilton vs. Regents on the ground that the state could impose any conditions it wished on the privilege of enrolling in its university. Nevertheless, despite these decisions, it is clear that the state may not act arbitrarily with respect to its own property; and may no more condition the use of its streets and parks on the relinquishment of the right to propagandize for religion, than it may condition the enrollment in a public school on the engaging in released-time religious instruction or on saluting the flag. In Jamison vs. Texas[51] the Supreme Court of the United States expressly rejected a contention by a city that "its power over its streets is not limited to the making of reasonable regulations for the control of traffic and the maintenance of order, but that it has the power absolutely to prohibit the use of the streets for the communication of ideas."

On the other hand, it is equally without doubt that the community is not powerless to regulate the use of its streets and parks for religious meetings. The Constitution does not impose anarchy on communities — even religiously motivated anarchy. This was made clear by the United States Supreme Court in Cox vs. New Hampshire.[52]

In that case it appeared that in July 1939 some 90 Witnesses met at a hall in Manchester, New Hampshire, "for the purpose of engaging in an information march." The company was divided into four or five groups, each with fifteen to twenty persons. Each group then proceeded to a different part of the city's business district and "there would line up in single-file formation and then proceed to march along the sidewalk in single-file." Each marcher carried a small staff with a sign reading, "Religion is a Snare and a Racket," and on the reverse, "Serve God and Christ the King." Some of the marchers carried placards reading, "Fascism or Freedom. Hear Judge Rutherford and Face the Facts." The marchers also handed out printed leaflets

676

announcing a meeting to be held at a later time in the hall from which they had started.

The marchers neither received nor applied for a permit to hold the procession; and they were prosecuted for violating a state statute requiring a permit to hold a parade or procession on a public street. The Supreme Court of New Hampshire, in affirming the conviction, interpreted the statute to confer no power on the licensing official to consider the purpose of the parade or to censor the signs carried or literature distributed, but only to consider the time, place, and manner of the proposed parade so as "to prevent confusion by overlapping parades or processions, to secure convenient use of the streets by other travelers, and to minimize the risk of disorder."

So construed, the statute was held constitutional by the United States Supreme Court, which affirmed the Witnesses' conviction. The Court said:

> Civil liberties, as guaranteed by the Constitution, imply the existence of an organized society maintaining public order without which liberty itself would be lost in the excesses of unrestrained abuses. The authority of a municipality to impose regulations in order to assure the safety and convenience of the people in the use of public highways has never been regarded as inconsistent with civil liberties but rather as one of the means of safeguarding the good order upon which they ultimately depend. The control of travel on the streets of cities is the most familiar illustration of this recognition of social need. Where a restriction of the use of highways in that relation is designed to promote the public convenience in the interest of all, it cannot be disregarded by the attempted exercise of some civil right which in other circumstances would be entitled to protection. One would not be justified in ignoring the familiar red traffic light because he thought it his religious duty to disobey the municipal command or sought by that means to direct public attention to an announcement of his opinions. As regulation of the use of the streets for parades and processions is a traditional exercise of control by local government, the question in a particular case is whether that control is exerted so as not to deny or unwarrantedly abridge the right of assembly and the opportunities for the communication of thought and the discussion of public questions immemorially associated with resort to public places.

Of course the Witnesses' religious liberty was restricted by requiring them to apply for a permit to hold their parade; and it would have been even more seriously restricted if, because of a prior permit to another group to use the streets for a parade on the day and hour sought by the Witnesses, the latter had been denied a permit for that time. Nevertheless, the necessity of avoiding disorder on the streets which would inevitably result if two or more groups were to seek to parade on the same street at the same time, justifies the relatively minor restriction on religious liberty imposed by the statute. The evil which the statute sought to avoid was obviously a substantial one; the danger that unrestricted exercise of religious liberty would bring on the evil was clear; and the method employed to avoid the evil was the only practicable one — that is, there was no alternative method which would have avoided the evil without restricting religious liberty.

What is true of parades and processions is true also of other types of religious gatherings. There can be little doubt of the constitutionality of a narrowly drawn statute requiring a permit to hold religious meetings in streets and parks — provided the licensing official has no discretion to refuse a permit because of the content of the meeting, but only to regulate time and place. Equally clear, on the other hand, is the unconstitutionality of a statute that enables a local official to refuse a permit to hold a religious (or political) assembly, either without any stated reason[53] or merely on his own opinion that refusal is necessary to prevent "riots, disturbances or disorderly assemblage."[54]

It is not that riots, disturbances, and disorderly assemblage do not constitute a sufficiently substantial evil to warrant the restriction of religious freedom for their avoidance — obviously they do. Broad licensing statutes are unconstitutional because it is not unmistakably clear that no other method is practicable for the avoidance of these evils. Though there may be circumstances under which disorder at a public assembly can be avoided only by prohibiting the assembly, those circumstances are abnormal and rare; ordinarily, disturbances can be avoided by adequate policing. Hence, a statute that would require the giving notice of an intent to hold a religious assembly in a street or park, so as to enable the community to provide adequate policing if the nature of the meeting appeared to require it, would be constitutional. A statute that enables the community to refuse to allow the meeting, merely because it is simpler and more economical to ban the meeting than to provide the necessary policing, would be unconstitutional.

The balancing of the conflicting interests of those seeking to use a park for rest and meditation and those for religious preaching would justify a municipal ordinance or an administrative regulation banning religious meetings from some parks or some parts of a park, provided some other parks or parts of a park were kept available for such meetings. (Of course, in administering such a statute or regulation municipal authorities may not discriminate in favor of conventional faiths and against unpopular ones, such as Jehovah's

Witnesses.[55]) So, too, the balancing of the conflicting uses of streets to get to work and to hold religious meetings would permit the municipal authorities to restrict religious meetings to streets less burdened with vehicular traffic.

The same considerations are present in judicial attacks on statutes prohibiting the distribution of leaflets on the public streets. The community's interest in keeping city streets open to traffic and clean and free of litter is universally recognized. On the other hand, leaflet distribution in public places has almost from the invention of printing been a means of communicating religious and political as well as commercial messages. These conflicting interests must be balanced in a scale which is weighted on the side of the free exercise of religion, speech, and press. This principle was thus expressed by the United States Supreme Court in Schneider vs. Irvington:[56]

> Municipal authorities, as trustees for the public, have the duty to keep their communities' streets open and available for movement of people and property, the primary purpose to which the streets are dedicated. So long as legislation to this end does not abridge the constitutional liberty of one rightfully upon the street to impart information through speech or the distribution of literature, it may lawfully regulate the conduct of those using the streets. For example, a person could not exercise this liberty by taking his stand in the middle of a crowded street, contrary to traffic regulations, and maintain his position to the stoppage of all traffic; a group of distributors could not insist upon a constitutional right to form a cordon across the street and to allow no pedestrian to pass who did not accept a tendered leaflet; nor does the guarantee of freedom of speech or of the press deprive a municipality of power to enact regulations against throwing literature broadcast in the street. . . .

> In every case . . . where legislative abridgment of the rights is asserted, the courts should be astute to examine the effect of the challenged legislation. Mere legislative preferences or beliefs respecting matters of public convenience may well support regulation directed at other personal activities, but be insufficient to justify such as diminishes the exercise of right [guaranteed by the First Amendment] so vital to the maintenance of democratic institutions. . . .

In the Schneider case the court invalidated ordinances in three cities, all of which prohibited the distribution of leaflets in the public streets. The court said:

> We are of the opinion that the purpose to keep the streets clean and of good appearance is insufficient to justify an ordinance which prohibits a person rightfully on a public street from handing literature to one willing to receive it. Any burden imposed upon the city authorities in cleaning and caring for the streets as an indirect consequence of such distribution results from the constitutional protection of the freedom of

speech and press. This constitutional protection does not deprive a city of all power to prevent street littering. There are obvious methods of preventing littering. Amongst these is the punishment of those who actually throw papers on the streets.

It should be noted that the court appears to have invalidated the ordinances on two grounds: first, the broad ground that the interest sought to be protected (unlittered streets) is not sufficiently important to warrant restriction of the rights secured by the First Amendment; and second, the narrow ground that the restriction was not necessary to avoid the evil legislated against (the constitutional way to prevent littering is to arrest litterers).

Jamison vs. Texas[57] illustrates the superior constitutional position held by the freedoms guaranteed by the First Amendment. In Valentine vs. Chrestensen[58] the Supreme Court in 1942 held that, notwithstanding the Schneider case, the state, in the interest of unlittered streets, can prohibit the use of the streets for the distribution of purely *commercial* leaflets. In Jamison vs. Texas, decided the following year, the Supreme Court followed the Schneider case; and — in reversing the conviction of a Witness for violating an ordinance of Dallas that prohibited the distribution of handbills in city streets — ruled that a state "may not prohibit the distribution of handbills in the pursuit of a clearly *religious* activity merely because the handbills invite the purchase of books for the improved understanding of the religion or because the handbills seek in a lawful fashion to promote the raising of funds for religious purposes."

The state has a legitimate interest in protecting the quiet of the users of city streets and parks and of home owners; but this interest may not be protected by barring all religious meetings in streets or parks, even if the noise of such meetings may disturb the quiet of the park user or adjacent home owner. The Supreme Court has gone even further than that: it has ruled that the state may not absolutely prohibit or arbitrarily refuse permission to use a loudspeaker or amplifying system in conducting street or park meetings,[59] although it may prohibit such use in specific parts of a city[60] — just as it may limit religious meetings generally to specific sections of a city. It has also ruled unconstitutional a city ordinance that prohibited ringing doorbells or knocking at doors for the purpose of summoning any inmate to the entrance to receive a handbill; and reversed the conviction of a Witness who violated the ordinance.

In the latter case, Martin vs. Struthers,[61] the court recognized that though "door to door distributors of literature may be either a nuisance or a blind for criminal activities, they may also be useful members of society engaged in the dissemination of ideas in the best tradition of free discussion." The interests of quiet and safety could be adequately protected by laws punishing "those who call at a home in defiance of the previously expressed will of the occupant"; but the state may not penalize the distribution of religious handbills to home occupants who might welcome the handbills.

Just as the state may not prohibit absolutely the distribution of handbills to street pedestrians or home occupants, or the conducting of religious meetings in streets and parks with or without loudspeakers, so too it may not condition these activities on the prior obtaining of a license or permit from a municipal official who has absolute discretion to grant or refuse the permit.[62] Such ordinances have the effect of conferring censorship powers on the municipal official in violation of the First Amendment. The Amendment, however, does not invalidate narrowly drawn ordinances which only regulate the time or place of these religious activities without relation to the content of the handbill or sermon.

### Public Buildings

In his dissent in Kunz vs. New York Justice Jackson said, referring to the McCollum case:

> Do we so quickly forget that one of the chief reasons for prohibiting use of "released time" of school students for religious instruction was that the Constitution will not suffer tax-supported property to be used to propagate religion? How can the Court now order use of tax-supported property, for the same purpose? In other words, can the First Amendment today mean a city cannot stop what yesterday it meant no city could allow?

It does seem paradoxical for the court to hold in the McCollum case that religion may not be propagated in a publicly owned school building, and yet to hold in the Kunz and Niemotko cases that the propagation of religion may not be prohibited in a publicly owned park or street. This appears to be another one of the cases in which the requirements of the separation of church and state seem to conflict with the requirements of religious liberty.

A distinction between a closed building and an open street or park may appear arbitrary; yet—as we have seen—it is real and has at least a historic basis. Streets have from time immemorial been used not merely for the transportation of pedestrians and vehicles but for the communication of ideas. The use of the streets by pedestrians has always been considered—at least in this country—as free as the use of the air above it. The function of the municipality in respect to streets has been primarily that of policing and regulation so as to assure their equal free use by all. Unpaved paths and open places are in some respects the gift of nature; and though technically the state as sovereign may have ultimate title to the land, so too it has ultimate title to the land on which rest churches and private houses. In neither case does the state's ultimate ownership of the land warrant the prohibition of its use to communicate religious ideas.

If the state may not prohibit missionary activity on unpaved highways and open places, it may not remove these from the domain of communication by paving and finishing them. Such improvements merely make them serve better their original purpose; and do not change their basic character or nature. The same is true of the landscaping which makes an open place into a park.

But the same is not true of public buildings. An unpaved path is usable to carry people from place to place; but a building until it is built is nothing at all. Buildings, whether publicly or privately owned, are property in the sense of economic assets. Public buildings are frequently sold and leased like private buildings; but public streets and parks are rarely sold or leased. The use of a public building is not free unless the state makes it free; and when it does so it acts in the same way as any other proprietor who permits the free use of his property. It is true that the state may—and frequently does—grant the free use of its buildings for political debates, dancing lessons, or groups singing. Such a grant of free use is constitutional, not because it does not constitute a grant of public funds, but because the Constitution permits a state to grant public funds to promote political discussion, dancing, or group singing. The state may not grant the free use of its buildings to propagate religion, because the constitutional requirement of separation bars a state from granting public funds for that purpose.

In any event, it is quite clear that the Supreme Court decisions that bar a state from prohibiting religious meetings in streets and parks do not require it to grant the free use of its buildings for religious purposes. In 1951 the court dismissed for want of a substantial Federal question an appeal from a decision that upheld the constitutionality of a state statute that limited the use of public school auditoriums to "associations formed for recreational, educational, political, economic, artistic or moral activities." By dismissing the appeal, the court held that the failure to include religious bodies among the beneficiaries of the free use of public school auditoriums did not constitute a violation of the First Amendment's guaranty of the freedom of religion.[63] The court also dismissed an appeal from a Pennsylvania decision that upheld the validity of a public school board's regulation that barred permits to sectarian institutions for the free use of school buildings. The board's refusal to allow the use of a high school auditorium for Bible lectures was held not to constitute an unconstitutional exercise of discretion.[64]

## PROTECTING AND REGULATING PRIVATE PROPERTY
### *Protecting Property*

The interest the state has in protecting the enjoyment of private property does not—as we have seen—justify a prohibition of distributing religious literature to home owners who have not indicated their unwillingness to be summoned to their home entrances for that purpose. Presumably the state may penalize a person who disregards a sign on the entrance of a home indicating that such solicitation is not welcome; but it does not follow that an owner's desire to exclude the exercise of religion from his property may always be given effect. Individuals have an interest in controlling the use of their own possessions, and the state has an interest in protecting the individuals' interest; but neither the individual nor the state interest is absolute. Where the exercise of the right to control the use of one's property competes with another's exercise of a right secured by the First Amendment, the courts must weigh the competing rights, and decide in the light of the principles we have already discussed.

This limitation of the right of exclusive dominion over one's private property is illustrated by the case of Marsh vs. Alabama.[65] The state of Alabama has a law making it a crime to enter or remain on private premises after being warned by the owner not to do so. The law was applied against a Jehovah's Witness who distributed religious literature in the streets of a company-owned town in disregard of a company rule, posted in store windows, reading: "This is Private Property, and Without Written Permission, No Street or House Vendor, Agent or Solicitation of Any Kind Will Be Permitted."

The town, a suburb of Mobile, Alabama, known as Chickasaw, was entirely owned by the Gulf Shipbuilding Corporation. Except for that fact it had all the characteristics of any other town; it consisted of residences, streets, sewers, and a "business block," and had as town policeman a deputy county sheriff. All residents of the town were company employees and their families; but the streets of the town were open for traveling by all persons.

In holding that the statute could not constitutionally be enforced against the Witness, the court ruled that the decisions that

683

held that a state may not prohibit the dissemination of religious literature in the publicly owned streets of the usual town are equally applicable to a case involving the privately owned streets of a company town. The court said:

> . . . Ownership does not always mean absolute domination. The more an owner, for his advantage, opens up his property for use by the public in general, the more do his rights become circumscribed by the statutory and constitutional rights of those who use it. . . .
>
> Many people in the United States live in company-owned towns. These people, just as residents of municipalities, are free citizens of their State and country. Just as all other citizens they must make decisions which affect the welfare of the community and nation. To act as good citizens, they must be informed. In order to enable them to be properly informed their information must be uncensored. There is no more reason for depriving these people of the liberties guaranteed by the First and Fourteenth Amendments than there is for curtailing these freedoms with respect to any other citizens.
>
> When we balance the Constitutional rights of owners of property against those of the people to enjoy freedom of press and religion, as we must here, we remain mindful of the fact that the latter occupy a preferred position. . . . In our view the circumstance that the property rights to the premises where the deprivation of liberty, here involved, took place, were held by others than the public, is not sufficient to justify the state's permitting a corporation to govern a community of citizens so as to restrict their fundamental liberties and the enforcement of such restraint by the application of a State statute. . . .

Marsh vs. Alabama is an extreme case. Ordinarily the right of an owner to the peaceable enjoyment of his property and the exclusion of unwelcome visitors is almost sacred in a democratic capitalist economic system. It was only because Chickasaw, Alabama, was for all practical purposes identical with all other towns that it was made subject to the constitutional restriction of the First Amendment to which other towns are subject.

Of course the restrictions are not greater. A public town may prohibit the free use of its buildings for the propagation of religion, and so too may a private town. In Watchtower Bible and Tract Society vs. Metropolitan Life Insurance Company[66] the New York courts refused to apply the holding of Marsh vs. Alabama to invalidate a regulation of the Metropolitan Insurance Company, owner of the large Parkchester housing project in the Bronx, which prohibited solicitation or handbill distribution in any of the 171 seven- to twelve-story apartment buildings of the project. An appeal was attempted to be taken to the United States Supreme Court. If the regulation had prohibited handbill distribution on the streets of Parkchester, it may well be that the court would have applied the Marsh doctrine, even though the project is wholly within the confines of New York City. There is no more reason for depriving the 35,000 residents of Parkchester of their constitutional right to receive political or religious literature than the residents of Chickasaw. Since the regulation was limited to the apartment buildings, the Supreme Court understandably refused to accept the appeal and denied the writ of certiorari.[67]

Though the court's denial of certiorari is understandable, it would have been equally understandable if it had accepted the appeal and reversed the New York court's decision. The Metropolitan Life Insurance Company could not be compelled to allow the free use of the project's auditoriums or meeting rooms for religious assemblies, any more than a board of education can be compelled to allow the free use of its school buildings for that purpose. On the other hand it would not have been an unreasonable extension of the decisions in Marsh vs. Alabama and Martin vs. Struthers to hold that the choice whether or not to receive religious or political handbills could not be made for the project dwellers by the landlord. The hallways of Parkchester apartment houses can be distinguished from the streets of Chickasaw, yet the two are more similar than dissimilar, and a judicial equalization of the two may well have been more consistent with the spirit of the First Amendment.

In 1949, however, the court again dismissed an appeal involving the same issue. A Jehovah's Witness was convicted of unlawfully trespassing in a large apartment building in violation of a Virginia statute making it a misdemeanor for a person to enter another's premises after having been forbidden to do so. The evidence showed that the Witness, after having been warned by the building owner not to, entered the apartment building and solicited tenants to appear at a religious meeting. The Supreme Court of Virginia affirmed the conviction,[68] and the United States Supreme Court refused to review its decision.[69]

### Zoning Regulations

The constitutional power of the state to regulate the use of property by zoning ordinances is well established. The purpose of these ordinances is to insure the most beneficial enjoyment of property by the most owners and residents. Zoning ordinances may—and usually do—set aside certain sections of a municipality exclusively for residential purposes; these ordinances are undoubtedly valid where the conflicting interest is commercial. A person seeking to establish a factory or store in a district zoned exclusively for residence cannot successfully attack the ordinance as unreasonable and arbitrary and hence invalid.

The result, however, is not as clear where the effect of the ordinance is to exclude houses of worship from the zoned district. Here the competing interest, religious freedom, enjoys a preferred status in our constitutional scheme of things. It might well be urged that whatever inconvenience or annoyance might be suffered by home owners because of the proximity of a church or synagogue is not sufficiently substantial to justify excluding such buildings from the area.

This in effect has been the conclusion of most zoning boards and courts faced with the problem. The approach of the framers of the zoning regulations of New York City was probably typical of that of most zoning boards. It has been described in the following words by Edward Basset, author of a Russell Sage monograph on zoning:

> When in 1916 the framers of the Greater New York building zone resolution were discussing what buildings and uses should be excluded from residence districts, it did not occur to them that there was the remotest possibility that churches, schools, and hospitals could properly be excluded from any districts. They considered that these concomitants of civilized residential life had a proper place in the best and most open localities.[70]

By and large the courts have concurred in this approach. In construing most ordinances since the advent of zoning, courts have held churches to be proper in residential districts. Both the early decisions and the recent ones frown on the exclusion of churches from residential neighborhoods, in spite of annoyances sometimes experienced in the parking of automobiles or the other temporary inconveniences incident to the gathering of crowds in residential areas.[71]

The view of these courts was well expressed by the Supreme Court of Texas:[72]

> To exclude churches from residential districts does not promote the health, the safety, the morals or the general welfare of the community, and to relegate them to business and manufacturing districts could conceivably result in imposing a burden upon the free right to worship and, in some instances, in prohibiting altogether the exercise of that right. An ordinance fraught with that danger will not be enforced.

The New York Court of Appeals, in upholding the sale at auction of certain city-owned property to Fordham University, a Jesuit institution, has even indicated that excluding religious organizations from the right to bid for property in a program of urban redevelopment might be unconstitutional.[73]

Lately, however, a number of state courts have construed ordinances that limit certain areas exclusively to residences as meaning what they say, *i.e.,* to exclude houses of worship or other communal buildings. So construed, these ordinances have been held not to violate either state or Federal constitutional guaranties of religious freedom. For example, the city of Porterville, California, was divided into four districts, in two of which only residences were permitted. The California courts sustained the action of the city authorities in refusing a permit to erect a Mormon church in one of these districts; and overruled the contention that the ordinance placed unwarranted restrictions on religious freedom in violation of the First and Fourteenth Amendments.[74] This holding was in effect sustained by the United States Supreme Court, when it dismissed an appeal from the decision for want of a substantial Federal question[75] and a similar holding by Wisconsin courts in a case involving a Lutheran parochial school received the same treatment from the United States Supreme Court in 1955.[76]

Since, as the California court said, "there is nothing in the record . . . to indicate that the church building could not be erected if located in the area zoned for that purpose," the resultant restriction on religious freedom was slight, amounting only to the inconvenience of traveling from home to another section of the town to engage in congregational worship. An entirely different situation is presented where the ordinance under consideration seeks to bar houses of worship from the entire municipality. Here the restriction on religious freedom is substantial; for if one town may bar churches, so too may the neighboring towns, and the would-be worshipper may find the distance to the closest hospitable town prohibitive for ordinary travel. The unconstitutionality of such an ordinance would seem to be as clear as the unconstitutionality of an ordinance barring religious meetings or leaflet distribution from all the streets of a town.

The United States Supreme Court has never specifically passed on this question, but the state courts that have been faced with it have uniformly declared invalid those ordinances whose practical effect is to bar churches from an entire village.[77] In the light of its decisions on laws barring leaflet distribution, religious meetings, and doorbell ringing, it is safe to predict that the United States Supreme Court, if called upon to decide, would invalidate a zoning ordinance that barred churches from an entire municipality.

## PREVENTING FRAUD

The duty of the state to prevent the commission of fraud would generally be conceded of sufficient importance to a tranquil society to justify restraints on the free exercise of religion, if such restraints are clearly necessary for the prevention of fraud. The difficulty faced by the courts in cases presenting a conflict between religious liberty and the prevention of fraud is twofold: First, the court must decide in each instance whether the liberty-restricting measure adopted by the state is really necessary for the avoidance of fraud; that is, whether the commission of fraud cannot be effectively prevented by measures that do not restrict religious freedom, or which restrict it to a substantially lesser extent than that adopted by the state. Second—and probably far more difficult—is the decision whether that which the state seeks to prevent is actually fraud and not religion. Put in other words, the court must determine in each case the propriety of the means and the justifiability of the end.

Fraudulent appeals are unfortunately sometimes made in the name of religion; persons occasionally abscond with funds solicited for a genuine religious cause. But these facts would not warrant the prohibition of all appeals for funds in the name of religion—at least in the absence of clear, convincing proof that fraud and embezzlement cannot otherwise be prevented. Fortunately no state or municipality in the United States is likely to make such an assertion, and the unconstitutionality of a statute or municipal ordinance seeking to prohibit solicitation of funds for churches or other religious causes is therefore hardly open to question.

Absolute prohibition is constitutionally impermissible; regulation may be valid. Validity would depend on whether the regulation restricts religious freedom no more than unavoidably necessary to prevent fraud. For example, a municipal ordinance requiring all persons seeking to solicit funds from the general public to register with the public official, and receive some card or document for identification purposes, is probably not invalid. It would, however, be invalid if it conferred absolute discretion on the official to grant or withhold the required document. As the Supreme Court said in Schneider vs. Irvington:[78]

> Conceding that fraudulent appeals may be made in the name of charity and religion, . . . a municipality cannot, for this reason, require all who wish to disseminate ideas to present them first to police authorities for their consideration and approval, with a discretion in the police to say some ideas may, while others may not, be carried to the homes of

citizens; some persons may, while others may not, disseminate information from house to house.

In Cantwell vs. Connecticut[79] the United States Supreme Court reversed the conviction of three Jehovah's Witnesses who solicited funds without obtaining the certificate required under a statute empowering the issuing official to refuse the certificate if he did not believe that the "cause is a religious one." The state of Connecticut sought to justify the statute on the ground that it "merely safeguards against the perpetuation of frauds under the cloak of religion."

The Supreme Court agreed that

> The general regulation, in the public interest, of solicitation, which does not involve any religious test and does not unreasonably obstruct or delay the collection of funds, is not open to any constitutional objection, even though the collection be for a religious purpose. Such regulation would not constitute a prohibited previous restraint on the free exercise of religion or interpose an inadmissible obstacle to its exercise.

The Connecticut statute went much further than that. It empowered a public official to determine whether or not a particular cause was religious as he defined that concept in his own mind.

> He is authorized to withhold his approval if he determines that the cause is not a religious one. Such a censorship of religion as a means of determining its right to survive is a denial of liberty protected by the First Amendment and included in the liberty which is within the protection of the Fourteenth. . . .
>
> Nothing we have said [the Supreme Court continued] is intended even remotely to imply that, under the cloak of religion, persons may, with impunity, commit frauds upon the public. Certainly penal laws are available to punish such conduct. Even the exercise of religion may be at some slight inconvenience in order that the state may protect its citizens from injury. Without doubt a state may protect its citizens from fraudulent solicitation by requiring a stranger in the community, before permitting him publicly to solicit funds for any purpose, to establish his identity and his authority to act for the cause which he purports to represent. The state is likewise free to regulate the time and manner of solicitation generally, in the interest of public safety, peace, comfort or convenience. But to condition the solicitation of aid for the perpetuation of religious views or systems upon a license, the grant of which rests in the exercise of a determination by state authority as to what is a religious cause, is to lay a forbidden burden upon the exercise of liberty protected by the Constitution.

More difficult than judging the propriety of the means to prevent the commission of fraud in the name of religion is the task of judging what in fact constitutes fraud. When the Supreme Court denied "that, under the cloak of religion, persons may, with impunity, commit frauds upon the public," it was stating rather than solving a problem. It is a relatively simple matter for a judge or jury to determine whether or not a certain brick sold for a large sum of money is gold or lead, or whether certain corporate shares are valuable or worthless; it is not as simple a matter to determine whether or not a solicitor of funds to build a spiritualist temple has actually communed with the physically dead.

State courts that have uniformly upheld convictions under statutes prohibiting fortune telling have disposed summarily if not contemptuously of charges that these statutes violated religious liberty;[80] yet one man's fraud may be another man's religion, and *vice versa*. A jury of Catholic priests would probably have little hesitation in finding astrology to be fraudulent and astrologists defrauders. But a jury of Jehovah's Witnesses would probably have less hesitation in making the same finding with respect to Roman Catholicism and Catholic priests. The New York judge who threatened to jail Father Divine for contempt of court did not believe that he was in fact God; but neither did Pilate believe that the Nazarene carpenter was the son of God in a sense different from any other human being; nor did Pharaoh believe that Jehovah, Lord of Hosts, had sent Moses to lead the Israelites out of Egypt.

The test cannot be what the majority believe. It may well be that the majority of Americans do not believe in the literal historicity of all events narrated in the Bible; that fact does not make a defrauder out of the fundamentalist preacher. Perhaps the test should be that of time—those faiths that have survived over a long period are religions; those that have not were frauds. This would set up a sort of Darwinian law of survival: all new faiths are presumptively fraudulent and should be so treated; those that nevertheless survive will thus establish their right to be deemed religions; those that do not will have thereby confessed their fraudulency.

It may safely be said that neither this trial by fire nor the test of numbers accords with the constitutional guaranty of religious freedom either as conceived by Jefferson or Madison or interpreted by the United States Supreme Court. What test does accord with the Constitution may not as confidently be stated. The issue has come before the Supreme Court only once, and in that case three disparate approaches were presented in the three opinions.

United States vs. Ballard[81] is an important case—though for technical reasons difficult to understand. The case involved the "I Am" movement organized by Guy W., Edna W., and Donald Ballard. The Ballards were indicted for using the mails to defraud. The indictments charged that the defendants had falsely and fraudulently represented "that Guy W. Ballard . . . alias Saint Germain, Jesus, George Washington . . . had been selected and designated . . . as a divine messenger;" that the words of "ascended masters and of the divine entity Saint Germain" would be communicated to the world through the "I Am" movement; that the Ballards had supernatural powers to heal the incurably ill — and that they had in fact cured hundreds of afflicted persons. The indictment charged that the Ballards knew that these representations were false, and made them solely for the purpose of obtaining for their own use the moneys of the credulous.

During the course of the trial it was testified that the Ballards had represented that the teachings of the "I Am" movement had been dictated from Heaven to the Ballards, who took down and transcribed them as spiritual stenographers; and that Jesus — in a commendably democratic spirit — had shaken hands with them. The trial judge instructed the jury that they should not decide whether or not these statements were literally true, but only whether the defendants honestly believed them to be true. On appeal, the Circuit Court held that this instruction was erroneous, and that the jury should have passed on the truth of the representation. The case was then appealed to the Supreme Court, where three opinions were written.

The majority of the court, in an opinion written by Justice Douglas, agreed with the trial judge. They held that under the constitutional principle of the separation of church and state and religious freedom, neither a jury nor any other organ of state has the power or competence to pass on whether certain alleged religious experiences actually occurred. The jury could no more constitutionally decide that Guy Ballard did not shake hands with Jesus than they could constitutionally determine that Jesus did not walk on the sea. The court said:

> . . . we do not agree that the truth or verity of respondents' religious doctrines or beliefs should have been submitted to the jury. Whatever this particular indictment might require, the First Amendment precludes such a course, as the United States seems to concede. "The law knows no heresy, and is committed to the support of no dogma, the establishment of no sect." The First Amendment has a dual aspect. It not only "forestalls compulsion by law of the acceptance of any creed or the practice of any form of worship" but also "safeguards the free exercise of the chosen form of religion." Thus the Amendment embraces two concepts, — freedom to believe and freedom to act. The first is absolute but, in the nature of things, the second cannot be. Freedom of

thought, which includes freedom of religious belief, is basic in a society of free men. It embraces the right to maintain theories of life and of death and of the hereafter which are rank heresy to followers of the orthodox faiths. Heresy trials are foreign to our Constitution. Men may believe what they cannot prove. They may not be put to the proof of their religious doctrines or beliefs. Religious experiences which are as real as life to some may be incomprehensible to others. Yet the fact that they may be beyond the ken of mortals does not mean that they can be made suspect before the law. Many take their gospel from the New Testament. But it would hardly be supposed that they could be tried before a jury charged with the duty of determining whether those teachings contained false representations. The miracles of the New Testament, the Divinity of Christ, life after death, the power of prayer are deep in the religious convictions of many. If one could be sent to jail because a jury in a hostile environment found those teachings false, little indeed would be left of religious freedom. . . . The religious views espoused by respondents might seem incredible, if not preposterous, to most people. But if those doctrines are subject to trial before a jury charged with finding their truth or falsity, then the same can be done with the religious beliefs of any sect. When the triers of fact undertake that task, they enter a forbidden domain. . . .

It appears—though not too clearly—that the court agreed that the honesty of the Ballards' beliefs was properly presented to the jury; the jury could determine whether or not the Ballards honestly believed in the truth of what they represented. The test of religion under the Constitution therefore is belief: that which is believed to be religiously true is religion, and constitutionally protected; that which is not believed to be true is not religion but fraud, and may be the subject of criminal prosecution.

Chief Justice Stone dissented. According to him, the truth or falsity of the defendants' representations could properly be determined by a jury. He said:

I am not prepared to say that the constitutional guaranty of freedom of religion affords immunity from criminal prosecution for the fraudulent procurement of money by false statements as to one's religious experiences, more than it renders polygamy or libel immune from criminal prosecution. I cannot say that freedom of thought and worship includes freedom to procure money by making knowingly false statements about one's religious experiences. To go no further, if it were shown that a defendant in this case had asserted as a part of the alleged fraudulent scheme, that he had physically shaken hands with St. Germain in San Francisco on a day named, or that, as the indictment here alleges, by the exertion of his spirtual power he "had in fact cured . . . hundreds of persons afflicted with diseases and ailments," I should not doubt that it would be open to the Government to submit to the jury proof that he had never been in San Francisco and that no such cures had ever been effected.

692

Justice Jackson too dissented, but from the other extreme. He believed that neither the truth of the Ballards' representations nor their belief in their truth should have been submitted to the jury, but that the entire case should have been thrown out; for him the truth of facts could not be divorced from the truth of belief. He said:

> The Ballard family claimed miraculous communication with the spirit world and supernatural power to heal the sick. They were brought to trial for mail fraud on an indictment which charged that their representations were false and that they "well knew" they were false. The trial judge, obviously troubled, ruled that the court could not try whether the statements were untrue, but could inquire whether the defendants knew them to be untrue; and if so, they could be convicted.
>
> I find it difficult to reconcile this conclusion with our traditional religious freedoms.
>
> In the first place, as a matter of either practice or philosophy I do not see how we can separate an issue as to what is believed from considerations as to what is believable. The most convincing proof that one believes his statements is to show that they have been true in his experience. Likewise, that one knowingly falsified is best proved by showing that what he said happened never did happen. How can the Government prove these persons knew something to be false which it cannot prove to be false? If we try religious sincerity severed from religious verity, we isolate the dispute from the very considerations which in common experience provide its most reliable answer.
>
> Belief in what one may demonstrate to the senses is not faith. All schools of religious thought make enormous assumptions, generally on the basis of revelations authenticated by some sign or miracle. The appeal in such matters is to a very different plane of credulity than is invoked by representations of secular fact in commerce. Some who profess belief in the Bible read literally what others read as allegory or metaphor, as they read Aesop's fables. Religious symbolism is even used by some with the same mental reservations one has in teaching of Santa Claus or Uncle Sam or Easter bunnies or dispassionate judges. It is hard in matters so mystical to say how literally one is bound to believe the doctrine he teaches and even more difficult to say how far it is reliance upon a teacher's literal belief which induces followers to give him money.

At first glance it would seem that the majority opinion presents an acceptable, workable compromise position. It does not empower state agencies to pass on the actuality of religious experiences; yet by requiring honest belief in their actuality it affords reasonable protection to the credulous and serves to prevent the more egregious frauds. When it is considered further, however, some difficulties appear. In the first place, the dichotomy between fact and belief, though tenable in commercial transactions, is much less real in religious experiences. It is a rare jury that would find that a defendant

693

honestly believed what to that jury was inherently incredible. In the second place, are all preachers of religion guilty of criminal fraud in accepting offerings if they privately do not believe in the literal truth of everything that they teach as truth? If so, there must be widespread criminality among the modern American clergy of all faiths. It would seem more consistent with the spirit of the First Amendment for civil courts not to take cognizance of the type of wrong committed by the Ballards. Justice Jackson's words are cogent:

> The chief wrong which false prophets do to their following is not financial. The collections aggregate a tempting total, but individual payments are not ruinous. I doubt if the vigilance of the law is equal to making money stick by over-credulous people. But the real harm is on the mental and spiritual plane. There are those who hunger and thirst after higher values which they feel wanting in their humdrum lives. They live in mental confusion or moral anarchy and seek vaguely for truth and beauty and moral support. When they are deluded and then disillusioned, cynicism and confusion follow. The wrong of these things, as I see it, is not in the money the victims part with half so much as in the mental and spiritual poison they get. But that is precisely the thing the Constitution put beyond the reach of the prosecutor, for the price of freedom of religion or of speech or of the press is that we must put up with, and even pay for, a good deal of rubbish.

Considerations similar to those presented in Justice Jackson's dissent would render unconstitutional such statutes as section 435-a of the New York Penal Law, which makes it a crime fraudulently to represent as kosher foods not "sanctioned by orthodox Hebrew religious requirements." The constitutionality of this statute was upheld by the United States Supreme Court in 1925,[82] but the First Amendment was neither invoked nor considered. The court stressed the fact that the critical consideration was fraudulent intent; and that if a vendor honestly believes that the food product he sells is kosher, he may not be prosecuted even though he was mistaken and the food was actually not kosher. It may well be therefore that under the majority opinion in the Ballard case the result would have been the same if the First Amendment had been invoked. Nevertheless, a prosecution under this statute could not succeed unless a jury found that the food product sold by a defendant was as a matter of fact not kosher. To this writer it is incongruous under our concept of the separation of church and state for a jury—often exclusively of non-Jews—to determine whether or not certain meats were prepared in accordance with the ritual requirements of Orthodox Jewish law. This situation is too reminiscent of the Anglican Church's unsuccessful petition to Parliament to allow changes in the Anglican prayer book.[83] It would seem more consistent with the spirit of the First Amendment and the principle of separation that spiritual obligations be enforced by exclusively spiritual sanctions.

### CHAPTER SEVENTEEN

# Freedom and the General Welfare

## THE PEOPLE'S HEALTH

THE WELFARE of the people in modern communal society is dependent on the public health; and preservation of the public health is almost everywhere accepted as a responsibility of government. Occasionally the state in fulfilling this responsibility comes into conflict with the religious convictions of some of its citizens. When this conflict reaches a court for determination, the court must weigh the importance to society of the preservation of the public health as against the importance of preserving religious freedom; and if it decides the issue in favor of the public health, it must decide whether that interest has been clearly and immediately endangered by the religious practice sought to be restrained, and whether the interest of public health may not be adequately protected by means other than that restriction of religious freedom.

Human life is precious in the eyes of society and the state — more precious than almost anything else. Irrespective of the intensity of a person's belief in the religious obligation of human sacrifice, it is hardly open to doubt that such belief would not absolve one from criminal responsibility if he sought to give practical effect to that belief. So too the prevention of the widespread loss of life through the spread of communicable diseases is an interest which must override any considerations predicated on religious convictions. As the United States Supreme Court said in Jacobson vs. Massachusetts,[1]

> Upon the principle of self-defense, of paramount necessity, a community has the right to protect itself against an epidemic of disease which threatens the safety of its members.

In that case, decided in 1905, the court upheld the constitutionality of a Massachusetts statute empowering communities to compel the vaccination of all residents against smallpox in the presence of a threatened outbreak of an epidemic. The statute was not attacked under the First Amendment; the court had not yet decided the cases which held that the restrictions of that amendment were applicable to the states. Nor is there any indication that the defendant's refusal to submit to vaccination was in any way motivated by religious considerations; hence the court did not discuss the freedom of religion guaranty. Nevertheless, later citations of the decision by the Supreme Court indicate clearly that the result would not have been different if religious freedom had been specifically invoked. For example, in 1943 the court unqualifiedly cited the Jacobson case for the proposition that one "cannot claim freedom from compulsory vaccination . . . on religious grounds."[2] So, too, Justice Rutledge in his dissent in the Everson case listed the Jacobson decision among a group of religious liberty cases to support the proposition that the First Amendment "secures all forms of religious expression . . . except conduct which . . . clearly and presently endangers the community's good order and security." Regardless of its origin, the Jacobson case now stands squarely for the principle that necessary health measures are of such paramount importance as to override the free exercise of religion.

Since vaccination may constitutionally be required of all persons, it is clear that it may be made a prerequisite of admission to public schools.[3] This was so held in 1950 by the Supreme Court of Ohio, in a decision that the United States Supreme Court refused to review.[4]

Smallpox is a serious and highly contagious disease, and there may be no practicable method of avoiding an epidemic except by compulsory, universal vaccination. In the presence of an outbreak of the disease in a particular community, the clarity and immediacy of the danger of epidemic is hardly open to serious dispute; and the disregard of the religious scruples of some members of the community to avert the danger does not violate the First Amendment. Where the disease is less serious or the danger of contagion less grave, the courts will be more strict in acquiescing in state restrictions on religious liberty to avert the danger. Obviously no rule of thumb is possible; each case must be decided in the light of the best medical knowledge available; and even then the court's decision is essentially subjective. Nevertheless, in view of the potentially tragic consequences of a wrong guess, it would seem reasonable here—as in cases involving the common defense against foreign enemies—to resolve doubts in favor of the decision of the health authorities. To a certain extent this is a deviation from the "clear and present danger" approach; for it allows restriction of religious liberty where—though the evil sought to be averted is unquestionably serious—the danger of that evil may be less than crystal clear or immediately present. Yet it is unrealistic to expect courts to take even slight gambles with large numbers of human lives.

In 1952 the Supreme Court of Washington was called on to determine the validity of a requirement of the state board of regents that all students registering at the University of Washington have their chests examined by X ray for the detection of tubercular infection.[5] The regulation was attacked by a member of the Christian Science church, who unsuccessfully requested an exemption from the examination because of her belief that submission would be contrary to the doctrines of the church and to her personal religious convictions. In upholding the validity of the regulation the court stressed the seriousness of tuberculosis and its high incidence among college students. It pointed out that the regents did not propose

> . . . that any person found to be infected take any prescribed treatment. The regulation is purely for the purpose of discovery. It does not say to this appellant, you must be treated if you are ill; it only says, if you are so unfortunate as to be ill and not know it, you cannot spread your infection to others at the university. Its primary concern is not for the possibly infected student, but is for those jeopardized by contact with such an individual. It is a preventive measure. Noncompliance with it for any reason by one or more of the group tends to make such a measure ineffective.

The validity of the regulation was upheld because tuberculosis is an "insidious, slow, and progressive disease and is infectious," and because discovery through X ray examination is the only practicable means of preventing the spread of the disease. The court said:

> . . . we cannot say the questioned regulation violates any constitutional inhibition. Here the public interest threatened is the health of all of the students and employees of the university. It may lawfully be protected. In this case, it is of more importance than the right of the appellant which is infringed. The danger to this interest is clear and present, grave and immediate. Infringement of appellant's rights is a necessary consequence of a practical attempt to avoid the danger. The questioned requirement utilizes the generally approved method of combatting the danger, and no practical method which might not possibly infringe a constitutional right is shown. . . .

Smallpox and tuberculosis are serious diseases, endangering life itself. Cavities in teeth do not generally endanger life nor present a serious hazard to health; does the prevention of tooth cavities constitutionally justify interference with religious freedom? The issue has arisen with the recent acceptance by many public health authorities of the finding that fluoridation of the public water supply has a markedly salutary effect on the incidence of tooth decay in the community. Many Christian Scientists have asserted that the fluoridation of water is medication, and therefore barred by the tenets of their church. Since there is no practicable way of separating the water

698

drunk by Christian Scientists from that consumed by the rest of the community, they have vigorously opposed all fluoridation as a violation of religious freedom.[6]

A number of suits have been brought to restrain municipal officials from adding fluorine to the public water supply. These have been uniformly unsuccessful in the state courts. In two the decisions were sought to be appealed to the United States Supreme Court but in both the appeals were dismissed for want of a substantial Federal question.[7] While tooth decay is not a grave disease in the sense that smallpox and tuberculosis are, it is far more widespread; and quantitative as well as qualitative factors should be considered in gauging gravity. Since the clarity and immediacy of tooth decay among the population is hardly open to question, and there appears to be no practicable alternative for its prevention other than the fluoridation of the water supply, it is reasonably safe to predict that most courts, including the United States Supreme Court, are likely to continue to decide the issue in favor of the general welfare rather than the Christian Scientists' religious liberty.

The cases we have discussed all involve restrictions on the religious freedom of some to safeguard the lives and health of others. True, a person vaccinated against smallpox is immunized not only as a transmitter but also as a victim of the disease; and the fluoridated water consumed by Christian Scientist children is likely to aid their oral health as well as that of other members of the community. But this aspect is incidental; in the Jacobson vs. Massachusetts and University of Washington cases the courts stated that their concern was only with the public health, not with that of the litigant's. (Indeed, in the Jacobson case the defendant contended that because of certain inherited physical characteristics vaccination was dangerous to him.) These cases did not decide whether the state may constitutionally restrict a person's religious liberty against his will to protect only his own life or health.

Where the life of a child is at stake, there can be little doubt of the state's power to intervene. Martyrdom may be a constitutional right, but if so it may be exercised only after attaining the age of reason; a parent, no matter what his religious convictions are, may not deprive his child of needed medical attention. This point was dramatically illustrated in Chicago in 1951. Cheryl Lynn Labrenz was born with an RH-negative factor, inherited from the mother, which causes a baby's red blood cells to destroy each other. Medical experts at the hospital agreed that her life could be saved only by a transfusion. The baby's parents, however, were Jehovah's Witnesses, who believed that a blood transfusion was the equivalent of eating or drinking blood, which is forbidden by the Bible, and accordingly refused to consent to the transfusion.

The hospital authorities brought the matter to the family court, and the judge took the child out of the technical custody of the parents and appointed a court official as her legal guardian. The official immediately consented to the transfusion and the infant's life was saved. The guardianship was then terminated and custody returned to the parents.[8]

Although the child's recovery made the issue academic, the parents appealed to the Supreme Court of Illinois, which affirmed the family court's decision.[9] The court quoted the following from Prince vs. Massachusetts:[10]

> The right to practice religion freely does not include liberty to expose the community or child to communicable disease or the latter to ill health or death. . . . Parents may be free to become martyrs themselves. But it does not follow they are free, in identical circumstances, to make martyrs of their children before they have reached the age of full and legal discretion when they can make that choice for themselves.

Unless we are prepared to sanction ritual filicide, the court's decision is hardly open to question, and has uniformly been followed in other states.[11] The issue, however, is far more difficult where the objecting Jehovah's Witness is a mature, mentally competent adult. Here the issue is whether religious freedom includes the right to commit suicide, or does society's interest in human life transcend in importance the individual's right to exercise his religion as he believes it?

The state has an interest in human life beyond that of the individual; human life is a societal asset that the state has the power and duty of preserving. Suicide is a crime at common law,[12] and even today attempted suicide is a crime under many state penal codes.[13] "Although suicide," says the New York Penal Law,[14] "is deemed a grave public wrong, yet from the impossibility of reaching the successful perpetrator, no forfeiture is imposed." If suicide is a "grave public wrong," the state has the right to prevent it if prevention is practicable.

The United States Supreme Court, in one of the Mormon polygamy cases,[15] had no doubt that "if a wife religiously believed it was her duty to burn herself upon the funeral pile of her dead husband," it would be within the "power of civil government to prevent her carrying her belief into practice." The question is far from academic. In 1949 the Supreme Court of North Carolina upheld a conviction against members of a snake-handling cult under a city ordinance prohibiting snake-handling.[14] The court held that the ordinance did not unconstitutionally impinge on the defendant's freedom of religious worship, and the United States Supreme Court dismissed an appeal for want of a substantial Federal question.[17]

It is true that the ordinance prohibited only the handling of poisonous reptiles "in such a manner as to endanger public health, safety and welfare," but it was clear that the only persons whose safety was endangered were other members of the cult voluntarily engaging in the same practice. So, too, state courts have sustained the constitutionality of statutes prohibiting paid or professional "faith healing";[18] and the United States Supreme Court has refused to review the one decision appealed to it.[19] Here also the only persons whose health is endangered are those who themselves believe in "faith healing" and voluntarily submit to the practice. Hence these decisions hold that the state may constitutionally preserve a person's life even against his will and religious convictions.

Most Americans today would probably accept as almost unarguable the proposition that the state has the constitutional power to prevent a person from committing even religiously motivated suicide, or other conduct that gravely endangered the person's own life. Yet a reasonable case may be made for the contrary position. As long as the state considers human life not so precious as to be willing to extinguish it against the owner's will in punishment of a capital crime, or in pursuit of international political policy, it may not be entirely unreasonable to suggest that the owner might be legally permitted to risk it in adherence to deeply felt religious conviction; religious martyrdom has at least as long and honored a history as political martyrdom.

A number of state and lower Federal courts have been faced with the problem of a hospital's application for authorization of a blood transfusion to an unwilling adult Jehovah's Witness, and most have decided in favor of authorization. The minority have stressed religious liberty and freedom of choice,[20] while the majority have offered a variety of reasons for their conclusion.[21] Thus, in one case,[22] the court noted that the Witness was 32-weeks pregnant and asserted that even if she could sacrifice her own life, she could not sacrifice the life of her unborn child. In another case,[23] the court reasoned that the Witness, being *in extremis*, was incompetent and like a child, so that the Labrenz decision is applicable. In the same case, the court also relied on the fact that the Witness was the mother of a seven-month-old child, and the state had an interest in

701

preventing parents from voluntarily abandoning their infant children.

Such reasoning appears to be highly artificial, rationalizing a judicial reluctance to allow the death of a person whose life physicians can save. Sooner or later the Supreme Court will find it necessary to pass on the issue and, should it, as is likely, uphold the state's power to order the transfusion, its decision would be more realistic if it were based frankly on society's interest in the continuance of life where this can medically be achieved.

Where the risk to life is not clear or immediate, or where health rather than life is at stake, a different result might be reached. A Christian Scientist may not prevent the community from adding fluorine to the public water supply, but it is doubtful that the community may compel him to drink the water; and it is likewise doubtful that an adult Christian Scientist may be legally compelled to consult a physician when he is physically ill, or perhaps even to accept a blood transfusion where physicians do not agree that his life cannot otherwise be saved. In 1964, the Supreme Court of California held that in the absence of clear proof that peyote, a hallucinogen, had a harmful effect on its users, Indian members of the American Native Church, who used the drug as a sacrament, could not constitutionally be prosecuted for violating the state's narcotics law.[24]

## Marriage and the Family

The state has a well-recognized interest in the marital status and the family relationship. As the United States Supreme Court stated in Reynolds vs. United States,[25]

> Marriage, while from its very nature a sacred obligation, is nevertheless, in most civilized nations, a civil contract, and usually regulated by law. Upon it society may be said to be built, and out of its fruits spring social relations and social obligations and duties, with which government is necessarily required to deal.

Since the monogamous family is the basis of western societal life, the state has the constitutional power to prohibit polygamy even if polygamous marriages are required by the dictates of religious conscience.[26] The state also has an important interest in the permanence of marriage, and may therefore take appropriate measures to avoid hasty and ill-considered marriages. It may prohibit marriages of persons below an age it deems proper. It may require the obtaining of a license to marry, and may compel a waiting period between the obtaining of the license and the marriage. It may prohibit ministers

702

from advertising or otherwise soliciting marriages; and in each case may disregard the religious convictions of the persons involved.[27] Similar considerations empower a state to require premarital medical examination for venereal disease, and perhaps even to prohibit the marriage of persons suffering from venereal disease. As early as 1914—when venereal diseases were not as amenable to curative medication as they are today, so that a victim of venereal disease could frequently be effectively barred from ever marrying—a state court refused to recognize the presence of a religious liberty issue, saying: "We know of no church which desires its ministers to profane the marriage tie by uniting a man afflicted with a loathsome disease to an innocent woman."[28]

State statutes generally provide that marriages may be validly performed by clergymen after a license has been obtained from a public official. What creates the marital relation is not the clergyman's ceremonial act, but the parties' expressed intent manifested by participation in the religious ceremony. It is for that reason that the civil recognition of the relationship growing out of the religious ceremony does not violate the constitutional mandate of the separation of church and state. On the other hand, since the First Amendment protects the nonbeliever no less than the believer, it is highly improbable that the courts would sustain the validity of a statute that required all marriages to be performed religiously.

Family planning, more popularly called birth control, through contraception, is a subject which in actuality, if not in technical constitutionality, is permeated with church-state conflicts.[29] Ever since enactment of the Comstock law in 1873 under Protestant sponsorship, Federal and state laws have in varying degrees forbidden or restricted the giving of contraceptive information and material. By the middle of the 20th century, however, these had become dead letter laws, a fact officially recognized by the United States Supreme Court in 1961.[30] Four years later, the court held that a law forbidding contraception even by married couples was an unconstitutional invasion of marital privacy and therefore unenforceable against officials of a birth control clinic who supplied information and materials to married couples.[31]

## THE WELFARE OF CHILDREN

### The Health of Children

We have noted that the religious convictions of parents—or even of children themselves—cannot stand in the way of the state's performance of its obligation to protect the lives of children. But the state may go even further: it may disregard religious convictions when it is immediately and clearly necessary to protect not only the lives but the health of children as well. Thus, for example, a statute making it a crime to neglect to provide medical attention for one's ill child is not unconstitutional, even if applied against a parent whose religious convictions preclude medical aid.[32] In Prince vs. Massachusetts[33] the United States Supreme Court upheld the validity of a conviction under a state child labor law of a member of Jehovah's Witnesses who allowed her two young children and nine-year-old ward to accompany her on the streets and help sell or distribute "Watchtower" and "Consolation." The particular statute that was violated prohibited boys under 12 and girls under 18 from selling newspapers, magazines, or periodicals on any street or public place, and made the adult who furnished the child with the publications subject to criminal punishment. At the trial it was testified that the defendant, Mrs. Prince, and the children considered themselves ordained ministers, and that they believed it was their religious duty to perform this work and that neglect would bring condemnation "to everlasting destruction at Armageddon."

The court acknowledged the "right of children to exercise their religion and of parents to give them religious training and to encourage them in the practice of religious belief, as against predominant sentiment and assertion of state power voicing it." It also recognized that "the custody, care and nurture of the child reside first in the parents, whose primary function and freedom include preparation for obligations the state can neither supply nor hinder."

> But [the Court continued] the family itself is not beyond regulation in the public interest, as against a claim of religious liberty. And neither rights of religion nor rights of parenthood are beyond limitation. Acting to guard the general interest in youth's well being, the state as parens patriae may restrict the parent's control by requiring school attendance, regulating or prohibiting the child's labor, and in many other ways. Its authority is not nullified merely because the parent grounds his claim to control the child's course of conduct on religion or conscience. Thus, he cannot claim freedom from compulsory vaccination for the child more than for himself on religious grounds. The right to practice religion freely does not include liberty to expose the community or the child to communicable disease or the latter to ill health or death. . . . The state has a wide range of power for limiting parental freedom and authority in things affecting the child's welfare; and . . . this includes, to some extent, matters of conscience and religious conviction.

The court conceded that a statute prohibiting street hawking could not constitutionally be applied against adult Jehovah's Witnesses selling their religious publications as an aspect of their missionary activities. But the court said:

> The State's authority over children's activities is broader than over like actions of adults. This is peculiarly true of public activities and in matters of employment. A democratic society rests, for its continuance, upon the healthy, well-rounded growth of young people into full maturity as citizens, with all that implies. It may secure this against impeding restraints and dangers, within a broad range of selection. Among evils most appropriate for such action are the crippling effects of child employment, more especially in public places, and the possible harms arising from other activities subject to all the diverse influences of the street. It is too late now to doubt that legislation appropriately designed to reach such evils is within the state's police power, whether against the parent's claim to control of the child or one that religious scruples dictate contrary action.

Missionary activities in the public streets present dangers which in the case of children the state may legitimately seek to prevent.

> Street preaching, whether oral or by handing out literature, is not the primary use of the highway, even for adults. While for them it cannot be wholly prohibited, it can be regulated within reasonable limits in accommodation to the primary and other incidental uses. . . . The zealous though lawful exercise of the right to engage in propagandizing the community, whether in religious, political or other matters, may and at times does create situations difficult enough for adults to cope with and wholly inappropriate for children, especially of tender years, to face. Other harmful possibilities could be stated, of emotional excitement and psychological or physical injury. . . . We think that with reference to the public proclaiming of religion, upon the streets and in other similar public places, the power of the state to control the conduct of children reaches beyond the scope of its authority over adults, as is true in the case of other freedoms, and the rightful boundary of its power has not been crossed in this case.

Justice Murphy dissented; to him it had not been clearly established that the action of the Witness children presented an immediate danger to their health or welfare. "The great interest of the state," he said, "in shielding minors from the evil vicissitudes of early life does not warrant every limitation on their religious training and activities." The bare possibility that harm "might emanate from distribution of religious literature is not, standing alone, sufficient justification for restricting freedom of conscience and religion. Nor can parents or guardians be subjected to criminal liability because of vague possibilities that their religious teachings might cause injury to the child. The evils must be grave, immediate, substantial."

Justice Murphy did not find the evils to be grave, immediate, or substantial; on the contrary, the evil influences that frequently accompany youth, such as gambling, truancy, and irregular habits, "are not consistent with the high moral character ordinarily displayed by children fulfilling religious obligations. [The] fact that the zealous exercise of the right to propagandize the community may result in violent or disorderly situations difficult for children to face is no excuse for prohibiting the exercise of that right."

The danger, Justice Murphy felt, lay not in the possible harm to the children, but to the principle of religious liberty by the use of laws enacted for a wholesome purpose to restrict the rights of unconventional and unpopular faiths. Justice Murphy concluded:

> No chapter in human history has been so largely written in terms of persecution and intolerance as the one dealing with religious freedom. From ancient times to the present day, the ingenuity of man has known no limits in its ability to forge weapons of oppression for use against those who dare to express or practice unorthodox religious beliefs. And the Jehovah's Witnesses are living proof of the fact that even in this nation, conceived as it was in the ideals of freedom, the right to practice religion in unconventional ways is still far from secure. Theirs is a militant and unpopular faith, pursued with a fanatical zeal. They have suffered brutal beatings, their property has been destroyed; they have been harassed at every turn by the resurrection and enforcement of little used ordinances and statutes. To them, along with other present-day religious minorities, befalls the burden of testing our devotion to the ideals and constitutional guarantees of religious freedom. We should therefore hesitate before approving the application of a statute that might be used as another instrument of oppression. Religious freedom is too sacred a right to be restricted or prohibited in any degree without convincing proof that a legitimate interest of the state is in grave danger.

## The Religious Upbringing of Children[34]

The free exercise clause of the First Amendment protects the right of parents to control the religious upbringing of their children.[35] Although the Supreme Court has spoken of the "right of children to exercise their religion,"[36] it is really the religious liberty of parents that is protected. Application of the free exercise clause to children within their parents' custody is at best meaningless, and may in fact be mischievous. In the McCollum case, the record showed that young Terry McCollum wanted to participate in the religious instruction, but his mother objected. What would have been the effect on the family life of the McCollums if the court had held that Terry had a constitutional right to participate which the court would enforce notwithstanding his parents' objection?

A child's interest in its temporal welfare will be protected by the law if its parents neglect to protect it; hence, it is appropriate to speak of a child's right to its temporal welfare. On the other hand, under the mandate of separation of church and state, if the child's religious welfare is neglected the state may not intervene to protect it. A judge convinced that a child will die if it does not receive an immediate blood transfusion can constitutionally direct the giving of a transfusion over the parents' objection. A judge equally convinced that the parents' refusal to baptize their dying child will deprive the child of eternal salvation is constitutionally without power to take legal action. It serves no useful purpose to speak of a legal right which the Constitution prohibits the state from recognizing or enforcing. And it is unrealistic to speak of the right of a child to determine its religious upbringing when it is subject to parental custody and control.

As has been suggested, the free exercise clause protects nonreligion as well as religion, and therefore secures the right of parents to bring up children without religion, or even as militant atheists. There can be little doubt that no American tribunal could constitutionally follow the precedent of the English court that deprived the poet Shelley of custody of his children because of his avowed atheism.[37] The First Amendment also secures the right of parents to bring up children in unconventional or unpopular religions.[38] If the parents' beliefs endanger the child's life or health, as, for example, their refusal to provide the child with needed medical aid, the courts will intervene to protect the child's health but will not otherwise interfere with the parents' religious upbringing of the child.[39]

In England until comparatively recent times, it was the father who had the right to determine in what faith a child should be reared.[40] In this country the parents' rights are equal,[41] and the courts will not intervene even if the parents cannot agree between themselves.[42] Where the marital unity is dissolved by divorce, separation, or death of one spouse, the parent who receives legal custody of the child has the right to determine its religious upbringing.[43]

The canon law of the Roman Catholic church provides that when a Catholic marries a non-Catholic the latter must sign a written contract that all children of the marriage will be brought up as Catholics. It often happens that upon the dissolution of the marriage custody of the children is awarded to the non-Catholic parent (usually the mother) who returns to her own faith and seeks to bring the children up in it in violation of the contract. Catholic spouses have often gone to court to get a judicial order compelling the non-Catholic to abide by the antenuptial agreement, but the courts have almost uniformly held that these agreements are not enforceable in a civil court.[44]

Several reasons may be suggested for this judicial policy. In the first place, if an unwilling parent is forced by a court of law to rear his child in a religion which he disbelieves, the child will suffer. Besides, there is a strong policy in a democracy in allowing persons to worship God as their conscience now dictates, a policy that is equally applicable to teaching their children how to worship God. It would be contrary to this policy judicially to enforce a contract not to change one's own religious beliefs or practices; and it is equally contrary to this policy judicially to enforce a contract not to change the religious upbringing of one's children. Finally, a sound argument can be made that if judicial enforcement of a promise not to sell one's land to a Negro would be state action violating the "equal protection" clause of the Fourteenth Amendment,[45] then such enforcement of a promise not to raise one's child in the faith held sacred by the promisor would be state action violating the free exercise clause of the First Amendment, which is equally applicable to the states under the Fourteenth.

## The Custody of Children

When a court is called upon to fix the custody of a child, as where the parents separate, the universal rule is that it should be guided exclusively by what it deems to be the child's best interests. Suppose the parents are of different faiths; may the courts consider that fact? Some courts have expressed the view that in fixing custody they will give no consideration to religion but will and necessarily must decide the controversy as if that factor were completely absent.[46] Such view, however, may be too broad. A more correct view, it is submitted, is this: In deciding upon the course most likely to secure the temporal welfare and happiness of a child whose custody a court is called upon to fix, all relevant, probative factors must be considered. In many instances the prior religious training of the child may be one of these factors, for in some children or under some circumstances a change in religious training may have traumatic psychic consequences. In such a case the court, to secure the child's probable temporal welfare and happiness, may and should consider the religious factor and may seek to match the child's previous religious training with that which it is likely to receive in the home of the would-be parent. Where, however, the child has had no religious training, or competent psychologists testify that a change in religious upbringing would not be harmful, the court should decide the custody question without regard to the religion of the parents.

A more difficult question arises when a child has lost both parents, through death, desertion, neglect, or other causes. In many states statutes have been enacted requiring the courts to give some consideration to the child's religion in fixing its custody. These statutes, frequently called "religious protection" laws, go back to the 18th century. Their language varies widely. Typical, though perhaps the broadest in scope and apparently the only one accorded constitutional sanction, is the provision in the New York constitution[47] that "whenever a child is committed to an institution or is placed in the custody of any person by parole, placing out, adoption, or guardianship, it shall be so committed or placed, when practicable, to an institution governed by persons or in the custody of a person, of the same religious persuasion as the child."

A number of policy considerations may be suggested to justify these "religious protection" statutes. Perhaps the most valid (and probably their original motivation) is that they prevent proselytization in the children's courts and neutralize the personal religious bias of the custody judges. In few areas are the personal predilections of the judge more intense and potent than in religious controversies, particularly those affecting children. By requiring the judge to match religions, the statutes remove or at least substantially minimize the temptation, consciously or unconsciously, to allow religious bias to affect the decision.

The difficulty with this argument is that unless religious identity between the natural and the would-be parents is adjudged desirable for its own sake, the effect of the statutes is merely to substitute one irrelevant factor for another. If temporal welfare rather than religious identity is the desired end, then by the laws of chance the desired end will be achieved as often where the judge's religious bias controls as where religious identity controls. Moreover, minimization of the judge's bias might be effected in the opposite direction, that is, by forbidding consideration of the religious issue or any questioning thereon by judge or court officer.

Another possible justification for the statutes is that they constitute some recognition of the place of religion in our national culture and that "we are a religious people."[48] They recognize that materialistic considerations are not necessarily the highest, and certainly not the exclusive value in our society; that religion, too, is important—a recognition particularly called for in an era when our traditions and concepts are threatened by an aggressive statism predicated solely on materialistic values.[49] The weakness of this argument lies in its irrelevancy to statutes requiring not that the would-be parent be religiously committed, but that his religion be identical with that of the natural parent.

Finally, and somewhat related to the last point, is the possible justification that these statutes recognize the church as possessing the right to exercise sovereignty over and claim the fealty of its members.

But in a democracy the church can rightfully claim sovereignty and fealty only if it recognizes and honors the principle of voluntary entry and free exit. Therein lies the fundamental objection to the "religious protection" statutes. Originally seen as a means whereby dissenting sects could protect themselves against forceable proselytization by a legislature or judiciary affiliated with and subservient to an established church, they have long since become vehicles whereby the church seeks to protect itself not from a predatory state, but from its own imperfect ability to retain through persuasion, the fealty of its subjects. If the church has had so little influence upon parents whose allegiance it claims that they have brought up their child without training in the religion of that church or have expressed the wish that the child be brought up by persons of a different faith, its invocation of a "religious protection" statute becomes an act not of self-defense but of aggression.

The basic objection to the "religious protection" statutes is that they rest on a concept alien to American traditions, the concept that religion is a matter of status. American culture, religious as well as social and political, is predicated upon the principle of voluntariness, that religion is acquired not through birth but through election. This principle, stated in a variety of ways, was the common philosophy that could unite the two disparate forces most responsible for the constitutional sanctification of religious liberty and the separation of church and state, the pietistic Protestant dissenters who followed Roger Williams and Jonathan Edwards, and the rationalist skeptics who received their inspiration from Jefferson, Paine, and the French Enlightenment. When religious status is imposed by the fiat of secular government, it offends not only principle and tradition, but constitutional mandate as well.

### The Adoption of Children

Perhaps even more than conflicts over custody, adoptions have caused grave interreligious tensions and have raised serious constitutional problems. As in the case of custody, it has been the general rule ever since the leading Massachusetts case of Purinton vs. Jamrock,[50] decided in 1907, that the test which a court should apply in passing upon a petition of a couple to adopt a child is whether the adoption would serve the best interests of the child. The fact that the child was born into a faith different from that of the adopting couple is not a bar if the child's welfare will be benefited by the adoption. Although many states have passed "religious protection" laws stating that "whenever practicable" or "whenever possible" a child should be placed for adoption with a family of the same faith, the courts in these states have interpreted the laws as being consistent with the principle of Purinton vs. Jamrock, that is, that religious difference does not constitute an absolute bar to adoption.[51]

This, in any event, is how the Supreme Judicial Court of Massachusetts interpreted the statute in 1952 when, in the Gally case, it approved the adoption by a Protestant couple of a child born to Roman Catholic parents.[52] The decision was bitterly criticized in the editorial columns of the *Pilot*, organ of the Boston archdiocese, which called it a "supreme tragedy" and a "victory for the current secularist philosophy, which considers religion, any religion, of secondary or minor importance and the material advantages of life as of prevailing consequence."[53]

Two years later the Goldman case came before the court. It involved illegitimate twins, born to Pearl L. Dome, a divorced Roman Catholic woman, in 1951. The natural father was also Roman Catholic. Two weeks after the birth of the children a Jewish couple, Reuben and Sylvia Goldman of Marblehead, took them for adoption. Pearl Dome consented in writing and was agreeable to their being raised in the Jewish faith. But at the adoption hearing Judge John V. Phelan found that, although the Goldmans were otherwise suitable adopters, many nearby Catholic couples had applications for similar children on file with the Catholic Charities Bureau. He ruled therefore that, even though these Catholic couples had never sought to adopt the Dome twins and had not in fact ever seen them, nevertheless it appeared "practicable" to give the twins to a Catholic couple. He accordingly denied the Goldmans' petition. The Supreme Judicial Court affirmed the decision, in effect thereby overruling the Gally decision, and the State Department of Public Welfare started proceedings to take the twins from the Goldmans and place them in a Catholic institution. The Goldmans thereupon abandoned their home and business, a clothing store in Boston, and departed with the twins to establish a new home in another state.[54]

Shortly after the Goldman case came the even more publicized "Hildy" case. Hildy was born in February 1951, to a Catholic student nurse, said to have been unmarried. Records indicate that the court had ascertained that the father of the child, an intern, was a Protestant. With the oral consent of the young mother, Hildy was placed by her physician with a Jewish couple, Mr. and Mrs. Melvin Ellis of Boston. When Hildy was five weeks old, the natural mother, who later married Mr. McCoy, claimed that she had learned for the first time that the adoptive parents were not Catholics and that both had been divorced previously. With the vigorous cooperation of the Roman Catholic Church, she began proceedings for Hildy's return. There followed a long battle in the courts, climaxed in February 1955, when the Supreme Judicial Court, following the Goldman decision, ruled in favor of Marjorie McCoy.[55] Like the Goldmans, the Ellises, defying the court, fled Massachusetts with Hildy. In 1957 they were discovered living in Florida, and the Massachusetts authorities sought to extradite them for trial on kidnapping charges, but Governor LeRoy Collins of Florida refused the extradition request. Periodic feature stories through the years since then have portrayed Hildy's apparent happiness with her adoptive parents.

Most state courts have refused to follow the lead of Massachusetts in interpreting their "when practicable" statutes as in effect barring all interreligious adoptions.[56] Typical of their approach to the problem is a case decided in the courts of Pennsylvania in 1954. The crazed neighbor of a young couple in Michigan entered their house and shot them both. The husband had been a Catholic, the wife a Protestant. They had one young child whom they had agreed to rear in the Catholic faith and accordingly had had him baptized as a Catholic. On the death of the couple, the child's (Protestant) maternal aunt came from Pennsylvania, took him, and brought him back with her with the intent to adopt him. The child's (Catholic) paternal grandparents followed her to Pennsylvania and, with the support and backing of the Roman Catholic Church, brought legal proceedings to recover the child for adoption by them. The Pennsylvania courts ruled in favor of the aunt and her husband on the ground that the welfare of the child dictated that he be brought up away from the scene of the tragedy and by a couple whose age relationship to him was that of the normal age relationship between parents and children. While the religious factor, the court said, is important and must be given consideration, it may not be allowed to override the demands of the child's welfare.[57]

The position of the Roman Catholic Church against interreligious adoptions is quite logical and understandable in the light of its dogmatic concepts and philosophical principles. Those particularly relevant here are that (1) religion is a matter of status and not of election; (2) Catholic baptism is immutable and accordingly there is no exit from the Catholic faith; (3) eternal salvation is more important than temporal happiness, and if a choice must be made the first must always be chosen over the second; (4) Catholicism is the one and only true faith, and membership therein is the surest if not the only certain road to eternal salvation; (5) voluntariness is not the ultimate test nor basic requirement in religion, and therefore the wishes of a Catholic mother that her child be adopted by a couple of a non-Catholic faith need not be honored (". . . no one," said a Catholic judge in a Massachusetts custody case, "not even the parents have the right to deny an immature child who has been baptized a Roman Catholic the privilege of being reared in Catholicity"); (6) the Church has a legitimate and legally recognizable interest in the faith of its members and has the right to call upon the state to use its machinery to protect that interest and preserve the sovereignty of the Church over its members.

None of these concepts or principles is acceptable to Protestantism,[58] and it was therefore no more than to be expected that the Catholic position was strenuously contested by Protestants. In the Hildy case the Massachusetts Council of Churches urged the Florida governor to base his decision in the extradition primarily on the welfare of the child. Methodist Bishop John Wesley Lord of Boston asserted that superior to the Massachusetts law was "moral judgment [which] must always be the last judge in any matter." "It is," he continued, "moral judgment that, for the welfare and good of this six-year-old adopted daughter, the law be superseded by the divine law of love. . . . This devout Jewish couple, at sacrifice of earthly possessions and with a devotion none can deny, wishes to continue to rear tɭe child in a home in which love and devotion are the paramount factors. No law of the land can supersede moral law." The United Presbyterian Church, in the statement on church and state that has already been referred to,[59] has taken a similar position and has urged that religion or race not be considered in adoptions except where pertinent to temporal benefits.

The United States Supreme Court, although it refused to review the Goldman decision, has never passed upon the constitutionality of a state statute or court decision which barred interreligious adoptions. The principles which it has announced and applied in other cases would seem to require that, when such a case does come before it, the prohibitory statute or decision will be adjudged unconstitutional under both the establishment and free exercise clauses.

## The Secular Education of Children

The judicial responsibility of weighing the conflicting interests of religious liberty and children's welfare has also been presented in cases where the state compulsory school attendance law has been enforced against parents whose religious convictions either forbid their children to receive any secular education, or permit secular education in an amount less than required by the law. In the Pierce and Everson cases the United States Supreme Court assumed the power of the states to require all children to receive a minimum secular education; but the issue was not squarely presented in either of those cases. Nevertheless, by 1951 the states' constitutional power was so clear that the court held an attack on it to be so lacking in merit as not to warrant consideration (though two of the nine justices disagreed and thought the case should be heard).

In People vs. Donner[60] a prosecution for the violation of New York's compulsory education law was brought against the parents of a number of children who attended a small Jewish religious school. The New York law requires all children to receive secular instruction in ten common branches of learning for a period equivalent to the time spent for that purpose in the public schools. In the religious school that they attended the children did not receive instruction in these ten common branches; nor was English the language of instruction, their education consisting entirely of the Bible, the Talmud, and elementary Jewish law.

In their defense the parents asserted that according to their religious belief all systematic, secular education is prohibited as a matter of Jewish law; they therefore asserted that the enforcement of the compulsory school attendance law against them violated their constitutional rights under the First Amendment. In overruling this contention and finding the parents guilty, Domestic Relations Court Justice Hubert T. Delany stated:

> The Court can take judicial notice that practically all Jewish children of school age in the United States receive secular instruction in the public schools, except some who attend Hebrew Parochial schools in which they receive both secular and religious instruction. It seems obvious that Respondents' interpretation of the fundamental Jewish law·is not in accordance with the normal interpretation of almost all Americans of the Hebrew faith. The Court does not question the *bona fides* of

Respondents' belief in this case in their interpretation of the Jewish law of their particular sect, and therefore cannot pass upon the validity of that interpretation. . . .

The United States Supreme Court has been diligent in protecting the right to religious liberty secured by the First Amendment. Some interests which a State would seem to have a right to protect have been held subordinate. Governmental power to prevent fraud, preserve cleanliness of streets, regulate highway traffic, raise revenue and require overt manifestations of loyalty, have in many instances been held subject to restrictions when their exercise interfered with the religious liberty of the people.

On the other hand, the courts have upheld legislative interference with religious liberty where such interference has been found clearly necessary for the protection of society. Since Western society is based upon the monogamous family, the interests of the state in the protection of our total society from polygamy was held superior to the religious conviction of Mormons in plural marriages. The courts have uniformly held that the duty required of every citizen to "support and defend the government against all enemies" takes precedence over certain religious convictions against armed warfare. The State's obligation to preserve peace and orderliness is superior to an individual's religiously motivated conduct which disturbs the peace of the community, and the State's interest in protecting the community from communicable diseases takes precedence over the individual's religious opposition to vaccination. Like illustrations need not be multiplied to show that Respondents' opposition to a secular education on religious grounds, does not necessarily exempt them from the obligations imposed by our Compulsory Education Laws requiring compliance therewith by Respondents. . . .

A restriction of religious liberty, like other liberties guaranteed by the Constitution, has been held by the courts to be justified if it is clearly and immediately necessary to protect our total society against the unrestricted exercise of a religious conviction of a particular sect of a religion.

In all cases where an individual seeks to invoke the protection of the constitutional safeguards of religious liberties the court is faced with the responsibility of weighing the interest of our total society in compelling compliance, as against the interest of our total society in permitting non-compliance.

In this case, therefore, the issue is whether it is more important to our total society, that all children within the realm of our democratic society shall receive a basic secular education in the English language as prescribed in Section 3204 of the Education Law, than that parents whose religious convictions preclude compliance with our secular education laws, shall be permitted to rear their children exclusively in conformance with their religious conviction. If the answer were in the negative, it might leave the door open to all sorts of abuses against society in the name of religion.

It seems clear . . . that the religious convictions of Respondents herein must yield to the total public interest. Compulsory education laws constitute but one of many statutes of a government, dedicated to the democratic ideal, which are universally enacted for the benefit of all of the children within the realm of government. Child labor laws and laws making it criminal to abandon or neglect children, are similar instances of governmental intervention for the protection of children. Religious convictions of parents cannot interfere with the responsibility of the State to protect the welfare of children. . . .

Judge Delany's decision was unanimously affirmed by the Appellate Division and the Court of Appeals, and the United States Supreme Court refused to review it. Its constitutional correctness is hardly open to question.[61] Less clear is the correctness of the decision of the Pennsylvania Supreme Court in an Amish case.[62]

In that case members of the Old Order Amish Church were prosecuted under the Pennsylvania compulsory school attendance law, which requires the secular instruction of children until they reach the age of 17. The Old Order Amish religion, according to a dictate by its ruling bishops, prohibits attendance at secular schools after the attainment of 14 years. The defendants removed their children from the public schools after they had graduated from the elementary grades and had reached the age of 14.

The court sustained the conviction, saying:

> . . . there is no interference with religious liberty where the State reasonably restricts parental control, or compels parents to perform their natural and civic obligations to educate their children. They may be educated in the public schools, in private or denominational schools, or by approved tutors; but educated they must be within the age limits and in the subjects prescribed by law. The life of the Commonwealth — its safety, its integrity, its independence, its progress — and the preservation and enhancement of the democratic way of life, depend upon the enlightened intelligence of its citizens. These fundamental objectives are paramount, and they do not collide with the principles of religious or civil liberty. Unless democracy lives religious liberty cannot survive.

The democratic state unquestionably has a vital interest in the secular education of its children. Unquestionably, too, a child who, through parental neglect or religious conviction, is denied a basic secular education is seriously handicapped throughout life; the interests of society and the welfare of children clearly outweigh the religious liberty of parents. Hence a state may constitutionally compel parents to supply their children with a basic, elementary secular education. When religious convictions oppose only secondary education, it is not so certain that — in view of the high position of the First Amendment in our constitutional democracy — the interest of society in the secondary school education of children clearly outweighs the religious liberty of the almost insignificant number of parents whose religious convictions bar secondary school education for their children.

Even more questionable is a 1950 decision of the same court,[63] in which it sustained the conviction of a Moslem couple who, because of their religious convictions, persistently refused to send their children to public school on Fridays, the sacred day of their religion, although the children attended regularly the other days. The court said:

> Our statute . . . permits attendance at private and parochial schools. All that it requires is continuous attendance at a day-school of the kind and character mentioned in the statute, or daily instruction by a private tutor. Since the parent may avail himself of other schools, including parochial or denominational schools, the statute does not interfere with or impinge upon the religious freedom of parents or the guarantees of either the Federal or State constitution. The requirement is within the constitutional power of the state.
>
> Having exercised the option provided by the statute and elected to send their children to the public schools, appellants are bound to perform all the requirements of the compulsory attendance provisions. They cannot send their children to the public schools under condition that they shall be excused on Fridays. They have no constitutional right to submit to only a part of the statute or to a part of regulations made pursuant to it.

It is extremely doubtful that there were any Moslem parochial schools in Pittsburgh, where the defendants lived; even if there were, they may well not have been able to pay the tuition fees. In a real sense they were probably compelled to send their children to public school, and the "option" the court spoke of was purely fictional. Hence they appear to have had no alternative but to violate their religious convictions or go to jail. It would not have been entirely impracticable for the children to make up the time lost on Fridays, and the disruption of the public school routine could not have been too serious—not more serious than the disruption that accompanies the released-time program. All in all, it may well be doubted that there was such a clear and present danger to a substantial public interest as would justify such a complete overriding of religious liberty.

The same considerations would preclude penalizing Catholic or Jewish parents of children who remain away from school on their holy days in accordance with their religious convictions.[64] Though a closer case is presented by the programs in some schools that require six-day attendance, it would seem clear that penalizing Jews or

Seventh Day Christians for refusing to send their children to school on Saturday would be inconsistent with constitutional guaranties of religious liberty.

## RELIGIOUS LIBERTY AND SOCIAL WELFARE[65]

The church has a long and honorable history in the field of social welfare. Time and time again the Bible commands that provision be made for the poor, the stranger, and the fatherless. From its very beginning the Christian church undertook the responsibility of caring for orphans and foundlings. With the legal recognition of Christianity under Constantine in the 4th century, church institutions for orphans and others in need became widespread throughout the empire, and church responsibility in this area continued through the Middle Ages.[66] In this country, sectarian groups have been first in the field of child welfare.[67] The first private orphan asylum in America was established by the Ursuline Convent in New Orleans in 1727. Today, the majority of institutions in the United States caring for children are operated by denominational groups.[68]

Church-operated institutions for the aged and infirm are also of long standing. Denominational homes for the aged and hospitals for the ill are an accepted part of American life. Today, for example, there are more than 1600 denominational hospitals in the United States.[69]

Beginning in the 19th century, however, government began to recognize its responsibility in areas which for centuries had been the exclusive domain of the churches. By the middle of the 19th century state governments in this country had taken over from the churches major responsibility for the education of the young. To a lesser but still substantial extent, responsibility for maintaining the aged poor and the infirm was assumed by Federal, state, and municipal governments. Still later, government undertook even greater responsibilities in the field of social welfare, enacting social security laws to afford some measure of financial protection against old age, unemployment insurance laws to protect against joblessness, laws for medical care for the aged, and laws aimed at poverty generally, such as the Economic Opportunity Act.

These manifold parallel and often competitive activities of church and state in social welfare have given rise to numerous problems under the no-establishment clause of the First Amendment, particularly out of governmental financing of denominational welfare institutions. These have already been discussed in this volume,[70] but they also give rise to serious questions under the free exercise clause. Is it constitutional, for example, to compel clergymen or persons having religious objection to participate in social security programs? Federal and state laws provide for collective bargaining by workers; can these laws constitutionally permit the discharge of a worker whose religious beliefs preclude joining a labor union?

Fortunately American legislatures, state and Federal, have been sympathetic to claims of religious liberty, and have been generous in enacting exemptions based upon religious belief. Exemptions of conscientious objectors from military service, Sabbatarians from Sunday closing laws, and children of Christian Scientists from school curriculum laws, insofar as they include teaching of the germ theory of disease, are but a few of the many examples that could be cited.

Religious exemptions, however, are not always granted, and where they are not it becomes the responsibility of the courts to decide between the competing claims of social welfare and religious liberty. Thus, the administration of unemployment compensation laws has given rise to one such serious question. Under these laws an unemployed applicant for insurance benefits must be willing to accept suitable employment; if he refuses, he forfeits his right to benefits. The problem has arisen whether a seventh-day observer — Baptist, Adventist, or Jew — who refuses to accept a proffered position that entails work on Saturday thereby forfeits his right to unemployment benefits.

Fortunately the unemployment insurance boards and courts[71] in the overwhelming majority of states have construed their laws not to require forfeiture in cases where the applicant has for religious reasons always abstained from work on Saturday, and is applying for benefits in a locality where it is generally feasible to obtain a suitable position not requiring work on Saturday — though at the particular time no such position is available. In a few states, however, the boards have taken a contrary position, and have disqualified conscientious seventh-day observers.

The issue reached the Supreme Court of Ohio in 1946. In that year the court affirmed a lower court decision that had refused to direct the board to grant benefits to an Orthodox Jewish applicant notwithstanding his refusal to accept a job requiring Saturday work. The lower court disposed of the religious liberty issue in the following statement:[72]

Nothing in the refusal to grant compensation to the plaintiff can be considered in any way an interference with his right to worship in any manner he sees fit or any interference with his rights of conscience. If he wishes to attend his church on Saturday that is his right. No one is attempting to interfere with that constitutional privilege. But what the plaintiff is saying is that, "although my conscience will not permit me to work on Saturday, I should receive the same compensation as if it did not, and that if you refuse to give me such employment compensation, you are discriminating against me." In passing it will be noted that the section of the Constitution referred to also provides "and no preference shall be given by law to any religious society." Only by the employment of inverse logic can the plaintiff claim discrimination in the refusal to grant him unemployment compensation.

If the [plaintiff's contention] be sustained, certainly, there would be discrimination, but in favor of the plaintiff. All other persons except those holding conscientious scruples would be required to accept employment and be barred from such compensation if they did not. Certainly, this could be nothing less than discrimination against them.

The predicament of the plaintiff is not overlooked. He is bound by his conscience to refuse work on Saturday. If work on that day is offered, he feels he must refuse it. If he accepts the work, he, of course, will not be entitled to unemployment compensation. If he refuses the work, then he has denied his availability for it and disqualified himself for compensation.

His solution is to refuse the work and still claim unemployment compensation. This he cannot do, for he has rendered himself not available.

Nothing in section 1, Art. XIV of the Constitution of the United States requires that unemployment compensation be given to one who refuses for any reason to work upon any given day of the week, not excluded by law as a day of labor.

Several years later, an appeal was sought to be taken to the United States Supreme Court from a similar decision,[73] but the court dismissed the appeal for want of a substantial Federal question, thus indicating its opinion of the complete lack of merit in the contention that the statute so applied violated the First Amendment.[74] However, like the Jehovah's Witnesses,[75] the Sabbatarians persisted, and ultimately in the 1963 case of Sherbert vs. Verner[76] their persistence was rewarded.

The case involved a Seventh Day Adventist who was discharged by her employer because, when the plant changed from a five-day to a six-day week, she would not work on Saturday. When she was unable to obtain other employment because of her unwillingness to work Saturday, she filed a claim for unemployment compensation benefits under the compensation law of the state (South Carolina). The law disqualified from benefits a person who "without good cause" refused to take a suitable position offered him. The state unemployment compensation commission ruled the claimant's refusal to accept a position requiring Saturday work was "without good cause" and therefore she was not entitled to unemployment benefits.

The ruling was affirmed by the state courts, and the claimant appealed to the United States Supreme Court.

With two Justices dissenting, the Supreme Court reversed the decision and ruled that the denial of benefits to the claimant constituted an infringement of her constitutional rights under the First Amendment. The disqualification for benefits, the Court held, imposed a burden on the free exercise of religion. The consequence of such a disqualification to religious principles and practices, it continued, may be only an indirect result of the state's action, but this fact does not necessarily render it immune from invalidation under the First Amendment. Here not only was the claimant's declared ineligibility for benefits derived solely from the practice of her religion, but the pressure upon her to forego that practice was unmistakable. The ruling forced her to choose between following the precepts of her religion and forfeiting benefits, on the one hand, and abandoning one of the precepts of her religion in order to accept work, on the other. Governmental imposition of such a choice puts the same kind of burden upon the free exercise of religion as would a fine imposed against the claimant for her Saturday worship, and both are equally unconstitutional.

## The Raising of Revenue

Providing for the general welfare, the common defense, and domestic tranquillity, as well as the other necessary functions of a modern state, requires considerable finances. These finances are raised primarily through the multifarious forms of taxation which the modern state has necessarily evolved to keep pace with the increasing numbers and varieties of state activities. Modern society is pretty well committed to the welfare state; and though the rate of progress toward that end may be slower in the United States than in most other countries less deeply committed to concepts of free economic enterprise, even the most conservative Americans recognize that social security, unemployment and disability insurance, universal education, publicly financed housing, and a variety of other manifestations of the welfare state are here to stay. They, as well as everybody else, recognize that these welfare benefits — and the even greater defense efforts — must be paid for out of tax-raised funds.

In a democratic society the tax burden should be borne by all segments of the community, in proportion to their ability to pay. When therefore a substantial segment of the community claims the right to share in the benefits provided by the community but to be excluded from sharing in the economic burden of providing these benefits, that claim requires careful scrutiny.

It is evident that it will be no easy task to reconcile the conflicting claims of religion to be free of the undeniable restrictions on its free exercise through compulsory taxation with that of the government to funds required for the carrying out of its necessary functions. It is therefore not surprising that the United States Supreme Court has split sharply on the issue, and that the same justices have reached different conclusions at different times.

We have more or less arbitrarily divided the subject of taxation and religion into two parts. The part dealing with the reconciliation of exempting church-owned property from taxation with the principle of the separation of church and state has already been discussed.[77] Here we shall consider the cases that seek to reconcile the state's power of taxation with its constitutional disability to restrict the free exercise of religion. On the basis of this consideration we shall offer some conclusions that we believe tenable.

In Jones vs. Opelika[78] the Supreme Court considered the constitutional validity of the application of city ordinances that impose license taxes on bookselling against Jehovah's Witnesses who were distributing their religious literature. The license taxes, varying in amounts from $10 to $300 a year, were not shown to be so unreasonably high as to interfere seriously with the Witnesses' activities; but the Witnesses refused to pay them on the ground that their sale of their literature constituted an exercise of religion that could not constitutionally be taxed.

In a five to four decision the court sustained the validity of the city's action in enforcing the license tax ordinances against the Witnesses. The majority viewed the Witnesses' action as primarily commercial rather than religious, and therefore subject to the nondiscriminatory taxes on commercial transactions. The majority said:

> When proponents of religious or social theories use the ordinary commercial methods of sales of articles to raise propaganda funds, it is a natural and proper exercise of the power of the state to charge reasonable fees for the privilege of canvassing. Careful as we may and should be to protect the freedoms safeguarded by the Bill of Rights, it is difficult to see in such enactments a shadow of prohibition of the exercise of religion or of abridgment of the freedom of speech or the press. It is prohibition and unjustifiable abridgment which is interdicted, not taxation. Nor do we believe it can be fairly said that because such proper charges may be expanded into unjustifiable abridgments they are therefore invalid on their face. The freedoms claimed by those

seeking relief here are guaranteed against abridgment by the Fourteenth Amendment. Its commands protect their rights. The legislative power of municipalities must yield when abridgment is shown. If we were to assume, as is here argued, that the licensed activities involve religious rites, a different question would be presented. These are not taxes on free will offerings. But it is because we view these sales as partaking more of commercial than religious or education transactions that we find the ordinances, as here presented, valid. A tax on religion or a tax on interstate commerce may alike be forbidden by the Constitution. It does not follow that licenses for selling Bibles or for manufacture of articles of general use, measured by extra-state sales, must fall. It may well be that the wisdom of American communities will persuade them to permit the poor and weak to draw support from the petty sales of religious books without contributing anything for the privilege of using the streets and conveniences of the municipality. Such an exemption, however, would be a voluntary, not a constitutionally enforced, contribution.

Jones vs. Opelika was decided in 1942. In 1943 Justice Byrnes, who had voted with the majority, was succeeded by Justice Rutledge. The issue was again presented to the court in 1943, and this time the court divided five to four against constitutionality. In Murdock vs. Pennsylvania[79] the court held that a tax ranging from $1.50 a day to $20 for three weeks for the privilege of canvassing or soliciting orders for articles could not constitutionally be applied to Witnesses who sold their religious literature from door to door.

It could hardly be denied, the court said, that a tax laid specifically on the exercise of religion would be unconstitutional, yet the license tax imposed by the city of Jeannette was in substance just that. The Witnesses spread their interpretations of the Bible and their religious belief largely through the hand distribution by full- or part-time workers, each of whom is ordained by the society as a minister. They assert that they follow the example of Paul, teaching "publickly, and from house to house" (Acts 20:20), and take literally the mandate of the Scriptures, "Go ye into all the world, and preach the gospel to every creature" (Mark 16:15). In doing so they believe that they are obeying a commandment of God.

The new majority then continued:

> The hand distribution of religious tracts is an age-old form of missionary evangelism—as old as the history of printing presses. It has been a potent force in various religious movements down through the years. This form of evangelism is utilized today on a large scale by various religious sects whose colporteurs carry the Gospel to thousands upon thousands of homes and seek through personal visitations to win adherents to their faith. It is more than preaching; it is more than distribution of religious literature. It is a combination of both. Its purpose

is as evangelical as the revival meeting. This form of religious activity occupies the same high estate under the First Amendment as do worship in the churches and preaching from the pulpits. It has the same claim to protection as the more orthodox and conventional exercises of religion. It also has the same claim as the others to the guarantees of freedom of speech and freedom of the press.

The majority in Jones vs. Opelika had not denied that purely religious practices, like preaching, could not constitutionally be subject to a license tax, but held that because the Witnesses' religious literature was sold the transaction was more commercial than religious and was therefore taxable. In the Murdock case the court met this argument by saying:

> . . . But the mere fact that the religious literature is "sold" by itinerant preachers rather than "donated" does not transform evangelism into a commercial enterprise. If it did, then the passing of the collection plate in church would make the church service a commercial project. The constitutional rights of those spreading their religious beliefs through the spoken and printed word are not to be gauged by standards governing retailers or wholesalers of books. . . . It should be remembered that the pamphlets of Thomas Paine were not distributed free of charge. It is plain that a religious organization needs funds to remain a going concern. But an itinerant evangelist however misguided or intolerant he may be, does not become a mere book agent by selling the Bible or religious tracts to help defray his expenses or to sustain him. Freedom of speech, freedom of the press, freedom of religion are available to all, not merely to those who can pay their own way.

Religious groups, the court stated, are not free from all the financial burdens of government. A tax on the income of one who engages in religious activities or a tax on property used in connection with those activities would be constitutional. But it is one thing to impose a tax on the income or property of a preacher; it is quite another thing to exact a tax from him for the privilege of delivering a sermon. A person cannot be compelled to purchase, through a license fee or a license tax, a privilege that is freely granted by the Constitution. The fact that the tax is nondiscriminatory does not render it constitutional; a license tax does not acquire constitutional validity "because it classifies the privileges protected by the First Amendment along with the wares and merchandise of hucksters and peddlers and treats them all alike. . . . Freedom of press, freedom of speech, freedom of religion are in a preferred position."

The court agreed that the Witnesses' activities could be subject to regulation, such as a registration requirement for the purpose of identification; and that a nominal fee could be imposed for the purpose of defraying the expense of such necessary and proper police measure. What was held unconstitutional was a flat license tax whose payment was a prerequisite to the exercise of religion.

On the same day that the decision in the Murdock case was announced the court reversed its own previous decision in Jones vs. Opelika, and likewise held unconstitutional the ordinances in the city involved in that case. And the next year the court, in Follett vs. Town of McCormick,[80] held that the rule of the Murdock case was applicable even where the Witness is not an itinerant colporteur or evangelist, but resides permanently in the town that has imposed the license tax, and earns his livelihood exclusively by selling religious literature. Preachers of the more orthodox faiths, the court pointed out, are not engaged in commercial undertakings merely because they are dependent on their calling for a living, nor because they reside permanently in the community in which they preach, and the same is constitutionally true of such unorthodox faiths as that of Jehovah's Witnesses.

On the other hand the court in 1950 refused to review a decision of the Circuit Court of Appeals that upheld the constitutionality of the action of the State of California in applying a general uniform tax statute against the religious pamphlets and books of Jehovah's Witnesses. The Circuit Court, following the Supreme Court dictum in the Murdock case, held that the imposition of a general uniform ad valorem property tax, for revenue purposes only, on religious literature does not violate the First Amendment guaranties of the freedom of religion and of the press.[81]

On the basis of these decisions and our previous discussions, the following would appear to be reasonable propositions with respect to the constitutional aspects of religion and taxation.

(1) The exemption of religious groups from the taxation of property is a fairly universal practice throughout the United States. Although its constitutionality under the principle of the separation of church and state is arguable, the practice is so well established that it is unlikely that the courts — including the United States Supreme Court — would disturb it if the issue were presented for judicial determination.

(2) The exemption is a matter of grace, not of constitutional right. A state is free to withdraw the exemption at any time; and as long as a property tax is not discriminatory against religious groups its constitutionality is hardly open to question. Church buildings — no less than office buildings — receive police and fire protection, and may be required, through real property taxation, to pay their share of the cost of these services. There can therefore be no doubt as to

the right of the state to limit (as they generally do) tax exemption to property used exclusively for religious purposes, and to exclude from that exemption property used for commercial purposes—even though its income be used exclusively for religious purposes.

(3) Exclusively religious practices, such as preaching or performing mass, may not be taxed, even under a nondiscriminatory tax law.

(4) Practices that are primarily religious, such as the evangelical sale of religious tracts, are likewise immune from taxation, even though they are income-producing, and the income inures to the benefit of an individual who earns his livelihood by engaging in the practice.

(5) Religious practices that are constitutionally subject to nondiscriminatory regulation in the interest of public order or safety, such as the requirement of obtaining a license to conduct a (religious) parade on the public streets, may be taxed a "nominal" amount to help defray the cost of such regulation.

(6) Purely commercial transactions engaged in by churches and religious groups, such as operating an ordinary business, are subject to nondiscriminatory license taxes even if the profits are used exclusively for religious purposes.

(7) The income of clergymen or others who earn their livelihood solely through the practice of religion is subject to general nondiscriminatory income tax laws.

# Ten Theses

AT THE CONCLUSION OF THIS STUDY I offer the following ten theses, which, I believe, find reasonable support in this volume.

(1) Probably ever since the institutions of religion and of secular powers were recognized as separate and distinct in human history, the two forces have competed for and struggled over human destiny. In this struggle the church has sought to dominate the state and use it as an engine for its purposes, and the state has sought to dominate the church and use it as an engine for its purposes.

(2) During temporary periods of history and in scattered areas, the church has dominated the state; but overwhelmingly in time and place, state has dominated church and used it for its own purposes.

(3) Before the launching of the American experiment, the concept of religious liberty and the separation of church and state was — for all practical purposes — unknown. The experiment embodied in the majestic words, "Congress shall make no law respecting an establishment of religion or prohibiting the free exercise thereof," was a uniquely American contribution to civilization, and one that the other countries of the world in increasing numbers have emulated and are continuing to emulate.

(4) The principle of separation and freedom was conceived as a unitary principle. Notwithstanding occasional instances of apparent conflict, separation guarantees freedom, and freedom requires separation. The experiences in other countries indicate clearly that religious freedom is most secure where church and state are separated, and least secure where church and state are united.

(5) The principle of separation and freedom was conceived to be as absolute as possible within the limitation of human communal society. Only where they were unavoidably necessary to prevent an immediate and grave danger to the security or welfare of the community were infringements on religious freedom to be justifiable, and only to the smallest extent necessary to avoid the danger. Likewise the separation aspect was conceived to be as absolute as could be achieved, predicated as it was on the concept that religion is outside the jurisdiction of government.

(6) When the constitutional fathers and the generation that

727

adopted the Constitution formalized the concept in the First Amendment, they thereby imposed—and intended to impose—on future generations of Americans in church and state a great moral obligation to preserve their experiment and adhere strictly to the principle they expressed. They were fully familiar with the religious wars, the persecutions, and all the other evils that had inevitably accompanied unions of church and state, and sought forever to keep those evils from our shores.

(7) Since man is imperfect, and does not lose all his imperfection when he enters the service of church or state, there have been deviations from the principle. Religious freedom has on occasions been interfered with, and the separation of church and state has on occasions been impaired. These impairments have incorrectly been urged as evidence that it was not the intent of the framers of the First Amendment that the principle be absolute and the separation complete.

(8) These impairments of the principle of absolute separation have inevitably brought with them, in greater or lesser degree, the very evils that the constitutional fathers sought to keep from the new republic; particularly when the impairments have occurred in the area of public education have the evils of interreligious disharmony and oppression been manifest.

(9) Nevertheless the American people have by and large been faithful to the obligation placed on them by the framers of the First Amendment; church and state have been kept separate, and religious freedom has been preserved. The people have willingly kept faith; whenever an opportunity has presented itself to obtain an expression of the voice of the people, that voice has clearly been expressed on the side of absolute separation and freedom.

(10) Under this system of the separation of church and state and religious freedom, religion has achieved in the United States a high estate unequalled anywhere else in the world. History has justified the great experiment, and has proved the proposition on which it was based—that complete separation of church and state is best for church and best for state, and secures freedom for both.

# Notes

### FOREWORD

1. Field, David Dudley, "American Progress" in *Jurisprudence*, New York, Martin B. Brown, 1893, p. 6.
2. Black, Jeremiah S., *Essays and Speeches*, New York, D. Appleton and Co., 1885, p. 53.

### CHAPTER ONE
### *Old World Antecedents*

1. Wieman, Henry Nelson, and Horton, Walter M., *The Growth of Religion*, Chicago, Willett, Clark & Co., 1938, p. 22.
2. *Ibid.*, p. 29.
3. Hopkins, E. Washburn, *Origin and Evolution of Religion*, New Haven, Yale University Press, 1923, pp. 68, 206.
4. Genesis 14:18.
5. Hopkins, p. 221.
6. *Cambridge Ancient History*, New York, Macmillan Co., 1928, I, pp. 512–528.
7. Clemen, Carl, *Religions of the World*, New York, Harcourt, Brace & Co., 1931, p. 47.
8. *Ibid.*, p. 61.
9. *Against Apion*, Book II, paragraph 17, in *Complete Works of Josephus*, New York, World Syndicate Publishing Co., X, p. 500.
10. Clemen, p. 44.
11. *Ibid.*, pp. 46–47.
12. Northcott, Cecil, *Religious Liberty*, New York, The Macmillan Co., 1949, p. 24.
13. Ruffini, Francesco, *Religious Liberty*, London, Williams & Norgate, 1912, p. 19. The point is also made by Guido de Ruggiero in his article on "Religious Freedom" in the *Encyclopaedia of Social Sciences*, New York, The Macmillan Co., 1942, XIII, p. 243.
14. Baron, Salo, *A Social and Religious History of the Jews*, New York, Columbia University Press, 1937, I, pp. 133-137.
15. "Proselyte," *Jewish Encyclopaedia*, New York and London, Funk & Wagnalls, 1905, p. 223.
16. Moore, George Foot, *Judaism*, Cambridge, Harvard University Press, 1946, II, p. 386.
17. *Encyclopaedia Britannica*, Socrates, 14th ed., XX, p. 916.
18. Exodus 32:28.
19. 1 Samuel 16:2.
20. 1 Kings 2:35.
21. Baron, I, p. 55.
22. 1 Kings 12:26–33.
23. Acton, Lord, "The History of Freedom in Antiquity," in *Essays on Freedom and Power*, Boston, Beacon Press, 1949, p. 33.

24. Baron, I, p. 65.
25. 2 Kings 22:8 – 23:3.
26. Baron, I, p. 158.
27. *Ibid.*, p. 165.
28. Nilsson, Martin P., *A History of Greek Religion*, London, Oxford University Press, 1925, pp. 242 – 244.
29. Reinach, Salomon, *Orpheus*, New York, Horace Liveright, 1930, p. 96.
30. Clemen, p. 186.
31. Nilsson, pp. 247 – 248.
32. Clemen, p. 193.
33. Nilsson, p. 266.
34. *Ibid.*
35. Clemen, p. 187.
36. Gowen, Herbert H., *A History of Religion*, London, Society for Promoting Christian Knowledge, 1934, pp. 283 – 285.
37. Kellett, E. E., *A Short History of Religions*, New York, Dodd, Mead & Co., 1934, p. 108.
38. Gowen, p. 286; Kellett, p. 110.
39. Kellett, pp. 112 – 113.
40. Wieman, pp. 134 – 135.
41. Kellett, p. 114.
42. Wieman, p. 135.
43. *History of Christianity in the Light of Modern Knowledge*, London, Blackie & Son, 1929, p. 464.
44. Walker, Williston, *A History of the Christian Church*, New York, Charles Scribner's Sons, 1940, p. 48.
45. *History of Christianity*, pp. 464 – 465.
46. *Ibid.*, p. 468.
47. Walker, p. 49.
48. *Ibid.*
49. *History of Christianity*, pp. 471 – 472.
50. *Ibid.*, pp. 475, 478.
51. Walker, p. 108.
52. *Ibid.*
53. *History of Christianity*, p. 481.
54. Bates, M. Searle, *Religious Liberty: An Inquiry*, New York and London, International Missionary Council, 1945, p. 134.
55. *Ibid.*
56. *Ibid.*, pp. 135 – 136.
57. *Ibid.*, p. 137. Compare Thomas Jefferson's statement fifteen centuries later: ". . . it does me no injury for my neighbor to say there are twenty gods, or no God. It neither picks my pocket nor breaks my leg." "Notes on Virginia," in Blau, Joseph L., *Cornerstones of Religious Freedom in America*, Boston, Beacon Press, 1949, p 78.
58. Bates, pp. 137 – 138.
59. *Ibid.*, p. 139.
60. Ruffini, p. 36.
61. Carlyle, Alexander J., *The Christian Church and Liberty*, London, J. Clarke, 1924, p. 96.
62. Bates, p. 140.

63. *Encyclopaedia Britannica*, "Charles the Great," 14th ed., V, p. 258.
64. Bates, p. 140.
65. Noss, John B., *Man's Religions*, New York, The Macmillan Co., 1949, pp. 645–646.
66. *Ibid.*, p. 646.
67. *Encyclopaedia Britannica*, "Stephen Langton," 14th ed., XIII, p. 695.
68. Bates, pp. 140–141.
69. *Encyclopaedia Britannica*, 14th ed., XIII, p. 695.
70. *Encyclopaedia Britannica*, "Papacy," 14th ed., XVII, p. 203.
71. Noss, p. 652–658.
72. *Encyclopaedia Britannica*, "Marsilius of Padua," 14th ed., XIV, p. 973.
73. Acton, "History of Freedom in Christianity," in *Essays on Freedom and Power*, pp. 64-65.
74. *Ibid.*, p. 65.
75. Ruffini, pp. 43–44.
76. Bates, pp. 142–143.
77. *Ibid.*
78. *Encyclopaedia Britannica*, "Inquisition," 14th ed., XII, pp. 377–383.
79. Sweet, William Warren, *Religion in Colonial America*, New York, Charles Scribner's Sons, 1942, p. 320.
80. Bates, p. 155.
81. Acton, "The Protestant Theory of Persecution," in *Essays on Freedom and Power*, p. 92.
82. Wace, Henry, and Bucheim, C.A., *Luther's Primary Works*, Lutheran Publication Society, Philadelphia, 1885, pp. 194-195, quoted in Noss, p. 661.
83. Acton, p. 103.
84. *Ibid.*, p. 102.
85. *Ibid.*, pp. 103–105.
86. *Ibid.*, p. 100.
87. *Ibid.*, p. 106.
88. *Ibid.*, pp. 112–113.
89. *Institutes of the Christian Religion*, quoted in Stokes, Anson Phelps, *Church and State in the United States*, New York, Harper & Brothers, 1950, I, p. 110.
90. Bates, p. 157.
91. *Ibid.*
92. Quoted in Stokes, I, p. 100.
93. *Ibid.*, p. 101.
94. *Ibid.*, p. 113.
95. *Encyclopaedia of Social Sciences*, "Religious Freedom."
96. *Ibid.*
97. Bates, pp. 163–164.
98. *Encyclopaedia of Social Sciences*, XIII, p. 243.
99. Garbett, Cyril (Archbishop of York), *Church and State in England*, London, Hodder & Stoughton, 1950, p. 93.
100. Noss, pp. 674, 675.
101. Garbett, pp. 61–62.
102. *Ibid.*, p. 63.
103. *Encyclopaedia of Social Sciences*, XIII, p. 243.

104. Bates, p. 172.
105. Quoted in Stokes, I, p. 122.
106. Jordan, Wilbur K, *The Development of Religious Toleration in England*, London, Allen & Unwin, 1938, III, p. 146.
107. *Encyclopaedia of Social Sciences*, XIII, p. 243.
108. Stokes, I, p. 132.
109. *Encyclopaedia of Social Sciences*, XIII, p. 243.
110. People ex rel. Everson vs. Board of Education, 330 U.S. 1 (1947).
111. Blau, p. 85.

CHAPTER TWO
## The Solution in Other Countries

1. Bates, p. 18.
2. *Religious News Service*, Feb. 11, 1952.
3. *Statesman's Year-Book* (1963 – 1964), pp. 1425, 1426.
4. Bates, pp. 18 – 19; Castiella, Fernando M., "Non-Catholics in Spain," *America*, August 24, 1963.
5. See, *e.g., Ibid.*, "Letter to the Editor," Dr. Roderick Wheeler, Editor of *The Americas*, New York *Times*, September 20, 1948; article in *The Tablet* (official organ of the Brooklyn diocese), March 5, 1949; article in *The Pilot* (official organ of the Boston diocese), March 12, 1949; "Letter to the Editor," Manuel Maestro, Spanish Embassy Press Attaché, New York *Herald Tribune*, March 20, 1949; *Religious News Service*, May 20, 1963.
6. Cavalli, F., S.J., *The Position of the Protestants in Spain*, quoted in *Information Service*, Federal Council of Churches of Christ in America, October 29, 1949.
7. Garrison, W.E., "Religious Liberty in Spain," *The Christian Century*, October 18, 1950, p. 1234. See also, generally, Hughey, J.O., *Religious Freedom in Spain*, Nashville, Broadman Press, 1955; Blanshard, Paul, *Freedom and Catholic Power in Spain and Portugal*, Boston, Beacon Press, 1962.
8. New York *Times*, February 8, 1951.
9. *Information Service*, October 29, 1949; New York *Herald Tribune*, February 23, 1949.
10. Pattee, Richard, *The Protestant Question in Spain*, Washington, D.C., National Catholic Welfare Conference, March 4, 1949.
11. *Religious News Service*, March 24, 1949.
12. New York *Times*, February 8, 1951.
13. *The Christian Century*, August 23, 1952, p. 966.
14. New York *Times*, March 10, 1952, p. 1; March 13, 1952, p. 10.
15. New York *Times*, May 11, 12, 1952; *Religious News Service*, August 18, 1952.
16. Garrison, p. 1234.
17. New York *Herald Tribune*, February 23, 1949.
18. Garrison, p. 1234; *Religious News Service*, May 17, 1949; *The Christian Century*, August 23, 1952, p. 966.
19. *Religious News Service*, June 19, 1950.
20. *Religious News Service*, September 23, 1952.
21. Garrison, p. 1234; *Information Service*, October 29, 1949.

22. *Information Service; The Pilot* (official organ of Boston Archdiocese), June 11, 1949, p. 1.
23. New York *Times*, February 8, 1951.
24. Garrison, p. 1234; *Information Service*, National Council of the Churches of Christ, January 13, 1951.
25. New York *Times*, June 19, 1955.
26. *Religious News Service*, February 23, 1962.
27. Garrison, p. 1234.
28. New York *Herald Tribune*, February 23, 1949.
29. Bates, p. 20.
30. *Ibid.; The Tablet*, February 4, 1950, p. 1.
31. *The Tablet*, February 4, 1950.
32. New York *Times*, February 11, 1952.
33. *Ibid.*, June 13, 1950.
34. *Ibid.*, February 8, 1951.
35. Castiella, *op. cit.*
36. New York *Times*, May 3, 1959.
37. *Religious News Service*, February 14, 1963, June 27, 1963, January 29, 1964, February 21, 1964.
38. *Religious News Service*, November 8, 1963.
39. *Religious News Service*, February 13, 1964.
40. *Religious News Service*, July 6, 1964.
41. *Religious News Service*, January 24, 1951, April 18, 1951.
42. Bates, p. 98.
43. *Religious News Service*, March 29, 1949.
44. Bates, p. 98.
45. *Ibid.*, p. 515.
46. *Documents and State Papers*, United States Department of State, April, 1948, pp. 46 *et seq.*
47. *Ibid.*
48. Attwood, William, "Church and State in Italy," *The Nation*, August 28, 1948, p. 223.
49. Bates, p. 43.
50. *Ibid.*, pp. 22–23.
51. Chicago *Daily Tribune*, November 1, 1951; New York *Times*, December 31, 1957; *Religious News Service*, December 31, 1958.
52. *Religious News Service*, July 20, 1956; July 10, 1959.
53. *Religious News Service*, March 23, 1959.
54. *Religious News Service*, February 27, 1951, September 25, 1951, December 24, 1951.
55. Chicago *Daily Tribune*, November 1, 1951; *Religious News Service*, September 16, 1952.
56. New York *Times*, September 15, 16, 1952; *Religious News Service*, September 15, 16, 25, 1952.
57. *Religious News Service*, May 29, 1953; December 1, 1953; November 12, 1954; June 25, 1956; March 19, 1957; New York *Times*, November 25, 1958.
58. Attwood, p. 223.
59. Letter of Pope Pius XI to Cardinal Gasparri, May 30, 1929, *Current History*, August, 1929, pp. 846–851.

60. Binchy, Daniel A., *Church and State in Fascist Italy*, London, Oxford University Press, 1941, p. 593.
61. New York *Times*, January 8, 1950, p. 1.
62. *The Catholic News*, January 14, 1950, p. 1.
63. *Treaty and Concordat between the Holy See and Italy*, National Catholic Welfare Conference, Washington, D.C., 1929, pp. 79–80.
64. Bates, p. 48.
65. Attwood, p. 223.
66. Chicago *Daily Tribune*, November 1, 1951.
67. *The Tablet*, July 2, 1964.
68. Constitution of Ireland, enacted July 1, 1937, Government Publications Sales Office, Dublin, 1945.
69. Bates, p. 106.
70. *Ibid.*
71. *Religious News Service*, August 4, 1950, August 11, 1950.
72. *Ibid.*
73. *Religious News Service*, January 25, 1956.
74. Bates, p. 106.
75. *Religious News Service*, February 21, 1950. For a more critical view of church and state in Ireland, see Blanshard, Paul, *The Irish and Catholic Power*, Boston, Beacon Press, 1953, particularly Chapter 4.
76. Quoted in Macfarland, Charles S., *Chaos in Mexico: Conflict of Church and State*, New York, Harper and Brothers, 1935, p. 237.
77. Mecham, J. Lloyd, *Church and State in Latin America*, Chapel Hill, University of North Carolina Press, 1934, p. 402.
78. Bates, p. 62.
79. *Religious Liberty in Mexico, Report of a Deputation to Mexico*, American Committee on Religious Rights and Minorities, September, 1935, p. 5.
80. Macfarland, p. 247–252.
81. Fitzgibbon, Russell H., *The Constitution of the Americas*, Chicago, University of Chicago Press, 1948, p. 505.
82. *Ibid.*, p. 507.
83. *Religious Liberty in Mexico*, p. 11.
84. Fitzgibbon, p. 550.
85. *Religious Liberty in Mexico*, p. 12.
86. *Ibid.*, pp. 13–14; Fitzgibbon, pp. 500, 550–552.
87. Fitzgibbon, pp. 498–499.
88. Bates, pp. 71–72.
89. New York *Times*, February 20, 1952, p. 12.
90. *Ibid.; Religious News Service*, December 26, 1950.
91. Mecham, p. 193.
92. Fitzgibbon, pp. 676, 681.
93. *Ibid.*, pp. 673, 693.
94. Mecham, pp. 193–219.
95. Fitzgibbon, pp. 680, 684.
96. Howard, George P., *Religious Liberty in Latin America?* Philadelphia, Westminster Press, 1944, p. 79; Mecham, pp. 246–274.
97. Mecham, pp. 354–359; Fitzgibbon, p. 234.
98. *Religious News Service*, March 14, 1963; December 19, 1963.
99. Dewart, Leslie, "The Church in Cuba: A Universal Dilemma," *The*

*Commonweal*, October 11, 1963.

100. New York *Times*, April 2, 1952; January 23, 1956; January 24, 1964; *Religious News Service*, September 12, 1952.

101. *The Tablet*, May 14, 1955; New York *Times*, May 14, 1955, July 10, 1955; *The Pilot*, May 7, 1955.

102. *Religious News Service*, October 19, 1955, November 14, 1955, December 14, 1955, October 10, 1961.

103. Bates, p. 88; "Religious Instruction in the Schools of Canada," *Information Service*, October 20, 1951; Regulations and Programme for Religious Education in the Public Schools, issued by Ontario Minister of Education, 1949; Phillips, C.E., "Religion and our Public Schools," pamphlet published by Ethical Education Association, Toronto, 1961; New York *Journal American*, July 17, 1961; *Canadian Jewish Weekly*, March 9, 1961, Toronto *Daily Star*, February 10, 1959, February 14, 1959; *Religious News Service*, January 18, 1957, April 15, 1961, May 9, 1961, November 24, 1961.

104. Toronto *Daily Star*, October 29, 1962; *The Tablet*, April 22, 1961; *America*, June 13, 1964; *Religious News Service*, November 1, 1962, November 15, 1962, December 18, 1962, February 12, 1963, February 25, 1963, July 12, 1963, October 18, 1963.

105. *Information Service*, October 20, 1951; Brickman, William W., and Lehrer, Stanley, ed., *Religion, Education and Government*, New York, Society for the Advancement of Education, 1961, pp. 241–245.

106. Goldstick, Isidore, "Where Jews Can't Pray," *Contemporary Jewish Record*, VI, pp. 587–597 (1943).

107. *Religious News Service*, October 26, 1951, December 24, 1951.

108. *Ibid.*, November 14, 1951.

109. *Ibid.*, November 16, 1951.

110. *Ibid.*, June 18, 1952; New York *Times*, June 18, 1952.

111. *Religious News Service*, October 31, 1950.

112. *Ibid.*, August 22, 1951.

113. See Sissons, C.B., *Church and State in Canadian Education: An Historical Study*, Toronto, Ryerson Press, 1959.

114. Fitzgibbon, p. 123.

115. *Religious News Service*, June 29, 1950.

116. This and the succeeding paragraphs are based on reports of the Canadian Jewish Congress; article by A.H.J. Zeitlin, in *The Menorah*, March 5, 1951, publication of the Mount Royal Lodge of B'nai B'rith; report of Committee Appointed to Study the Outremont School Situation, of the Quebec Federation of Home and School Associations, March 28, 1947; and pamphlet of the Inter-Racial Committee for Democratic Action, *Race Discrimination in Education*, February 4, 1946. See also *The Churchman*, March 15, 1952, p. 19.

117. New York *Times*, October 7, 1956.

118. *Ibid.*

119. *The Pilot*, March 23, 1963.

120. *Religious News Service*, April 3, 1962.

121. New York *Times*, February 9, 1964.

122. See *e.g.*, Justice Frankfurter's concurring opinion in People ex rel. McCollum vs. Board of Education, 333 US 203 (1948); Corwin, Ed-

735

ward S., *A Constitution of Powers in a Secular State*, Charlottesville, Va., Michie Co., 1951, p. 114.

123. See discussion of this point *infra*, p. 354.
124. See *infra*, pp. 105 ff.
125. Bates, pp. 87 – 88.
126. Garbett, p. 5.
127. *Ibid.*, pp. 119 – 120.
128. *Church and State*, Report of the Archbishop's Commission on the Relations between Church and State (1935) I, p. 41.
129. Garbett, p. 120.
130. *Ibid.*, p. 146.
131. Hope, Norman V., "Church and State: The Scottish Solution," *The Christian Century*, August 18, 1948, pp. 826 – 828.
132. *Religious News Service*, January 25, 1952.
133. *The Christian Century*, February 13, 1952, p. 180.
134. New York *Herald Tribune*, November 16, 1955.
135. *Religious News Service*, July 13, 1961.
136. *Ibid.*, November 18, 1955, December 8, 1955.
137. *Ibid.*, December 21, 1962.
138. Garbett, pp. 123 – 127, 148 – 149.
139. *Religious News Service*, July 9, 1962.
140. *Ibid.*, December 21, 1962.
141. Garbett, pp. 135 – 137.
142. Brickman and Lehrer, p. 159; Giannella, Donald A., ed., *Religion and the Public Order*, Chicago, University of Chicago Press, 1964, pp. 176 – 181.
143. *Religious News Service*, July 27, 1962.
144. See below pp. 64–65.
145. See, *e.g.*, "Letter to the Editor" Dr. Roderick Wheeler, New York *Times*, September 20, 1948; *The Tablet*, December 3, 1949, p. 1.
146. *Religious News Service*, June 5, 1951, January 4, 1952; New York *Times*, June 17, 1949.
147. Bates, p. 524.
148. *Religious News Service*, June 5, 1951.
149. Bates, pp. 108, 524.
150. New York *Times*, September 9, 1962; *Religious News Service*, September 11, 1962.
151. Bates, p. 332.
152. *Religious News Service*, January 4, 1952.
153. *Ibid.*, February 6, 1952.
154. *Ibid.*
155. New York *Times*, September 9, 1962.
156. Constitution of Norway, Royal Norwegian Government Information Office, p. 1.
157. *Religious News Service*, November 1, 1956.
158. Constitution of Denmark, State Minister's Department.
159. Bates, pp. 108 – 109, 332, 523 – 524.
160. Constitution of the French Republic, French Press and Information Service, New York, p. 2.
161. *Ibid.*, p. 1.

162. *Infra*, pp. 496 ff.
163. Bates, p. 343.
164. New York *Times*, September 10, 22, 1951.
165. Brickman and Lehrer, p. 172.
166. Bates, p. 508.
167. Brickman and Lehrer, pp. 174–175.
168. Bates, p. 331.
169. Vandenbosch, Amry, and Eldersveld, Samuel J., *Government of the Netherlands*, Bureau of Government Research, University of Kentucky, 1947, p. 136.
170. Reller, Theodore L., "Public Funds for Religious Education," in Giannella, p. 187.
171. *Ibid.*, p. 189.
172. *Ibid.*
173. *Ibid.* For a more sympathetic view of the Dutch system, see Brickman and Lehrer, pp. 175–183.
174. Bates, pp. 110, 507.
175. *Religious News Service*, June 21, 1949.
176. Knauth, Theodore W., "The Church and State in Germany," New York *Herald Tribune*, April 20, 1950, editorial page.
177. New York *Herald Tribune*, January 20, 1949.
178. New York *Times*, March 27, 1957; *The Pilot*, June 10, 1961.
179. Knauth.
180. Lewis, Harold O., *New Constitutions in Occupied Germany*, Washington, D.C., Foundation for Foreign Affairs, 1948, p. 29.
181. *Basic Law for the Federal Republic of Germany*, Military Government, Bonn, Germany, May, 1949.
182. Bates, p. 7.
183. Northcott, p. 54.
184. Wood, H.G., *Religious Liberty Today*, Cambridge, England, University Press, 1949, pp. 39–40; Spinka, Matthew, *The Church in Soviet Russia*, New York, Oxford University Press, 1956, pp. 80–82.
185. Northcott, pp. 56–57; Wood, pp. 40–41; Bates, p. 7.
186. Northcott, p. 57.
187. *Information Bulletin*, Embassy of USSR, Washington, D.C., 1947, p. 34. See also, *Freedom of Religion in the USSR* (pamphlet), *USSR Information Bulletin*, Washington, D.C., December, 1951.
188. The text of the agreement, as released by the National Catholic Welfare Conference, was printed in *The Pilot* (organ of Boston Archdiocese), May 13, 1950.
189. New York *Times*, October 25, 1950. See also, Gsovski, Vladimir, ed., *Church and State Behind the Iron Curtain*, New York, Frederick A. Praeger, 1955, pp. 199–203.
190. *Religious News Service*, March 30, 1951.
191. *Ibid.*, December 10, 1956; New York *Times*, December 1, 1956; Chicago *Sun-Times*, December 8, 1956.
192. *Religious News Service*, March 20, 1961.
193. New York *Times*, January 31, 1957, March 19, 1957.
194. *Religious News Service*, June 4, 1964.
195. New York *Times*, August 31, 1950; Gsovski, pp. 107–108.

196. *Religious News Service*, October 7, 1948; Gsovski, pp. 102–103.
197. Rumania: *Religious News Service*, July 10, 1950, October 11, 1950, April 6, 1951; Czechoslovakia: *Religious News Service*, December 4, 1950, January 15, 1951, July 16, 1951; Gsovski, pp. 39–40; Bulgaria: *Religious News Service*, December 12, 1949, December 27, 1950; *Information Service*, Federal Council of Churches, June 18, 1949; Albania: *Religious News Service*, August 6, 1951, Gsovski, pp. 27–28, 275.
198. "The Churches in Czechoslovakia," *Christianity and Crisis*, February 20, 1950, pp. 11–13; *Religious News Service*, August 6, 1951.
199. Constitution of the Federal Peoples Republic of Yugoslavia, Yugoslav Embassy, Washington, D.C., 1946, p. 13; New York *World-Telegram and Sun*, April 6, 1951; "Church and State," *Yugoslav Review*, March, 1952, p. 12.
200. See, generally, Solberg, Richard W., *God and Caesar in East Germany*, New York, Macmillan Co., 1961.
201. Bates, pp. 9–10; Wood, pp. 110–113; Northcott, pp. 87–91.
202. *Ibid.*
203. *The Catholic Messenger*, February 18, 1950.
204. *Religious News Service*, July 6, July 24, September 10, 1956.
205. *Ibid.*, December 19, 1951.
206. *Ibid.*, July 18, 1961.
207. New York *Times*, December 26, 1949; Bates, p. 13.
208. Bates, p. 511. See, generally, Badi, Joseph, *Religion in Israel Today: The Relation between State and Religion*, New York, Bookman Associates, 1959.
209. *Religious News Service*, March 29, 1949; June 23, 1950.
210. *Time*, June 13, 1949; *The Sentinel* (Chicago), March 10, 1949.
211. *Religious News Service*, August 8, 1949.
212. *Ibid.*, December 12, 1950.
213. *Ibid.*, July 17, 1961, March 10, June 25, 1964.
214. New York *Times*, May 22, 1958.
215. *Religious News Service*, October 17, 1951, February 25, 1963; New York *Times*, October 15, 1961.
216. *Religious News Service*, December 2, 1949.
217. The Constitution of India, Government of India, New Delhi, 1949, Articles 25–30, pp. 13–15; *Religious News Service*, September 11, 1962.
218. Bates, pp. 119–121; Northcott, pp. 83, 97.
219. *Religious News Service*, October 6, 1949, December 7, 1949.
220. *Ibid.*, October 4, 1949.
221. Bates, pp. 50–51.
222. U.S. Department of State, Publication 2836, Far Eastern Series 22.

### CHAPTER THREE
#### The Colonial Period in America

1. Beard, Charles A. and Mary R., *The Rise of American Civilization*, New York, The Macmillan Co., 1947, I, pp. 9–10.
2. Goodman, Abram Vossen, *American Overture*, Philadelphia, Jewish Publication Society, 1947, p. 83.
3. Mecklin, John M., *The Story of American Dissent*, New York, Harcourt,

Brace & Co., 1934, p. 201.

4. Greene, Evarts B., *Religion and the State*, New York, New York University Press, 1941, pp. 24−25.
5. People ex rel. Everson vs. Board of Education, 330 U.S. 1.
6. Beard, I, p. 30.
7. Cobb, Sanford H., *The Rise of Religious Liberty in America*, New York, The Macmillan Co., 1902, pp. 70−71.
8. Cobb, p. 139.
9. Jordan, II, p. 21.
10. Bates, p. 155.
11. Cobb, pp. 138−140; Greene, p. 37.
12. *Ibid.*
13. Greene, p. 39.
14. Cobb, p. 174.
15. *Ibid.*, pp. 176−177.
16. Stokes, I, p. 172.
17. *Dictionary of American Biography*, IX, p. 436.
18. Stokes, I, pp. 176−178; Sweet, pp. 92−94.
19. Stokes, I, p. 177.
20. Clinchy, Everett R., *All in the Name of God*, New York, John Day & Co., 1934, p. 27.
21. *Ibid.*; Cobb, pp. 191−194; Sweet, pp. 92−94.
22. Stokes, I, p. 195.
23. Cobb, p. 216.
24. Myers Gustavus, *History of Bigotry in the United States*, New York, Random House, 1943, p. 5.
25. Cobb, p. 217; Sweet, pp. 146−147.
26. Myers, p. 81; Cobb, p. 177.
27. Cobb, p. 233.
28. Greene, pp. 44−45.
29. Greene, p. 32; Beard, I, p. 10.
30. Stokes, I, p. 164.
31. Cobb, p. 78.
32. *Ibid.*, p. 79.
33. Greene, p. 33−35.
34. *Ibid.*, p. 64.
35. *Ibid.*, pp. 59−60; Cobb, pp. 116−117.
36. Cobb, pp. 311−312.
37. *Ibid.*, p. 315.
38. Goodman, p. 72.
39. Cobb, pp. 313−314.
40. *Ibid.*, pp. 317−318.
41. Goodman, p. 73.
42. Butts, R. Freeman, *The American Tradition in Religion and Education*, Boston, Beacon Press, 1950, p. 27.
43. Cobb, pp. 326−327.
44. *Ibid.*, pp. 333−334, 338−340, 361.
45. *Ibid.*, pp. 408−418.
46. *Ibid*, pp. 418−421
47. Beard, I, p. 60.

48. Greene, p. 53.
49. Beard, I, pp. 60–61.
50. *Ibid.,* p. 61.
51. Greene, p. 54.
52. Cobb, p. 372.
53. Clinchy, p. 40.
54. *Ibid.,* p. 41.
55. Cobb, p. 373.
56. "Religious Freedom," *Encyclopaedia of Social Sciences.*
57. Beard, I, p. 63.
58. *Ibid.,* pp. 63–64; Stokes, I, p. 191.
59. Beard, I, p. 64.
60. *American State Papers on Freedom in Religion,* Washington, D.C., Religious Liberty Association, 1949, pp. 43–47.
61. Goodman, pp. 141–143.
62. *Ibid.,* pp. 138–139.
63. Myers, Chap. II.
64. Stokes, I, pp. 193–194.
65. Beard, I, p. 65.
66. Stokes, I, p. 195.
67. Greene, p. 47.
68. *Ibid.,* p. 51.
69. *American State Papers,* p. 53.
70. Greene, p. 51.
71. Blau, pp. 50–51.
72. Greene, p. 51.
73. Blau, p. 43.
74. Parrington, Vernon, *Main Currents in American Thought,* New York, Harcourt, Brace & Co., 1930, I, p. 62.
75. Quoted in Ernst, James, *The Political Thought of Roger Williams,* p. 244; Mecklin, p. 89.
76. Justice Brewer, in Church of Holy Trinity vs. United States, 143 U.S. 457 (1892), discussed *infra,* pp. 243–244.
77. Sunday Law cases discussed *infra,* pp. 282–287.
78. Hosmer, J. K., ed., *Winthrop's Journal,* New York, Charles Scribner's Sons, 1908, I, pp. 61–62.
79. Stokes, I, p. 197.
80. The pamphlet in full may be found in the *Publications* of the Narragansett Club, Providence, 1866–1874, III, pp. 3 *et seq.* Abridged, but without the substance affected, it may be read conveniently in Blau, pp. 36 *et seq.*
81. See *infra,* pp. 135–137.
82. Blau, p. 43. Note how Williams anticipated Locke, Rousseau, and Jefferson.
83. Blau, p. 48.
84. See *infra,* pp. 106 ff.
85. Blau, p. 46.
86. See *infra,* p. 132.
87. Greene, p. 56.
88. Beard, I, pp. 70–71.

89. Greene, pp. 56–57.
90. Sweet, p. 159.
91. Greene, pp. 57–58.
92. Beard, I, p. 72.
93. Greene, p. 58.
94. *Ibid.;* Sweet, pp. 162–163.
95. Bates, p. 211.
96. Arnold, S. G., *History of Rhode Island, 1636–1790,* Providence, Preston & Rounds, 1894, II, p. 494.

CHAPTER FOUR
*The Principle Is Born*

1. Myers, p. 94.
2. Clinchy, p. 47.
3. Greene, p. 58.
4. Myers, p. 48.
5. Humphrey, Edward F., *Nationalism and Religion in America, 1774–1789,* Boston, Chipman Law Publishing Co., 1924, pp. 368–369.
6. *Writings of James Madison,* ed. Gaillard Hunt, New York, G. P. Putnam's Sons, 1900–1909, I, pp. 18–21.
7. *Ibid.,* p. 369.
8. Greene, p. 69.
9. Mecklin, p. 202.
10. Greene, p. 63.
11. Stokes, I, p. 200.
12. Mecklin, p. 54.
13. Sweet, pp. 297–298.
14. Stokes, I, p. 215.
15. *Ibid.,* I, p. 400; Greene, p. 63.
16. Beard, I, p. 30.
17. See *supra,* pp. 42 ff.
18. U.S. Department of Commerce, Census of Religious Bodies, 1936.
19. Sweet, p. 323.
20. *Ibid.,* pp. 323–324.
21. Humphrey, p. 13.
22. See, *e.g.,* Greene, pp. 64–65; Sweet, pp. 323–324; Stokes, I, p. 228; Beth, Loren P., *American Theory of Church and State,* Gainesville, Fla., University of Florida Press, 1958, pp. 55–56.
23. Stokes, I, p. 228; Sweet, p. 338.
24. Sweet, p. 339.
25. *Ibid.,* p. 334.
26. *Ibid.,* p. 229.
27. Garrison, W. E., "History of Anti-Catholicism in America," *Social Action,* Jan. 15, 1948, p. 9; Moehlman, Conrad H., "In Defense of McCollum v Board of Education," *American Bar Association Journal,* April 1952 (Vol. 39), p. 345.
28. *World Almanac* (1964), p. 622.
29. Stokes, I, p. 256.
30. Sweet, p. 332.
31. *Ibid.,* p. 332; Stokes, I, p. 255.

32. Ruffini, p. 289.
33. Beth, p. 58.
34. Greene, p. 76.
35. Humphrey, p. 373.
36. *Ibid.,* p. 234.
37. Stokes, I, p. 459; Greene, p. 77.
38. Williams, Michael, *The Shadow of the Pope,* New York, McGraw-Hill, 1932, pp. 36–37.
39. Stokes, I, pp. 460–461.
40. Greene, p. 77.
41. Sweet, p. 326.
42. Stokes, I, p. 231.
43. Everson case, 330 U.S. 1 (1947).
44. Davis vs. Beason, 133 U.S. 333 at 342 (1890).
45. Sweet, pp. 323, 326; Humphrey, p. 330.
46. Greene, p. 66.
47. Sweet, p. 333.
48. *Ibid.,* p. 130.
49. Stokes, I, p. 205.
50. See *supra,* pp. 86–88.
51. Humphrey, pp. 119–120.
52. Mecklin, p. 297.
53. See *infra,* pp. 106 ff.
54. Eckenrode, N.J., *The Separation of Church and State in Virginia,* Richmond, Virginia State Library, 1910, p. 107.
55. Mecklin, p. 223.
56. Humphrey, pp. 331–332.
57. *Ibid.,* p. 363.
58. *Ibid.,* p. 466.
59. Mecklin, p. 291.
60. Morison, S. E., and Commager, H. S., *Growth of the American Republic,* New York, Oxford University Press, 1930, p. 123.
61. Stokes, I, p. 209.
62. *American State Papers,* p. 110.
63. See, *e.g.,* Mecklin, p. 342; Stokes, I, pp. 141, 146.
64. Locke, John, *A Letter Concerning Toleration,* New York, Liberal Arts Press, 1955, p. 20.
65. *Ibid.,* p. 17.
66. *Ibid.,* pp. 17–18.
67. Humphrey, p. 332.
68. Beth, p. 29.
69. Mecklin, p. 293.
70. *Ibid.,* pp. 188–189; Greene, pp. 65–66.
71. Greene, p. 66; Cobb, p. 485.
72. Mecklin, p. 36.
73. Beard, I, p. 449.
74. Laski, Harold J., *The American Democracy,* New York, Viking Press, 1948, p. 267.
75. Mecklin, p. 35.
76. Stokes, I, pp. 318–319.

77. Everson case, 330 U.S. 1; Reynolds vs. United States, 98 U.S. 145 (1878); Watson vs. Jones, 13 Wall 679 (1872); Davis vs. Beason, 133 U.S. 333 (1890).

78. Henry, M. W., *The Part Taken by Virginia in Establishing Religious Liberty as a Foundation of the American Government,* Papers of the American Historical Association, II, p. 26, cited by Mecklin, p. 266.

79. Humphrey, p. 366.

80. Greene, pp. 85 – 86.

81. Cobb, pp. 108 – 11; Eckenrode, pp. 22 – 28.

82. Malone, Dumas, *Jefferson the Virginian,* Boston, Little, Brown & Co., 1948, p. 275.

83. Padover, Saul K., *The Complete Jefferson,* New York, Duell, Sloan & Pearce, 1943, p. 943.

84. Blau, pp. 78 – 79.

85. Jefferson's "Notes on Virginia," in Blau, pp. 77 – 78; Humphrey, p. 368.

86. Humphrey, p. 370.

87. The struggle for religious liberty and separation in Virginia has received considerable attention from historians. Perhaps the best account is Eckenrode's. Others include Cobb, Sweet, Humphrey, James, Charles F., *Documentary History of the Struggle for Religious Liberty in Virginia,* Lynchburg, 1899; Thom, W. F., *The Struggle for Religious Freedom in Virginia,* Baltimore, Johns Hopkins Press, 1900; Semple, R. B., *History of the Rise and Progress of the Baptists in Virginia,* Richmond, published by the author, 1810.

88. Humphrey, p. 373.

89. *Ibid.;* James, p. 52.

90. Semple, p. 62.

91. Padover, p. 109.

92. Butts, pp. 46 – 47.

93. Mecklin, pp. 268 – 269; *American State Papers,* pp. 103 – 105.

94. Humphrey, p. 379.

95. *Writings of Thomas Jefferson,* ed. P. F. Ford, New York, G. P. Putnam's Sons, 1892, I, p. 54.

96. Humphrey, p. 378.

97. *American State Papers,* pp. 106 – 107.

98. Humphrey, p. 381; Mecklin, p. 271.

99. Semple, p. 27.

100. Eckenrode, p. 53.

101. Butts, pp. 53 – 56.

102. The text of this bill is printed as an appendix to Justice Rutledge's dissent in the Everson case, 330 U.S. 1.

103. Eckenrode, p. 86.

104. Everson case, 330 U.S. 1.

105. Eckenrode, p. 102.

106. U.S. Bureau of Census, *A Century of Population Growth,* 1790 – 1900 (1909), p. 116; Goodman, pp. 148–149.

107. Stokes, I, p. 390.

108. Eckenrode, p. 107.

109. Semple, p. 71.

110. *American State Papers*, p. 110.
111. Eckenrode, p. 100.
112. James, p. 231.
113. Howe, Mark de Wolfe, *Cases on Church and State in the United States*, Cambridge, Harvard University Press, 1952, p. 16.
114. Rives, *History of the Life and Times of James Madison*, I, p. 632, cited in Luzzatti, Luigi, *God in Freedom*, New York, The Macmillan Co., 1930, pp. 679–680.
115. *American State Papers*, p. 129.
116. Blau, pp. 74–75.
117. *Jefferson's Writings*, ed. Ford, I, p. 62.
118. Humphrey, pp. 405–406.
119. Thorpe, Francis N., *Federal and State Constitutions, Colonial Charters and other Organic Laws*, Government Printing Office, Washington, D.C., 1909, III, pp. 1889–1890.
120. Thorpe, IV, p. 2454.
121. Stokes, I, p. 411.
122. Cobb, p. 482.
123. Thorpe, V, pp. 2636–2637.
124. Humphrey, p. 490.
125. Thorpe, V, pp. 2597–2598.
126. *Ibid.*, I, pp. 566–568.
127. *Ibid.*, VI, pp. 3082–3085.
128. *Ibid.*, III, p. 1689.
129. *Ibid.*, V, p. 2793.
130. Stokes, I, p. 434.
131. Thorpe, VI, pp. 3255–3257; Humphrey, pp. 494–495; Cobb, pp. 505–507.
132. Thorpe, II, pp. 779–784.
133. Cobb, p. 507; Humphrey, pp. 499–500; Stokes, I, p. 444.
134. Greene, p. 82.
135. Humphrey, pp. 330–334, 415–416.
136. *Ibid.*, pp. 407–408.
137. *Ibid.*, pp. 408–427.
138. *Ibid.*, pp. 410, 414.
139. *Ibid.*, p. 426.
140. *Ibid.*, pp. 412, 421, 428, 430.
141. Butts, pp. 68–71.
142. Stokes, I, pp. 478–479.
143. Humphrey, p. 439.
144. Farrand, Max, ed., *Records of the Federal Convention of 1787*, New Haven, Yale University Press, 1911, I, pp. 450–452; Scott, E.H., ed., *Journal of the Constitutional Convention of James Madison*, Chicago, Scott & Co., 1893, pp. 259–261.
145. See *supra*, p. 119.
146. Humphrey, pp. 462–463.
147. Greene, p. 83.
148. Madison, V, p. 176.
149. Farrand, III, p. 310.
150. *Ibid.*, III, p.122, Appendix; Elliot, Jonathan, *The Debates in the Several*

*State Conventions on the Adoption of the Federal Constitution,* 2d ed., Philadelphia, J. B. Lippincott & Co., 1888, V, p. 131.

151. Stokes, I, pp. 526–527; Butts, p. 71; Humphrey, p. 458.
152. Hamilton, Alexander, *Federalist Papers,* Modern Library ed., 1937, p. 559; *Annals of the Congress of the United States,* Washington, Gales and Seaton, 1834–1856, I, p. 729.
153. Madison, V, p. 105.
154. Farrand, II, pp. 461, 468.
155. See *infra,* p. 159. See also Pfeffer, Leo, "No Law Respecting an Establishment of Religion," *Buffalo Law Review,* Spring, 1953.
156. Story, Joseph, *Commentaries on the Constitution of the United States,* Boston, Hillard, Gray & Co., 1833, III, p. 705.
157. Farrand, III, p. 227.
158. Humphrey, pp. 463–464.
159. Madison, V, p. 176.
160. Elliot, *Debates,* II, pp. 118–120, 148–149.
161. *Ibid.,* IV, pp. 195–198.
162. *Ibid.,* pp. 175, 200.
163. Kohler, Max J., "The Fathers of the Republic and Constitutional Establishment of Religious Liberty," in Luzzatti, Luigi, *God in Freedom,* New York, The Macmillan Co., 1930, pp. 692–693.
164. Humphrey, p. 478.
165. Butts, p. 72.
166. *Jefferson's Writings,* ed. Ford, V, pp. 371–372.
167. Madison, V, p. 176.
168. *Jefferson's Writings,* ed. Ford, V, p. 371.
169. Elliot, *Debates,* II, pp. 435–437.
170. *Federalist Papers,* Modern Library ed., 1937, p. 559.
171. Elliot, *Debates,* III, p. 318.
172. Butts, p. 72.
173. Madison, V, p. 320.
174. Stokes, I, p. 538; Butts, p. 78.
175. Stokes, I, pp. 538–539.

CHAPTER FIVE
*The Meaning of the Principle*

1. Madison, V, pp. 132, 176.
2. Schaff, Philip, "Church and State in the United States," *Papers of the American Historical Society,* 1888, p. 137.
3. Beard, Charles, *The Republic,* New York, Viking Press, 1944, pp. 166, 170.
4. "Letter to the Editor," New York *Times,* November 12, 1951. A fuller discussion of this subject appears below, pp. 302 ff.
5. *Annals,* I, p. 451.
6. See *infra,* pp. 287–289.
7. See *infra,* pp. 266–267.
8. 330 U.S. 1, 333 U.S. 201.
9. *America,* February 15, 1947.
10. New York *Times,* November 21, 1948.
11. St. Louis *Globe-Democrat,* November 6, 1951; St. Louis *Post-Dispatch,*

November 6, 1951.

12. O'Neill, James M., *Religion and Education under the Constitution,* New York, Harper & Brothers, 1949, pp. 4, 82.
13. New York *Times,* March 31, 1951, p. 16.
14. Corwin, Edward S., *Constitution of Powers in a Secular State,* Charlottesville, Va., Michie Co., 1951, p. 98. See, also, Brady, Joseph H., *Confusion Twice Confounded,* South Orange, N.J., Seton Hall University Press, 1955, *passim;* Griswold, Erwin, "Absolute is in the Dark," *Utah Law Review,* 8 (1963), p. 167.
15. Fleet, Elizabeth, "Madison's 'Detached Memoranda,' " *William and Mary Quarterly,* 3rd Series, 1946, p. 555.
16. McCollum, 333 U.S. 203; Zorach vs. Clauson, 343 U.S. 306; McGowan vs. Maryland, 366 U.S. 420; Torcaso vs. Watkins, 367 U.S. 488; Engel vs. Vitale, 370 U.S. 421; School District of Abington Township vs. Schempp, 374 U.S. 203.
17. Padover, Saul K., *The Complete Jefferson,* New York, Duell, Sloan & Pearce, 1943, pp. 518—519.
18. O'Neill, p. 83.
19. Corwin, p. 106.
20. *Jefferson's Writings,* ed. Ford, IX, pp. 346, 347, quoted by Butts, p. 94.
21. Reynolds vs. United States, 98 U.S. 145.
22. Ryan, John A., and Boland, Francis J., *Catholic Principles of Politics,* New York, The Macmillan Co., 1948, p. 312.
23. See *infra,* pp. 174 ff.
24. Murray, John Courtney, "Law of Prepossession?" *Law and Contemporary Problems,* XIV, No. 1 (Winter, 1949), p. 32.
25. Reed, George E., "Separation of Church and State—Its Real Meaning," *Catholic Action,* March 1949, p. 9.
26. Keehn, Thomas B., "Church-State Relations," *Social Action,* November 15, 1948, p. 31.
27. Griswold, *op. cit.,* p. 167.
28. Kauper, Paul G., "Church and State: Cooperative Separation," *Michigan Law Review,* 60, p. 1 (1960); *"Church, State, and Freedom:* A review," *Michigan Law Review,* 52 (1954), p. 829.
29. Katz, Wilber, "Freedom of Religion and State Neutrality," *University of Chicago Law Review,* 20, (1953), p. 426. For an account of the Columbus conference, see Wogaman, Philip, "The WCC National Study Conference on Church and State," in Giannella, Donald A., *Religion and the Public Order,* 1964, Chicago, University of Chicago Press, 1965, p. 121.
30. Katz, Wilber, "The Case of Religious Liberty," in Cogley, John, ed., *Religion in America,* New York, Meridian Books, 1958, p. 97.
31. Parsons, Wilfred, *The First Freedom,* New York, Declan X. McMullen Co., 1948, pp. 28—29.
32. Corwin, p. 114.
33. *Supra,* p. 52.
34. See *supra,* Chapter 2.
35. See *infra,* pp. 161 ff.
36. See *infra,* p. 266.
37. Reynolds vs. United States, 98 U.S. 145 (1878).
38. 330 U.S. 1 (1947).

39. Ruffini, p. 16.
40. 343 U.S. 306 (1952).
41. See *infra*, p. 224.
42. See *infra*, p. 157.
43. See Kunz vs. New York, 340 U.S. 290 (1951), particularly Justice Jackson's dissent, discussed below, pp. 657 ff.
44. Madison, V, p. 288.
45. See note, *Yale Law Journal*, 61, No. 3, March, 1952, pp. 406–407.
46. Warren, Charles, "The New Liberty under the Fourteenth Amendment," *Harvard Law Review*, 39 (1926), pp. 434–435.
47. 7 Peters, (U.S.) 243 (1833).
48. Warren, p. 436.
49. Permoli vs. First Municipality of New Orleans, 44 U.S. 589 (1845).
50. Levinger, L. J., *History of the Jews in the United States*, Cincinnati, Union of American Hebrew Congregations, 1930, pp. 134–136; Blau, p. 89.
51. Butts, p. 42.
52. Meyer, Jacob C., *Church and State in Massachusetts*, Cleveland, Western University Press, 1930, pp. 201–220.
53. Quoted in appendix to Justice Black's dissent in Adamson vs. California, 332 U.S. 46 (1947).
54. *Ibid.*, p. 105.
55. Flack, Horace E., *The Adoption of the Fourteenth Amendment*, Baltimore, Johns Hopkins Press, 1908, p. 94.
56. Fairman, Charles, "Does the Fourteenth Amendment Incorporate the Bill of Rights?", *Stanford Law Review*, II, 5 (1949).
57. Slaughter House Cases, 16 Wall (U.S.) 36 (1873).
58. 332 U.S. 46 (1947).
59. See Justice Frankfurter's concurring opinion, Adamson case, *ibid.*
60. Prudential Insurance Co. vs. Cheek, 259 U.S. 530 (1922).
61. Meyer vs. Nebraska, 262 U.S. 390 (1923), discussed below, p. 517.
62. *Ibid.* (italics added).
63. Pierce vs. Society of Sisters of the Holy Name, 268 U.S. 510 (1925), discussed below, pp. 514–517.
64. Gitlow vs. New York, 268 U.S. 652 (1925).
65. See Green, John R., "Liberty under the Fourteenth Amendment," *Washington University Law Quarterly Review*, 27 (1942), pp. 497 ff.
66. Among these cases are: Cantwell vs. Connecticut, 310 U.S. 296 (1940); Minersville School District vs. Gobitis, 310 U.S. 586 (1940); Murdock vs. Pennsylvania, 319 U.S. 105 (1943); West Virginia State Board of Education vs. Barnette, 319 U.S. 624 (1943); Marsh vs. Alabama, 326 U.S. 501 (1946). These cases are discussed in Part III of this volume.
67. Warren, p. 463.
68. But see Justice Jackson's dissent in Beauharnais vs. Illinois, 343 U.S. 250 (1952).
69. O'Neill, pp. 124–126; Meyer, Alfred W., "The Blaine Amendment and the Bill of Rights," *Harvard Law Review*, 64, p. 939 (1951).
70. Parsons, pp. 70–73.
71. Appellees' brief in McCollum case, p. 109; Corwin, pp. 113–114; Meiklejohn, Alexander, "Educational Cooperation between Church and State," *Law and Contemporary Problems*, 14, 70 (1949); Howe, Mark

DeWolfe, "The Constitutional Question," *Religion and the Free Society* (pamphlet), Fund for the Republic, 1958, p. 59 ff.

72. Corwin, p. 114.
73. Meyer, *The Blaine Amendment . . .* , Parsons, pp. 70–71; O'Neill, pp. 123–124.
74. Pfeffer, Leo, "Religion, Education and the Constitution," *Lawyers Guild Review*, 8 (1948), p. 393.
75. 4 *Congressional Record* (44th Congress), 175 (1875).
76. *Ibid.*, p. 5580 (1876).
77. *Ibid.*, 5595 (1876).
78. Ames, Herman V., *The Proposed Amendments to the Constitution of the United States during the First Hundred Years of its History*, Government Printing Office, Washington, D.C., 1897, pp. 277–278, cited in concurring opinion of Justice Frankfurter in McCollum case, 333 U.S. 203.
79. McCollum case, Justice Frankfurter's concurring opinion, 333 U.S. 203.
80. 310 U.S. 296 (1940) (italics added).
81. 310 U.S. 586 (1940) (italics added).
82. 319 U.S. 105 (1943) (italics added).
83. 293 U.S. 245 (1934) (italics added).
84. See, *e.g.,* Bridges vs. California, 314 U.S. 252 (1941).
85. 330 U.S. 1.
86. See, *e.g.,* Murray, John C., "The Court Upholds Religious Freedom," *America*, March 8, 1947, p. 628.
87. See, *e.g.,* editorial, "Now Will Protestants Awake?" *The Christian Century,* February 26, 1947, p. 262; editorial, "The Protestants Get a Licking," *The Churchman,* March 1, 1947, p. 4; Dawson, Joseph M., *Separate Church and State Now,* New York, Richard R. Smith, 1948, p. 75.
88. O'Neill, p. xii.
89. 333 U.S. 203.
90. New York *Times,* November 21, 1948, p. 63.
91. "Law or Prepossessions?" *Law and Contemporary Problems,* 14, p. 23.
92. "Religion, Education and the Supreme Court," *ibid.*, p. 73.
93. Brady, *passim.*
94. 63, p. 451.
95. New York *Times,* March 31, 1951, p. 16.
96. Corwin's article, "The Supreme Court as National School Board," was originally published in *Thought,* 43, p. 665 (1948), then in *Law and Contemporary Problems,* 14, p. 3 (1949), and finally in *A Constitution of Powers in a Secular State.* Meiklejohn's article, "Educational Cooperation between Church and State," appeared in *Law and Contemporary Problems*, 14 (1949), p. 61.
97. Parsons, p. 79.
98. See *e.g., ibid.,* p. 136.
99. Zorach vs. Clauson, 198 Misc. (N.Y.) 631 (1950); Gordon vs. Board of Education, 78 Cal. App. 2d 464 (1947).
100. U.S. Department of Commerce, *Census of Religious Bodies,* p. 17 (1936).
101. Cochran vs. Louisiana State Board of Education, 281 U.S. 370 (1930). The case is discussed below, pp. 558–561.

102. Blau, p. 78.
103. *Papers of the American Historical Association,* II (1888), p. 10.
104. 98 U.S. 145 (1878).
105. Lieber, Francis, *On Civil Liberty and Self Government,* Philadelphia, J. B. Lippincott, 1859, p. 99 (italics added).
106. *The American Commonwealth,* 3rd ed., 1894, II, p. 766.
107. *The Republic,* pp. 165, 166, 170.
108. O'Neill, p. 204. Substantially similar definitions are found *ibid.,* p. 56; Corwin, p. 104; Catholic bishops' statement; Parsons, p. 46; McCollum brief, p. 57; Fahy, p. 80; Brady, pp. 7–9.
109. Morrison, Charles C., *The Separation of Church and State in America* (pamphlet), p. 4.
110. Terrett vs. Taylor, 9 Cranch (U.S.) 43 (1815).
111. Fleet, Elizabeth, "Madison's 'Detached Memoranda,' " *William and Mary Quarterly,* October, 1946, Third Series, 3, p. 559 (italics added).
112. Butts, pp. 122–123.
113. See *infra,* p. 506.
114. *Annals,* I, p. 732.
115. Richardson, J. D., *Messages and Papers of the Presidents,* New York, *Bureau of National Literature,* 1900, I, pp. 489, 490 (italics added). Note plural "societies."
116. Fleet, pp. 560–562; Stokes, I, p. 697; Butts, p. 94. A fuller discussion appears below, pp. 265 ff.
117. Stokes, I, pp. 260–264.
118. *Journal of Proceedings of the First Session of the United States Senate,* pp. 63, 67 (August 25, September 3, 1791).
119. Story, Joseph, *Commentaries on the Constitution of the United States,* Boston, Hillard, Gray (1833), III, pp. 724–726.
120. 9 Cranch (U.S.) 43 (1815).
121. *Ibid.,* p. 49. Note use of word "establishing."
122. 333 U.S. 203 (1948).
123. 4 *Congressional Record,* 5245, 5561 (1876), quoted in Meyer, *The Blaine Amendment . . . ,* pp. 942–943.
124. *Annals,* I, p. 434.
125. *Ibid.,* p. 729.
126. Fleet, p. 558.
127. Stokes, I, p. 351.
128. *Annals,* I, p. 731.
129. Stokes, I, p. 317 (italics added).
130. *Annals,* I, pp. 729–731.
131. Dissenting in Everson, 330 U.S. 1 (1947).
132. Eckenrode, p. 85.
133. *American State Papers,* p. 193.
134. See *infra,* pp. 476–478.
135. Everson, 330 U.S. I, 14.
136. Alaska Constitution (1959) Article VII Section 1. Hawaii Constitution (1959) Article IX Section 1.
137. DeTocqueville, Alexis, *Democracy in America,* 1851, I, p. 332.
138. Bryce, James, *The American Commonwealth,* New York, The Macmillan Co. (1889), II, p. 561.

139. Schaff, p. 55.
140. See *supra,* p. 95.
141. Sweet, William W., "The Protestant Churches," *Annals,* March, 1948, p. 45.
142. Dissenting in Everson, 330 U.S. 1.
143. McCollum brief, pp. 53–54; Corwin, p. 102; Murray, p. 43.
144. Schwegmann Bros. vs. Calvert Distillers Corp., 341 U.S. 384, 394 (1951).
145. Humphrey, p. 479; Brant, Irving, "Madison On Separation of Church and State," *William and Mary Quarterly,* Third Series, 8, No. 1, Jan. 1951, p. 17.
146. Fleet, p. 561.
147. 143 U.S. 457 (1892).
148. See *infra,* pp. 185 ff.
149. Stokes, III, p. 602.
150. See *infra,* pp. 618 ff.
151. See *infra,* pp. 721 ff.
152. Fleet, pp. 555, 558, 559.
153. Stokes, I, p. 491.
154. *Ibid.,* p. 500.
155. Eckenrode, p. 53.
156. *Supra,* p. 110.
157. O'Neill, p. 103.
158. Brant, pp. 18–19.
159. Murray, p. 29.
160. See *supra,* pp. 125–126.
161. 333 U.S. 203.
162. For another explanation, see Louisell, David W., "The Man and the Mountain: Douglas on Religious Freedom," *Yale Law Journal* 73 (1964), pp. 995–996.
163. 343 U.S. 306.
164. Kauper, Paul, *"Church, State, and Freedom:* A Review," *Michigan Law Review,* 52 (1954), p. 839.
165. 366 U.S. 420 (1961), discussed more fully *infra* pp. 281–287.
166. *Ibid.* at p. 563.
167. 367 U.S. 488 (1961), discussed more fully *infra* pp. 469 ff.
168. School District of Abington Township vs. Schempp, 374 U.S. 203 (1963), discussed more fully *infra* pp. 469–473.
169. Sunday Law Cases, discussed *infra* pp. 281–287.
170. For a more complete discussion of the interpretation of the Establishment Clause of the First Amendment set forth in this subsection, see Pfeffer, Leo, "Court, Constitution and Prayer," *Rutgers Law Review* 16 (1962), pp. 743–752.
171. Madison, II, p. 185.
172. Black, p. 53.

CHAPTER SIX
*State Aid to Religion*

1. For other similar state constitutional prohibitions, see *Constitutions of the States and United States,* New York State Constitutional Convention

Committee, 1938, Index, p. 1799; Anticau, C.J., Carroll, P.M., Burke, T.C., *Religion Under the State Constitutions,* Brooklyn, Central Book Co., 1965, Appendix.

2. See Everson, 330 U.S. 1.
3. *Ibid.*
4. 343 U.S. 306.
5. See *infra,* pp. 537 ff.
6. *E.g.,* People vs. Friedman, discussed below, pp. 281 ff.
7. *E.g.,* Pierce vs. Society of Sisters, discussed below, pp. 514 ff.
8. *E.g.,* Kunz vs. New York, discussed below, pp. 657 ff.
9. Discussed below, pp. 545 ff.
10. See, *e.g.,* People ex rel. Lewis vs. Graves, 245 N.Y. 195 (1927); Lewis vs. Spaulding, 193 Misc. (N.Y.) 66 (1948); Lewis vs. Board of Education, 275 N.Y. 480 (1937); Lewis vs. Board of Education, 157 Misc. (N.Y.) 520 (1935); Lewis vs. Mandeville, 201 Misc. (N.Y.) 120 (1952); New York League for Separation of Church and State vs. Graves, 170 Misc. (N.Y.) 196 (1939); Lewis vs. Allen, 195 N.Y.S. 2d 807 affirmed 207 N.Y.S. 2d 862 affirmed 200 N.E. 2d 767 (1964) certiorari denied 379 U.S. 923 (1964).
11. McCollum, Vashti, *One Woman's Fight,* New York, Doubleday & Co., 1951, chap. 13, pp. 95 ff.
12. *Religious News Service,* March 7, 1963.
13. Massachusetts vs. Mellon, 262 U.S. 447 (1923).
14. Elliott vs. White, 23 F. 2d 997 (1928).
15. Bull vs. Stichman, 273 App. Div. 311, affirmed 298 N.Y. 516 (1948).
16. New York League for Separation of Church and State vs. Graves, 170 Misc. (N.Y.) 196 (1939).
17. See *infra,* pp. 308–310.
18. Letter of Edward S. Corwin to Editor of New York *Times,* November 12, 1955; Howe, Mark De Wolfe, "Diplomacy, Religion and the Constitution," *The Nation,* January 12, 1952. *Information Service,* National Council of Churches of Christ in the United States, December 1, 1951.
19. Massachusetts vs. Mellon, 262 U.S. 447 (1923).
20. People ex rel. McCollum vs. Board of Education, 396 Ill, 14 (1947).
21. Brief *Amici Curiae* of Synagogue Council of America and National Community Relations Advisory Council, pp. 30–31.
22. Sutherland, Arthur E., "Due Process and Disestablishment," *Harvard Law Review,* 62 (1949), pp. 1343–1344. See also, McCloskey, Robert G., "Principles, Powers and Values," in Giannella (1964), p. 3.
23. See *infra,* pp. 479 ff.
24. See *infra,* pp. 436 ff.
25. See *infra,* p. 638.
26. See *supra,* p. 92.
27. Madison's Remonstrance, paragraph 8.
28. *Ibid.,* paragraph 3.
29. McLaurin vs. Oklahoma, 339 U.S. 637 (1950); Brown vs. Board of Education, 347 U.S. 483 (1954).
30. Cooper vs. Aaron, 358 U.S. 1 (1958).
31. See note, "Taxpayer's Action against State Officials to Prevent Alleged Unconstitutional Use of State Funds," *Fordham Law Review,* 17 (1948), pp. 107, 110; Arthur Garfield Hays Civil Liberties Conference: "Public

Aid to Parochial Schools and Standing to Bring Suit," *Buffalo Law Review*, 12 (1962) pp. 35 ff; Jaffe, Louis, "Standing to Secure Judicial Review: Public Actions," *Harvard Law Review*, 62 (1961), pp. 1265 ff.

32. Bradfield vs. Roberts, 175 U.S. 291 (1899), discussed below, pp. 199–200.
33. 342 U.S. 429 (1952).
34. Cochran vs. Louisiana Board of Education, 281 U.S. 370 (1930), discussed below, pp. 558–560.
35. 330 U.S. 1 (1947), discussed below, pp. 563 ff.
36. Discussed below pp. 597–604.
37. See *Congressional Record*, October 15, 1963, p. 18493 ff.; Boston *Pilot*, December 28, 1963.
38. 370 U.S. 421 (1962).
39. People ex rel. Lewis vs. Graves, 245 N.Y. 195 (1927); Lewis vs. Board of Education, 157 Misc. (N.Y.) 520 (1935); New York League for Separation of Church and State vs. Graves, 170 Misc. (N.Y.) 196 (1939); Lewis vs. Board of Education, 275 N.Y. 480 (1937); Lewis vs. Spaulding, 193 Misc. (N.Y.) 66 (1948); Lewis vs. Mandeville, 201 Misc. (N.Y.) 120 (1952); Lewis vs. Allen, 195 N.Y.S. 2d 807 affirmed 207 N.Y.S. 2d 862 affirmed 200 N.E. 2d 767 certiorari denied 379 U.S. 923 (1964).
40. 198 Misc. (N.Y.) 631; brief of Board of Education in Court of Appeals, p. 38; briefs of Coordinating Committee, *passim*.
41. 303 N.Y. 161.
42. 343 U.S. 306.
43. 333 U.S. at p. 211.
44. 370 U.S. 421.
45. 374 U.S. 203.
46. See *infra* pp. 476–478.
47. Note, *Yale Law Journal*, 50 (1941), pp. 917, 923.
48. See *infra*, p. 451.
49. Hackett vs. Brooksville Graded School District, 120 Ky. 608 (1905).
50. Billard vs. Board of Education of Topeka, 69 Kans. 53 (1904).
51. Reichwald vs. Catholic Bishop, 258 Ill. 44 (1913).
52. See *supra*, p. 157.
53. See *infra*, pp. 199–200.
54. See *infra*, pp. 558 ff.
55. See *infra*, pp. 563 ff.
56. See *infra*, pp. 432 ff.
57. See *infra*, pp. 282–284.
58. See *e.g.*, Sholes vs. University of Minnesota, 54 N.W. 2d 122 (1952); Lewis vs. Board of Education, 258 N.Y. 117 (1932).
59. 175 U.S. 291 (1899); see *infra*, pp. 199–200.
60. 193 Misc. (N.Y.) 66 (1948).
61. 273 App. Div. 311, affirmed, 298 N.Y. 516 (1948).
62. Stokes, II, p. 255.
63. Stokes, I, p. 693.
64. *Constitution of the States*, p. 1816.
65. Dunn vs. Chicago Industrial School, 280 Ill. 613 (1917).
66. Craig vs. Mercy Hospital–Street Memorial, 209 Miss. 427 (1950).
67. Abernathy vs. City of Irvine, 355 S.W. 2d 159, certiorari denied, 371

U.S. 831 (1962).

68. American Law Reports, 22, p. 1319.
69. 175 U.S. 291.
70. *Supra,* pp. 178–180.
71. See *infra,* pp. 526–529.
72. New York *Times,* May 24, 1952.
73. "Report from the Capital," Newsletter of Baptists' Joint Conference Committee on Public Relations, December, 1949, p. 4; *Religious News Service,* November 6, 1959, February 1, 1961, March 4, 1963.
74. *Religious News Service,* December 13, 1962.
75. *Ibid.,* January 31, 1961.
76. New York *Times,* February 1, 1952.
77. *America,* February 16, 1952.
78. New York *Times,* February 2, 1952.
79. *Ibid.,* June 19, 1961.
80. *Ibid.,* June 21, 1961.
81. *Religious News Service,* August 21, 1961, January 31, 1962, January 25, 1963; *Christian Century,* July 12, 1961.
82. *Religious News Service,* June 26, 1961; Brooklyn *Tablet,* December 23, 1961.
83. *Religious News Service,* June 26, 1961.
84. Brooklyn *Tablet,* December 2, 1961; *Religious News Service,* December 18, 1961.
85. See *infra,* p. 577.
86. *Infra,* pp. 583–592.
87. *Religious News Service,* August 10, 1964, August 18, 1964.
88. Kunz vs. New York, 340 U.S. 290 (1951); Tucker vs. Texas, 326 U.S. 517, (1946). These cases are discussed below, pp. 657 ff.
89. Hague vs. C.I.O., 307 U.S. 496 (1939).
90. See *infra,* pp. 675.
91. See, *e.g.,* McNight vs. Board of Public Education, 365 Pa. 422 (1951), appeal dismissed for want of a substantial Federal question, 341 U.S. 913 (1951); Lyon vs. Compton Union High School (Calif.), appeal dismissed for want of a substantial Federal question, 341 U.S. 913 (1951).
92. See *infra,* pp. 537 ff.
93. See, *e.g.,* School District No. 8 vs. Arnold, 21 Wisc. 665 (1867), where the court said: ". . . although the schoolhouse is the property of the district, it does not follow that the electors may divert it from its original use. . . . Certainly the schoolhouse is not the property of the electors in such sense that they may control its use as they would that of their own property."
94. Wright vs. Board of Education, 106 Kan. 469 (1920). In that case the court refused to enjoin the construction of a school building merely because it was proposed to use it as a community house when not used for school purposes.
95. Act of March 10, 1949, art. VII, sec. 775.
96. Chamberlin vs. Dade County Board of Public Instruction, 142 So. 2d 21 (1962).
97. Cochran vs. Louisiana State Board of Education, 281 U.S. 370 (1930) (italics added), discussed below, pp. 558–560.

98. 396 Ill. 14 (1947).
99. 333 U.S. 203.
100. Davis vs. Boget, 50 Iowa 11 (1878).
101. Southside Estate Baptist Church vs. Board of Trustees, 115 So. 2d 697 (1959).
102. Matter of Lewis vs. Mandeville, 201 Misc. (N.Y.) 120 (1952).
103. Law Pamphlet 6, "Use of School Building," No. 1260, January 3, 1944, p. 5.
104. Lewis vs. Board of Education, 157 Misc. (N.Y.) 520 (1935).
105. New York League for Separation of Church and State vs. Graves, 170 Misc. (N.Y.) 196 (1939).
106. Justice Jackson, dissenting in Everson, 330 U.S. 1.
107. Genesis 47:26.
108. Ezra 7:24.
109. Baron, I, p. 287.
110. Danby, Herbert, *The Mishnah,* London, Oxford University Press, 1933, p. 450.
111. Stokes, III, p. 419.
112. Paulsen, Monrad G., "Preferment of Religious Institutions in Tax and Labor Legislation," *Law and Contemporary Problems,* 14 (Winter, 1949), p. 148.
113. Zollman, Carl, *American Church Law,* St. Paul, West Publishing Co., 1933, p. 329; note "Constitutionality of Tax Benefits Accorded Religion," *Columbia Law Review,* 49, p. 969 (November, 1949).
114. Franklin Street Society vs. Manchester, 60 N.H. 342 (1880).
115. Note, *Columbia Law Review,* 49, p. 969.
116. See, *e.g.,* O'Neill, pp. 224–225; Fahy, p. 81; Parsons, p. 124; Bennett, John C., *Christians and the State,* New York, Charles Scribner's Sons, 1958, p. 234–235.
117. Note, *Columbia Law Review,* pp. 969–970; Gabel, Richard J., *Public Funds for Church and Private Schools,* Washington, D.C., Catholic University, 1947, p. 566.
118. Hurley, Mark J., *Church-State Relationships in Education in California,* Washington, D.C., Catholic University, 1948, Chaps. 3, 4; Fey, Harold J., "Should Parochial Schools be Taxed?" *The Christian Century,* August 8, 1951; Bloom, Hannah, "California's Church School War," *The Nation,* May 31, 1952.
119. Note, *Columbia Law Review,* 49, pp. 973–974.
120. New York Constitution (1938), art. 16, sec. 1; New York Tax Law, sec. 4, subdiv. 6.
121. Note, *Columbia Law Review,* 49, p. 972.
122. *Ibid.,* pp. 974, 981.
123. Paulson, pp. 144–145; *Villanova Law Review,* 5 (1959), pp. 269–274.
124. City of Hannibal vs. Draper, 15 Mo. 634 (1852).
125. Stokes, III, p. 422; Paulsen, p. 150.
126. Paulsen, pp. 154–155.
127. *Ibid.,* p. 155.
128. Tannen, Andrew P., *The Question of Tax Exemption for Churches* (pamphlet), National Conference of Christians and Jews (undated), p. 17.
129. Larson, Martin A., "You, the Church and Tax-exempt Wealth," *Liberty,*

September—October, 1965, p. 7.

130. See, *e.g.*, "Churches Feel 'Tax Squeeze,'" *America,* August 22, 1964, p. 185; Larson, Martin A., *Church Wealth and Business Income,* New York, Philosophical Library, 1965, *passim.*

131. See concurring opinion of Justice Douglas in Engel vs. Vitale, footnote 1.

132. Quoted in Paulsen, p. 149.

133. Young Men's Christian Association vs. Douglas County, 60 Neb. 642 (1900).

134. Zollman, p. 327; Paulsen, p. 149; Saxe, John G., *Charitable Exemption from Taxation in New York State,* 1933, pp. 45—46; Van Alstyne, Arvo, "Tax Exemption of Church Property," *Ohio State Law Journal,* 20 (1959), p. 462.

135. Bennett, John C., *Christians and the State,* New York, Charles Scribners Sons, 1958, p. 232.

136. Stokes, III, p. 423.

137. Fleet, p. 555.

138. Editorial, "Churches Should Pay Taxes," *The Christian Century,* April 9, 1947.

139. See *e.g.*, Ream, Norman S., "The State, the Church and Taxes," *The Christian Century,* November 9, 1949; Votaw, Heber H., "Shall We Tax Church Properties?" *Liberty,* 46, No. 3, p. 17, Third Quarter, 1951; *Religious News Service,* January 19, 1962, February 2, 17, 1964, May 28, 1964.

140. *Relations between Church and State* (pamphlet), United Presbyterian Church, Philadelphia, May, 1962, pp. 19—20.

141. "Tax Exemption and the Churches," *Christianity Today,* August 3, 1959, pp. 6—8. This position was supported by Dr. Edwin T. Dahlberg, Dr. Blake's successor as president of the National Council of Churches; Drinan, Robert F., S.J. *Religion, the Courts and Public Policy,* New York, McGraw-Hill Book Company, 1965, p. 12.

142. See *e.g.*, Drinan, pp. 13—14.

143. Brown, William A., *Church and State in Contemporary America,* New York, Charles Scribner's Sons, 1936, p. 161.

144. Rian, pp. 1326—1327; Paulsen, p. 149; Brown, p. 175.

145. *Congressional Record,* 4, p. 175 (1875).

146. Paulsen, p. 151.

147. *Ibid.*, p. 152.

148. Zollman, p. 327; Adler, Phillip, "Historical Origin of the Exemption from Taxation of Charitable Institutions," in Westchester County Chamber of Commerce, *Tax Exemptions on Real Estate,* p. 76 (1922); Stimson, Claude W., "The Exemption of Churches from Taxation," *Taxes,* 18, p. 364 (1940); Stimson, Claude W., "The Exemption of Property from Taxation in the United States," *Minnesota Law Review,* 18, p. 422 (1934). In the last cited article the author writes: "Since the fundamental laws that have been accepted in the United States provide for separation of Church and State, and since the exemption of church property from taxation constitutes a subsidy to the church associations, it is clear that what has been expressly prohibited is being indirectly carried on and that the courts and a large part of the public are sanc-

tioning it."

149. Zollman, p. 327.
150. Orr vs. Baker, 4 Ind. 86 (1853).
151. Trustees of Griswold College vs. Iowa, 46 Iowa 275 (1877).
152. Garrett Biblical Institute vs. Elmhurst State Bank, 331 Ill. 308 (1928).
153. Note, *Columbia Law Review,* 49, p. 992; Paulsen, p. 147. The same conclusion is reached by the author of the note, "Establishment of Religion by State Aid," *Rutgers Law Review,* 3, p. 115 (1949).
154. Sperry, Willard L., *Religion in America,* Cambridge, Eng., University Press (1946), p. 60.
155. 343 U.S. 306.
156. See Drinan, p. 11; Van Alstyne, p. 507; Tanner, pp. 48–49.
157. Heisey vs. County of Alameda, 352 U.S. 921 (1956), dismissing appeal from Lundberg vs. County of Alameda, 46 Cal. 2d 644 (1956).
158. General Finance Corp. vs. Archette, 176 A. 2d 73 (1961), appeal dismissed, 369 U.S. 423 (1962).
159. Murray v. Comptroller, 216 A. 2d 897 (1966).
160. Act of October 30, 1951, Chap. 531, Title I, sec. 2, 65 Stat. 672; 39 U.S.C.A. 289a (a).
161. See, *e.g., The Christian Century,* April 4, 1951.
162. See *infra,* pp. 718–720.

CHAPTER SEVEN
*Church Intervention in State Affairs*

1. Humphrey, p. 408.
2. See *supra,* pp. 118–119.
3. Stokes, I, p. 622.
4. Thorpe, V, p. 2637.
5. Thorpe, VI, p. 3253.
6. *Supra,* pp. 117–118.
7. Stokes, I, p. 622.
8. Madison, V, p. 288.
9. Stokes, I, p. 624.
10. Maryland Constitution, article 3, section 11; Tennessee Constitution, article 9, section 1.
11. *To Secure These Rights,* Report of the President's Committee on Civil Rights, U.S. Government Printing Office, Washington, D.C., 1947, p. viii.
12. See *infra,* pp. 496 ff.
13. Isaiah 1:11–17.
14. Taft, Philip, "The Popes Point the Way to Social Justice," *America,* April 22, 1950, pp. 81–82; Masse, Benjamin L., "The Popes and the Industrial Revolution," *America,* May 12, 1951, p. 157.
15. High, Stanley, *The Church in Politics,* New York, Harper & Brothers, 1930, *passim.*
16. Stokes, III, pp. 18–21.
17. Nichols, James H., *Democracy and the Churches,* Philadelphia, Westminster Press, 1951, pp. 217–218.
18. Wise, Stephen, *Challenging Years,* New York, G. P. Putnam's Sons, 1949, p. 109.

19. Stokes, III, p. 674.
20. Lawrence, David, "Mixing Religion and Politics," *U.S. News*, March 28, 1947, cited in Ebersole, Luke E., *Church Lobbying in the Nation's Capital*, New York, The Macmillan Co., 1951, p. 1.
21. Furfey, Paul H., "The Church and Social Problems," *Annals of the American Academy of Political and Social Science*, March, 1948, p. 105.
22. Beard, I, p. 259.
23. Sweet, William Warren, *Religion in the Development of American Culture*, New York, Charles Scribner's Sons, 1952, p. 18.
24. Humphrey, pp. 413–414.
25. Stokes, II, p. 121.
26. Ebersole, p. 2.
27. *Ibid.*, p. 6.
28. Stokes, II, p. 246.
29. See Ahmann, Matthew, ed., *Race and Challenge to Religion*, Chicago, Henry Regnery Co., 1963.
30. Ebersole, pp. 12–15.
31. Cited in Stokes, III, p. 68.
32. Ernst, Morris L., and Lindley, Alexander, *The Censor Marches On*, New York, Doubleday, Doran & Co., 1940, p. 144.
33. Ebersole, *passim;* Nichols, Chap. VIII.
34. Ebersole, Chap. II.
35. Flynn, John T., *The Road Ahead*, New York, Devin-Adair, 1949.
36. Dawson, pp. 209–210.
37. Ebersole, p. 69.
38. Moscow, Warren, *Politics in the Empire State*, New York, Alfred A. Knopf, 1948, p. 201.
39. New York *Times*, March 13, 1952.
40. Ebersole, p. 54.
41. *Ibid.*, Chap. V.
42. 396 Ill. 14 (1947), discussed below, pp. 401 ff.
43. 303 N.Y. 161 (1951), discussed below, pp. 667 ff.
44. 143 U.S. 457 (1892).
45. Howe, pp. 8–11.
46. See *supra,* p. 114.
47. See his concurring opinion in Engel vs. Vitale, 370 U.S. 421 (1962).
48. *Ibid:* "At the opening of each day's Session of this Court we stand while one of our officials invokes the protection of God. Since the days of John Marshall our crier has said, 'God save the United States and this Honorable Court.' Both the Senate and the House of Representatives open their daily sessions with prayer. Each of our Presidents, from George Washington to John F. Kennedy, has upon assuming his Office, asked the protection and help of God."
49. *Supra,* p. 122.
50. Schaff, p. 433.
51. *Religious News Service,* August 14, 1964.
52. Humphrey, p. 430.
53. See *supra,* p. 114.
54. McAllister, David, *The National Reform Movement*, Allegheny, Christian Statesman Co., 1898, p. 16.
55. *American State Papers*, p. 237. The italicized matter is the proposed

addition.

56. *Ibid.*, pp. 252–253.
57. *Ibid.*, pp. 251–252.
58. Ebersole, pp. 57–58.
59. *Congressional Record,* February 14, 1951.
60. Senate Joint Resolution 87, 83d Congress, 1st session.
61. *Religious News Service,* June 11, 1959.
62. *Ibid,* May 19, 1954.
63. Stokes, I, p. 498.
64. 143 U.S. 457 (1892).
65. Paulsen, p. 156.
66. See *e.g.,* Fahy, p. 82; Zorach vs. Clauson, 303 N.Y. 161 (1951).
67. See *infra,* p. 665.
68. 2 How. 127 (1844).
69. *Supra,* p. 159.
70. See *infra,* pp. 673 ff.
71. But see discussion of Sunday laws *infra,* pp. 270 ff.
72. Howe, pp. 8–13.
73. *American State Papers,* pp. 652–653.
74. *Supra,* p. 86.
75. See *supra,* p. 120.
76. Brant, Irving, *James Madison, Father of the Constitution,* Indianapolis, Bobbs-Merrill Co., 1950, pp. 272–273.
77. Stokes, I, p. 457, III, pp. 133, 135.
78. *Ibid.,* III, pp. 135–136.
79. Stokes, I, p. 457.
80. Fleet, p. 559.
81. *Ibid.,* pp. 558–559.
82. Stokes, III, p. 138.
83. *Ibid.,* III, pp. 130, 136.
84. 370 U.S. 421 (1962).
85. Elliott vs. White, 23 F 2d 997 (1928).
86. Fleet, p. 559.
87. *Ibid.,* pp. 559, 560.
88. See *supra,* p. 169.
89. Schenck vs. United States, 249 U.S. 47 (1919).
90. Deuteronomy 20:1–4.
91. 1 Eliz. 1, c. 1, Sect. 19.
92. 5 Eliz. 1, c. 1, Sect. 5.
93. 3 Jac. 1, c. 5.
94. 13 Car. 2, Stat. 2 c. 1, Sect. 12, 25 Car. 2 c. 2. See, generally, article on "non-Conformity," in *Encyclopedia of Religion and Ethics* (Hastings, ed., 1928) IX, pp. 381–393.
95. *Supra,* p. 85.
96. Greene, p. 51.
97. Farrand, III, 122.
98. *Ibid.,* II, p. 468.
99. *Ibid.,* III, p. 227.
100. *Ibid.,* II, pp. 461, 468.
101. Ford, Paul L., *Essays on the Constitution of the United States,* pp. 168–171.

102. See Ferrand, III, pp. 122, 227, 314; Elliot, II, pp. 118, 119, 148, 149, 193–200.
103. *Supra*, pp. 144–149.
104. 367 U.S. 488 (1961).
105. See *infra*, pp. 708 ff.
106. Hartogensis, B. H., "Denial of Equal Rights to Religious Minorities and Non-Believers in the United States," *Yale Law Journal*, 39 (1930), p. 667.
107. Torpey, William George, *Judicial Doctrines of Religious Rights in America*, Chapel Hill, N.C., University of North Carolina Press, 1948, p. 277.
108. Torpey, p. 278; Zollman, p. 616.
109. Biggs, J. C., "Religious Belief as Qualification of a Witness," *North Carolina Law Review*, 8 (1929), p. 31. Biggs erroneously omits Arkansas, though section 26 of article I of the Arkansas constitution contains a provision similar to that contained in the New York constitution.
110. Delaware, Maryland, New Hampshire, New Jersey, North Carolina, Pennsylvania, and South Carolina.
111. Li Sing vs. United States, 180 U.S. 486 (1900).
112. See *supra*, pp. 255–256.
113. New York *Times*, November 8, 1949, p. 1.
114. New York *Herald Tribune*, November 8, 1949.
115. *Time*, November 21, 1949.
116. People ex rel. Bernat vs. Bicek, 405 Ill. 510 (1950).
117. *Religious News Service*, June 2, 1950.
118. *Annals*, I, 1106–1108.
119. Foster, Charles R., *A Question of Religion* (pamphlet), University, Ala., University of Alabama Press, 1961, p. 3.
120. United States Code, Title 13, Section 225(2).
121. Foster, p. 9.
122. New York *Times*, July 15, 1957; Washington *Post*, July 16, 1957. See also Pfeffer, Leo, "Is It the Government's Business?", *Christian Century*, October 30, 1957.
123. Quoted in Healey, Robert M., *Jefferson on Religion in Public Education*, New Haven, Yale University Press, 1962, p. 127.
124. Foster, p. 12.
125. *Ibid.*

## CHAPTER EIGHT
### State Intervention in Church Affairs

1. Humphrey, p. 408.
2. Stokes, I, pp. 486–487.
3. Fleet, pp. 561–562.
4. Stokes, III, p. 181.
5. *Jefferson's Writings*, Monticello ed., 1905, XI, pp. 428–430.
6. See *supra*, pp. 128 ff.
7. Fleet, pp. 560–561.
8. Stokes, I, pp. 488–489.
9. Stokes, III, pp. 181–183.
10. *United States Code*, Title 5, Section 87B.
11. Stokes, III, p. 199.

12. *Religious News Service,* March 24, 1952.
13. H. J. Res. 188, 82nd Congress, 1st Session, March 7, 1951.
14. St. Louis *Register,* June 6, 1952; see *infra,* p. 553.
15. Information received from Board of Education.
16. Exodus 31:14, 15.
17. Yost, Frank H., "Sunday Laws are Religious Laws," *Congress Weekly,* March 3, 1952, p. 12.
18. Johnson, Alvin W., and Yost, Frank H., *Separation of Church and State in the United States,* Minneapolis, University of Minnesota Press, 1948, pp. 210 – 220.
19. *Ibid.,* p. 222.
20. *Ibid.,* pp. 221 – 222.
21. *Ibid.,* p. 224.
22. *American State Papers,* p. 30.
23. Goodman, p. 92.
24. People vs. Hoym, 20 How. Pr. (N.Y.) 76 (1860).
25. *Ibid.*
26. Lindenmuller vs. People, 33 Barb. (N.Y.) 548 (1861).
27. Matter of Rupp, 54 misc. 1, 105 N.Y.S. 407 (1907).
28. Shover vs. State, 10 Ark. 259 (1850).
29. Note, "Sunday Statutes in a Modern Community," *Yale Law Journal,* 61, March, 1952, p. 427.
30. Laws of 1952, chap. 301.
31. Held illegal in People vs. Friedman, 302 N.Y. 75 (1950); appeal dismissed 341 U.S. 907 (1951).
32. Note "Sunday Statutes . . . ," p. 430.
33. People vs. Hesterburg, 43 Misc. (N.Y.) 510 (1904).
34. Koelble vs. Woods, 92 Misc. (N.Y.) 254 (1916).
35. Stokes, III, p. 173.
36. Murdock vs. Pennsylvania, 319 U.S. 105 (1943); Follett vs. Town of McCormick, 321 U.S. 573 (1944); discussed below, pp. 725–726.
37. New York *Daily News,* October 19, 1951; *Brooklyn Eagle,* October 18, 1951.
38. Shreveport vs. Levy, 26 La. Ann. 671 (1874).
39. People vs. Friedman, 302 N.Y. 75 (1950); People vs. Adler, 174 App. Div. (N.Y.) 301 (1916); People vs. Rudnick, 259 App. Div. 922 (1940); State vs. Haining, 131 Kan. 853 (1930); Komen vs. City of St. Louis, 316 Mo. 9 (1926); Commonwealth vs. Has, 122 Mass. 40 (1877); State vs. Weiss, 97 Minn. 125 (1906).
40. Krieger vs. State, 12 Okla. Cr. App. 566 (1916); Robbins vs. State, 19 Ohio N.P. (N.S.) 606 (1915).
41. 302 N.Y. 75 (1950); appeal dismissed 341 U.S. 907 (1951).
42. The statutes are listed in Justice Frankfurter's concurring opinion in McGowan vs. Maryland, 366 U.S. 420 (1961).
43. Hennington vs. Georgia, 163 U.S. 299 (1896).
44. Petit vs. Minnesota, 177 U.S. 164 (1900).
45. Friedman vs. New York, 341 U.S. 907 (1951).
46. 366 U.S. 420 (1961).
47. 366 U.S. 582 (1961).
48. 366 U.S. 617 (1961).

49. 366 U.S. 599 (1961).
50. Perhaps it indicates only that Catholic concepts of proper Sabbath observance have displaced those of Puritan Protestantism, as they have done in respect to consumption of intoxicating liquors and are doing in respect to bingo and other forms of gambling. See, Pfeffer, Leo, *Creeds in Competition*, New York. Harper & Bros., 1958, pp. 93 – 111.
51. Reynolds vs. United States, 98 U.S. 145 (1878)., Discussed more fully *infra*, pp. 645–646.
52. Prince vs. Massachusetts, 321 U.S. 158 (1944). Discussed more fully *infra*, pp. 704–706.
53. See Ferguson vs. Skrupa, 372 U.S. 726 (1963).
54. McGowan vs. Maryland, 366 U.S. 420 (1961).
55. 80 U.S. 679 (1871).
56. Illustrative cases are to be found in Howe, pp. 94 – 227. Fairly comprehensive discussions of the numerous cases are in Zollman, Chap. 9, and Torpey, Chap. 4.
57. Gartin vs. Penick, 68 Ky. 110 (1868).
58. Watson vs. Avery, 2 Bush (Ky.) 332 (1869).
59. Article 3, section 2, of the United States Constitution allows suits to be brought in the Federal courts in controversies between citizens of different states.
60. Watson vs. Garvin, 54 Mo. 353 (1873).
61. See *supra*, p. 229.
62. "*Testem Benevolentiae*," *Catholic Encyclopedia*.
63. Quoted in Stokes, I, p. 808.
64. Dignan, Patrick J., *History of the Legal Incorporation of Catholic Church Property in the United States*, New York, P. J. Kenedy & Sons, 1935, p. 75.
65. Guilday, Peter, *The Life and Times of John Carroll*, New York, Encyclopaedia Press, 1922, p. 783.
66. Dignan, p. 82.
67. Stock, Leo F., *Consular Relations between the United States and the Papal States*, Washington, D.C., American Catholic Historical Association, 1945, pp. xxv – xxvi.
68. Billington, p. 40.
69. Krauczunas vs. Hoban, 221 Pa. 213 (1908).
70. Mazaika vs. Krauczunas, 229 Pa. 47 (1910).
71. Mazaika vs. Krauczunas, 233 Pa. 138 (1911).
72. Novickas vs. Krauczunas, 240 Pa. 248 (1913).
73. Novicky vs. Krauczunas, 245 Pa. 86 (1914).
74. St. Casimir's Polish Roman Catholic Church case, 273 Pa. St. 494 (1922).
75. Dignan, p. 148.
76. New York Religious Corporation Law, section 90.
77. St. Nicholas Cathedral vs. Kedroff, 302 N.Y. 1 (1950).
78. Kedroff vs. St. Nicholas Cathedral, 344 U.S. 94 (1952). For a later development in this case, see Kreshik vs. St. Nicholas Cathedral, 363 U.S. 190 (1960). See also the interesting case of Gonzalez vs. Archbishop 280 U.S. 1 (1929). See generally, Note, *Yale Law Journal*, 74 (1963) 1113.

79. This account is based on two pamphlets published by the Melish Case Defense Committee, "The Melish Case: Challenge to the Church"; "The Story of a Congregation," and the petition for writ of certiorari filed with the United States Supreme Court in Melish vs. The Rector, Church Wardens and Vestrymen of the Church of the Holy Trinity, all presenting the pro-Melish side; and on a memorandum "Church of the Holy Trinity" and the opinion of Justice Meir Steinbrink in Rector, Church Wardens and Vestrymen of Holy Trinity Church vs. Melish, 194 Misc. (N.Y.) 1006 (1949), presenting the pro-vestry side. I have not seen the memorandum itself but rely upon Stokes' summary, III, pp. 395 – 403.

80. 301 N.Y. 679, affirming 278 App. Div. 1088, affirming 194 Misc. 1006.

81. 340 U.S. 936 (1951).

82. Cadman Memorial Congregational Society vs. Kenyon, 197 Misc. (N.Y.) 124 (1950).

83. 279 App. Div. 1015 affirmed 306 N.Y. 151.

84. 340 U.S. 936 (1951).

85. Katz vs. Goldman, 168 N.E. 2d 763 (Ohio App., 1929); Katz vs. Singerman, 241 La. 103 (1961); Solomon vs. Congregation Tiffereth Israel, 183 N.E. 2d 492 (Mass. 1962).

86. Stock, *Consular Relations*, p. xxiii.

87. *Ibid.*, p. xxv.

88. Rush, Alfred C., "Diplomatic Relations, the United States and the Papal States," *American Ecclesiastical Review*, January, 1952, p. 13.

89. Stock, *Consular Relations*, p. 95.

90. Stock, Leo F., *United States Ministers to the Papal States,* Washington, D.C., Catholic University Press, 1933, p. xxii.

91. Billington, Ray A., *The Protestant Crusade,* New York, The Macmillan Co., 1938, p. 268.

92. Stock, *United States Ministers . . .* , p. xxii.

93. Feiertag, Loretta C., *American Public Opinion on the Diplomatic Relations between the United States and the Papal States,* Washington, D.C., Catholic University, 1933, pp. 6 – 12.

94. Stock, *United States Ministers . . .* , p. xxii.

95. Richardson, IV, p. 551.

96. Rush, pp. 16 – 17.

97. Stock, *United States Ministers . . .* , pp. 2 – 3.

98. Graham, Robert A., and Hartnett, Robert C., *Diplomatic Relations with the Vatican* (pamphlet), America Press, p. 7.

99. Stokes, I, p. 835.

100. *Ibid.,* II, p. 96.

101. Blau, Joseph L., "The Lesson of the Past," *The Nation,* January 12, 1952, pp. 30 – 33; Rush, pp. 19 – 25; Stock, *United States Ministers,* Introd.

102. *Reference Manual on U.S. Diplomatic Representation at the Vatican* (pamphlet), National Council of the Churches of Christ in the United States of America, p. 5.

103. New York *Times,* December 24, 1939.

104. Stokes, II, p. 97.

105. *Reference Manual,* p. 5.

106. *The Christian Century,* January 3, 1940.
107. *Reference Manual,* pp. 7 – 10.
108. *Time,* October 29, 1951.
109. Graham and Hartnett, p. 6.
110. *America,* November 3, 1951, p. 118; *The Living Church,* November 4, 1951.
111. *Congress Weekly,* December 3, 1951, p. 15.
112. *Look,* March 3, 1959.
113. Corwin, Edward S., "Letter to the Editor," New York *Times,* November 12, 1951.
114. *Reference Manual,* p. 34.
115. *Ibid.,* p. 35.
116. *Ibid.,* p. 34.
117. *Information Service,* National Council of Churches of Christ in the United States, December 1, 1951.
118. See *supra,* pp. 185 ff.
119. See United States vs. Lovett, 328 U.S. 303 (1946).
120. November 12, 1951.
121. Howe, Mark De Wolfe, "Diplomacy, Religion, and the Constitution," *The Nation,* January 12, 1952, p. 29.
122. *Supra,* pp. 129 ff.
123. Everson case, 330 U.S. 1 (1947); McCollum case, 333 U.S. 203 (1948); McGowan vs. Maryland, 366 U.S. 420 (1961); Torcaso vs. Watkins, 367 U.S. 488 (1961).
124. City of Ponce vs. Roman Catholic Apostolic Church, 210 U.S. 296 (1908).

CHAPTER NINE

*The Public School and Religious Education*

1. Standard volumes on the history of public education in the United States include Cubberley, Elwood P., *Public Education in the United States,* New York, Houghton Mifflin Co., 1919; Knight, Edgar W., *Education in the United States,* Boston, Ginn & Co., 1951; Graves, Frank P., *A History of Education in Modern Times,* New York, The Macmillan Co., 1928; Finney, R. L., *A Brief History of the American Public School,* New York, The Macmillan Co., 1946.
2. Beard, *Rise of American Civilization,* I, p. 177.
3. 333 U.S. 203.
4. Moehlman, Conrad H., *The Church as Educator,* New York, Hinds, Hayden & Eldredge, 1947, p. 56; Thayer, V. T., *Religion in Public Education,* New York, Viking Press, 1947, p. 139.
5. Finney, p. 3.
6. Cubberley, p. 22.
7. Rian, Edwin H., *Christianity and American Education,* San Antonio, The Naylor Co., 1949, p. 4.
8. *Ibid.,* p. 15.
9. Brown, Samuel W., *The Secularization of American Education,* New York, Columbia University Press, 1912, p. 17.
10. Finney, p. 4.
11. Cubberley, pp. 44 – 45.

12. Thayer, *Religion in Public Education*, p. 28.
13. Rian, p. 17.
14. *Ibid.*, pp. 19–20.
15. Commager, Henry Steele, *Documents of American History*, New York, F. S. Crofts, 1935; Cubberley, pp. 58–59; Knight, pp. 144–146.
16. Moehlman, Conrad H., *School and Church: The American Way*, New York, Harper & Brothers, 1944, p. 87.
17. Arrowood, Charles F., *Thomas Jefferson and Education in a Republic*, New York, McGraw Hill Co., 1930, p. 49; Healey, Robert M., *Jefferson on Religion in Public Education*, New Haven, Yale University Press, 1962, Ch. 9.
18. Honeywell, Roy J., *The Educational Work of Thomas Jefferson*, Cambridge, Mass., Harvard University Press, 1931, p. 24.
19. Curti, Merle E., *The Social Ideas of American Educators*, New York, Charles Scribner's Sons, 1935, p. 44.
20. Honeywell, pp. 13, 148.
21. Thayer, V. T., *The Attack upon the American Secular School*, Boston, Beacon Press, 1951, pp. 26–27.
22. Beard, *Rise of American Civilization*, I, p. 810.
23. Stuart vs. School District No. 1 of Kalamazoo, 30 Mich. 69 (1874); Interstate Ry. vs. Massachusetts, 207 U.S. 79 (1907); Cochran vs. Louisiana State Board of Education, 281 U.S. 370 (1930).
24. See *infra*, pp. 714 ff.
25. Moehlman, *School and Church*, p. 91.
26. Smith, Sherman M., *The Relation of the State to Religious Education in Massachusetts*, Syracuse, N.Y., Syracuse University, 1926, p. 95.
27. Rian, p. 42.
28. Moehlman, *School and Church*, p. 92.
29. Culver, Raymond B., *Horace Mann and Religion in the Massachusetts Public Schools*, New Haven, Yale University Press, 1929, p. 225.
30. Hay, Clyde L., *The Blind Spot in American Education*, New York, The Macmillan Co., 1950, p. 31.
31. Culver, p. 207.
32. Blau, pp. 179–182.
33. Fleming, W. S., *God in our Public Schools*, Pittsburgh, National Reform Association, 1942, p. 29.
34. Blau, pp. 185–186.
35. See *infra*, pp. 436 ff.
36. "Baltimore, Provisional Councils of," *Catholic Encyclopedia.*
37. Silcox, C. E., Fisher, G. M., *Catholics, Jews and Protestants*, New York, Harper & Brothers, 1934, p. 164. For an account, factually objective, of Catholic contributions to the secularization of New York's public schools, see Connors, Edward M., *Church-State Relationships in the State of New York*, Washington, D.C., Catholic University, 1951, Chaps. 2 and 3.
38. See, Thayer, *The Attack upon the American Secular School*, particularly Chap. 3.
39. McCollum case, 333 U.S. 203.
40. *Ibid.*
41. H. Res. 1, 44th Congress, 1st Session, 1876.

42. *Supra,* p. 147.
43. Rian, pp. 52 – 53.
44. Gibbons, Ray, "Protestantism and Public Education," *Social Action,* February 15, 1949, pp. 18 – 19.
45. See Griswold, Erwin, "Absolutism is in the Dark," *Utah Law Review,* 8 (1963), p. 166.
46. Gibbons, p. 17.
47. See Dawson, Joseph M., *Separate Church and State Now,* New York, Richard R. Smith, 1948, *passim.* See also the issues of *Report from the Capital,* monthly newsletter of the Baptists Joint Conference Committee on Public Affairs.
48. See *infra,* pp. 389–391.
49. Gibbons, pp. 15, 18.
50. *Public Education and Religion* (pamphlet), address delivered at 1940 Annual Meeting of the International Council of Religious Education.
51. Blanshard, Paul, *American Freedom and Catholic Power,* Boston, Beacon Press, 1949, pp. 80, 81.
52. Hearings before Subcommittee No. 1 of the Committee of Education and Labor of the House of Representatives, 80th Congress, First Session, on Federal Aid to Education, I, pp. 344 – 345.
53. *America,* April 3, 1948, p. xv, Supplement.
54. Quigley, Thomas J., "The Relationship Between Government and Church Sponsored Education," *Religious Education,* July – August, 1948, pp. 221 – 222.
55. *Five Great Encyclicals,* New York, Paulist Press, 1947, p. 40.
56. Redden, John D., and Ryan, Francis A., *A Catholic Philosophy of Education,* Milwaukee, Bruce Publishing Co., 1942, pp. 107, 118.
57. Johnson, George, "The Catholic Schools in America," *Atlantic Monthly,* April, 1940, p. 500.
58. Rian, p. 128; see *infra,* pp. 530 ff.
59. *Religious Education,* July – August, 1948, p. 227.
60. *Central Conference of American Rabbis Yearbook,* 14 (1904), pp. 120, 151. See also Fink, Joseph L., *Summary of C.C.A.R. Opinions on Church and State as Embodied in Resolutions adopted at Conferences Through the Years* (pamphlet), Central Conference of American Rabbis, 1948.
61. Brief *Amici Curiae* of Synagogue Council of America and National Community Relations Advisory Council in McCollum case, pp. 1 – 2.
62. Meyer, Agnes E., "The Clerical Challenge to the Schools," *Atlantic Monthly,* March, 1952, p. 46.
63. *The Status of Religious Education in the Public Schools* (pamphlet), National Education Association, Washington, D.C., 1949, pp. 13 – 15.
64. Weigle, Luther A., "The American Tradition and the Relation between Religion and Education," *Religion and Public Education, American Council on Education Studies,* Washington, D.C., IX, No. 22, February, 1945.
65. Fleming p. 226, quoted in Thayer, *The Attack upon the American Secular School,* pp. 54 – 55.
66. See, *e.g.,* Hay, Clyde L., *The Blind Spot in American Education,* New York, The Macmillan Co., 1950, Chap. 1, "Signs of the Times."
67. Quoted in Thayer, *Religion in Public Education,* p. 102.
68. "The Relation of Religion to Public Education," *American Council on*

*Education Studies,* Washington, XI, April, 1947, No. 26, p. 19.

69. Little, Lawrence C., "The Relation of Religion to Contemporary Public Education," *Religious Education,* 46, No. 4, July–August, 1951, p. 237.

70. Weigle, *Public Education and Religion,* p. 14.

71. Rian, p. 135; Guilday, Peter, *A History of the Councils of Baltimore,* New York, The Macmillan Co., 1932, p. 237.

72. Besides the authorities already cited in the notes to this section, the following may be helpful: American Council on Education, *The Study of Religion in the Public Schools: An Appraisal,* Washington, D.C., 1958; Bell, Bernard I., *Crisis in Education—A Challenge to American Complacency,* New York, McGraw Hill and Co., 1949; Bower, William C., *Church and State in Education,* Chicago, University of Chicago Press, 1944; Bryson, Lyman, and others, *Goals for American Education,* New York, Harper & Brothers, 1950; Gauss, Christian, "Should Religion Be Taught in Our Schools?" *Ladies Home Journal,* September, 1948, p. 40; Henry, Virgil, *The Place of Religion in the Public Schools,* New York, Harper & Brothers, 1950; Mattox, F. W., *The Teaching of Religion in the Public Schools,* Nashville, George Peabody College for Teachers, 1948; Trager, Frank N., *Religion, Intercultural Education and the School,* New York, National Community Relations Advisory Council, 1948; Van Dusen, Henry P., *God in Education: A Tract for Our Times,* New York, Charles Scribner's Sons, 1951; Worell, E. K., *Restoring God to Education,* Wheaton, Illinois, Van Kempen Press, 1910. The Bimonthly official organ of the Religious Education Association, *Religious Education,* should be particularly helpful.

73. Knowlton vs. Baumhover, 182 Iowa 691 (1918).

74. See Thayer, *Religion in Public Education,* pp. 109–111; Thayer, *The Attack upon the Secular School,* pp. 152–157.

75. Williamson, Henry J., "Religion and the Public Schools," *The Churchman,* August, 1947, p. 10.

76. Golden, Harry L., "Jews in the South," *Congress Weekly,* December 31, 1951, p. 11.

77. Weigle, *Public Education and Religion,* p. 17.

78. Johnson and Yost, p. 94.

79. *Ibid.,* pp. 97–98.

80. New York *Post,* May 13, 1962.

81. 102 Wash. 369 (1918).

82. Weigle, *The American Tradition . . . ,* pp. 33–34.

83. Henry, p. 81.

84. Bower, p. 60.

85. See Fink, p. 13.

86. "The Relation of Religion to Public Education," p. 15.

87. *Moral and Spiritual Values in the Public Schools,* National Education Association, Washington, D.C., 1951, pp. 77–79.

88. 374 U.S. 203 (1963).

89. Dierenfeld, Richard B., *Religion in American Public Schools,* Washington, Public Affairs Press, 1962.

90. "Transcript of Record," in McCollum case, pp. 99–103.

91. *Ibid.,* pp. 219–220.

92. Henry, p. 81.

93. Quoted in Thayer, *The Attack Upon the American Secular School,* p. 166.
94. Bower, William Clayton, *Moral and Spiritual Values in Education,* Lexington Ky., University of Kentucky Press, 1952; Hartford, E. F., *Moral Values in Public Education: Lessons from the Kentucky Experience,* New York, Harper and Brothers, 1958.
95. New York *Times,* January 30, 1956.
96. New York *Times,* June 27, July 30, September 13, 14, October 5, 1956; New York *Herald Tribune,* July 30, 1956.

CHAPTER TEN
*Released Time*

1. Rian, p. 219.
2. Davis, Mary Dabney, *Weekday Classes in Religious Education,* Bulletin 1941, No. 3, United States Office of Education, p. 1.
3. Quoted in Justice Frankfurter's concurring opinion in McCollum case, 333 U.S. 203.
4. Quoted in Collins, Joseph B., "Released Time for Religious Education," *American Ecclesiastical Review,* 115, No. 1, July, 1946, p. 14.
5. McCollum case, 333 U.S. 203.
6. A full bibliography on released time would be too large to incorporate in this volume. Besides the many authorities cited in Justice Frankfurter's concurring opinion in the McCollum case, which itself contains one of the best short summaries, the following might be consulted: Fine, Morris, "The Released Time Plan of Religious Education," *Contemporary Jewish Records,* February, 1941, p. 13; Collins, Joseph B., "Released Time for Religious Education," *American Ecclesiastical Review,* July, 1946, p. 11, and No. 2, August, 1946, p. 121; Pfeffer, Leo, *Religion and the Public Schools* (pamphlet), American Jewish Congress, 1949; Minsky, Louis, "The Released Time Plan of Religious Education," *Religion in Life,* Autumn 1943 issue, p. 1; Gove, Floyd S., *Religious Education on Public School Time,* Cambridge, Mass., Harvard University Press, 1926; Franer, William A., *Religious Instruction on Released School Time,* unpublished M.A. dissertation, Catholic University, 1942; *Religious Education and the Public Schools* (pamphlet), American Association for Jewish Education, undated; *The State and Sectarian Education* (pamphlet), National Education Association, Research Bulletin, 24, No. 1, February, 1946; Waterhouse, Howard A., "Is Released Time Worthwhile?" *The Christian Century,* October 2, 30, December 4, 1957. Particularly valuable are the 1941 United States Office of Education survey report by Mary Dabney Davis, the National Education Association 1949 report, *The Status of Religious Education in the Public Schools* (pamphlet), and the three reports of surveys conducted under the auspices of the Public Education Association of New York in 1943, 1945, and 1949, the last conducted under the direction of Dan W. Dodson. The National Education Association 1949 report contains a bibliography that is valuable for specific states.
7. McCollum case, 333 U.S. 203.
8. Howlett, Walter M., "Released Time for Religious Education in New York City," *Religious Education,* March—April, 1942, p. 104; Fine, p. 20.

9. People ex rel. Lewis vs. Graves, 245 N.Y. 195 (1927).
10. Howlett, p. 106.
11. Zorach vs. Clauson, 198 Misc. (N.Y.) 631.
12. New York *World-Telegram and Sun,* January 19, 1952.
13. *Religious News Service,* January 16, 1964.
14. Collins, p. 15.
15. Shaver, Erwin L., *Remember the Weekday to Teach Religion Thereon* (pamphlet), International Council of Religious Education, Chicago, Ill., 1949, Question 4.
16. Davis, Mary Dabney, *Weekday Religious Instruction,* Office of Education Pamphlet No. 36, Washington, D.C., 1933.
17. Davis, *Weekday Classes in Religious Education,* p. 12.
18. *The State and Sectarian Education,* p. 36.
19. Thayer, *Religion in Public Education,* pp. x–xi.
20. *Status of Religious Education,* p. 8.
21. Dierenfeld, p. 79.
22. *E.g.,* Hay, p. 22; Henry, p. 5.
23. Hay, p. 22.
24. *Religious News Service,* February 13, 1952.
25. New York *Times,* June 13, 1947.
26. Bureau of Census, U.S. Government Printing Office, Washington, D.C., p. 116.
27. In 1945, the average daily register of children in New York City's public schools was 845,817, in 1962 it had risen to 992,590. *World Almanac* (1964), p. 232.
28. *Religious News Service,* January 16, 1964.
29. "Religious Instruction on Time Released from Public School," *The Humanist,* VII, No. 4, Spring, 1948.
30. *The Weekday Church School* (pamphlet), Educational Bulletin No. 601, 1945, p. 2.
31. Blau, p. 86.
32. *1949 Study,* p. 31.
33. Stein vs. Brown, 125 Misc. N.Y. 692 (1925).
34. *1943 Report,* p. 10.
35. McPherson, Imogene M., "The Protestant Program of Teaching," *Religious Education,* January—February, 1943, p. 16.
36. Collins, p. 133.
37. *Remember the Weekday,* paragraph 3.
38. "The Weekday Church School—Opportunity and Challenge," *Information Service,* Federal Council of Churches of Christ in America, 21, No. 22, May 29, 1943.
39. Pierce vs. Society of Sisters, 268 U.S. 510 (1925).
40. For a fuller discussion of the religious liberty claim see, Kauper, Paul G., "*Church, State and Freedom:* A Review," *Michigan Law Review,* 52 (1954), pp. 829–49; Pfeffer, Leo, "Released Time and Religious Liberty: A Reply," *Michigan Law Review,* 53 (1954), pp. 91—98; Kauper, Paul G., "Released Time and Religious Liberty: A Further Reply," *Michigan Law Review,* 53 (1954), pp. 223—235.
41. 198 Misc. (N.Y.) 631.
42. New York *Times,* November 16, 1949.

43. Quoted in Hay, p. 24; see also Rian, p. 222.
44. Pp. 106, 112–113.
45. See *infra*, pp. 397, 404.
46. New York *Times,* April 12, 1949; Providence *Journal,* November 1, 1949.
47. Gabel, Richard J., *Public Funds for Church and Private Schools,* Washington, D.C., Catholic University, 1937, p. 737.
48. See *infra*, pp. 450, 461–462.
49. "Twenty-five Years of Jewish Education in the United States," *American Jewish Year Book,* 1936–1937, p. 107; Hurwich, Louis, "Religious Education and the Release Time Plan," *Jewish Education,* 1941, pp. 103–107.
50. The position of the Jewish organizations was arrived at after a three-day national conference of representatives of all major Jewish national and local organizations, religious and secular, held in New York City in November, 1947, under the direction of Jules Cohen, National Coordinator of the National Community Relations Advisory Council.
51. Shaver, Erwin L., "They Reach One-Third," *International Journal of Religious Education,* December, 1943, p. 11.
52. Blair, W. Dyer, "A Case for the Weekday Church School," *Frontiers of Democracy,* December 15, 1950, pp. 75–76.
53. Hay, p. 23.
54. "Religious Education on Time Released from Public School," *The Humanist,* Spring, 1948.
55. Davis, *Weekday Classes,* p. 19.
56. *The Status of Religious Education,* p. 10.
57. Davis, *Weekday Classes,* p. 20.
58. *1949 Report,* p. 27.
59. Beckes, Isaac K., *Weekday Relgious Education: Help or Hindrance to Inter-Religious Understanding,* National Conference of Christians and Jews, Human Relations Pamphlet No. 6, 1946.
60. Educational Code of California (Deering, 1944) sec. 8286; 6 Indiana Statutes Annotated (Burns, 1934) 1945 Supplement, sec. 28–505a; 1 Code of Iowa, Chap. 299, sec. 299.2 (1946); Kentucky Revised Statutes (1946) sec. 158–220; Revised Statutes of Maine (1944), Chap. 37, sec. 131; 2 Annotated Laws of Massachusetts (1945), Chap. 76, sec. 1; Michigan, Sec. 732 (G) of Act 296 P.A. 1955, as amended by Act 270 P.A. 1964; Minnesota Statutes (1945), sec. 132–05; New York Education Law, sec. 3210 (1); 8 Annotated Laws of Oregon (1940), sec. 111–3014; 24 Pennsylvania Statutes Annotated (Purdon, 1930), 1947 Supplement, sec. 1563; 1 Code of South Dakota (1939), sec. 15.3202; 1 Code of West Virginia (1943), sec. 1847.
61. People ex rel. Lewis vs. Graves, 245 N.Y. 195 (1927); People ex rel. Latimer vs. Board of Education, 394 Ill. 228 (1946).
62. Stein vs. Brown, 125 Misc. (N.Y.) 692 (1925).
63. People ex rel. Lewis vs. Graves, 245 N.Y. 195.
64. People ex rel. Latimer vs. Board of Education, 394 Ill. 228 (1946).
65. Gordon vs. Board of Education, 78 Cal. App. 2nd Series 464 (1947).
66. McCollum case, 333 U.S. 203 (1948).
67. Transcript of record in McCollum case, pp. 1–2.

769

68. *Ibid.,* pp. 121, 162.
69. *Ibid.,* pp. 96–97.
70. See Olson, Bernhard E., *Faith and Prejudice,* New Haven, Yale University Press, 1963, pp. 195–222.
71. *Religious News Service,* July 7, 1948.
72. See, *e.g.,* opinion of California Attorney General No. 48/83, April 21, 1948; opinion of Attorney General of Virginia, July 9, 1948; opinion of Attorney General of Florida, 48–209, June 23, 1948.
73. *The Churchman,* August, 1948, p. 24.
74. Balazs vs. Board of Education of St. Louis, Circuit Court, St. Louis, Mo., No. 18369, Div. No. 3, Opinion per Koerner, J., filed May 25, 1948.
75. Matter of Lewis vs. Spaulding, 193 Misc. N.Y. 66; appeal withdrawn, 299 N.Y. 564 (1948).
76. Transcript of record in Zorach case, pp. 15–16.
77. *Ibid.,* pp. 16–18.
78. Extracts from some of these affidavits appear in a note, "Released Time Reconsidered: The New York Plan is Tested," *Yale Law Journal,* 61, No. 3, March, 1952, pp. 405–416.
79. This and the succeeding affidavits are on file in the office of the County Clerk of Kings County in the case of Zorach vs. Clauson, Index No. 10327/1948.
80. *New York Law Journal,* August 23, 1950, p. 299.
81. 198 Misc. (N.Y.) 631.
82. 278 App. Div. 573.
83. 303 N.Y. 161.
84. 343 U.S. 306 (1952).

CHAPTER ELEVEN
*Bible and Prayer in the Public School*

1. Billington, p. 220.
2. Williams, Michael, *The Shadow of the Pope,* New York, McGraw-Hill Book Co., 1932, p. 75.
3. Billington, pp. 220–230; Williams, pp. 75–76; Myers, pp. 175–179.
4. Billington, pp. 231, 295.
5. *Ibid.,* pp. 413–414.
6. Johnson and Yost, p. 33.
7. 38 Me. 376 (1854).
8. Williams, pp. 85–86.
9. Donahoe vs. Richards, 38 Me. 376 (1854).
10. Commonwealth vs. Cooke, 7 Am. L. Reg. 417 (1859); Howe, pp. 316–321. For somewhat similar incidents in New York, see Connors, p. 68.
11. Whipple, Leon, *The Story of Civil Liberty in the United States,* New York, Vanguard Press, 1927, p. 64.
12. Beale, Howard K., *A History of Freedom of Teaching in American Schools,* New York, Charles Scribner's Sons, 1941, p. 211.
13. The account that follows is based in large part on Helfman, Harold M., "The Cincinnati 'Bible War,' 1869–1870," *Ohio State Archaeological and Historical Quarterly,* 60, No. 4, October, 1951, pp. 369–386.
14. Board of Education of Cincinnati vs. Minor, 23 Ohio St. 211 (1872).

15. Brief *Amicus Curiae* of City of New York in Doremus case, p. 2.
16. Dierenfeld, p. 51.
17. National Education Association, *The State and Sectarian Education,* pp. 26–27.
18. North Dakota Compiled Laws (1913), sec. 1388.
19. See, *e.g.,* Revised Statutes of New Jersey (1937), 18:14–17.
20. See, *e.g.,* ibid., 18:14–78.
21. See North Dakota laws, quoted above.
22. Keesecker, Ward W., *Legal Status of Bible Reading,* United States Office of Education, Bulletin No. 14 (1930); Johnson and Yost, Chap. 4.
23. See *supra,* pp. 350 ff.
24. Stokes, II, p. 566.
25. West Virginia Board of Education vs. Barnette, 319 U.S. 624 (1943), discussed below, pp. 640 ff.
26. Synagogue Council of America, *Report of Conference on Religious Education and the Public School,* 1944, p. 26.
27. People ex rel. Ring vs. Board of Education, 245 Ill. 334 (1910).
28. State ex rel. Weiss vs. District Board, 76 Wisc. 177 (1890).
29. 370 U.S. 421 (1962).
30. 374 U.S. 203 (1963).
31. Stokes, II, p. 571.
32. "Another Tradition at Stake," *Catholic Action,* February, 1950, p. 4.
33. 284 U.S. 573 (1930).
34. 159 Wash. 519 (1930).
35. 342 U.S. 429 (1952).
36. That this was the sole ground for the dismissal of the parent's appeal is not clear from the opinion in the Doremus case, but it was made clear in the court's opinion in the Zorach case that this was the only ground for dismissal.
37. Carden vs. Bland, 288 S.W. 2d 718 (1956).
38. The cases are summarized in Johnson and Yost, Chap. 4, in Keesecker, and in Boles, Donald E., *The Bible, Religion and the Public Schools,* Ames, Iowa, Iowa State University Press, 1961. See also note, "Bible Reading in Public Schools." *Michigan Law Review,* 28, (1930), p. 430.
39. These cases include Donahoe vs. Richards, 38 Me. 376 (1854); Spiller vs. Inhabitants of Woburn, 94 Mass. 127 (1866); Hackett vs. Brooksville Graded School District, 120 Ky. 608 (1905); Billard vs. Board of Education, 69 Kans. 53 (1904); Church vs. Bullock, 104 Tex. 1 (1908); Wilkerson vs. City of Rome, 152 Ga. 762, 110 S.E. 895 (1922); People vs. Stanley, 81 Colo. 276 (1927); Kaplan vs. Independent School District, 171 Minn. 142 (1927); Doremus vs. Board of Education, 5 N.J. 435 (1950); Carden vs. Bland, 288 S.W. 2d 722 (1956).
40. 120 Ky. 608.
41. People ex rel. Ring vs. Board of Education, 245 Ill. 334 (1910); State ex rel. Weiss vs. District Board, 76 Wisc. 177 (1890); State ex rel. Freeman vs. Scheve, 65 Nebr. 853 (1902); Herold vs. Parish Board, 136 La. 1034 (1915).
42. 245 Ill. 334 (1910).
43. Evans vs. Selma Union High School Board, 193 Calif. 54 (1924).
44. *Religious News Service,* May 11, 1950.

45. *Catholic Bulletin,* May 28, 1950.
46. *Religious News Service,* May 17, 1950.
47. *Ibid.,* December 6, 1950.
48. *Ibid.,* November 8, 1949.
49. *Ibid.,* November 3, 1949.
50. November 2, 1949.
51. 14 N.J. 31 (1953) certiorari denied 348 U.S. 816 (1954).
52. Orange County Board of Public Instruction vs. Brown, 155 So. 2d 371 (1963).
53. Arizona: OAG 61-14 (1961); California: 25 Cal. Ops. A/G 316 (1955); Colorado: 1955 – 1956 Colo. A/G Rept. 62 (1955). Pennsylvania: Op. Att. Gen., May 31, 1956; Washington: AGO 61-62 No. 118 (1962) Contra: Maine, 1951 – 1954 Me. A/G Rept. 217 (1953).
54. *E.g.,* Hackett vs. Brooksville Graded School District, 120 Ky. 608 (1905); Wilkerson vs. City of Rome, 152 Ga. 762 (1922); Church vs. Bullock, 104 Tex. 1 (1908).
55. 94 Mass. 127 (1866).
56. 69 Kans. 53 (1904).
57. See, *e.g.,* Doremus case, 5 N.J. 435 (1950); State ex rel. Finger vs. Weedman, 55 S.D. 343 (1929); Billard vs. Board of Education of Topeka, 69 Kans. 53 (1904); Moore vs. Monroe, 64 Iowa 367 (1884).
58. See, *e.g.,* Doremus case, 5 N.J. 435 (1950).
59. New York *Times,* December 1, 1951.
60. *Ibid.*
61. New York *Times,* January 9, 1952.
62. Peekskill *Evening Star,* January 16, 1952.
63. New York *Times,* December 15, 1961, January 4, 17, 1952; New York *Herald Tribune,* December 19, 1951, January 4, 1952.
64. New York *Times,* December 10, 1951; New York *Herald Tribune,* December 18, 1951; New York *Compass,* February 10, 1952.
65. The *Tablet,* December 8, 1951; New York *Times,* December 1, 1951; January 13, 1952.
66. New York *Herald Tribune,* March 18, 1952.
67. Engel vs. Vitale, 18 Misc. 2d 659 (1959).
68. 11 App. Div. 2d 340. 10 N.Y. 2d 174 (1961).
69. 370 U.S. 421 (1962).
70. New York *Times,* July 1, 1962.
71. *Ibid.*
72. Washington *Post,* July 7, 1962.
73. New York *Times,* July 4, 1962.
74. New York *Times,* July 1, 1962.
75. *Ibid.*
76. Abington School District vs. Schempp, 374 U.S. 203 (1963).
77. *Religious News Service,* March 7, 1963.
78. House Judiciary Committee Hearings on "School Prayers," April 22 – June 3, 1964, p. 742. (These Hearings contain a wealth of information on reactions to the Schempp-Murray decision.)
79. *Ibid.,* p. 572.
80. *Ibid.,* pp. 566 – 567.
81. *Religious News Service,* June 18, 1963.

82. *Ibid.*
83. *Religious News Service,* June 17, 1963.
84. *Religious News Service,* June 18, 1963.
85. *Ibid.*
86. *Religious News Service,* June 19, 1963.
87. *Ibid.*
88. *Religious News Service,* June 21, 1963.
89. *Religious News Service,* June 18, 1963.
90. *Ibid.*
91. New York *Times,* June 18, 1963.
92. The most complete and convenient source for materials on the Becker Amendment is the three-volume House Judiciary Committee Hearings on "School Prayers."
93. *Ibid.,* p. 212. The texts are set forth, *ibid.,* pp. 1–59.
94. *Ibid.,* pp. 212–213; *Religious News Service,* September 9, 1963.
95. This summary is based on a survey conducted by the American Jewish Congress in the organization's *Information Bulletin* No. 27, October 1, 1963; and on a similar survey conducted by the American Jewish Committee and reported in December 1963 in that organization's *Research Report* entitled "Bible Reading after the Schempp-Murray Decision."

CHAPTER TWELVE
*Religious Practices in the Public Schools*

1. New York *Herald Tribune,* December 6, 1947.
2. *Religious News Service,* December 8, 1947.
3. New York *PM,* December 6, 1947.
4. *Ibid.,* December 5, 1947.
5. *Ibid.,* December 5, 1947.
6. New York *Herald Tribune,* December 6, 1947; New York *PM,* December 14, 1947.
7. The details of the Chelsea incident have been obtained from reports to the writer by Gerald Berlin, local counsel of the American Jewish Congress, and Robert E. Segal, director of the Jewish Community Council of Boston, both of whom personally interviewed the principal participants, and from newspaper reports in the Chelsea *Record,* the Boston *Globe* and the Boston *Post.*
8. Report to the National Community Relations Advisory Council and to the Synagogue Council of America from the Jewish Community Council of Camden, N.J. The report is in the files of the National Community Relations Advisory Council. For a humorous account of how one Jewish family solved this difficulty, see Sharnik, John S., "O Hum, All Ye Faithful," *The New Yorker,* December 25, 1948.
9. *National Jewish Post,* December 30, 1949.
10. Hayman, Julius, "Christmas Observance and the Jewish Community," *Jewish Standard* (Toronto), January, 1951, p. 6.
11. Suffern *Journal News,* December 14, 1950; *Ramopo Valley Independent,* December 14, 1950, December 21, 1950.
12. *Long Island Review-Star,* December 12, 1951.
13. This account of the White Plains incident is based on a background memorandum prepared by the American Jewish Committee, supple-

mented by reports from local members of the American Jewish Congress and newspaper reports in the New York *World Telegram and Sun,* December 19, 1950; *The Tablet,* December 23, 1950; New York *Herald Tribune,* December 10, 1950; New York *Times,* December 20, 1950; *National Jewish Post,* January 12, 1951.

14. The details of the Dade County case related herein are taken from the transcript of the Record on Appeal in the case of Chamberlin vs. Dade County Board of Public Instruction, 142 So. 2d 21 (1962) and from personal interviews by the author in his capacity as council for the plaintiffs in that case.

15. Blau, p. 86.

16. Trager, Frank N., *Religion, Intercultural Education and the School* (pamphlet), National Community Relations Advisory Council, New York, 1948, p. 15.

17. Vincent, Sidney, *The Hanukah Manual for Public School Teachers* (pamphlet), Jewish Community Council of Cleveland, undated. See also *Sharing the December Holidays* (pamphlet), St. Paul Council of Human Relations, undated.

18. December 1950, p. 554.

19. The author is Turkel, Roma Rudd. See also Clemente, Thomas A., "Double or Nothing," *Commonweal,* December 22, 1950, p. 273.

20. Benard, Edmond Durvil, "The 'Meaning' of the Springfield Plan," *American Ecclesiastical Review,* February, 1945, p. 1.

21. By Chatto, Clarenee I., and Halligan, Alice L.

22. Alland, Alexander, and Wise, James Waterman, *The Springfield Plan: A Photographic Record,* New York, Viking Press, 1945.

23. Italics in original. See also *American Ecclesiastical Review,* September, 1948, p. 219; October, 1949, p. 341.

24. O'Connor vs. Hendrick, 184 N.Y. 421 (1906).

25. Zellers vs. Huff, 55 N.M. 501 (1951).

26. Gerhardt vs. Heid, 66 N.D. 444 (1936): State ex rel. Johnson vs. Boyd, 217 Ind. 348 (1940); Hysong vs. Gallitzin Borough School District, 164 Pa. 629 (1894); Sargent vs. Board of Education, 177 N.Y. 317, 69 N.E. 722 (1904).

27. Gerhardt vs. Heid, 66 N.D. 444; Rawlings vs. Butler, 290 S.W. 2d 801 Ky. (1956).

28. Hysong vs. Gallitzin Borough School District, 164 Pa. 629 (1894).

29. Commonwealth vs. Herr, 229 Pa. 132 (1910).

30. *E.g.,* Arizona Code Annotated, 1939, sec. 54:1006; Oregon Statutes, 1943, sec. 111–2106, 2109.

31. *The State and Sectarian Education,* p. 36. The report lists North Dakota, New Mexico, and Missouri among the states permitting the practice; but after the report was written North Dakota enacted a law prohibiting the wearing of religious garb; the New Mexico state education department issued a similar regulation; and judicial decisions in Missouri would appear to bar the employment of all nuns as public school teachers.

32. Gerhardt vs. Heid, 66 N.D. 444; Zellers vs. Huff, 55 N.M. 501; Rawlings vs. Butler, 290 S.W. 2d 801 (Ky. 1956).

33. Gerhardt vs. Heid, 66 N.D. 444.

34. O'Connor vs. Hendrick, 184 N.Y. 421.

35. Zellers vs. Huff, 55 N.M. 501.

36. 349 Mo. 808 (1942).

37. These canons were quoted in part in Justice Jackson's dissent in the Everson case; see *supra*, p. 345.

38. Berghorn vs. Reorganized School District No. 8; Circuit Court of Franklin County, Missouri, No. 1291, Opinion per Crouse, J., April 21, 1952, affirmed 364 Mo. 121 (1953).

39. U.S. Constitution, Article II, section 2. During World War I a Quaker was discharged from employment as teacher in the public schools of New York, but the evidence disclosed that she had refused to urge her pupils to do Red Cross work or buy thrift stamps. McDowell vs. Board of Education, 104 Misc. (N.Y.) 564 (1918).

40. Dissent in Hysong vs. Gallitzin Borough School District, 164 Pa. 629 (1894).

41. California: San Francisco *Chronicle,* June 2, 1961; Maine: New York *Times,* March 25, 1958, Boston *Pilot,* March 29, 1958, Washington *Post-Times Herald,* June 2, 1959; Minnesota: Minneapolis *Star,* June 7, 1955, March 11, 1958, St. Paul *Pioneer Press,* May 21, 1957; New Jersey: New York *Times,* June 16, 1956, New York *Herald Tribune,* June 5, 1959; New York: Catholic *Universe Bulletin,* June 29, 1951, *Religious News Service,* Nov. 3, 1952, July 6, 12, 1954; North Carolina: *Religious News Service,* May 27, 1953, *Catholic Light,* April 9, 1953; Oregon: *Religious News Service,* December 9, 1960; Pennsylvania: Pittsburgh *Post Gazette,* May 30, 1952, *Religious News Service,* March 4, 1957, May 31, 1960; Vermont: *Religious News Service,* November 20, 1963; West Virginia: New York *Post,* April 21, 1957, *Religious News Service,* May 21, 23, 1957, February 17, 1958, February 15, 1960, February 18, 1963; Wisconsin: *Religious News Service,* June 10, 1952.

42. Washington *Post and Times Herald,* June 9, 1959.

43. *Religious News Service,* June 7, 1950; New York *Times,* June 15, 1950.

44. New York *Herald Tribune,* June 6, 1950.

45. *Religious News Service,* June 8, 1950.

46. Opinion of Hon. Lewis A. Wilson, Commissioner of Education, in the Matter of the Appeal of Rt. Rev. Msgr. Edward V. Dargin, June 12, 1951.

47. Miller vs. Cooper, 56 N.M. 355 (1952). See also, Balgooyen vs. Board of Trustees, Calif. Super. Ct., No. 156913 (1964); Chamberlin vs. Dade County Board of Public Instruction, 142 So. 2d 21 (1962).

48. Pittsburgh *Post-Gazette,* May 30, 1952.

49. *Church and State Newsletter,* July, 1952, p. 3.

50. Pope, Liston, "Religion and our Schools," *The American Magazine,* May, 1952.

51. On this subject see generally: Allen, Henry E., ed., *Religion in the State University: An Initial Exploration,* Minneapolis, Burgess Publishing Co., 1950; Walter, Erich A., *Religion in the State University,* Ann Arbor, University of Michigan Press, 1958; Littell, Franklin H., "Church, State and University," in Giannella, Donald A., ed., *Religion and the Public Order, 1963,* Chicago, University of Chicago Press, 1964.

52. Shedd, Clarence Prouty, "Religion in the American State University: Its History and Present Problem," in Allen, Henry E., ed., *Religion in*

*the State University: An Initial Exploration,* Minneapolis, Burgess Publishing Co., 1950, pp. 24 – 25.

53. McCollum case, 333 U.S. 203.
54. Butts, pp. 121 – 130.
55. State ex rel. Sholes vs. University of Minnesota, 54 N.W. 2d 122 (Minn. 1952).

CHAPTER THIRTEEN
*State Aid to Religious Education*

1. According to the United States Office of Education, nine out of ten children attending nonpublic schools are enrolled in Catholic parochial schools. *The State and Nonpublic Schools,* Washington, D.C., U.S. Government Printing Office, 1958, p. 2.
2. In 1947 there were 35,219 children enrolled in Seventh Day Adventist Schools, Stokes, II, p. 645; the total membership of the church was estimated at 208,030. *Annals of the American Academy of Political and Social Sciences,* March, 1948, p. 165. In the same year there were 2,607,879 children enrolled in Catholic schools, Stokes, II, p. 645. The total church membership was estimated at 25,268,173, *Annals,* p. 168. The absolute figures have increased substantially since then, but the ratios remain substantially the same. See *Yearbook of American Churches,* 1964.
3. See almost any issue of *Liberty,* organ of the General Conference of Seventh Day Adventists.
4. Stokes, II, p. 645.
5. Rian, p. 214.
6. *Ibid.,* pp. 208 – 209; Stokes, II, p. 645; *The State and Nonpublic Schools,* U.S. Office of Education, 1958, p. 2.
7. Silcox and Fisher, p. 201.
8. Jewish Education Association of New York, "Twenty-five Years of Jewish Education in the United States," *American Jewish Year Book,* 1936 – 1937, p. 37.
9. *American Jewish Year Book,* 1964 p. 86.
10. See General Summary of *The Official Catholic Directory (1963);* Hearings before Senate Subcommittee on Education at S. 370, Eighty-ninth Cong., First Session, p. 2548.
11. New York *Times,* March 30, 1952.
12. *Supra,* p. 345.
13. Redden, John D., and Ryan, Frances A., *A Catholic Philosophy of Education,* Milwaukee, Bruce Publishing Co., 1942, pp. 107, 118.
14. *Ibid.,* p. 29.
15. Fichter, Joseph H., *Parochial Schools: A Sociological Study,* Notre Dame, Ind., University of Notre Dame Press, 1958, p. 86.
16. Burns, J. A., *The Catholic School System in the United States,* New York, Benziger Brothers, 1908, p. 249.
17. *Ibid.,* p. 374.
18. Silcox and Fisher, p. 170.
19. Burns, J. A., *The Growth and Development of the Catholic School System in the United States,* New York, Benziger Bros., 1912, p. 195.
20. Hearings before House Committee on Education and Labor on H.R. 6074, Eighty-eighth Congress, p. 540.

21. *Ibid.*
22. Stokes, II, p. 659; Cushing, Archbishop Richard J., "The Case for Religious Schools," *The Saturday Review,* May 3, 1952, p. 14; Heely, Allan V., "A Call for Diversity," *ibid.,* p. 15; Rian, Chap. VIII; McGucken, William H., *The Philosophy of Catholic Education* (pamphlet), New York, America Press; Hartnett, Robert C., *The Right to Educate* (pamphlet), New York, America Press, 1949; McCluskey, Neil G., S.J., *Catholic Viewpoint of Education,* Garden City, N.Y., Hanover House, 1959; Ward, Leo, C.S.C., *Federal Aid to Private Schools,* Westminster, Md., Newman Press, 1964.
23. Stokes, II, pp. 659–660; Silcox and Fisher, pp. 178–184; Conant, James B., "The Threat of the Private School," *Saturday Review,* May 3, 1952, p. 11; Moehlman, *School and Church: The American Way,* Chaps. 5 and 6; Ryan, Mary, P., *Are Parochial Schools the Answer?,* New York, Holt, Rinehart and Winston, 1964.
24. 268 U.S. 510 (1925).
25. Myers, p. 293.
26. The religious liberty aspect of the Pierce case is discussed below, pp. 629 ff.
27. The Court cited Hitchman Coke and Coal Co. vs. Mitchell, 245 U.S. 229, and American Steel Foundries vs. Tri-City Central Trades Council, 257 U.S. 184. Both cases sustained injunctions against picketing and boycotts by labor unions.
28. 262 U.S. 390 (1923).
29. *Ibid.*
30. 273 U.S. 284 (1927).
31. Carr, Matter of (St. Johns University), 231 N.Y.S. 2d 410 (1962) affirmed 235 N.Y.S. 2d 834 (1962).
32. 342 U.S. 884 (1951); discussed below, pp. 714 ff.
33. Blanshard, p. 73.
34. This and the following statements in this section are based on the 1946 study of the National Education Association, *The State and Sectarian Education,* pp. 38–41. See also, *The State and Nonpublic Schools,* pp. 8–11.
35. *E.g.,* Kentucky, New Hampshire, and New Mexico.
36. *E.g.,* Kentucky.
37. *E.g.,* Maine, Michigan.
38. *E.g.,* Nebraska, North Dakota.
39. *E.g.,* Michigan, Nebraska, South Dakota.
40. Hearings on H.R. 6074, p. 539.
41. New York *Times,* August 9, 1952.
42. Hearings on H.R. 6074, p. 539.
43. *Ibid.,* p. 540.
44. Callahan, Daniel, ed., *Federal Aid and Catholic Schools,* Baltimore, Helicon Press, 1964; Blum, Virgil C., S.J., *Freedom of Choice in Education,* New York, Macmillan, 1958; McCluskey; Brickman and Lehrer; Hearings on Federal Aid to Schools, H.R., 4970, 87th Congress, March 1951; National Catholic Welfare Conference, "The Constitutionality of the Inclusion of Church-Related Schools in Federal Aid to Education," *Georgetown Law Journal,* Vol. 50, No. 2, 1961.

45. For other examples see Hearings on H.R. 6074, pp. 32–48.

46. Brickman and Lehrer, pp. 144–247. Australia, like the United States, does not grant any financial assistance to confessional schools, though it did so until 1880. Keane, William, "Australia: A Study in Courage," in Hartnett, Robert C., ed., *The Right to Educate* (pamphlet), New York, America Press, 1949, p. 25.

47. See *supra*, p. 52.

48. See *infra* pp. 601–603.

49. Thayer, *The Attack upon the American Secular School*, Chap. 6, "Should the Public Support Non-Public Schools"; Childs, John L., "New Threats to the Principle of Separation," *Progressive Education*, February, 1949; Konvitz, Milton R., "Whittling Away Religious Freedom," *Commentary*, June, 1946; Hearings on H.R. 4970.

50. Arnold, James W., "Religious Textbooks; Primers in Bigotry," *Ave Maria*, October 10, 17, 1964.

51. Dawson, *Separate Church and State Now, passim;* Gibbons, *Protestantism and Public Education;* Dana, Ellis H., *Storm Clouds over our Public Schools* (pamphlet), Wisconsin Council of Churches, Madison, Wisconsin, 1948; statement of Dr. Samuel McRea Cavert, Hearings before Subcommittee No. 1 of the House Committee on Education and Labor on Federal Aid for Education, Eightieth Congress, First Session, 1947, pp. 423–427.

52. Hearings before House Subcommittee on Education on H.R. 2361 and 2362, 89th Congress, First Session, p. 740.

53. "The Catholic Schools in America," *Atlantic Monthly*, 165 (April, 1940), p. 504.

54. Hearings before Subcommittee No. 1., pp. 310–311.

55. Note, "Catholic Schools and Public Money," *Yale Law Journal*, 50, p. 917 (1941); National Education Association, *The State and Sectarian Education;* U.S. Office of Education, *The State and Nonpublic Schools.*

56. Sargent vs. Board of Education, 177 N.Y. 317 (1904).

57. Rian, pp. 123–126; Butts, p. 133.

58. Billington, p. 145.

59. Rian, pp. 124–126.

60. Burns, *Catholic School System*, p. 370.

61. *Ibid.*, pp. 370–372; Billington, pp. 130–131.

62. Rian, p. 128.

63. New York Laws of 1844, Chap. 320, sec. 12.

64. Gabel, pp. 348–470; Brown, Samuel W., *The Secularization of American Education*, New York, Columbia University Press, 1912, pp. 48-74.

65. New York State Constitutional Convention Committee, *Problems Relating to the Bill of Rights and General Welfare*, Albany, 1938, p. 267.

66. Judd vs. Board of Education, 278 N.Y. 200 (1938).

67. Root, Elihu, *Addresses on Government and Citizenship*, Cambridge, Mass., Harvard University Press, 1916, p. 140.

68. Justice Frankfurter concurring in McCollum case, 333 U.S. 203.

69. Citations of the relevant provisions are listed in Note, "Catholic Schools and Public Money," *Yale Law Journal*, 50, pp. 920–921; National Education Association, *The State and Sectarian Education*, pp. 11–12.

70. Everson case, 330 U.S. 1. The state cases are discussed in National

Education Association, *The State and Sectarian Education,* pp. 14–17; *American Law Reports,* V, pp. 879 ff., CXLI, pp. 1148 ff.

71. Dunn vs. Chicago Industrial School, 280 Ill. 613 (1917); People ex rel. Roman Catholic Orphan Asylum Society vs. Board of Education, 13 Barb (N.Y.) 400 (1851); Sargent vs. Board of Education, 177 N.Y. 317 (1904); New Haven vs. Town of Torrington, 132 Conn. 194 (1945); Crain vs. Walker, 222 Ky. 828 (1928).

72. Cook County vs. Chicago Industrial School, 125 Ill. 540 (1888); State ex rel. Nevada Orphan Asylum vs. Hallock, 16 Nev. 385 (1882).

73. 175 U.S. 291 (1899); see *supra,* pp. 199–200.

74. 210 U.S. 50 (1908).

75. By act of June 7, 1897, Congress made this declaration of policy.

76. At p. 17.

77. Senate Subcommittee Hearings on S. 370, p. 115.

78. New York *World-Telegram,* August 6, 1949.

79. 197 Va. 419 (1955).

80. 122 Vt. 177 certiorari denied 366 U.S. 925 (1961).

81. National Education Association, *The State and Sectarian Education,* p. 17.

82. Burns, *Growth and Development,* pp. 243–247, 261.

83. Silcox and Fisher, p. 173.

84. Note, "Catholic Schools and Public Money," *Yale Law Journal,* 50, p. 917.

85. This account of the North College Hill incident is based on the following: *North College Hill, Ohio* (pamphlet), *Report of an Investigation by National Commission for the Defense of Democracy through Education of the National Education Association,* Washington, D.C., 1947; Petition of Frieda Reckman in case of Reckman vs. Frank, Court of Common Pleas, Hamilton County, Ohio; Fey, Harold E., "Preview of a Divided America," *The Christian Century,* May 28, 1947, p. 682; Fey, Harold E., "They Stand for Free Schools," *The Christian Century,* July 2, 1947; contemporary reports in Cincinnati press (Cincinnati *Post,* Cincinnati *Enquirer,* and Cincinnati *Star Times*), particularly statement of Msgr. Clarence G. Issenman, chancellor of Cincinnati Archdiocese of the Catholic Church, appearing in full in Cincinnati *Post,* July 17, 1947; contemporary *Religious News Service* reports; Stokes, II, pp. 662–668; editorial comment in *America,* August 2, 1947, p. 479, and February 7, 1948, p. 508; New York *Times,* July 11, 1947 (report by Benjamin Fine); New York *PM,* April 30, 1947.

86. This account of the New Mexico case is based on the following: decision of District Court of Sante Fe County in Zellers vs. Huff (March 10, 1949); decision of Supreme Court of New Mexico in the same case, 55 N.M. 501 (1951); complaint in the same case; Mead, Frank S., "Shadows over Our Schools," *The Christian Herald,* February, 1948; *Religious News Service* contemporary reports; *Catholic Messenger,* November 20, 1948; reports in New York *Times;* Garber, Lee O., "Supreme Court Defines Church-State Separation," *The Nation's Schools,* February, 1952, p. 69.

87. For the converse of the situation, see *supra,* pp. 502 ff.

88. 349 Mo. 808.

89. Zellers vs. Huff, 55 N.M. 501.

90. It does not violate the Federal Constitution; see Cochran vs. Louisiana, discussed below, pp. 558–560.
91. The latter part of this statement is erroneous; see Everson case, discussed below, pp. 563 ff.
92. Harfst vs. Hoegen, 349 Mo. 808 (1942).
93. *Religious News Service,* July 9, 11, August 2, 1951, March 14, July 16, 1952.
94. Minneapolis *Tribune,* September 7, 1951; *Religious News Service,* September 13, 17, October 17, 22, 1951, July 17, 1952.
95. Scripture vs. Burns, 59 Iowa 70 (1882); Dorner vs. School District No. 5, 137 Wisc. 147 (1908).
96. Nance vs. Johnson, 84 Tex. 401 (1892). This case involved a Baptist rather than a Catholic school.
97. Dorner vs. School District No. 5, 137 Wisc. 147 (1908).
98. See note, *Yale Law Journal,* 50, p. 723.
99. State ex rel. Johnson vs. Boyd, 217 Ind. 348 (1940); see also Millard vs. Board of Education, 121 Ill. 297 (1887).
100. Harfst vs. Hoegen, 349 Mo. 808 (1942); Knowlton vs. Baumhover, 182 Iowa 691 (1918); Williams vs. Board of Trustees, 173 Ky. 708 (1917); Zellers vs. Huff, 55 N.M. 501 (1951); Berghorn vs. Reorganized School District No. 8, Circuit Court, Franklin County, Missouri, No. 1291, affirmed 364 Mo. 121 (1953); Sterling, Colorado, case reported in *Religious News Service,* September 2, 1952.
101. Zellers vs. Huff, 55 N.M. 501 (1951); Berghorn vs. Reorganized School District (1953).
102. Note, *Yale Law Journal,* 50, p. 923.
103. Harfst vs. Hoegen, 349 Mo. 808 (1942).
104. Berghorn vs. Reorganized School District No. 8.
105. Petition in Kuper, *et al.* vs. Taylor, *et al.,* Circuit Court, Cole County, Mo. 1950.

CHAPTER FOURTEEN

*Indirect and Federal Aid*

1. National Education Association, *The State and Sectarian Education,* p. 36.
2. Zellers vs. Huff, 55 N.M. 501 (1951); Dickman vs. Oregon School District, 366 P. 2d 533 certiorari den. 371 U. S. 823 (1962).
3. R.I. Laws of 1963 ch. 12; N.Y. Laws of 1965 ch. 320.
4. Smith vs. Donahue, 202 App. Div. (N.Y.) 656 (1922).
5. *Ibid.*
6. 168 La. 1005 (1929).
7. 168 La. 1030 (1929).
8. Loan Association vs. Topeka, 20 Wall (U.S.) 655 (1875).
9. Cochran vs. Louisiana State Board of Education, 281 U.S. 370 (1930).
10. Judd vs. Board of Education, 278 N.Y. 200 (1938); this case involved bus transportation; discussed below, pp. 561 ff.
11. Zellers vs. Huff, 55 N.M. 501 (1951).
12. Dickman vs. Oregon School District, 366 P. 2d 533, certiorari denied 371 U.S. 823 (1962).
13. Chance vs. Mississippi State Textbook Board, 190 Miss. 453 (1941).
14. Gurney vs. Ferguson, 190 Okla. 254 (1941) (a school bus case).

15. National Education Association, *The State and Sectarian Education*, p. 36. Since the NEA study was made, transportation laws were enacted in Connecticut, Michigan, Ohio, Pennsylvania, and Wisconsin.

16. State ex rel. Traub vs. Brown, 36 Del. 181 (1934); Gurney vs. Ferguson, 190 Okla. 254 (1941); Judd vs. Board of Education, 278 N.Y. 200 (1938); Mitchell vs. Consolidated School District, 17 Wash. 2d 61 (1943); Zellers vs. Huff, 55 N.M. 501 (1951); Silver Lake School District vs. Barker, 238 Iowa 984 (1947); McVey vs. Hawkins, 258 S.W. 2d 927 (Mo., 1953); Matthews vs. Quinton, 362 P. 2d 932 (Alaska, 1961); Board of Education vs. Antone, 384 P. 2d 911 (Okla., 1963); Reynolds vs. Nussbaum, 115 N.W. 2d 761 (Wisc., 1962].

17. Bowker vs. Baker, 73 Cal. App. 2d 653 (1946); Nichols vs. Henry, 301 Ky. 434 (1945); Board of Education vs. Wheat, 174 Md. 314 (1938); Everson vs. Board of Education of the Township of Ewing, 133 N.J.L. 350 (1946); Snyder vs. Newton, 161 A. 2d 770 (Conn. 1961, appeal dismissed 365 U.S. 299).

18. Judd vs. Board of Education, 278 N.Y. 200 (1938).

19. Gurney vs. Ferguson, 190 Okla. 254 (1941).

20. Judd vs. Board of Education, 278 N.Y. 200 (1938).

21. Everson case, 330 U.S. 1 (1947).

22. Prince vs. Massachusetts, 321 U.S. 158 (1944); discussed *infra*, pp. 704–706.

23. Connell vs. Kennett Township Board of School Directors, 356 Pa. 585 (1947), affirming an opinion of court below.

24. New York *Times,* August 30, 1947.

25. *Religious News Service,* October 8, 1947.

26. Visser vs. Nooksack Valley School District, 33 Wash. 2d 699 (1949); Zellers vs. Huff, 55 N.M. 501 (1951); McVey vs. Hawkins, 258 S.W. 2d 927 (Mo., 1953); Matthews vs. Quinton, 362 P. 2d 932 (Alaska, 1961); Reynolds vs. Nussbaum, 115 N.W. 2d 761 (Wisc. 1962); Silver Lake School District vs. Barker, 29 N.W. 2d 214 (Iowa, 1947); Board of Education vs. Antone, 384 P. 2d 911 (Okla. 1963); Dickman vs. Oregon School District, 366 P. 2d 533 (1961). The last cited case involved textbooks, but the court's decision indicated that bus transportation was likewise unconstitutional; the state authorities have so construed it and have discontinued bus transportation to parochial schools.

27. Snyder vs. Newton, 161 A. 2d 770 (Conn. 1961); Squires vs. City of Augusta, 155 Me. 151 (1959). In the Maine case the court held that a city had no power to enact bus legislation but stated that the state legislature could constitutionally do so. See also Quinn vs. School Comm., 332 Mass. 410 (1955) wherein the constitutional issue was not considered.

28. 370 U.S. 421 (1962).

29. 365 U.S. 299 (1961).

30. Although interest in the shared time plan is hardly more than five or six years old, it has already given rise to an extensive and rapidly growing bibliography. Among others the following sources are available: Hearings on H.R. 6074, ("Shared Time"), 88th Cong., 2nd session; Hearings on H.R. 2361 and H.R. 2362, 89th Cong., 2nd session; Hearings on S. 370, 89th Cong., 1st session; "Shared Time: A Symposium", *Religious Education,* January–February, 1962; Cassels, Louis, "A Way

Out for our Parochial-Public School Conflict," *Look,* August 28, 1962; *Dual Enrollment in Public and Nonpublic Schools,* U.S. Department of Health, Education and Welfare, Washington, D.C., U.S. Government Printing Office, 1965; Croft Educational Services, "The Pros and Cons of Shared Time," *Education Summary,* April 1, 1964; Library of Congress, *Proposed Federal Promotion of "Shared Time Education,"* Washington, D.C., U.S. Government Printing Office, 1963; Pfeffer, Leo, "Second Thoughts on Shared Time," *Christian Century,* June 20, 1962; Wakin, Edward, and Powell, Theodore, "The Shared Time Experiment," *Saturday Review,* March 15, 1964; "We're Not Sold on Shared Time, Majority Says; School Administrators' Opinion Poll," *The Nation's Schools,* July, 1964; Powell, Theodore, "Shared Time, 1964," in Giannella, Donald A., ed., *Religion and the Public Order, 1964,* Chicago, University of Chicago Press, 1965, p. 62.

31. *Supra* p. 506.
32. State vs. Milquet, 180 Wis. 109 (1923).
33. Hearings on H.R. 6074, p. 288.
34. Jefferson's Works, Washington, ed., vol. 6 p. 389.
35. See *infra,* pp. 601–604.
36. See "The Pennsylvania School Bus Fight," *Christian Century,* August 25, 1965.
37. Hearings on H.R. 2361 and 2362, p. 737.
38. See testimony of Msgr. Frederick G. Hochwalt for National Catholic Welfare Council, Hearings on H.R. 6074 pp. 261–264.
39. Hearings on H.R. 6074, p. 525.
40. *The Nation's Schools,* July, 1964.
41. The New York statute (Education Law section 3210), for example, permits absence for religious instruction (released time), but this obviously would not authorize absence for instruction in secular subjects available within the public school.
42. See Katz, Wilber G., "Note on the Constitutionality of Shared Time," in *Religion and the Public Order, 1964.*
43. Pierce vs. Society of Sisters, 268 U.S. 510 (1925).
44. 343 U.S. 306 (1952).
45. See American Civil Liberties Union, "Position on Shared Time," adopted by the Board of Directors, April 4, 1965.
46. This account of the historical background of Federal aid to education is based largely on Mitchell, William A., "Religion and Federal Aid to Education," *Law and Contemporary Problems,* 14, No. 1, Winter, 1949, pp. 113 ff.; supplemented by Quattlebaum, Charles, *Federal Educational Activities and Educational Issues before Congress* (pamphlet), *Legislative Reference Service Report of the Library of Congress,* United States Government Printing Office, Washington, D.C., 1951.
47. Msgr. Michael J. Ready, General Secretary of the National Catholic Welfare Conference, and Rev. George Johnson, Secretary General of the National Catholic Education Association.
48. Mitchell, p. 125.
49. *Hearings: Public School Assistance Act of 1949—*House Education and Labor Committee, p. 748, quoted in Quattlebaum, p. 117.

50. Mitchell, p. 133.
51. Quoted in Mitchell, p. 137.
52. *Ibid.,* p. 138.
53. *Federal Aid to Sectarian Education?* (pamphlet), Federal Council of the Churches of Christ in America, New York, April, 1947, p. 4.
54. This account of the controversy around the Barden bill is based on contemporary reports in the New York papers, particularly the New York *Times, Religious News Service* reports, reports in the Catholic press, particularly the Brooklyn *Tablet,* editorial comment in *The Christian Century, The Churchman,* and *America,* an article by Father William E. McManus of the National Catholic Welfare Conference, *America,* October 29, 1949, entitled "Roadblock to Federal Aid," and two by Father Robert C. Hartnett in *America* of July 9 and August 6, 1949, entitled "Who's Blocking Federal Aid?" and "Central Issue in Federal Aid."
55. H.R. 4643, 81st Congress, 1st session.
56. H.R. 7160, 81st Congress, 2nd session.
57. See New York *Times* of July 23, 1949 for the full text.
58. See, *e.g.,* editorial in New York *Times,* July 26, 1949.
59. New York *Times,* July 28, 1949.
60. *Ibid.,* August 6, 1949.
61. New York *World Telegram,* August 23, 1949.
62. New York *Times,* March 7, 1950.
63. Quattlebaum, p. 49.
64. *Ibid.,* pp. 97, 106, 112.
65. New York *Times,* September 14, 1960.
66. Senate Document 29, 87th Congress.
67. House Report 143, 89th Congress, 1st Session, p. 17; Senate Report 146, 89th Congress, 1st Session, p. 28.
68. See, *e.g.,* Senate Hearings on S. 370, 89th Cong. 1st Session, pp. 146–157.
69. Public Law 347, 78th Congress; 38 U.S.C. 1601 et. seq.
70. Public Law 550, 82nd Congress.
71. Public Law 85-857.
72. Public Law 396, 79th Congress; 42 U.S.C. 175, et. seq.
73. Senate Hearings on S. 370, p. 155.
74. Public Law 85-864; 20 U.S.C. 421 et. seq.
75. Public Law 88-204.
76. *Supra,* p. 190.
77. Public Law 88-452.
78. Hearings on S. 370 p. 2634.
79. Public Law 89-10.
80. N.E.A., Special Report, "The Elementary—Secondary Education Act of 1965," April 22, 1965, p. 1.
81. Senate Report on H.R. 2362 p. 10–11.
82. House Committee Hearings on H.R. 2361 and 2362, pp. 1610–1611.
83. La Noue, George R., "A Critical Look at the Education Bill," *Christianity and Crisis,* March 8, 1965, pp. 36–37.
84. Section 304(a).
85. See *infra* pp. 623–624.

CHAPTER FIFTEEN
*Freedom and the Common Defense*

1. 122 U.S. 333 (1890); see also George vs. United States, 196 F. 2d 445 (1952).
2. Church of Latter Day Saints vs. United States, 136 U.S. 1 (1890).
3. "Memorial and Remonstrance," in Blau, p. 83.
4. People vs. Ashley, 184 App. Div. (N.Y.) 520 (1918); State vs. Durham, 21 Del. 105 (1904); State vs. Neitzel, 69 Wash. 567 (1912); City of St. Louis vs. Hellscher, 295 Mo 293 (1922).
5. 85 S. Ct. 850 (1965).
6. 367 U.S. 488 (1961).
7. Washington Ethical Society vs. District of Columbia, 249 F. 2d 127 (1957).
8. See symposium on "The Meaning of Religion in the First Amendment," *Catholic World,* August, 1963. See also, University of Chicago Law Review, XXXII, p. 533 (1965); American Political Science Review, LVII, p. 865 (1963).
9. Scopes vs. State, 154 Tenn. 105 (1927).
10. Burstyn vs. Wilson, 343 U.S. 495 (1952); discussed *infra,* pp. 673 ff.
11. Lovell vs. Griffin, 303 U.S. 444 (1938); Schneider vs. Irvington, 308 U.S. 147 (1939).
12. Prince vs. Massachusetts, 321 U.S. 158 (1944).
13. Thomas vs. Collins, 323 U.S. 516 (1945).
14. "Notes on Virginia," in Blau, p. 78.
15. *Ibid.,* p. 75.
16. *In re* Robert Harold Scott, F.C.C. Memorandum Opinion and Order, No. 96050, July 19, 1946. See, generally, Loevinger, Lee, "Religious Liberty and Broadcasting," *George Washington Law Review,* March, 1965, p. 631.
17. United States vs. Ballard, 322 U.S. 78 (1944); discussed below, pp. 690 ff.
18. In re Jenison, 120 N.W. 2d 515 (Minn. 1963).
19. In re Jenison, 375 U.S. 14 (1963).
20. In re Jenison, 125 N.W. 2d 588 (Minn. 1964). A similar result was reached in United States vs. Hillyeard, 52 F. Supp. 612 (1943).
21. Blau, p. 75.
22. Schenck vs. United States, 249 U.S. 47 (1919).
23. See, *e.g.,* Abrams vs. United States, 250 U.S. 616 (1919).
24. See *e.g.,* Dennis vs. United States, 341 U.S. 494 (1951).
25. See Yates vs. United States, 354 U.S. 298 (1957).
26. Feiner vs. New York, 340 U.S. 315 (1951).
27. Kunz vs. New York, 340 U.S. 290 (1951).
28. Thomas vs. Collins, 323 U.S. 516 (1945).
29. Pierce vs. Society of Sisters, 268 U.S. 510 (1925).
30. Martin vs. City of Struthers, 319 U.S. 141 (1943).
31. In re Jenison, 125 N.W. 2d 588 (Minn. 1964).
32. Sherbert vs. Verner, 374 U.S. 398 (1963).
33. People vs. Donner, 199 Misc. (N.Y.) 643; affirmed 278 App. Div. 705; affirmed 302 N.Y. 857; appeal dismissed for want of a substantial Federal question 342 U.S. 884; (1951); discussed below, pp. 714 ff. See also, Meyerkorth vs. State, 115 N.W. 2d 585 (Neb. 1962) appeal dismissed

372 U.S. 705 (1963) (unlicensed parochial school teachers).

34. Pierce vs. Society of Sisters, 268 U.S. 510 (1925).

35. Schneider vs. Irvington, 308 U.S. 147 (1939).

36. See particularly: West Virginia State Board of Education vs. Barnette, 319 U.S. 624 (1943); Prince vs. Massachusetts, 321 U.S. 158 (1944); Thomas vs. Collins, 323 U.S. 516 (1945) (not a religious liberty case); Marsh vs. Alabama, 326 U.S. 501 (1946); Schneider vs. Irvington, 308 U.S. 147 (1939); Cantwell vs. Connecticut, 310 U.S. 296 (1940).

37. See particularly his dissent in Prince vs. Massachusetts, 321 U.S. 158.

38. See particularly his dissent in West Virginia State Board of Education vs. Barnette, 319 U.S. 624 (1943).

39. Hirabayashi vs. United States, 320 U.S. 81 (1943); Korematsu vs. United States, 323 U.S. 214 (1944).

40. Selective Draft Law cases (Arver vs. United States), 245 U.S. 366 (1918).

41. United States vs. Macintosh, 283 U.S. 605 (1931). This statement is not affected by the overruling of the Macintosh decision in Girouard vs. United States, 328 U.S. 61 (1946); discussed below, p. 621.

42. 293 U.S. 245 (1934).

43. 325 U.S. 561 (1945).

44. See West Virginia State Board of Education vs. Barnette, 319 U.S. 624; and Justice Frankfurter's dissent in that case.

45. Wieman vs. Updegraff, 344 U.S. 183 (1952); Torcaso vs. Watkins, 367 U.S. 488 (1961).

46. 279 U.S. 644 (1929).

47. 283 U.S. 605 (1931).

48. 328 U.S. 61 (1946). The Girouard decision itself might not be followed today; two of the five justices who constituted the majority in that case, Justices Rutledge and Murphy, have since died, and have been succeeded by Justices Clark and Minton, who are generally more conservative in interpreting the guaranties of the First Amendment.

49. Gara vs. United States, 178 F 2d 38 (1949); affirmed by an equally divided court, 340 U.S. 857 (1951).

50. Schenck vs. United States, 249 U.S. 47 (1919).

51. The standard and classic work on the problem is Chafee, Zechariah, Jr., *Free Speech in the United States,* Cambridge, Harvard University Press, 1946.

52. Warren vs. United States, 177 F 2d 596 (1949); certiorari denied, 338 U.S. 947 (1950).

53. See Justice Cardozo's concurring opinion in Hamilton vs. Regents of the University of California, 293 U.S. 245 (1934).

54. Gara vs. United States, 178 F 2d 38 (1949); affirmed 340 U.S. 857 (1951); Richter vs. United States, 181 F 2d 591 (1950).

55. Summers, Clyde W., "The Sources and Limits of Religious Freedom," *Illinois Law Review,* 41, p. 53, May—June, 1946; citing *Report of Bureau of Prisons,* June 30, 1944.

56. See *United States Code,* 50, Appendix, sec. 301; United States vs. Mroz 136 F 2d 221 (1943), appeal dismissed 320 U.S. 805 (1943).

57. United States vs. Kauten, 133 F 2d 703 (1943).

58. 367 U.S. 488 (1961).

59. United States vs. Seeger, 380 U.S. 163 (1965). The court appears to

have adopted the test for tax exemption as a religious organization formulated in Fellowship of Humanity vs. County of Alameda, 315 P. 2d 395 (Cal. App. 1957), wherein the test was stated to be "whether or not the belief occupies the same place in the lives of its holders that orthodox beliefs occupy in the lives of believing majorities."

60. Sherbert vs. Verner, 374 U.S. 398 (1963); Commonwealth vs. Arlan's Department Store, 357 S.W. 2d 708 (Ky., 1962), appeal dismissed for want of a substantial Federal question, 371 U.S. 218 (1962); In re Jenison, 375 U.S. 14 (1963). Compare Kunz vs. New York, 340 U.S. 290 (1951) with Feiner vs. New York, 340 U.S. 315 (1951). See also Saladin, Peter R., "Relative Ranking of the Preferred Freedoms, Religion and Speech," in Giannella, Donald A., ed., *Religion and the Public Order, 1964,* Chicago, University of Chicago Press, 1965.

61. Torcaso vs. Watkins, 367 U.S. 488 (1961).

62. Selective Draft cases (Arver vs. United States) 245 U.S. 366 (1918); see also United States vs. Stephens, 245 Fed. 956 (1917); George vs. United States, 196 F. 2d 445 (1952).

63. 262 U.S. 390.

64. Bartels vs. Iowa, Bohning vs. Ohio, 262 U.S. 404 (1923).

65. Hazen, Charles D., *Alsace-Lorraine under German Rule,* New York, H. Holt & Co., 1917, pp. 172 – 173.

66. Tims, Richard W., *Germanizing Russian Poland,* New York, Columbia University Press, 1941, p. 78; *Encyclopaedia of Social Sciences,* IX, p. 167.

67. Lemkin, Raphael, *Axis Rule in Occupied Europe,* Washington, D.C., Carnegie Foundation for International Peace, 1944, p. 79.

68. Hayes, Carleton J., *Essays in Nationalism,* New York, The Macmillan Co., 1926, pp. 239 – 240.

69. Meyer vs. State, 107 Neb. 657 (1922).

70. 268 U.S. 510.

71. 273 U.S. 284.

72. Blauch, L. E., and Reid, C. F., *Public Education in the Territories and Outlying Possessions,* Washington, D.C., Government Printing Office, 1939, p. 80.

73. Prince vs. Massachusetts, 321 U.S. 158 (1944); discussed below, pp. 704 ff.

74. Transcript of record in Stainback vs. Po, 336 U.S. 368 (1949), *passim.*

75. Practically invalidated in Oyama vs. California, 332 U.S. 633 (1948).

76. Invalidated in Takahashi vs. Fish and Game Commission, 334 U.S. 410 (1948).

77. *Report of California Senate Fact Finding Committee on Japanese Resettlement,* May 1, 1945.

78. Transcript of record in Stainback vs. Po, p. 85.

79. Stainback vs. Po, 336 U.S. 368 (1949).

80. Act 72 S.L. 1949, H.B. No. 1000; approved April 25, 1949.

81. 319 U.S. 624 (1943). For a thorough study of the flag salute controversy, see Manwaring, David R., *Render unto Caesar,* Chicago, University of Chicago Press, 1962.

82. *Reasons Why a True Follower of Jesus Christ Cannot Salute the Flag;* quoted in Stokes, II, p. 602. See also, Manwaring, pp. 30 – 33.

83. 302 U.S. 656.

84. Hering vs. State Board of Education, 303 U.S. 624 (1938).
85. Gabrielli vs. Knickerbocker, 306 U.S. 621 (1939).
86. Johnson vs. Town of Deerfield, 306 U.S. 621 (1939); rehearing denied, 307 U.S. 650 (1939).
87. 21 F. Supp. 581.
88. 24 F. Supp. 271.
89. 108 F. 2d 683 (1940).
90. Minersville School District vs. Gobitis, 310 U.S. 586 (1940).
91. Fennell, William G., "The 'Reconstructed Court' and Religious Freedom: The Gobitis Case in Retrospect," *New York University Law Quarterly Review,* XIX, p. 35, November, 1941.
92. *The Christian Century,* June 19, 1940, quoted in Barber, Hollis W., "Religious Liberty vs. Police Power: Jehovah's Witnesses," *American Political Science Review,* XLI, April, 1947, p. 232.
93. New York *Herald Tribune,* July 21, 1940, quoted in Fennell, p. 35.
94. See, Manwaring, Chap. 7.
95. This account of the violence following the Gobitis decision is based on an article by two members of the Federal Department of Justice, Rotnem, Victor W., and Folsom, F. G., Jr., "Recent Restrictions upon Religious Liberty," *American Political Science Review,* XXXVI, December, 1942, p. 1053, and Manwaring, Chapter 8.
96. Blau, pp. 77–78.
97. *The Christian Century,* November 20, 1940, quoted in Stokes, II, pp. 612–613.
98. See, *e.g., In re* Reed, 262 App. Div. (N.Y.) 814 (1941).
99. New Hampshire vs. Lefebvre, 91 N.H. 382 (1941).
100. 47 F. Supp. 251.
101. West Virginia State Board of Education vs. Barnette, 319 U.S. 624 (1943).
102. The reference is to the 1942 law referred to above.
103. 319 U.S. 583 (1943).

CHAPTER SIXTEEN
### *Freedom and Domestic Tranquillity*

1. Delk vs. Commonwealth, 166 Ky. 39 (1915), in which a preacher was convicted for using obscene language in a sermon; Knowles vs. United States, 170 Fed. 409 (1909), sustaining a conviction for sending through the mails obscene matter religiously motivated; and Dill vs. Hamilton, 137 Neb. 723 (1940), involving immoral conduct asserted to be a religiously required practice, are rare exceptions.
2. 98 U.S. 145.
3. See *supra,* p. 133.
4. 133 U.S. 333 (1890).
5. 341 U.S. 494 (1950).
6. 136 U.S. 1 (1890).
7. II, pp. 279–280, citing Lecky, William Edward, *Democracy and Liberty,* I, p. 548.
8. Quoted in Stokes, III, p. 527.
9. *In re* Black, 3 Utah 2d 315, certiorari denied, 350 U.S. 923 (1955).
10. *United States Code,* Title 18, sec. 398.

11. Cleveland vs. United States, 329 U.S. 14 (1946).
12. Rotnem and Folsom, pp. 1055 – 1056; Manwaring, Chapter 2.
13. Quoted in Waite, Edward F., "The Debt of Constitutional Law to Jehovah's Witnesses," *Minnesota Law Review*, XXVIII, March, 1944, p. 213.
14. Douglas vs. City of Jeannette, 319 U.S. 157 (1943).
15. Cantwell vs. Connecticut, 310 U.S. 296 (1940).
16. 315 U.S. 568 (1942).
17. Niemotko vs. Maryland, 340 U.S. 268 (1951).
18. Hague vs. C.I.O., 307 U.S. 496 (1939).
19. Fowler vs. Rhode Island, 345 U.S. 67 (1953).
20. 340 U.S. 290 (1951).
21. See, generally, Lincoln, C. Eric, *The Black Muslims in America,* Boston, Beacon Press, 1961.
22. Pierce vs. LaVallee, 293 F. 2d 233 (1963); Bryant vs. Wilkins, 265 N.Y.S. 2d 455 (1965).
23. *Ibid;* Sostre vs. McGinnis, 334 F. 2d 906 certiorari denied 379 U.S. 892 (1964); Sewell vs. Peyelow, 291 F. 2d 196 (1961); Banks vs. Havener, 234 F. Supp. 27 (1964); Brown vs. McGinnis, 180 N.E. 2d 791 (N.Y., 1962).
24. *In re* Ferguson, 55 Cal. 2d 663 (1961) certiorari denied 368 U.S. 864 (1961); People ex rel Wright vs. Wilkins, 26 Misc. 2d 1090 (N.Y. Sup. Ct., 1961); Bryant vs. Wilkins, 265 N.Y.S. 2d 455 (1965).
25. Sherbert vs. Verner, 374 U.S. 398 (1963); *In re* Jenison, 375 U.S. 14 (1963).
26. Fowler vs. Rhode Island, 345 U.S. 67 (1953). See Cooper vs. Pate, 378 U.S. 546 (1964).
27. But cf. Lanza vs. New York, 370 U.S. 139 (1962).
28. Swancara, Frank, *The Separation of Religion and Government,* New York, Truth Seeker Co., 1950, p. 96.
29. In a letter to the writer Professor Kallen says: "The story of my indictment on blasphemy rang around the world in 1928. The blasphemous address is what is reserved for posterity in my book *The Liberal Spirit.* I am told that there were memorial services for me in Moscow, and that somebody said Kaddish for me in Jerusalem. The warrant was withdrawn before I could return to Boston to take service. The full story is as comic as it is catholic."
30. Stokes, III, p. 153.
31. Commonwealth vs. Kneeland, 20 Pick. (37 Mass.) 206 (1838); State vs. Mockus, 120 Me. 84 (1921).
32. People vs. Ruggles, 8 Johns (N.Y.) 290 (1811).
33. State vs. Mockus, 120 Me. 84 (1921).
34. Updegraph vs. Commonwealth, 11 Serge. & R. (Pa.) 394 (1824).
35. State vs. Mockus, 120 Me. 84 (1921).
36. 3 Keb. 607. I am indebted to my colleague Philip Baum for the research into the early history of blasphemy.
37. Holdsworth, W. S., *History of English Law,* Boston, Little, Brown, 1926. VIII, p. 403.
38. 2 Lewin C.C. 237.
39. 8 Johns. (N.Y.) 290 (1811).
40. Although not officially reported, this opinion is reprinted in *The Truth*

*Seeker's Annual* for 1895; see Schroeder, Theodore, *Constitutional Free Speech Defined and Defended,* New York, Free Speech League, 1919, p. 60.

41. See *supra,* p. 106.
42. This account of "The Miracle" case is based on Crowther, Bosley, "The Strange Case of 'The Miracle,' " *Atlantic Monthly,* April, 1951, p. 35, on contemporary newspaper reports, particularly in the New York *Times* and *Herald Tribune,* and on the transcript of record in Burstyn vs. Wilson, 343 U.S. 495 (1952).
43. 278 App. Div. 253 (1951).
44. 303 N.Y. 242 (1951).
45. Mutual Film Corporation vs. Ohio Industrial Commission, 236 U.S. 230 (1915).
46. Burstyn vs. Wilson, 343 U.S. 495 (1952).
47. Letter to the writer by Joseph Burstyn.
48. Tucker vs. Texas, 326 U.S. 517 (1946); Niemotko vs. Maryland, 340 U.S. 268 (1951).
49. Marsh vs. Alabama, 326 U.S. 501 (1946).
50. Scopes vs. State, 154 Tenn. 105 (1927).
51. 318 U.S. 413 (1943).
52. 312 U.S. 569 (1941).
53. Niemotko vs. Maryland, 340 U.S. 268 (1951).
54. Hague vs. C.I.O., 307 U.S. 496 (1939); Kunz vs. New York, 340 U.S. 290 (1951).
55. Fowler vs. Rhode Island, 345 U.S. 67 (1953).
56. 308 U.S. 147 (1939).
57. 318 U.S. 413 (1943).
58. 316 U.S. 52 (1942).
59. Saia vs. New York, 334 U.S. 558 (1948).
60. Geuss vs. Pennsylvania, 368 Pa. 290 (1951); appeal dismissed for want of a substantial Federal question, 342 U.S. 912 (1952).
61. 319 U.S. 141 (1943).
62. Lovell vs. Griffin, 303 U.S. 444 (1938); Schneider vs. Irvington, 308 U.S. 147 (1939); Saia vs. New York, 334 U.S. 558 (1948); Kunz vs. New York, 340 U.S. 290 (1951).
63. Lyon vs. Compton Union High School, 341 U.S. 913 (1951).
64. McNight vs. Board of Public Education, 365 Pa. 422, appeal dismissed, 341 U.S. 913 (1951). To the same effect see Greisiger vs. State of Ohio, 153 Ohio St. 474 (1950); certiorari denied, 340 U.S. 820 (1950).
65. 326 U.S. 501 (1946).
66. 297 N.Y. 572 (1948).
67. 335 U.S. 886 (1948).
68. Hall vs. Commonwealth of Virginia, 188 Va. 72 (1948).
69. 335 U.S. 875 (1948).
70. Quoted in City of Sherman vs. Simms, 143 Tex 115 (1944).
71. See, *e.g.,* Ellsworth vs. Gercke, 62 Ariz. 198 (1945); Roman Catholic Archbishop vs. Baker, 140 Oreg. 600 (1932); State ex rel. Synod of Ohio vs. Joseph, 139 Ohio St. 229 (1942); Western Theological Seminary vs. Evanston, 325 Ill. 511 (1927); Diocese of Rochester vs. Planning Board, 1 N.Y. 2d 508 (1956).

72. City of Sherman vs. Simms, 143 Tex. 115 (1944).
73. 64th St. Residences vs. City of New York, 4 N.Y. 2d 268 (1958) certiorari denied 357 U.S. 907 (1958).
74. Corporation of Presiding Bishop vs. City of Porterville, 90 Cal. App. 2d 563 (1949).
75. 338 U.S. 805 (1950).
76. State ex rel Wisconsin Lutheran Conference vs. Sinar, 267 Wis. 91 appeal dismissed 349 U.S. 913 (1955).
77. See, *e.g.*, Roman Catholic Archbishop vs. Village of Orchard Lake, 332 Mich. 389 (1952).
78. 308 U.S. 147 (1939).
79. 310 U.S. 296 (1940).
80. People vs. Ashley, 184 App. Div. (N.Y.) 520 (1918); McMasters vs. State, 21 Okla. App. 318 (1922); see also New vs. United States, 245 Fed. 710 (1917).
81. 322 U.S. 78 (1944).
82. Hygrade Provision Co. vs. Sherman, 266 U.S. 497 (1925).
83. See *supra*, p. 520.

CHAPTER SEVENTEEN

*Freedom and the General Welfare*

1. 197 U.S. 11 (1905).
2. Prince vs. Massachusetts, 321 U.S. 158 (1944).
3. Zucht vs. King, 260 U.S. 174 (1922).
4. State ex rel. Dunham vs. Board of Education, 154 Ohio St. 469 (1950); certiorari denied, 341 U.S. 915 (1951).
5. State ex rel. Holcomb vs. Armstrong, 39 Wash. 2d 860 (1952).
6. *Religious News Service,* May 15, June 27, October 19, 1951, July 30, 1952.
7. Birnel vs. Town of Firecrest, 361 U.S. 10 (1959) dismissing for want of a substantial Federal question 53 Wash. 2d 830; Kraus vs. City of Cleveland, 351 U.S. 935 (1956) dismissing for want of a substantial Federal question, 163 Ohio St. 559; Baer vs. City of Bend, 206 Oreg. 221 (1956); Dowell vs. City of Tulsa, 273 P. 2d 859 (Okla. 1954) certiorari denied 348 U.S. 912 (1955); See generally, Nichols, "Freedom of Religion and the Water Supply," *University of Southern California Law Review,* XXXII, p. 158 (1959).
8. New York *World Telegram and Sun,* April 18, 1951; *Religious News Service,* April 25, July 23, 1951.
9. People ex rel. Wallace vs. Labrenz, 411 Ill. 618 (1952); certiorari denied, 344 U.S. 824 (1952).
10. 321 U.S. 158 (1944); discussed below, p. 704.
11. *In re* Clark, 21 Ohio 2d 86 (1962); State vs. Perricone, 37 N.J. 463 (1962).
12. Blackstone's *Commentaries,* IV, p. 190; Cited in Darrow vs. Family Fund Society, 116 N.Y. 537 (1889).
13. Modern legislators generally consider it a problem for medical rather than penal attention. New York's statute making attempted suicide a felony was repealed in 1919; Laws of 1919 Chap. 414.
14. Sec. 2301.

15. Reynolds vs. United States, 98 U.S. 145 (1878); see *supra*, pp. 645–646.
16. State vs. Bunn, 229 N.C. 734 (1949). To the same effect, see Lawson vs. Commonwealth, 291 Ky. 437 (1942); Harden vs. State, 188 Tenn. 17 (1949).
17. Bunn vs. North Carolina, 336 U.S. 942 (1949).
18. Smith vs. People, 51 Colo. 270 (1911); State vs. Verbon, 167 Wash. 140 (1932); People vs. Handzik, 410 Ill. 295 (1952).
19. Handzik vs. Illinois, 343 U.S. 927 (1952).
20. Erickson vs. Delgard, 252 N.Y.S. 2d 705 (1962); *In re* Brooks' Estate, 205 N.E. 2d 435 (Ill., 1965).
21. Application of Georgetown College, Inc., 331 F 2d 1000, certiorari denied 377 U.S. 978 (1964); Raleigh Fitkin Hospital vs. Anderson, 42 N.J. 421 certiorari denied 377 U.S. 985 (1964); United States vs. George, U.S. Law Week, April 14, 1965 (U.S.D.C., Conn.).
22. Raleigh Fitkin Hospital vs. Anderson, 42 N.J. 421 certiorari denied 377 U.S. 985 (1964).
23. Application of Georgetown College, Inc., 331 F. 2d 1000, certiorari denied 84 S. Ct. 1883 (1964).
24. People vs. Woody, 394 P. 2d 813 (1964).
25. 98 U.S. 145 (1878).
26. Reynolds vs. United States, 98 U.S. 145 (1878); Davis vs. Beason, 133 U.S. 333 (1890).
27. State vs. Hopkins, 69 A. 2d. 456 (1950); appeal dismissed for want of a substantial Federal question, 339 U.S. 940 (1950).
28. Peterson vs. Widule, 157 Wisc. 641 (1914).
29. On the subject generally, see St. John-Stevas, Norman, "Birth Control: Morals, Law, and Public Policy" in Giannella, Donald A., ed., *Religion and the Public Order,* 1964.
30. Poe vs. Ullman, 367 U.S. 497 (1961).
31. Griswold vs. Connecticut, 381 U.S. 479 (1965).
32. People vs. Pierson, 176 N.Y. 201 (1903).
33. 321 U.S. 158 (1944).
34. The discussion in this and the two following subsections is based largely on Pfeffer, Leo, "Religion in the Upbringing of Children," *Boston University Law Review,* XXXV, 333 (1955). Other treatments of the subject are to be found in Friedman, Lee M., "The Parental Right to Control the Religious Education of a Child," *Harvard Law Review,* XXIX, 485 (1960); Ramsey, Paul, "The Legal Imputation of Religion to an Infant in Adoption Proceedings," *New York University Law Review,* XXXIV, 649 (1959); Paulsen, Monrad G., in Oaks, *The Wall Between Church and State,* p. 117.
35. Prince vs. Massachusetts, 321 U.S. 158 (1944).
36. *Ibid.,* at 165–166. See also West Virginia Board of Education vs. Barnette, 319 U.S. 624 (1943).
37. Shelley vs. Westbrooke, 37 Eng. Rep. 850 (1821).
38. Lindsay vs. Lindsay, 257 Ill. 328 (1913); People ex rel Sisson vs. Sisson, 271 N.Y. 285 (1936). Cf. Matter of Auster vs. Weberman, 198 Misc. 1005 affirmed 278 App. Div. 656 affirmed 302 N.Y. 855 appeal dismissed 342 U.S. 884 (1951); *In re* Black, 3 Utah 2d 315 certiorari denied 350 U.S. 923 (1955).

39. Levitsky vs. Levitsky, 190 A. 2d 621 (Md. 1963).
40. *In re* Agar-Ellis, 24 Ch. D. 317 (1883); D'Alton vs. D'Alton, L. R. 4 P.D. 87 (1878).
41. Donahue vs. Donahue. 142 N.J. Eq. 701 (1948); DeLaney vs. Mount St. Joseph's Academy, 198 App. Div. 75 affirmed 234 N.Y. 565 (1922).
42. People ex rel Sisson vs. Sisson, 271 N.Y. 285 (1936).
43. People ex rel Portnoy vs. Strasser, 303 N.Y. 539 (1952).
44. *In re* Butcher's Estate, 266 Pa. 479 (1920); Denton vs. James, 107 Kan. 729 (1920); *In re* Dixon, 254 Mo. 683 (1914); Martin vs. Martin, 308 N.Y. 136 (1954).
45. Shelley vs. Kramer, 334 U.S. 1 (1948).
46. *E.g.,* Describes vs. Wilmer, 69 Ala. 25 (1881); Jones vs. Bowman, 13 Wyo. 79 (1904).
47. Article VI Section 18.
48. Zorach vs. Clauson, 343 U.S. 306 (1952).
49. See editorial in Boston *Pilot,* June 28, 1952.
50. 109 Mass. 187 (1907).
51. *E.g., In re* Walsh's Estate, 100 Cal. App. 2d 194 (1950); State ex rel Baker vs. Bird, 253 Mo. 569 (1913); *In re* Butcher's Estate, 266 Pa. 479 (1920).
52. Matter of Gally, 329 Mass. 143 (1952).
53. Boston *Pilot,* June 28, 1952, July 5, 1952.
54. *Religious News Service,* April 26, 1955; Petitions of Goldman, 33 (Mass. 64), certiorari denied 348 U.S. 942 (1955).
55. Ellis vs. McCoy, 332 Mass. 254 (1955).
56. See, *e.g.,* Matter of Maxwell, 4 N.Y. 2d 424 (1958); Cooper vs. Hinrichs, 10 Ill. 2d 269 (1957).
57. Commonwealth ex rel Kuntz vs. Stackhouse, 176 Pa. Super 361, certiorari denied, 348 U.S. 981 (1955).
58. See Ramsey, op. cit.
59. *Supra,* p. 474.
60. 199 Misc. 643 (1950); affirmed 278 App. Div. 705 (1951); affirmed 302 N.Y. 857 (1951); dismissed for want of a substantial Federal question, 342 U.S. 884 (1951).
61. See also State vs. Hershberger, 150 N.E. 2d 671 (1958).
62. Commonwealth vs. Beiler, 168 Pa. Sup. 462 (1951).
63. Commonwealth vs. Bey, 166 Pa. Sup. 136 (1950).
64. Ferriter vs. Taylor, 48 Vt. 444 (1897). See also Zorach vs. Clauson, 303 N.Y. 161 (1951).
65. See generally, Coughlin, Bernard J., *Church and State in Social Welfare,* New York, Columbia University Press, 1965; Keith-Lucas, Alan, *The Church and Social Welfare,* Philadelphia, Westminster Press, 1962.
66. Stridley, Leonard A., *Sectarian Welfare Federation Among Protestants,* New York, Association Press, 1944, p. 3.
67. *Ibid.,* p. 147.
68. Encyclopedia of Social Sciences, III, 410.
69. Coughlin, p. 160.
70. *Supra,* pp. 196–202.
71. See, *e.g.,* Swenson vs. Michigan Employment Security Commission, 340 Mich. 430 (1954); *In re* Miller, 243 N.C. 509 (1956).
72. Kut vs. Bureau of Unemployment Compensation, 76 Ohio App. 51

(1945) *affirmed* 146 Ohio St. 522 (1946).

73. Heisler vs. Board of Review, 156 Ohio St. 395 (1951).
74. Heisler vs. Board of Review, 343 U.S. 939 (1952).
75. See *supra* p. 634.
76. 374 U.S. 398.
77. See *supra,* pp. 210 ff.
78. 316 U.S. 584 (1942).
79. 319 U.S. 105 (1943).
80. 321 U.S. 573 (1944).
81. Watchtower Bible and Tract Society vs. County of Los Angeles, 181 F. 2d 739 (1950); certiorari denied, 340 U.S. 820 (1950).

# Selected Bibliography

Acton, Lord, *Essays on Church and State*, New York, Viking Press, 1953

Acton, Lord, *Essays on Freedom and Power*, Boston, Beacon Press, 1948

Ahmann, Matthew, ed., *Race Challenge to Religion*, Chicago, Henry Regnery Co., 1963

Alland, Alexander, and Wise, James Waterman, *The Springfield Plan: A Photographic Record*, New York, Viking Press, 1945

Allen, Henry E., ed., *Religion in the State University: An Initial Exploration*, Minneapolis, Burgess Publishing Co., 1950

*American State Papers on Freedom in Religion*, Washington, D.C., Religious Liberty Association, 1949

Antieau, C.J., Carroll, P.M., and Burke, T.C., *Religion Under the State Constitutions*, Brooklyn, Central Book Co., 1965

Badi, Joseph, *Religion in Israel Today: The Relation between State and Religion*, New York, Bookman Associates, 1959

Bates, M. Searle, *Religious Liberty: An Inquiry*, New York, International Missionary Council, 1945

Beale, Howard K., *A History of Freedom of Teaching in American Schools*, New York, Charles Scribner's Sons, 1941

Beckes, Isaac K., *Weekday Religious Education: Help or Hindrance to Interreligious Understanding?* (pamphlet), New York, National Conference of Christians and Jews, 1946

Bell, Bernard I., *Crisis in Education: A Challenge to American Complacency*, New York, McGraw-Hill Book Co., 1949

Bennett, John C., *Christians and the State*, New York, Charles Scribner's Sons, 1958

Beth, Loren P., *American Theory of Church and State*, Gainesville, Fla., University of Florida Press, 1958

Billington, Ray A., *The Protestant Crusade*, New York, The Macmillan Co., 1938

Binchy, Daniel A., *Church and State in Fascist Italy*, London, Oxford University Press, 1941

Blanshard, Paul, *American Freedom and Catholic Power* (2d ed.), Boston, Beacon Press, 1958

Blanshard, Paul, *God and Man in Washington*, Boston, Beacon Press, 1960

Blanshard, Paul, *The Irish and Catholic Power*, Boston, Beacon Press, 1953

Blanshard, Paul, *Religion and the Schools: The Great Controversy*, Boston, Beacon Press, 1963

Blau, Joseph L., ed., *Cornerstones of Religious Freedom in America*, Boston, Beacon Press, 1949

Blum, Virgil C., S.J., *Freedom of Choice in Education*, New York, Macmillan, 1958

Boles, Donald E., *The Bible, Religion and the Public Schools,* Ames, Iowa, Iowa State University Press, 1961

Bower, William C., *Church and State in Education,* Chicago, University of Chicago Press, 1944

Bower, William Clayton, *Moral and Spiritual Values in Education,* Lexington, Ky., University of Kentucky Press, 1952

Brady, Joseph H., *Confusion Twice Confounded,* South Orange, N.J., Seton Hall University Press, 1955

Brickman, William W., and Lehrer, Stanley, ed., *Religion, Government and Education,* New York, Society for the Advancement of Education, 1961

Brown, Samuel W., *The Secularization of American Education,* New York, Columbia University Press, 1912

Brown, William A., *Church and State in Contemporary America,* New York, Charles Scribner's Sons, 1936

Burns, J. A., *The Catholic School System in the United States,* New York, Benziger Brothers, 1908

Burns, J. A., *The Growth and Development of the Catholic School System in the United States,* New York, Benziger Brothers, 1912

Butler, Richard, *God on the Secular Campus,* Garden City, New York, Doubleday & Company, 1963.

Butts, R. Freeman, *The American Tradition in Religion and Education,* Boston, Beacon Press, 1950


Callahan, Daniel, ed., *Federal Aid and Catholic Schools,* Baltimore, Helicon Press, 1964.

Carlyle, Alexander J., *The Christian Church and Liberty,* London, J. Clarke, 1924

Carrillo de Albornoz, A. F., *The Basis of Religious Liberty,* New York, Association Press, 1963

*Church, State and Education: A Selected Bibliography* (pamphlet), New York, American Jewish Committee, 1951

Cobb, Sanford H., *The Rise of Religious Liberty in America,* New York, The Macmillan Co., 1902

Cogley, John, ed., *Religion in America: Original Essays on Religion in a Free Society,* New York, Meridian Books, 1958

Connors, Edward M., *Church-State Relationships in the State of New York,* Washington, D.C., Catholic University, 1951

Corwin, Edward S., *A Constitution of Powers in a Secular State,* Charlottesville, Va., Michie Co., 1951

Coughlin, Bernard J., *Church and State in Social Welfare,* New York, Columbia University Press, 1965

Cousins, Norman, ed., *"In God We Trust": The Religious Beliefs and Ideas of the American Founding Fathers,* New York, Harper & Brothers, 1958

Cubberley, Ellwood P., *Public Education in the United States,* Boston, Houghton Mifflin Co., 1919

Culver, Raymond B., *Horace Mann and Religion in the Massachusetts Public Schools,* New Haven, Yale University Press, 1929


Dana, Ellis H., *Storm Clouds Over Our Public Schools* (pamphlet), Madison,

Wis., Wisconsin Council of Churches, 1948

Davis, Mary Dabney, *Week-Day Classes in Religious Education* (pamphlet), Washington, D.C., U.S. Office of Education, U.S. Government Printing Office, 1941

Dawson, Joseph M., *Separate Church and State Now*, New York, Richard R. Smith, 1948

Dierenfeld, Richard B., *Religion in American Public Schools*, Washington, Public Affairs Press, 1962

Dignan, Patrick J., *History of the Legal Incorporation of Catholic Church Property in the United States*, New York, P. J. Kenedy & Sons, 1935

Douglas, William O., *The Bible and the Schools*, Boston, Little, Brown, & Co., 1966.

Drinan, Robert F., S.J., *Religion, the Courts and Public Policy*, New York, McGraw-Hill Book Company, 1963

Drouin, Brother Edmond G., *The School Question: A Bibliography of Church-State Relationships in American Education 1940–1960*, Washington, The Catholic University of America Press, 1963

Dunn, William Kailer, *What Happened to Religious Education? The Decline of Religious Teaching in the Public Elementary School*, 1776–1861, Baltimore, Johns Hopkins Press, 1958

Ebersole, Luke E., *Church Lobbying in the Nation's Capital*, New York, The Macmillan Co., 1951

Eckenrode, H.J., *The Separation of Church and State in Virginia*, Richmond, Va., Virginia State Library, 1910

Edwards, Newton, *The Courts and the Public Schools* (rev. ed.), Chicago, University of Chicago Press, 1955

Ehler, Sidney Z., and Morrall, John B., *Church and State Through the Centuries*, Westminster, Md., The Newman Press, 1954

*Federal Aid to Sectarian Education?* (pamphlet), New York, Federal Council of the Churches of Christ in America, 1947

Feiertag, Loretta C., *American Public Opinion on the Diplomatic Relations Between the United States and the Papal States*, Washington, D.C., Catholic University, 1933

Fichter, Joseph H., *Parochial Schools: A Sociological Study*, Notre Dame, Ind., University of Notre Dame Press, 1958

Fink, Joseph L., *Summary of CCAR Opinions on Church and State as Embodied in Resolutions Adopted at Conferences Through the Years* (pamphlet), New York, Central Conference of American Rabbis, 1948

Finney, R. L., *A Brief History of the American Public School*, New York, The Macmillan Co., 1946

Fleet, Elizabeth, *Madison's "Detached Memoranda,"* Williamsburg, Va., William and Mary Quarterly, October, 1946

Fleming, W.S., *God in Our Public Schools* (3d ed.), Pittsburgh, National Reform Association, 1947

Flynn, John T., *The Road Ahead*, New York, Devin-Adair Co., 1949

Foster, Charles R., *A Question of Religion* (pamphlet), University, Ala., University of Alabama Press, 1961

Friedlander, Anna Fay, *The Shared Time Strategy*, St. Louis, Missouri, Concordia Publishing House, 1966

Freund, Paul A., and Ulich, Robert, *Religion and the Public Schools,* Cambridge, Mass., Harvard University Press, 1965

Gabel, Richard J., *Public Funds for Church and Private Schools,* Washington, D.C., Catholic University, 1937

Garbett, Cyril (Archbishop of York), *Church and State in England,* London, Hodder & Stoughton, 1950

Giannella, Donald A., ed., *Religion and the Public Order, 1963,* Chicago, University of Chicago Press, 1964

Giannella, Donald A., ed., *Religion and the Public Order, 1964,* Chicago, University of Chicago Press, 1965

Gibbons, Ray, *Protestantism and Public Education* (pamphlet), New York, Social Action, 1949

Gove, Floyd S., *Religious Education on Public School Time,* Cambridge, Mass., Harvard University Press, 1926

Graham, Robert A., *Vatican Diplomacy: A Study of Church and State on the International Plane,* Princeton, N.J., Princeton University Press, 1959

Graham, Robert A., and Hartnett, Robert C., *Diplomatic Relations with the Vatican* (pamphlet), New York, America Press, 1952

Graves, Frank P., *A History of Education in Modern Times,* New York, The Macmillan Co., 1928

Greene, Evarts B., *Religion and the State in America,* New York, New York University Press, 1941

Gsovski, Vladimir, ed., *Church and State Behind the Iron Curtain,* New York, Frederick A. Praeger, 1955

Hanley, Thomas O'Brien, S.J., *Their Rights and Liberties,* Westminster, Md., The Newman Press, 1959

Hartford, E. F., *Moral Values in Public Education: Lessons from the Kentucky Experience,* New York, Harper and Brothers, 1958

Hartnett, Robert C., *Equal Rights for Children* (pamphlet), New York, America Press, 1948

Hartnett, Robert C., *Federal Aid to Education* (pamphlet), New York, America Press, 1950

Hartnett, Robert C., *The Right to Educate* (pamphlet), New York, America Press, 1949

Hay, Clyde L., *The Blind Spot in American Public Education,* New York, The Macmillan Co., 1950

Healey, Robert M., *Jefferson on Religion in Public Education,* New Haven, Yale University Press, 1962

Henry, Virgil, *The Place of Religion in the Public Schools,* New York, Harper and Brothers, 1950

High, Stanley, *The Church in Politics,* New York, Harper and Brothers, 1930

Howard, George P., *Religious Liberty in Latin America?* Philadelphia, Westminster Press, 1944

Howe, Mark De Wolfe, *Cases on Church and State in the United States,* Cambridge, Harvard University Press, 1952

Howe, Mark De Wolfe, *The Garden and the Wilderness: Religion and Government in American Constitutional History,* Chicago, University of Chicago Press, 1965

797

Hudson, Winthrop S., *The Great Tradition of the American Churches,* New York, Harper and Brothers, 1953

Humphrey, Edward F., *Nationalism and Religion in America, 1774–1789,* Boston, Chipman Law Publishing Co., 1924

Hurley, Mark J., *Church-State Relationships in Education in California,* Washington, D.C., Catholic University, 1948


James, Charles F., *Documentary History of the Struggle for Religious Liberty in Virginia,* Lynchburg, Va., J. P. Bell Co., 1900

Johnson, Alvin W., and Yost, Frank H., *Separation of Church and State in the United States,* Minneapolis, University of Minnesota Press, 1948

Johnson, F. Ernest, ed., *American Education and Religion,* New York, Harper and Brothers, 1952

Jordan, Wilbur K., *The Development of Religious Toleration in England,* London, Allen & Unwin, 1938


Keehn, Thomas B., *Church-State Relations* (pamphlet), New York, Social Action, 1948

Keesecker, Ward W., *Legal Status of Bible Reading* (pamphlet), U.S. Office of Education, Washington, D.C., U.S. Government Printing Office, 1930

Keith-Lucas, Alan, *The Church and Social Welfare,* Philadelphia, Westminster Press, 1962

Kerwin, Jerome G., *Catholic Viewpoint on Church and State,* Garden City, N.Y., Hanover House, 1960

Klineberg, F. J., *A Free Church in a Free State,* Indianapolis, National Foundation Press, 1947

Knight, Edgar W., *Education in the United States,* Boston, Ginn & Co., 1951

Kurland, Philip B., *Religion and the Law,* Chicago, Aldine Publishing Co., 1962


Larson, Marrin A., *Church Wealth and Business Income,* New York, Philosophical Library, 1965

Lecler, Joseph, *The Two Sovereignties,* New York, Philosophical Library, 1952

Lincoln, C. Eric, *The Black Muslims in America,* Boston, Beacon Press, 1961

Littel, Franklin H., *From State Church to Pluralism,* Garden City, N.Y., Doubleday & Co., 1962

Locke, John, *A Letter Concerning Toleration,* New York, Liberal Arts Press, 1955

Lotz, P. H., ed., *Orientation in Religious Education,* New York, Abingdon-Cokesbury Press, 1950

Loughery, Sister M. Bernard Francis, *Parental Rights in American Educational Law: Their Bases and Implementation,* Washington, D.C., Catholic University, 1952

Luzzatti, Luigi, *God in Freedom,* New York, The Macmillan Co., 1930


Macfarland, Charles S., *Chaos in Mexico: Conflict of Church and State,* New York, Harper and Brothers, 1935

Marnell, William H., *The First Amendment,* Garden City, N.Y., Doubleday & Co., 1964

McAllister, David, *The National Reform Movement,* Allegheny, Pa., Christian

Statesman Co., 1898

McCluskey, Neil Gerard, S.J., *Catholic Viewpoint on Education*, Garden City, N.Y., Hanover House, 1959

McCluskey, Neil Gerard, S.J., *Public Schools and Moral Education: the Influence of Horace Mann, William Torrey Harris and John Dewey*, New York, Columbia University Press, 1958

McCollum, Vashti, *One Woman's Fight*, New York, Doubleday & Co., 1951; Boston, Beacon Press, 1953

McGrath, John J., ed., *Church and State in American Law: Cases and Materials*, Milwaukee, Bruce Publishing Co., 1962

McGucken, William J., *The Philosophy of Catholic Education* (pamphlet), New York, America Press, no date

McManus, William E., *The Non-Sectarian Bus* (pamphlet), Washington, D.C., National Catholic Welfare Conference, 1947

Manwaring, David R., *Render Unto Caesar: The Flag Salute Controversy*, Chicago, University of Chicago Press, 1962

Mattox, F. W., *The Teaching of Religion in the Public Schools*, Nashville, George Peabody College for Teachers, 1948

Mecham, J. Lloyd, *Church and State in Latin America*, Chapel Hill, University of North Carolina Press, 1934

Mecklin, Joseph M., *The Story of American Dissent*, New York, Harcourt, Brace & Co., 1934

Meyer, Jacob C., *Church and State in Massachusetts*, Cleveland, Western University Press, 1930

Moehlman, Conrad H., *The Church as Educator*, New York, Hinds, Hayden & Eldredge, 1947

Moehlman, Conrad H., *School and Church: The American Way*, New York, Harper and Brothers, 1944

*Moral and Spiritual Values in the Public Schools* (pamphlet), Washington, D.C., Educational Policies Commission, National Education Association, 1951

Morrison, Charles C., *The Separation of Church and State in America* (pamphlet), Indianapolis, International Convention of Disciples of Christ, 1947

Myers, Gustavus, *History of Bigotry in the United States*, New York, Random House, 1943


Nettleton, Tully, *Church, State and School* (pamphlet), Boston, Beacon Press, 1949

Nichols, James H., *Democracy and the Churches*, Philadelphia, Westminster Press, 1951

Nielsen, Niels C., *God in Education: A New Opportunity for American Schools*, New York, Sheed and Ward, 1966

*North College Hill, Ohio: Report of an Investigation* (pamphlet), Washington, D.C., National Commission for the Defense of Democracy Through Education, National Education Association, 1947

Northcott, Cecil, *Religious Liberty*, New York, The Macmillan Co., 1949


Olson, Bernhard E., *Faith and Prejudice*, New Haven, Yale University Press, 1963

O'Neill, James M., *Religion and Education Under the Constitution*, New York, Harper and Brothers, 1949

Parsons, Wilfred, *The First Freedom*, New York, Declan X. McMullen Co., 1948

Pattee, Richard, *The Protestant Question in Spain* (pamphlet), Washington, D.C., National Catholic Welfare Conference, 1949

Pfeffer, Leo, *Creeds in Competition*, New York, Harper & Bros., 1958

Phenix, Philip H., *Education and the Worship of God*, Philadelphia, Pennsylvania, The Westminster Press, 1966

Politella, Joseph, ed., *Religion in Education: An Annotated Bibliography*, Oneonta, N.Y., American Association of Colleges for Teacher Education, 1956


Quattlebaum, Charles A., *Federal Educational Activities and Educational Issues before Congress* (pamphlet), Washington, D.C., U.S. Government Printing Office, 1951


Raab, Earl, ed., *Religious Conflict in America*, Garden City, N.Y., Doubleday & Co., 1964

Redden, John D., and Ryan, Francis A., *A Catholic Philosophy of Education*, Milwaukee, Bruce Publishing Co., 1942

*Reference Manual on U.S. Diplomatic Representation at the Vatican* (pamphlet), New York, National Council of the Churches of Christ in the United States of America, no date

*Relation of Religion to Public Education, The* (pamphlet), Washington, D.C., American Council on Education Studies, 1947

*Released Time for Religious Education in New York City Schools* (three pamphlets), Public Education Association, 1943, 1945, 1949

*Religion and Public Education: Proceedings of a Conference* (pamphlet), Washington, D.C., American Council on Education, 1945

*Religion and the State*, Durham, N.C., Duke University, Law and Contemporary Problems, Winter, 1949

*Religious Liberty in Mexico: Report of a Deputation to Mexico* (pamphlet), American Committee on Religious Rights and Minorities, 1935

*Report of Conference on Religious Education and the Public School*, New York, Synagogue Council of America, 1944

Rian, Edwin H., *Christianity and American Education*, San Antonio, Texas, The Naylor Co., 1949

Ruffini, Francesco, *Religious Liberty*, London, Williams & Norgate, 1912

Ryan, John A., and Boland, Francis J., *Catholic Principles of Politics*, New York, The Macmillan Co., 1948

Ryan, Mary P., *Are Parochial Schools the Answer?*, New York, Holt, Rinehart and Winston, 1964


Schachner, Nathan, *Church, State and Education* (pamphlet), New York, American Jewish Committee, 1947

Schaff, Philip, *Church and State in the United States*, Papers of the American Historical Society, 1888

Schroeder, Theodore, *Constitutional Free Speech Defined and Defended*, New York, Free Speech League, 1919

Semple, R. B., *History of the Rise and Progress of the Baptists in Virginia*, Richmond, the author, 1810

*Sharing the December Holidays* (pamphlet), St. Paul Council of Human Relations, no date

Silcox, C. E., and Fisher, G. M., *Catholics, Jews and Protestants,* New York, Harper and Brothers, 1934

Sissons, C. B., *Church and State in Canadian Education: An Historical Study,* Toronto, Ryerson Press, 1959

Smith, Sherman M., *The Relation of the State to Religious Education in Massachusetts,* Syracuse, N.Y., Syracuse University, 1926

Solberg, Richard W., *God and Caesar in East Germany,* New York, Macmillan Co., 1961

Sperry, Willard L., *Religion in America,* Cambridge, England, Cambridge University Press, 1946

Spinka, Matthew, *The Church in Soviet Russia,* New York, Oxford University Press, 1956

*State and Sectarian Education, The* (pamphlet), Washington, D.C., National Education Association, 1946

*Status of Religious Education in the Public Schools, The* (pamphlet), Washington, D.C., National Education Association, 1949

Stidley, Leonard A., *Sectarian Welfare Federation Among Protestants*, New York, Association Press, 1944

Stock, Leo F., *Consular Relations Between the United States and the Papal States,* Washington, D.C., American Catholic Historical Association, 1945

Stock, Leo F., *United States Ministers to the Papal States,* Washington, D.C., Catholic University Press, 1933

Stokes, Anson Phelps, *Church and State in the United States,* New York, Harper and Brothers, 1950

Swancara, Frank, *The Separation of Religion and Government,* New York, Truth Seeker Company, 1950

Sweet, William Warren, *Religion in Colonial America,* New York, Charles Scribner's Sons, 1942

Sweet, William Warren, *Religion in the Development of American Culture,* New York, Charles Scribner's Sons, 1952


Thayer, V. T., *The Attack Upon the American Secular School,* Boston, Beacon Press, 1951

Thayer, V. T., *Religion in Public Education,* New York, Viking Press, 1947

Thom, W. F., *The Struggle for Religious Freedom in Virginia,* Baltimore, Johns Hopkins Press, 1900

Torpey, William George, *Judicial Doctrines of Religious Rights in America,* Chapel Hill, University of North Carolina Press, 1948

Trager, Frank N., *Religion, Intercultural Education and the Public Schools* (pamphlet), New York, National Community Relations Advisory Council, 1948

Tussman, Joseph, ed., *The Supreme Court on Church and State,* New York, Oxford University Press, 1962


Van Dusen, Henry P., *God in Education: A Tract for Our Times,* New York, Charles Scribner's Sons, 1951

Vincent, Sidney, *The Hanukah Manual for Public School Teachers* (pamphlet), Jewish Community Council of Cleveland, no date

Walter, Erich, *Religion and the State University*, Ann Arbor, University of Michigan Press, 1958

Ward, Leo, C.S.C., *Federal Aid to Private Schools,* Westminster, Md., Newman Press, 1964

Weigle, L.A., *Public Education and Religion* (pamphlet), New York, Greater New York Federation of Churches, 1940

Williams, J. P., *The New Education and Religion,* New York, Association Press, 1945

Williams, Michael, *The Shadow of the Pope,* New York, McGraw-Hill Co., 1932

Wood, H. G., *Religious Liberty Today,* Cambridge, England, Cambridge University Press, 1949

Worell, E. K., *Restoring God to Education,* Wheaton, Ill., Van Kempen Press, 1910


Zollmann, Carl, *American Church Law,* St. Paul, West Publishing Co., 1933

# Table of Legal Cases

Updegraph vs. Commonwealth, 11 Serg. & R. (Pa.) 394 (1824): 788

Valentine vs. Chrestensen, 316 U.S. 52 (1942): 680
Vidal vs. Girard's Executor, 2 How. 127 (1844): 244, 245
Visser vs. Nooksack Valley School District, 33 Wash. 2d 609, 207 P. 2d 198 (1949): 781

Wall Case. *See* Commonwealth vs. Cooke
Wallace, People ex rel., vs. Labrenz, 411 Ill. 618, certiorari denied 344 U.S. 824 (1952): 701, 790
Walsh's Estate, *In re,* 100 Cal. App. 2d 184, 223 P. 2d 578 (1950): 792
Warren vs. United States, 177 F. 2d 596, certiorari denied 338 U.S. 947 (1950): 785
Washington Ethical Society vs. District of Columbia, 249 F. 2d 127 (1957): 784
Watchtower Bible and Tract Society vs. County of Los Angeles, 181 F. 2d 739, certiorari denied 340 U.S. 820 (1950): 793
Watchtower Bible and Tract Society vs. Metropolitan Life Insurance Co., 297 N.Y. 339, certiorari denied 335 U.S. 886 (1949): 684
Watson vs. Avery, 2 Bush (Ky.) 332 (1869): 761
Watson vs. Garvin, 54 Mo. 353 (1873): 761
Watson vs. Jones, 13 Wall 80 (U.S.) 679 (1872): 288, 290, 291, 296, 297, 298, 299, 300, 301, 743
Weiss, State ex rel., vs. District Board, 76 Wisc. 177, 44 N.W. 967 (1890): 771

West Virginia State Board of Education vs. Barnette, 319 U.S. 624 (1943): 634, 640, 641, 643, 747, 771, 785, 787, 791
Western Theological Seminary vs. Evanston, 325 Ill. 511 (1927): 789
Wieman vs. Updegraff, 344 U.S. 183 (1952): 785
Wilkerson vs. City of Rome, 152 Ga. 762, 110 S.E. 895 (1922): 771, 772
Williams vs. Board of Trustees, 173 Ky. 708, 191 S.W. 507 (1917): 780
Wisconsin Lutheran Conference, State ex rel., vs. Sinar, 267 Wis. 91, 65 N.W. 2d 43, appeal dismissed 349 U.S. 913 (1955): 790
Wright vs. Board of Education, 106 Kan. 469 (1920): 753
Wright, People ex rel., vs. Wilkins, 26 Misc. 2d 1090 (N.Y. Sup. Ct., 1961): 788

Yates vs. United States, 354 U.S. 298 (1957): 784
Young Men's Christian Association vs. Douglas County, 60 Neb. 642, 83 N.W. 924 (1900): 755

Zellers vs. Huff, 55 N.M. 501, 236 P. 2d 949 (1951): 185, 497, 498, 499, 505, 545, 550, 554, 774, 779, 780, 781
Zorach vs. Clauson, 198 Misc. (N.Y.) 631, affirmed 278 App. Div. 573, affirmed 303 N.Y. 161 (1951): 768, 792; 343 U.S. 306 (1952): 135, 138, 174, 175, 176, 177, 178, 184, 185, 189, 192, 194, 196, 218, 239, 240, 249, 250, 262, 355, 386, 387, 389, 400, 412, 413, 414, 435, 451, 459, 460, 464, 535, 536, 552, 553, 578, 622, 634, 665, 746, 748, 758, 770, 771, 792
Zucht vs. King, 260 U.S. 174 (1922): 790

# Index

584–592; and Barden Bill, 588–590; and 1965 education act, 595; and Gobitis decision, 638; and Jehovah's Witnesses, 652–653, 655; and "The Miracle," 669–671; and religious education of children, 707–708; antenuptial agreements and courts, 707–708; and interreligious adoption, 713. *See also* Catholics

Catholic Church. Third Plenary Council: statement on public schools and religion, 352

Catholic Sisters of Charity, 195, 199

Catholic Truth Society, 131

Catholic War Veterans, 231

Catholic War Veterans·of N. Y., 479

Catholic Welfare Committee, N. Y., 237

Catholics: in England, 27–29; in Massachusetts Bay Colony, 76–77; in Virginia Colony, 78; in Rhode Island, 85; in Pennsylvania, 89; in Colonial period, 90; in 18th century America, 91; and English Act of Toleration, 93; and Continental Congress, 97–98; and Revolutionary War, 97–98; and Oregon statute, 630–631. *See also* Catholic Church

Cato, 10

Cavert, Samuel McCrea, 235

Celestine III, Pope, 18

Celler, Emanuel, 477

Census, 1960: proposed inquiry on religion, 263–264

Census of Religious Bodies, 261–262

Central Conference of American Rabbis, 393; "Declaration of Social Principles" quoted, 226; and birth control legislation, 230; on separation of church and state, 347

Chafee, John H., 478

Chamberlin, Harlow, 488

Chandler, Porter R., 192, 414

Chapin, Mae, 404, 407; testimony quoted, 404–405

Chaplains: in armed forces, 169; to Congress, 170, 248

Charlemagne, 16

Charles II, 28, 99, 271

"Charter of Liberties," N. Y.: quoted, 80

Chelsea, Mass., 482–485

Chelsea *Record,* 483, 485; quoted, 484

Chicago: participation in released time in, 377

Chickasaw, Ala., 683–684

*Child at Home:* quoted, 331

Child-benefit theory: court opinions quoted, 562–563

Child labor amendment: Catholic opposition to, 232

Child welfare: and church groups, 718

Children: custody of in Ireland, 41; and medical attention, 699–700; state's right to protect, 700; state authority over, 703–708; and street selling, 705; religious education of, 706–708; determining custody of and religion, 708–710; adoption of and religion, 710–714

Children, Jewish: effect of Christmas celebrations on, 490

Childs, John L.: quoted, 365

Chile, 46–47

China, 68–69

Christancy, Senator, 161

Christian Amendment: movement, 241–242, 244; House Judiciary Committee report on quoted, 242

*The Christian Century,* 228, 234, 339, 340, 361, 468; on state churches, 53; demand for McGrath's removal, 152; and tax exemption, 215; on Taylor appointment to Vatican, 307; editorial "Public Schools Can Teach Religion" quoted, 362; opposition to released time, 389–390; quoted on Gideons Bible offer, 457–458; and N. Y. Regents' prayer, 462; on *America* editorial and Engel decision, 468; on aid to parochial schools, 526; on Gobitis decision, 638

*Christian Education of Youth* (encyclical): quoted, 344

Christian Scientists, 616; and census, 261; and X-ray for tuberculosis, 698; and fluoridation of water supply, 698–699, 702; exemption of from school curriculum laws, 719

Christians: in ancient Rome, 11–13; in Israel, 67–68

Christmas: as public holiday, 268; and public schools, 479–487, 490–492; and Hanukah, 493

Chrysostom, St. John, 15

*Church and State in Education,* 365

*Church and State in England:* quoted, 52

*Church and State in the United States,* 154

*Church and State Newsletter,* 390

*The Church as Educator:* quoted, 388

*Church Lobbying in the Nation's Capital,* 237

133; letter to Levi Lincoln quoted, 134; and proclamations, 137, 170, 266; and clergymen and public office, 138, 223; on neutrality, 154; use of term "establishment," 156–157; on Christianity and common law, 239, 246–247; and treaty with Tripoli, 243; and chaplains to Congress, 247–248; quoted on privacy of religious opinion, 263; and public education, 326–327; quoted on religion in state universities, 506; and federal aid to education, 580; and freedom to attack religion, 610; *Notes on Virginia* quoted, 638–639

Jehovah's Witnesses, 145, 148, 180, 188, 407, 447, 615, 617, 690; in Quebec Province, 51; and Sunday laws, 285; belief on flag saluting quoted, 634; and saluting of flag, 634–644; attacks on following Gobitis decision, 638; history of, 650–651; statement of purpose quoted, 651; and Catholics, 652; and disturbing the peace, 654–658; in Manchester, N.H., 676–677; and Chickasaw, Ala., 683–684; and blood transfusions, 699–700; adults and medical attention, 701–702; and street hawking, 705; and license taxes, 722–725

Jeroboam, 7

Jesus, 11, 225, 660; references to in official documents, 241

Jews: in ancient Rome, 11; in England, 29, 96; in Spain, 31, 34; in Italy, 40; in Montreal, 48, 50–51; in Quebec City, 48; in West Germany, 60; in New Amsterdam, 71; in Maryland, 84; in Rhode Island, 85; in Pennsylvania, 89; in Colonial period, 90; in Virginia, 110; and social problems, 226–227; and immigration laws, 232; and political issues, 235–236; and Sunday laws, 280, 616–617; and ambassador to Vatican, 309; and public schools, 346–348; and McCollum case, 347–348; in the South, 355; educational system of, 369, 510; and released time, 376, 378, 384, 388, 389, 392–393; and school Bible reading, 450; and Gideons Bible, 457; and Lord's Prayer, 461; and N. Y. Regents' prayer, 462; and Engel decision, 469; and school Christmas celebrations, 479–487; and Miami Beach schools, 487; effect of Christmas celebrations on children, 490; and aid to parochial schools, 529;

and shared-time programs, 577; and Barden Bill, 593; and 1965 education act, 593; and work on Saturday, 616

John, King, 18

John XXIII, Pope, 40, 62, 226, 235, 310, 496, 525, 594; effect on Spain, 35

Johnson, Alvin W., 356–357

Johnson, Andrew, 168

Johnson, F. Ernest, 315, 317

Johnson, George, 586; quoted on aid to parochial schools, 527

Johnson, Lyndon B., 594, 601

Johnston, Gov. Samuel, 124

Joint Baptist Committee on Public Affairs: and Engel decision, 469

Jorgensen, Sarah, 404

Joseph II of Austria, 29

Josephus, 4

Juarez, 42

Judaism: and the state, 8

Judea, 8

Justin Martyr, 15; on observance of Sunday as Sabbath, 270

Justinian Code, 21

Kallen, Horace M., 663

Kansas: court quoted on use of public buildings, 207

Katz, Wilber: quoted, 135–136

Kauper, Paul, 135, 176

Kennedy, John F., 203, 592, 593; and ambassador to Vatican, 303–310

Kenrick, Francis, 436, 437

Kent, Chancellor, 244; quoted in blasphemy case, 665

Kentucky: and Presbyterian church, 289–290

Khrushchev, Nikita, 62

King, Martin Luther, 221; quoted on Engel decision, 468–469

King: and religion in ancient times, 3; and priest in ancient times, 3; and religion in ancient Greece, 8–9; and religion in ancient Rome, 10

Knights of Columbus, 231; N. Y. state council on Bildersee letter, 480

Know-Nothing Party: in Massachusetts, 437–438

Koran, 66

Kosher foods: and fraud, 694

Kunz, Carl Jacob, 658

Labrenz, Cheryl Lynn, 699–700

Langer, William, 278

Morals: and religious education in
schools, 351–352, 354, 365–366
Mormons, 645–650; declaration of submission to federal law quoted, 649; and
polygamy today, 650
Morrill Act: of 1862, 581; of 1890, 581
Morrison, Charles Clayton, 234
Mosaic code, 5
Moses, 4, 5, 7; and religious persecution,
6; laws of, 8; quoted, 251
Motion pictures: and First Amendment,
673
Mount Vernon, N.Y.: court opinion on
released-time program, 399
Murphy, Frank, 175; and McCollum case,
408; and Everson case, 564; and Barnette case, 640; opinion in Barnette
case quoted, 642–643; dissent in Prince
case quoted, 705, 706
Murray, John Courtney, 131, 135, 151;
quoted, 174
Murray, Madalyn, 185, 219, 470
Mussolini, Benito, 37, 38, 136, 319

Nantes, Edict of, 27
Nast, Thomas, 442
National Apostleship of Prayer, 479
National Catholic Educational Association, 131, 152, 586
National Catholic Welfare Conference:
statement on "separation" phrase, 131;
quoted on meaning of First Amendment, 151; defends Peace Corps contracts with religious groups, 204; statement on scope of its interest quoted,
237; on judges and divorce, 258–259;
department of education, 342; on religion in school, 344–345; on savings to
taxpayers by parochial schools, 520;
statement on aid to parochial schools
quoted, 528; quoted on constitutionality of state aid, 536; quoted on federal
aid to education, 586, 587–588; and
Barden Bill, 590
National Community Relations Advisory
Council: brief in McCollum case
quoted, 347–348; on teaching of moral
values, 367; on joint holiday celebrations, 495
National Conference of Christians and
Jews: quoted on Catholics and secularization of schools, 335–336; quoted on
textbooks used in released-time classes,
397; and Bildersee letter, 479

National Congress of Parents and Teachers: and aid to parochial schools, 529;
and Barden Bill, 593
National Council of Catholic Men, 450
National Council of Churches, 226, 389;
statement of conference on church and
state quoted, 132; and social issues, 233–
234; and POAU, 235; and ambassador to
Vatican, 309, 312, 315–316; policy statement on "common core" proposal, 360–
361; statement on Bible reading quoted,
449, 474; statement on aid to parochial
schools, 526; statement on shared time,
576–577; and 1965 education act, 603
National Council of Evangelical
Churches: report on Mexico quoted, 42
National Defense Education Act, 523
National Education Association, 365, 588;
1948 survey of superintendents of
schools, 349–350; description of teaching about religion quoted, 361; report
on released time, 373, 374, 375, 377, 382,
394–395; survey on Bible reading, 445;
quoted on supervision of private
schools, 520; and aid to parochial
schools, 529; and North College Hill
case, 544; survey on textbooks for parochial schools, 556–557; and shared time,
573–574, 577; and Mead-Aiken Bill,
587; and Barden Bill, 593
National Municipal League: model state
constitution quoted, 197
National Reform Association: purpose
of, 241; its amendment to constitution
quoted, 241
National School Boards Association, 529
National university: support for in early
years, 580
National Youth Administration Program,
523
The Nation's Schools: survey on shared
time, 577
Nebraska: bill, 229; law on teaching of
foreign languages, 627–628
Negroes: and Fourteenth Amendment,
171
Nero, 11
Nestor, Bishop of Constantinople, 14
Netherlands: religious liberty in, 29; constitution of, 58; government aid to private schools in, 529
New Catholic Dictionary: quoted on
birth control, 230–231